THE VIRTUAL WINDOW

THE VIRTUAL WINDOW

FROM ALBERTI TO MICROSOFT

ANNE FRIEDBERG

THE MIT PRESS CAMBRIDGE, MASSACHUSETTS LONDON, ENGLAND

MIT Press books may be purchased at special quantity discounts for business or sales promotional use. For information, please email special_sales@mitpress.mit.edu or write to Special Sales Department, The MIT Press, 55 Hayward Street, Cambridge, MA 02142.

This book was set in Adobe Caslon and HTF Gotham by Graphic Composition, Inc.

Printed and bound in Spain.

Library of Congress Cataloging-in-Publication Data

Friedberg, Anne.
The virtual window : from Alberti to Microsoft / Anne Friedberg.
p. cm.
Includes index.
ISBN-13: 978-0-262-06252-7 (hc : alk. paper)
ISBN-10: 0-262-06252-6 (hc : alk. paper)
1. Image (Philosophy)—History. 2. Mass media—Philosophy—History. I. Title.

B105.I47F75 2006
701—dc22

2006044876

10 9 8 7 6 5 4 3 2 1

FOR
HOWARD
AND
TRISTAN

To live in a glass house is a
revolutionary virtue par excellence.

—Walter Benjamin

CONTENTS

ACKNOWLEDGMENTS

This book would not have been possible without the help of many generous colleagues and supportive institutions. Its interests and methodology were formed while I was engaged in the proposal, launch, and first years of a PhD program in Visual Studies at the University of California, Irvine. My colleagues in Art History—especially David Joselit, Sally Stein, and Jim Herbert—were exceptional comrades in this endeavor. Support from the UC Humanities Research Institute and the UCI Humanities Center was also vital to this project in its initial stages.

During a crucial stage in the formation and writing of this book, I had the great fortune to be a scholar-in-residence at the Getty Research Institute. I am particularly indebted to Thomas Crow, Charles Salas, and Gail Feigenbaum for the opportunity to benefit from the Getty's generous programs and activities. This book was indelibly marked by the lively debate among the participants in the 2001–2002 "Frames of Viewing" Scholar Year—Mieke Bal, Benjamin Buchloh, S. M. Can Bilsel, Cloe Chard, John Elderfield, Charles Harrison, Marian Hobson, Melissa Hyde, John Hyman, Kajri Jain, Lawrence Kruger, Jacqueline Lichtenstein, Michael Lobel, Maria Hsiuya Loh, Jerry Moore, Andrew Perchuk, Deanna Petherbridge, Lisa Pon, Dennis Sepper, Terry Smith, and Ernst Van Alphen. While at the Getty, I was also fortunate enough to benefit from the friendship and curatorial beneficence of Rani Singh, who programmed, among other things, a live mix of Mike Figgis's *Time Code* and the newly restored version of Harry Smith's *Mahagonny*.

A network of friends, colleagues, and critics have helped to sharpen my thinking and provide intellectual subsidy. Sylvia Lavin, with her cool insight into questions of space and transparency, and Vivian Sobchack, with her challenging questions about the window and frame, both provided me with early and continued support. The work of Miriam Hansen and Annette Michelson continue to provide extraordinary models of scholarship and intellectual determination. Many of my ideas have developed in dialogue with the groundwork laid by their thinking about the cinema and modernity. Other friends and colleagues have contributed to the book with conversations along the way: Anthony Vidler, Ricky Jay, Gertrud Koch, Barbara Kruger, Jon Wiener, Judy Fiskin, Tiahna Skye, Lev Manovich, Jeremy Kagan, James Schamus, Ken Brecher, Akira Lippitt, Peggy Phelan, Raiford Guins, and Edward Dimendberg.

In addition, the graduate students in Visual Studies at UCI—especially Sheila Murphy, Janice Neri, Joanna Bouldin, Beth Rayfield, Rene Bruckner, Rachel Thompson, Nicole Woods, Jenny Rogers, Tobey Crockett, and Heidi

Cooley—helped me to work through many of the ideas in this book. Discussions in two particular seminars—Theories of Vision and Visuality, and Cinematic and Televisual Space: The Architecture of Spectatorship—were paradigmatic of productive dialogue and still influence my thinking. Sheila Murphy was an exemplary and tireless research assistant in the early stages. Heidi Cooley, a graduate student who took the risk of following me from UCI to USC, has been an unflagging supporter and eager reader at the book's last stages.

In 2003, I left UCI for the University of Southern California, and wish to thank Dean Elizabeth Daley, Rick Jewell, and Marsha Kinder for allotting me a sabbatical semester in advance of my teaching. I am also grateful to a faculty cabal at USC—Vanessa Schwartz, Marita Sturken, Richard Meyer, Leo Braudy, and Nancy Troy—who provided a welcoming climate for interdisciplinary work; and to the Digital Research Group led by Mimi Ito for many astute conversations on the turns of new media. Michael Renov and Tara McPherson lent institutional support to these interdisciplinary ventures.

Others gave of their time and wisdom above any conceivable obligation. Edward Dimendberg read the first draft of this manuscript and offered expert editorial and scholarly advice. I also wish to thank my editor, Roger Conover, for his early support of this project, his patience as its writing took longer than anticipated, and his astute commentary in its final stages.

The Margaret Herrick Library at the Academy of Motion Picture Arts and Sciences and the Research Library and Special Collections at the Getty Research Institute provided essential research resources. Portions of this book were given as talks at MIT, University of California/Berkeley, Queen's University/Kingston, Ontario, Society of Cinema Studies, George Mason University, University of California Digital Research Group, Getty Research Institute, USC, Freie Universität Berlin, Haus der Kulturen der Welt/Berlin, and Brown University. In all instances, I am grateful to the colleagues who invited me as well as to the audiences who provided constructive response. This book would have been inconceivable without the contributions of the people and institutions listed above. Any shortcomings, errors, or omissions are, of course, my own.

It is to the following that I owe my deepest gratitude:

To Carly Eiseman and Mayola Pinelo, childcare providers extraordinaire, without whose indulgence and good humor the time and space for writing would not have been possible.

To Arthur Leroy Friedberg, my late father, a glass and ceramic scientist whose research, writing, and teaching had a deeper impact on my thinking than I knew at the time. His enthusiasm for the visualization of science and technology led to regular childhood excursions to the Museum of Science and Industry in Chicago, family trips to the New York World's Fair in 1964, and to Expo '67 where I was exposed at a formative age to a wide variety of multiple-screen experimentation. I'm certain that he would have had his own ideas about the relation between the glass window, the silicon chips of the computer, and the screen; and I sorely miss our ongoing dialogue about technological innovation.

To the architect John Lautner—living in a house of his design is living inside a viewing machine. Many of the insights and arguments in this book came from the play of light and shadow, the framing of the view, encountered in daily movement through a house with more windows than walls.

To Tristan Rodman—who grew up in that glass house, who has come of age on a computer screen, and who knows deeply about the technologies of mobility. At age five, while riding on a narrow-gauge steam railway in Wales—at the culmination of a trip enabled by high-speed trains hurtling across Europe and through the tunnel to England—he was asked why he liked trains so much. Leaning back, he looked out the window and said with profound measure: "It's all the moving pictures."

And to Howard A. Rodman—whose eloquence as both a writer and a reader helped me to chisel my language to its most lapidary; his love, encouragement, and sly wit sustained me over the long *durée.*

And of course, the noble canine Nemo—who literally licked the windows.

Portions of this book have been published as articles in other form: "Gerahmte Visualität" (Framed Visuality), trans. Claudia Neumann, in *Der Sinn der Sinne,* Kunst- und Ausstellungshalle der Bundesrepublik Deutschland (Bonn: Stroemfeld/Roter Stern, 1997), 433–457; "The End of Cinema: Multi-Media and Technological Change," in Christine Gledhill and Linda Williams, eds., *Reinventing Film Studies* (London: Arnold, 1999), 438–452 (reprinted in Leo Braudy and Marshall Cohen, eds., *Film Theory and Criticism,* 6th ed. [New York: Oxford University Press, 2004]); "The Virtual Window" (1999), in David Thorburn and Henry Jenkins, eds., *Rethinking Media Change: The Aesthetics of Transition* (Cambridge: MIT Press, 2002), 337–353; "Urban Mobility and Cinematic Visuality: The Screens of Los Angeles—Endless Cinema or Private Telematics," *Journal of Visual Culture* 1, no. 2 (June 2002): 183–204; "Interfacing the Screen: CDs, CD-ROMs, DVDs," in Dan Harries, ed., *The New Media Book* (London: BFI Publications, 2002), 30–39; "*Trottoir Roulant:* The Cinema and New Mobilities of Spectatorship," in Jan Olsson and John Fullerton, eds., *Allegories of Communication: Intermedial Concerns from Cinema to the Digital* (London/Sydney: John Libbey, 2003), 263–276; "Virilio's Screen: The Work of Metaphor in the Age of Technological Convergence," *Journal of Visual Culture* 3, no. 2 (August 2004): 183–194.

INTRODUCTION

THE VIRTUAL WINDOW

FRAMING VISUALITY: FROM ALBERTI TO MICROSOFT

Vision itself has a history.

—Heinrich Wölfflin, *Principles of Art History*

The window is an opening, an aperture for light and ventilation. It opens, it closes; it separates the spaces of here and there, inside and outside, in front of and behind. The window opens onto a three-dimensional world beyond: it is a membrane where surface meets depth, where transparency meets its barriers. The window is also a frame, a proscenium: its edges hold a view in place. The window reduces the outside to a two-dimensional surface; the window becomes a screen. Like the window, the screen is at once a surface and a frame—a reflective plane onto which an image is cast and a frame that limits its view. The screen is a component piece of architecture, rendering a wall permeable to ventilation in new ways: a "virtual window" that changes the materiality of built space, adding new apertures that dramatically alter our conception of space and (even more radically) of time.

WE KNOW the world by what we see: through a window, in a frame, on a screen. As we spend more of our time staring into the frames of movies, television, computers, hand-held displays—"windows" full of moving images, text, icons, and 3-D graphics—how the world is framed may be as important as what is contained within that frame.

In his 1435 treatise on painting and perspective, *De pictura,* Leon Battista Alberti—painter, architect, scholar of antiquity, quintessential Renaissance man—famously instructed the painter to "regard" the rectangular frame of the painting as an open window (*aperta finestra*).[1] Alberti's text serves as my starting point, not because his is the first account of the transformation of three-dimensional space to the planes of two-dimensional representation, but because of his striking use of the architectural figure of the window. Alberti's Renaissance metaphor of the window has haunted centuries of subsequent thinking about the humanist subject of perspective, and has remained a defining concept for theories of painting, architecture, and moving-image media.

Unlike the metaphor of the window as a frame for perspectival view, the metaphor of the window in computer software relies on a different set of assumptions about the viewer and the view that the window provides. An early component of the graphical user interface, the computer "window" referred not to the full expanse of the computer screen, but rather to a subset of its screen surface: an inset screen within the screen of the computer, one of many nested on its "desktop."[2] The computer "window" shifts its metaphoric hold from the singular frame of perspective to the multiplicity of windows within windows, frames within frames, screens within screens.

In the centuries since Alberti, single-point perspective and its concomitant symbolic system have been challenged on many fronts: by changes in perspective in modern painting; by modern architecture's replacement of the "perspectival" window with the horizontal window or "picture wall"; by moving-image technologies that provide a temporal exponent to spatial perspectivalism. Yet these challenges to perspective occurred with a stuttering anachrony in different media. In *The Origin of Perspective* (1995), Hubert Damisch chronicled many challenges to the "perspective paradigm" in painting and architecture and yet maintained: "Without any doubt, our period is much more massively informed by the perspective paradigm, thanks to photography, film and now video, than was the fifteenth century, which could boast of very few correct perspective constructions."[3] This insight may hold true for many uses of photography, film, and video (if one accepts the camera as an apparatus that renders mechanically produced perspective), but does not address the perspectival "shifts" when images move or follow each other in sequential display. Although it may seem that cinematic, televisual, and computer-based representations continue to rely on perspectival positioning, a key component of my argument is to suggest otherwise. The complex relation between perspective and the moving image necessitates a more refined account of the viewer's position in space in relation to a fixed frame with either static, moving, multiply layered, obliquely angled, abstract, sequential, or multiple-frame images. As moving images follow each other, the shifts of editing offer the viewer multiple perspectives but sequentially and within a fixed frame. Here it will be important to consider how, through most of the cinematic century, the dominant form for the moving image was, with striking consistency, a single image in a single frame. The fractured modernisms of cubist painting, photographic collage, architectural transparency—post-perspectival techniques that multiply and layer the planes of representation spatially and temporally—were strategies that remained only exceptions, experiments, the "avant-garde," in the vernacular forms of moving-image media.[4]

Perspective may have met its end on the computer desktop. As computing devices added a screen for the display of data, the graphical user interface (GUI) introduced an entirely new visual system—a text or image in one "window" meets other texts or images in other "windows" on the same screen. Above, below, ahead, and behind are simultaneous on the computer display, where each element in composition is seen separately with no systematic spatial relationship between them. Although the algorithmic constructions found in video games, in QuickTime panoramas, in virtual reality systems continue to rely on digital simulacra of perspectival space, not all digital space is designed to suggest three dimensions.[5] Instead, the vernacular "space" of the computer screen has more in common with surfaces of cubism—frontality, suppression of depth, overlapping layers—than with the extended depth of Renaissance perspective. In this way, computer-generated virtual spaces coexist with the vernacular daily virtual spaces that we inhabit (or at least sit in front of) as viewers and users, in the same way that perspectival painting coexisted with its challengers. Microsoft, the corporate Goliath, figures not so much as the endpoint of this account but as a marker of the commercial alchemy of metaphor turned to commodity capital, making "windows" proprietary. (Indeed, the Microsoft version of windows has in many ways overtaken its architectural referent. A quick Google search will bring up more references to Windows than to architectural apertures.)

As I will detail in a later chapter, there have been sporadic examples of multiple-frame images and multiple-screen display throughout the century-long history of cinematic and televisual media. And yet aside from some notable historical anomalies, only in the last two decades—markedly with the advent of digital imaging technologies and new technologies of display—did the media "window" began to include multiple perspectives within a single frame.[6] And as a coincident development, the interface of computer display made this "new" multiple-"window"/multiple-screen format a daily lens, a vernacular system of visuality.[7] This remade visual vernacular requires new descriptors for its fractured, multiple, simultaneous, time-shiftable sense of space and time. Philosophies and critical theories that address the subject as a nodal point in a communicational matrix have failed to consider this important paradigm shift in visual address.

Underneath this layer of argument lurks another one, equally historically situated, yet perhaps more difficult to chronicle. In the last two decades, with accelerating speed, the media-specific distinctions between cinematic, televisual and computer media have been eroded beyond recognition by the digital technologies that have transformed them. While the development of digital technologies of image production, delivery, and display have helped to remake the visual syntax of the screen, many formal strategies (composites, multiple-frame images, multiple-screen projections) existed before digital technology. Hence it may be important to soften the agonistic claims of a technologically determined digital break.[8] Digital compositing technology eased the combination of live action, animated, and computer-generated images in cinematic and televisual production, and yet the turn-of-the-century magician-turned-filmmaker Georges Méliès could equally be considered as a compositing technician—conjuring a world that did not exist outside of the filmmaking apparatus, a world with its own physical laws. Méliès's predigital trick films could be tagged with one of the common descriptors for digital compositing—"postindexical." (Or, more precisely, given our historical vantage, they might be considered *proto*-post-indexical.)[9] Here, a taxonomy marking the specificities and lost specificities of the film, television, and computer screen seems necessary. How do we parse the media distinctions between image production (shot on film, video, "born digital"?); postproduction (transferred from film to video to computer-generated digital effect or in the reverse direction from CGI to video or film?); and "screen practice" (projected on a large screen, transmitted via broadcast, cable, satellite, or seen on computers, portable DVD screens, or streaming online on WebTV)? The movie screen, the TV screen, and the computer screen may still occupy separate spaces (their very location changes our concept of spectatorship—the place of the computer in the home or in the workplace is quite different from the domestic lodging of the TV set), but their cross-purposed interaction poses new questions about medium-based specificity. As Nicholas Negroponte asserted a decade ago: "The medium is no longer the message in the digital age."[10]

To situate the technical underpinnings of this convergence requires a yet-to-be-written intermedial history of cinema, television, and computer technologies. Siegfried Zielinski's exemplary intertwined history of cinema and television, *Audiovisions: Cinema and Television as Entr'actes in History* (1988), eloquently demonstrates the development of these two media, in reaction to or in concert with each other.[11] As the media of movies, television, and the Web now routinely interact among themselves, a history of moving-image technologies segregated from histories of electricity, telephony, telegraphy, photography, radio, and computing technologies denies the intermedial complexity of technological development.

Virtual images radically transformed the twentieth-century understanding of reality. A long list of writers struggled to assess the changes in scale, time, space, and consciousness produced by technological enhancements to human vision—Paul Valéry, Walter Benjamin, Sigfried Giedion, and Lewis Mumford; Marshall McLuhan, Raymond Williams, Jean Baudrillard, and Paul Virilio; Donna Haraway, Nicholas Negroponte, Vivian Sobchack, and Lev Manovich.[12] My debts to these and other theorists should be evident in my methodological mix of historiographical exegesis with theoretical inquiry and polemic. The screens of cinema, television, and computers open "virtual windows" that ventilate the static materialities and temporalities of their viewers. A "windowed" multiplicity of perspectives implies new laws of "presence"—not only here and there, but also *then* and *now*—a multiple view—sometimes enhanced, sometimes diminished—out the window.

WINDOW FRAME SCREEN

WINDOW

> *What one can see in the light of day is always less interesting than what happens behind a pane of glass.*
>
> —Charles Baudelaire, "Windows"

From the mid-fifteenth-century writings of Leon Battista Alberti to the late-twentieth-century computer software trademarked by Microsoft as Windows, the window has a deep cultural history as an architectural and figurative trope for the framing of the pictorial image. An opening in architectural space, the window supplies a common metaphor for the various frames that form its virtual analogs—the frame of the painting and the photograph, the screens of movie, television, and computers. Alberti's Renaissance metaphor drew upon the window as an analog for the perspectival frame of the painting; since then, the window and its common metaphysical corollary—perspective—have remained central figures in theorizations of the space of vision. The following study examines the figure of the window as a key measure of epistemic changes in representational systems from painting to photography to moving-image media and computer display.[13]

FRAME

Like the frame of the architectural window and the frame of the painting, the frame of the moving-image screen marks a separation—an "ontological cut"—between the material surface of the wall and the view contained within its aperture.[14] Starting at the end of the nineteenth century, the projection of moving images—the cinema as it was developed and exhibited—relied on the immobility of its spectators and the aperture of a fixed frame. This newly wrought combination of mobile and virtual visualities provided a *virtual mobility* for immobile spectators who witnessed movement confined to a frame.[15] As cinema "spectators" we sit immobile in front of moving images; our bodies do not move, but our "point of view" may change. Film theorists have long sought to account for the immobile spectator's experience of cinematic space. Theorizations of televisual space and the television "viewer" require many of the same distinctions between the mobile/immobile, mediated/"real."[16] As a viewer of *virtual* images, the moving-image spectator has a bodily presence in material architectural space, yet engages with virtually rendered immaterial space framed on the screen. As computer "users," we spend hours immobile in front of the flat, multicapable, framed virtual space of the computer screen. The frame becomes the threshold—the liminal site—of tensions between the immobility of a spectator/viewer/user and the mobility of images seen through the mediated "windows" of film, television, and computer screens. But the frame also separates the *materiality* of spectatorial space from the *virtual immateriality* of spaces seen within its boundaries.[17]

While the tensions between mobility and stasis, materiality and immateriality, may seem at first to be purely spatial paradoxes, they also have a temporal component. As a unique tool of modernity, the cinema freed its spectators not only from the bindings of material space but also from the bindings of time.[18] The cinema spectator engages in the fluid temporalities of cinematic construction—flashbacks, ellipses, achronologies—as well as in time frames other than the spectator's moment in historical time, whether she is watching the diegetic fiction of a period drama or a film from an earlier period. And as television and VCR-based (and now PVR-based) televisuality began to take the cinema's essential temporal *flânerie* to even more time-shifted extremes, our access to history and to the past changed dramatically.[19] These emerging habits of cinema and televisual spectatorship, visual practices that routinely engaged with virtual and mobile visualities, have helped to shape a newly mediated *episteme.*[20] As a measure of the frame's metaphysical consequence, it will be necessary to question both the discursive and material practices of "framing" the visual field.[21]

SCREEN

As the twentieth century ended, new systems of circulation and transmission began to replace the cinema's projection screen and to link, as well, the screens of the television and computer with the dialogic interactivity of the telephone. "Convergence"—once merely a discursive buzzword—has become a literal description of the codependency of the movie screen, TV screen, and computer screen. Once seen as the paradigmatic twentieth-century medium, the "cinema" has become embedded in—or perhaps lost in—the new technologies that surround it. Cinema now merely forms an originary visual system for a complexly diverse set of "postcinematic" visualities.

Screens have become a pervasive part of daily experience. Buildings are adorned with screens as exterior walls, sports stadiums add Jumbotrons to the proscenium space of spectacle, screens show games to sport spectators in a time loop of instant replay and a crosscut to its fans, fighter pilots and military strategists conduct maneuvers on screens with global positioning, televisions have gaming consoles and eye-toys, computers interface with other screens and digital archives, PDAs browse the Web, cell phones take and transmit photos. Our physically embodied and subjectively disembodied relation to the screen changes as we engage with the distant, large cinema screen with projected images; the closer and light-emanating television screen; and the even closer computer screen, one that we put our faces very close to, often touch, one that sits on our laps or in our beds. Camera phones, BlackBerries, and other "mobile screenic devices" add mobility to the screen's face.[22]

Production techniques, display technologies, and delivery platforms have jumbled the predigital/digital divide into uncertain convergences in a rapidly shifting technological terrain. As screens multiply in a proliferation of "display technologies," an equally daunting number of "delivery platform(s)" compete to supply images and sounds: videotapes, CDs, CD-ROMs, DVDs, MP3, "streaming" audio and video on the Web. A variety of screens—long and wide and square, large and small, flat and fat, composed of grains, composed of pixels, lit by projected light, cathode-ray tube, plasma, LCD—all compete for our attention without any convincing arguments about hegemony.

Here it might be useful to extend Wittgenstein's incisive epigram, "The limits of my language are the limits of my world," to its visual corollary: the limits and multiplicities of our frames of vision determine the boundaries and multiplicities of our world. As the beholders of multiscreen "windows," we now receive images—still and moving, large and small, artistic and commercial—in spatially and temporally fractured frames. This new space of mediated vision is post-Cartesian, postperspectival, postcinematic, and posttelevisual, and yet remains within the delimited bounds of a frame and seen on a screen.

THE VIRTUAL AND ITS WINDOW

In the glare of a jargon-ridden present, the term "virtual" may have lost its descriptive power. As the term gained wide currency in debates about cyberspace and virtual reality in the 1980s and 1990s, it became a routinely and reflexively deployed adjective. By returning to the term's definition and etymology, I hope to reclaim its considerable utility for making distinctions about the ontological status—and the materiality versus the immateriality—of an object. In this way, I find it necessary to challenge accounts that assume that "virtual" refers only to electronically mediated or digitally produced images and experiences, and to decouple the term from its unquestioned equation with "virtual reality."

> **Virtual** (Latin, *virtus,* for strength or power) of, relating to, or possessing a power of acting without the agency of matter; being *functionally or effectively but not formally* of its kind.[23]

The virtual is a substitute—"acting without agency of matter"—an immaterial proxy for the material. The term becomes a key marker of a secondary order in the relationship between the real and its copy, the original and its reproduction, the image and its likeness. Here it is necessary to clarify the relation between "virtual" and the Latin term *simulacrum*—where the image has no referent in the real. "Virtual" refers to the register of representation itself—but representation that can be either simulacral or directly mimetic.[24]

The Platonic dismissal of the image as untrue, a "false claimant" to the real, receded as the term "virtual" entered into writings on optics and became less charged with negative associations. By the seventeenth century, theories of light rays and their refraction—geometric principles first devised in antiquity by Euclid—were reformulated as optical researchers learned more about the physiology of the eye, the crystalline lens, and the retinal screen. Working within the tradition of medieval geometers, Johannes Kepler described how the crystalline "lens" of the eye focused intromitted light rays from many points in the visual field to form a point-to-point correspondence on the retina as an inverted image. Kepler's *Ad Vitellionem paralipomena* (1604) distinguished between two kinds of images—the *imago,* which could be seen but not measured, and the *pictura* which could be focused on walls and other surfaces and could be measured.[25] While the optical principles delineated by Kepler, Galileo, Snel, Descartes, and others did not make the exact distinction between "virtual" and "real," these thinkers did distinguish between the *imago,* the image without physical substance, and the *pictura,* the reflection on the retina. The *pictura* had a materiality of its own, but one quite different from that of the object in the world. Despite the inherent differences in their materialities and how they were produced, the retinal *pictura* was, like the painting (*pictura*), already in the register of representation. In order to explain how and why the image on the retina was inverted, Kepler—and later, Descartes—invoked the apparatical model of the camera obscura to describe the principles of the eye, the lens, and the retinal wall.[26]

In seventeenth- and eighteenth-century optics, "virtual" was used to describe an image that was seen by looking through a lens or that appeared in a mirror.[27] The term "virtual" first appears in English in the writings of Sir David Brewster about the properties of refraction in his *Treatise on Optics* (1831).[28] Best known for his 1816 invention of the kaleidoscope (an optical device that demonstrated the principles of reflective symmetry), Brewster described the differing properties of an image seen by the eye and an image seen through the mediation of a lens. A "real image" is formed by the convergence of rays of light and is visible to the eye, but will also appear on a surface that is placed in a plane with the image. A "virtual image"—perceived in the brain—is visible to the eye but will not appear on a surface placed in its plane. Hence a "virtual image" in Brewster's optics is not recuperable to representation. This meaning of "virtual" suggests an intangible, uncapturable, ineffable appearance—more *imago* than *pictura.*[29]

Although the virtual image was first described as a purely retinal image, it also became tied to representation as a descriptor for the secondary register of representation, the *pictura.* A "virtual image" may also be produced through the refracting mediation of a lens or the reflecting mediation of a mirror. Both of these optical meanings for "virtual"—an image produced in the brain without referent in the world, and an image produced out of some optical mediation—form precedents to the use of the term in the contemporary vernacular. Both meanings (that of the simulacral and the mimetic) imply a separate ontological register, an immaterial form that is *functionally but not effectively* material. The semantic slippage between the virtual image that has no material existence (appears in the brain, on the retina) and the virtual image that is formed in representation signifies a subtle shift in its materiality.

A virtual image begins to have its own liminal materiality, even if it is of a different ontological order. And, of course, both of these meanings were in use centuries before electronic or digital optical systems of representation. As Elizabeth Grosz bluntly states: "We did not have to wait for the computer screen or the movie projector in order to enter virtual space; we have been living in its shadow more or less continually."[30]

At the end of the nineteenth century, the notion of "the virtual" played a crucial role in the philosophy of Henri Bergson.[31] In *Matter and Memory* (1896), Bergson uses the term "virtual" to depict the immateriality of memory.[32] The recent revival of interest in Bergson's writing, largely due to the interest taken in him by Gilles Deleuze, may also be attributed to the number of concepts that he deployed—"virtuality," "difference," "multiplicity," "mobility"—which resonant with contemporary philosophical debate.[33] (I will discuss Bergson's concept of the virtual at greater length in "Lens III: Bergson's Virtual.")

Deleuze reworks Bergson's biological metaphor of "creative evolution," using the virtual as a key difference: "Evolution takes place from the virtuals to the actuals."[34] To Deleuze, the virtual and the actual both have a reality: "The virtual as virtual has a reality."[35] Félix Guattari describes the virtual as one of "four ontological functors"—the virtual, the actual, the real, and the possible.[36] In *Becoming Virtual,* Pierre Lévy also appeals to a model of evolution, yet with the arrow in the other direction—away from the actual, toward the virtual. Arguing that the "virtual is by no means the opposite of the real," Lévy traces the "accelerated cultural transition" toward virtualization—virtual identities, virtual communities, virtual realities—"the very process of humanity's 'becoming other'—its heterogenesis."[37] In Lévy's "cartography of the virtual," the term "virtual" supplies what Deleuze, Baudrillard, and Virilio describe (in spatial terms) as derealization, disappearance, deterritorialization, and changes in the materiality of space.[38]

These uses of the term "virtual"—in the science of optics, in the philosophical discourse of Bergson and, later, Deleuze, Guattari, Lévy, and others—have proceeded in a separate discursive arena from the developing use of the term in information and computer science.[39] Computer terminology invokes "virtual" to refer to a digital object or experience without physical existence. Hence, computer discourse more exactly links the virtual with the effects of a constructed simulacrum, unhinged from a referent in the real. "Virtual memory" refers to the use of a hard drive to augment RAM.[40] In the computer lexicon, where terms already inhabit the realm of metaphor, "virtual" joins other connotatively laden terms like "memory" and "language."

As the above discussion illustrates, despite the assertions of those who equate virtuality with the changes wrought by digital technology in the early 1990s, the term long existed in the discourse of optics, and was an operable philosophical concept in the late nineteenth century. As Brian Massumi aptly puts it, "Nothing is more destructive for the thinking of the virtual than equating it with the digital. All arts and technologies envelop the virtual, in one way or another. Digital technologies in fact have a remarkably weak connection to the virtual, by virtue of the enormous power of their systemization of the possible."[41] While this may seem a simple point, it is surprising how many contemporary writers base their discourse about the "virtual" on the conflation of the digital with the virtual and who assume, in the blindness of the present, that all mediated reproductions—by virtue of their *re*-presentation—must be electronic or digitally reproduced.[42] These more recent uses have overtaken and obscured the previous meanings and implications of the virtual.[43] Perhaps understandably, scholars who take information theory rather than theories of visual representation as their source for a definition of "virtuality" routinely neglect the tradition of predigital forms of virtual representation. For N. Katherine Hayles, for example, "virtuality" is a term that arose in the historically specific context of post–World War II cybernetics, and its meaning is inseparable from the technologies of "information." Hayles defines "virtuality" as "the cultural perception that material objects are interpenetrated by information patterns."[44]

Seen in this way, Hayles's virtuality is technologically determined, dependent upon the machinic dematerialization of "bodies" into information.[45]

Perhaps a polemic is needed: before the digital age, there was virtuality—painterly, photographic, cinematic, and televisual—and its aesthetics and visual systems cannot be reduced simply to information. There is a long prehistory to the "virtual" image: mirrors, paintings, images produced by the camera obscura, photographs, and moving-picture film all produce mediated representations in a "virtual" register. Once the term "virtual" is free from its enforced association with the "digital," it can more accurately operate as a marker of an ontological, not a media-specific, property.

We also need to disentangle the term "virtual" from its associations with the rhetoric of an immersive—and hence unframed—"virtual reality." In a recent study, *Virtual Art: From Illusion to Immersion* (2003), Oliver Grau aims to expand art historical analysis to include the spaces and experiences that intend to "seal off the observer from external visual impressions." Grau's history of immersive "spaces of illusion"—the panorama, *cinéorama,* stereoscope, Sensorama, and 3-D IMAX—describes visual systems that supply a totality of image space, a 360-degree space of illusion with an infinite number of perspectives, not fixed but dynamic.[46] But Grau makes a clear distinction between such immersive works and the representational strategies and traditions that otherwise are concerned with the frame. Framed images organize and structure perception and cognition in a very different way.[47] As the cinema screen, and later the television "set," became a framed delivery system for virtual images, the screen began to rely on an observer on the "outside," not the "inside." Once the "virtual" is separated from its reflexive association with immersive "realities," we can also account for the range of "virtual" images (still or moving) that are found in frames—paintings, photographs, images produced by a camera obscura, images projected by the magic lantern, and the subsequent moving-image media of film and television.[48]

For the purposes of this study, then, the term "virtual" serves to distinguish between any representation or appearance (whether optically, technologically, or artisanally produced) that appears "functionally or effectively *but not formally*" of the same materiality as what it represents. Virtual images have a materiality and a reality but of a different kind, a second-order materiality, liminally immaterial. The terms "original" and "copy" will not apply here, because the virtuality of the image does not imply direct mimesis, but a transfer—more like metaphor—from one plane of meaning and appearance to another.

A crucial component of my argument—that the cinematic, television, and computer screens have become substitutes for the architectural window—relies on the virtuality of representational images. A portion of this argument is metaphoric: the window has become a metaphor for the screen. But a portion is also literal: the screen has become an actual substitute for the window. While my argument does not attribute causality, the coincidence of these changes is marked: the architectural role of the window changed alongside the development of its virtual analogs. Hence the "virtual" in my construction "virtual window" suggests both a metaphoric window and an actual window with a virtual view.

And the use of metaphor itself takes us into the realm of the virtual.

VISUAL METAPHORS AND REVERSE EKPHRASIS

Metaphors are proxies, aliases. As a rhetorical trope, metaphor relies on the substitution of one thing for another, a transfer of properties from the plane of the literal to the plane of the figurative.[49] Metaphors themselves are virtual; they reside in the immateriality of language, yet they refer to the material world. A *visual* metaphor functions in a complex circuit of rhetorical exchange and substitution: as a metaphor, it operates first as a language-based analogy for a literal object (as metaphor); as a visual metaphor, it relies on the description of a visual object rendered in words (ekphrasis).[50]

In order to unravel some dominant assumptions about Alberti's window metaphor, we need to examine the slippage of meaning occasioned by metaphor itself. Alberti invokes the image of the window as an instructive substitute for the rectangular frame of the painting. As a visual metaphor, the window functions to reinscribe its image onto another image, the painting. The relation of images in this circuit is bidirectional: the window is like a painting (it frames an opening onto the world) and the painting is like a window (as a technique to construct perspective, the painter should frame the view). But, I will argue, Alberti used the window predominately as a metaphor for the frame—the relation of a fixed viewer to a framed view—and not as a "transparent" "window on the world," as has been suggested widely by art historians and media theorists. Its frame was to be used to position the viewer in relation to its perspectival construction of space. Although Alberti's metaphor conflates the literal window with its figurative aspects, the architectural window and the painting developed separately as registers of constructed vision, separate worldviews but with similar frames.[51] Alberti may have meant to use the window metaphor as an instructional device and not as a philosophical paradigm, and yet, as a metaphoric figure, it performs a coy slippage. It is important to "out" the hidden rhetoric of metaphor because it is here, in the sliding signifiers of language, that they perform their sly discursive tricks: metaphors construct our cultural realities.

Many of the key terms in this book—window, perspective, frame, screen, architecture—operate in both metaphoric and literal registers, and their meanings frequently slip between the dual functions of philosophical paradigm and representational device. Here, to serve as a brief prologmenon to the necessity of unpacking the use of metaphor in discourses about painting, architecture, and the frame, I want to turn to a section of Jacques Derrida's densely metaphoric *The Truth in Painting* (1978). Deeply nested in this text is a compelling polemic.

In *The Truth in Painting,* Derrida describes the *parergon* (*par-*, around; *ergon,* the work), the boundaries or limits of a work of art. Philosophers from Plato to Hegel, Kant, Husserl, and Heidegger debated the limits of the intrinsic and extrinsic, the inside and outside of the art object. In Derrida's discussion, the *parergon* is a Möbius-like boundary—a frame marking what is inside the work but, paradoxically, demarcating its outside in order to constitute what it contains.[52] To interrogate this "discourse on the frame,"[53] Derrida offers his discussion of the *parergon* as a nested commentary on Kant's *Third Critique,* a *mise en abyme* of frames:

> *Parerga* have a thickness, a surface which separates them not only (as Kant would have it) from the integral inside, from the body proper of the *ergon,* but also from the outside, from the wall on which the painting is hung, from the space in which statue or column is erected, then, step by step, from the whole field of historical, economic, political inscription in which the drive to signature is produced. . . . *No "theory," no "practice," no "theoretical practice" can intervene effectively in this field if it does not weigh up and bear on the frame, which is the decisive structure of what is at stake,* the invisible limit to (between) the interiority of meaning (put under shelter by the whole hermeneuticist, semioticist, phenomenologicalist, and formalist tradition) and (to) all the empiricisms of the extrinsic which, incapable of either seeing or reading, miss the question completely.[54]

In this passage, Derrida zooms out—from the frame to the wall to the architectural space that vaults itself around the wall, to the historical, economic, and political context of the work. His fiery assertion that "no theory, no practice, no theoretical practice can intervene effectively in this field if it does not weigh up and bear on the frame" forms a justification for this study. The everyday frames through which we see things—the "material" frames of movie screens, television sets, computer screens, car windshields—provide compelling evidence of the dominance of the frame and its visual system. A study of the frame itself ("the decisive structure of what is at stake") will tell us more than a study of the intrinsic and extrinsic meanings of what the frame contains.[55]

But it is also worth investigating the role of metaphor here. Derrida's interrogation of the metaphysics of the frame relies on a metaphoric claim: a metaphysician is a "good architect," and "philosophy is an art of architecture."[56] Philosophers have had, as Mark Wigley details, a lengthy history of reliance on the metaphor of architecture.[57] One of the plates that accompanies the above-quoted section of *The Truth in Painting* is an engraving of a doorway, an ornate portal with Louis XIV-style ornamentation on its lintels and frames. Inside the doorway is another door, and inside that door another, and inside that another, as they recede inward in *mise en abyme.*[58] The illustration here forms a visual analog to Derrida's discussion of the Kantian *Critique,* a philosophical text which itself embeds its remarks on the *parergon* inside many other frames and which Derrida surrounds with his own commentary.[59] The image of this nested doorway, embedded in a text full of metaphors and wordplay, forms its own metaphoric relation to the text, but in a visual register, a sort of reverse ekphrasis—a pictorial representation of a textual *parergon.*[60]

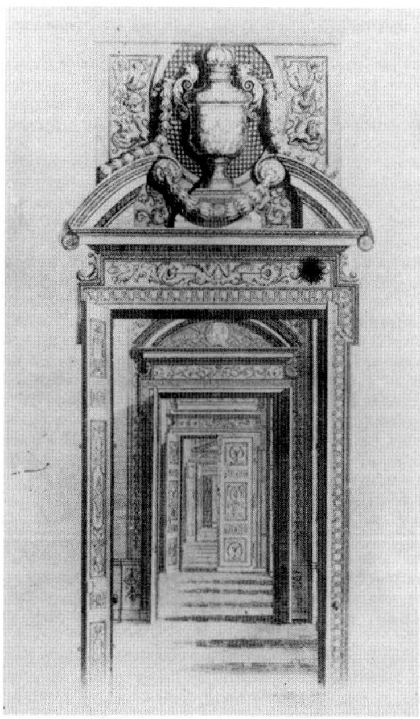

I.1 *Encadrement de porte,* plate from Jacques Derrida, *La vérité en peinture* (Paris: Flammarion, 1978).

The metaphysician-as-architect may rely on one register of metaphor—invoking tectonic structures and architectural forms as discursive figures for the immaterialities of thought—but the *image* of the doorway, a material architectural figure, operates in another register of metaphoric translation.[61] In the Derridean example above, the *parergon* conducts a metaphoric transfer from the frame of a painting (literal) to the framed structure of a philosophical argument (figurative). While Derrida's text is densely metaphoric, and its transfers and references complexly nested, once the visual image of the framed doorway is introduced, the transfer that had been conducted in the pure immateriality of language has found, in the image, a figurative and literal referent.

Derrida's discussion of the *parergon* offers a model for the disciplinary and philosophical boundaries of this study *and* of its object. A visual metaphor, such as the window, functions in a complex circuit of rhetorical exchange and substitution. Because metaphors are transfer devices, conduits for meaning from one frame of reference to another, metaphor may itself offer a discourse of translation between the traditions, debates, and objects of study of separate disciplinary domains.[62] As new media are introduced, metaphor functions as accommodation, wrapping the newly strange in the familiar language of the past. Architecture, long a metaphor for philosophy, was also adopted as an early model for software design. In the culture of interface, we live in the realm of metaphor. An interrogation of the cultural valences of metaphor may build "bridges" (another metaphor) between the disciplines of philosophy, art history, film studies, and new media studies.

METAPHORS FOR THE SCREEN

As a metaphor for the screen, the window proposes transparency, a variable size, and the framed delimitation of a view. In this regard, it is worth comparing at the outset another metaphor for the screen—one well trodden in contemporary Lacanian-inflected film theories—the mirror.[63] The mirror's opacity, reflected light, and inverse image suggest a visual system quite opposed to that of the window's transparency, transmitted light, and seemingly unmediated image.

These two competing visual systems are at the very root of perspectival theory: Alberti's window and Brunelleschi's mirror. In a 1425 experiment, Filippo Brunelleschi crafted an apparatus designed to demonstrate the correlation between perspectival painting and a mirrored image of the Baptistry of San Giovanni in Florence, as if the painting of the Baptistry were comparable to the flat plane of its mirror reflection rather than to the three-dimensional view of the building itself. Biographer Antonio di Tucci Manetti described Brunelleschi's experiment in a 1475 account: "the spectator felt he saw the actual scene when he looked at the painting."[64] (A key discrepancy between the mirror and the painting will be discussed later: movement—of the wind and clouds—was visible on the mirrored surface but not on the painted one.) Hubert Damisch writes at length about the Brunelleschi experiment that forms the basis of our historical understanding of perspective, and leaves open the question of whether the mirror was a tool for constructing perspective or just for the demonstration of its mimetic effect.[65] But either way, the mirror served as a verifier of the "truth" of perspective. In Damisch's historiography, the Brunelleschi experiment enacts the "mirror stage of painting," as if painting formed its identity in relation to the flat planes of a mirror image. The metaphor of the mirror—producing substitutive, deceptive, illusory vision—and the metaphor of the window—producing direct, veridical, unmediated vision—imply very different epistemological consequences.

In the context of film theory, the mirror and the window have quite separate discursive histories.[66] The following synoptic survey draws upon the metaphors in contemporary film theoretical accounts. In her 1992 book *The Address of the Eye: A Phenomenology of the Film Experience,* Vivian Sobchack isolates three metaphors that have dominated and delimited film theory: picture frame, window, and mirror.[67] In her account, Sobchack adopts the familiar binary opposition between formalism and realism, and finds the metaphors of frame and window as "emblematic" of each.[68] In this way, the frame and the window not only "represent the opposing poles of classical film theory," but the two metaphors also neatly illustrate the theoretical opposition between "perception" and "expression," the very poles that a phenomenological approach will resolve as a "systematic exchange." The mirror metaphor, as a third term, "represents the synthetic conflation of perception and expression that characterizes most contemporary film theory."[69] Here it should be noted that Sobchack uses each metaphor as "emblematic" of a theoretical position but does not suggest (or supply examples which might indicate) that these theories use the metaphors directly. Yet the crux of Sobchack's critique of classical and contemporary film theory is located in the "non-dynamic activity of viewing" implied by each of these metaphors: "What is interesting to note is that all three metaphors *relate directly to the screen rectangle and to the film as static viewed object,* and only indirectly to the dynamic activity of viewing that is engaged in by both the film and the spectator, each *as viewing subjects*."[70] Here, it is precisely Sobchack's non-metaphoric use of the frame that becomes important for her phenomenological discussion of the viewing subject. Sobchack asserts that the geometric rectangularity of the film frame "is invisible to the seeing that is the film."[71] The frame "functions for the film as the field of our bodies does for us."[72] The frame is, in Sobchack's account, an "organ of perception." Yet its "lived logic" is one of duping the body's senses in the act of viewing. The frame is not a metaphor here; it is a component of an embodied visual field both literal and phenomenal.[73]

Other writers have used the metaphor of the window to describe cinematic spectatorship. In *Technology as Symptom and Dream* (1989), Robert D. Romanyshyn offers an account of the "condition of the window" as a constituent component of film spectatorship. Instead of assuming the window's unmediated transparency, Romanyshyn's window relies on assumptions about its mediated separation of inside and outside: "The condition of the window implies a *boundary* between the perceiver and the perceived. It establishes as a condition for perception a formal *separation* between a subject who sees the world and the world that is seen, and in so doing it sets the stage, as it were, for that retreat or withdrawal of the self from the world which characterizes the dawn of the modern age. Ensconced behind the window the self becomes an observing *subject,* a *spectator,* as against a world which becomes a *spectacle,* an *object* of vision."[74]

While Romanyshyn's characterization of the boundary separation between the "subject who sees the world and the world that is seen" seems to invoke Heidegger's philosophical discourse of the setting-forth (*Vorstellen*) of the "world picture," he is less concerned with the philosophical consequences produced by modern technology and relies, instead, on accounts of the social effects of technological change in Marshall McLuhan, Harold Innis, Walter Ong, and Donald Lowe. Romanyshyn invokes the metaphor of the window in order to emphasize the removed position of the viewer, in "retreat" and "withdrawal."[75]

To philosopher Stanley Cavell, the cinema screen serves as a metaphoric barrier, like Romanyshyn's boundary window: "A screen is a barrier. What does the silver screen screen? It screens me from the world it holds—that is, makes me invisible. And it screens that world from me—that is, screens its existence from me."[76] Cavell turns the screen on its linguistic side: its noun form is turned into a verb: "what does the silver screen *screen*?" As an action verb, the screen renders the spectator invisible, keeps the spectator from the world it holds in its frame.

The screen—as a filtering or distorting device—is frequently used as a metaphor for the function of the film screen itself. In this way, the English translation of the title of Freud's 1899 paper "Über Deckerinnerungen" as "Screen Memories" may be responsible for the common conflation of screen as mediating device and as a surface for representation.[77] Freud's short paper described how an early memory could serve as a "screen" for a later event. But the German term that Freud used—*Deckerinnerungen*—emphasizes the manner in which an early memory "covers" or "blankets" rather than filters or distorts. (The compound noun *Deckerinnerung* includes the root for memory [*Erinnerung*] and for cover or blanket [*Decke*].) Strachey's translation "screen memories" carries the potential double meaning of screen as both a filtering/distorting device and as the material surface of projection. In 1899, Freud certainly was not referring to a film screen or even to the screens of magic lantern projection. But in the slippage of metaphor, the double-entendre forms the basis for readings of how films, seen on the screen, "screen" memories.[78]

While psychoanalyst Jacques Lacan invoked the metaphor of the mirror as a model for the visual scenario of identity formation, his most elaborate theorization of the constitutive scenario of vision relies on the metaphor of the screen (*écran*).[79] In Lacan's interlaced triangular diagrams of vision in *Le séminaire,* the screen figures as a metaphor for intersubjective mediation, the relation between the subject and the "gaze" (*regard*).[80] In *The Threshold of the Visible World* (1996), Kaja Silverman deploys Lacan's use of screen—as both a verb and noun—to describe the mediation between the spectator and spectacle, the subject and representation.[81] Although Silverman proposes "that the screen is the site at which social and historical difference enters the field of vision," she means "the screen" in the Lacanian sense as "category" or metaphor for intersubjective mediation and *not* as a material surface for the projection of moving images or for the screenic display of televisual images.[82] Screens interpose themselves between the subject and the gaze, but the "shifting social or historical variability" to which Silverman refers remains in an imaginary psychic register and does not account for the material registers of the frame, or the complicated multiplicity seen within its boundaries. While engaged in a call to meet discursive formation with material practice, Silverman retains the metaphoric use of the terms "camera" and "screen" and resists describing cinematic, televisual, or computer interfaces as material practices framing the view.[83]

The metaphors of windows, mirrors, frames, screens fall into a slippery discursive tumble of synecdoche and displacement. With all of these metaphoric figures it will be important to underline the dynamic interaction between the place of the viewing subject and the framed view. As images move across the screens of cinema, television, and the computer, the viewer's immobility meets a paradoxical and compensatory mobility when moving images are seen within a frame. As screens contain other screens in a nested *mise en abyme* of multiple frames, as quattrocento perspective is both fractured and multiplied, the "virtual window" opens onto a new logic of visuality, a time-architecture, framed and virtual, on a screen.

THE WINDOW AND THE BOOK

> *[T]he printed book has not simply been played out, but rather this unique medium was what made its own high-technological outdoing possible in the first place.*
>
> —Friedrich Kittler, "Perspective and the Book"

In a recent essay, "Perspective and the Book," German media scholar Friedrich Kittler argues that the very technologies that led to the book have also led to its undoing.[84] Kittler constructs a teleology beginning with two devices from the Renaissance that, he argues, have lead to the contemporary "end" of the book: Leon Battista Alberti's use of the camera obscura for linear-perspective drawing, and Johannes Gutenberg's invention of the printing press with movable type. For Kittler, these two devices illustrate the Renaissance roots of technical reproducibility, respectively, of image and text. Each apparatus was able to produce copies without the interference of the human hand. Kittler uses this historically confluent "media-union" between printing and linear-perspective drawing to launch a historical trajectory that hurtles headlong toward computer-assisted writing and reading and the inevitable demise of the printed book. "From the *camera obscura* have come the photographic camera and the computer screen," he writes, "from movable type, movable electrons in silicon chips."[85] While Kittler's argument is a forceful polemic linking the technologies of the text and the image and noting the fatal intertwining of their destinies, the leap between the camera obscura, the photographic camera, and the computer screen is an enormous one, one that elides details of technology and history. How do we account for the complex set of forces that have led to the computer display screen and its referential relation to the archives of image and text and databases of knowledge?

Walter Benjamin may have had some inkling of the book's eventual demise when he wrote, in "One-Way Street" (1928): "Now everything indicates that the book in [its] traditional form is nearing its end."[86] Benjamin noted the postural change from the "archaic stillness" of the book to the "dictatorial perpendicular" of the newspaper, the advertisement, and the film: "The newspaper is read more in the vertical than in the horizontal plane, while film and advertisement force the printed word entirely into the *dictatorial perpendicular.* And before a child of our time finds his way clear to opening a book, his eyes have been exposed to such a blizzard of changing, colourful, conflicting letters that the chances of his penetrating the archaic stillness of the book are slight."[87] Benjamin's complaints about book writing and the changing habits of reading now seem uncannily prescient, as if he had already imagined the mechanical potentials and pitfalls of computer writing and reading. The "Arcades Project" now appears as a precursor to the nonlinear logic of computer writing and hypertext.[88]

The computer screen is both a "page" and a "window," at once opaque and transparent. It commands a new posture for the practice of writing and reading—one that requires looking into the page as if it were the frame of a window. The computer screen adds new depth to the perpendicular surface. Its overlay of "windows"—open to different applications for word-processing, Web browsing, emailing, downloading—transforms the screen surface into a page with a deep virtual reach to archives and databases, indexed and accessible with barely the stroke of a finger.[89]

This is a book about windows, their virtual substitutes, and the fractured multiplicity of the multiple "windowed" screen. It was written while looking into a screen fractured into many windows—overlapping and simultaneous applications, some hermetically sealed, some wired to the outside. And until there is a hyperlinked electronic edition, it will be read while held with the "archaic stillness" of a book.

BOOK ARCHITECTURE AND FRAME

The structure of this book is accretive and refractive, rather than linear. I examine the window in three separate and sometimes converging registers: the metaphoric window, the architectural window, and the virtual window of the film, television, and computer screen. Although the chapters follow a loosely chronological schema, the book does not paint a continuous cultural history. Rather, it offers a series of aperçus that slowly unravel dominant assumptions about the histories of media, and about perspective and its relation to the frames of moving images, and about the status of virtual images in our lives and experience.

I have drawn upon a variety of philosophers and critical theorists each with a separate mediating "optic." I've positioned their theories as dioptric devices, "lenses" between chapters. Each "lens" takes a philosopher's metaphor—window, frame, virtual, screen—as a refractive skrim to our contemporary use of these terms. If, as Marshall McLuhan suggests, we see the world best in a rearview mirror, we need to examine the past with a deeper refractive lens, adjust our lenses to a history that stretches to vanishing points deeper than the last century.[90]

Chapter 1, "The Window," introduces Leon Battista Alberti's metaphor of the picture as "an open window [*aperta finestra*] through which the subject to be painted is seen."[91] As a metaphor for the painting, the window implied subjective and representational consequences for the viewer with a fixed position in relation to the picture. Alberti's text and the subsequent debates about the perspectival image and its centered subject have served as an underpinning for theories that align the perspective frame with the frame of the photograph and the cinema screen. This chapter will argue that Alberti's window was *not* a "transparent" "window on the world," but rather that Alberti used the window predominately as a metaphor for the frame. Alberti's metaphor emphasizes the fixed relation of a viewer to a framed view.

In "Lens I: Descartes's Window" Descartes's seventeenth-century meditations on dioptrics form a basis for the still-ongoing debate about disembodied versus embodied vision.

Chapter 2, "The Frame," examines the role of the camera obscura as a scientific instrument and as a device for illusion. The camera obscura has served as an orginary apparatus for those who trace a continuity between quattrocento codes of perspective and the frames of photography and cinema, and yet, for more recent writers, it has also served to mark a rupture in such genealogies. The optical principle of the camera obscura is architectural: it translates a three-dimensional view from outside an enclosed space onto a two-dimensional surface inside. As projected light forms a virtual image on the inside wall, the wall boasts a "virtual window." In this chapter, I underline the camera obscura's relation to techniques of light and magic lantern projection and the emergence of "screen practices" that rely, not on the image's verisimilitude, but on its virtuality.

"Lens II: Heidegger's Frame" introduces the concept of a "framed visuality," which, considered through a Heideggerian lens, assumes that there are subjective consequences to the "enframing" implicit in modern thought and experience.

Chapter 3, "The 'Age of Windows,'" begins and ends with a telling prediction found in William Cameron Menzies's 1936 film adaptation of H. G. Wells's *Things to Come.* In the imagined world of 2054, a character offers an architectural tutorial as he describes images of twentieth-century buildings seen on a flat screen. With a tone of retrospective certainty, he asserts: "The age of windows lasted three centuries." In the film's streamlined image of the future, the architectural window has been replaced by its virtual substitute, a screen. This chapter frames a history of the architectural window in terms of developing technologies of glass and materials of transparency in order to demonstrate how the window as an architectural opening for light and ventilation ceded its priorities to the modern function of the window: to frame a view. Two case studies illustrate symptomatic changes in the architectural window and in its frame: first, the 1920s debate between the architects Auguste Perret and Le Corbusier on the size, shape, and function of the window, and second, the late 1920s polemic between Sergei Eisenstein and the Academy of Motion Picture Arts and Sciences about the shape of the movie screen.

In "Lens III: Bergson's Virtual," Henri Bergson's nineteenth-century use of the term "virtual" is held up to its uses in present discourse. Bergson's debate with Einstein about time and the observer, his notions of "virtuality" and "multiplicity," serve as a refracting optic to contemporary debate about these topics.

Chapter 4, "The Screen," explores the tension between the material reality of built space and the dematerialized imaginary space that cinematic, televisual, and computer-based media provide. Here, the historical specificity of the cinema screen—and the luminous moving images projected upon it—forms a transitional surface as light became a building element in a newly *immaterial* architecture. As an architectonic element, the screen negotiates the paradoxical relations between mobility and immobility, materiality and immateriality in "the architecture of spectatorship."

"Lens IV: Virilio's Screen" takes Virilio's prophetic theorization of the screen as a "temporal window" and begins to amplify the effects of the fracture of the screen into multiple "windows."

Chapter 5, "The Multiple," examines the limited use of split-screen or multiple-screen compositions and multiple-screen display in the century-long history of film and the half-century-long history of television. In their dominant forms through most of the twentieth century, the media of film and television were viewed in a single frame, seen on a single screen. In the last two decades, with the advent of digital technologies, cinematic, televisual, and computer-based forms of imaging and display began more commonly to fracture screen space into multiple screens. Coincident with the introduction of the inset "windows" of the graphical user interface, a new visual vernacular has taken hold of the film and television screen: one that is multiple, adjacent, postperspectival. This chapter begins to theorize the technical base and subjective consequences of a multiply windowed screen.

The conclusion, "The Future of Windows: Smart Glass, Streaming Portals, and Screenless Images," offers some projections about the future of windows—buildings with image-bearing glass skins; computer screens within screens streaming with images from multiple sources; virtual reality alternatives that expand the gaming world into entertainment and daily services. As flat-screen technology improves and screens replace real windows with a kind of "inhabited TV," a "windows environment" may give way to virtual "window-walls," an image not far from the shape of H. G. Wells's *Things to Come.*

1

THE WINDOW

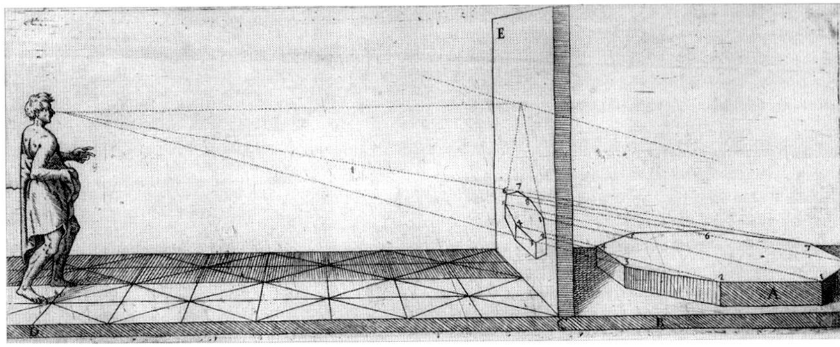

1.1 Drawing from Giacomo Barozzi da Vignola, *Le due regole della prospettiva practica* (Rome, 1583).

1 PERSPECTIVE AND ITS FRAME

Alberti's 1435 metaphor for the painting (*pictura*) as an "open window" (*aperta finestra*) remains a pivotal trope in debates about the origins, practices, and traditions of perspective, debates that continue to pose key questions about visual representation itself. Is perspective a practical formula (as Martin Kemp, Samuel Edgerton, and Cecil Grayson describe)? An epistemological metaphor (as James Elkins eloquently denotes)? A transhistorical "symbolic form" (as Erwin Panofsky contends)? A visual system unique to Italy and distinct from the more aggregate system of visual representation relied upon by northern Dutch painters (as Svetlana Alpers argues)? The dominant visual system in Western culture, or one of several (as suggested by Martin Jay)? A technique for painters (*perspectiva artificialis*), as evidenced in the writings of Alberti, or for architects (*costruzione legittima*), as evidenced in the experiments of Brunelleschi (described in the work of Hubert Damisch, Alberto Pérez-Gómez, and Louise Pelletier)?[1] James Elkins depicts the conceptual and historiographical impasse between the many positivist accounts of perspective that revel in practice and not philosophy (i.e., resist metaphor) and the philosophical accounts that situate perspective within a history of Western thought (i.e., revel in metaphor).[2] The window serves as a symptomatic trope in these debates, because it has functioned both as a practical device (a material opening in the wall) and an epistemological metaphor (a figure for the framed view of the viewing subject).

In *De pictura,* Alberti demonstrates his attraction to the illustrative powers of metaphor to enrich his abstract reduction of the phenomenal world of vision to the mathematics of point, line, and surface.[3] He writes: "Mathematicians measure the shapes and forms of things in the mind alone and divorced entirely from matter. We, on the other hand, who wish to talk of things that are *visible,* will express ourselves in cruder terms."[4] Alberti's "cruder terms" were supplied through language, not image; he supplied no diagrams for *De pictura*.[5] His geometrical account of vision was, instead, retold in a variety of translations—in the descriptors of the Latin language, in the vernacular Tuscan, in the language of metaphor.

Here it is instructive to compare Alberti's metaphor-laden *De pictura,* written early in his scholarly career (1435), with his lengthy disquisition on architecture, *De re aedificatoria* (On the Art of Building) written in 1452.[6] An examination of both texts will demonstrate several important differences between the fifteenth-century representational "picture" and the fifteenth-century architectural window. While *De pictura* has been the subject of extensive exegesis, I find it necessary to return to this text in order to ground a discussion of the window, perspective, and its frame. If read carefully, the famous passage that contains the window metaphor reveals some key assumptions about the "picture":

> Let me tell you what I do when I am painting. *First of all, on the surface on which I am going to paint, I draw a rectangle of whatever size I want, which I regard as an open window through which the subject to be painted is seen;* and I decide how large I wish the human figures in the painting to be. I divide the height of this man into three parts, which will be proportional to the measure commonly called a *braccia;* for, as may be seen from the relationship of his limbs, three *braccia* is just about the average height of a man's body. With this measure I divide the bottom line of my rectangle into as many parts as it will hold; and this bottom line of the rectangle is for me proportional to the next transverse equidistant quantity seen on the pavement. Then I establish a point in the rectangle wherever I wish; and as it occupies the place where the centric ray strikes, I shall call this the centric point. The suitable position of this centric point is no higher from the base line than the height of the man to be represented in the painting, for in this way both the viewers and the objects in the painting will seem to be on the same plane.[7]

In this paragraph Alberti outlines a formula for perspectival painting that entails (1) a variable rectangular frame, (2) the window as a metaphor for the frame of the painting, (3) the "subject" that is seen through this frame, (4) the human figure as a standard of measure and as determinant of the "centric point," and (5) the immobility of the viewer.

I. GEOMETRICS OF VISION: THE RECTANGLE AND THE PICTURE PLANE

Alberti was a geometer of vision; he recast the visual coordinates of space into the geometrics of triangle, pyramid, and intersection. Relying on the Euclidean optical principles of the "visual pyramid" and "visual cone," Alberti described the operation of vision in terms of visual rays that stretch between the eye of the beholder and the object seen—a triangular pyramid formed by rays that converge from the eye as vertex.[8] While Alberti was quick to "set aside" ancient debates about the visual process—whether rays were emitted from the eyes or from the visual plane—he stalwartly described vision as emanating from a fixed monocular point.[9]

Alberti applied this "cold logic of optical geometry" to painterly representation.[10] The "picture" was a surface, a plane that intersected the visual pyramid of sight at its perpendicular axis. The picture plane was thus imagined as a flat vertical surface between the artist (and viewer) and the scene depicted. The planar surface of the painting formed a material support for the painting's virtual representation: "A painting is the intersection of a visual pyramid at a given distance, with a fixed centre and a defined position of light, represented by art with lines and colours on a given surface."[11]

Hence, the artist and the viewer of the painting were in a fixed position in relation to the picture plane—a position that implied the artist's and the viewer's upright posture facing a picture plane also in an upright position.[12] In a later chapter, I will compare this concept of the picture plane to the film and television screen and to the computer "window," which also imply an upright viewer facing a vertical planar surface, Benjamin's "dictatorial perpendicular."[13] Unlike perspectival space which extends beyond the surface, computer space flattens the spatial differences between near and far, supplying no perspectival depth.

The perspectival image constructed from this single viewpoint also needed to be viewed from a single point, encoding the position of its viewer into its representation. Perspectival representation was dependent on two important divergences from human vision. The mobility and binocularity of vision was reduced to a static, monocular "point" of view.[14] The vertex of single-point perspective took on the monocular view of the painter and positioned the viewer to share its vantage. Contemporary art theorist Norman Bryson deems the scene viewed by the painter as the "Founding Perception," a perception to be united with two other "points" of view: the point from which the painting is viewed (the "Viewpoint") and the imagined horizon where perspective rays converge (the "Vanishing Point").[15] The viewer apprehends from this vantage—as the monocular endpoint of converging visual rays.[16]

The "intersection" *(intersegazione)* of the converging rays of vision and the picture plane led Alberti to another related figurative construction for the planar surface. In a passage of *De pictura* that precedes his direct invocation of the window, Alberti describes the planar painting surface as "transparent and like glass": "They should understand that, when they draw lines around a surface, and fill the parts they have drawn with colours, their sole object is the representation on this surface of many different forms of surfaces, just as though this surface which they colour were so transparent and like glass [*admodum vitrea et perlucida huiusmodi*], that the visual pyramid passed right through it from a certain distance and with a certain position of the centric ray and of the light, established at appropriate points nearby in space. . . . Consequently the viewers of a painted surface appear to be looking at a particular intersection of the pyramid."[17]

The surface of transparent glass serves as a vivid figure for the rays of vision passing—as if they were rays of light—through the picture plane toward a vanishing point. Many scholars have assumed that this passage invokes the trope of the window, even though Alberti refers to the transparency of the planar surface of the painting and not to the containment of its rectangular frame.

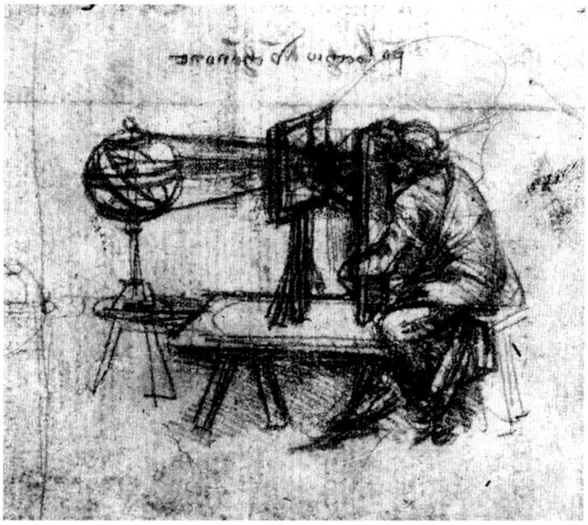

1.2 Leonardo da Vinci drawing (1480–1482), captioned "perspectival window," from Kim H. Veltman, *Linear Perspective and the Visual Dimensions of Science and Art: Studies on Leonardo da Vinci*, vol. 1 (Munich: Deutscher Kunstverlag, 1986).

Here it is important to decouple the figure of transparent glass from the metaphor of the window and its frame of vision. Leonardo da Vinci later described techniques of perspective by imagining a "pane of glass, quite transparent, on the surface of which the objects behind that glass are drawn."[18] This oft-quoted passage led one scholar to conflate Alberti's window with da Vinci's prescription for a transparent glass surface and to deem this the "Leonardo window."[19]

One of Leonardo's drawings (from 1480–1482) shows a rather cumbersome perspective framing device that may be holding a transparent pane of glass. In a notebook of 1492, Leonardo drew an eye looking at an object through a transparent plane of glass (*pariete di vetro*) and provided this definition: "Perspective is nothing else than seeing a site behind a flat transparent plane, on the surface of which are marked all the things which are behind that glass and which can be conduced by mean of pyramids to the point of the eye and these pyramids intersect the said pane."[20] Leonardo emphasizes the transparency and flatness of the plane as crucial components of the instrument but does not invoke the figure (or term) of the window or the importance of the frame.

The metaphor of the window may have functioned to situate the artist and the viewer in relation to the flat plane of representation, but—as I will further demonstrate in a moment—for Alberti, at least, the fifteenth-century window did not imply transparency. Given the architectural nature of fifteenth-century windows and the technical specifications of fifteenth-century glass, Alberti's mention of glass (*admodum vitrea*) in *De pictura* merely implied a surface that was transparent and not a window-view. This distinction will be important because it will challenge the assumption that Alberti's formula implied a subject matter for painterly representation. The painting was not intended to copy a literal view out the window but to recreate a spatial reconstruction of such a view. Hence, Alberti's window emphasized the rectangular frame of viewing, a frame for the spatial realism of perspective. The frame was what mattered, not the view from a window.

"First of all, on the surface on which I am going to paint, I draw a rectangle of whatever size I want." Alberti instructed the artist to begin with a rectangular frame that formed lines around the painting surface. As for the size and shape of the picture's frame, Alberti specified "a rectangle of whatever size I want." Hence, he had no exact codification for the size or proportion of the painterly frame, but, as we will see, its human subjects—both as viewer and as subjects in the painting—become proportional measures for its size.[21]

2. THE WINDOW AS METAPHOR

Alberti "regards" *(quod quidem)* this rectangle as an "open window" (*aperta finestra)*—not a glazed or closed one. In his later study of architecture, *On the Art of Building*, he describes the window as an opening (*apertio*) that functions for light and ventilation.[22] Alberti's window is an aperture, an opening distinguished from a door: "There are two types of opening, one for light and ventilation, and the other to allow man or object to enter or leave the building. Windows serve for light; for objects there are doors, stairs, and spaces between the columns. . . . Every part of the house should have a window to allow the air within to breathe and be regularly renewed, otherwise it will decay and become stale."[23]

Alberti's windows were either opened or shuttered or, if sealed by a protective pane, covered with a translucent stone like gypsum. Alberti describes the window of a temple:

> The windows that provide the temple with light would have, instead of leaves, *either fixed, thin slabs of translucent alabaster* or a lattice of

> bronze or marble, to keep out the frost and wind. In the latter case the spaces *were filled, not with fragile glass, but with transparent stone,* imported mainly from the Spanish town of Segovia, or from Boulogne in Gaul. These are *sheets of translucent and extremely pure gypsum* rarely larger than a foot in size and with the natural capacity not to deteriorate with age.[24]

And the window of a basilica:

> The openings of the windows should be latticed, but not glazed with gypsum, like those of a temple. Obviously they must contain something to ward off the bitter wind and keep out the irksome cold, to prevent any damage. On the other hand they must also provide continuous and unobstructed ventilation, to prevent the dust disturbed by the numerous feet from irritating eyes or lungs. I would therefore strongly *advise the use of thin sheets of bronze or lead, patterned with numerous tiny perforations, to admit light and breezes to purify the air.*[25]

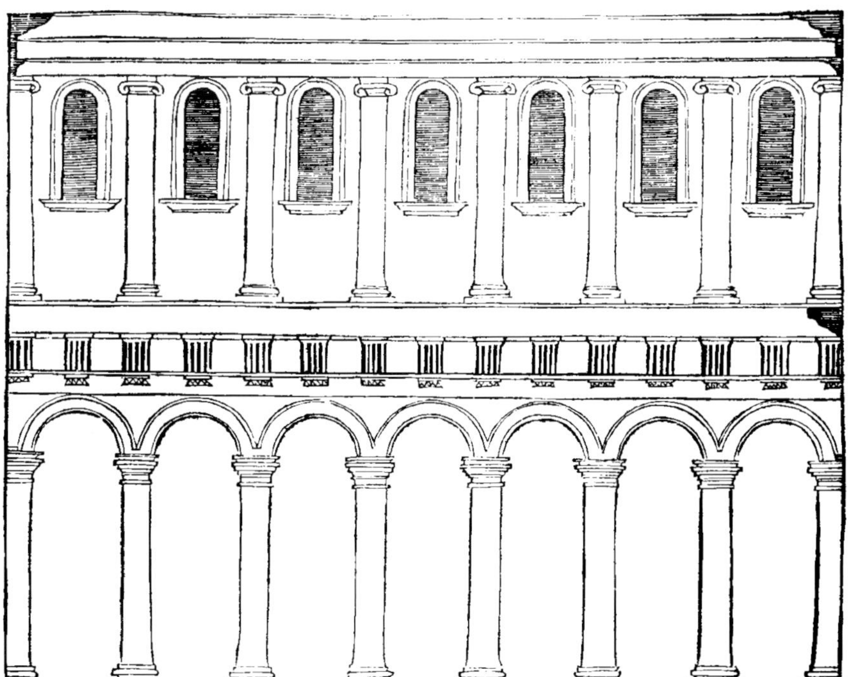

1.3 Drawing from Leon Battista Alberti, *De re aedificatoria* (1452).

For Alberti, the architectural window was to serve for light and ventilation. Windows were *translucent,* not transparent.[26] This will be an important component of the window's eventual function—in relation to the mobility and virtuality of the images *seen through* "virtual" windows. I will discuss the history of glass and issues of transparency further but suffice it to say here that fifteenth-century windows did not necessarily use glass nor were they necessarily transparent.[27] Alberti's window was a metaphoric trope,[28] at odds with his own account of an architectural window. Whereas for Alberti the painting was like a window, paintings are less like the open window of *De pictura* and more like the translucent window of *De re aedificatoria.*

3. "THE SUBJECT TO BE PAINTED"

"The subject to be painted" was, in Alberti's Latin text, *historia.*[29] *Historiae* were imaginative narrative paintings of great events and classical heroes, and were not landscapes or direct records of nature.[30] The Latin text is important here because it indicates that what has been translated as "the subject to be painted" is, in Latin, *historia:* "quod quidem mihi pro aperta finestra est ex qua historia contueatur." Alberti's text has frequently been misunderstood on this point: he boldly meant it as a formula for representation of narrative *historia,* not of empty landscapes or window-views.[31] Hence the window was deployed as a figure for the frame and did not imply that the "subject to be painted" should be a mimetic rendition of what one would see out of an architectural window, looking onto the natural world. I will return to this point because, contrary to the common and flawed use of Alberti's window as a model for realist representation, Alberti supplies us with a Renaissance root for the concept of a windowed "elsewhere"—not a realism of subject matter but a separate spatial and temporal view.

In the introduction to a 1972 translation of *De pictura,* Cecil Grayson addresses the window's metaphoric function as descriptive of the picture surface: "Hence his [Alberti's] famous visualization of painting as a window through which the observer, from a certain fixed viewpoint on this side, looks at the scene 'outside.' The painter's object is to represent on the surface corresponding to that window (the picture surface) the three-dimensional space 'beyond,' which is continuous with that in which he himself stands. The window is the intersection of the visual pyramid. . . ."[32] To Grayson, the observer looks "outside" and "beyond" from a fixed viewpoint (these are Grayson's words, not Alberti's). Grayson corrects the common assumption that Alberti meant for the window to open onto an un-tampered view of nature: "Although Alberti recommends this sort of activity for training and for studying the outlines and proportions of Nature, he is not, generally speaking, advocating a kind of through-the-window representation as the subject of art. The artist's object is certainly to give the spectator the spatial experience of window-gazing, in which the mathematics of vision and the general appearances and proportions of Nature will dictate basic relationships and attitudes. It does not follow from this methodological realism that the spectator should see a scene of 'real life.'"[33] Grayson's introduction draws out this oft-neglected distinction—between the window-view as determinant of the realism of representation and the window-view as the determinant of the spatial experience of the spectator. The nuance of this distinction is apparent in Erwin Panofksy's opening paragraph of his 1924 essay "Perspective as Symbolic Form": "We shall speak of a fully 'perspectival' view of space not when mere isolated objects, such as houses or furniture, are represented in 'foreshortening,' but rather only when the entire picture has been transformed—to cite another Renaissance theoretician—into a 'window' and when we are meant to believe we are looking through this window into a space."[34] The spectator's experience of "gazing" through the window had its own spatial effect—and yet this new perspectival realism of representational space did not imply realism of subject matter, nor, as we will see in a moment, did it imply a temporal realism.

"Alberti's all-too-famous Renaissance idea of a painted image as window-like does not simply apply to the (overall) surface of a painting, assumedly framed," argues Joseph Masheck in his critique of the persistent art historical misreading of the Albertian window.[35] The assumption that the painting was a window through which the world is seen is, in Masheck's account, a troubling "misprision" that became a key tenet of antimodernist critics who charged modernist painting with the violation of this "Renaissance-validated pictorial sense."[36] What is important about the Albertian window, Masheck argues, is not its view onto a natural world, but its metaphoric index of the frame. I will return to Masheck's correction of the Albertian metaphor because I too wish to emphasize the importance of the frame of the window as the grounding metaphysic of its view.[37]

4. THE BODY AS MEASURE: THE HUMAN AS CENTRIC POINT

Alberti places the human figure in this frame as the key measure, a calculable element for correct proportion. The *braccia* of the human body serves as the standard of reference for the relative size of all objects in the frame that "stand to each other in a determined relationship."[38] In Alberti's schema, the human figure is three *braccia* tall, and human height establishes the centric point "no higher from the base line than the height of the man to be represented in the

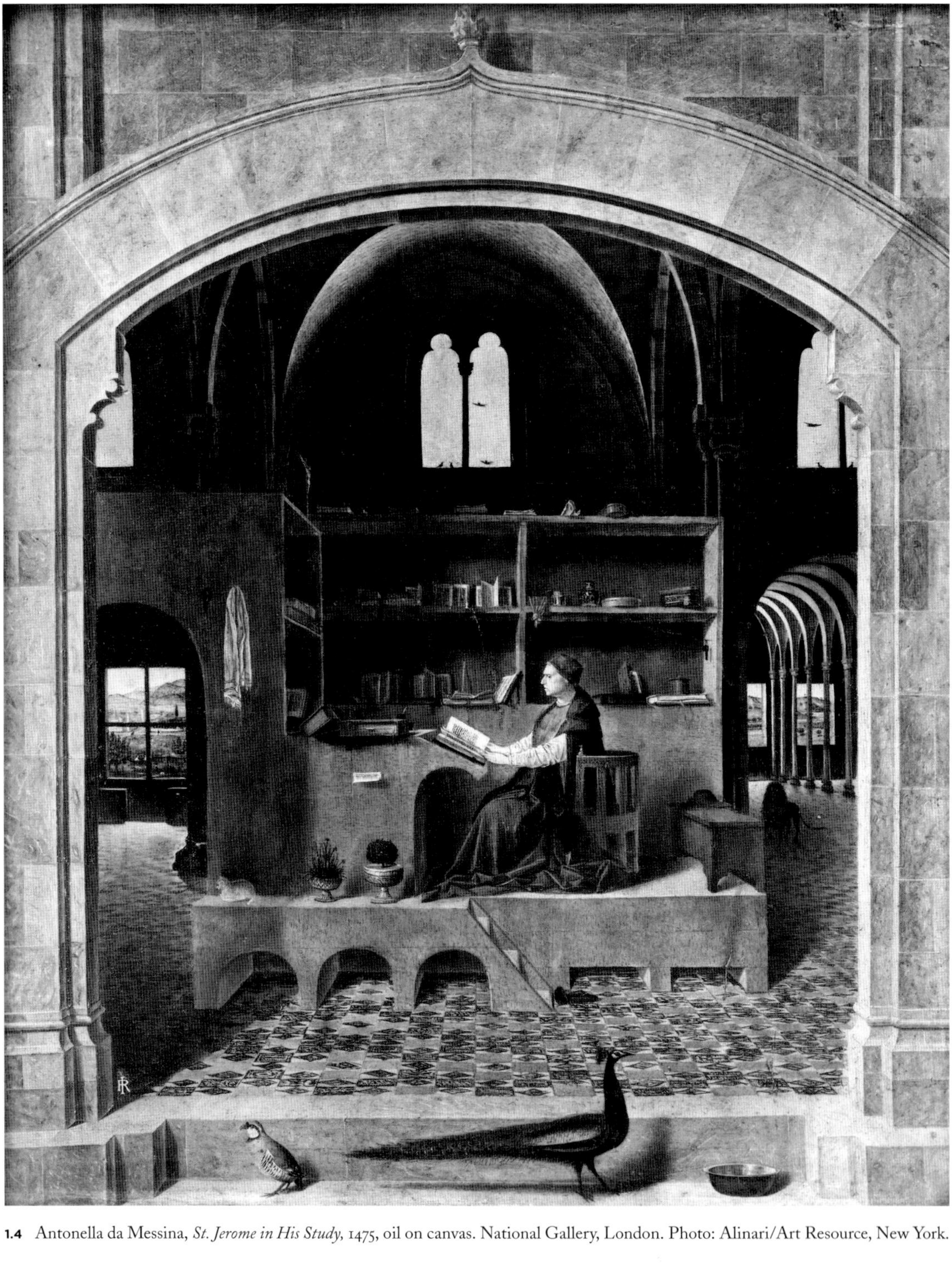

1.4 Antonella da Messina, *St. Jerome in His Study,* 1475, oil on canvas. National Gallery, London. Photo: Alinari/Art Resource, New York.

painting." The viewer is to be at the same height as the figure *in* the picture so that "both the viewers and the objects in the painting will seem to be on the same plane."[39] In this way, the body of the observer suggests a scale for the bodies in the representational confines of the painting. The human was in a central position as a spectator in front of a pictorial world but was also the measure of that world.[40] The painter's position was also to be the position of the viewer, framing and delimiting the image.

The mid-fifteenth-century painting *St. Jerome in His Study* provides an example of the idea of a picture as a view through a window: the painting is framed as if seen through an arched stone frame and ledge. Panofksy describes this painting as "an architectural exterior with the front removed"—a definitive "open" window.[41] Yet the painter, Antonella da Messina—almost as if to playfully taunt Alberti—places in the background of the painting a framed window with transparent glass, one that conforms to the mathematics of the perspectival vanishing point.[42] In the fifteenth-century study, the scholar does not look out of his window or into a screen, but holds a manuscript close for its illuminations.

In sum, Alberti's metaphoric "window" was a framing device for the geometrics of his perspective formula. While it implied a fixed position for the viewer of single point perspective, it did not assume or imply that the "subject to be painted" should be the exact view of what one would see out of an architectural window onto the natural world, as in a "window on the world." As a representational system, linear perspective was a technique for reproducing the space of what was seen on the *virtual* plane of representation. But if the logic of perspective produced a representation of pictorial space with the effect of window-gazing, it also placed new restrictions on a viewer who was, as one writer will describe, "immobilized by the logic of the system."[43]

5. IMMOBILITY OF THE VIEWER

In his study *Story and Space in Renaissance Art: The Rebirth of Continuous Narrative* (2001), Lew Andrews challenges traditional accounts of the spatial innovations of Renaissance perspective, symptomatically summarized by German art historian Dagobert Frey's assertion that the "simultaneous unity of content of painting is scientifically attained in perspective."[44] In Frey's account in *Gotik und Renaissance,* the immobility of the Renaissance spectator is drawn in sharp contrast to the Gothic viewer. The Gothic painting, according to Frey, "scrolls off, as it were, like a film before the observer, except that the successive pictorial impressions do not depend upon the mechanical movement of the film, but upon the intellectual movement of the viewer."[45]

This passage from Frey's 1929 study deploys a striking metaphor for the viewer's relation to the multiple time frames implied by multiple scenes within the single frame of a Gothic painting: "like a film before the observer." Frey is comparing the pre-Renaissance viewer of a painting with the mid-twentieth-century cinematic spectator. In Frey's account, the Renaissance painting was thought to be rooted in a fixed moment of time, more like a photograph with its viewer fixed and its image motionless. The Renaissance viewer, Frey maintains, "must not stray from [the fixed position of the beholder] if the illusion of space is to remain convincing."[46] The assumption here about Renaissance painting and one-point perspective is that it was "mono-scenic," that it detailed a single image in a single frame, a unified pictorial space frozen in a single moment of time.

Yet Andrews notes a troubling paradox in the representational logic of single-point perspective: he finds a striking persistence of "polyscenic" frescoes, panels, and reliefs in the Renaissance. Ghiberti's Baptistry doors in Florence and Masaccio's *Tribute Money* (1427), Andrews suggests, provide telling examples of representations that conform to the new dictates of a spatial realism, but oddly, do not adhere to a temporal realism. They contain a repetition of figures seen in a variety of narrative moments—a "continuous narrative" in a single frame. This form of "polyscenic painting" is consistent with Alberti's window metaphor as I've just discussed it—as a mathematical formula for realist space, in no way precluding the *historia* of a continuous narrative.

Andrews challenges Frey and generations of art historians who describe the "polyscenic" paintings of the Renaissance as only a residual "mistake," a carry-over from earlier systems of representation. Instead, Andrews finds that "continuous narrative" or "polyscenic" painting—long considered an anachronism in the Renaissance—not only remains present after the introduction of linear perspective but becomes perhaps even more prominent. Read backward from a teleology that assumed Renaissance perspective found its ultimate end with the invention of the mechanical apparatus of the photographic camera, the multiple time frames of polyscenic "continuous narrative" painting may have seemed a mistake. What is significant here for my larger argument is that Renaissance painting, long thought to be the rational representation of a single moment in a single space—the proto-equivalent of a photograph—may not have had this "snapshot" quality, but instead contained a fracturing of times within a single space. This single insight challenges the common belief in a teleology leading from Renaissance perspective to the photographic camera, and will profoundly alter theories of the perspectival functioning of the cinematic image.

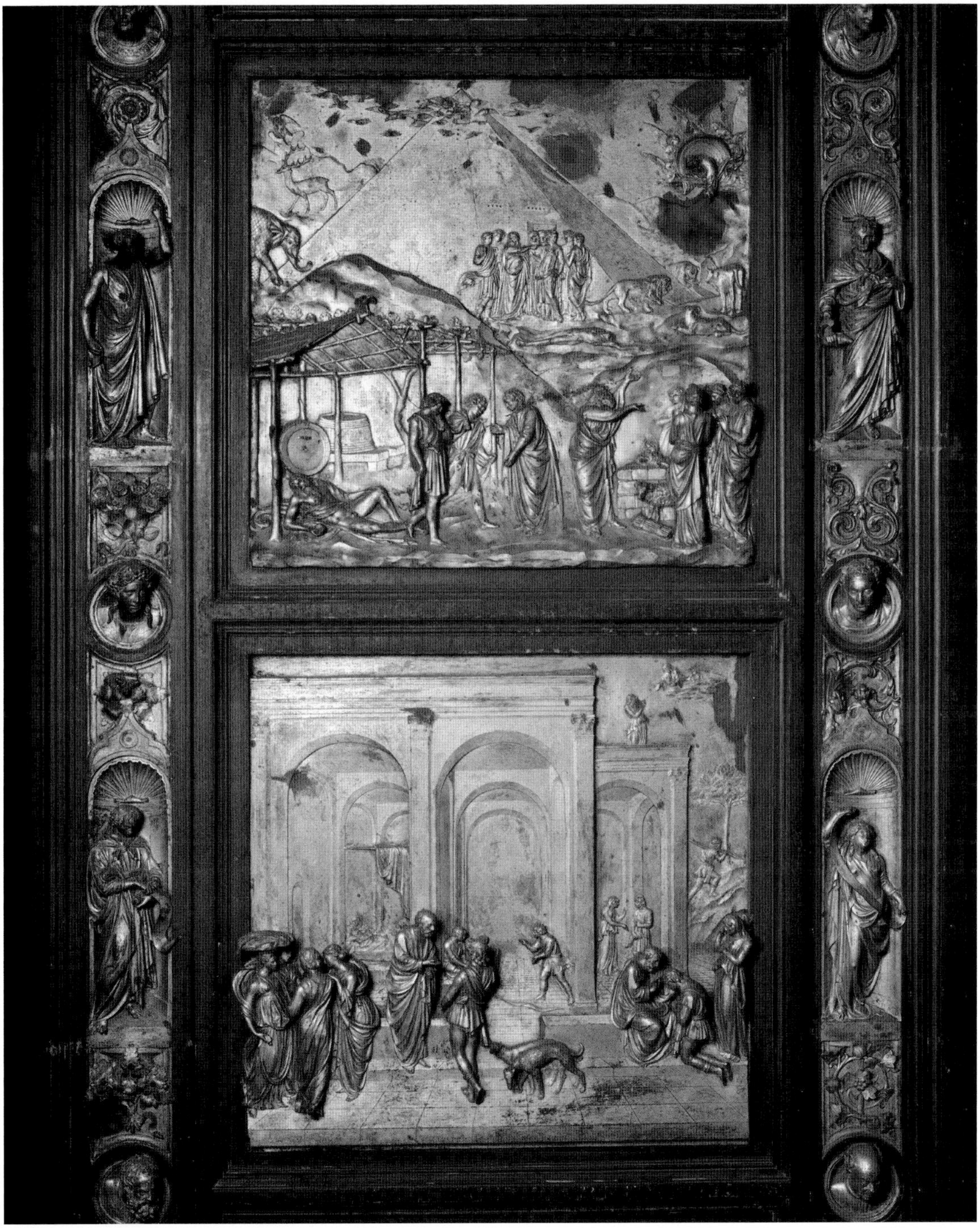

1.5 Detail of Lorenzo Ghiberti's *Gates of Paradise* (east doors), 1403–1424: story of Noah and Esau. Baptistry, Florence. Photo: Scala/Art Resource, New York.

The histories of perspective practice and its theories—the treatises, manuals, and mechanical and illusionistic devices that proliferated after Alberti—complicate any assumption of a perseverance of a single representational technique.[47] And, as many commentators on Renaissance painting have detailed, the rules of perspective proffered by Alberti and other theoretical advocates were not necessarily followed by painters, and did not imply the fixed viewer often assumed. Michael Kubovy argues, for example, that the Renaissance painting may have been viewed from other positions than the apex of the visual pyramid.[48] As Leo Steinberg has masterfully demonstrated in his analysis of *The Last Supper,* Leonardo violated his own rules on the correspondence between the center of projection and the viewer's vantage.[49] And Svetlana Alpers has contrasted the framed picture surface of Italian painting with the surfaces of paintings by northern European artists (Vermeer, van Eyck, de Hooch), whose impulses, she claims, are more descriptive than narrative, less interested in the frame, more entranced with surfaces than depth.[50] The litany of questions that began this chapter remain testimony to the unease scholars have with reductive caricatures of the Renaissance representational system implied by perspective and its frame. Yet two points remain clear: (1) the frame of the window was an important metaphor for constructing the coherent spatial arrangement of objects on the picture surface, and (2) the single spatial frame of perspectival representation did not always imply a single frame of time.

THE WINDOW, THE *VELO*-GRID, THE FRAME

As we've just seen, in Alberti's geometric formula for creating the representational space of perspective, the window served as a metaphor for the rectangle of perspectival rendering, the frame of the picture plane. In *De pictura,* Alberti also described another framing device that, while not named as a window, functions in a similar way. The "veil" (*velo*) is "a grid-like netting stretched on a frame": "It is like this: a veil loosely woven of fine thread, dyed whatever colour you please, divided up by thicker threads into as many parallel square sections as you like, and stretched on a frame. I set this between the eye and the object to be represented, so that the visual pyramid passes through the loose weave of the veil."[51] But while Alberti suggested the rectangular frame and planar surface of a metaphoric "window" as a device for geometrical calculation, his *velo* did not require the calculation of orthogonals and vanishing points. It was, instead, dependent solely on its frame and its inset quadrants as a device to "map" the three-dimensional world onto a two-dimensional plane. "This veil affords the greatest assistance in executing your picture," Alberti instructed his readers, "since you can see any object that is round and in relief, represented on the flat surface of the veil."[52] With the *velo,* the artist divided the image into separate squares of a reticulated net. The grid of Alberti's *velo* forms a direct antecedent to the "bit-mapped" computer screen where picture elements—pixels—are "mapped" onto digital "bits."[53]

Leonardo described a similar perspective aid—with a plane of glass encased in the frame—which is illustrated with the drawing shown in figure 1.2. In a note from 1490, he explained: "the eye is to be placed at a distance from the glass of 2/3 *braccio* and the head is fixed by an instrument in such a way that the head may not be moved at all."[54] Leonardo's perspective frame used the transparency of glass as surface for the artist, an aid for reducing the proportions and forms of solid bodies to a planar surface. A variety of perspective "frames" are illustrated in the woodcut illustration in the first and second editions of Dürer's *Underweysung der Messung* (Treatise on Measurement) of 1525 and 1538. Unlike Alberti's unillustrated, pre-Gutenberg treatise, Dürer's woodcut illustrations of drawing devices illustrate the use of this *velo*-like frame for draftsmen. It was primarily through the reproductive technologies of print (in print, via print) that image-making devices like the perspective window were disseminated and held their power.[55]

As Dürer explained it: "*Perspectiva* is a Latin word which means 'seeing through.'" This is also the first sentence of Erwin Panofksy's seminal essay, "Die Perspektive als 'symbolische Form'": "Item Perspectiva ist ein lateinisch Wort, bedeutt ein Durchsehung."[56] The *velo*-frame did not rely on the geometric formulas for perspective delineated in Alberti's window metaphor, and yet it did posit a transparent plane for "seeing through." In one Dürer woodcut, the artist sits in front of a window-like grid through which he measures his subject. The latticework of the *velo*-frame aided the artist in translating the three-dimensional natural world onto the two-dimensional virtual plane of the picture surface. This well-known image—with the artist, male; the subject, voluptuous, reclining, and female—has often been used to indicate the

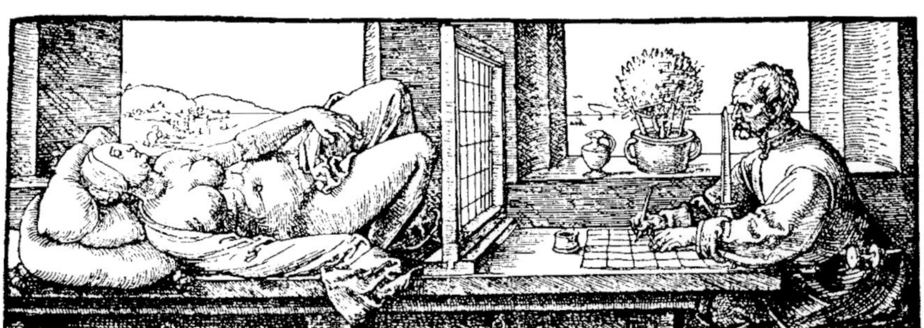

1.6 Woodcut illustration from Albrecht Dürer, *Underweysung der Messung* (Nuremberg, 1538).

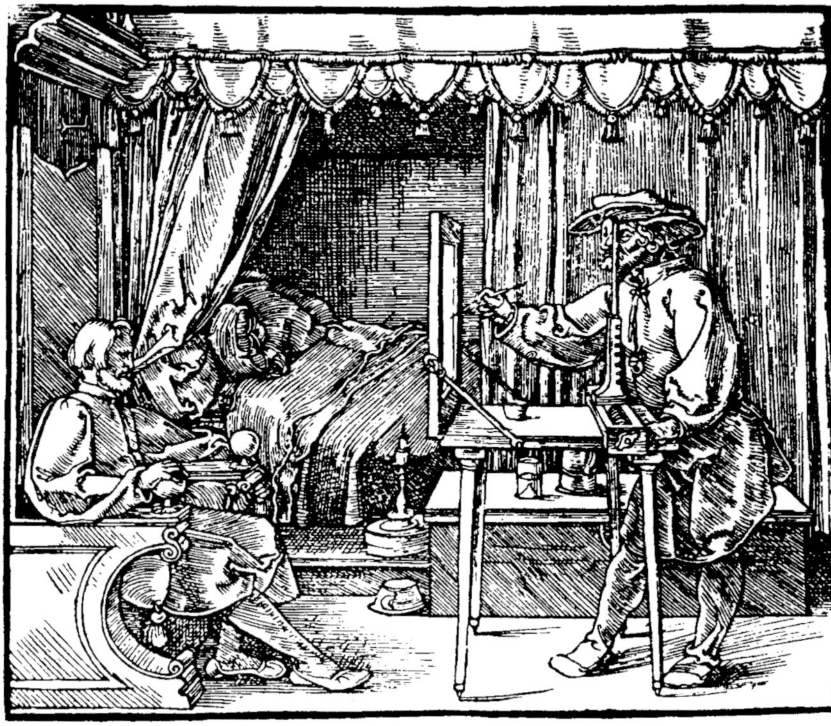

1.7 Woodcut illustration from Albrecht Dürer, *Underweysung der Messung* (Nuremberg, 1525).

gendered difference between the holder of focal-point perspective and the massive three-dimensional subject of this perspective. While the window served as perspective's practical metaphor, the *velo* served as its practical instrument. Both relied on a frame, a rectangular aperture that was to hold the two-dimensional plane of the picture.

Although another sixteenth-century woodcut (figure 1.8) provides an excellent illustration of the use of the window itself as an aid in representation, it should be noted that the artist here uses the gridlike sections of the window as his drawing aid (the *velo* as window) instead of the mathematical formulas for perspective outlined by Alberti. Despite the different techniques of perspectival rendering, the common attribution of these devices as "windows"—often with marked neglect of their very different techniques—was based in the shared feature of a framed image—framed by the artist, seen in a frame by the viewer—facing a coherent spatial arrangement of objects in depth.

While the transparency of "seeing through" (*durchsehen*) the picture plane was shared by both the window and the *velo,* the picture surface was itself materially opaque.[57] A picture plane covered with layers of pigment became the

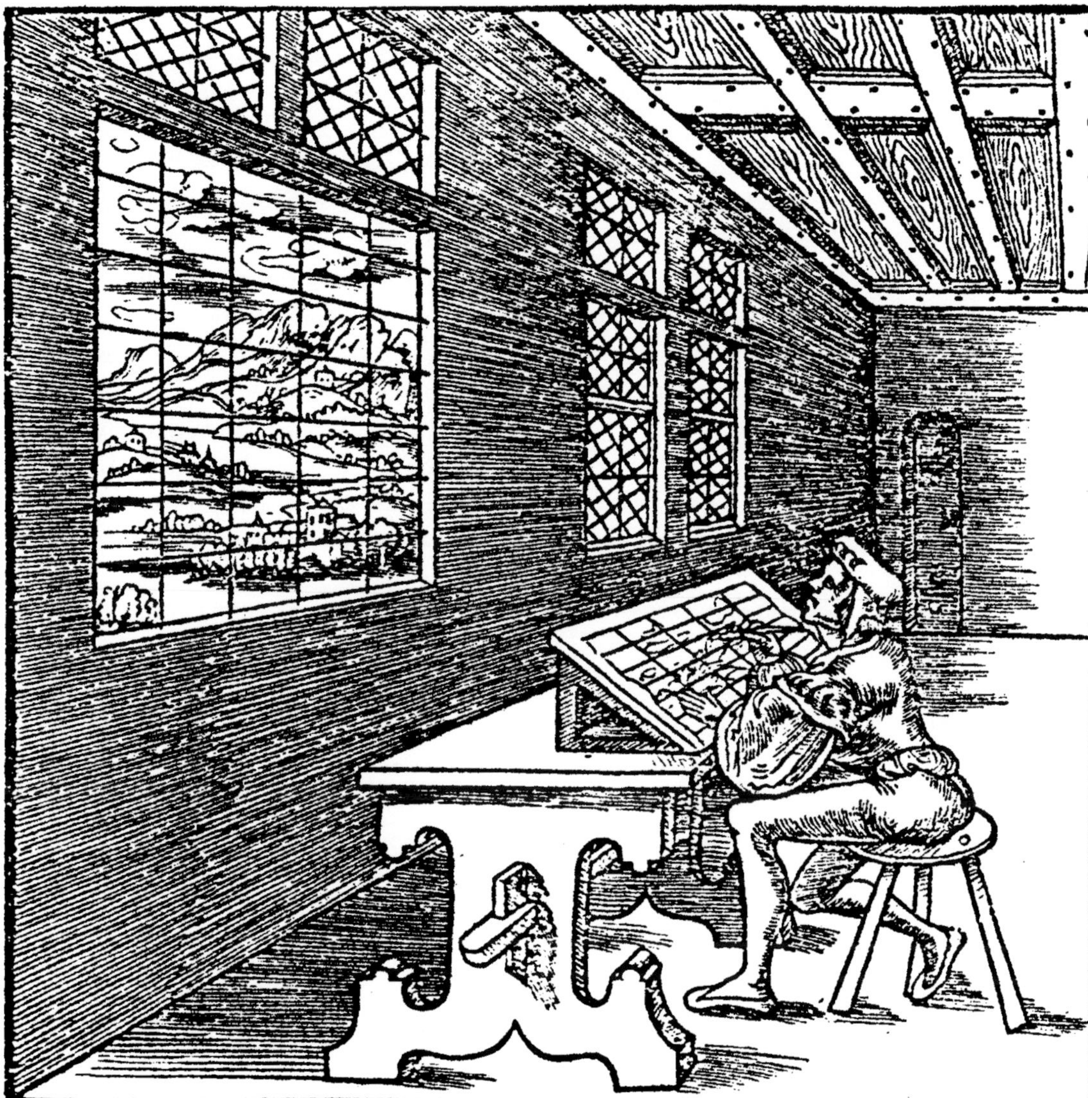

1.8 Woodcut illustration from Johann II of Bavaria and Hieronymus Rodler, *Ein schön nützlich büchlein und unterweisung der Kunst des Messens* (Siemern, 1531).

material logic of Western oil painting: the painter, following what Norman Bryson has termed an "erasive imperative," applied a thickness of paint that eclipsed the surface of the picture plane.[58] Hence the metaphoric transparency of the picture plane belied its material opacity. The opacity of the picture plane, and later—as I will discuss—the material opacity of screenic surfaces of the cinema, television, and computer screen form the necessary precondition for virtual representation. The material opacity of the painting surface was already a step in the direction of a window with only a *virtual* transparency.

While the window was more of a metaphor than a mechanical apparatus, like other perspective devices, it served to transfer the skills of image-making from the artist to a mechanical aid. As Martin Kemp notes in *The Science of Art,* the "mechanical artlessness" of these "perspective machines" was criticized when they first appeared.[59] Alberti's and Brunelleschi's attraction to mechanical aids for drawing may have been an extension of their reliance on other medieval instruments—the quadrant and the astrolabe—used for surveying and measurement. As Kemp further notes, "sighting" devices for mapping and measurement led to later drawing machines like Cigoli's perspectograph and Scheiner's pantograph, devices which further automated the mechanics of representation for the draftsman. Although there were numerous treatises that described and illustrated the many variations of drawing devices and perspective "machines," their actual use in pictorial practice remains a matter of art historical debate.

THE METAPHYSICS OF PERSPECTIVE

PERSPECTIVE AS "SYMBOLIC FORM"

Erwin Panofsky, writing in 1924, found the metaphysics of perspective clearly recognizable. Although many writers have challenged crucial elements of Panofksy's account, his argument about perspective as "symbolic form" forcefully posits a modern sense of space (*Raumgefühl*) and sense of the world (*Weltfühl*) conditioned by "habituation" to looking at perspective constructions.[60] Borrowing a "felicitous" term from Ernst Cassirer, Erwin Panofsky describes perspective as a historically specific system of spatial representation, a "symbolic form."[61] In his "Perspective as Symbolic Form," Panofsky suggests that rather than presenting a correct rendition of reality, *perspectiva artificialis* presented instead a "rather bold abstraction from reality": "'central perspective' makes two tacit but essential assumptions: first, that we see with a single and immobile eye, and second, that the planar cross section of the visual pyramid can pass for an adequate reproduction of our optical image. In fact these two premises are rather bold abstractions from reality."[62] With such a "fundamental discrepancy between 'reality' and its construction," perspective transformed "psychophysiological space" into a "mathematical space," ordered and rational.[63] This new mathematical space was—to Panofsky—an "evolution" from the aggregate multiplicity of medieval and Gothic visual systems and at the same time a "return" to ancient variations on perspective.[64] In a sharp, descriptive passage on the representational surface, Panofsky suggests the transformative effects of this new sense of space on the picture plane:

> The surface is now no longer the wall or the panel bearing the forms of individual things and figures, but rather is once again that transparent plane through which we are meant to believe that we are looking into a space, even if that space is still bounded on all sides. We may already define this surface as a "picture plane," in the precise sense of the term. The view that had been blocked since antiquity, the vista or "looking through," has begun to open again; and we sense the possibility that the painted picture will once again become a section cut from infinite space, only a more solid and more integrally organized space than the antique version.[65]

And, in a remarkable comment delivered almost in passing, Panofksy suggests that our perceptual habituation to flat, noncurvilinear surfaces is "reinforced by looking at photographs": "And indeed, if even today only a very few of us have perceived these curvatures, that too is surely in part due to our habituation—further reinforced by looking at photographs—to linear perspectival construction: a construction that is itself comprehensible only for a quite specific, indeed specifically modern, sense of space [*Raumgefühl*], or if you will, sense of the world [*Weltfühl*]."[66] The fixity of the viewer's vantage—the picture seen from only one point in space—was an essential component of this new representational system of objects in space.[67] In the final section of his essay, Panofsky restates the import of perspective's translation of psychophysiological space into mathematical space—"In other words," he asserts boldly, "an objectification of the subjective."[68] Panofksy reduces this epistemological claim to an aphorism of twin "triumphs": "Thus the history of perspective may be understood with equal justice as a triumph of *the distancing and objectifying sense of the real* and as a triumph of the *distance-denying human struggle for control*."[69] The transformation of space, and its newfound unity through perspective, takes on a metaphysical significance and "finds its theoretical analogue in the view of space of contemporary philosophy."[70] Perspective, he writes, "is as much a consolidation and systematization of the external world, as an extension of the domain of the self. . . . [Through perspective] the 'claim' of the object . . . confronts the ambition of the subject."[71] Although Panofsky does not make the direct equation between the "ambition of the subject" and the Cartesian *cogito,* he hints at it: "And yet this view of space, even with its still mystical coloring, is the same view that will later be rationalized by Cartesianism and formalized by Kantianism."[72]

Panofsky's 1924 essay positions perspective as a change of human perception in a historical context—a cultural topos comparable to Thomas Kuhn's notion of "paradigm," Foucault's "episteme," or what Martin Jay (via Christian Metz) will call a "scopic regime."[73] But if perspective was a historically specific "symbolic form," it too could pass as complex historical conditions change. In 1924, Panofsky writes about perspective on the cusp of the form's symbolic decline.

Here, it is striking how—as perhaps the only historian of perspective to also write about the moving image—Panofsky shied away from making the same forceful claims about the cinema as the new mode of viewing and representation of his century. If, as Panofsky suggests, perspective habituated its viewers, conditioning their perception of space and time, it would seem that his various talks and essays on the "movies," the "moving picture," or the "motion picture" might suggest that the moving image heralds a new "symbolic form." Yet Panofksy never makes this claim.

In November 1936, as a recent émigré to the United States and as a renowned art historian with a European pedigree, Panofsky gave a lecture entitled "The Motion Picture as an Art" in the bastion of tradition and high culture, the Metropolitan Museum of Art in New York. In June 1936, he published "On Movies" (taken from an informal lecture given in 1934), an essay that was revised and retitled "Style and Medium in the Moving Picture" and published in Eugene Jolas's expatriate American "little magazine" *transition* in 1937 alongside *Finnegans Wake* as a "work in progress." Panofsky revised the essay again in 1947 as "Style and Medium in the Motion Picture," and this widely circulated revision served to further legitimate the "motion picture as an art."[74] "Style and Medium in the Motion Picture" (1947) has long been included in film anthologies as a canonical example of the early theorization of cinema's specificity as a "medium," and yet it has only recently been brought into contrastive relation to Panofsky's art historical writing. Thomas Y. Levin notes the "virtually complete lack of serious scholarly work on Panofsky's film essay in the art historical secondary literature" and the corollary neglect in film studies where Panofksy's essay is "almost completely absent from the canonical historiography of film theory."[75]

Panofsky's interest in the newly evolving "moving" image figures in the larger historical confluence of the technical development of the moving image with the foundations of art history as a discipline in the late nineteenth century. Panofsky's essay begins: "Film art is the only art the development of which men now living have witnessed from the very beginnings."[76] His role alongside Siegfried Kracauer, another German émigré, at the first annual meeting of the Society of Cinematologists at the NYU faculty club in April 1960 suggests that Panofsky was an early representative of the changes to disciplinary boundary and method.

Although the title of Panofksy's essay indicates his concern with film "style," the essay has, as Levin points out, "a focus on content which almost completely disregards questions of cinematic form."[77] Nevertheless, Panofsky's incisive isolation of the twin qualities of cinematic specificity—the "dynamization of space" and the "spatialization of time"—suggests that he also had insights into the "medium." Panofsky tosses off his diagnosis of these "unique and specific possibilities" as "self-evident to the point of triviality."[78] But when held up to his writing on perspective as "a concrete expression of a contemporary advance in epistemology or natural philosophy," these chiasmic opposites begin to posit "the movies" as a new form of space-time perception, a post-perspectival "symbolic form."[79]

Another essay from 1936 made dramatic claims about the medium-specific qualities of film and consequent changes in perception. While not received as such at the time, Walter Benjamin's "Work of Art in the Age of Mechanical Reproduction" essay became a central piece of twentieth-century cultural criticism, a canonical essay marking new configurations of time and space in the "age" (read "episteme," "paradigm," "symbolic form") of "technical reproducibility." Panofsky's essay "On Movies" (written in English and published in June 1936) and Walter Benjamin's "Work of Art" essay (written in German in January/February 1936 and published in French in *Zeitschrift für Sozialforschung* later in 1936) seem in retrospect to mark a shared cultural moment of insight into the new medium.[80] Not only were both authors writing in a language that was not their own, they each were attempting to isolate the specificities of another new, and somewhat foreign, visual language.

Like Panofsky, Benjamin asserts the historicity of vision, that changes in perception are determined by and, in turn, determine their historical context. Benjamin's essay contains a sharp critique of the Viennese school of art historians (Alois Riegl and Franz Wickhoff) for not drawing conclusions about the social effects of these changes in perception:

> During long periods of history, the mode of human sense perception changes with humanity's entire mode of existence. *The manner in which human perception is organized, the medium in which it is accomplished, is determined not only by nature but by historical circumstances as well.* The fifth century, with its great shifts of population, saw the birth of the late Roman art industry and the Vienna Genesis, and there developed not only an art different from that of antiquity but also a new kind of perception. The scholars of the Viennese school, Riegl and Wickhoff, who resisted the weight of classical tradition under which these later art forms had been buried, were the first to draw conclusions from them concerning the organization of perception at the

time. However far-reaching their insight, these scholars limited themselves to showing the significant, formal hallmark which characterized perception in late Roman times. They did not attempt—and perhaps, saw no way—to show the social transformations expressed by these changes of perception. The conditions for an analogous insight are more favorable in the present.[81]

Benjamin locates these changes in the "apperceptive apparatus" in the material conditions of urban life. "The film corresponds to profound changes in the apperceptive apparatus," he writes in a footnote, "changes that are experienced on an individual scale by the man in the street in big-city traffic, on a historical scale by every present-day citizen."[82]

In this regard, it is interesting to consider what Panofsky's essay did not claim: Panofsky did not suggest anything about the film viewer's perception, nor did he speculate on film's metaphysical or metapsychological effects. Rather, his film essay is often cited for an aphorism drawn in contradiction to the auteurist claim of single authorship: "It might be said that a film, called into being by a co-operative effort in which all contributions have the same degree of permanence, is the nearest modern equivalent of a medieval cathedral."[83] By contrast, Benjamin's invocation of architecture as an analogy for the film medium interrogated the "use and perception" of such buildings. His much-contested assertion that "Architecture has always represented the prototype of a work of art the reception of which is consummated by a collectivity in a state of distraction" led to his theorization of the "profound changes in apperception" represented in the film spectator.[84] I will return to Benjamin's discussion of the "distracted person" (*der Zerstreute*) when I discuss "multitasking" and its potential consequences for the contemporary "apperceptive apparatus."

Panofksy's writing on perspective had a split critical optic: he could clearly assert that perspectival representation conditioned the viewer's perception of space and time, but he would not make the same claims about the representational practices of his own age. Panofsky's visual acuity may have been a determinative: he was nearsighted in one eye and farsighted in the other. His eyesight may have formed a critical corollary to his own vision of the historical near and the historical far.[85]

THE CARTESIAN COINCIDENCE: "CARTESIAN PERSPECTIVALISM"

The "single and immobile eye" of perspective, as Panofsky terms it, enacted a fiction, a visuality at odds with vision. Its Cyclopean viewer remained fixed, focused, immobile. The frame of perspective produced a separation of the represented world from its viewer who, at an objectifying distance from it, was still able to measure its near and its far.

In this regard, the positioned view of single-point perspective has been frequently conflated—in a posited historical "coincidence"—with the metaphysical position of the Cartesian subject: centered and stable, autonomous and thinking, standing outside of the world. In all cases, the language of this equation—whether used by philosophers, art historians, or film theorists—bespeaks a historical elision, what I will call the Cartesian coincidence.[86]

Martin Jay notes this common equation between Cartesian metaphysics and the metaphysics of perspective and, "for convenience," names it—even as he marks its "radical dethroning"—as "Cartesian perspectivalism."[87] In his essay "The Scopic Regimes of Modernity," Jay characterizes a widespread and ongoing critique of perspective's implicit metaphysic for its "privileging of an ahistorical, disinterested, disembodied subject entirely outside of the world it claims to know only from afar."[88] Although perspective was, in Jay's account, "in league with" the "dispassionate eye" of "a scientific world view" and complicit with the bourgeois ethic of Florentine business, as the painting became a portable commodity in capitalist exchange, the oversight of the perspectivalist regime was such that "the bodies of the painter and viewer were forgotten in the name of an allegedly disincarnated, absolute eye."[89] Hence, the similarity between the viewer of perspective and the Cartesian "subject" is based on the implied separation of the viewer from the world viewed, the spectator from the spectacle. Jay challenges those who have invoked the combined optic of "Cartesian perspectivalism" as "*the* reigning visual model of modernity" and suggests, instead, that it was only one of several "scopic regimes" or "visual subcultures" in the modern era.[90]

Nevertheless, the combinant metaphysic "Cartesian perspectivalism" is a somewhat shaky conflation. The forced homology between perspective's fifteenth-century representational system and Descartes's seventeenth-century meditations on the separation of subject and object all too tidily elides the two centuries between Alberti and Descartes.[91] Unlike that of Alberti and other Renaissance theorists, Descartes's interest in optical processes and devices was deeply rooted in a philosophical skepticism about knowledge attained through the senses, particularly vision.[92] Deeply distrustful of perspective, Descartes was more interested in optical trickery and anamorphosis—how representations depart from reality—than in representations that attempt to offer a veridical reinstatement of it.

The devices and techniques for perspective that relied on the monocular "point" of view of the artist also assumed that the viewer would occupy an equivalent position in relation to the image; that the viewer must apprehend the image from the same vantage as the painter. This conflation of "points" of view became of key importance to philosophers and is perhaps the reason that the philosophical paradigm of perspective may have overtaken its use as a practical device. For Descartes, and later for Heidegger, the "standing in front of"—observing from a fixed point in relation to a framed image—became equated with a philosophical position, a *Weltbild,* which transformed the world into a measurable object.[93]

Many recent debates about visuality have pitted Cartesian-based theories of *disembodiment*—which hold that the viewer is separate from the world, disincarnated in vision—against phenomenologically based theories of *embodiment,* which root sight in its bodily organ. But the term "embodiment" also cuts across theories of virtuality and accounts of how we experience realities that are mediated and virtual.[94]

In the next chapter, I will return to the representational transfer of the three-dimensional space of the phenomenal world onto the two-dimensional virtual plane of representation and examine the camera obscura—a perspective device often conflated with Alberti's window. The camera obscura will lead us to examine competing historiographical accounts of the relationship between Renaissance perspective and the photographic and moving image.

LENS I

DESCARTES'S WINDOW

IN HIS treatise on lenses and their refraction, *La dioptrique* (1637), Descartes draws upon the camera obscura as an analogy for the operation of the eye: "Now it is said that this room represents the eye; the hole, the pupil; the lens, the crystalline humour." As exemplar of this "ingenious comparison," Descartes recommends a macabre experiment using the cross-section of the eye of a newly dead man or another large animal to illustrate the operation of vision.[1] He instructs:

> Take an eye of a newly dead man (or failing that, of an ox or some other large animal); carefully cut away the three enveloping membranes at the back, so as to expose a large part of the humour without shedding any; then cover the hole with some white body, thin enough to let daylight through (e.g. a piece of paper or eggshell). Now put this eye in the hole of a *specially made shutter*, so that its front faces a spot where there are a number of objects lit up by the sun, and the back where the white body is, faces the inside of the room you are in. (No light must enter the room except through the eye. . . .) If you now look at the white body, you will see (I dare say with surprise and pleasure) a picture representing in natural perspective all the objects outside. . . . Further the images of objects are not only produced in the back of the eye but also sent on to the brain.[2]

In this description of the eye as a camera obscura, Descartes uses the word *fenestre*—window—to describe the hole in the eye—the "shutter" or lens—that lets light through and focuses it onto the retina. While most translations of Descartes eliminate the window reference and use another term to describe the opening, I mention it here to underline this key etymological root for the window as mediating lens to vision—a window-lens producing a *pictura*.[3]

Descartes drew his epistemological conclusions about vision from Kepler's work on the optical principles of the retinal screen. In *Ad Vitellionem paralipomena* (1604), Kepler invoked the apparatical model of the camera obscura in order to explain how and why the image on the retina—the *pictura*—was inverted.[4] In the camera obscura model for vision, the aperture forms a *pictura* through the crystalline lens of the eye. The *pictura* has a materiality of its own, but one quite different from that of the object in the world. Although Kepler was the first to describe the inverted "pictura" on the back of the retina in his 1604 *Ad Vitellionem paralipomena,* he had no drawing to illustrate it. The 1637 Leiden edition of Descartes's *La dioptrique* included an illustration of this theory of the retinal image.

Descartes's interest in optics, perspective, painting, automata, telescopes, and mirrors suggests his investment in the distinction between the image and its representation.[5] Vision was determined by the perceiving eye, a concept that gave a powerful priority to the viewing subject.[6] To constitute subjectivity through vision meant not just *cogito ergo sum,* but also *video ergo sum.* Descartes's epistemological skepticism—his doubt about the reliability of knowledge derived from the senses—had a direct bearing on his mechanical, physiological, and geometric account of vision in *Dioptrics.* He wrote *Dioptrics* as an illustration of the philosophical method detailed in his *Discourse on Method* (1637). Descartes's distrust of knowledge acquired through sight and his scientific interest in pinpointing the optical and veridical properties of vision suggest both its denigration and its veneration.

Although Descartes does not taxonomize the different registers of unmediated vision, vision mediated by representation, and vision mediated by instrument, he does assign a priority to the viewer-perceiver's response to the object perceived. In his account, a picture depicts an object by causing a sensory perception of its qualities—light, color, position, distance, size, and shape. Resemblances do not explain representation: "in order to be more perfect *qua* images, and to represent the object better, it is necessary for the engravings not to resemble it."[7] Clearly Descartes has an ambivalent position toward the mimetic relation of the object of vision to its representation. Lenses are useful for "making vision more perfect" and yet, to be more perfect, engraving/representation should not resemble the object.[8]

Discourse on Method served as a self-reflexive preamble to *Meditations on First Philosophy* (1641). In this passage from *Meditations,* we find Descartes at his window, in a contemplative mode about the epistemologies of vision: "I chanced, however, to look out of the window, and see men walking in the street; now I say in ordinary language that I 'see' them . . . [But] what can I see besides hats and coats which may cover automata?"[9] Here, the window separates Descartes from direct knowledge of what is on the street below, and hence from certainty. Descartes may be "seeing" men on the street below, but their hats and coats might also conceal that they are not men, but their machine-others, soulless automatons. Vision out the window is not unlike vision through the glass lens of a telescope or microscope—mediated, and producing questionable knowledge.

Descartes's meditation on the *mediation* of the window reveals an anxiety basic to the Cartesian premise: How does one distinguish between "man" and machine, automata without soul or consciousness? Indeed, one might at first think Descartes meant to distinguish between the "human" (not "man") and the machine, but the anecdote which follows may suggest otherwise.

Descartes himself was no stranger to automatons.[10] Here, a piece of apocryphal biography—which might be placed in a lengthy footnote—seems important to draw forth: Descartes, it is said, traveled with a life-sized female automaton named after his illegitimate daughter Francine. (That his daughter was produced by a one-night liaison with a chambermaid during his study of fetuses in *Anatomica* 1634,[11] and—as another source claims—that she was named after the Francini Brothers, makers of mechanical moving statues, lead us to conclude that the so-called *father* of modern philosophy was also a "seminal" thinker about artificial intelligence and the kinkier pleasures of cyber-sex.) One source claims Descartes had this companionate female doll constructed to "show that animals are only machines and have no souls," while others maintain that this story was used as a piece of sexual innuendo to discredit Descartes and his eighteenth-century followers. Either way, the anecdote seems to extend Descartes's theory of animals as soulless nonthinkers to women and to conflate the body of woman with the machine. Animals, to Descartes, may have perceptual cognition (unlike clocks and other machines), but they functioned only in mechanical terms and, hence like machines, had no souls. Women, it would seem, hover nearer to the bestial side of this *bête*-machine versus human divide. If women are not animals, they are not thinkers either. As Genevieve Lloyd asserts: "We owe to Descartes an influential and pervasive theory of mind, which provides support for a powerful version of the sexual division of mental labour. Women have been assigned responsibility for that realm of the sensuous which the Cartesian Man of Reason must transcend, if he is to have true knowledge of things."[12]

In fact, Descartes's question at the window (*but what can I see besides hats and coats which may cover automata?*) suggests that he was asking some of the same questions—how to distinguish between "man" and machine—that preoccupied Alan Turing and others conducting mid-twentieth-century cybernetic research.[13] The "Turing test"—the "imitation game" proposed by Alan Turing in his 1950 article "Computing Machinery and Intelligence"—proposed to answer the question "Can machines think?" Of course, most often the Turing test is remembered as a way to separate humans from androids, thinkers from machines.[14] But if we add the gender components of Turing's original proposal, the question of gender becomes as it has with Descartes—an oft-repressed but crucial term of difference in the differential calculus of "men" and machine.

Imagine the Turing test as a TV game show: backstage, unseen contestants teletype their answers to questions posed by an onscreen interrogator. Their object is to stump the interrogator: to conduct a textual masquerade so that the interrogator cannot tell who is male and who is female. Turing insisted on the mediation of response—visual clues are reduced to type: no voice, no image, only text. After the male/female test is completed, Round Two: Turing suggests that a machine assume the masquerade: "We now ask the question, 'What will happen when a machine takes the part of A [the man] in this game?' Will the interrogator decide wrongly as often when the game is played like this as he does when the game is played between a man and a woman? These questions replace our original, 'Can machines think?'"[15]

The logic here takes a curious form. In order to answer the question "Can machines think?" Turing asks the interrogator to see if machines can be distinguished from humans in the same manner that women can be distinguished from men—through language, but not through visual appearance. Turing directly parallels gender masquerade with the masquerade of the machine.

N. Katherine Hayles begins her account *How We Became Posthuman* by recalling the Turing test: "Here, at the inaugural moment of the computer age," Hayles writes, "the erasure of embodiment is performed so that 'intelligence' becomes a property of the formal manipulation of symbols rather than enaction in the human life-world."[16] Hayles is drawn to the Turing test because it exemplifies the type of disembodiment she finds in the "cybernetic tradition." She has a passionate stake in arguing against the "posthuman" assumption that consciousness can be separated from the fleshy materiality of the human body—that it could be "downloaded" into a bodiless substrate. The Turing test pits an "enacted" body against a "represented" body—yet a body that is represented only by verbal and semiotic signifiers. Hayles hints at the subversive challenge implicit in posing this game: If you solve the riddle of gender disguise—match the represented body with the correct enacted body — then you have reunited the two into a single correct gender identity. If you fail, you have only acknowledged the possibility that identity has become contingent to or dependent upon its technological mediation.

Information may have "lost its body," as Hayles suggests, and Turing's test may indeed be a telling instance of this loss.[17] Hayles asks: "Why does gender appear at this primal scene of humans meeting their evolutionary successors, intelligent machines?" Here I read into Turing's "game" a primal wish that may explain his alignment of gender masquerade with the Pinocchio-into-real-boy masquerade of the machine. In both tests, the enigma of identity acknowledges identity's dependence on its technological mediation but also identity's new freedom from the body. Imagine Turing as one of the contestants, wishing to be neither man nor woman, but machine. "What does Turing want?" His answer may have come a decade or so later from a much more flagrant but no less tortured Andy Warhol, who whined: "I want to be a machine."

So: let's bring Descartes at his window and Alan Turing behind the teletype "screen" onto the register of virtuality for a moment and ask some contemporary questions about how we know what we know.

Descartes premised his own epistemological skepticism by questioning knowledge inferred from the senses. The newly fashioned term "tele-epistemology"[18] helps to describe the technological extensions of the original Cartesian separation of the subject outside of/in front of the world. In contemporary terms, our relation to the world is mediated by diverse and various electronic prostheses linking us to distances across time and space. To extend Descartes's windowsill to the screen — much of our knowledge of the world is derived from what we *see* on a screen. It is indirect and virtual, inferred from the mediated transmission of images, sounds and, (yes) information.

DESCARTES.COM

The contemporary legacy of Descartes's disembodiment could not be imagined more perfectly if I had invented it or written it as a parodic endnote — Descartes.com. To quote the discursive patois of this website:

> Descartes Systems Group is a world leader in collaborative logistics management, providing customers with the Internet-based technological capabilities to manage the end-to-end supply chain.

> The logistics process begins with enterprises that need to manage the delivery of goods, and extends to the transportation carriers they hire and the third-party logistics providers that mediate.

In the telecommunication infrastructure of the new millenium, Descartes.com offers remote (wireless) control of the delivery of goods and information. Is this the teleology of Descartes at his window, “bringing real-time visibility” to the “third-party logistics providers that mediate”?

2

THE FRAME

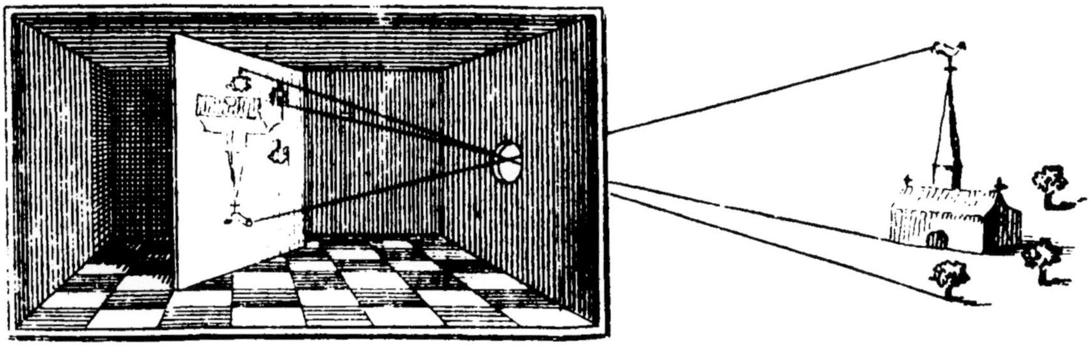

2.1 Drawing of a camera obscura, from Athanasius Kircher, *Ars magna lucis et umbrae* (Amsterdam, 1671).

2 PERSPECTIVE AND THE CAMERA OBSCURA

The principles of pinhole projection, known in antiquity by Aristotle and Euclid, were described in the writings of the Arabic scholar Alhazen in the tenth century and in John Pecham's perspective treatise *Perspectiva communis* of 1279.[1] Although Alberti may have been familiar with the principles of the camera obscura, he did not mention the device in *De pictura.* Nevertheless, Alberti's metaphor of the window bears consideration in relation to the camera obscura as a device used to translate the phenomenal space of vision onto the virtual plane of representation. In this chapter, I examine the camera obscura, its relation to the window metaphor, and its pivotal position in philosophical and historiographic debates about the production of images. Like the window, the camera obscura acquired the discursive weight of metaphor and, over centuries, its identity as a philosophical paradigm developed alongside—although somewhat separately from—its use as a technical apparatus. My concern here is not so much to provide an account of the camera obscura's complex technical and discursive history, which has been discussed at length elsewhere, but rather to underline the functions of the camera obscura that exceeded its use as a drawing tool or a scientific instrument for veridical observation.[2] Here it will be important to emphasize the camera obscura's relation to the long tradition of devices that relied on projected light in a darkened room and on a projected image produced for a viewer's delight—due not to its versimilitude, but to the *illusion* of versimilitude. I will argue that it was the fascination with *virtuality*—the approximation of the real—that drove these inventions.

Like both Alberti's window metaphor and the reticulated net, the camera obscura helped the artist to transform the three-dimensional space of vision to the two-dimensional *virtual* plane of representation. But the nuance of difference between their techniques will become an important pivot as we consider their implications for producing and viewing photographic and moving images. The window frame and the *velo*-grid both positioned the artist to look *through* a frame in a frontal relation to the painterly surface. As Alberti describes the *velo:* "I set this up *between the eye and the object to be represented,* so that the visual pyramid passes through the loose weave of the veil."[3] While Alberti used the rectangular frame of his "window" as a means of geometric calculation, the camera obscura was a mechanical device that could render a perspectival image onto a picture plane without the need of mathematical calculation or geometric formula. And, unlike the Albertian window metaphor and the *velo*-net, the camera obscura projected its images—inverted and laterally reversed—onto a planar surface. As we have seen in the last chapter, Alberti's window was a metaphor predominantly for the frame, a rectangle for seeing through. His window had only a virtual transparency and hence was not an actual "window on the world."

The camera obscura functioned much more like an architectural window: its pinhole aperture brought light from the outside into a darkened interior. Relying on light and its opposite—darkness—the camera obscura conducted the following piece of optical commerce: in a dark chamber penetrated by a tiny opening, a ray of light will carry—project onto the wall opposite the opening— an exact image, moving and in full-color, of the scene outside. The darkness and opacity of the wall becomes a receptacle for the light and transparency of the window aperture. Never mind that in this unmediated instance, the image will be inverted and laterally reversed: the outside is brought inside. The optical principle of the camera obscura performs an architectural exchange: the wall exchanges places with the window.[4] The projective light of the camera obscura produced a virtual image, a frame of light that—via this "natural magic"— formed a virtual window upon the wall.[5] It is important to foreground this architectural model of visuality, the basic spatial construct of the camera obscura's visual system. As projected light images became an entertainment medium, the optical principle of the camera obscura illustrates how light could carry images to this newly virtual window.

Philosophers, art historians, film historians, and cultural theorists have debated the epistemological and phenomenological effects of the camera obscura according to its two most commonly ascribed functions—as a scientific instrument and as a device for illusion. As an instrument used for celestial observation, the camera obscura had a veridical role in observation, recording, and research. As a drawing tool, its use by painters as a "perspective machine" followed the same epistemic assumptions about its use as a device for making an accurate record of the visual world. But, as a device for illusion, the optical principles of the camera obscura took on a different function, one that led to a different aspect of its virtual destiny.

As a projection device, the camera obscura repositioned the artist in relation to the picture plane. In his notebooks of 1490, Leonardo proposes a solution to the left-right reversal of the camera obscura image: he suggests that the artist deploy a translucent paper screen viewed from the back, thus positioning the artist on the other side of the projection surface. This technique corrects the left-right reversal, but not the inversion. The artist still sees an inverted image, but the artist's head will not block the incoming light.[6]

In the centuries after Leonardo, the techniques of the camera obscura were detailed in a range of treatises on optics, light, and perspective: Daniele Barbaro, *La practica della prospettiva* (1569); Giambattista della Porta, *Magiae naturalis* (1558); Johannes Kepler, *Ad Vitellionem paralipomena* (1604); Athanasius Kircher, *Ars magna lucis et umbrae* (1646). Kepler may have been the first to name the optical principle with the architectural description "camera obscura"—an incisive term that indicated the reductive simplicity of the behavior of light entering a dark room.[7] As we have seen, Kepler's theory of the retinal image, as described in *Ad Vitellionem paralipomena,* explained the optical principle of image-inversion, the retinal "picture" as a reverse and inverted version of the visual field.[8]

In the late sixteenth century, as lenses were added to its aperture, the camera obscura became a dioptric device that—like other optical instruments, such as the microscope and telescope—negotiated vision by the use of lenses.[9] In his 1637 treatise on lenses and refraction, *Dioptrics,* Descartes drew upon the camera obscura as model to demonstrate the analogy between the eye and the behavior of light in pinhole projection—a literal example of argument *ad oculum.* ("Now it is said that this room represents the eye; the hole, the pupil; the lens, the crystalline humour. . . ."[10]) The shutter aperture—or as one translator indicates, the *fenestre*—was a refracting medium for the light which travelled through it forming a virtual image. (See "Lens I: Descartes's Window" for a further discussion of the window and lens in Descartes's epistemology.)

Dioptric instruments were crafted from the same brass, wood, and glass materials as the measuring instruments of astrolabes, quadrants, thermometers, and barometers. And yet instruments that used lenses served an additional function separate from those designed simply for geographical or astronomic measurement. Dioptric instruments served to extend human vision, to magnify vision of the near or the far, but also to transform—or even distort—the objects within their view. Robert Hooke's careful drawings of specimens seen through the microscope in *Micrographia; or, Some Physiological Descriptions of Minute Bodies Made by Magnifying Glasses* (London, 1665) illustrate both a refined precision of detail and his use of remarkably aestheticized pictorial strategies.[11] And Galileo's observations through the telescope led him to reject the reigning cosmology of geocentrism, thus transforming the visual significance of the earthbound view toward the heavens.[12]

Here, in the most material sense, the technologies of glass and transparency—aided by developments in lens-grinding and glass-making technique—played a determinant role in the scientific transformation of the modern world. As Lewis Mumford would proclaim from a mid-twentieth-century vantage: "Without the use of glass for spectacles, mirrors, microscopes, telescopes, windows and containers, the modern world as realized by physics and chemistry could scarcely have been conceived."[13] Mumford notably places windows alongside dioptric instruments in his list of transformations implemented by glass. Drawing an analogy between the glass instruments of scientific observation and the easel painting, he invokes the metaphor of the window, not as a technique for perspective, but as a metaphor for aperture: "The world as conceived and observed by science, the world as revealed by the painter, were both worlds that were seen through and with the aid of glasses: spectacles, microscopes, telescopes, mirrors, windows. What was the new easel picture, in fact, but a removable window opening upon an imaginary world?"[14]

The next chapter will examine developments in glass technology and the role of glass and its transparency in the context of the window's architectural history. But here, as we consider the optical principles of lenses and apertures, it is necessary to emphasize the nonscientific role of the glass-enabled instrument. The telescope and the microscope may have served largely as instruments for scientific research, but they also began to serve another—albeit limited—use by amateurs as parlor entertainment.[15] The entertainment function of these optical devices relied not only on the versimilitude of the images seen and the recording capacities of mediated vision, but also on the illusion of versimilitude, the very *virtuality* of the experience produced.

By the seventeenth century, knowledge of the camera obscura was widespread.[16] The recent controversy about whether—and to what degree—painters relied on the camera obscura and other optical devices points us to a slightly different, but related, set of historiographic concerns.[17] For decades, art historians have debated whether Dutch painter Johannes Vermeer used lenses or optical devices like the camera obscura.[18] As Philip Steadman asserts about the paintings of Vermeer: "I can think of no plausible explanation as to why any mathematical perspective method should produce [these] results . . . which are so straightforwardly and simply accounted for by a camera technique."[19] Quite simply, as a drawing device, the camera obscura was a much simpler tool than the book-laden geometrics of perspectival technique. David Hockney's 2001 study, *The Secret Knowledge: Rediscovering the Lost Techniques of the Old Masters*, proposes that by the sixteenth century artists were routinely using the apparatus of a camera obscura.[20] Hockney asserts that linear perspective techniques cannot explain the folds of fabric or the shine on metals in paintings such as Jan van Bylert's *Man in Armour holding a Pike* (c. 1630) and that Dürer's 1525 perspective machine could not have aided in Holbein's *The Ambassadors* (1533). In this controversy, the common rejoinder to the claims of Hockney and others is to question whether there is any evidence—other than an analysis of painterly stylistics—that would offer testimony to the use of an optical device.[21] The debate about the putative or prevalent use of the camera obscura serves to illustrate the differences between the representational device of the camera obscura and the perspectival "window," how each technique bears its own representational consequences, and how each has met a separate historiographical fate.

While somewhat suspicious of claims about its actual use as a picture-making device, art historian Svetlana Alpers claims that the camera obscura was a "source of style" for Dutch artists in the seventeenth century.[22] In her 1983 book *The Art of Describing: Dutch Art in the Seventeenth Century*, Alpers draws a broad distinction between the narrative "perspectival" art of the Italian Renaissance—often the defining tradition of Western art—and that of the more descriptive "optical" art of northern Dutch painters. In Alpers's account, the "northern mode" of painting is distinct from the "Albertian mode" and can be characterized by "the absence of a prior frame—that rectangle or framed window which Alberti offers as his initial definition of the picture—so that the image spread out on the pictorial surface appears to be an unbounded fragment of the world that continues beyond the canvas."[23] Dutch or "northern" visuality, on the other hand, presented "an aggregate of views," fragmentary, arbitrary framing unlike Italian or "southern" visuality represented by the Albertian rectangle of an open window.[24] Although Dutch painters might share the cartographic grid and mapping impetus of Mercator with the painters of the Italian Renaissance, Alpers asserts, "they do not share the positioned viewer, the frame, and the definition of the picture as a window through which an external viewer looks."[25]

Alpers bases much of her argument on "the sweep of a panoramic landscape that continues beyond the arbitrary rectangle of the canvas" in the paintings of Pieter Saenredam, Jan van Eyck, and others, yet she grounds her claim that the camera obscura is "paradigmatic of Dutch images" in a specifically northern "cultural ambience" that imparts "a trust to devices, to intermediaries that represent nature to us."[26] In her reading, it was the Dutch trust in lenses that, while not a direct influence on painters, became a determinant factor in painterly style.[27] At stake in Alpers's broad oppositions—narrative/descriptive, perspectival/optical, Albertian/Keplerian—is the concept of a specifically "Dutch visual culture," a regional subvariant to art historical generalizations radiating from the Italian Renaissance.[28] Alpers finds this "cultural ambience" evident in the writings of Constantijn Huygens and in the optical research of Johannes Kepler.[29] While she does not claim that Kepler had a direct influence on Dutch painters (in fact she argues to the contrary—Alpers admits that Hoogstraten and Huygens doubted his findings), Alpers asserts that Dutch art was produced in "the Keplerian mode."[30]

While the unbounded "descriptive" aspects of northern painting may form a stark contrast to paintings by their Italian counterparts, the Keplerian optics of mediation through lenses and optical devices also points to another effect, other than easel painting, of seventeenth-century representational practices. Dutch artists used the principles of the camera obscura to create peep-boxes (*perspectifkas*), into which viewers "outside the box" would look to see a perspectivally constructed room.[31] Peep-boxes perform a complex set of illusions, creating an attraction to looking in and not out; to miniatures reduced in spatial verisimilitude; and to using the monocular eye, not the frame, as a determinant of vision.

Whether or not the camera obscura was a widely used optical tool for painting, the viewing practices associated with it will become an important component of cinematic and "post-cinematic" viewing. As Alpers notes: "We are so accustomed by now to associating the image cast by the camera obscura with the real look of Dutch painting (and after that with photography) that *we tend to forget that this was only one face of the device. It could be put to quite different uses.* . . . One of the other wondrous devices . . . was *a magic lantern show* similar in construction to the camera obscura but with a human performance in view."[32]

THE CAMERA OBSCURA: PERSPECTIVE MACHINE OR PROJECTION DEVICE

Here I turn from a consideration of the representational consequences of techniques for perspective and the optical device of the camera obscura to an assessment of the position of its viewer. In his landmark 1990 book *Techniques of the Observer,* Jonathan Crary draws an explicit distinction between the effects of the camera obscura and linear perspective based on the position of the viewer of its images:

> Obviously the two [camera obscura and linear perspective] are related, but *it must be stressed that the camera obscura defines the position of an*

> *interiorized observer to an exterior world, not just a two-dimensional representation, as is the case with perspective.* Thus the camera obscura is synonymous with a much broader kind of subject-effect: it is about far more than the relation of an observer to a certain procedure of picture making. Many contemporary accounts of the camera obscura single out as its most impressive feature its representation of movement. . . . Thus the phenomenological differences between the experience of perspectival construction and the projection of the camera obscura are not even comparable.[33]

For Crary, the camera obscura is "inseparable" from this "metaphysic of interiority."[34] In the engraved illustration to Kircher's *Ars magna lucis et umbrae* (figure 2.2), the artist or viewer is shown to be on the *inside* of a cross-sectioned boxlike chamber. We will return to this "interiorized observer" in a moment when we examine the range of sizes and material manifestations that the camera obscura took on as a device. In its larger format—the tent or booth—the camera obscura would have an enclosed observer as Crary suggests, but the smaller devices position the observer outside of its box. Either way, the observer was positioned in front of the camera obscura's projected light; and as light was brought through its aperture, it carried moving images on its rays. The second "phenomenological difference" between the camera obscura and linear perspective provides a more important distinction. The images produced by the camera obscura—whether seen from inside its box or in front of the box's projected light—offered more than the rendition of three-dimensional space onto a two-dimensional plane: they were moving images. And this image of movement was distinctly separate from its source: it was *virtual* movement watched by an immobile viewer.

And it is here—in the moving images produced by the camera obscura—that I return to the polemic that began this chapter. As a drawing tool, the camera obscura aided the artist in the static rendition of its projected image. But in the late sixteenth to early seventeenth century, the camera obscura began to take on quite another function. In Giambattista della Porta's treatise *Magiae naturalis* (1558) and in Athanasius Kircher's *Ars magna lucis et umbrae* (1646), the camera obscura is celebrated for its potential to project images that could confuse and delight. A citation from the 1658 English edition of della Porta's 1558 Latin text provides insight into the method and intention of its use. In an instructive section, "How in a Chamber you may see Hunting, Battles of Enemies, and other delusions," della Porta writes:

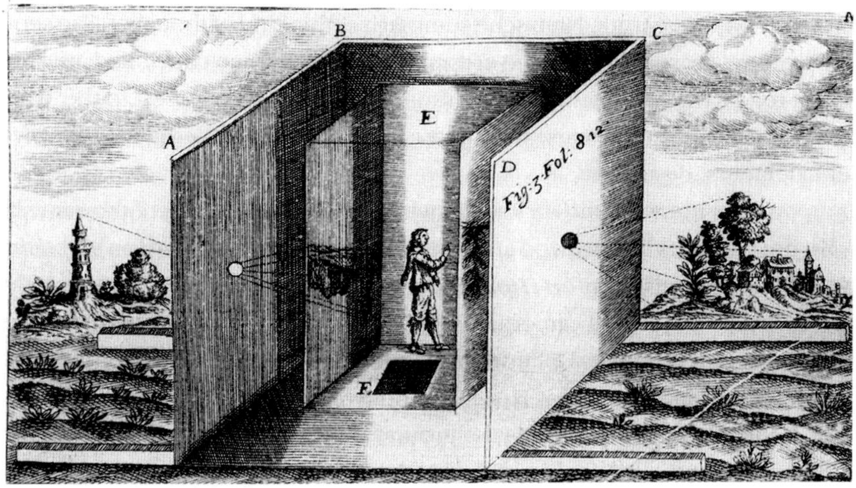

2.2 Drawing from Athanasius Kircher, *Ars magna lucis et umbrae* (Rome, 1646). Getty Research Institute Library, Special Collections.

Now for a conclusion I will add that, then which nothing can be more pleasant for great men, Scholars, and ingenious person to behold; That in a dark chamber by white sheets objected, one may see as clearly and perspicuously, as they were before his eyes, Huntings, Banquets, Armies of Enemies, Plays, and all things else that one desireth. Let there be overagainst that Chamber, where you desire to represent these things, some spacious Plain, where the Sun can freely shine: Upon that you shall set Trees in Order, also Woods, Mountains, Rivers, and Animals, that are really so, or made by Art, of Wood, or some other matter. You must frame little children in them, as we bring them in when Comedies are Acted: and you must counterfeit Stages, Bores, Rhinocerets, Elephants, Lions, and what other creatures you please: Then by degrees they must appear, as coming out of their dens, upon the Plain: The Hunter he must come with his hunting Pole, Nets, Arrows, as other necessaries, that may represent hunting: Let there be Horns, Cornets, Trumpets sounded: *those that are in the Chamber shall see Trees, Animals, Hunters Faces, and all the rest so plainly, that they cannot tell whether they be true or delusions:* Swords drawn will glitter in at the hole, that they will make people almost afraid. I have often shewed this kind of Spectacle to my friends, who much admired it, and took pleasure to see such a deceit; and I could hardly by natural reasons, and reasons from the Opticks remove them from their opinions, when I had discovered the secret.[35]

Della Porta's insistence on the "counterfeit" and the "pleasure to see such a deceit" illustrate that the camera obscura was not merely a scientific instrument; it was a device for illusion and entertainment.

In the seventeenth century, as portable versions became more common, the camera obscura was crafted into a variety of forms—wooden boxes fitted with lenses used as drawing aids, but also as devices for illusion. As is evident in the illustrations to Johannes Zahn's *Oculus artificialis teledioptricus,* the magic lantern and camera obscura had very similar construction.[36]

Having underlined the historical emergence of the projective aspect of the camera obscura's optical principle, let's return to Crary's *Techniques of the Observer.* In the last decade or so, in the wake of Crary's book, the camera obscura has acquired a newly valenced position. Crary's methodological stake in the "historical construction" of vision marked an important shift from the art historical tradition of stylistic or iconographic analysis (as evidenced in accounts from Wölfflin to Panofsky) to a new assessment of an "observing subject."[37] Crary's attention to the "observer" as "a subject who is both the historical product and the site of certain practices, techniques, institutions and procedures of subjectification . . . one who sees within a prescribed set of possibilities, one who is embedded in a system of conventions and limitations" forms an exemplary model for describing the visual practices and habits of vision of the contemporary movie-goer, TV-viewer, computer user, or driver.[38]

Crary's supple argument effectively challenges the familiar lineage that led from the camera obscura to photography and cinema, productively questioning the reductive teleologies that had been the core narratives in the histories of photography, modernist painting, and cinema.[39] And yet I need to question Crary's account of the broad epistemic differences between the optical system of the camera obscura (which he locates as the model for the seventeenth- and eighteenth-century observer) and the optical systems of the stereoscope and the phenakistoscope (which he locates as the model for the nineteenth-century observer) in order to demonstrate that cinematic visuality was a combination of both of these models of vision—a visual system more complex than Crary's model of rupture and discontinuity might suggest.[40] Here it seems that Crary's model of two successive epistemes—seventeenth century/eighteenth century versus the nineteenth century—becomes nearly as reductive as the model he criticizes. Crary's dismissal of the coexistent and continuous use of the camera obscura model of vision—through the nineteenth century and well into the twenty-first—effectively obscures the importance of the projective tradition of the camera obscura, of the architectural model of visuality and its place in the production of virtual images.[41] Crary avows that the camera obscura's principle

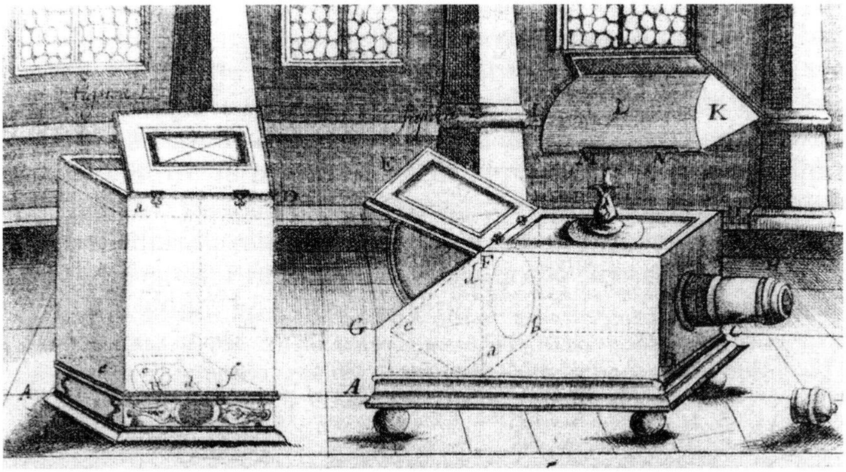

2.3 Detail of a camera obscura from Johannes Zahn, *Oculus artificialis teledioptricus* (Würzburg, 1685). Getty Research Institute Library, Special Collections. In the same text as the magic lantern device, Zahn includes designs of portable camera obscuras, devices with similar wooden boxes and lenses.

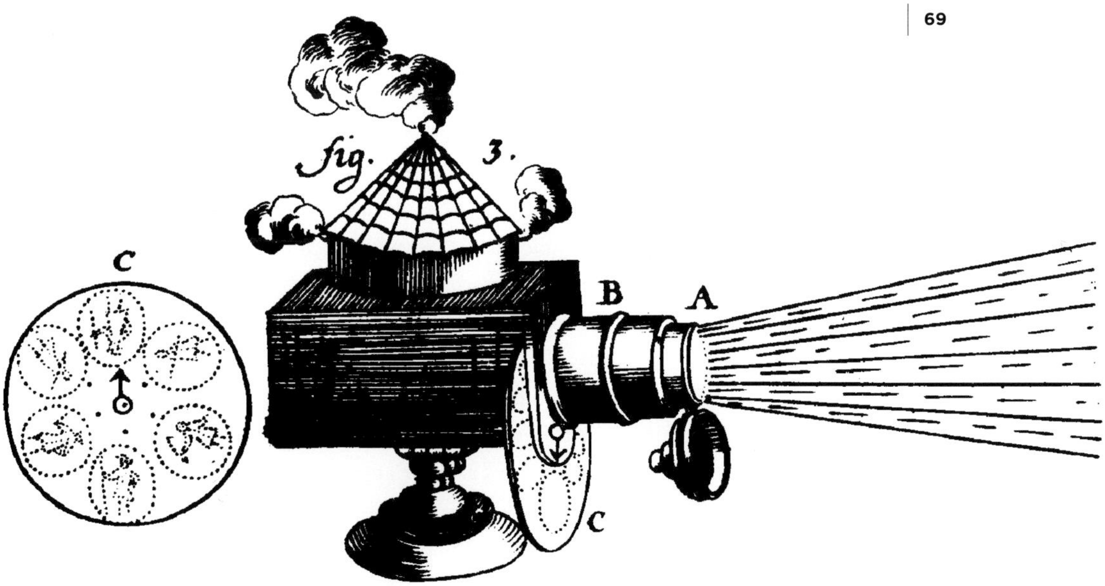

2.4 Drawing from Johannes Zahn, *Oculus artificialis teledioptricus* (Würzburg, 1685). Getty Research Institute Library, Special Collections. Zahn perfected Kircher's optical lantern with a device that used glass slides mounted on a circular disk; when the disk revolved, the projected images could provide the impression of movement.

of projected light was used as a device for illusion, but dismisses the importance of these devices: "The magic lantern that developed alongside the camera obscura had the capacity to appropriate the setup of the latter and subvert its operation by infusing its interior with reflected and projected images using artificial light. However, this counter-deployment of the camera obscura *never occupied an effective discursive or social position from which to challenge the dominant model I have been outlining here*."[42] Yet it is precisely this "counter-deployment" of the camera obscura, the centuries-long tradition of projected images, that has been at the core of recent film historical writing and research.[43] The magic lantern tradition has long been a component in prehistories of cinema.[44] From the magic lantern shows of the mid-seventeenth century (detailed in Kircher's text) to the *eidophusikon* of the late eighteenth century (Philip Jacob de Loutherberg, 1781), the *phantasmagoria* (Etienne Gaspar Robertson, 1797–1800), and on to the projection of photographic slides and illustrated lectures of the 1850s and 1860s, projection devices that relied on the darkened room and the projection of light onto a surface held for viewing had continuous use by scientists and showmen alike. Charles Musser calls this tradition of screen-based entertainments "screen practice," a term that maintains the importance of the screen as a key component of the cinema's visual system.

Laurent Mannoni's recently translated *The Great Art of Light and Shadow* (2000) and Deac Rossell's *Living Pictures: The Origins of the Movies* (1998) provide ample evidence of an "effective discursive or social position," that is, the continued cultural and epistemic centrality of the projection of light and images. While Mannoni is careful to correct many erroneous historical attributions—della Porta did not invent the camera obscura, Kircher did not invent the magic lantern, Robertson did not invent the *phantasmagoria*—his account is emphatic about the continuous tradition of projected light images (dark room, white screen, illuminated image) from the seventeenth century through the nineteenth.[45]

Importantly, the projected light images of the camera obscura retained the elements of movement missing in painting.[46] As lantern techniques were developed for projecting painted slides and for animating painted images by moving slides and moving the lantern, a live entertainment form was adapted for audiences who sat in front of projected images. Although these visual practices were inaugurated in the seventeenth century, they continued to develop as a cultural practice well into the nineteenth century and beyond. As Mannoni asserts: "The lantern was never so much in demand, so widely sold, so much *à la mode* as in the second half of the nineteenth century."[47] The continuation of projected light entertainment based on the visual model of the camera obscura troubles Crary's tidy account of a shift in visuality.[48] The camera obscura may have provided the artist with a "perspective machine" (indeed, the resistant reaction to the prevalence of its use may point to a contemporary anxiety about machine-aided representation), but it also became a "viewing machine" that imported—reproduced—exact, full color, moving images onto a two-dimensional surface for viewing.

In 1845–1846 Karl Marx and Friedrich Engels famously drew upon the camera obscura as an optical metaphor in *The German Ideology:* "If in all ideology men and their circumstances appear upside-down as in a *camera obscura,* this phenomenon arises just as much from their historical life-process as the inversion of objects on the retina does from their physical life-process."[49] The inversion of "men and their circumstances" in the camera obscura implies that there might be a positivist alternative to illusions of ideology. Many commentators have remarked on the timing of Marx and Engel's metaphor.[50] Marx ridicules the camera obscura at the very moment that its apparatical extension—the photographic camera—was seen as veridical. In 1845 and 1846, the years that *The German Ideology* was written, William Henry Fox Talbot had just produced *The Pencil of Nature* (1844–1846). A few sentences before this passage of *The German Ideology,* Marx and Engels assert that the production of ideas is "directly interwoven with the material activity and material intercourse of men [sic], the language of real life."[51] Marx finds the dual nature of the camera obscura—as scientific instrument and device for illusion—to be a perfect visual analog for the invisible workings of ideology. While 1845 was a year that marked photography's introduction as an instrument for exact drawing of the natural world (the "pencil of nature") and hence it would seem odd to question the mediating effects of the camera obscura, that year was also the height of the magic lantern's popularity as a projective technique for illusion.

The darkened chamber of the camera obscura—whether the size of a room or the size of a portable box—contained transient images projected onto one of its walls by light from the exterior. While teleologists may debate a centuries-long desire to "fix" the transient image, it wasn't until the perfection of light-sensitive chemicals in the early nineteenth century that it was possible to retain the rays of light on a surface. "It is often said that it was the painters who invented Photography (by bequeathing it their framing, the Albertian perspective, and the optic of the *camera obscura*)," declares Roland Barthes. "I say: no, it was the chemists."[52]

> *The decisive moment undoubtedly came with the discovery of the first scientific and already, in a sense, mechanical system of reproduction, namely perspective: the camera obscura of Da Vinci foreshadowed the camera of Niépce. The artist was now in a position to create the illusion of three-dimensional space within which things appeared to exist as our eyes in reality see them.*
>
> —André Bazin, "The Ontology of the Photographic Image"

Nicéphore Niépce's view from his window, a view captured on pewter plate in 1826, has become the canonical "first image," claimed by many photo historians as the earliest extant photograph. For Niépce's eight-hour exposure, the window was convenient as a site, its view framed and held static to be fixed in a virtual fashion. As Niépce wrote to his brother while experimenting with the process: "I placed the apparatus in the room where I work facing the birdhouse and the

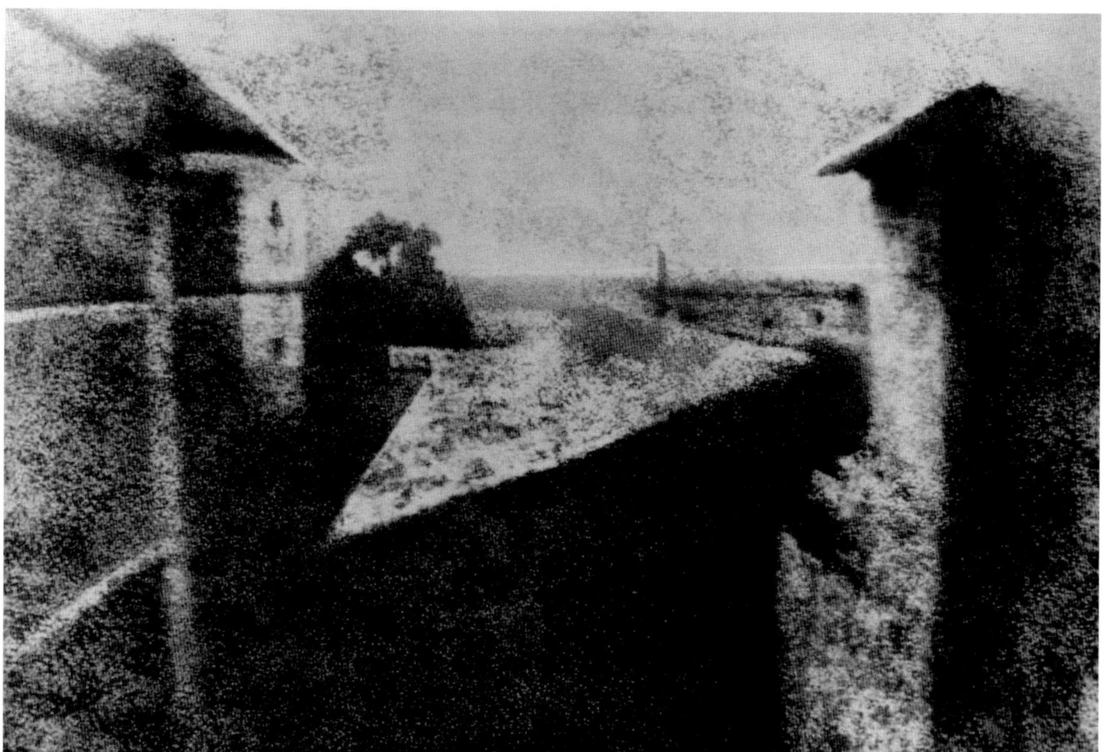

2.5 Gelatin silver print reproduction of Joseph Nicéphore Niépce's *View from the Window at Le Gras* (1826), taken at Kodak Research Library, Harrow, England, March 1952. Image courtesy of Harry Ransom Humanities Research Center, The University of Texas at Austin.

open casement . . . and I saw on the white paper all that part of the birdhouse which is seen from the window and a faint image of the casement which was less illuminated than the exterior objects."[53] Niépce, who named his process "heliography" to emphasize the determinant role of sunlight in image inscription, placed his camera box at the best source of light—his window. In the resultant photograph, the frame of the window becomes the frame of the image; its open casement is transformed into a framed image of a window. And yet Niépce's "view from his window" may too easily encourage a conflation between the perspectival metaphor of Alberti's window and the camera obscura. The opacity of the photosensitive surface captured the window's view on a picture plane possessing only a virtual transparency. Here, as elsewhere, transparency serves as a metaphor for opacity. In this case, the photograph of Niépce's window did not frame a transparent plane for *seeing through* but, rather, uses its frame to encase a surface, its virtual substitute.[54]

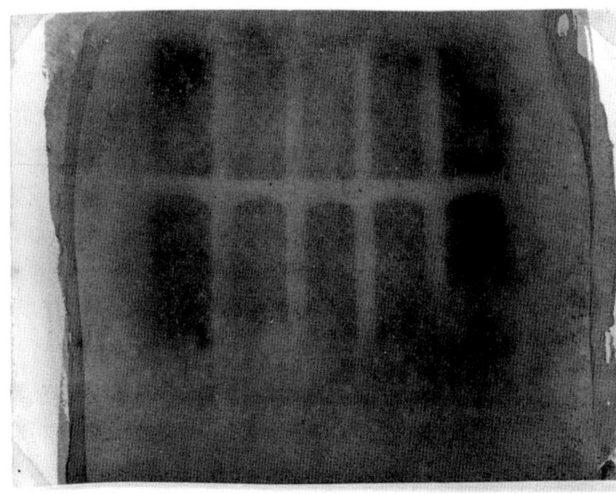

2.6 William Henry Fox Talbot, *The Oriel Window, South Gallery, Lacock Abbey,* 1835. Image courtesy of The Metropolitan Museum of Art, New York. Accession no. 1997.382.1.

The image of another window forms one of the earliest surviving paper negatives: Talbot's view of the oriel window from the south gallery of Lacock Abbey, Wiltshire dated August 1835. Talbot put photosensitive paper inside a camera obscura constructed from a large box and placed the camera outside, facing the building's window. The resulting image shows the negative effect of light in the leaded glass panes of the window; the mullions are white, the panes are black.

In his 1945 essay "The Ontology of the Photographic Image," film theorist André Bazin concisely recites the common equation between the representational ontology of the camera obscura and the image produced by the photographic camera: "the *camera obscura* of Da Vinci foreshadowed the camera of Niépce."[55] Bazin's passage offers a symptomatic account—often repeated by historians and theorists of photography and moving-image media—of the headlong teleology between the camera obscura and the cinematic camera.[56] Because Bazin's "ontology" held its faith in film's referential realism, his writing has served as a theoretical benchmark for the claim that the cinematic medium was an evolving component of a technological grail—the representation of the "real." In another short essay written the following year, "The Myth of Total Cinema,"

Bazin asserts that there was a "guiding myth," an "idée fixe," that led to cinema's invention. "In their imaginations," Bazin writes of cinema's inventors, "they saw the cinema as a total and complete representation of reality . . . an *integral realism,* a recreation of the world in its own image."[57] Bazin makes a special case for the "true realism" of photography over and against painting, which he variously characterizes as having a "resemblance complex," an "obsession with likeness," an "appetite for illusion." "Perspective was the original sin of Western painting," Bazin declares. "It was redeemed from sin by Niépce and Lumière."[58] In Bazin's logic, the photographic camera fulfilled a redemptive ontology: the "sin" of perspective's illusion was redeemed by the camera's reality. As a device with an "impassive lens" that could "lay bare the realities," the photographic camera—not Alberti's metaphoric window—threw open the sash to an unmediated view of the world.[59]

While Bazin's version of the genealogy from perspective to the camera obscura to the photographic image was drawn in service of an argument about the realism of the photographic image and the "transparent" unmediating role of the photographic camera, his formulations were echoed in service of a very different—and much less celebratory—set of arguments by "apparatus" film theorists Christian Metz, Jean-Louis Baudry, Jean Comolli, Stephen Heath, and others in the 1970s.[60] Theories of the "apparatus" sought to characterize the specificities of a cinematic *dispositif*—its instrumental "technical base" but also its metapsychological effects on the spectator.[61] Emerging from the post-1968 force fields of structural linguistics, Althusserian Marxism, and psychoanalysis, apparatus film theory of the 1970s turned away from the reigning auteurist, new critical, and sociological approaches to film analysis and offered instead a theoretical account of the film spectator as "subject." While each of the apparatus theorists emphasized a different aspect of cinematic signification, like Bazin, they each assumed a direct and unquestioned genealogical continuity between Renaissance perspective, the camera obscura, and the photographic camera. Bazin and apparatus theorists assigned the same spectatorial effects to perspective (its "manmade" codifications to vision) and to its less mathematically rule-bound apparatical cousin, the camera obscura. Let us return to these premises in order to untangle the common conflations and confusions between three separate representational devices of perspective: the camera obscura, the photographic camera, and the moving-image camera.

PERSPECTIVE AND THE CAMERA OBSCURA OF "APPARATUS THEORY"

The camera obscura, Jean-Louis Baudry proclaims in his 1970 essay "The Ideological Effects of the Basic Cinematographic Apparatus," "coincides exactly" with the birth of Western science and "will serve in the same period to elaborate in pictorial work a new mode of representation, *perspectiva artificialis*."[62] Baudry's statement of dramatic coincidence may have confounded the historical relation between the camera obscura and perspective. The "birth" of Western science (commonly situated in the seventeenth century) and the instrument of the camera obscura (most widely known by the seventeenth century) occurred two centuries after *perspectiva artificialis*, a fifteenth-century development. The subtle differences between the geometric formulas of *perspectiva artificialis* as exemplified by Alberti's window metaphor and the projective light of the camera obscura require uncoupling from the historical conflation "coincides exactly."

In "Ideological Effects," Baudry offers a densely reductive account of a genealogy that locates the photographic camera in direct descent from the camera obscura and images organized in Renaissance perspective: "Fabricated on the model of the *camera obscura*, it permits the construction of an image analogous to the perspective projections developed during the Italian Renaissance."[63] Unlike the "discontinuous and heterogeneous" space of the Greeks "based on a multiplicity of points of view," the "centered space" of the Renaissance painting presents a "motionless and continuous whole," a "virtual image" that, Baudry writes, "provides a tangible representation of metaphysics."[64] The photographic camera takes the optical principle of the camera obscura to produce its images, which are then seen as "analogous" to perspective projection. The phrase from *The German Ideology* ("If in all ideology men and their circumstances appear upside-down as in a *camera obscura* . . .")—circulating as an idiom of Althusserian Marxism—played a key role in imagining the ideological nature of the cinema as an optical device.[65] For Baudry and other apparatus theorists of the 1970s, the image produced by perspective and by the camera was implicitly tainted with the ideology of the producing device.

It is necessary to underline two essential components of Baudry's account that subtend his analogy between perspective and photography: (1) that the centered space of perspective and the monocular aperture of the camera both have a singular "point of view," instead of multiple viewpoints for the spectator; and (2) that perspective and the photographic camera both produce—Baudry used the term taken from optics—a virtual image. Baudry accompanies his discussion with a geometric diagram using diagonal lines and arrows to indicate the disposition of the spectator, screen, projector, and "objective reality."[66] By emphasizing the relation between the fixed position of the viewer of Renaissance perspective and the fixed position of the cinematic spectator, Baudry argues that this *fixity*, inscribed into the camera's apparatus, carried with it an ideological positioning for the spectator.

Historian and theorist of perspective Hubert Damisch archly protested this ideological reading. In the preface to his book *The Origin of Perspective*, Damisch seems to target Baudry, among others:

> A curious polemical debate took shape in these fields in Paris in the 1970s. . . . Basing their arguments . . . on the fact that the photographic box, and the camera which is its technical extension, function optically in a way wholly consistent with so-called one-point perspective . . . some maintained that photography and film disseminate spontaneously and so to speak mechanically, bourgeois ideology (because perspective, having appeared at the dawn of the capitalist era, must of necessity be essentially "bourgeois") while others (sometimes the same individuals) celebrated the pallid attempts of would-be experimental cinema to free itself from the "tyranny" of the single point of view and from the general constraints of perspective. Against which still others protested vigorously, citing perspective's scientific status as a means of defending it against accusations of its being an ideological tool.[67]

Damisch succinctly (yet without naming names) summarizes Baudry's account of the "ideological effects" of the "basic cinematographic apparatus":

> This debate is now an old story. But it has left copious traces behind it. It is frequently misclaimed that perspective, through the intermediary of the camera obscura, functions like ideology as understood by Marx. While both of these, in the last analysis, rely on similar reasoning, *the operation of perspective nonetheless differs from that of the camera obscura* in two fundamental respects: first, it is not based on the play of shadow, but rather requires bright light if it is to produce its effect; second, it in no way dictates an upside-down reversal, only the simple possibility of turning the image from left to right, which poses an entirely different problem.[68]

In Baudry's account, the camera obscura was undifferentiated from other techniques for perspective that did not produce a lateral or upside-down reversal. Damisch's reaction to this debate seems largely concerned with disentangling the effects and operation of the camera obscura from those of perspectival technique, but he also holds a larger stake in decoupling ideological critique from its historical vicissitudes: "To discuss perspective in terms of ideological critique is to foreclose all possibility of understanding its historical fortune, as well as the efforts of humanism, over almost a century, to bring it into conformity with its own standards, those—precisely—of ideology."[69] For Damisch, perspective is a "paradigm," a structure that can "traverse history—or collide with it." His mention of "the pallid attempts of would-be experimental cinema to free itself from the 'tyranny' of the single point of view" likely refers to the late 1970s filmwork of "structural-materialist" filmmakers and their claims for challenging the ideological holds of classical spectatorship.[70] Without invoking "ideological critique," American filmmaker Stan Brakhage had earlier, in 1963, polemically defied the "man-made law" of perspective in his manifesto *Metaphors on Vision:* "Imagine an eye unruled by man-made laws of perspective, an eye unprejudiced by compositional logic, an eye which does not respond to the name of everything but which must know each object encountered in life through an adventure of perception."[71]

Brakhage's project imagined the perceptual expansions of "an eye unruled." In his handpainted or nonphotographic films, Brakhage eliminated the perspectival taints of the photographic camera and lens as mediator to the movement of projected light. Yet his filmmaking was still reliant on the spectatorial conditions of a darkened room and a viewer facing framed, luminous moving images projected onto a screen. As films complicit with the conditions of exhibition and display, they rely on the projective properties of light in a dark room.

Although I've isolated Baudry in the discussion so far, he was not alone in invoking the direct teleology from Renaissance perspective to the cinema or in suggesting that it required fundamental critique. The relation of the photographic camera to Renaissance perspective was a broadly circulating axiom in much French and British post-1968 film theory. Christian Metz allied his account of the spectator as an "all-perceiving subject" (*le sujet tout-percevant*) with "analyses of quattrocento painting or of the cinema itself which insist on the role of monocular perspective (hence the camera) and the 'vanishing point' that inscribes an empty emplacement for the spectator-subject."[72] In his 1976 essay "Narrative Space," Stephen Heath summarizes this position by quoting from a 1969 interview with Marcelin Pleynet in which he describes the camera as "productive of a perspective code directly constructed on the model of the scientific perspective of Quattrocento."[73] In this way, Heath claims Renaissance perspective as a foundational basis for both photographic and cinematic camera, "a machine for the reproduction of objects (of solids) in the form of images realized according to the laws of the rectilinear propagation of light rays, which laws constitute the perspective effect."[74] Maintaining that quattrocento codes of perspective were inherent in the camera, he declares: "photography and cinema share the camera."[75]

Like Baudry's, Heath's account of the Renaissance roots of cinematic representation emphasizes the role of "central projection" and its "fixed centrality" for the spectator.[76] Although the Albertian metaphor of the window may have been lurking in some of the other apparatus accounts of perspectival positioning, Alberti's window makes a manifest appearance in Heath's "Narrative Space": "What is fundamental is the idea of the spectator at a window, an *aperta finestra* that gives a view on the world—framed, centred, harmonious (the *istoria*)."[77] For Heath, the frame of the camera reproduces the frame of Alberti's metaphoric window, offering a view that is framed and centered. He continues with the window metaphor, citing Leonardo da Vinci's passage about the transparent pane of glass: "The pane is at once *a frame, the frame of a window, and a screen,* the area of projection on which what is seen can be traced and fixed; from the Quattrocento on, the 'pane' delimits and holds a view, the painter's canvas as a screen situated between eye and object, point of interception of the light rays."[78] In the critique of Baudry and Heath, it is the film *frame* that organized the spectator's vision. As if in a relay of reference, the frame of perspective, the frame of the camera, the frame of the screen all form a fixed and "centered" view for the spectator.

As Heath writes: "In so far as it is grounded in the photograph, cinema will contribute to the circulation of this currency, will bring with it monocular perspective, the positioning of the spectator-subject in and identification with the camera as the point of a sure and centered embracing view."[79] Even if the equation between the eye and the camera is not exact—vision is binocular, and the eye's scanning movements means that vision is not static—Heath asserts that it has been the "ideological force of the photograph" to "ignore" these aspects of vision. In a key insight into the paradoxical nature of the moving image, Heath notes: "It may well be that classically cinema acquires the mobility of the eye while preserving the contained and delimited visual field on which 'correct' perspectives depend, but mobility is nevertheless difficult: movements in figures 'in' film, camera movement, movement from shot to shot. . . ."[80] I will return to the tension between the fixity of the frame and the mobility of the image in a moment, after considering the fixed position implied by the frame itself.

THE FRAME

The exact origins of the picture frame are somewhat indistinct, but the frame became a component element of the painting when the painting became independent from its wall. The technique of fresco painting—in which pigments are applied directly onto the wet lime plaster of a wall—had been a practice for fifteen thousand years, evidenced in the cave paintings of Lascaux, France, and Altamira, Spain, in dynastic Egypt, and in the Roman frescoes of Pompeii in the first century AD; it was prevalent in both Asian and eastern European civilizations. In a material sense, fresco painting meant that the painted surface remained fixed to the original site on which it was painted. As historian Claus Grimm has written: "The question whether in classical times or in the early Middle Ages there were 'frames' in our sense of the word, cannot be answered."[81] Paintings on wooden panels or stone slabs were portable and could be set up in public meeting halls, thermal baths, and temples. In the thirteenth century, once a painting was set on or in front of an altar table (*tabular antependia*), it became a movable object, separate from the wall. And, when panel paintings were detached from their base on altars to be carried in a religious processional, the frame permitted the painting to become not only separate from the wall, but mobile as well.[82] In the thirteenth century, as Grimm indicates, even if the form of the frame consisted only of flat and beveled pieces, its representational tendencies exceeded its function as "mere spatial demarcation."[83] The painting's frame acquired its own representational function—matching the motifs and materials of portal surrounds, doors, and window jambs. The frame became, in a sense, its own form of architectonic structure.[84]

The practice of easel painting played an important role in the changing practices of painting in the fifteenth century. Along with the rise of oil-based paint, available and storable in tubes, the easel freed the painter not only from the wall as a surface to paint on, but also from the studio as the enclosed site for painting. The easel was a perpendicular mount, an upright surface separate from the wall on which to paint an image.[85] And, as the commerce of oil painting began in the fifteenth century, paintings would travel from the artist's easel to the distant wall of the owner.

John Berger invokes a metaphor for the frame of western European oil painting as it was placed on the wall belonging to its new owner: "It is not so much a framed window open on to the world," he writes, "as a safe let into the wall, a safe in which the visible has been deposited."[86] The commercial value of the oil painting imbued the edges of its frame with a new meaning—the frame served as an opening to a virtual vault. Stephen Heath cites an etymology of the word "frame" that indicates the term was first used in an artistic sense around 1600. In this way, Heath targets a key transition in the history of painting: "Before the 15th century frames hardly exist, other than as the specific architectural setting that is to be decorated (wall, altarpiece, or whatever); it is during that century that frames begin to have an independent reality."[87] In this Heath finds "a step in the direction of the camera": "Easel painting . . . established along with perspective system and camera obscura (the latter itself rapidly becomes a portable apparatus for the mobile painter) is a step in the direction of the camera, a camera that will provide screen and frame and the image reflected, fixed, painted with light: a camera that will culminate this whole vision."[88] As we have seen, perspective and the camera obscura were widely different representational techniques for painters. But whatever the techniques, whether perspectival or optical, Albertian or Keplerian, "narrative" or "descriptive," the frame of the painting was a key component of a representational system dependent on the limitations of its frame. This representational system was maintained in the camera's delimitation of a view. Here, let's recall an element of perspective underlined by Damisch in *The Origin of Perspective.* Perspective, Damisch writes, is a "structure of exclusion, the coherence of which is based on a set of refusals."[89] In a relay of frames, the framed view of the camera becomes a framed image seen by an observer.

As we saw in the last chapter, not only the painter but the viewer of perspective was "immobilized by the logic of the system."[90] While the viewer's immobility had a degree of leeway to it, the visual system of easel painting assumed a fixed viewing position: the viewer stands in front of the painting and looks into its frame. Even if paintings like Holbein's *The Ambassadors* (1533) relied on the subtle shifting of the viewer's vantage in order to catch its play with anamorphosis, the frame itself suggests a common position for viewing: separate from yet facing it.

THE CAMERA AND THE EYE OF THE VIEWER: PRIMARY IDENTIFICATION?

The ideological project of "apparatus film theory" read the *cinematic dispositif* as a culmination of a Western philosophical tradition of a transcendental idealist—hence disembodied—observing subject. In this account, the cinema spectator both takes on the view of the camera and remains outside of the framed view. As Metz writes, the "eye" of the observer is monocular and in exact identity with the camera's aperture: "And it is true that as he [*sic*] identifies with himself as look, the spectator can do no other than identify with the camera, too, which has looked before at what he is now looking at and whose stationing (= framing) determines the vanishing point."[91]

In Heath's account, as in Metz's, the cinema spectator is positioned in identification with the camera. Heath describes how the quattrocento "system" transforms "scenographic space" ("space set out as spectacle for the eye of the spectator") to photographic and cinematic space: "The ideal of space remains that of photographic vision which brings with it the concern to sustain the *camera as eye;* in the sense of the *detached untroubled eye . . . an eye free from the body, outside process, purely looking.*"[92] Detached and outside: Baudry's argument also hinges upon the disembodied position of the spectator. Baudry writes: "If the eye which moves is *no longer fettered by a body*, by the laws of matter and time, if there are no more assignable limits to its displacement—conditions fulfilled by the possibilities of shooting and film—the world will be constituted not only by this eye but for it."[93] Disregarding the implied monocularity of single-point perspective, apparatus theorists isolated two essential elements of cinematic representation: (1) the essential immobility of the spectator in relation to the screen, and (2) the relation of this fixity to the movement of the image on the screen.

Kaja Silverman targets the premise implicit in these accounts of "primary identification" with the camera—the alignment of the spectator with the camera's vantage and vision, the "smooth meshing of spectator with . . . apparatus."[94] The post-1968 French film theorists of "suture" had, according to Silverman, a more disjunctive account of the match between eye and camera, between spectatorial look and the camera. For suture theorists—Oudart, Dayan, Miller—the moment that the spectator becomes aware of the frame, the *jouissance*/pleasure in an image is lost, reduced to an awareness of the enunciative presence of the apparatus.[95] The frame serves as the "prick" to the bubble of illusion.

Theorists of suture certainly have a different account of the cinematic text from the apparatus theorists—its pleasures are contained in its illusion of a *diegesis*, pleasures only to be ruined by the reminders of an enunciative presence. Nevertheless, suture theory contends with the shifts in perspective *between* shots—something that is only tangentially mentioned in Metz, Baudry, and Heath. For suture theorists, the shot/reverse shot repositioning of the spectator places him or her both inside and outside of the spectacle, and "sutures" the spectator into narrative diegetic space. And yet, for suture theorists, the overarching effect of continuity editing—and, in fact, of "suture" itself—is to restitch the ruptures in the seams of a spatially and temporally intact diegesis, to realign any fractures in perspective/points of view.

Following the spatial codes of Renaissance perspective, apparatus theorists maintained that the film frame imbricated—interpellated—the spectator into its philosophical program and ideological consequences. In fact, it was the uniformity of film frame size and its aspect ratio as distinct from the variable sizes of frames in painting that Heath argues was crucial for setting the conditions of spectatorship. The film frame remained, in Heath's account, in the 1.33:1 aspect ratio or was limited to a very few ratios.[96]

As a key component of the "basic cinematic apparatus"—consisting of the film, the film projector, the screen, and the spectator in a fixed relation—the film *screen* was cast as a conflationary substitute for the film frame.[97] Apparatus theory may have been dismantled by feminist (and other) correctives to its ahistoric generalizations about spectatorship, its disregard for oppositional strategies of style or exhibition.[98] And yet for apparatus theorists the screen was the locus of fascination, the site of enfolding psychic space onto physical space—perhaps more aligned with the Lacanian metaphor of the mirror (and its reflective surface) than with the metaphor of the window (and its transparency).[99]

THE FRAME AND THE FIXED POSITION OF THE VIEWER

In his 1985 study *Narration in the Fiction Film,* David Bordwell refutes many of the tenets of apparatus theory's reliance on perspectival positioning: "The motion picture camera is constructed to produce an image by virtue of the central projection of light rays. Many film theorists have taken this to imply that the film image is condemned to repeat the single spatial schema, and thus the 'positionality' of Albertian linear perspective. This conclusion is utterly unwarranted."[100] As an example of nonperspectival "positionality," Bordwell suggests that the mise-en-scène found in German expressionist film belies this fixed position. (His primary example is the false perspective painted on the set design of *The Cabinet of Dr. Caligari* [1919].) Bordwell's other challenge to perspectival positionality is based on variations in lens length: "Theorists who see the camera as doomed to replicate central perspective tend to wave aside variations in lens length. . . . If lens length has the capacity to create effects of 'nonscientific' perspective systems, it does not matter that the camera is built on the Albertian model."[101]

And yet, if Bordwell was a forceful critic of apparatus theory and its reliance on the perspectival frame, his section entitled "Perspective as Narration" seems to claim otherwise. In the opening section of *Narration in the Fiction Film,* Bordwell describes how "mimetic" theories of narration—storytelling by showing, rather than telling—depend on a perspectival model of vision.[102] Relying primarily on the accounts of perspective rendered by Erwin Panofsky and John White, Bordwell describes—in almost exact agreement with apparatus theorists—how perspective "creates . . . not only an imaginary scene but a fixed imaginary witness."[103] Bordwell both claims that perspective "emerges as a central concept for explaining narration," and asserts that perspective is a "central and fully elaborated concept within the mimetic tradition."[104] Bordwell invokes Alberti's discussion of *istoria* to illustrate how the "story space" of perspective maintained a separate space from its viewer. In tracing a history of the *theatron,* the seeing space and sightlines of the theater, Bordwell provides an excellent account of the positioned relation of the viewer to the framed delimitations of the proscenium stage. Here he suggests that the framed story space of the stage was organized according to Albertian principles of perspective. While Bordwell indicts the "positionality" implied in apparatus theory, his account of the position of the theater and cinema spectator seems uncannily in alignment with it.[105] (The distinction between the terms "seeing through" [*perspective*] and "seeing in front of" [*prospettiva*] might be important here.)[106]

THE PERSPECTIVE FRAME AND THE MOVING IMAGE

Does motion disrupt perspectival fixity? The camera obscura produces, as one of its uncanny effects, a moving image distinctly separate from its source—a virtual two-dimensional image that *moves*. The photographic camera could not capture this movement, it could only reproduce a virtual snapshot of it—still time, still space.

The cinematic moving image is produced by a series of "frames" traveling at a precise speed through a fixed aperture of projected light. The film frame may remind us of Alberti's axioms for perspectival representation. But while the photographic camera's mechanical capture of objects in depth follows the logic of perspectival positioning and the photographic conventions of depth of field and framing, and hence may support the relation between the filmed image and Renaissance perspective, the cinematic movement of objects within the frame, to its edges, and off-frame, suggests its radical contradiction.[107]

The moving image—with its successive frames linked by various codes of editing—produces multiple perspectives over time. Hence, in the sequential series of frames and in the succession of "shots," the single point of perspective is transformed into a series of shifting positions. Indeed, the movement of the image and the mechanics of editing and montage contradict the idea of a consistent, positioned "single-point" perspective frame. In this regard, it is necessary to have a taxonomy of the changes in perspective produced (1) by movement within the single frame of a single shot, which can be either movement of objects within a fixed frame or camera movement that makes the edges of the frame movable; (2) by spatial and temporal shifts between shots in a multiple-shot film (the variation of angle and distance between shots); and (3) by multiple frames within a single shot.[108] For the moment, it will be necessary to suspend a stylistic or historically situated analysis of film form in order to consider the essential multiplicity of spatial and temporal perspective inherent in the cinematic moving image. The moving image provides multiple instances of time *within* each frame as well as a complex temporality *between* frames.

While apparatus theory assessed the perspectival heritage of the fixed frame of the cinematic image, its theorists also had to account for the mobility of the image—movement in a marked contrast to its fixed frame. Baudry acknowledged this problem: "It might thus seem to counter the unifying and 'substantializing' character of the single-perspective image, taking what would seem to be instants of time or slices from 'reality.' . . . This might permit the supposition, especially since the camera moves, of a multiplicity of points of view which would neutralize the fixed position of the eye-subject and even nullify it."[109] But equally he denied its effect. In a section of "Ideological Effects" entitled "Projection: Difference Denied," Baudry argues that projection effectively effaces the difference between the multiple frames of the film: "The projection operation (projector and screen) restores the continuity of movement and the temporal dimension to the sequence of static images."[110] As images are seen sequentially at a speed that produces the illusion of movement (the optics of persistence of vision), the differences between the separate still images is "denied." In his disavowal of the sequential multiplicity of viewpoints, Baudry offers, instead, an explanation that holds the viewpoint and its viewer as fixed. He subordinates the impact of these changes in perspective to the overall "ideological positioning" of the spectator. The single-viewpoint of the camera eye is maintained; film lives on the "denial of difference"—all attempts at continuity are attempts to preserve "at any cost the synthetic unity of the locus where meaning originates."[111]

Stephen Heath's solution to this issue of shifting perspectives is to argue that narrative (not the film's projection) functions to recenter/reposition the spectator as a chain of shots produces radical perspective shifts between shots.[112] In this argument, the storytelling drives of narrative film mask the incoherence of space with the unity of story: "on the basis of a narrative organization of look and point of view that moves space into place through the image-flow: the character, figure of the look, is a kind of *perspective within the perspective system*, regulating the world, orienting space, providing directions for the spectator."[113] Here I would suggest, in service of my larger argument, that it is not narrative and not the optics of projection that recenter the spectator, but the frame itself. It is the consistency of the frame that performs the unity of space, not narrative.[114] Even in films where shots are geometrically variant, the frame positions the viewer. The frame is equally present in Bruce Conner's *Valse Triste* and Hollis Frampton's *Zorn's Lemma*, in Stan Brakhage's *Mothlight* and Hans Richter's *Rhythmus 21*, in Orson Welles's *Citizen Kane* and Michelangelo Antonioni's *L'avventura*, in Georges Méliès's *Trip to the Moon* and Edwin S. Porter's *Great Train Robbery*, in George Lucas's *Star Wars* and Steven Soderbergh's *Schizopolis*.

Heath almost asserts this primacy of the frame when he cites Pierre Francastel's phenomenological account of film movement: "the spectator is not just responsive to what is moving but also to what stays in place and the perception of movement supposes fixed frames."[115] "*What stays in place*": the frame of the image, the frame of the screen serves as the boundary demarcation between the screen world and the material world of the spectator. Although systems of multiple-frame, multiple-screen representation will be the subject of my final chapter, the overarching convention of moving-image technologies—of cinema and television—is the containment of the moving image within a frame.

To return for a moment to Heath's suggestion about the role of narrative as a spatial ameliorative, let's examine one of his key claims, that the narrative character, "the figure of the look," is a "kind of perspective within the perspective system."[116] Perspective, seen as a system that maintains subject position, is described here as a system that also regulates the space of narrative in a mobile and metaphoric manner. Even the shifting "perspectives" of sequential shots can be "orienting" to the spectator, if regulated by a character in the film's fiction.

While not claiming the same figure of "perspective within the perspective system" as Heath, David Bordwell and Kristin Thompson also argue that "techniques of narration" work to produce a unifying effect for the spectator, who, despite the shifts in shot-to-shot position, is not unmoored. In her discussion of the development of the continuity system of "classical Hollywood cinema," Kristin Thompson claims that the use of editing, composition, and staging combined to provide a unified viewpoint as the action shifts. "The spectator as invisible onlooker at the ideal vantage point," Thompson writes, "underlies the development of the classical system."[117] Adhering to the principles of Renaissance perspective theory, Thompson also asserts: "The space of the scene both in painting and in the classical film is organized outward from the spectator's eye." In the continuity system, the "knot hole in the fence" "is not stationary but moves to the ideal place for viewing."[118]

I don't want to venture too far afield from the line of my own argument about the cinematic frame as a container for the fractured multiplicity of spatial and temporal perspectives inherent in the cinematic moving image. Even when shots follow in spatial and temporal "continuity," they are from differently positioned views. As Rudolf Arnheim points out in his defense of the formal specificities that separate film from reality in *Film as Art* (1932), "there are no jerks in time or space." By contrast, in film time and film space, there are "jerks."[119] The spatial and temporal disjunctions of montage produce more radical fractures in this fixed view. (Indeed, André Bazin's defense of deep focus and the long take was rooted in his emphatic rejection of montage and its "violations" to the "realism" of space and time.)[120]

Cinematic images implicitly have multiple temporal and spatial frames seen in sequence, *not in simultaneity.* Sequential images fracture the single-point positioning of the image in a single spatial frame. I will return to this issue in the final chapter when I discuss the tenacious hold of single-frame images in the history of filmmaking and the gradual use of (and comfort with) multiple-frame images.[121]

> *The* camera obscura, *with its monocular aperture, became a more perfect terminus for a cone of vision, a more perfect incarnation of a single point than the awkward binocular body of the human subject.*
>
> —Jonathan Crary, *Techniques of the Observer*

In Jonathan Crary's account, the camera obscura implanted its observer with an "*in*corporeal," "apparatically produced" visuality that ignored the "awkward binocular body," while nineteenth-century social practices and optical devices like the phenakistoscope and the stereoscope produced a new system of visuality, where vision became "corporeal," located in the "body of the observer." The broad category of visual experiences and optical devices that rely on light and projected images, visual practices which as I've demonstrated exist in a continuum from the mid-seventeenth century through to the present, are not easily defined as "corporeal."

The "cinema" combined optical trickery with the projective illusions of the camera obscura—the projection of light in a darkened room. I have sustained my critique around this point: the cinema was a device that combined both of these models of vision. Televisual visuality confounds this further. Based less on optically produced moving images, its light-emanating transmissions—while not relying on projection—certainly command a disembodied noncorporeal mode of viewing.[122] To illustrate this point, I'd like to locate a different rupture that fractures these two models even further, one that occurred between 1891 and 1896.

In 1891, Thomas Edison applied for a patent for his kinetoscope, an individual peepshow viewer. The kinetoscope, it would seem, conforms neatly with Crary's model of a "corporeal" observer. One imagines the body of the viewer draped over these wooden boxes, leaning in to see rolls of film produce motion. The kinetoscope box was as much a prosthetic seeing device as the hand-held toys and viewing apparatuses placed against the face and eye. As we know, Edison was not—at first—interested in projection devices, but rather in the arcade novelty of the individual viewing machine. It took Edison a few years to perfect his moving-picture camera—the kinetograph—and to manufacture enough kinetoscope viewing boxes, but by April 1894 the first kinetoscope parlor opened in New York.[123] Edison's device proved to be a popular novelty, and yet it was the development of systems that *projected* moving images that became the determinative visual practice of the "cinema."

Certainly, as was evident by the anniversaries dramatically celebrated in 1995, the "cinema" has been regarded as being "born" on the dates in 1895 (March 22, the scientific introduction; December 28, the commercial exploitation) when the French *frères* Auguste and Louis Lumière used their invention, the Cinématographe, to project moving images onto a screen.[124] The switch from the kinetoscope viewer to a projection device implied a convergence of "physiological optics" with the "noncorporeal" viewing of the camera obscura, and a radical shift in the viewer's position, now seated in front of a screen. The continuous tradition of projected light and illusory images suggests that important aspects of "noncorporeal" visuality remained constant through the cinematic century.

The cinema as a public projection device was a form of popular entertainment for a full century, and yet many of its key components—the delimited screen, the reliance on projection display, the photographic basis of its images—have dramatically changed. Here we need to return to Crary's comments about his own historical vantage. Crary opens *Techniques of the Observer* (1990) with the proclamation: "[we are] in the midst of a transformation in the nature of visuality . . . more profound than the break that separates medieval imagery from Renaissance perspective."[125] Although this assertion elides the profound "break" that is at the core of his study—between the visual systems of the seventeenth to eighteenth century and those of the nineteenth—and locates by analogy a break two centuries earlier, Crary suggests that the digital image will "relocate vision" back onto "a place severed from the human observer," that is, return us to an apparatically produced visuality more like that of the camera obscura. Here I agree with Crary, but with the added caveat that there have been visual practices that were apparatically produced and noncorporeal continuously through the nineteenth and twentieth centuries. A key component of the viewer's position in the cinematic century was to be immobile in front of the frame of the screen. In this new century, the "postcinematic" viewer is ever more subject to an apparatically produced visuality, facing a screen. But screens are now everywhere—on our wrists, in our hands, on our dashboards and in our backseats, on the bicycles and treadmills at the gym, on the seats of airplanes and buses, on buildings and billboards. Our position is no longer fixed in relation to the virtual elsewheres and elsewhens seen on a screen. As the screen has become ubiquitous, the virtual window is mobile and pervasive.

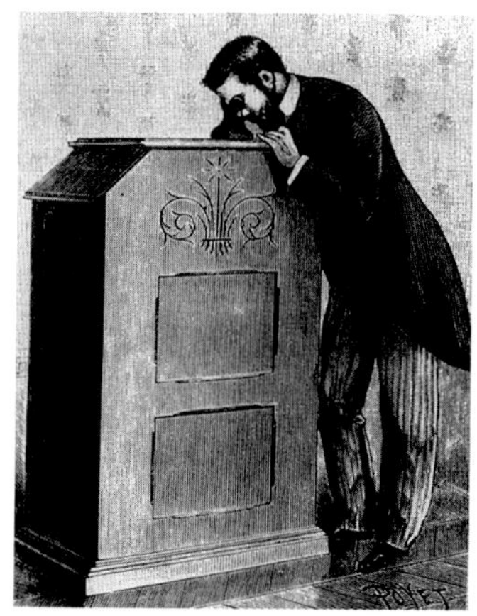

2.7 Thomas Edison's kinetoscope, 1891.

They were the first images to effectively rupture the perspectival code that had dominated painting since the Renaissance. . . . Chronophotography provided a language for representing simultaneity.

—Marta Braun on Etienne-Jules Marey in *Picturing Time*

The normative still photograph, the snapshot, purports to be an ideal, infinitely thin, wholly static cross-section through a four-dimensional solid, or tesseract, of unimaginable intricacy.

—Hollis Frampton[126]

The geometric, geophysical delineations of the perspective frame were based on the spatial codes of human vision—the representation of the near and far on the flat plane of representation. In *La géométrie*—one of the appendices to *Discourse on Method* (1637)—Descartes offers a conceptualization of space as a system of coordinates. "Cartesian space" had a physical dimensionality, its positions could be graphed and measured—*x, y, z,* for height, width, and depth. Perspective, as a rectilinear, geometrically isotopic system, fit perfectly into this rationalized model of space. "Linear," "central," "single-point," "focal-point" perspective created a spatial logic of depth—arranging the above, below, ahead, and behind seen from a viewer's positioned view.

The photographic camera, relying upon the optical principle of the camera obscura, captured its image in the fixed position of monocular perspective. As we have seen in our earlier discussion of "polyscenic" painting, the single spatial frame of perspectival representation did not always imply a single frame of time. But even as a mechanical reproduction of the Albertian principles of space, the photograph had an important counterdistinction to the painting: a new potential for preserving a single instant of time. The chemical processes that fixed the image of the camera obscura fixed an image of both a single perspectival space and a single moment of time. And, as exposure times became shorter and film speed became faster, the photograph reduced the time of the image to an ever more fractional instant. Just as the Cartesian model of space held until the physics of relativity unmoored it, perspectival space began to unravel as *time* was introduced as a dimensional element.

Before it was possible to represent movement with moving images, the representation of motion required its reduction to its graphically static form. In the fourteenth century, mathematician Nicolas Oresme tabulated and graphed intensities in an attempt to represent movement. His method was, at best, a symbolic displacement, a graphic map of how movement operated, but not a mimetic rendition of it. The optical principle of the camera obscura made it possible to bring movement onto a surface separate from its origin—and even as its representational essence was flattened to two dimensions, its motion (of the wind in the trees, for example) remained a key part of the virtual transfer. Photography may have provided a means to record and represent the images of the camera obscura, but the resulting image subtracted the liveliness, immediacy, and movement of the camera obscura's projected image.

In this way the late-nineteenth-century "motion studies" conducted by the physiologist Etienne-Jules Marey and by the photographer Eadweard Muybridge offer two separate models for how the photographic camera was deployed to record movement. While recent studies have examined these two photographers in sumptuous detail, the differences between their goals and methods provide important distinctions between the use of the single-frame image and a more "polyscenic" representation of time.[127]

As a physiologist, Marey came to photography twenty years into his struggle to record, measure, and quantify movement. His earliest attempts to record heartbeats (the sphygmograph, 1860), the movement of muscle (the myograph, 1866), the flight of insects and birds (in 1868, he harnessed a pigeon to a device that connected its wings to a pneumatic drum, recording their movement on a cylinder) involved instruments that were designed to "graph" the movement of living physiology as the sinuous curves of analog measurement. Marey's book *Animal Mechanism: A Treatise on Terrestrial and Aerial Locomotion,* published in 1874, illustrated the elaborate attachments that he used to tether insects, horses, and birds as he struggled to measure their movements.[128]

Marey's machines graphed animal locomotion but could not provide a mimetic rendition of it. It was not until after Marey saw the photographs by Muybridge that he turned to photography as a less encumbering means to record and analyze motion. In 1882, Marey adapted Jules Jansen's photo-revolver (*revolver-photographique*) to "shoot" a bird in flight.[129] Marey's mechanism (*fusil photographique*) was more than metaphoric; it cannily deployed the exact registration of the gun-barrel mechanism to register the phases of a bird in flight. Although the gun apparatus had distinct advantages over the graphic method of tethering his moving subjects, Marey needed to cut out and arrange its postage-stamp-sized images from its revolving photosensitive disk in order to measure the trajectory of the wing's intermittent movement. As a next step, Marey constructed a camera mechanism that reversed the logic of the *fusil photographique:* instead of having the photographic plate revolve, exposing light through the shutter of a fixed barrel, it had a fixed plate and a revolving shutter mechanism. As Marta Braun describes: "As the slot—or *window,* as Marey called it—passed the lens, a phase of the movement was registered on the plate; as the subject moved to a new position, the plate was masked by the shutter; and then as the slot passed the lens again, the subject's new position would be registered on a fresh portion of the plate immediately next to the first, and so on. . . . Marey had created a systematic multiple exposure on a single plate."[130] Marey continued to make adjustments to his camera setup—a black background, a mobile camera wagon—all designed to produce sharper multiple images on a single plate. Marey called his procedure time-photography—*chronophotographie.*[131]

By contrast, Muybridge's endeavors as a photographer and stereographer capturing landscape views of the American West were far from the scientific laboratory experiments of Marey. Yet they became integrally related. As is well known, Muybridge was hired to work for Leland Stanford, the avid horse enthusiast and governor of California, to settle a bet about the gait of a horse in full trot. Marta Braun cites a Muybridge letter that indicates that Stanford had access to a copy of Marey's *Animal Mechanism,* which had been published in English in 1874. In 1878, Muybridge arrayed a battery of cameras with trip-wires to their shutters to photograph successive frames of a horse in motion. The resulting images, when placed side by side, formed a sequence that analyzed movement into its constituent single-frame elements.

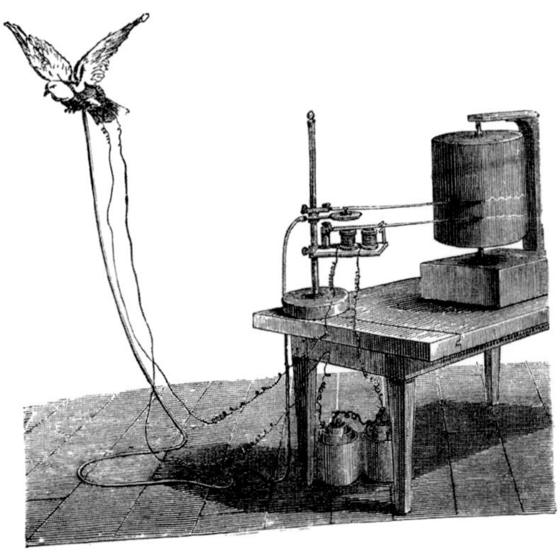

2.8 Illustration from Etienne-Jules Marey, *Animal Mechanism: A Treatise on Terrestrial and Aerial Locomotion* (1874).

Hence, Muybridge and Marey chose two quite different modes to represent movement. Marey's chronophotography recorded movement in a single representation, on a single plate, seen from a single view—a multiple exposure over time (figure 2.9).[132] The resulting image is a composite of layers of time within a single frame. Filmmaking (and now digital) strategies that include layers of superimposition, double exposure, or stop-action substitutions follow this lineage. Contemporary exemplars from the predigital composites of Zbigniew Rybczynski to Robert Zemeckis's *Who Framed Roger Rabbit?* to Michel Gondry's digitally enabled multiple-layered Kylie Minogue all extend from Marey's model of spatially contained but temporally fractured moving images.

Muybridge, on the other hand, set his cameras side by side; each camera recorded an isolated movement on a discrete frame (figure 2.10). As "motion

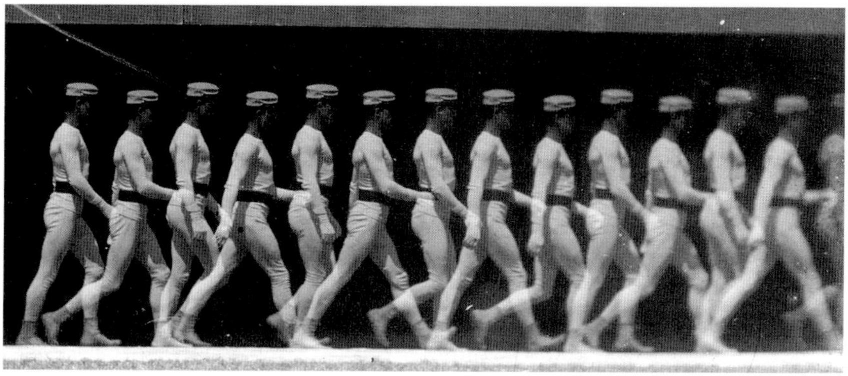

2.9 Etienne-Jules Marey, Georges Demeny walking at the Station Physiologique, c. 1883.

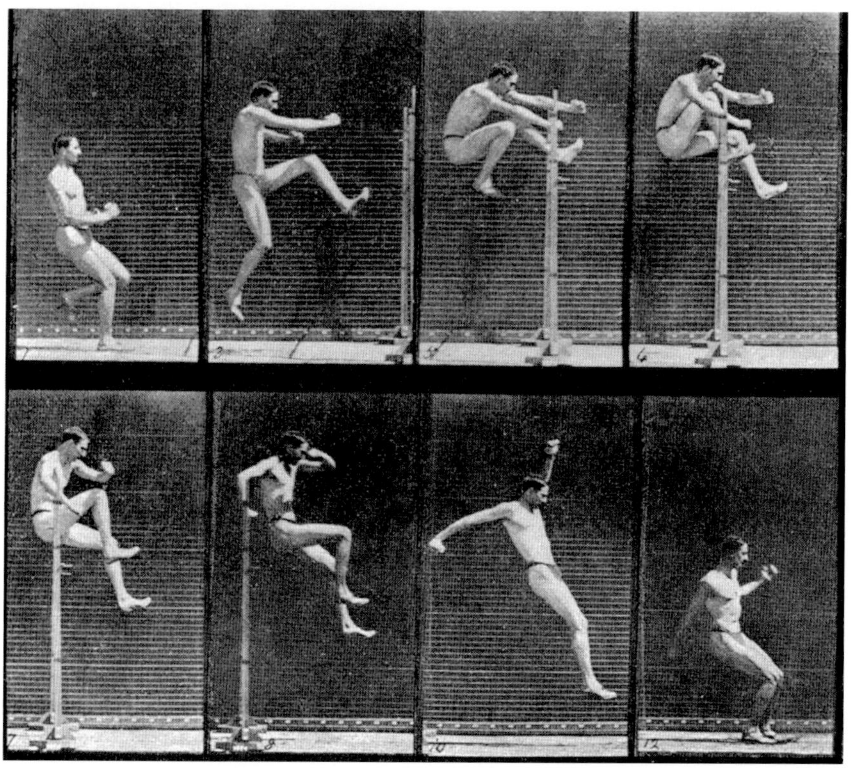

2.10 Illustration from Eadweard Muybridge, *Animal Locomotion* (1887).

studies," Muybridge's images, viewed in a series of successive and adjacent frames, were a set of multiples that parsed movement into constituent shots. Muybridge's 1879 Zoöpraxiscope device combined a rotating disk that spun images in rapid succession with a biurnal (two-stage) projecting lantern. Spun at the proper speed, the sequence of successive spatially fractured, temporally sequential single-frame images gave an illusion of fluid motion.[133] This apparatus did not—at first—use Muybridge's photographs, but became a key transitional device for producing the illusion of movement, movement now seen in its virtual form. Nevertheless, one key aspect of the transition from Muybridge's still images to their reanimation needs to be underlined here. The analytic insights made visible from the array of images in adjacent synchronic display were lost when the multiples were projected in sequence and in the confines of a single frame. Filmmaking (and now digital) strategies that combine multiple framed images in adjacent display—whether it be split screens, multiple screens, or the overlapping "windows" of computer display—follow this other lineage of movement and the frame.

Here too, if the still photograph provided a "tesseract of unimaginable intricacy," the moving image produces a further exponent of the complicated temporality of the photographic record. In *The Emergence of Cinematic Time: Modernity, Contingency, the Archive,* Mary Ann Doane has eloquently detailed the paradox essential to the cinematic production of time: movement is produced from frozen instants in separate frames.[134]

As the motion studies of Muybridge and Marey proved, the still photograph could see and record what the eye could not.[135] And yet, for motion to be reconstituted, its virtual rendition relies on a missing element, a perceptual process that depends on the darkness between the frames. The apparatus of the moving image made this darkness invisible, hiding what the eye might see. The photographic fixing of the image of the camera obscura removed its movement; the still image captured a static instant. The analytic insight that is made visible in the "snapshot" or the frozen moment is lost when the frozen moment is returned to motion. As projection commences, the visibility of moving-image projection depends on a form of invisibility. Film theorist Thierry Kuntzel has called this invisibility a *défilement*—the spectator sees only the projected movement on the screen, not the hidden frames of film passing through the projector.[136]

Casting moving images onto a wall or screen, projection reconstructs the movie camera's view, but in the camera's absence. (The Lumières' Cinématographe cannily used the same apparatus as both camera and projector.) The separation of these two instances—the time of recording and the time of projection—became the core determinant to the fluid temporalities of cinematic spectatorship. As the time of filming was shifted onto the time of the film's projection, the cinematic apparatus enacted a tesseract as a time machine of inherent delay and playback.[137] The moving image opened the representational frame to the temporal analog of near and far—the now and then.

The cinematographically produced moving image could reproduce the perspectival space of the photographic camera, and yet, from its first uses, the movement of elements within the frame, the movement of the camera, movement between frames, and between shots challenged the fixed position of the single-frame "window" view. The photographic or cinematic image cannot be experienced outside of the movement of time (*durée*). The photograph and the moving image are perceived in duration, with an interval between perception and response. Additionally, the mechanical reproduction of moving images allows the exact repetition of these images over time.

As we trace the evolution of challenges to perspectival fixity, the moving image adds a new—but virtual—mobility to the framed view. Certainly motion and mobility were key terms for early writers about the "kinematics" of the moving image. Vachel Lindsay's *The Art of the Moving Picture* (1915) contained sections titled "Architecture-in-Motion," "Painting-in-Motion," and "Sculpture-in-Motion,"[138] and Erwin Panofsky's writing "On Movies" (1936) emphasized the addition of "movement to works of art originally stationary" and characterized early filmmaking's "sheer delight in the fact that things seemed to move, no matter what things they were" and the "recording of 'movement for movement's sake.'"[139] Although he left these incisive phrases largely unelaborated, Panofsky coined the twin specificities of the "motion picture" as the "dynamization of space" and "spatialization of time," as we have seen.[140]

While the moving image in a single frame retains some of perspective's fixity, as single frames follow each other sequentially to produce movement, the moving image produces a complex and fractured representation of space and time. And once two or more moving images are included within a single frame—split-screen or multiple-screen films, inset screens on television, multiple windows on the computer screen—an even more fractured spatiotemporal representational system emerges. What Paul Virilio described as the "battle of geometers"—those who struggled to map the world into a geographic, geometric, geocentric dimension—now cedes to a battle of the *temporameters* as we attempt to measure the entirely new temporal dimensions produced by these multiple and virtual mobilities.[141] The "virtual window" is a fixture of this newly mediated "time architecture."

LENS II

HEIDEGGER'S FRAME

PHILOSOPHICAL PARADIGM AND AESTHETIC DEVICE

> *The fundamental event of the modern age is the conquest of the world as picture.*
>
> —Martin Heidegger, "The Age of the World Picture"

HEIDEGGER and his contemporaries were deeply concerned about the effects of modernity—industrialization, commodification, mass entertainment—and the technologies that were darkening its skies. In his 1938 lecture "The Establishing by Metaphysics of the Modern World Picture" (later retitled "The Age of the World Picture"),[1] Heidegger located the metaphysical shift into the "modern age" (*Neuzeit*) at the moment, loosely historicized, when "the world becomes picture."[2] To Heidegger, this transformation of the world (*Welt*) into "picture" (*Weltbild*) "is one and the same event" with the Descartes's seventeenth-century *Meditations* on the *subjectum* who represents the world through thought—*ego cogito* [*ergo*] *sum.*[3] While Heidegger does not mention perspective as a component factor for this standing-outside-of representation, he equates this new form of mental "representation" (*Vorstellung*) with the visual metaphor of the "picture" and its implied frame.

Heidegger asserts: "That the world becomes picture is one and the same event with the event of man's becoming *subjectum* in the midst of that which is."[4] "Now," he writes, "for the first time is there any such thing as a 'position' (*Stellung*) of man."[5] "The word 'picture' (*Bild*)," Heidegger continues, "now means the structured image (*Gebild*), that is the creature of man's producing which represents and sets before."[6]

A decade later, in a series of lectures he gave in Bremen in 1949–1950, Heidegger introduced a new component of the picture—the frame (*das Ge-stell*)—as a metaphor for "representational thought."[7] For Heidegger, the *Ge-stell* became a key figure in his portrait of the world "conceived and grasped as a picture"—a world picture in a world set-before (*vorstellen*).[8] The *Ge-stell* organizes perception, sets everything in place, orders the world.[9] Heidegger did not assess the visual aspects of this framing; for him the *Ge-stell* was a philosophical "enframing" which transforms the world into objects, into a "standing reserve" (*Bestand*) awaiting its representation, ready for its close-up.[10]

In Heidegger's loosely historicized "modern age," the effects of industrialization and commodification were succinctly illustrated in his description of the hydroelectric plant on the Rhine:

> The hydro-electric plant is not built into the Rhine River as was the old wooden bridge that joined bank with bank for hundreds of years. Rather the river is dammed up into the power plant. What the river is now, namely, a water power supplier, derives from out of the essence of the power station. In order that we may even remotely consider the *monstrousness* (*das Ungeheuere*) that reigns here, let us ponder for a moment the contrast that speaks out of the two titles, "The Rhine" as dammed up into the *power* works, and "The Rhine" as uttered out of the *art* work in Hölderlin's hymn by that name. But, it will be replied, the Rhine is still a river in the landscape, is it not? Perhaps. But how? In no other way than as an object on call for inspection by a tour group ordered there by the vacation industry.[11]

Here, the landscape of the natural world is no longer a river and its banks, but a "water power supplier" transformed into a "standing reserve" for technology's instrumentalization. The relation between the river and the wooden bridge changes with industrialization; the power plant transforms the Rhine. And, as evident in Heidegger's snide quip about the tourist group "ordered there by the vacation industry," the river becomes a tourist site, an "object on call." Heidegger's "frame" here is metaphysical, not literal. But we might easily carry forth his thought to include the metaphysics of the literal frame. Consider a *post*modern visitor to a river, as described by the artist Robert Smithson:

> Noonday sunshine cinema-sized the site, turning the bridge and the river into an over-exposed *picture.* Photographing it with my Instamatic 400 was like photographing a photograph. The sun became a *monstrous* light-bulb that projected a detailed series of "stills" through my Instamatic into my eye. When I walked on the bridge, it was as though I was walking on an enormous photograph that was made of wood and steel, underneath the river existed as an enormous movie film that showed nothing but a continuous blank.[12]

Heidegger did not walk on the bridge that joins the banks of the Rhine, but he knew that something "monstrous" has transformed the river. For Smithson, this "monstrous" something has transformed nature even further. The sun "became" a "monstrous light-bulb." Smithson walks on the bridge which is now a photograph, and the river has become a moving-image film. Smithson's river is a prestructured image, a *Ge-bild,* a picture that is not merely a preframed still photograph but also a "movie film" of moving images. The transformation of nature into representation is now more complete — the sun is a "monstrous lightbulb" that "cinema-sizes" the site, projecting images through the "Instamatic" camera back into the eye of Smithson.

Heidegger was certainly aware of the subjective changes produced by communication technologies. (He describes his contemporaries as "we whose hearing and seeing are perishing through radio and film under the rule of technology.")[13] Witness his opening comments in the first of his 1949 Bremen lectures, "The Thing":

> All distances in time and space are shrinking. Man now reaches overnight, by plane, places which formerly took weeks and months of travel. He now receives instant information, by radio, of events which he formerly learned about only years later, if at all. The germination and growth of plants, which remained hidden throughout the seasons, is now exhibited publicly in a minute, on film. Distant sites of the most ancient cultures are shown on film as if they stood this very moment amidst today's street traffic. Moreover, the film attests to what it shows by presenting the camera and its operators at work. The peak of this abolition of every possibility of remoteness is reached by television, which will soon pervade and dominate the whole machinery of communication.[14]

Despite his constant questioning of unquestioned terms, when Heidegger addresses the technological apparatuses of radio, television, and film, he avoids questioning their literal frames — the film or television screen.[15] For Heidegger, the frame is only a metaphor for the "enframing" implicit in modern thought and experience. Heidegger does not address the visual system of perspective, yet Panofksy's claim for perspective as a "triumph of the distancing and obectifying sense of the real and . . . of the distance-denying human struggle for control" seems to bear an uncanny similarity to the Heideggerian *Gestell.*[16]

Heidegger's questioning of technology and the metaphysics of the frame will set the stage for our questioning of the everyday frames through which we see things — the "material" frames of computer screens, car windshields, television sets, movie screens — because the frame itself carries with it some subjective consequences. Like perspective, both the window and the frame serve as philosophical paradigms and aesthetic devices. To invoke Heidegger here, at the cusp of new paradigms of thought and representation, provides a grounding metaphysic for the dominance of the frame and its visual system.

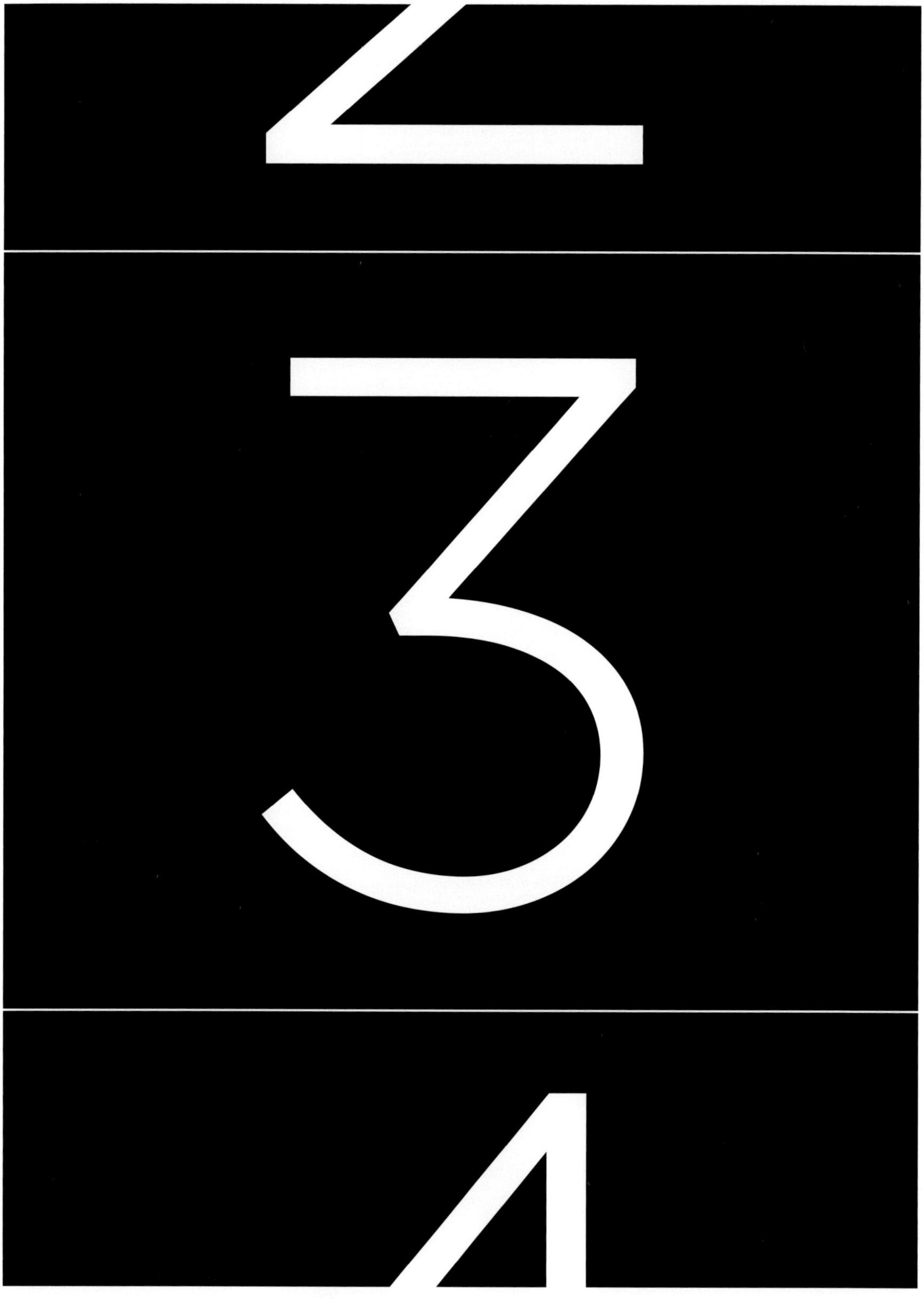
3

THE "AGE OF WINDOWS"

The incidental newness and developments that are accompanying the present transition have also their vistas of promise. . . . The screen will be transformed into a window, through which we shall look in stereoscopic perspective upon a living and audible world.

CLIFFORD HOWARD, "WHAT OF THE FUTURE?"

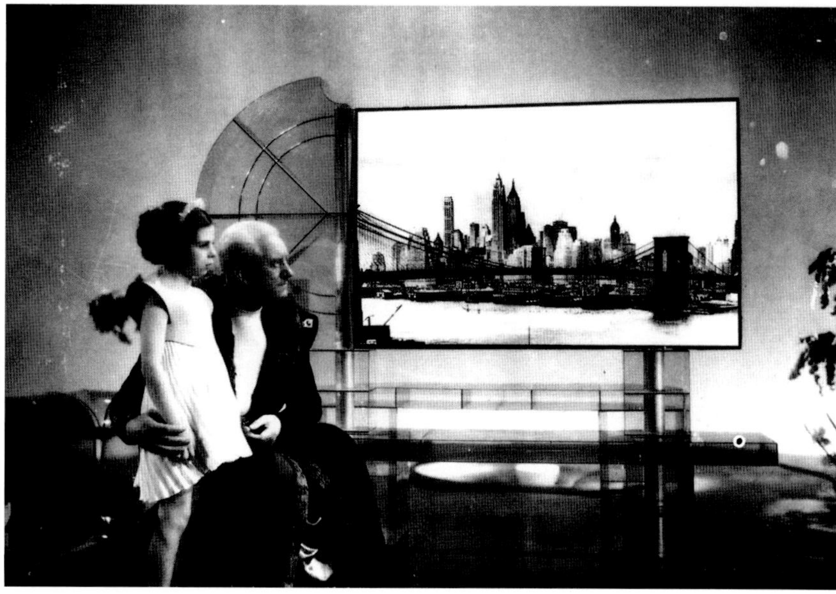

3.1 Frame enlargement from *Things to Come,* London Film Productions, directed by William Cameron Menzies, 1936.

3 THE "AGE OF WINDOWS"

H. G. Wells's 1933 novel *The Shape of Things to Come* offered a wild prophecy of many dark years at the end of the twentieth century, of global war, of salvation by technocracy. In the Vincent Korda and William Cameron Menzies 1936 film adaptation, buildings in the year 2036 look like late-twentieth-century shopping mall atriums or John Portman hotel lobbies, with elevator tubes, moving walkways, and terraced balconies. In one scene in this city of the future, a young girl stands in a room with austerely streamlined decor. Facing a framed screen supported almost invisibly by Plexiglas, she declares somewhat leadenly: "I like these history lessons."[1] A picture of the New York skyline appears on the screen: "What a funny place New York was," she shrieks, "all sticking up and full of windows!" Ralph Richardson, her wizened great-grandfather, attempts to supply an explanatory caption to the view: "They opened and shut those windows to let in the wind and the wet and the cold. I don't know how to describe these windows to you but perhaps there are pictures. . . . The age of windows," he goes on to explain, "lasted four centuries."

In H. G. Wells's fictional imaginary, the buildings of the future do not have windows, but instead have the virtual windows of telescreens. As the above "picture" illustrates, "pictures" render "history" through their evidentiary power, providing the only record of windows. In *Things to Come,* these screen "pictures" also *serve* as windows—as the architectural window has been replaced by the screen, its virtual substitute.

"The age of windows lasted four centuries." If we conduct a rough historical calculation: large sheets of cast glass, rolled and poured, were first available as a building material in the mid-seventeenth century. With this as a starting point, four centuries of windows would conclude in the middle of the twenty-first century, a moment in the not-so-far-off future.

This chapter will trace a history of the "age of windows" by examining the role of fenestration, the materials of glass and transparency, and debates about the size, shape, and function of the "modern" window. The architectural role of the window has changed, I will argue, alongside the development of its virtual analogs—the screens of film, television, and the computer.[2] As moving images were projected and transmitted, the window became an equally compelling metaphor for the screen. In the quotation that serves as an epigraph to this chapter, Clifford Howard, the Hollywood correspondent to the European-based film journal *Close Up*, predicted in 1929: "the screen will be transformed into a window."[3] While he did not predict the corollary—that the window would be transformed into a screen—the convergence of these functions, an exchange between the architectural and virtual window, is now a critical component of twenty-first-century visuality.

A BRIEF HISTORY OF FENESTRATION

> **window,** *n. [ME.* windowe, *a. ON.* vindauga, *f.* vindr WIND *n.*[1] + auga EYE *n. . . .*
> *The Scand. word replaced and finally superseded OE.* éagþyrel EYETHURL, éagduru, *but the French-derived FENESTER was in concurrent use down to the beginning of the modern period.]*
>
> —*Oxford English Dictionary*

The English word "window" derives from the Old Norse *vindauga* (from *vindr,* "wind," and *auga,* "eye") and emphasizes the etymological root of the eye, open to the wind. The window aperture provides ventilation for the eye. The Latin *fenestra* evolved into the Italian, French, and German words, *finestra, fenêtre,* and *Fenster.* A brief history of fenestration will demonstrate how the window as an architectural opening for light and ventilation ceded its priorities to the modern function of the window: to frame a view.

The window began as an opening slit for light and ventilation (a *clostra*) and developed in Roman times as glazing was introduced. Representations of windows appear in wall paintings in Egypt and in reliefs from Assyria. As evident in

Vitruvius and later in Alberti, the window's architectural purpose was—at first—only as an aperture for light or fresh air. In Alberti's Florence, windows were commonly covered with wooden shutters, hinged in several places to regulate the amount of light or air. In some Florentine houses, *impannate*—frames stretched with oiled linen—were used to moderate the amount of light and air through the porous and translucent membrane of fabric. As I indicated in my earlier discussion of Alberti's metaphoric window in *De pictura* (1435) compared with his discussion of the architectural window in *De re aedificatoria* (1452), in fifteenth-century Florence the use of glass for windows was rare. The use of transparent glass for windows was even rarer.

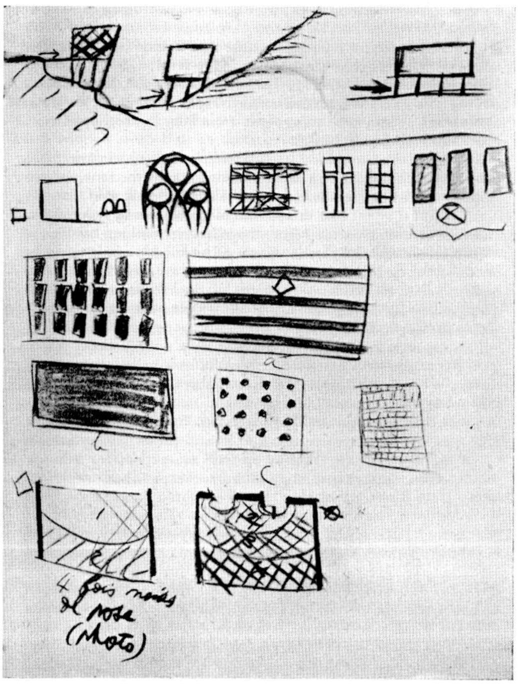

3.2 Le Corbusier, sketches from lecture "Techniques Are the Very Basis of Poetry," October 5, 1929, Buenos Aires, published in *Précisions sur un état présent de l'architecture et de l'urbanisme* (Paris: Crès, 1930).

L'histoire matérielle de l'architecture montre qu'à travers tous les siècles ce fut une lutte inlassable en faveur de la lumière contre l'obstacle imposé par le loi de la pesanteur: histoire des fenêtres.

—Le Corbusier, "Techniques Are the Very Basis of Poetry"

In the sketches for a 1929 lecture, the architect Le Corbusier describes the "history of architecture" as a "history of windows throughout the ages." His drawings provide a reductive caricature of "the little classical window, then the big opening, unglazed with nothing to close it, of Pompeii, the pretty Romanesque window, the gigantic Gothic effort toward the light that ends in the pointed arch." In the Middle Ages, Le Corbusier writes, "they glazed all they could, using all the resources of wood," and Renaissance builders used "stone mullions in a window that was made as big as possible."[4]

The following survey of a "history of windows throughout the ages" is in some ways as selective as the sketches by Le Corbusier. A comprehensive account of the techniques of glass production, the regional specificities of glassmaking, and the global architectural variations in fenestration can be found in more detail elsewhere.[5] A material history of glass and the window can be constructed from written documents on glassmaking techniques and in treatises on architecture.[6] Another—perhaps less reliable—history of glass and the window can be found in an examination of the visual archive of paintings and the windows that appear in them. And, although an analysis of the representation of windows in paintings is outside the scope of this study, there are significant insights to be drawn from such an analysis. Seventeenth-century Dutch painting, for example, provides tell-tale evidence of the appearance and use of the window in a secular domestic space.

In Vermeer's *Music Lesson* (1662–1665), *Woman Reading a Letter* (1659), *Officer and Laughing Girl* (1658), and *The Geographer* (1669), the leaded glass window opened at the hinge not only plays a prominent role in illustrating Vermeer's skill at detailing the suffusive nature of light, the reflective planes of window glass, and the perspectival angles of the room; it also provides a record of the size of a transparent glass pane and the use of leaded glass, wooden frames, the casement hinge, etc. Admittedly, to rely on paintings to provide an architectural record suggests a method devoid of analysis of representational style, of reading paintings as illustration rather than expression. More broadly, a history of the window as a motif in painterly representation reveals that the window is often weighted with more symbolic significance than appears on the surface of the painting.[7]

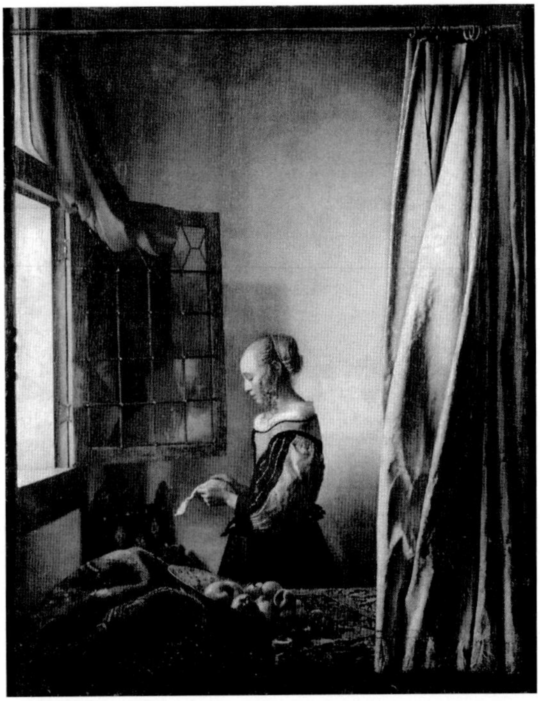

3.3 Jan Vermeer, *Woman Reading a Letter at the Open Window,* 1659, oil on canvas. Gemäldegalerie, Staatliche Kunstsammlungen, Dresden. Photo: Erich Lessing/Art Resource, New York.

A MATERIAL HISTORY OF GLASS

As a material, glass is both solid and potentially transparent. To produce glass, crystalline materials—oxides of sand (silica), soda, potash, lime—need to be melted at very high temperatures.[8] Yet in order to use glass successfully for windowpanes, it was necessary to develop the qualities of transparency and flatness which were dependent on variations in chemical composition and on developments of techniques for its production. A technical history of glassmaking and the use of glass for fenestration will emphasize how these developments had varying effects on the experience of the built environment, from both inside and out. The glass window performed many functions before it took the modern role of framing a view.

Glass was an ancient material. Obsidian, a natural glaseous material formed in the heat of a volcanic eruption, was used by the Aztecs to form

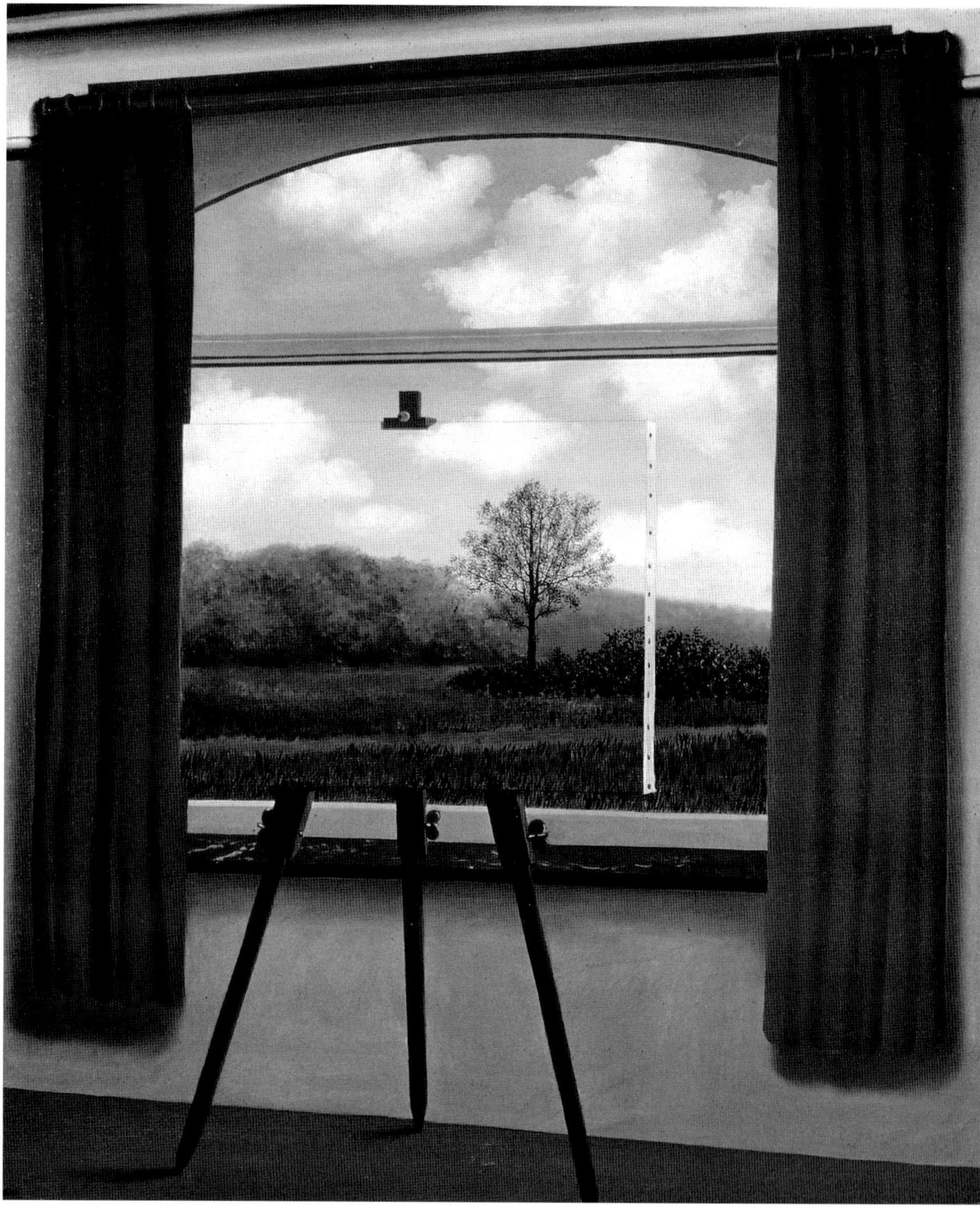

3.4 René Magritte, *La condition humaine,* oil on canvas, 1933. © ARS, NY. Photo: Herscovici/Art Resource, New York.

weapons, jewelry, and tools. Glassmaking began in Mesopotamia—now Iraq—where there is evidence of solid glass beads as early as 2500 BC. In China, in the Chou dynasty (1122–221 BC), glass was used to make jadelike figures and jewelry. Egyptian glass objects—hollow glass vessels (cups, bottles, bowls) dating back to 1500 BC—were formed by pouring molten glass around a clay core. In this process, threads of colored glass were wrapped around the core of a glass vessel as the glass cooled. In addition to this core technique, Egyptian and Islamic glassmakers also made glass objects by pouring melted glaseous materials into sand molds. This "cast glass" was then cut and polished. The Romans developed techniques for glass blowing, where molten glass was gathered onto the end of a blowpipe and blown outward into a variety of shapes. Glass blowing made glass easier to produce, with the result that the material took on utilitarian purposes; it was commonly used in Roman times for drinking cups, bottles, and vessels. During the Roman Empire, the Romans spread glass to Italy, France, Germany, and China through trade and conquest.

There is some evidence of Roman window glass, but the panes were thick and greenish-blue and produced in disks no larger than six to eight inches wide. With the decline of the Roman Empire, the use of glass for windows also declined. Although the term "Dark Ages" emerged in the Enlightenment to describe the relatively undocumented period following the end of the Roman Empire in the fifth century AD, the Dark Ages may have been literally dark because there were no glass windows to admit light.[9]

In the eleventh century, German glassmakers began to blow glass into elongated balloon shapes—cylinders—which were cut and the ends laid flat. The glass from this process had many imperfections; it was of an uneven thickness and fairly opaque. In early Christian and Byzantine churches, small pieces of glass were inserted into a masonry frame. Colored glass was easier to produce than clear crystalline glass, and the imperfections—bubbles and striations—increased its refractive quality. Experiments with colored glass produced the brilliant colors of cobalt blue (made from cobalt ore) and ruby red (made from copper, zinc, and ferric oxides). Techniques emerged using different colors of glass to produce ornamental patterns and to join pieces of glass by lead cames. Fine details or coats of colors could be "stained" onto glass by firing on an enamel pigment.

As light coursed through its patterned panes, the stained-glass window became an illuminated painting. With their translucent patterns and figures, the windows of stained glass demonstrate a more exacting use of the window to illustrate the *historia*—biblical stories, lives of saints—invoked in Alberti's metaphor. Yet the surface of a stained-glass window functions as a nonperspectival picture plane. The mid-twelfth-century window in the Chartres cathedral, "Notre Dame de la Belle Verrière," exemplifies the complex polyscenic fragmentation arrayed in separate panels of the leaded window panes, rather than a continuous narrative in a single frame. In the twelfth and thirteenth centuries, the church maintained a protective role in the custody of glass-making knowledge; its patrons and libraries held many of the processes and formulas for glass production.[10]

Glass properties were altered by changing its ingredients: for example, soda lime instead of lead alkali materials made a glass of greater transparency and strength. Glassblowing required physical strength, strong lungs, and technical knowledge. To make "crown" glass, a bubble of glass was blown thin and, using centrifugal force, was spun until it flattened. This glass had a fire-polished surface and was distinguished by the "crown," a little knob left by the glasspipe that remained in the center. The glass was then cut into squared pieces to be placed in lead frames. Like the crown process, the cylinder process (the slit-cylinder method) was a glassblowing procedure: glass was blown into elongated cylinders, cut open while still hot, then placed flat in an annealing oven and allowed to cool slowly.

The technologies for glass production were highly guarded secrets between the fourteenth and seventeenth centuries, when Venetian glassmakers dominated the European glass industry. Histories of Venetian glassmaking have all of the intrigue of industrial espionage. In 1291, an ordinance moved all glassmaking from the city of Venice to the island of Murano. In some accounts, the exile of the glass furnaces with their high temperatures was to protect the mostly wooden buildings in the crowded city of Venice from the threat of conflagration. In other accounts, the resulting isolation of glass artisans was a much more straightforward spatial regulation of the proprietary techniques of Venetian glass production. As Murano glassmaking became the leading source for fine glass in Europe (and a major source of income for the republic of Venice), its artisans were forbidden from leaving, enforced by threats to self and family. Early in the sixteenth century, Murano glassmakers began to manufacture a clearer glass, *cristallo,* by using manganese as a decolorizer, increasing the soda, and reducing the lime. Venetian—or Murano—imports became a major source of fine glass, largely mirrors and glass vessels.[11]

Improvements in glass technology and lens-grinding technique enabled instruments like microscopes, telescopes, magnifying lenses, and flat mirrors to produce new forms of vision. By the mid-fifteenth century, Samuel Y. Edgerton suggests, the flat glass mirror encouraged a new view of a two-dimensional visual field, priming the conditions for Brunelleschi's 1425 experiment.[12]

The demand for flat glass increased in France under Louis XIV, who directed his minister Jean Baptiste Colbert to install mirrors in his Versailles palace. Completed in 1684, the Galerie des Glaces was the most ambitious mirrored interior of its time. The mirrors magnified the light in the gallery as they reflected sunlight that streamed in from the transparent panes of the glass windows. But the mirrors also formed "false windows," as they were placed in frames identical to the glass windows opposite: a symmetrical arcade of light, transmitted and reflected. The mirrors in Versailles produced a *mise en abyme* of representation, reflecting the glass windows framing the pictorial space of the landscape outside. In this configuration, the mirrors also frame an empty pictorial space: the image inside each mirror is an image of the window. In the Galerie des Glaces, the mirrors supply a virtual plane of reflection and representation, and hence they form, in a direct sense, *virtual* windows.

Just as the mirror emerged in a conceptual system that lay the foundation for the "humanist" epistemologies of the seventeenth century, the plate glass window suggests an equivalent—but opposite—epistemological reconfiguration.[13] If the plane mirror and its reflection was an optical illusion, a trompe l'oeil, in the manner of mimesis and the simulacrum, the plate glass window and its transparency suggests its contrary—an optical veracity, an unmediated (yet still framed) view of the world.

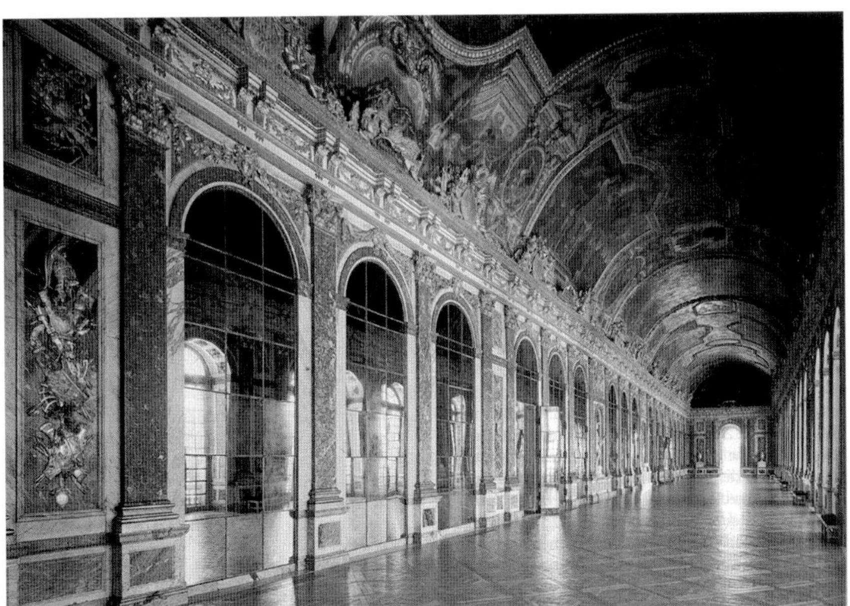

3.5 Galerie des Glaces, Versailles, completed 1684.

The optical "revolution" of the seventeenth century was dependent upon advances in glassmaking technology. Descartes devotes sections of *La dioptrique* (1637) to a discussion of lens grinding to create parabolic, ellipsoidal, or hyperbolic surfaces. And an entire section of Johannes Zahn's *Oculi artificialis teledioptrici sive telescopii* (1675) is devoted to engravings and techniques for the grinding of lenses.[14] In his discussion of the conceptual transformations implemented by glass, Lewis Mumford lists glass windows as dioptric instruments alongside the microscope and telescope.[15] Glass was a transformative material, a key component of catoptric and dioptric devices. Its use for lenses, mirrors, and windows demonstrates its wide utility for scientific, philosophical, and architectural purposes.

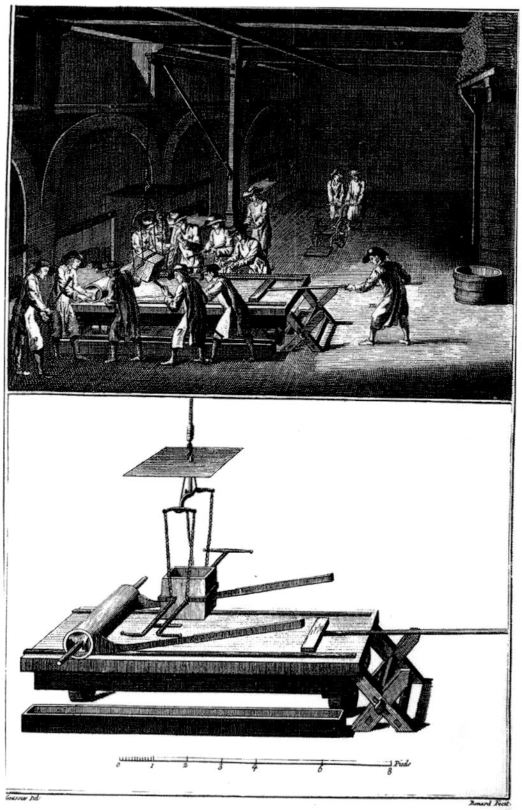

3.6 Plate from *Glaces* volume of Denis Diderot and Jean Le Rond d'Alembert, *Encyclopédie, ou Dictionnaire raisonné des sciences, des arts et des métiers* (Paris, 1751–1772).

By the late 1680s, the French had perfected a process for producing polished plate glass. Molten glass was poured onto a table, rolled flat, cooled, ground with rotating cast-iron disks and abrasive sands, then polished with felt disks. This plate-pouring process produced sheets of cast glass in larger sizes, with good optical properties. When coated with low-melting-point metals, mirrors of high quality could be produced. The plane mirror reflected a resemblance undistorted by the imperfections of glass. In 1695, a factory in the Faubourg Saint-Gobain became the official Manufacture Royale des Glaces de France with sole rights to French mirror production, the production of *grandes glaces.* The French court placed heavy duties on glass imports and, in an attempt to corner the European market on fine glass, offered incentives to lure Venetian glassmakers.

Hence, by the mid- to late seventeenth century—the beginning of H. G. Wells's "age of windows"—the French had developed a process for fine polished plate glass. In Diderot's *Encyclopédie,* one entire volume of engravings was devoted to the technique for making sheet glass. While other volumes illustrating the trades of the ceramicist, fisherman, tanner, casemaker, etc., are exacting records of craft technique, the making of plate glass was somehow like the *Encyclopédie* itself—its product was transparent and illuminating, its process was both revealed and propaedeutically inscribed. The forty-seven plates in the *Glaces* volume illustrate how the *Encyclopédie*'s detailed representation of knowledge—both textual and visual—was central to its demystifying transparency as an Enlightenment project.[16] (And yet, perhaps as an indication of the alternatives to the use of glass for windows, Diderot's *Encyclopédie* also includes a definition for a *chassisier*—a craftsman who covers windows with oiled paper or linen.)

Even as the Germans and English began to discover and refine their own glassmaking methods in the eighteenth century, glass remained a luxury used for public buildings and optical instruments. Between 1696 and 1851 property tax in England was assessed not by the square footage of property but by the number of windows, enforcing both the measure of glass as a taxable luxury and the number of windows as a measure of privilege. The British taxing of windows set the precedent for the French door and window tax between 1798 and 1917. Windows were a measure of property and wealth, indicating the privilege of those possessing a window view.[18] The window tax may have also exemplified the British equation of privilege with a clear window view. Poor-quality glass was exported to British colonies—the grade of crown glass just above "coarse" became known as "Irish."

So far, I have been tracing concordant and competing developments in European glass production. The predominant histories of glass provide accounts of glass production in Europe and North America, as if glassmaking were a European technology spread by colonial expansion from the sixteenth century onward. But here there is a disturbing irony, the global consequences of which I will save for a brief discussion in my epilogue. Glassmaking first emerged in the sands of Mesopotamia and was developed by Islamic countries. The work of the great Islamic optical theorists—Abu Yusuf Ya'qub ibn Ishaq al-Kindi (circa 790–866; known in the West as Al-Kindi), Abu 'Ali al-Husayn ibn 'Abdullah ibn Sina (980–1037; known as Avicenna), and Abu 'Ali al-Hasan ibn al-Haitham (965–1040; known as Alhazen), all eager to translate Greek learning to the Islamic world—demonstrates how actively Islamic scholars advanced theories of vision. Alhazen was interested in the passage of light, the laws of refraction, the workings of the eye, and catoptrics. He provided many of the fundamental principles for Kepler's visual theory.[17] Yet the Islamic roots of glass and optical theory have been too often lost in the accounts of the windows and mirrors of Western visuality.

The window was a membrane between inside and outside, and light was the material that modulated this relation. In the late eighteenth century and into the nineteenth century, middle- and upper-class residences in Europe demonstrated an ambivalence toward the invasion of light into the domestic interior.

Crystal-clear windowpanes were heavily curtained openings, as if to enact the separation between private and public space. Many tenement houses had windows that only received light indirectly via interior wells; residential space may have been private but also quite dim.[19] German cultural critic Dolf Sternberger notes the nineteenth-century ambivalence about the role of the window and the intrusion of light in domestic space. Well-lit interiors were acceptable in public buildings—in train stations, exhibition halls, winter gardens, and glass houses. What Sternberger called the "troublesome window" (*störende Fenster*) began to change its function.[20]

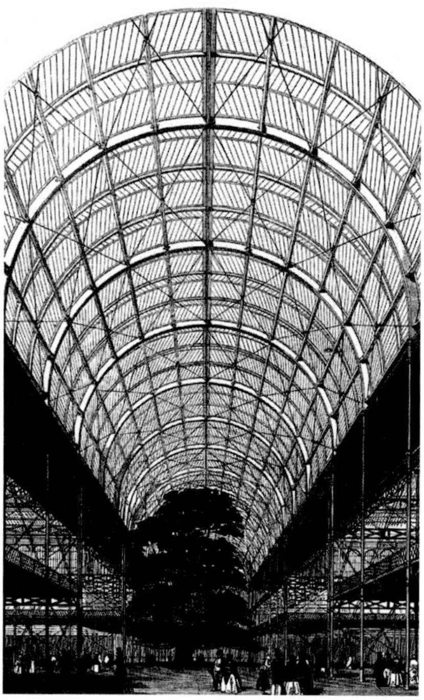

3.7 Joseph Paxton, Crystal Palace, London, 1851.

Glass emerged as an important building material when new building types—factories, horticultural hothouses, exhibition halls, winter gardens, department stores—required copious amounts of light. Improvements in cast-iron architecture—the rolled wrought-iron sash bar and section—enabled the construction of complete glass structures like the Crystal Palace (Joseph Paxton, 1851) and the glazed roofs of train stations (King's Cross Station by Lewis Cubitt, 1851–1852), market halls (Les Halles by Victor Baltard, 1853–1858), and department stores (Bon Marché by Boileau and Eiffel, 1869–1887). All of these structures allowed blazing light into an uncurtained, undraped, and hence well-lit interior space.[21]

In England, Robert and Lucas Chance improved on a German cylinder sheet method to produce glass of fine quality in large panes. The Chance brothers produced nearly one million square feet of glass to glaze and enclose the Crystal Palace in 1851—eight thousand square feet, fourteen acres, were covered by glass.[22] As the Crystal Palace demonstrated, a glass canopy could turn a large expanse of exterior space into an interior.[23]

When the Crystal Palace opened in 1851, German writer Lothar Bucher commented on the altered visual system for the "spectator" in an all-glass building:

> In contemplating the first great building which was not of solid masonry construction *spectators* were not slow to realize that here the standards by which architecture had hitherto been judged no longer held good. . . . We see a delicate network of lines without any clue by means of which we might judge their distance from the eye or the real

size. Instead of moving from the wall at one end to that at the other, *the eye sweeps along an unending perspective which fades into the horizon. . . . the transept . . . dissolves into a distant background where all materiality is blended into the atmosphere.*[24]

The spectator amid such a construction of glass was somehow lost, no longer in a position to judge distance or size as the perspectival viewer might have been. Glass buildings like the Crystal Palace posed a new visual system. Although the glass panes were encased in a skeletal structure that had iron frames, the sense of a framed window as a perforation of the wall was lost. Instead, the spectator's gaze traced the wall as "the eye sweeps along an unending perspective."[25]

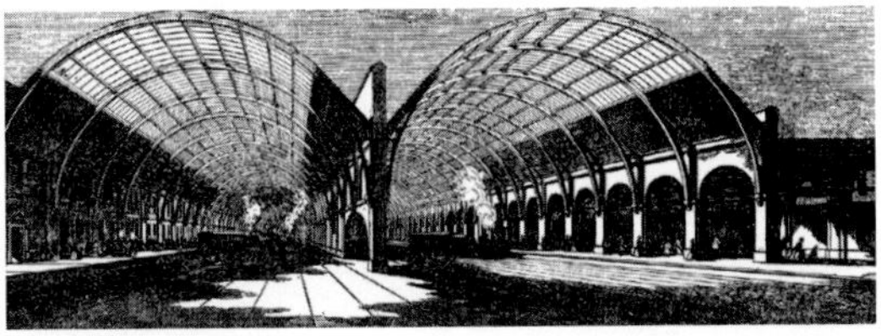

3.8 Lewis Cubitt, King's Cross Station, London, 1851–1852.

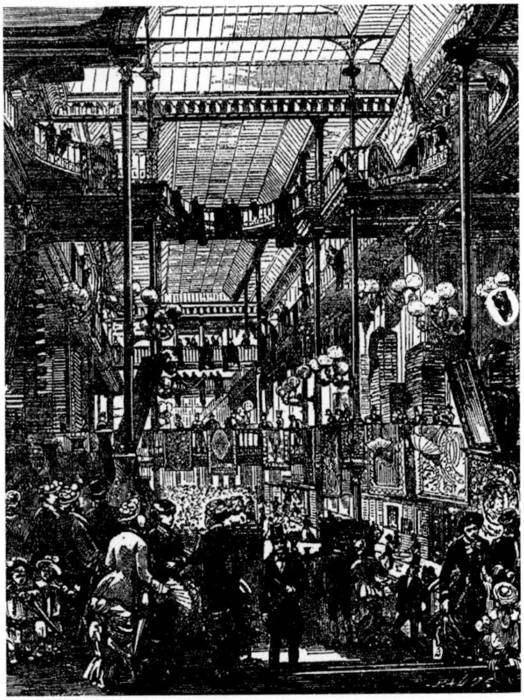

3.9 L. A. Boileau and Gustave Eiffel, Bon Marché, Paris, 1869–1887.

Glass was a material that featured both transparency and protection, could keep the outside *out* and at the same time bring it *in.* As the window grew in relation to the wall—shedding its mullions and posts—it became more and more of a permeable interface. Its transparency enforced a two-way model of visuality: by framing a private view outward—the "picture" window—and by framing a public view inward—the "display" window.

The shop window was a consequence of improved glass technology and the commercial exploitation of its visual display, framing the gaze of passing *flâneurs* and *flâneuses* at commodities seductively displayed. The pane of the shop window enacted the *entre libre* principle of the department store, where the consumptive mode of "just looking" had its own price, not in the obligation but in the desire for purchase.[26] Between 1830 and 1860, for example, the size of shop window panes in England expanded from seven feet high by three feet wide, to fourteen feet high by eight feet wide.[27] Atget's many photographs of shop windows provided exacting records of the practices of window display.[28] "Show windows led to larger openings in the wall," Sigfried Giedion writes. "It was from these store windows that we first learned how to use large glass areas in dwelling houses."[29]

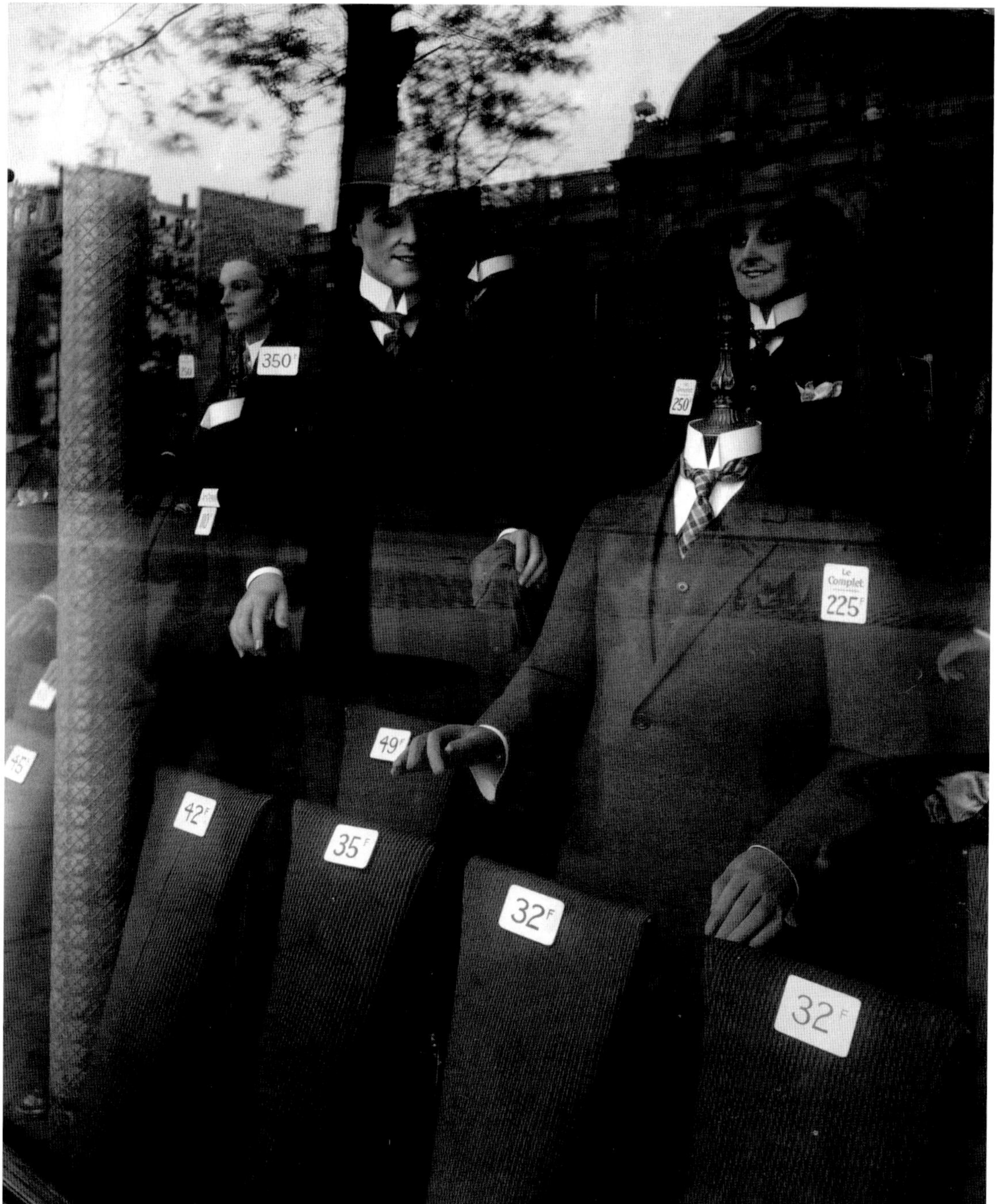

3.10 Eugène Atget, *Magasin, avenue des Gobelins,* 1925, albumen-silver print from a glass negative. The Museum of Modern Art, New York, Abbott-Levy Collection. Partial Gift of Shirley C. Burden. Digital image © The Museum of Modern Art/Licensed by Scala/Art Resource, New York.

The window could become a display frame or, as developments in "modern" architecture demonstrate, the window could also become a *wall.*

GLASS: THE MATERIAL OF "DEMATERIALIZATION"

> *When glass architecture comes in, there will not be much more talk of windows either; the word "window" will disappear from the dictionaries. Whoever wants to look at nature can go onto his balcony or his loggia, which of course can be arranged for enjoying nature as before. . . . These are visions of the future, which we must none the less keep in mind, if the new age is ever to come about.*
>
> —Paul Scheerbart, *Glasarchitektur*

Berlin poet and novelist Paul Scheerbart's vision of a utopian future was based in a near-messianic belief in the material properties of glass. Scheerbart's aphoristic manifesto *Glasarchitektur* began: "If we want our culture to rise to a higher level, we are obliged, for better or worse, to change our architecture," and concluded: "The new glass environment will completely transform mankind."[30] *Glasarchitektur* envisioned cities of the future covered in glass; glass houses with glass furniture; interior rooms with movable glass partitions, exterior glass walls. Glass architecture "lets in the light . . . not merely through a few windows, but through every possible wall, which will be made entirely of glass."[31] Ventilators would "supplant everything window-like."[32] As Scheerbart envisioned it, glass architecture would mean the end of the window. The window would effectively become the wall.

Glasarchitektur was dedicated to Bruno Taut, an architect whose glass pavilion for the 1914 Werkbund exhibition in Cologne served as a promotion for its sponsors—the German glass industry. Taut's glass dome used rhomboid sections of colored glass vaulting a fourteen-sided barrel. Scheerbart provided fourteen phrases to be inscribed on the sides of the building, each one proclaiming a material benefit to glass:

> Glass brings us the new age
> Brick culture does us only harm
>
> *Das Glas bringt uns die neue Zeit*
> *Becksteinkultur tut uns nur Leid*[33]

When Scheerbart died in 1915, Taut carried on the vision of a *Glaskultur.* In 1919, Taut began an epistolary manifesto, written collaboratively in a series of pseudonymous letters, known as the crystal chain (*Die gläserne Kette*). In this correspondence, Taut (whose pseudonym was *Glas*) extolled the properties and potentials of glass.[34] Scheerbart's glass manifesto and Taut's chain of correspondence remained largely ignored in histories of modern architecture until Reyner Banham reassessed the "genealogy of the glass legend" in "The Glass Paradise," a polemical essay for *Architectural Review* in 1959.[35]

Frank Lloyd Wright took up the "cause" of glass with a comparable utopian zeal. In 1928, Wright wrote a series of essays for *Architectural Record* on the "meanings of materials" (stone, wood, the kiln, glass, concrete, sheet metal). "Each material has its own message,"[36] Wright wrote, as if anticipating Marshall McLuhan's 1964 aphoristic insight that the "medium is the message." "Every new material means a new form, a new use if used according to its nature." About glass, he declared: "Had the ancients been able to enclose interior space with the facility we enjoy because of glass, I suppose the history of architecture would have been radically different, although it is surprising how little this material has yet modified our sense of architecture beyond the show-windows the shop keeper demands and gets."[37] Wright's instincts about a glass city, using glass for more than the commodified displays of the shop window, seem to echo Scheerbart: "Imagine a city iridescent by day, luminous by night, imperishable! Buildings—shimmering fabrics—woven of rich glass—glass all clear or part opaque and part clear—patterned in color or stamped. . . . Such a city would clean itself in the rain, would know no fire alarms nor any glooms."[38]

Glass was a material, a medium, with its own specificities to be exploited. Wright complained about the limited use of glass as a transparent material: "As glass has become clearer and clearer and cheaper and cheaper from age to age, about all that has been done with it architecturally is to fill the same opening that opaque glass screened before, with a perfect visibility now, except for the use to which the shop-man demands that it be put. The shop! That is where glass has almost come into its own."[39] The shop window utilized the broadest panes of transparent glass, maximized visibility out, in, and *through* the building: "The machine has given to architects, in glass, a new material with which to work. Were glass eliminated now from buildings, it would be, so far as our buildings have gone, only like putting our eyes out. We could not see or see into the building. We have gone so far with it as to make it the eyes of the building."[40]

With glass for windows, glass for walls, Wright, like Scheerbart in *Glasarchitektur,* extolled the property of glass to dematerialize space: "But now the walls might disappear, the ceilings too, and—yes—the floors as well."[41] As the "eyes of the building," new visualities were produced by large panes of transparent glass.

TRANSPARENCY, "DEMATERIALIZATION," AND THE END OF PERSPECTIVE

As Walter Benjamin noted in "Paris, Capital of the Nineteenth Century," glass was a material component in the building of the nineteenth-century *passage*, the glass-roofed arcades built in the 1820s and 1830s. But he notes: "The social conditions for its intensified use as a building material do not arrive, however, until a hundred years later. Even in Scheerbart's 'glass architecture' (1914) it appears in utopian contexts."[42] One hundred years later: In the 1920s and 1930s, the glass curtain wall, the continuous glass facades of Peter Behrens and Walter Gropius, the glass-clad skyscrapers of Mies van der Rohe, and the ribbon windows of Le Corbusier exploited the distinct material potentials of glass.[43]

The concept of transparency takes on a new set of meanings in the utopian turns of architectural modernism. As Anthony Vidler has noted, the modernist discourse of transparency and its ideologies of visibility—from the "universal transparency" of Jeremy Bentham to André Breton's *maison de verre* with "a bed of glass and glass sheets" to Le Corbusier's "ineffable space [*espace indicible*]"—make varying claims about an architecture of visibility and its "psycho-geographic" effect on the subject.[44]

While the use of a structural membrane of transparent glass in modern buildings performs a visual dematerialization, the material barriers of glass also isolate the other senses. "Fully apprehending the outside from within, yet feeling neither cold nor wind nor moisture, is a modern sensation," argues Richard Sennett, which produced "a complete visibility without exposure of the other senses."[45] This association of visibility with isolation developed, Sennett maintains, as air-conditioning and thermal glass were perfected a half a century later, culminating in the paradigmatic modernist "glass box." Plate glass performed this separation of the senses, one which also contributes to the virtuality of experience.

Transparency has an odd effect on the discursive "materiality" of glass. Glass is described paradoxically as a "material" that is also "dematerializing" because of its transparency. "Such a union of glass and iron demands by its nature," Sigfried Giedion wrote of the Crystal Palace, "an extensive dematerialization of the building."[46]

Giedion, in his now canonical *Space, Time and Architecture* (1941), constructs a periodization of architectural history based on three broadly distinct conceptions of space.[47] In Giedion's account, the first "space conception" was manifested in the Egyptian and Greek concern with volumetric solidity; the second, commencing in the Roman period and ending after transitional spaces in the nineteenth century, was concerned with the hollowing out, or vaulting, of interior space. In the twentieth century, a third space conception "set in" and represented a dissolution of perspective and the single viewpoint: "The third space conception set in at the beginning of this century with the optical revolution that abolished the single viewpoint of perspective. This had fundamental consequences for man's conception of architecture and the urban scene."[48]

Giedion does not pinpoint this twentieth-century "optical revolution" in terms of its scientific or technological advances in the way that historians of the seventeenth-century "optical revolution" describe the coalescence of optical research with technical developments in the making of glass lenses. While Giedion underscores that the impulse for new architectural forms was derived from both new technical materials (iron, glass, steel, reinforced concrete) and from a new consciousness of social responsibility, he draws a more determinant relation between the "art methods" of cubist and futurist painters and a "new" architectural conception of space.[49] Extending the formal ways in which cubist painting had challenged—or dissolved—the fixed position of perspectival space, Giedion declared that the "essence of space" in this new conception "is its many-sidedness, infinite positionality for relations within it."[50] Modern space was cubist.[51]

The project of Giedion's massive (almost nine-hundred-page) *Space, Time and Architecture* was to draw the sometimes determinant, sometimes merely analogic, relation between the spatial conceptions of painters and those of architects.[52] And yet, Giedion added a third term to this coincident development: the physics of relativity, the conception of "space-time":

> Space in modern physics is conceived of as relative to a moving point of reference, not as the absolute and static entity of the baroque system of Newton. And in modern art, for the first time since the Renaissance, a new conception of space leads to a self-conscious enlargement of our ways of perceiving space. . . . Cubism breaks with Renaissance perspective. It views objects relatively that is from several points of view, no one of which has exclusive authority. And in so dissecting objects it sees them simultaneously from all sides—from above and below, from inside and outside.[53]

The philosophical undertow of Giedion's project occurred in this triple superimposition: the layers of painting, architecture, and physics overlapping upon each other in coincident determinancy, all indicative of a new conception of "space-time."[54]

As a pivotal contrast, Giedion described the Bauhaus building in Dessau (Walter Gropius, 1926) as the "only large building of its date which was a com-

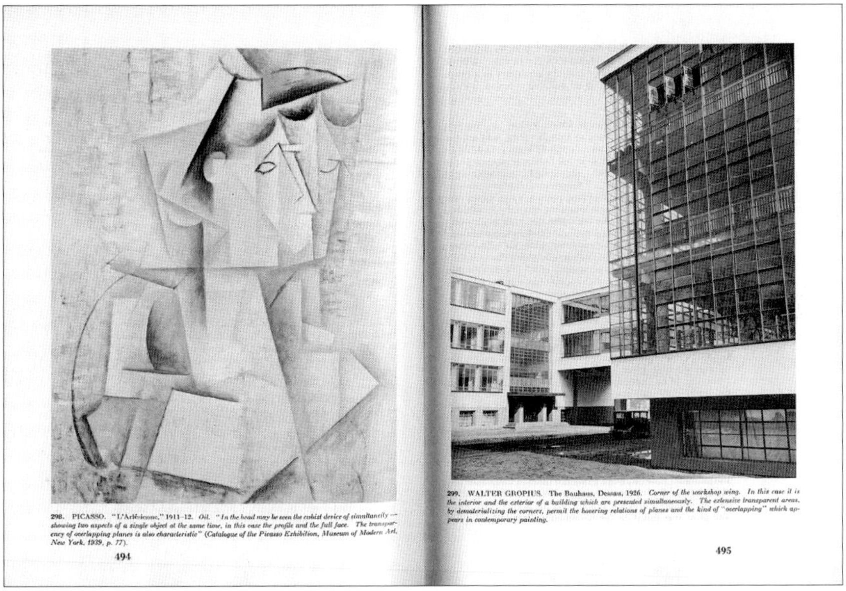

3.11 "New space conception," from Sigfried Giedion, *Space, Time and Architecture* (Cambridge: Harvard University Press, 1941): the Bauhaus building, Dessau, and Picasso's *L'Arlésienne.*

plete crystallization of the new space conception."[55] The extensive use of glass and "transparent areas" of the building had the effect of "dematerializing the corners" and illustrated the "dematerializing quality" of glass.[56] For Giedion, this use of glass produced new overlapping spatial planes, comparable to cubist changes to the painterly surface. His discussion of the Dessau Bauhaus draws it into direct comparison with Picasso's *L'Arlésienne:* "there is the hovering, vertical grouping of planes which satisfies our feeling of a relational space, and there is the extensive transparency that permits interior and exterior to be seen simultaneously, *en face* and *en profile,* like Picasso's 'L'Arlésienne' of 1911–12: variety of levels of reference, or of points of reference, and simultaneity—the conception of space-time, in short."[57] Here the material of glass and the plane of the painterly surface are brought into confluent contrast, near superimposition. Giedion relied on a theory of transparency more spatial than optical: the interior and exterior are seen "simultaneously." Frederick Kiesler's insight about glass seems particularly useful here: "Glass is the only material in the building industry which expresses surface and space at the same time."[58]

In *Language of Vision,* a text written a few years later (1944) with an endorsing foreword by Giedion, Gyorgy Kepes provided this succinct definition: "Transparency means simultaneous perception of different spatial locations."[59] Kepes's profusely illustrated volume made its case for transparency and the

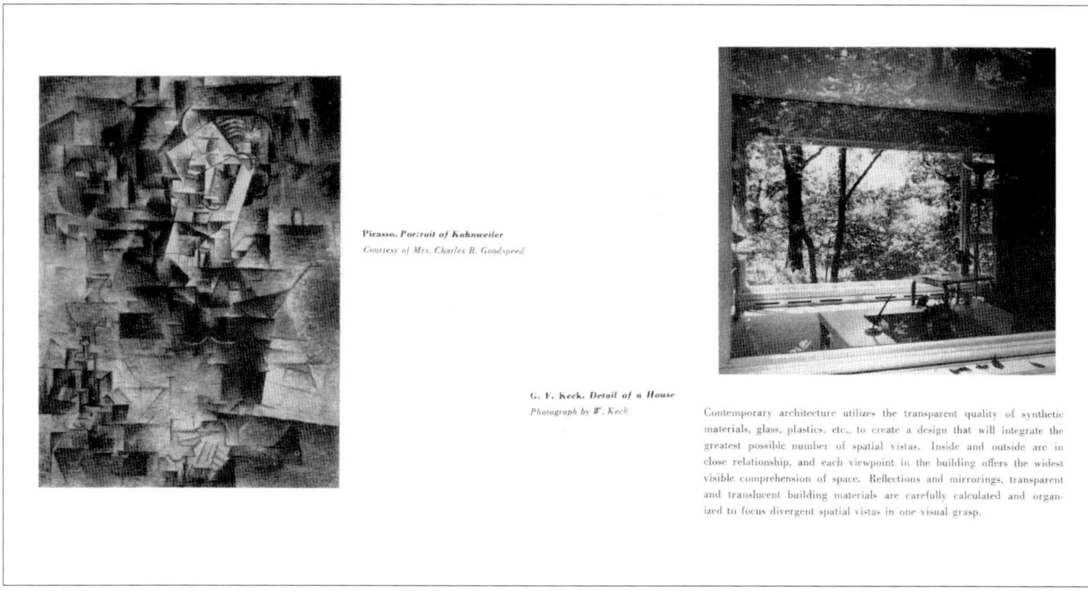

3.12 From Gyorgy Kepes, *Language of Vision* (Chicago: Paul Theobald, 1944): Picasso's *Portrait of Kahnweiler* and G. F. Keck's *Detail of a House.*

"breakdown of fixed perspective" by juxtaposing paintings, architectural photographs, advertising designs, and photomontage. In a page layout that bears striking similarity to Giedion's visual comparison of the Dessau Bauhaus with Picasso's *L'Arlésienne,* Kepes placed a reproduction of Picasso's *Portrait of Kahnweiler* across the page from an architectural photograph from a house by G. F. Keck. The photograph, taken from outside one plate-glass window, looking into and through the house to another plate-glass window that frames the landscape outside, illustrates the transparent and reflective layers of plate glass in a modern house. Kepes's caption reads: "Reflections and mirrorings, transparent and translucent building materials are carefully calculated and organized to focus divergent spatial vistas in one visual grasp."[60]

Kepes's *Language of Vision* was a Bauhausesque visual essay: its text is surrounded by images that supply evidence of his argument that "the fixed perspective order" has been "eliminated" by a new "language of vision."[61] While he asserts that "the invention and perfection of the camera was by no means the only factor tending to break down the absolute validity of linear perspective," Kepes nevertheless argues that that "vision" was "unchained" by photography and cinematography.[62] Whereas Giedion had fixed cubist painting as the exemplar of the break with perspective ("Cubism breaks with Renaissance perspective"), Kepes adds the optical properties of the photographic camera and "motion picture photography" as apparatical agents that produce a new post-perspectival "language of vision":

> Not only the accustomed frontal and profile-views but also the view from above, the bird's eye view, and that from below, the frog's eye view, were recorded. The vanishing point which, in the traditional space representation, had usually been in the middle of the picture place was shifted left, right, up and down, into almost all possible positions. Motion picture photography still further increased the elasticity of foreshortening. . . . The "close-up" broke up the transitional continuous space unity inherited through painting and theatre and extended the picture space to an amplified dimension. In a sequence a "close-up," "medium shot," and "long shot" bring a living, moving variety of expanding and condensing space.[63]

Kepes illustrates this section, entitled "Multiple, Simultaneous Perspective," with photographs by Moholy-Nagy taken from above, below, and an odd angle to the side. "Painters shifted the point of vision," Kepes writes, "into a kind of cinematographic sequence, and represented the projection of several points of view in one picture."[64] In Kepes's argument, painters took the sequential multiplicity of perspective inherent in the "cinematographic sequence" and reduced it to the "multiple, simultaneous perspective" in one "picture."[65]

But let's return, for a moment, to our discussion of the relation between the material transparency of glass and the figurative transparency of the painterly surface. The concept of transparency was parsed further in "Transparency—Literal and Phenomenal" (written in 1955–1956; published in 1963) by architectural historian Colin Rowe and painter Robert Slutzky.[66] While Slutzky and Rowe parallel the representational newness of "modern" painting with "modern" architecture, their critique draws a more nuanced distinction between uses of transparency. Slutzky and Rowe set "literal" and "phenomenal" transparency in opposition: literal transparency is a condition of nonopaqueness, seeing through transparent materials; whereas phenomenal transparency is a means of spatial ordering.

In a close analysis of buildings by Gropius and Le Corbusier, Slutzky and Rowe compare the planar qualities of glass used by Le Corbusier and the translucent attributes of glass as deployed by Gropius. Gropius, whom Giedion extolled for his overlapping transparent areas in the Dessau Bauhaus, is invoked as an example of "literal" transparency for his use of transparent materials—of large panes of glass, glazing around the corners of the building free from masonry piers. Le Corbusier, on the other hand, frames his horizontal windows in relation to the wall—using the planar surface of glass, not the transparency of the building. "Although one can obviously see through his windows," Slutzky and Rowe write, "it is not here that the transparency of his building is to be found."[67] Le Corbusier's use of glass, framed and frontal, fixed and orthogonal, is, in this distinction, a "phenomenal" transparency.

In the tradition of pairing glass architecture with cubist painting, Slutzky and Rowe compare Le Corbusier's window to Léger's *Three Faces,* a painting that emphasizes many of the features they define as analytic cubism: frontality, suppression of depth, contracting of space. The horizontal frame of Le Corbusier's window, they argue, disallows a view of the foreground and sky, conventional markers of perspectival depth. Gropius's Bauhaus building, on the other hand, as Slutzky and Rowe emphasize, relies on a diagonal view of the glass corner; its transparency functions not for seeing out of the frame of the window, but for seeing through the building. In one case, glass makes the building itself transparent; in the other, glass is a surface for framing a view. Glass expresses both surface and space: its planar surfaces are used for reflection, for transparency, and for the multiple planes produced by both. The distinction between "literal" and "phenomenal" transparency offers a parallel model for a consideration of the window as a literal architectural aperture and as a phenomenal space of viewing.

Here I need to bring to the surface the undertow of my own argument, which has been bobbing beneath this detailed discussion of the material developments in glass and its architectural use. As Giedion, Hitchcock, Kepes, and Slutzky and Rowe argue, architectural changes in the window were *roughly* coincident to changes in perspective in modern painting early in the century. I say "roughly" because in Giedion (and in Hitchcock and Slutzky and Rowe) there is a lag of a decade or so between the cubist "optical revolution" ("around 1910") and the architectural one in the 1920s. Nevertheless, Giedion suggests a determinant coincidence. Hence, for my discussion of perspective and the frame of moving-image media, it is important to establish that the painterly and architectural challenges to the perspectival frame occurred in the early part of the twentieth century.

In the same period, the cinematic moving image offered a unique challenge to perspective, one that involved temporality: perspectival single images in the sequential array. If we crosscut here to developments in film history, we might see the development of continuity editing as a counterposed struggle to build a coherent space out of its cubist shards. Multiple, shifting perspectives were seen shot-by-shot in the serial variants of editing. The emerging codes of narrative cinema struggled with these modernist influences, as if to reposition the spectator in relation to new-found slippages in space and time. As I will argue in the last chapter, although there were some film "experiments" with multiple images or with multiple perspectives in a single frame, the dominant practice for moving-image media was to retain a single (and arguably perspectival) frame through the "modern" period.[68]

THE SHAPE OF WINDOW, THE SHAPE OF THE SCREEN: TWO CASE STUDIES

So far in this chapter, I've traced a history of glass as a material and the role of the window in architectural built space. As the boundaries between interior and exterior dissolved in transparency, as the opacity of the wall *dematerializes,* glass *materialized* the architectural exchange between window and wall, wall and window. In his social history *The Americans: The Democratic Experience* (1973), Daniel Boorstin remarks on this transmutation between wall and window in order to speculate on the effects on privacy and individuality as "Glass gave a new, uncertain, meaning to the wall."[69] If we put these developments in confluence with the corresponding history of moving images and their *framed virtuality,* a remarkable set of exchanges begins to appear: as the window becomes the wall and the wall becomes a window, the wall also becomes a screen and the screen becomes a window. In the last chapter, I described a comparable piece of optical commerce performed by the camera obscura. The projective light of the camera obscura produces a *virtual* image. A beam of light forms a *virtual window* upon the wall.

In the next sections of this chapter, I examine two debates (one about the shape of the window, one about the shape of the screen) as case studies in this exchange. As Le Corbusier would declare in 1929, "a window is made for lighting, not for ventilation."[70] If the modern house was, in Le Corbusier's terms, a "dwelling machine," it was also a *viewing* machine. Modern architecture's revisions to the function of the window—no longer for ventilation, but for increased visibility and light—produced changes in the window's frame and shape—its "aspect ratio." The debate about the shape of the window took on an equivalent rhetorical force in a debate about the shape of the screen. These changes had profound effects on its users, the viewers in front of the window or in front of the screen.

CASE STUDY I: THE MODERN WINDOW: PERRET V. LE CORBUSIER

In the 1920s, a public and polemical debate between the architects Auguste Perret and Le Corbusier centered on the size, shape, and function of the window. Perret was an ardent proponent of the *porte-fenêtre,* the vertical "French window," an inward-opening hinged casement window that, while glazed and transparent, also functioned as a door. Perret criticized Le Corbusier for his use of the *fenêtre en longueur*, an elongated horizontal window. This debate—ostensibly about horizontal versus vertical fenestration—had an important philosophical undertow: it was more directly about the subjective effect of the window's frame on the human viewer.[71]

Le Corbusier first visited French architect and builder Auguste Perret in his Paris studio in 1908. Perret, who had pioneered the use of the ferroconcrete frame and was considered to be an early partisan of the "modern movement" in architecture, became Le Corbusier's mentor and, given the caustic nature of their eventual exchange, perhaps his tormentor. From 1909 to 1910, Le Corbusier remained in Paris to learn from Perret; the relationship that formed between the two was deep and complicated. As Le Corbusier would later note, the "paradox of Perret" was his simultaneous belief in both tradition and innovation.[72] Perret was didactic, combative, and bombastic and, as Le Corbusier would suggest, at times, "categorical to the point of absurdity."[73] Perret's opinions were feared and respected; his aphoristic pronouncements had a declaratory authority in Parisian architectural and intellectual circles.

Perret's innovative use of new materials and techniques was evident in his early factory, theater, and apartment designs.[74] Trained in his father's Parisian construction firm, he developed an early commitment to reinforced concrete as a building material.[75] The ferroconcrete frame made it possible to vault a large interior space without the obstruction of pillars or columns. Perret's church of Notre Dame, Le Raincy (1922), for example, relied on a load-bearing ferroconcrete skeleton to vault its massive interior. Ironically, these changes in construction materials—particularly the development of reinforced concrete—led to Le Corbusier's expansion of the window to a wide horizontal span.

Vertical casement windows, having made their first appearance in Versailles in the 1680s, had acquired the status of a national idiom, the "French window."[76] In his punning *détournement* of the architectural figure of the French window, Marcel Duchamp performed a knowing affront to this idiom in his readymade work *Fresh Widow,* a miniature-scale wooden casement window shrouded in black leather. It serves for neither light nor ventilation, is neither transparent nor openable. As "widow," the window takes on a gender—a tragic bride, perhaps having lost her transparency.[77] Duchamp's window cannily replaces Alberti's *aperta finestra*—and his foreclosure of classical representation attacks notions of the painting, the artist, the framed view of the world. Yet his ironic play on the French window only underlines its iconic stature.

The controversy between Perret and Le Corbusier ensued from a comment about fenestration and proper illumination that Perret had made in an interview

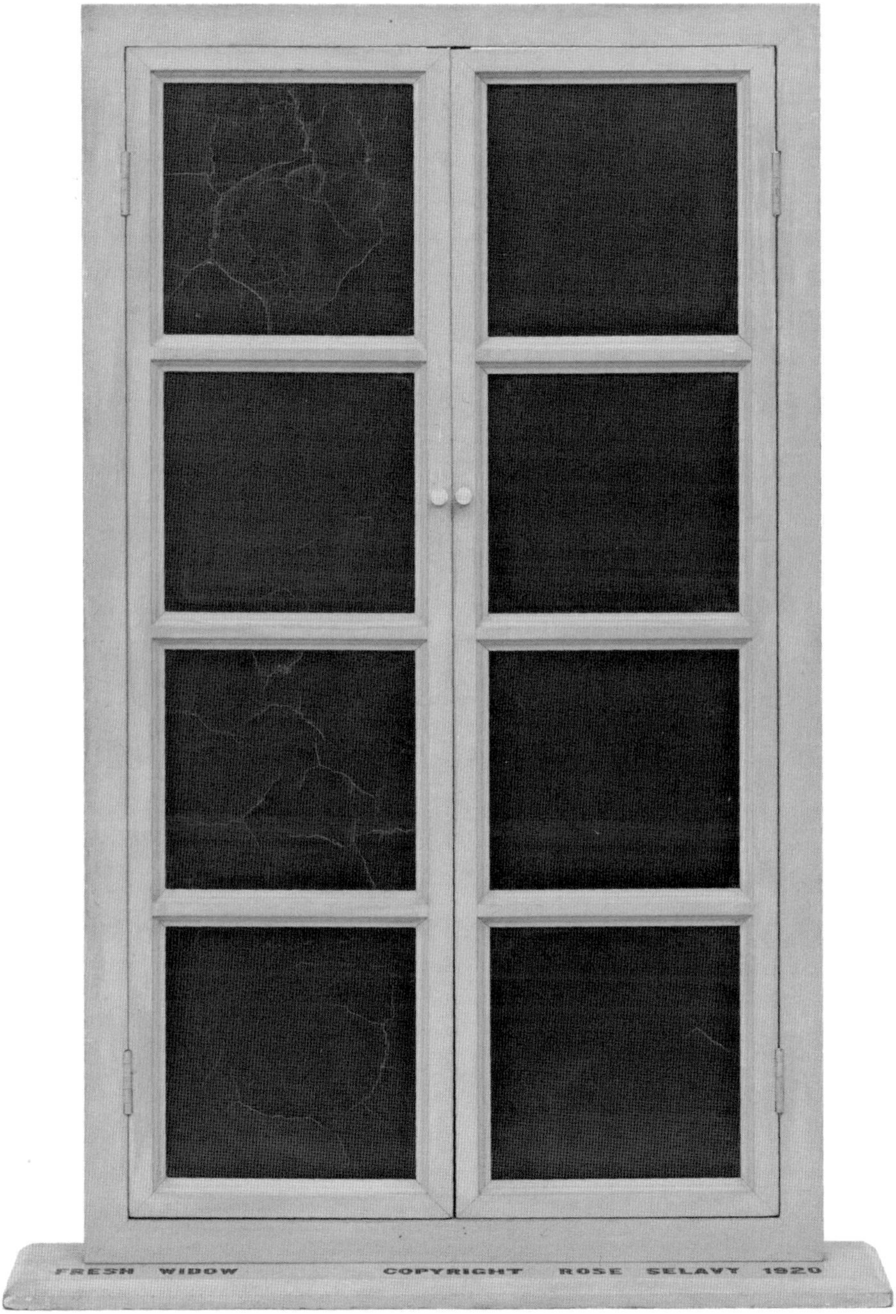

3.13 Marcel Duchamp, *Fresh Widow,* 1920, miniature French window, painted wood frame, and eight panes of glass covered with black leather on wood sill. The Museum of Modern Art, New York, Katherine S. Dreier Bequest. © ARS, NY. Digital image © The Museum of Modern Art/Licensed by Scala/Art Resource, New York.

with a journalist for *Paris Journal* in 1923. "A window is made to illuminate, to let light into an interior, and this is the reason for its existence, its prime quality," declared Perret:

> Then it has other secondary qualities, one of which, for instance, is to embellish the façade with the different forms that its opening can take; but this is no more than a detail and it would be absurd and tantamount to confusing the part with the whole, to regard a window solely as an ornamental motif. Now this is somewhat the tendency of Le Corbusier: . . . he tortures the openings by stretching them to an exaggerated degree in a vertical or in a horizontal direction.[78]

Le Corbusier was incensed by the criticism that his window did not allow for light. He responded in two successive subsequent issues of the *Paris Journal,* emphasizing that his windows were made possible by "the new conditions" of Perret's own prized ferroconcrete:

> All my architecture is conditional upon the windows. Windows totally suited to the new conditions brought about by reinforced concrete and metallurgy, but also adapted in turn to human functions. The windows are the main concern—concern of the technician and the aesthetician. I would like Perret to know that, after years of study, my windows will at last be mass produced by a large ironworks, they will work like precision machines, and this in itself was not easy to achieve.[79]

The horizontal window expanded the frame of the traditional French window not only by admitting more light, but also by encasing a panorama that, in essence, brought more of the outside in.

While the material dictates of the window's size and shape were a key factor in Le Corbusier's justification of his fenestration, the window's relation to "human functions" took the debate to its more philosophical (and perhaps snidely nationalist) extremes. As a proponent of the *porte-fenêtre,* Perret took Le Corbusier's horizontal window as an affront to the "fine French tradition" of the vertical window.[80] The upright rectangle of the vertical window embodied a cultural topos akin to the human measure of Alberti's window. "The horizontal window is not a window at all," Perret declared. Perret's attachment to the verticality of the French window came down to his belief in the anthropomorphic measure of the human habitant. Le Corbusier retorts: "the following sentence has been thrown at me: 'A window is a man, it stands upright!'"[81] If we return to two of the components of the window in Alberti's instructional passage in *De pictura*—the geometry of the rectangle and the human measure—the insistence that the vertical "French" window stand "upright" like a man makes a presumptive equation between the Gallic and the phallic. Le Corbusier's counterdefense of his horizontal window also anthropomorphized its function as the "chief protagonist of the house" (*l'acteur primordial de la maison*) but without the erectile chauvinism.[82]

In a 1984 article "The Pros and Cons of the Horizontal Window," Bruno Reichlin describes the debate between these two architects as an embodiment of "two distinct cultures."[83] In Reichlin's reading, Perret's defense of the *porte-fenêtre* was also a defense of traditional perspectival representation and the position of the viewer in relation to its depth. Le Corbusier's horizontal window served to challenge this traditional "perspectival window" with a window that—by cutting out the foreground and the sky—flattened the perspectival depth of the view. Reichlin compares Le Corbusier's window to the challenges made to perspective by modern painting: "With regard to the conception and effect of space, the horizontal window thus plays a similar role as the artistic experiments which, proceeding from the 'window motif,' brought about the transformation of the panel painting into an emphatically two-dimensional art form."[84]

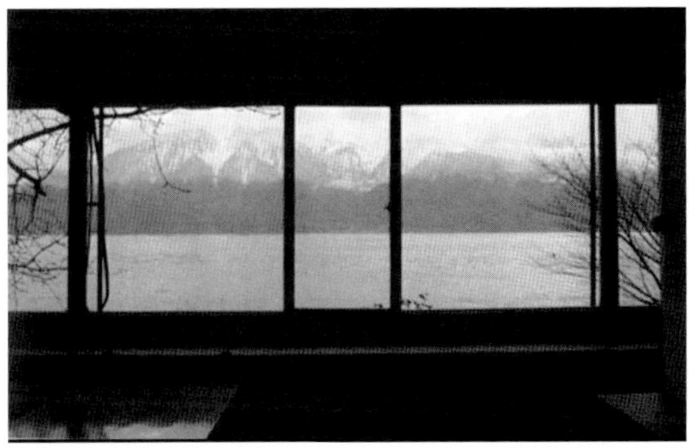

3.14 View of Lake Geneva through Le Corbusier's eleven-meter horizontal window, from *Une petite maison* (1923; Zurich: Editions d'Architecture, 1954).

Beatriz Colomina comes to a slightly different conclusion about the fenestration debate between Perret and Le Corbusier. While Reichlin reads the expansive horizontality of Corbusier's eleven-meter window as a challenge to the traditional fixity and proportion implied by the perspectival frame, Colomina restates the opposition between the vertical and horizontal window in terms of an opposition between perspective's "impression of complete space" and the "pictorial frontality" of purist painting.[85] But in Colomina's discussion, Le Corbusier's horizontal window also "corresponds . . . to the space of photography"[86] and represents an "architectural correlative of the space of the movie camera."[87] In this way, the house becomes a "system for taking pictures"; "no more than a system of views choreographed by the visitor, the way a filmmaker effects the montage of a film."[88] To Colomina, the "epistemological break between photography and perspective" occurred when the mechanical "eye" of the camera replaced the human(ist) eye. Her reading emphasizes the "eye" of the camera, its ability to move or be moved in a panoramic sweep ("the dispersal of the eye in Le Corbusier's villas of the twenties, effected through the architectural promenade").[89]

Here, Colomina's suggestion that the horizontal window is an "architectural correlative of the space of the movie camera" contains some assumptions that need to be clarified.[90] The "space of photography" and the "space of the movie camera" are not only different from each other but both are also significantly different from the space of the screen. If we unpack the implications of Colomina's analogy, the architectural "visitor" is likened to a camera (taking either still or moving images), but not to the viewer of a photograph or to the spectator of a film. (There may be a more radical assumption lurking beneath Colomina's analogy: that Le Corbusier's houses themselves, as viewing "machines," do not have human viewers at all; the inhabitor instead becomes a cyborg cameradroid.) Yet, unlike the camera's framed, mechanically recorded and reproduced view, the experience of architecture by a human viewer is unframed, unrepeatable, transient. Both the "space of photography" and the "space of the movie camera" are virtual spaces, framed, time-shifted, reproduced.

To return to the debate about fenestration, the frame of the window and its glass expanse become only one element in the inhabitor's or camera's mobile view. The constantly changing play of light and shifting point(s) of view are still framed by the camera itself—viewed through its delimited frame. A key paradox of the movie camera's mobility is that its fluid "panning," its mechanically aided movement through space, is reduced to the fixed frame of the screen. The movie viewer looks not at a horizontal panorama but at a fixed rectangular frame. Simply put, the camera's "eye" is not the same as the view of its recorded moving images.

I will return to this paradoxical tension between the camera's movement and the fixed frame of the screen in the next chapter when I discuss the "architecture of spectatorship." But, for now, let me invoke a passage from the beginning of Gilles Deleuze's *L'image-mouvement* to help underline this distinction:

> On the one hand, the viewpoint [prise de vue] was fixed, the shot was therefore spatially and strictly immobile; on the other hand, the apparatus for shooting [appareil de prise de vue] was combined with the apparatus for projection [appareil de projection], endowed with uniform abstract time. The evolution of the cinema, the conquest of its own essence or novelty, was to take place through montage, the mobile camera and the emancipation of the viewpoint, which became separate from projection. The shot would then stop being a spatial category and

become a temporal one; and the section [la coupe] would no longer be immobile, but mobile.[91]

While Deleuze is largely concerned with the temporal categories that the image gains when movement is added to the fixed view of the photographic camera, he importantly separates the view of the camera (*appareil de prise de vue*) from the view of the projector (*appareil de projection*). The space of photography, framed and fixed for the viewer, struggles to represent the experience of architectural space—inhabited by a moving body with a shifting visual field.[92] The mobile view of the movie camera—whether made mobile by combining static shots in sequence, by panning or tracking through space, or by intercutting separate spaces and times—is still reduced to the fixed frame of the screen in front of an immobile viewer.

CASE STUDY 2: THE MODERN SCREEN: EISENSTEIN V. THE ACADEMY OF MOTION PICTURE ARTS AND SCIENCES

While controversies about the size and shape of the architectural window were occurring among architects, similar debates about the size and shape of the cinema screen were being waged by filmmakers. The Perret-Le Corbusier debate about horizontality versus verticality strikingly prefigures a polemic about screen size and format by Soviet filmmaker and theorist Sergei Eisenstein only a few years later.[93]

On 17 September 1930, Eisenstein gave a speech at a meeting of the Technicians Branch of the Academy of Motion Picture Arts and Sciences in Hollywood. The text of his speech was published in the film journal *Close Up* in March 1931 as "The Dinamic Square."[94] In a rollicking and intently polemical style, Eisenstein eschews the shape of the frame—the 3 × 4, 3 × 5, and 3 × 6 aspect ratios—which "for thirty years," he claims, "has bent us and obliged us to a passive horizontalism." In reaction, Eisenstein passionately champions (upholds!) vertical, upright compositions. "It is my purpose," Eisenstein proclaims, "to defend the cause of this 50 percent of compositional possibilities exiled from the light of the screen. It is my desire to chant the hymn of the male, the strong, the virile, active, *vertical* composition!" He continues:

> I am not anxious to enter into the dark phallic and sexual ancestry of the vertical shape as symbol of growth, strength, or power. It would be too easy and possibly too offensive for many a delicate hearer! But I do want to point out that the movement towards a vertical perception led our hairy ancestors on their way to a higher level. This vertical ten-

> dency can be traced in their biological, cultural, intellectual and industrial efforts and manifestations.
>
> We started as worms creeping on our stomach. Then we ran horizontally for hundreds of years on our four legs. But we became something like mankind only from the moment when we hoisted ourselves onto our hind legs and assumed the vertical position.[95]

Of course, Eisenstein's plea for the phallic verticality of the screen—even if tongue-in-cheek, and as an acting out of his self-cast part as bad-boy-in-Hollywood—is not only a reflection on the relation of the objects on the screen to the screen's aspect ratio, but also a speculation on the broader implications of its otherwise unquestioned horizontality. While Eisenstein partly demurs from providing "an outline of the whole influence of the biological and psychological revolution and shock which followed from that paramount change of attitude," he claims that human progress "to a higher level of social, cultural, or intellectual

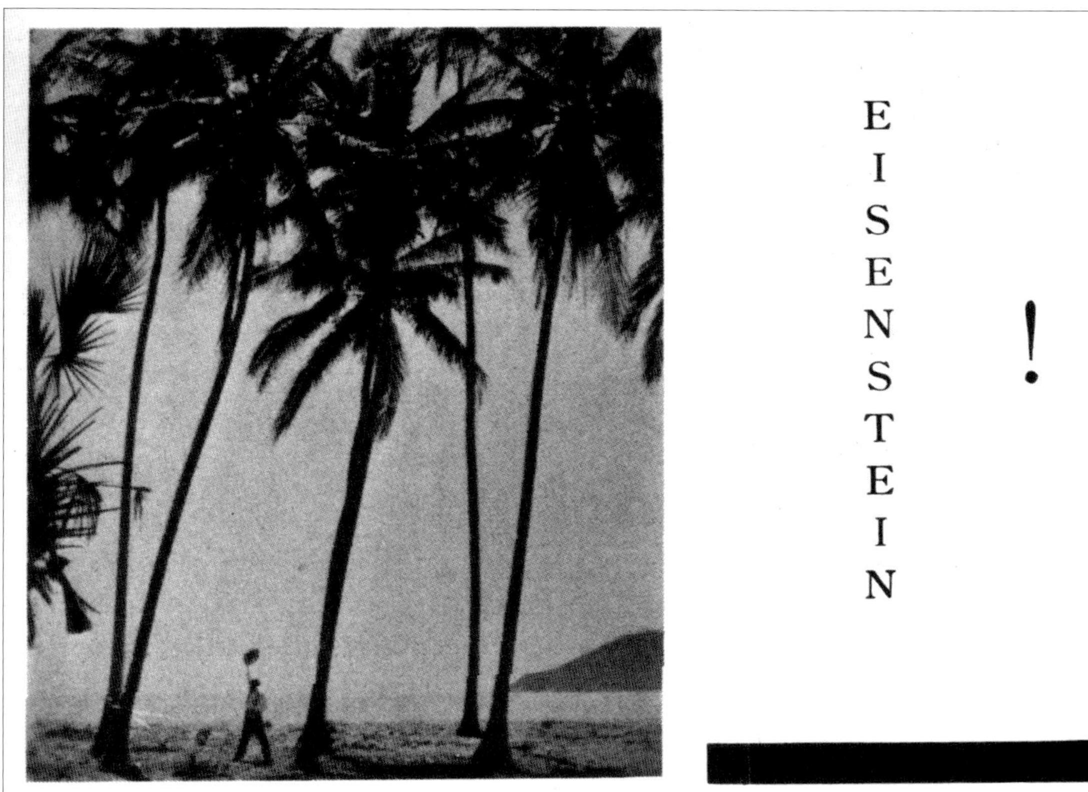

3.15 Page from *Close Up*, 1931.

development" has been marked in "vertical milestones" from the obelisks of Egyptian astrologers to the Gothic ogive arch and spire to the Eiffel Tower to the "huge skylines . . . armies of skyscrapers and the infinite rows of smoking chimneys or trellised oil pumps of our great industries."[96] (Much of this text was punctuated with vertical exclamation marks—and in *Close Up*, Eisenstein's name was placed in a vertical typography next to a large vertical exclamation mark!)

Yet, after several pages of derisive declamation of the horizontal, Eisenstein coyly claims a "nostalgia of infinite horizons"—for "'big trails,' 'fighting caravans,' 'covered wagons,' and the endless breadth of 'old man rivers,' and concludes with sarcastic diplomacy that "neither the horizontal nor the vertical proportion of the screen alone is ideal for it."[97] Instead of the stabilized format of the film screen, Eisenstein contraposes an alternative: the "dinamic square," a screen with changeable proportions of the projected picture. Eisenstein's appeal for a dynamic square, while consistent with the frame of the screen as a "window on the world," was keyed to the idea of a window with mobile sashes and sills.

The standardization of the physical characteristics of screen size had both technical and economic determinants in the competing formats for aspect ratio and film gauge size. The origins of the 1.33:1 aspect ratio for a rectangular frame and screen can be traced back to the 35mm format developed by Thomas Edison and W. K. L. Dickson in 1889.[98] Photographic camera mechanisms determined many of the early film gauges and aspect ratios, but the need for standardization of a photographic format became more pressing once film stock was manufactured in standard gauges. Unlike photographers who needed to match film stock to a camera mechanism, filmmakers needed to rely on a standard projection gauge for their films if they wished their films to be distributed to projection systems in theaters around the world.[99] In this regard, the aspect ratio of the projected image also determined the shape of the screen. In fact, it was the uniformity of film frame size, its aspect ratio—as distinct from the variable sizes of frames in painting—that Stephen Heath argues was crucial for setting the conditions of spectatorship.[100] Hence it should be emphasized that while there never was a standard ratio for rectangular size or shape in painting, the film frame retained remarkable consistency in the 1.33:1 aspect ratio.

When Eisenstein spoke to the Technicians Branch of the Academy of Motion Picture Arts and Sciences in September 1930, the Academy was still a relatively new organization (it had formed in May 1927, and had given out its first awards in 1929). The Academy was in the midst of formulating its own standards for film gauge and aspect ratio. In 1932, after extensive research and review, the Academy established the 1.33:1 (4 × 3) aspect ratio as standard. The

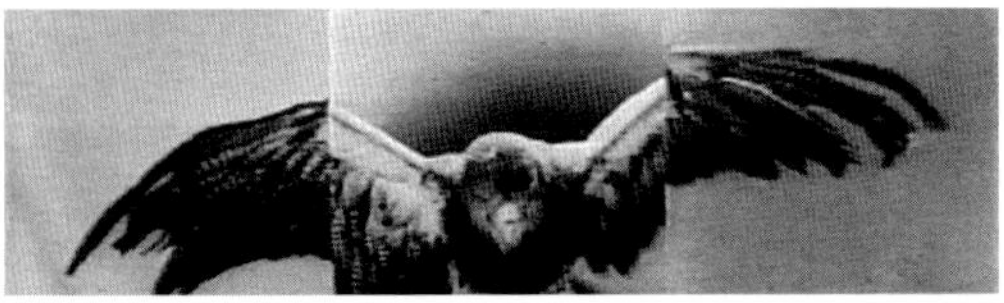

3.16 *Napoléon,* directed by Abel Gance, 1927: triptych effect.

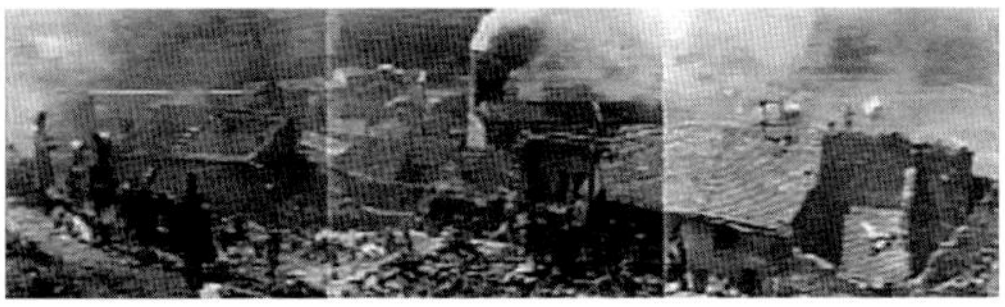

3.17 *Napoléon,* directed by Abel Gance, 1927: panoramic continuity.

"Academy ratio," "Academy Aperture," or "Academy Standard" became the standard for camera, projection, and screen apertures worldwide.[101]

The "dynamism" of Eisenstein's screen was found in its potential to fluidly reframe the image, an effect that had been demonstrated in the epic unfurling of the frame's edges at the end of Abel Gance's 1927 three-screen *Napoléon.* While Gance's three-camera, three-screen "Polyvision" system is generally discussed as a precursor to the "widescreen" formats of the 1950s, his use of three horizontally arrayed screens both as a continuously expansive panorama and as separate triptych panels marks the film as an unusual experiment in multiple-screen narrative.

Gance's Polyvision was not the first multiple-camera/multiple-projector system. Raoul Grimoin-Sanson's ten-projector panoramic screen, the Cinéorama, which debuted at the Paris 1900 Exposition, used ten 70mm projectors in a dramatic experiment in 360-degree panoramic display.[102] The immersive 360-degree Cinéorama poses a dramatic contrast to the 4:3 paradigm that emerged once the conventions of moving-picture exhibition settled on theatrical projection and display. The cinema camera recorded moving images by framing them through the lens of the camera and then replayed them as moving pictures in a framed viewer or on a screen. Movement was captured but at the same time confined.

Gance filmed using three interlocked cameras and yet reserved this multiple-screen Polyvision format for the dramatic finale of the film, Napoleon's Italian campaign. The complex spatial and temporal relations between the three screens include a daunting array of shot combinations in both sequential and serial array. In some cases, for example, three separate shots are arranged as if they were contemporaneous crosscuts. (One example is a triptych with Napoleon in the center screen panel flanked by hundreds of soldiers in the two side panels. Another example of such simultaneity arrayed across the three screens is when the army divides into three lines of troops, each in a separate screen panel. More complex sequences use rapid montage, dissolves, and superimpositions in some panels and not in others.) In other instances in *Napoléon,* three shots are arranged in matched continuity to expand the limits of one screen into an expansive panorama, as Napoleon surveys the expanse of his army's encampment at Albenga, for example, or as an eagle extends its wings across the three screens.[103] The consummate image of Gance's *Napoléon* is formed when the three screens—separately hand-tinted in blue, white, and red—unfurl as a *tricouleur* to join together in one continuous panoramic French flag. It is as if Gance's 1927 film culminates in a horizontal screen equivalent of the *fenêtre en longueur,* a cinematic (and equally nationalist) retort to Auguste Perret.

Gance's Polyvision experimentation and Eisenstein's interest in a "dynamic square" may have been part of the redefinition of the basic cinematic apparatus caused by the addition of sound. In the 1950s, debates around screen format emerged as a reaction to the commercial introduction of television. But the widening horizontal stretch of the screen was predominantly explored in the direction of the ontology of realism, not in the "Polyvision" mode of multiple screens that could complicate the spatial and temporal "scope" of the screened image. I will return to this discussion of the use of the multiple split-screen in my final chapter, but here wish to emphasize that the dominant use of this expanded screen "real estate" was to expand the frame, not to multiply the images or perspectives within it.

THE VIRTUAL WINDOW

The H. G. Wells pronouncement, "the age of windows lasted four centuries," posits a postfenestration architecture of the twenty-first century, an architecture imagined in the set design of a 1936 William Cameron Menzies film. His *Things to Come* envisions the "Everytown" of 2036 as an interior space resembling many planned public spaces of the late twentieth century—shopping malls, hotel lobbies, air terminals. In *Things to Come,* the interiors are strikingly absent of windows, as if air circulation and lighting are unseen functions in the breathing apparatus of the twenty-first-century building.[104] "Everytown" anticipates the type of "mutation in built space itself" that Fredric Jameson found in John Portman's 1976 Los Angeles Bonaventure Hotel, built only forty years after the 1936 *Things to Come.* Jameson assesses the perceptual disjunctions in such a "postmodern hyperspace"—the visitor shoots vertically up and through the atrium to visit a revolving cocktail lounge with another moving vantage on the city and its views. A "new sensorium" is needed, Jameson maintains, in order to contend with the building's "unimaginable, perhaps ultimately impossible, dimensions."[105]

The following discussion of the set design in *Things to Come* will accentuate the embodied difference between the architectural visitor (whose mobility through space has perceptual consequences) and the spectator of a framed screen image (whose immobility is compensated for in the virtual mobilities of the moving image). The "Everytown" of the future in *Things to Come* has many modes of moving transport, but they are shown to spectators only in the fixed frame of viewing. Its elevator tubes and moving walkways form vectors of movement solely within and through the frame. While cinematic set design could posit imaginary spaces without the material constraints of the built world, these newly fashioned spaces could be experienced only in a framed view. Hence the film has rapid montage sequences designed to emulate a sensorium of movement within the frame.

In fact, like other science fiction films, *Things to Come* self-reflexively serves as a "history picture," a fictional postulate about a future imagined from (what is now) the past.[106] *Things to Come* traces the last decades of the twentieth century—from the darkening fears of war on Christmas eve in 1940 onward through the war-ravaged years 1945, 1955, 1960, 1964, and 1966. By 1966, Everytown is in ruins. A "wandering sickness," a "new fever of mind and body" has spread throughout the world, and by 1967, this plague of peripetia has "like the black death . . . killed more than half the human race." In 1970, "the pestilence has ceased," and the film's arch dialogue of exasperation speaks the foreclosure of all hope: "what's the use . . . there's no petrol . . . flying is finished . . . everything's over . . . civilization's dead."[107]

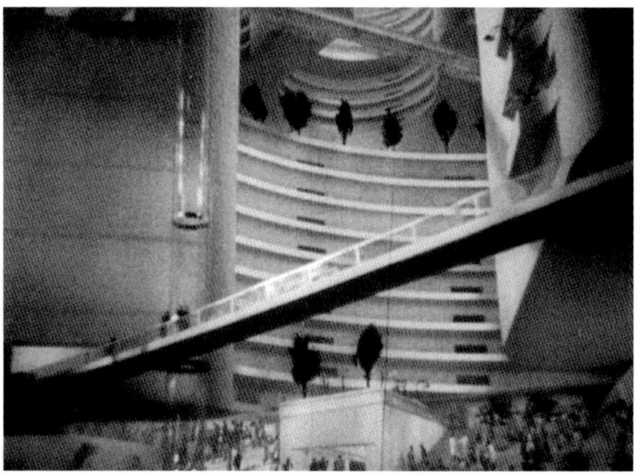

3.18 Frame enlargement from *Things to Come,* London Film Productions, directed by William Cameron Menzies, 1936.

Wells imagines a late-twentieth-century postapocalyptic interlude—the world run by a barely literate warlord, broken-down automobiles drawn by horses. Women wash their children in tubs in the street; the midcentury advances of transportation and communications are all but lost. The hopes for a utopian future (following many of the tenets of Wells's Fabian politics) are found in the character of John Cabal (played by Raymond Massey), who promotes a government of common sense and world communication, a "New Order" of freemasons, a "Brotherhood of Efficiency," who seek salvation through the communally deployed aircraft of "Wings over the World." The rebuilding of the once-decimated Everytown is shown in a five-and-a-half minute dialogue-free sequence—a montage of conveyor belts, factory production, drilling, spinning, neon bulbs, machines with many abstract light patterns, machinery moving in diagonals across the frame. The final scenes of the film take place in the strikingly streamlined spaces of 2036.[108]

The production team for *Things to Come* drew upon a variety of talents to construct its mise-en-scène of the future. In a recent monograph on the film, Christopher Frayling provides a detailed account of the film's production design.[109] Producer Alexander Korda hired director William Cameron Menzies, whose experience as art director, storyboard artist, illustrator, and "visualizer" was intended to counterbalance the wordy abstractions of H. G. Wells. In Frayling's account, Wells made dictatorial attempts to participate in every aspect of the film from script to casting to soundtrack to costume and set design. Wells first approached artist Fernand Léger (who had done the sets for Marcel L'Herbier's *L'inhumaine* in 1924) to do the set design; but when Léger provided sketches for the film, Wells found them to be "too kinetic" and too much like Léger's abstract film *Ballet mécanique* (1924). Wells then approached Le Corbusier (whose 1925 *Urbanisme* contained a compelling vision of the city of the future). According to Frayling, while Le Corbusier's writings may have influenced the production designer Vincent Korda and his son Michael, Le Corbusier himself was not taken with Wells's vision of the future and did not work on the film. Hungarian futurist and Bauhaus member László Moholy-Nagy was also asked if he would develop ideas for the rebuilding of the Everytown sequence. The Kordas had known Moholy-Nagy since 1930 and had seen his short abstract film *Light-Play* (1930). Moholy-Nagy worked on various special effects of light and movement using models built with a new transparent plastic material, Rhodoid. The final set design relied heavily on this new Plexiglas material to build the furniture, desks, couches, chairs, and transparent screen supports, but only ninety seconds of Moholy-Nagy's special effects made the final cut.[110]

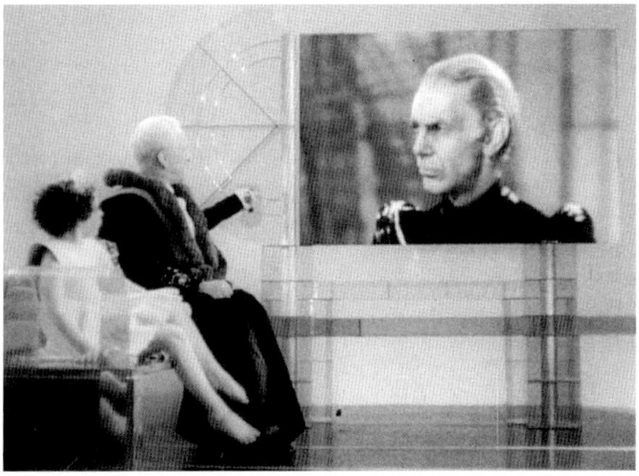

3.19 "You can see him in the pictures." Frame enlargement from *Things to Come*, London Film Productions, directed by William Cameron Menzies, 1936.

The stilted dialogue of *Things to Come* ("Why does it come to this? Why do we have to murder each other?"), delivered with stentorian staginess by performers wearing togas and sandals, stands in stark contrast to a setting that is sparse, sleek, and modern.[111] In the scene discussed at the opening of this chapter, the "screen" displaying "history pictures" floats atop transparent Rhodoid supports in a sparsely minimalist room with polished floors and transparent furniture. The first image on this screen is the shot of the New York skyline that evokes the remark, "what a funny place . . . all sticking up and full of windows." There is no projection mechanism in the room, only a surface that "transmits" moving images. In the shot before the young girl and her great-grandfather sit down to look at the "pictures," we see them from the back of screen through its transparent planar surface. As other shots of windows follow in this architectural tutorial, Ralph Richardson narrates: "they didn't seem to realize we could light the interior of our houses with sunshine of our own . . . there was no need to stick them up so high into the air." As the sequence of windows concludes, the young girl says rather leadenly: "They keep on inventing new things now don't they? And making life lovelier and lovelier."

Wells's concept of "history pictures" drew upon the archival documentary qualities of film—its ability to preserve images that no longer exist, histories that had since become invisible, like these now-strange images of windows. "History pictures" also served as a photographic album of ancestors long dead. As the dialogue proceeds:

> Great-grandfather: Go back to your history pictures . . .
> Girl: Did you see John Cabal, great-grandfather?
> Great-grandfather: You can see him in the pictures.
> Girl: You saw him when he lived.
> Great-grandfather: Yes, I saw the great John Cabal with my own eyes when I was a little boy . . . [He turns and adjusts the knob to a picture of John Cabal]

The pictures are adjusted by a dial on a transparent mount next to its transparent frame. Here the cut from the image of Raymond Massey as John Cabal on the "history" screen, to Raymond Massey as his great-grandson Oswald Cabal in the next shot enacts the fictional conceit of casting the same actor as his ancestor.

The "history picture" screen, sized for the domestic interior, is only one of many screens in *Things to Come.* As the film enters into its final rhetorical debate about technology, the character Theotocopulos (Sir Cedric Hardwicke) readies to make a speech against the symbol of technological progress, a "Space Gun" designed to propel two young humans into space. A large transparent surface descends into the public atrium space of Everytown, and a large crowd gathers to watch his five-story-tall "televised" speech against "progress." Cut to Oswald Cabal (Raymond Massey) at his desk pushing back a smaller transparent screen device, bemoaning the broadcast signal: "And that voice is sounding to the whole world." The image of Theotocopulos appears in a subsequent shot on another (vertically oriented) room-sized screen, stared at by two young viewers. In the final shot of the sequence, on the big screen in the public atrium, Theotocopulos declares: "Make an end to progress now; let this be the last day of the scientific age." Wells was certainly aiming for the irony implicit in the use of this advanced telecommunications device to broadcast a call to stop progress.

The televisual screens seen in the 1936 film *Things to Come* had appeared in several earlier films that also envisioned a future with screenic devices for telecommunicating. In Marcel L'Herbier's *L'inhumaine* (1924; with set designs by Fernand Léger, Robert Mallet-Stevens, and Pierre Chareau and costumes by Paul Poiret), the scientist Norsen invents a televisual machine in his laboratory (designed by Robert Mallet-Stevens and Léger) that could put a scene from anywhere in the world on the screen at the flick of a switch.[112] Fritz Lang uses para-cinematic surveillance "monitors" in *Der Spinnen* (1919), *Dr. Mabuse* (1922), and *Metropolis* (1926). In Lang's films, technologies of vision are deployed as regulatory devices, instrumental necessities for characters mad for the power made possible by a controlling gaze. The giant control panel (*Herzmaschine* or Heart Machine, HM2) that regulates the underground city in *Metropolis* is a television apparatus.[113]

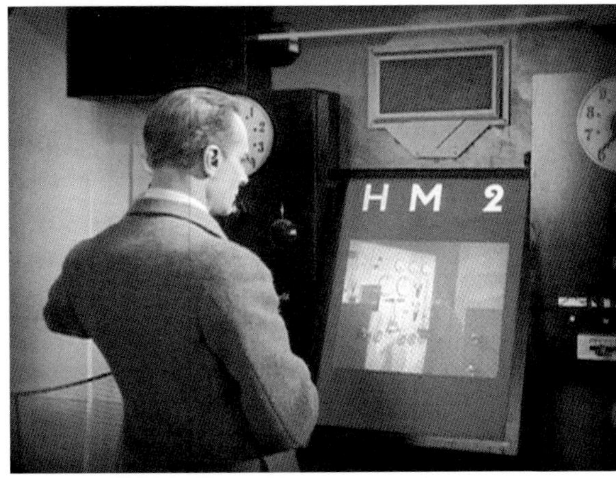

3.20 Frame enlargement from *Metropolis*, UFA Films, directed by Fritz Lang, 1927.

The architect Friedrich (later Frederick) Kiesler used an optical—not electronic—televisual device in his sets for the stage play of Karel Čapek's *R.U.R. (Rossum's Universal Robots)* in 1923. The special effect of this "Tanagra Apparat" relied on a mirror placed in small inset screen in the center of the stage:

> I had a big, square panel window in the middle of the stage drop which could be opened by remote control. When the director of the human factory in the play pushed a button at his desk, the panel opened and the audience saw two human beings reflected from a mirror arrangement backstage. The actors appeared in this window as a foot-and-a-half tall, casually moving and talking, heard through a hidden loud speaker. It was quite an illusion because a minute later you saw the same actors appear on stage in full size.[114]

In 1926–1927 Kiesler also constructed a "modern room," a "TELEVISION ROOM" for a Société Anonyme exhibition—in which visitors could see masterpieces from museums of the world at the touch of a button.[115]

In the fictions of these works, the para-cinematic, prototelevisual screens serve as both cautionary and awe-inspiring projections of the screens of the future. The "history pictures" of *Things to Come* conflate the architectural tutorial given by Ralph Richardson in the film's fiction with the film *Things to Come* itself, as a "history picture" of a 1936 vision of the future. If we draw back for a moment and gaze across the temporal timeline of 1936, we see that Walter Benjamin's "Work of Art" and Erwin Panofsky's "On Movies" form visions related to the telecommunicating projections of *Things to Come.*[116]

Large-screen televisions and high-resolution flat-screen displays illustrate how contemporary screens have gotten big enough and flat enough to substitute for windows. In 1995, the *New York Times* described the wall-sized screens in Bill Gates's $30 million home in Seattle: "Instead of traveling the world to collect great art for his nooks and sky-lighted reception rooms," the *Times* remarked, cyber-baron Gates "bought the electronic rights to art from museums like the National Gallery in London. With the press of a switch, the bathroom walls will become Rembrandts."[117] (If masterpieces can hang in your bathroom in electronically reproduced form, one can easily imagine a subscription service that would display the originals—a true masterpiece theater.) As flat-screen technology improves and screens replace real windows with a kind of "inhabited TV," a "windows environment" may give way to virtual "window-walls," an image not far from the shape of H. G. Wells's *Things to Come.*

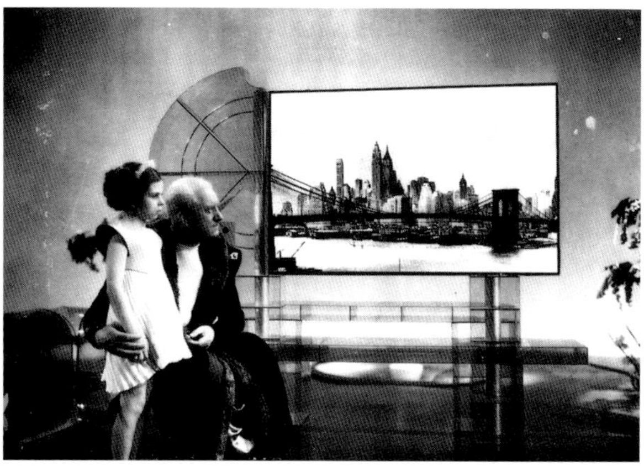

3.21 Frame enlargement from *Things to Come,* London Film Productions, directed by William Cameron Menzies, 1936.

The cinema screen transferred the sensual isolation produced by the plate glass window onto a virtual register. The cultural force of the cinematic and televisual screen produced an ingrained virtuality of the senses, removing our experience of space, time, and the real to the plane of representation, but in the form of delimited vision, in a frame. In this way, the screen—the film screen, the TV screen, the computer screen—is a component piece of architecture, a "virtual window" that renders the wall permeable to light and "ventilation" and that dramatically changes the materialities (and—perhaps more radically—the temporalities) of built space. A *virtual* window is reliant not on its transparency but on its opacity; its highly mediated modulation of light provides an aperture: not to a reality, but to a delimited *virtuality.* The "age of windows" may have lasted four centuries, but the "virtual window" will continue to transform our concept of architectural space.

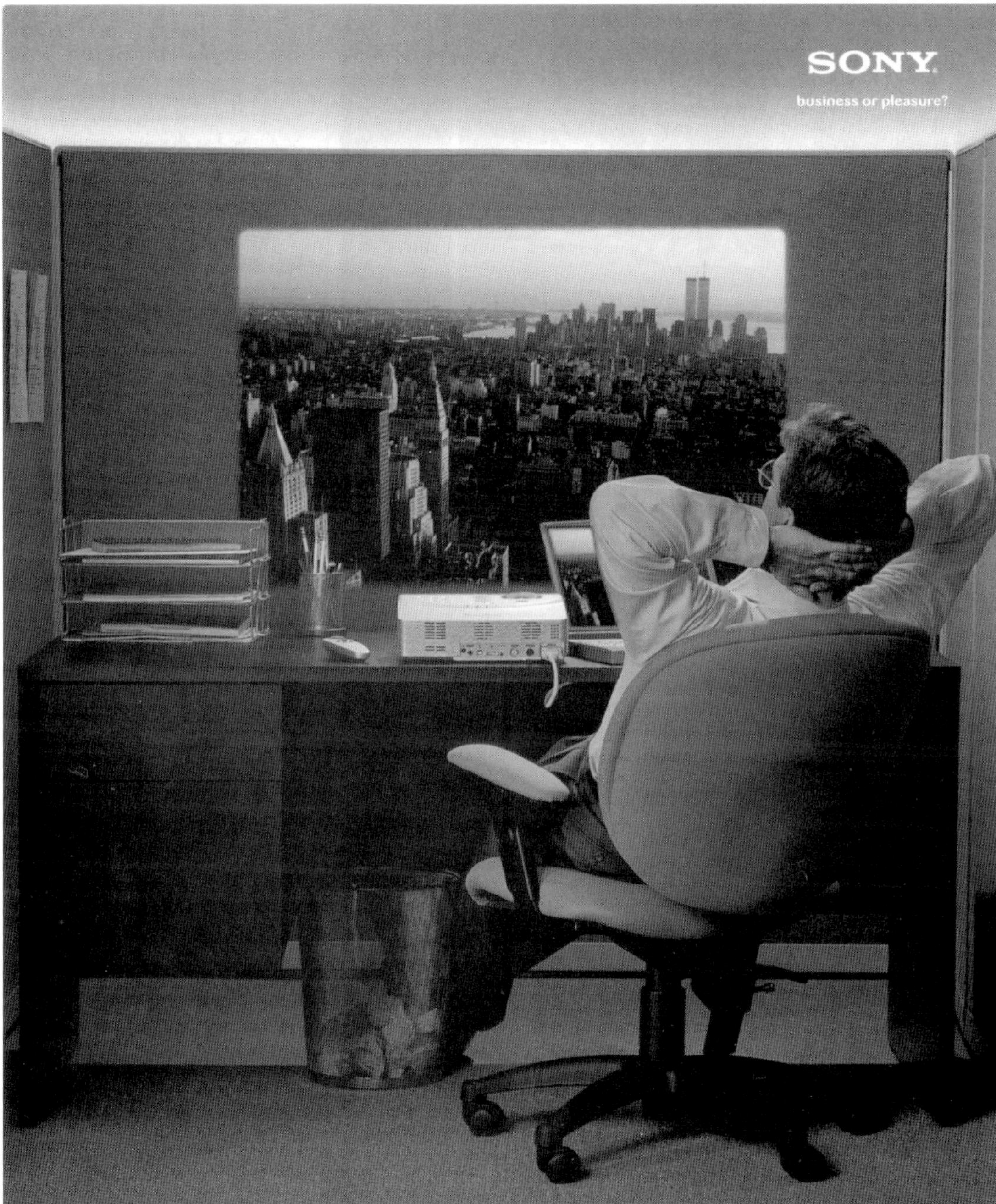

3.22 Sony LCD projector ad, November 2000.

LENS III

BERGSON'S VIRTUAL

DESPITE the assertions of those who equate virtuality with the late-twentieth-century changes wrought by digital technology, Bergson's writing profoundly illustrates that the term was an operable philosophical concept in the late nineteenth century.[1] An intellectual celebrity in Europe and America, Bergson was a philosopher who grappled with the changing experiences of time and space on the brink of a new century. Although Bergson is most frequently remembered for his concept of lived time (*durée*) and *élan vital* (creative impulse), his use of the term "virtual" provides a remarkably prescient insight into the philosophical consequences of photographic and cinematographic technologies.

The term first appears in *Time and Free Will* (1889) and soon after in *Matter and Memory* (1896).[2] For Bergson, the "virtual" served as an ontological distinction between the possible and the actual; aligned with the possible, the virtual was posed over and against the actual and the real. In *Matter and Memory,* Bergson's use of "virtual" seems to be taken directly from its optical definition, as if he were familiar with the Keplerian distinction between *imago* and *pictura.* Bergson turns the optics of light rays into a metaphor for perception: "To obtain this conversion from the virtual to the actual," he writes,

> it would be necessary, not to throw more light on the object, but, on the contrary to obscure some of its aspects, to diminish it by the greater part of itself, so that the remainder, instead of being encased in its surrounds as a *thing,* should detach itself from them as *picture.* . . . When a ray of light passes from one medium into another, it usually traverses it with a change of direction. But the respective densities of the two media may be such that, for a given angle of incidence, refraction is no longer possible. Then we have total reflection. The luminous point gives rise to *a virtual image* which symbolizes, so to speak, the fact that the luminous rays cannot pursue their way. . . . The objects merely abandon something of their real action in order to manifest their virtual influence . . . this is as much to say that *there is for images merely a difference of degree, and not of kind, between being and being consciously perceived.*[3]

The difference emphasized by Bergson here—"between being and being consciously perceived"—becomes the difference between the real and the virtual.

Bergson uses the term "virtual" to describe the nonmaterial properties of memory: "the memory-image itself, if it remained pure memory, would be ineffectual. Virtual, this memory can only become actual by means of the perception which attracts it. Powerless, it borrows life and strength from the present situation in which it is materialized."[4] The virtual here is latent until actualized by perception; memory is immaterial, not representable, until it is materialized in the present, becomes matter. The term "virtual" serves as a descriptor not only for the immateriality of memory but for the image that is mediated by "medium" (his word). In *Matter and Memory,* Bergson intends to resolve the dualist "intersection of mind and matter":[5] "Matter, in our view, is an aggregate of images. And by image we mean a certain existence which is more than that which the idealist calls a representation, but less than that which the realist calls a thing—an existence placed halfway between the 'thing' and the 'representation'"[6] *Matter and Memory* is structured as a treatise on the selection, recognition, survival, delimiting, and fixing of images.[7] As the above citation demonstrates, the "image" was "halfway" between the materiality of a "thing" and its immateriality in "representation."

In several remarkable passages of *Matter and Memory,* Bergson invokes the photograph as a metaphor for perception:

> we imagine *perception to be a kind of photographic view of things,* taken from a fixed point by that special apparatus which is called an organ of perception—*a photograph which would then be developed in the brain-matter* by some unknown chemical and psychical process of elaboration.[8]

As in much of Bergson's writing, he borders here on irredeemable abstraction, using the photographic camera—its lens and photosensitive plate—as a grand metaphysical metaphor. The virtual fits tidily as a photographic record:

> Only if, when we consider any other given place in the universe, we can regard the action of all matter as passing through it without resistance and without loss, and the photograph of the whole

as translucent: here there is wanting *behind the plate the black screen on which the image could be shown.* Our "zones of indetermination" play in some sort the part of the screen. They add nothing to what is there: they effect merely this: *the real action passes through, the virtual action remains.*[9]

This passage seems to describe a photosensitive surface ("behind the plate the black screen on which the image could be shown"/"il manque, derrière la plaque, un écran noir sur lequel se détacherait l'image") where the real action "passes through" (*passe*) the lens and the "virtual action" is all that remains (*l'action virtuelle demeure*).[10] In another striking passage at the beginning of the chapter entitled "Of the Survival of Images, Memory and Mind," Bergson draws upon the metaphor of the camera lens to describe the act of recollection:

> Whenever we are trying to recover a recollection, to call up some period of our history, we become conscious of an act *sui generis* by which we detach ourselves from the present in order to replace ourselves, first, in the past in general, then in a certain region of the past—*a work of adjustment, something like the focusing of a camera.* But our recollection still remains virtual.[11]

Gilles Deleuze has refered to this section as "the admirable passage where Bergson summarizes the whole of his theory."[12]

Between 1900 and 1904, Etienne-Jules Marey and Henri Bergson were both at the Collège de France. As Marta Braun notes, both were members of a small group dedicated to the scientific investigation of psychic phenomena, so that Bergson was undoubtedly familiar with Marey's work.[13] Marey's chronophotography is mentioned four times in Bergson's 1907 book *Creative Evolution.* But Marey's premises, rooted in scientific positivism and a belief in the machinic measurement of human movement, led him to different conclusions from those of Bergson. For Bergson, chronophotographs were not images of movement but motion made immobile, fixed in discrete sections. Chronophotography was, in a sense, the opposite of the cinematography: the freezing of motion into immobility instead of the "animation" of its immobile sections (*coupes*) into movement.

By the time Bergson wrote *Creative Evolution* (1907), he was taken with the "cinematographical" aspects of thought. In fact, in a footnote to a chapter of the book entitled "The Cinematographical Mechanism of Thought," Bergson notes that the chapter is "a very succinct résumé of views that we developed at length from 1900 to 1904 in our lectures at the Collège de France, especially in a course on the *History of the Idea of Time.* We then compared the mechanism of conceptual thought to that of the cinematograph."[14]

His choice of the term "cinematograph" is not accidental. By the year 1907, the Lumière brothers had taken their Cinématographe device around the globe, frequently recording the military review.[15] "Suppose we wish to portray on a screen a living picture, such as the marching past of a regiment," Bergson writes toward the end of *Creative Evolution.* "This is what the cinematograph does," he continues: "to take a series of snapshots of the passing regiment and to throw these instantaneous views on the screen, so that they replace each other very rapidly. . . . With photographs, each of which represents the regiment with a fixed attitude, it reconstitutes the mobility of the regiment marching."[16] Bergson's analysis is attuned to the *immobility* (his word) of the photograph: "It is true that if we had to do with photographs alone, however much we might look at them, we should never see them animated: *with mobility set beside immobility, even endlessly, we could never make movement.*"[17] Bergson appeals to the cinematograph as an apparatus based on a succession of photographic immobilities. "The movement does indeed exist here," he writes, "it is in the apparatus."[18] By proclaiming that "The mechanism of our ordinary knowledge is of a cinematographical kind," Bergson compares the apparatus of the intellect to persistence of vision, grasping mobility by synthesizing mobile objects.[19] While he describes the single moment fixed by the photographic image as a "mobile section"—an image congruent with Marey's "motion studies" conducted at the Station Physiologique—movement is produced only by the "apparatus" of the cinematograph.

I am not convinced, as other scholars seem to be, that Bergson's account of the cinematograph is a critque or condemnation of the cinema. Deleuze begins his first book on film, *Cinema 1: The Movement-Image,* with a lengthy exegesis of Bergson's "theses on movement" found in *Matter and Memory* and *Creative Evolution.* Deleuze points to a historical event that is frequently elided in discussions of Bergson's two texts: "Bergson was perfectly aware of the existence of mobile sections or movement-images. This happened before *Creative Evolution,* before the official birth of the cinema: it was set out in *Matter and Memory* in 1896. . . . Had Bergson forgotten it ten years later?"[20] Deleuze attempts to reclaim Bergson's treatment of the "cinematographic" by claiming this "memory lapse": "The cinema would rediscover that very movement-image of the first chapter of *Matter and Memory*."[21] Deleuze coins his own composite terms, derived from Bergson's opposition of movement and the image: "Movement as physical reality in the external world, and the image, as psychic reality in consciousness, could no longer be opposed. The Bergsonian discovery of a movement-image and still more profoundly of a time-image still retains such richness today that it is not certain that all of its consequences have been drawn."[22] Deleuze's two volumes on cinema took these hyphenated terms as their broad titles. Here, I will repeat an insight cited earlier in this volume, one that remains at the crux of my own argument about the spectatorial paradox of mobility and immobility and its reduction to a framed surface made "virtual":

> On the one hand, the view point [*prise de vue*] was fixed, the shot was therefore spatial and strictly immobile; on the other hand, the apparatus for shooting [*appareil de prise de vue*] was combined with the apparatus for projection, endowed with a uniform abstract time. The evolution of the cinema, the conquest of its own essence or novelty, was to take place through montage, the mobile camera and the emancipation of the view point, which became separate from projection. The shot would then stop being a spatial category and become a temporal one, and the section would no longer be immobile, but mobile.[23]

Although the "virtual" components of the cinema and its moving images were not part of Bergson's direct analysis, the writings of Deleuze and others have introduced Bergson's virtual as an ontological distinction, a new register of representation for the movement-image and the time-image.[24]

In *Duration and Simultaneity* (1922), the philosopher Bergson—whose concept of *durée* was a rejection of ideas of absolute quantifiable time—directly addressed the physicist Einstein, whose theory of relativity challenged the notion of objective time and recast the physical universe as measurable only by relative frames of reference.[25] On April 6, 1922, at a special reception for Einstein hosted in Paris by the Société de Philosophie, Bergson presented Einstein with a bold compliment: "I believe that we are being presented here not only with a new realm of physics, but also, in a certain respect, with a new way of thinking." After sketching his concept of "an intuitively established simultaneity," Bergson threw down a bold gauntlet: "When one accepts that the theory of relativity is a theory of physics, everything is left unfinished. There remains the need to determine the philosophical sense of the concepts that the theory has introduced."[26] Einstein restated the challenge: "So, the question before us is this: Is the philosopher's time the same as the physicist's?" Einstein's response tersely rejects an account of the subjectivity of the observer: "There are however objective events that are independent of all individuals. . . . There is therefore no philosopher's time; there is only a psychological time that differs from the time of the physicist."[27]

Bergson intended to give Einstein's theory of relativity the metaphysics it lacked, an intention that Deleuze found to be the "least appreciated aspect of his thought."[28] Bergson's encounter with Einstein was the culmination of his thinking about the idea of multiple time, a concept he had introduced as "multiplicity" to account for the *durée* of lived time. Put simply, Bergson's challenge to Einstein was that the human observer can't be—subjectively—in two places or times at once. Einstein's rebuttal, equally straightforward, was to counter with the nonsentient observer: two clocks can measure two times, with no need for the human observer.

In the next chapter, I will turn to the concept of multiplicity in order to distinguish between the representation of moving images as simultaneous or successive, multiple or sequential. The film technique of the crosscut, or "parallel editing"—the cinematic equivalent of "meanwhile"—posits sequential images as simultaneous events. By contrast, split-screen, multiple-screen, or multiply "windowed" representational systems produce distinctly different effects. And "multitasking," while giving the appearance of simultaneity, is sequential and very fast. As the technologies of the VCR and the DVR keep pace with physics and philosophy, multiple times can be experienced in more and more technologically mediated ways. Multiplicity, I will argue, allows us—in ways that neither Bergson nor Einstein could have foreseen—to inhabit, in a *virtual* sense, two or more spaces at once, and equally, two or more times.[29]

4

THE SCREEN

Mobile or immobile, everything that occupies space belongs to the domain of architecture.

AUGUSTE PERRET, *CONTRIBUTION TO A THEORY OF ARCHITECTURE*

Going to the cinema results in an immobilization of the body. Not much gets in the way of one's perception. All one can do is look and listen. One forgets where one is sitting. The luminous screen spreads a murky light throughout the darkness. Making a film is one thing, viewing a film another. Impassive, mute, still, the viewer sits. The outside world fades as the eye probes the screen. Does it matter what film one is watching? Perhaps. One thing all films have in common is the power to take perception elsewhere.

ROBERT SMITHSON, "A CINEMATIC UTOPIA"

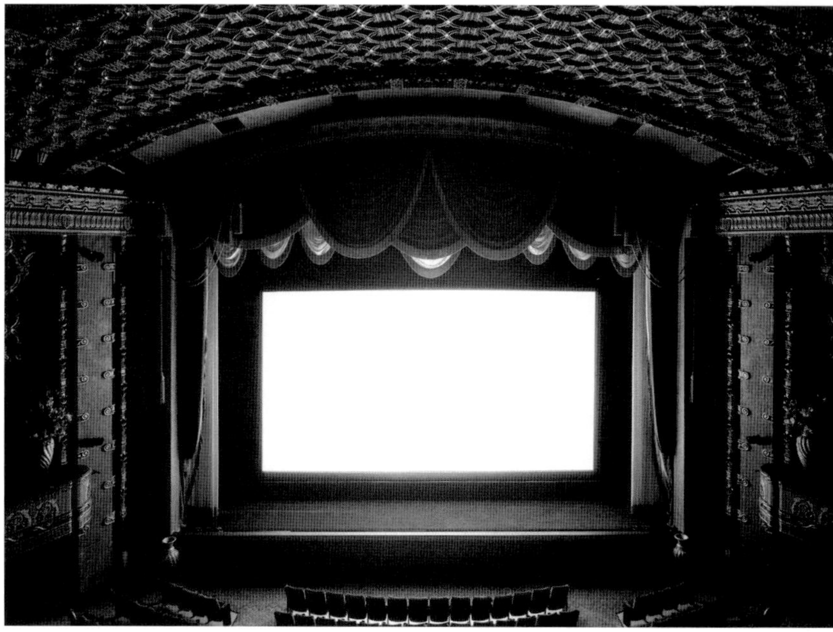

4.1 Hiroshi Sugimoto, *El Capitan,* 1993. Photo courtesy of Sonnabend Gallery, New York.

4 THE ARCHITECTURE OF SPECTATORSHIP

Architecture is experienced in a complex matrix of space. Using, visiting, inhabiting a building involves movement in, through, up, down, out. But as film spectators, as television viewers, as computer users, we are immobile in front of screens full of images and sounds.[1] Facing a screen, the spectator/viewer/user is caught in a phenomenological tangle—twin paradoxes—of mobility and immobility (the mobility of images; the immobility of the spectator) and of materiality and immateriality (the material space of the theater, domicile, or office and the immateriality of the cinematic, televisual, or computer image). The screen functions as an architectonic element, opening the materiality of built space to virtual apertures in an "architecture of spectatorship."[2]

Prevailing accounts of the relationship between film and architecture have typically held to some basic assumptions about the materiality of architectural space and the immateriality of cinematic space. In the most commonly theorized relation, cinematic space is conceptualized in terms of a pro-filmic "real" (filmed architecture) or a material "built environment" (set design). Hence, recent discussions of set design and the use of architecture within the film frame have focused on an emerging canon of historically disparate films (*The Cabinet of Dr. Caligari, Metropolis, L'inhumaine, Things to Come, The Fountainhead, Play-*

time, Blade Runner, Body Double) that illustrate how a range of architectures are rendered or imagined in cinematic mise-en-scène.[3] Other writers have explored how the fluid topographies built by montage and the moving camera were uniquely able to portray modern urban space and the visual cacophony of the city. The cinema, in these accounts, is a representational system commensurate with the new space and time of modernity.[4] Still others have described how montage and the moving camera had determinant effects on architects and their conception of architectural space.[5] Filmic space is seen, as Anthony Vidler has characterized it, "as a sort of laboratory for the exploration of the built world."[6]

The filmic representation of architectural space and the work of architects on film decor and mise-en-scène have been the predominant manners in which architecture and the cinema have been joined. A theory of spectatorship that describes the shifting views of a spectator engaged in an imaginary and *virtual mobility*, however, relies on a different concept of the space of spectatorship—one that emphasizes the relation between the bodily space inhabited by the spectator and the virtual visuality presented on the space of the screen. Instead of describing the use of architecture *within* the filmic or televisual image, the following account will consider the screen *as* architecture, as an expansion of material built space through the "virtual window" of the film, television, or computer screen.[7] The historical specificity of the cinema screen—and the luminous moving images projected upon it—forms a transitional surface as light becomes a building element in a newly *immaterial* architecture.

LIGHT AS A BUILDING MATERIAL: THE WALL BECOMES A SCREEN

> *Images have become a new form of light.*
>
> —Paul Virilio, interview in *Flash Art* (1988)

In the transfer of three-dimensional outside "sights" to a two-dimensional inside "wall," the camera obscura conducted a transformation from three-dimensional materiality to two-dimensional virtuality. The beams of light that pierced through the camera obscura's aperture carried images that were not static but moving. With the camera obscura, *virtual* movement was viewed by an immobile viewer.[8]

The camera obscura required strong outdoor solar illumination in order to project its image in a dark chamber. Since antiquity, both light and its primordial shadow, darkness, have been imbued with metaphysical properties. In Plato's allegory of the cave, Hans Blumenberg writes, "the *metaphorics* of light already has a *metaphysics* of light implicit in it."[9] As the late-sixteenth- and seventeenth-century lantern projections of della Porta, Kircher, Huygens, Walgenstein, Sturm, and Zahn began to demonstrate, light could also be harnessed and deployed as an entertainment medium.[10] In the tradition of projected light entertainments, the spectator's liminal confusion between veracity and illusion was both the lure and the rewarding delight.[11]

The metaphysics of light changed as projected light images became an entertainment medium. In his cultural history of the "industrialization" of light in the nineteenth century, Wolfgang Schivelbusch describes the relation of the darkened room to the illuminated images of light-based media: "*The power of artificial light to create its own reality only reveals itself in darkness.* . . . The spectator in the dark is alone with himself and the illuminated image because social connections cease to exist in the dark. Darkness heightens individual perceptions, magnifying them many times. *The darkened auditorium gives the illuminated image an intensity that it would not otherwise possess.* Every lighted image is experienced as the light at the end of the tunnel—the visual tunnel, in this case—and as a liberation from the dark."[12] Light could carry images, light could draw in space. In architectural terms, the window brought light into a darkened interior. But the window left its images outside, framed for the view. As glass began to replace opaque construction materials in the nineteenth century, a new transparency was added to public buildings. Yet the "intensity" of artificial light images was dependent on the dark, windowless space in which they were seen. This new mode of viewing light images in the dark had its own pleasures, demanded its own distinct architecture.

The darkened windowless interiors of nickel theaters and store-front cinemas began to demonstrate the need for a new building type to "house" the projection screen. Virilio notes this transition: "Why have historians focused on the iron and glass architecture of Paxton's 1851 Crystal Palace, ignoring the architecture of light of the darkrooms of the same period? On the one hand, the development of transparence was established as a result of the materiality of large surfaces of glass, held up by an impressing array of metal scaffolding. On the other hand, *transparence entered secretly in the unnoticed architectonic mutation of a wall-screen.*"[13] This "architectonic mutation of a wall-screen" takes us back to that end-of-century crossroad in 1895 when the individual viewing of moving images ceded its popularity to the collective viewing of projected images on a screen. Light was a building material as dark rooms were transformed by a screen-filled wall of light. Manonni writes of these "11th hour" transformations which would lead from individual viewers to projection: "1895 was the year when one of the oldest dreams of humanity was finally realized. *The human being and its chronophotographic alter ego found themselves face to face, one sitting in a seat in a darkened room, the other moving on a screen,* albeit in silence. It was as though an eye whose lids had been lifting, slowly across the centuries, now opened completely to the world. It was a very sharp eye, not only capable of capturing the slightest details of life, which Marey and Edison had known to do for some time, *but above all able to project that life onto a screen.*"[14] With an image of dramatic historiography—an eyelid opening slowly across centuries—Manonni describes this "face to face" moment in the dark when illuminated images were projected onto a screen by the brothers named Lumière. As the viewing of moving images switched from individual viewing devices like the kinetoscope to projection devices like the Cinématographe, Vitascope, and Bioskop, an important architectural and bodily shift occurred—a radical shift in the viewer's position, now seated in front of a screen. Film historian Douglas Gomery has announced this switch to a determinative visual practice with assured force: "By the year 1896 the movies were permanently on the screen."[15]

"ARCHITECTURE-IN-MOTION"

Early film theorists offered differing accounts of the relation between architecture and film and the spectatorial paradoxes of materiality and immateriality, mobility and immobility. Writing in 1915, poet and painter Vachel Lindsay devoted one chapter of his book *The Art of the Moving Picture* to the concept of "Architecture-in-Motion." Lindsay's book has the emphatic tone of a manifesto, a declaration of utopian goals for the future of the photoplay: "America is in the state of mind where *she* must visualize herself again," he writes, and "*architects, above all, are the men* to advance the work in the ultracreative photoplay."[16] Clearly, Lindsay feminized an America to be retooled by the masculine builder-architect. Architects were "crusaders" who should "appropriate the photoplay as *his* means of propaganda." Lindsay was an ardent partisan of the new "art" of the moving picture, and yet his enthusiasm for architectural transformations were limited to set design and models. He gave little thought to the architectural context of spectatorship. In a discussion of the thirty differences between photoplays and the stage, he notes that, unlike the stage audience where a late-comer is glared at, "In the motion picture art gallery . . . the audience is around two hundred, and these are not a unit, and the only crime is to obstruct the line of vision."[17]

On the other hand, in his 1916 book *Film: A Psychological Study of the Photoplay,* Hugo Münsterberg notes the spectatorial tension between the two-dimensional surface of the screen and three-dimensional "impression of depth." Münsterberg's study of the "means by which the photoplay influences the mind of the spectator" begins with his account of why "the surroundings appear to the mind plastic and the moving pictures flat." "To begin at the beginning," Münsterberg writes, "the photoplay consists of a series of flat pictures in contrast to the plastic objects of the real world which surround us." He continues: "Of course, when we are sitting in the picture palace we know that we see a flat screen and that the object which we see has only two dimensions, right-left, and up-down, but not the third dimension of depth, of distance toward us or away from us."[18] And yet, he remarked: "We have no right whatever to say that the scenes which we see on the screen appear to us as flat pictures." Münsterberg's perceptual explanation of this effect takes a detour through an explanation of stereoscopy and binocularity of vision, concluding that the "psychological causes" for the perception of depth are due to "differences of apparent size, the perspective relations, the shadows and actions performed in space."[19] Münsterberg poses an oddly Albertian experiment to explain the impression of surface and depth of the film screen: "Yet we need only to imagine that a large glass plate is put in the place of the curtain covering the whole stage. . . . This is exactly the case of the screen. If the pictures are well taken and the projection is sharp and we sit at the right distance from the picture, we must have the same impression as if we looked through a glass plate into a real space."[20] Münsterberg does not argue that this "same impression" is an impression of reality. "*Nevertheless,*" he writes in italics, "*we are never deceived; we are fully conscious of the depth and yet we do not take it for real depth.*"[21] He describes this impression of both depth and movement in terms of the "mental mechanism" that supplies what is not actually there: "the motion which he see appears to be a true motion, and yet it is created by his own mind." While he doesn't use the term "virtual" to describe this "suggestion of depth" and "suggestion of movement," Münsterberg underlines the ontological paradox of virtuality: "*They are present and yet they are not in the things.*"[22]

In *Film as Art* (*Film als Kunst,* 1932), Rudolf Arnheim makes the argument that the specific limitations of filmic representation—the projection of solids onto a plane surface, the reduction of depth, lighting and the absence of color, the limitations of the frame, the absence of the space-time continuum, and the absence of the nonvisual world of the senses—are the very qualities that make film an art. Arnheim was a champion of film's departure from direct mimesis, its absence of a "strong spatial impression." "If film photographs gave a very strong spatial impression," he argues, "montage probably would be impossible. It is the partial unreality of the film picture that makes it possible."[23] Film, according to Arnheim, is "neither absolutely two-dimensional nor absolutely three-dimensional, but something between."[24] Contemporary theorist Gertrud Koch reads this passage from Arnheim as directly descriptive of the viewer's perspectival positioning. Film reception is "governed precisely," Koch has written, "by the laws of one-point perspective, since the spectator, unlike the camera, cannot change the angle from which he or she sees the two-dimensional picture. Any such attempt would only trap the spectator in the most uncomfortable parts of the screening room—too near the screen, let's say, or in some corner that stretches the angle in a bizarre way."[25] Koch imagines the Arnheimian spectator in a fixed seat, facing a two-dimensional screen, positioned by its perspectival view. The screen may contain shifting camera angles, a montage of spaces and times, but the spectator does not move. Arnheim measured the film's dimensionality as a liminal mode of virtual space, "something between."

PARADOX 1: MATERIALITY OF THE THEATER, VIRTUALITY OF THE IMAGE

In order to examine how these tensions between materiality and immateriality, mobility and immobility were first negotiated, it will be instructive to revisit one of the key myths of cinema's spectatorial origin and recast it in architectural terms. The question of whether spectators really fled in terror and panic at the projected image of an approaching train—the "train effect"—has been at the center of historiographical and theoretical debate about early film spectatorship. As the Lumières' train approached the station at La Ciotat or as Edison's Black Diamond Express rounded the bend, did unsophisticated spectators confuse the image of a speeding locomotive with a real train barreling into the projection hall? Historians and theorists alike have invoked this apocryphal reaction in order to underscore the spectator's confusion between reality and the uncanny realism of its representation. Whether the "train effect" was a historically specific response of the first spectators of projected films or whether it was symptomatic of the disavowals of spectatorship itself, the projected two-dimensional moving image of a moving train poses an exacting instance of the twin paradoxes of spectatorship.[26]

In "An Aesthetic of Astonishment" (1989), film historian Tom Gunning challenges readings of this "primal scene" as a reaction to the realism of screened images, or a misrecognition of the imaginary as real: "Rather than mistaking the image for reality, the spectator is astonished by its transformation through the new illusion of projected motion. . . . The astonishment derives from a magical metamorphosis rather than a seamless reproduction of reality."[27] Gunning indicates that early projectionists were aware of the tension between stasis and movement as a dramatic component of this new entertainment, and often began with a frozen still image of the train in order to increase the drama of its lurch into movement. In Gunning's account, the practice of accentuating the switch between the photographic still image and the moving image convincingly contradicts the myth that spectators believed that the train was real enough to hurtle into the hall. His argument eloquently turns away from the myth of a panicked audience to an account of a spectator in the astonished thrall of a contrived illusion: "The movement from still to moving images accented the unbelievable and extraordinary nature of the apparatus itself. But in doing so, it also undid any naïve belief in the reality of the image."[28] Hence, the "train effect" was less an indication of the "reality effect" of moving images than it was a kind of "movement effect" resulting from the shock of movement itself.

The moving image of a moving train is perhaps an overdetermined example. The size and speed of a powerful machine hurtling across the screen toward the audience and off the edges of the frame had its own perceptual force. In *Film as Art,* Arnheim suggests that the boundary of the frame itself participates in the magnification of movement within it: "The nearer the engine comes the larger it appears, the dark mass on the screen spreads in every direction at a tremendous pace (a dynamic dilation toward the margins of the screen), and the actual objective movement of the engine is strengthened by this dilation."[29]

In a single-shot film, as the train approached the station, for example, or as workers left the Lumière factory, as a congress of photographers stepped toward and past the Cinématographe camera, the frame functioned as a limit for all movement within it and to its edges. Arnheim describes the "delimitation" of the image as one of the markers of film's representational separation from reality. ("The pictured space is visible to a certain extent, but then comes the edge which cuts off what lies beyond.")[30] Other film theorists have variously described this "off-frame" or "offscreen" space as either a confirmation of the inherent realism of film, or as an indication of its sutured illusionism. In the realist ontology of André Bazin, for example, the screen is a "mask which allows only a part of the action to be seen." The spectator's concept of a contiguous real space just offscreen allows Bazin to make a succinct distinction between the space of the theater and the space of the screen: "There are no wings to the screen."[31]

For historians of continuity editing and for theorists of "suture," when movement off the edge of one shot is met by the movement into the frame of the next, the spectator is effectively "cut" out of cinematic space while, at the same time, being sutured into it.[32] As filmmakers began to negotiate the spatial and temporal relations between shots, the perspectival frame and the fixed positionality of its viewers were radically undermined. The photographic camera's mechanical capture of objects in depth may have followed some axioms of perspectival positioning, but, as I argued in chapter 2, the movement of objects within the frame, to its edges and off-frame, suggests its contradiction.[33]

Here it might be instructive to turn again to Erwin Panofsky's account of the "motion picture," a description that prefigures Gunning's coinage of an "aesthetic of astonishment" and a "cinema of attractions."[34] Panofsky describes the relation between the moving image and the static spectator who takes "sheer delight in the fact that things seemed to move, no matter what things were."[35] "The spectator," Panofsky writes,

> *occupies a fixed seat, but only physically,* not as the subject of an aesthetic experience. Aesthetically, he is in permanent motion as his eye identifies itself with the lens of the camera, which permanently shifts in distance and direction. *And as movable as the spectator is, as movable is, for the same reason, the space presented to him. Not only bodies move in space, but space itself does, approaching, receding, turning, dissolving and re-crystallizing as it appears through the controlled locomotion* and focusing of the camera and through the cutting and editing of various shots—not to mention such special effects as visions, transformations, disappearances, slow-motion and fast-motion shots, reversals and trick films. This opens up a work of possibilities of which the stage can never dream.[36]

Here Panofsky is writing, of course, about a much later moment in cinema history than the first one-shot images of trains arriving in stations. His discussion of the "motion picture" emphasizes the relation between the "controlled locomotion" of the image and the spectator in a "fixed seat." His description of the "movable" spectator does not address the frame or the screen.[37]

From its first instances, the visual logic of the projected moving image presented its spectator (and subsequent theorists of spectatorship) with a simultaneously mystifying and demystifying set of pleasures. The frame of the screen marks a separation—an "ontological cut"—between the material surface of the wall and the view contained within the frame's aperture.[38] We might consider how the "train effect" operates along the lines of another set of tensions—not just between the mobility of the image and the immobility of the spectator, but also between the materiality of the theater and the virtuality of the moving image when spectators, either credulous or incredulous, witnessed the massive machine of iron and steam as a two-dimensional shadow.

As I will continue to emphasize, the virtuality of this two-dimensional framed cinema screen was as much the locus of spectatorial fascination as was its movement. Let's examine an early instance of these tensions as pictured in the familiar 1902 Edwin S. Porter and Thomas Edison film *Uncle Josh at the*

Moving Picture Show, an opportunistic remake of R. W. Paul's 1901 film *The Countryman and the Cinematograph.*[39] Both of these early films have a spectator enacting the shock and recoiling awe of the "train effect."

UNCLE JOSH AT THE MOVING PICTURE SHOW (1902)

This short film, often cited as exemplary of the spectator's confusion between offscreen and on-screen reality, also illustrates some originary tension between the *material* space of the theater and the *virtual* space on the screen.[40] The movie-goer Uncle Josh stands in his "box," an ornately framed loge at an oblique angle to the left of a film screen. The frame is almost exactly halved—on its left side, painted cardboard scenery denotes the proscenium surrounds of the stage and screen; on the right side, an inset film screen with the title "Edison Projecting Kinetoscope" announces itself reflexively.[41]

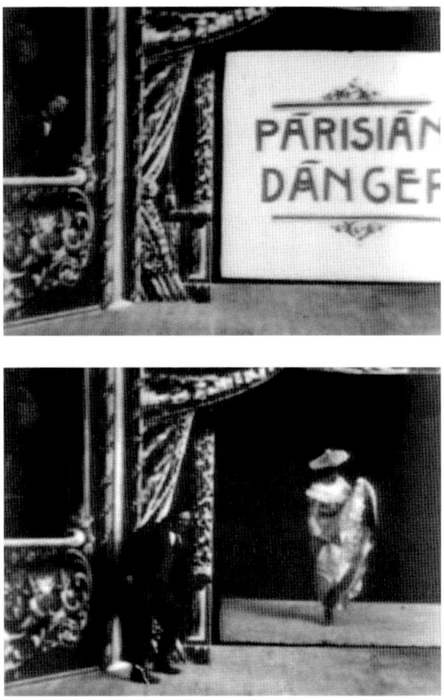

4.2, 4.3 Frame enlargements from *Uncle Josh at the Moving Picture Show,* directed by Edwin S. Porter, 1902.

The compositional logic of *Uncle Josh* illustrates the differential between the material space of the theater and the virtual space of the screen. As a tableau-style shot, taken from a camera set in the position of a good theater seat facing the stage, the mise-en-scène of the shot posits a *mise en abyme* of frames and screens. The three-dimensional material surrounds of the theater are represented by the flimsiest of painted sets. By contrast, the two-dimensional surface of the screen seems uncannily realistic compared to the false cardboard of Josh's loge and the painted proscenium curtains. From his box vantage, Uncle Josh telegraphs his spectatorial reactions by broad gesticulation. He looks in two directions—first toward the screen and then upward and away from the screen, as if he is looking for the source of the image, or perhaps to us, the other spectators of the same image.

As the first short film, *Parisian Danger,* commences, a woman enters the frame of the inset screen and begins to lift her skirts, revealing her legs with high kicks. Uncle Josh applauds and then quickly jumps out of his loge seat, shaking the flimsy boards of the theater set that frames him. As the woman dances in the space of screen, Josh remains on stage in the narrow space between his now-abandoned framed loge and the frame of the projection screen. The moving bodies of Josh and his female screen "other" are matched in scale as he mirrors her movements in a complex parody of transgendered identification and blatant gender difference. The dancer faces Uncle Josh and an imagined audience. But the two spaces are linked in a matched continuity because the floor of the theater and the floor where the dancer performs extend the material space of the theater into the virtual space of the screen. (Of course, to the viewer of *Uncle Josh,* both spaces appear as two-dimensional surfaces.)

Josh shows some surprise when *Parisian Danger* abruptly ends and the next film, *Black Diamond Express* (itself an Edison film from 1896), begins. His jolt of reaction enacts the loss of spatial orientation in the sudden discontinuity of shot-to-shot editing. Josh becomes a diegetic surrogate for the spectator of a multiple-shot "moving picture show," even while the spectators of *Uncle Josh* view the short film as an unedited shot in tableau style.

As he watches the approach of the locomotive, Uncle Josh stands slightly in front of the screen and—for a brief moment—his body becomes oddly transparent when he crosses the boundary of the frame and steps in front of the moving-picture screen. As a spectator, he is now permeated by the moving image, as if this moment of transparency—the overlap of two layers of moving images—indicates the spectator-effect of being in two places at once. When the train approaches him, he jumps back into his loge box for safety. The "train effect" may have been the intended comedy here, but the off-register "mistake" that turns Josh briefly into a spectral figure seems a more accurate portrait of the paradoxical spatiality of spectatorship. Josh is doubly exposed: he is projecting his presence into a remote location, a prescient illustration of the subjectivities suggested by telepresence.

When the last film, *The Country Couple,* begins, Josh jumps out of his loge again. This time he takes off his jacket, rolls up his sleeves, and attempts to battle with a similarly attired but slightly larger-scale male. His reaction to this film suggests that it posed a different, more potent threat than the cosmopolitan female in *Parisian Danger. The Country Couple* evokes a rivalry with Josh's own identity—a "country" man—now represented on screen in mirror fashion as a competitive other.[42]

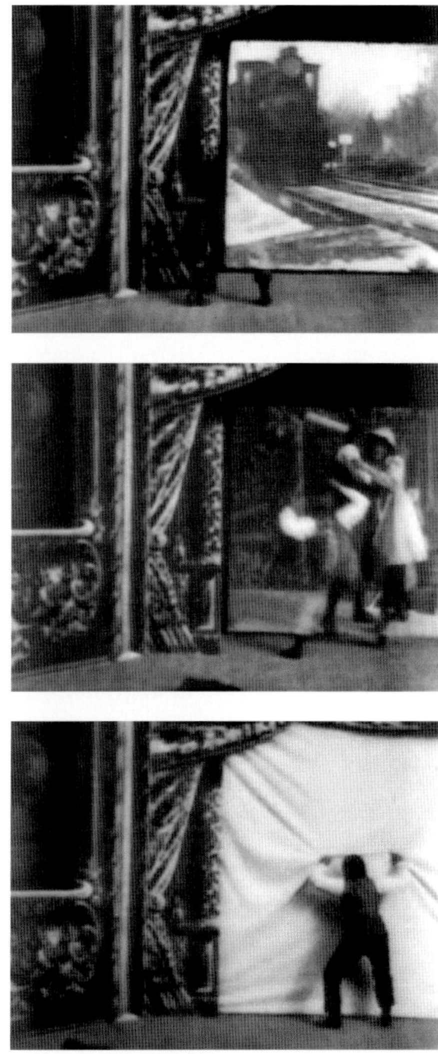

4.4, 4.5, 4.6 Frame enlargements from *Uncle Josh at the Moving Picture Show,* directed by Edwin S. Porter, 1902.

Even without a psychoanalytic reading of Josh's intent, his attempt to interact with the couple leads to his unveiling the mechanism and ending the illusion of their screen world. As he shadow-punches toward the image, he pulls the screen down to reveal its surface, the projectionist, and the apparatus behind it. This sudden unmasking, revealing the projecting mechanism behind the screen, engages in a knowing historical anachrony. Rear-screen projection was a common exhibition practice for concealing the projection apparatus in phantasmagoria spectacles in the eighteenth and nineteenth centuries, but much less common as an exhibition practice in 1902. The logic behind this must have been that, in order to expose the projecting mechanism, it would need to be visible on the screen—and not in the unseen 180-degree reverse position of the Edison Projecting Kinetoscope used to project *Uncle Josh at the Moving Picture Show.*[43] The final comic gag in *Uncle Josh* is about the screen surface and the realization that it is a material surface after all. The gesticulating Uncle Josh tugs so hard at the screen that it falls down, exposing its artifice, the empty materiality of its two dimensions, and the virtuality of its three-dimensional mobility. Unlike the painting or the photograph, the projected image has no materiality. Josh can attack the screen but the image remains untouched.

PARADOX 2: MOBILITY OF THE IMAGE, IMMOBILITY OF THE SPECTATOR

Many nineteenth-century exhibition devices strove to deliver the sensations of mobility, but in virtual terms.[44] As I've argued, the cinema provided a virtual mobility—the illusion of transport to other places and times for its spectators—but as the conventions of moving-picture exhibition settled on theatrical projection and display, another key representational paradigm emerged: movement was captured but at the same time confined.

Early panoramic films illustrate how the visual system of the panorama—the large-scale representational painting designed to be viewed by a spectator

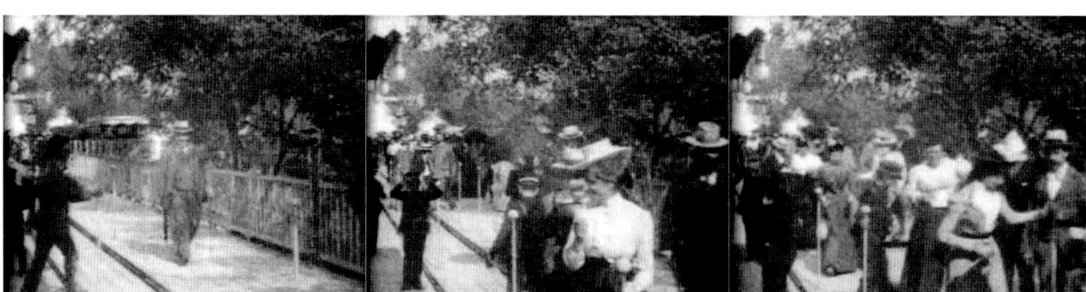

4.7 Frame stills from *Panorama of Moving Boardwalk,* filmed by James Henry White for the Thomas Edison Company, July 1900.

placed in the center, turning one's head—became reduced to framed images recorded by a moving ("panning") camera.[45] The filmed records of the Paris Universal Exposition of 1900 provide remarkable visual evidence of this effect. In July 1900, Thomas Edison sent one of his producers, James Henry White, to visit and film the Paris Exposition.[46] (Edison himself had visited the 1889 Exposition, but without a movie camera.) White was equipped with the then-new panning-head tripod, and many of the films that he recorded are remarkable panoramic records.

White's panoramic film *Panorama of Moving Boardwalk* uses the movement of the boardwalk to produce its "panning" movement. As described in the Edison catalog:

> This picture was taken from the stationary platform, showing the rapidly moving board walk on the outer edge, which has a speed of five miles per hour; also shows the middle platform moving two and a-half miles per hour, the third platform being stationary. At intervals there are upright posts to steady passengers passing from one platform to the other. By watching these uprights passing by the camera and passing each other, a good idea of the speed is obtained. The structure is crowded with passengers, some gliding by, standing still, others walking and running and stepping from one platform to the other.[47]

The still frames here provide some anticipation of the actual mobility that fairgoers had, measuring their steps against their stillness and the movement of the pavement itself. The catalog description emphasizes the relative movements of "passengers" moving toward the camera and away from it.

Another companion panorama, *Panorama from the Moving Boardwalk,* was taken *from* the walkway. In this short film, the camera is static again but the

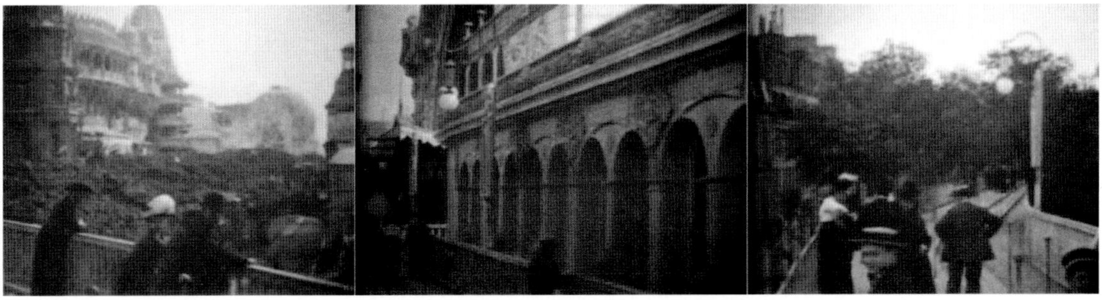

4.8 Frame stills from *Panorama from the Moving Boardwalk,* filmed by James Henry White for the Thomas Edison Company, July 1900.

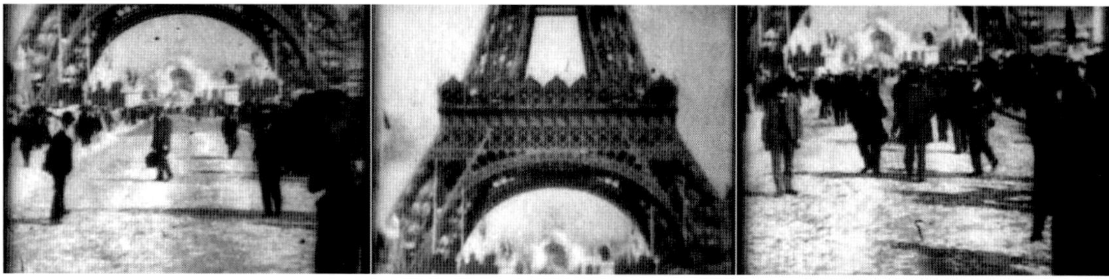

4.9 Frame stills from *Panorama of Eiffel Tower,* filmed by James Henry White for the Thomas Edison Company, July 1900.

"Platform Mobile" becomes a vehicle for a "tracking shot"—a glissando through the space of the exposition. White filmed the moving boardwalk from a stationary position, recording its movement, and from a mobilized position, recording its mechanization of the view. Similarly, White's two films of the Eiffel Tower, *Panorama of Eiffel Tower* (which panned up the tower in perhaps the first vertical pan) and *Elevator Ascending Eiffel Tower* (which placed the camera on the tower's elevator as it rose above the roofs and skylights of the buildings below), illustrated his fascination with the relativity of movement.

By 1900, many of the films that were projected onto screens demonstrated this propensity for recording pure movement. As these two panoramas illustrate, movement took on two distinct modalities—either recorded by static camera or provided by placing the camera on a mobile apparatus. Tom Gunning's descriptions of this early fascination with movement as a fascination with spectacle and sensation—an "aesthetic of astonishment," a "cinema of attractions."[48]—can be reframed if we think about the virtuality and relativity of such movement. The spectator is not really moving—his or her head and body remain relatively immobile.[49] The visuality here is compensatory, along the lines of the paradox I've emphasized elsewhere: as the mobilized gaze became more virtual, it grew to involve less physical mobility, and became located within the confines of a frame.[50]

WINDOWLESS ARCHITECTURE: THE THEATER AS BUILDING TYPE, SPECTATORS IN FRONT OF SCREENS

The word "theater," as many theorists remind us, has the same root as the word "theory" (*theoria*); both emphasize the importance of vision, speculation, looking with great attentiveness.[51] In the architecture of the classical Greek amphitheater, the audience was arrayed in concentric tiers of elevated seating to insure a clear view of the stage for performance. The Greek theater at Epidauros (designed by Polycleitus, 4th century BC) was built into a hillside so that the

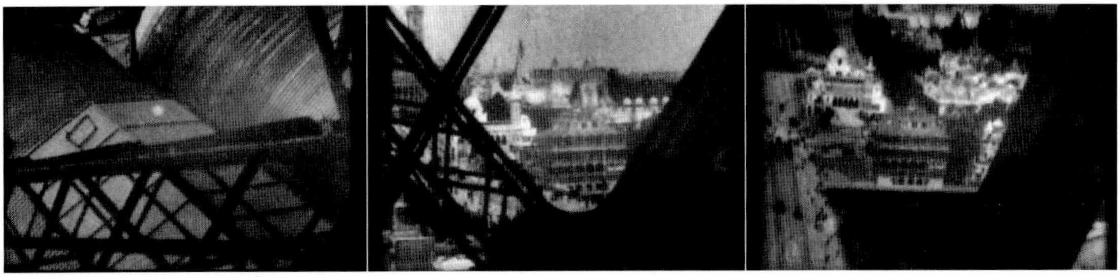

4.10 Frame stills from *Elevator Ascending Eiffel Tower,* filmed by James Henry White for the Thomas Edison Company, July 1900.

seating for spectators (the *theatron*) would be at an elevated angle for the view. The proscenium space of theatrical action was separate from its audience. The Roman Coliseum (AD 70–82) had tiers of seating for fifty thousand spectators around a central elliptical arena; the seating was raised by concrete vaulting, with corridors and stairs beneath.[52] These outdoor auditoria were built for multitudes of spectators, beholders with multiple vantage points onto a spectacle in the center below. In the Renaissance, theatrical performance was moved indoors and the stage was raised above the audience. Although the Renaissance theater spectator was not seated with the single-point positioning of Renaissance perspective, theatrical architecture began to favor a frontal view toward the proscenium frame. As theatrical architecture developed, the proscenium "arch" served to frame the space of action. Restoration theaters were rectangular with a stage at one end and rows of seats facing the proscenium. While the depth of action in the proscenium did not depend on a fixed point of view, the viewpoint of the spectators became more and more frontal and framed.[53]

Theaters for live performance (opera, concert, dramatic theater) developed according to their differing requirements for acoustics, stage size, seating, orchestral space, and backstage needs. The basic building type was a skeletal frame with cantilevers and trussed girders to support balconies for the audience. As outdoor amphitheaters switched to indoor architectural spaces, and as the angle of view from the audience switched from in-the-round to frontal, the illuminated stage and spectators in the dark became a prevailing convention to separate the audience from the proscenium world. Curtains covered and revealed the stage opening with a ritual deliberateness that signaled the beginning and ending of performance. The theatrical stage had depth and a frame for the live movement of dramatic action and was viewed by a seated audience of rapt and immobile viewers.[54]

The architectural requirements for viewing moving images on individually oriented devices like the kinetoscope were quite different from those for the collective viewing of projected images on a screen. (The kinetoscope—from the Greek *kineto,* "movement," and *scopos,* "to watch"—was the viewing mechanism for Edison's patented moving-image camera, the kinetograph.) Thomas Edison's initial business plan for his moving-image device was based on the business model for the phonograph as an individually oriented apparatus. Edison first installed his kinetoscope viewers in storefront phonograph "parlors"—spaces already designated for public "rental" of a mechanically reproduced experience—where customers would pay a nickel to listen privately to a variety of recordings on earphones. Dedicated kinetoscope parlors had rows of machines arranged so that the viewer could move sequentially from one machine to the next, watching separate or sometimes serially sequenced short films.[55]

The first venues for projected moving images were converted spaces—town halls, churches, lodges, schools, storefronts, courthouses, vaudeville theaters—rather than buildings dedicated for the showing of film.[56] Films were shown by itinerant exhibitors who would rent available local spaces, often adding folding chairs as seating.[57] Fixed-site cinemas emerged only when the economic logic of film distribution (rental or sale by film exchanges) began to take hold. As the new international commerce in moving images and patented devices began, film production was commonly autonomous from its distribution and its exhibition. Producers, distributors, and exhibitors were locked into an ongoing struggle for industrial control.[58]

Nevertheless, once projection devices were deployed to cast moving images onto framed flat surfaces, onto screens hung in darkened (windowless) halls, storefronts, or vaudeville theaters, the architectural paradigm for cinema spectatorship implied an increasingly fixed bodily position for the viewer to allow for new habits of engagement with the virtual image.

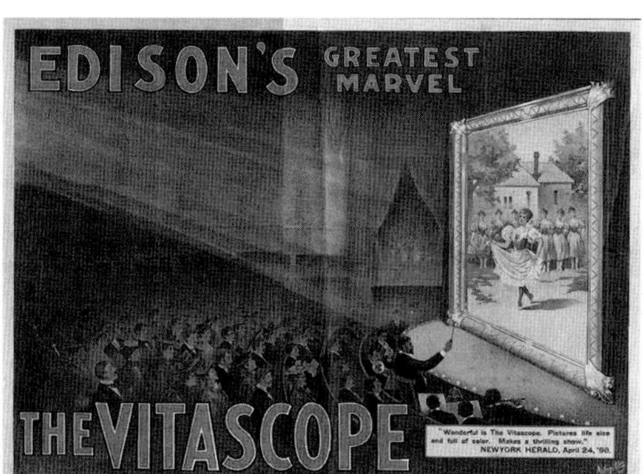

4.11 Thomas Edison, Vitascope ad, 1896.

The spaces that would house projected light images had definitive requirements: (1) they must be dark enough to allow for the projection of light from a mechanism at one end to a screen surface at the other; (2) they must have room to accommodate a collective number of immobile (preferably seated) viewers; and (3) the view of the screen must be clear of pillars and posts. In spaces designed for projection onto a screen, the size and depth of the stage was not important, neither was it necessary to have backstage space for dressing rooms or props, or catwalks of scaffolding for lighting or stage equipment.

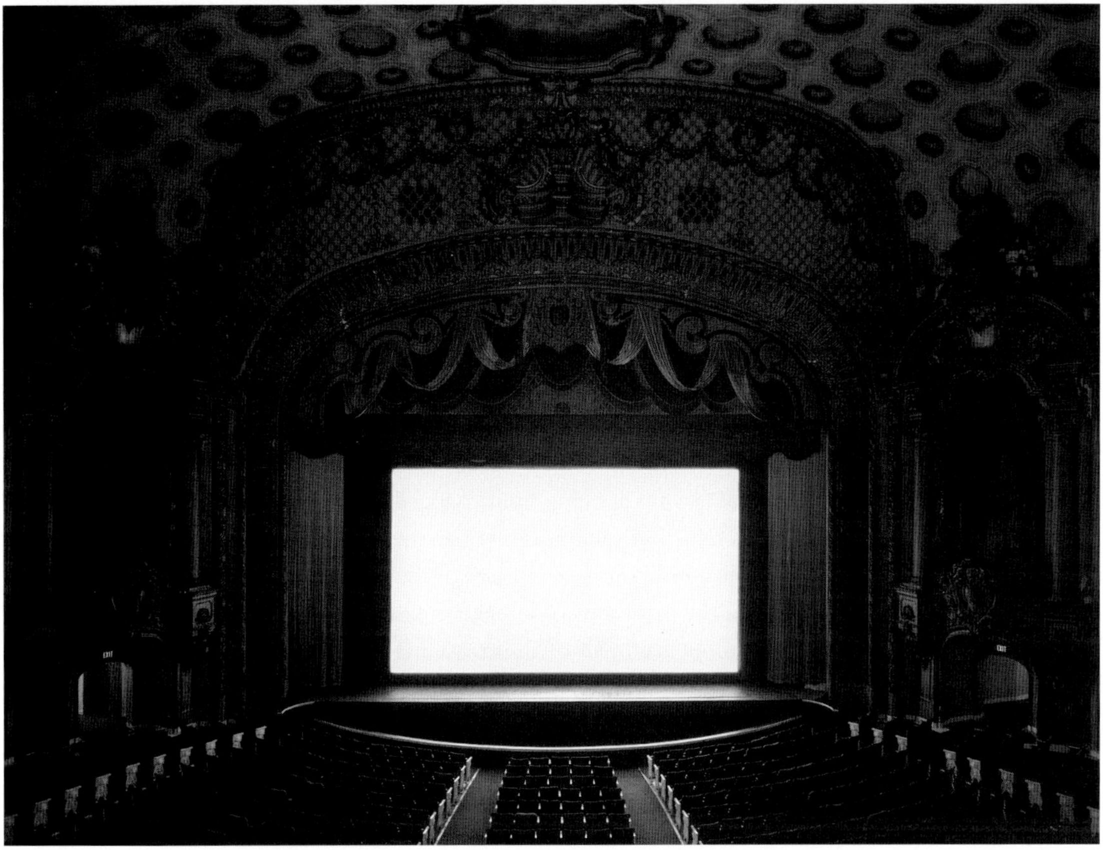

4.12 Hiroshi Sugimoto, *Metropolitan,* 1993. Photo courtesy of Sonnabend Gallery, New York.

THE MATERIALITY OF THE SCREEN

When we look at a painting or a photograph, we usually see the frame in a well-lit space. Its edges are as significant as its center. For the film spectator, the frame of the screen forms a tableau-like proscenium, forcing our vision to center its gaze, while implying a continuum of space lingering just offscreen/off-frame. The darkness that surrounds the luminous screen both minimizes its borders and calls us to play upon its boundaries. The darkened room and the screen "bordered with black like a letter of condolence," Baudry has written, "already present privileged conditions of effectiveness—no exchange, no circulation, no communication with any outside."[59]

Hiroshi Sugimoto's photographs, each of a blank and yet luminous cinema screen, help us to visualize the role of the screen itself. To capture the screen in its luminous emptiness, Sugimoto used an extended exposure time, holding his aperture open so long that the screened images vanish, leaving only the projection light on an empty white screen to cast its eerie glow on the surrounding architecture of the theater. Sugimoto's screens *expose* time: the length of each exposure was the length of a feature-film projection. Over time, projected moving images produce an abstract frame of light, an image that we cannot see in the time frame of our spectatorial vision, as if—to extend Dziga Vertov's claim for the "Kino-eye"—it is not just the camera but also the projector that is "more perfect than the human eye."[60] Sugimoto's photographs manage to capture the elusive absent presence of an intangible "imaginary signifier."

But what remains here, despite the ephemeral instability of the cinematic image, is the materiality of the theater. Sugimoto photographed a series of theaters—in New York, New Jersey, Pennsylvania, Ohio, Indiana, Florida, California (San Diego, Orange, San Francisco, Oakland, Los Angeles), and in Auckland, Tokyo, Sydney, Milan, and Paris. Hans Belting describes the "interiors" in Sugimoto's photographs as being "reintroduced as metaphors." The "screen is empty," he writes, "and thus qualifies either as the everything of all possible images or else as their nothingness as vehicles of illusion."[61] The photographs, when seen together in the diachrony of a series, reveal a structural similarity: each theater is a synchronic exemplar of the constants in the architecture of spectatorship. Sugimoto's photographs return us to the tension between the bodily stasis of the cinematic spectator and the virtual mobilities presented on the screen.

The film screen is a surface, a picture plane caught in a cone of light, dark and empty until projected images are caught on its veneer. Despite variations in theater architecture and films projected, what remains—constant and haunting—is the screen.[62]

THE THEATER OF "ATTRACTIONS"

During the "Nickelodeon era" (1905–1914), the common venues for the exhibition of moving images were dark spaces with poor ventilation and poorly planned exits.[63] The illicit connotation of public darkness only amplified the concerns for safety. But as new patterns of exhibition began to emerge, so did new styles of filmmaking. Tom Gunning has pinpointed 1906 to 1907 as the years when the "cinema of attractions"—a filmmaking style that relied on performative exhibitionism and the spectacle of pure movement—began to cede its hold to a "cinema of narrative integration."[64]

Between 1914 and 1922, four thousand new theaters opened in the United States. Many of these newly constructed "palaces" were attractions themselves. The grand architecture for spectatorship provided, as Douglas Gomery and others have shown, material evidence of the industrial and economic forces that shaped cinema-going.[65] The movie "palace" was the architectural embodiment of the shifting taste and class distinctions accorded to the moving image. (No wonder Panofsky so easily compared the production of a film to that of a medieval cathedral.) In the prevailing theater architecture of the 1920s and 1930s, the movie-goer entered a regal surround, an ornately appointed space in the guise of an opulent elsewhere—an Egyptian tomb, a Mayan temple, a Chinese palace. The newly narrativized format of the feature film was viewed in a theatrical space of pure exhibitionism, architectural hyperboles designed for the spectacle of pure visibility.[66] As the American movie exhibitor Marcus Loew quipped in the 1920s: "we sell tickets to theaters, not to movies." The lost "cinema of attractions" was replaced by newly built *theaters of attractions*.[67]

The architectural and urban context to these screens—the relation to the city, the sidewalk, pedestrian *flânerie*—forms an important phenomenological prologue and postlogue to the spectatorial moment.[68] As the title of Maggie Valentine's book about movie theater architect S. Charles Lee states, *The Show Starts on the Sidewalk*. The relation between the urban exterior and the theatrical interior was negotiated by the facade, marquee, and signage. In Roland Barthes's description, the cinema screen becomes the endpoint of an urban itinerary, a final destination or restful respite for the footsore *flâneur*. Barthes describes the acts of entering or exiting the movie theater in his short piece "En sortant du cinéma" (Leaving the Cinema). Entering, the subject is drawn from street to street, poster to poster, to "abandon himself into an anonymous, indifferent cube of darkness."[69] Once inside, the body of the spectator is seated, fixed, confined, facing a frame, a screen, a flat surface for projection.

"ELEGANT SURFACE SPLENDOR" AND THE PLAY OF LIGHT (*LICHTSPIEL*)

While Panofsky was writing about the sense of space (*Raumgefühl*) of perspective in his 1924 essay "Perspective as Symbolic Form," his German contemporaries deployed spatial images (*Raumbilder*) to write about the space of modernity. Material spaces were both metaphors and analytic instruments—for Adorno (*intérieur*), Benjamin (*passage*), and Kracauer (*Hotelhalle*). "Spatial images [*Raumbilder*]," German theorist Siegfried Kracauer wrote, "are the dreams of society. Wherever the hieroglyphs of any spatial image are deciphered, there the basis of social reality presents itself."[70]

In his now-well-known 1926 *Frankfurter Zeitung* article "The Cult of Distraction," Kracauer turned to the inherent spatial tensions between the two-dimensionality of the screen and the opulent three-dimensional architecture of the "picture palaces" (*Lichtspielhäuser*) of Berlin. (The English translation "picture palace" neglects the architecture designed for the "play" [*Spiel*] of "light" [*Licht*].) For Kracauer, the "cult of distraction" was equally a cult of surfaces. He describes the "elegant surface splendor" *(Prunk der Oberfläche)* of the theater, the "surface glamour of the stars" (*Oberflächenglanz der Stars*), the "white surface" (*weisse Fläche*) of the screen:

> until finally the white surface descends and the events of the three-dimensional stage imperceptibly blend into two-dimensional illusions.[71]
>
> *bis zuletzt die weisse Fläche herabsinkt und die Ereignisse der Raumbühne unmerklich in die zweidimensionalen Illusionen übergehen.*[72]

The architectural context of the film screen in these "optical fairylands" (*optischen Feenlokale*) undermined the potential power of the film itself. "The interior design of the movie theater serves one sole purpose," Kracauer contends, "to rivet the audience's attention to the peripheral so that they will not sink into the abyss."[73] The screen should suffice as the locus of spectator attention: "The two-dimensionality of film produces the illusion of the physical world without any need for supplementation."[74] Instead of conveying the disorder of society on the streets of Berlin, the film's "motley sequences of externalities" (*die bunte Reihe der Ausserlichkeiten*) are drawn into a unity, a *Gesamtkunstwerk* of surface splendor. Kracauer decrees that the movie theater—if it is to "fulfill" its "vocation"—should be free of all trappings that "deprive film of its rights [to] a kind of distraction which exposes disintegration [*Zerfall*] instead of masking it."[75] In Kracauer's critique, movie theater architecture is not about the screen, but about everything else.

As Heide Schlüpmann pointed out upon its first translation in 1987, Kracauer's essay moved his critique of film toward an "aesthetic of reception," but it also stalled at the "external layers" of film itself—the picture palaces, the UFA studios.[76] In retrospect, Kracauer's tirades against artifice and his distrust of surfaces (*Oberfläche*), his complaints about the "calico-world" of UFA city—film sets where "the old and the new, copies and originals . . . piled up in a disorganized heap like bones in catacombs"—seem now to have acted out an anxiety about the impending shift to the virtual, nonmaterial realities of the two-dimensional screen. Kracauer's complaint about the jumbled heap of "the old and the new, copies and originals" prefigured our current cohabitation with the virtual on our screens and in our lives. In fact, as CGI replaces the materialities of set design in contemporary filmmaking, the "derealization" of film's synthetic space-time has reached an ever more resisted, ever more compelling virtuality.

While Kracauer's cranky reaction to the ornate decor of the movie palace may have been at odds with a movie-going public (in the 1920s and 1930s) that took as much comfort from architectural hyperbole as from screen spectacle, his critique *was* consistent with the modern architectural urge for functionalism as found in the work of architects like Viennese-born Frederick Kiesler. For Kiesler, the movie theater required new designs. "Present day cinema or motion picture houses," he wrote in 1928, "are not cinemas, but merely imitations of old European theatres into which a screen was hung." Previous theater architecture (and Poelzig was a prime example) was, to Kiesler, "stuck fast in decoration."[77]

Kiesler's 1928 design for the Film Guild Theatre in New York was "designed solely for the projection of the cinema": "The most important quality of the auditorium is, on the one hand, its power of suggesting concentration of attention. Even more important is its power of destroying the sensation of confinement which may be involved in the focal concentration of the spectator on the screen. I mean that the reflex which the film creates in the psyche of the spectator must make it possible for him to lose himself in imaginary, endless space, to feel himself alone in universal space, even though the projection surface, the screen, implies the opposite: all for one point, the SCREEN."[78] And Kiesler, as if in dialogue with Kracauer, argues in a 1929 manifesto, "Building a Cinema Theatre": "The first radical step toward the creation of an ideal cinema is the abolition of the proscenium and all other stage platforms' resemblance to the theatre. . . . My invention, the screen-o-scope, takes the place of these theatrical elements and supplies a new method of opening the screen which eliminates curtains. The interior lines of the theatre must focalize to the screen compelling unbroken attention on the spectator."[79] Kiesler's design called for still and moving pictures to be shown on the walls and ceiling as well as on the main screen, which could be adjusted in size and shape. The theater's walls and ceiling sloped toward the front screen and were covered with black projection screens. (Kiesler had designed special machines to project onto a black surface.) Kiesler's plan—never fully realized—was for a theater that surrounded the spectator with filmed images—an imaginary, *endless space*.

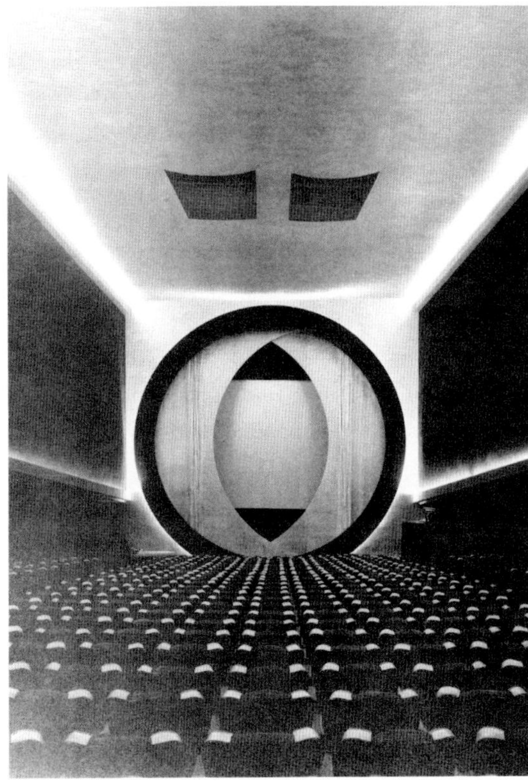

4.13 Frederick Kiesler, Film Guild Theatre, New York, 1928.

Kiesler was not the only architect to argue against the distracting ornamentation of the movie palace and for the immersion of the spectator. In 1933, A. V. Pilichowski wrote in the pages of *Close Up:*

> What seems required for a cinema to be truly cinematic is a more immediate contact between the screen and the audience. My suggestion is for *a panoramic screen;* the idea being that the screen should encircle the audience and thus make it part of a complete system. Mobile multiple projectors would throw pictures on the screen, the action being started at one end and terminated at the other. Visibility would not be required to be perfect from every seat at the same time, a certain element of interest being aroused by hiding, revealing, and hiding again the picture as it sweeps around the screen.[80]

These plans—whether with multiple mobile projectors and a spectator encircled by the screen, or a theater with walls, ceiling, and an adjustable main screen as projection surfaces—were designed to abolish the proscenium frame and allow the spectator to be lost in the imaginary space of the screen: not in distraction but immersion.

The difference between the "perspective" of the camera view and the spectator position in relation to the screen was also a topic of debate for motion-picture camera operators in late 1920s. In a 1928 article for the Society of Motion Picture Engineers, "Perspective Considerations in Taking and Projecting Motion Pictures" (1928), the authors describe the importance of the position of the viewer in the theater: "If he occupies a seat for which the perspective is correct, he will imagine himself viewing the scene from the position occupied by the camera when the exposure was made. . . . In other words, *the screen might be likened to a plate-glass window through which the observer looks with one eye at the actual scene.* From any other point in the theater, the perspective is distorted and the observer makes an erroneous estimate of his apparent distance from the objects in the picture area."[81]

PARADOX 2 REDUX: MOBILITY OF IMAGES, IMMOBILITY OF THE SPECTATOR

To return to a discussion of the paradox between the mobility of images and the stasis of the spectator, we might revisit Beatriz Colomina's analogy between Le Corbusier's architecture and the movie camera. Le Corbusier's horizontal window implied an expanded panoramic vista for the architectural spectator; his plan for a *promenade architecturale* addressed the architectural spectator's peripatetic vision. But the experience of Le Corbusier's buildings—moving through three-dimensional space—is not the same as the movie spectator's view of space confined to the frame.

Sigfried Giedion wrote of the difficulty representing "new architecture" in the limited fixed frame of still photography: "Still photography does not capture them [buildings] clearly. One would have to accompany the eye as it moves: only film can make the new architecture intelligible."[82] Pierre Chenal's film of Le Corbusier's Villa Savoye, *Architecture d'aujourd'hui* (1930–1931), used tracking camera movements and montage to approximate the experience of the mobile approach to and movement through the villa. But while Chenal's camera may have been able to "accompany the eye as it moves" and to capture a more dynamic and mobile record than a still photograph could, the implicit analogy between the architectural spectator and the mobile space of the moving image is complicated by a crucial component of the architecture of spectatorship: moving images are framed by the camera and seen from the *immobile* position of a spectator facing the frame of a screen.

Soviet filmmaker and theorist Sergei Eisenstein reenters our discussion here as a key interlocutor in the theorization of filmic and architectural space. In a 1937 essay, Eisenstein succinctly described the paradox between the "point of view of the moving spectator"—"that which is dispersed in reality, unseizable to a single gaze, scattered about"—and the fixed frame of the screen. Eisenstein quotes a description of the Athenian Acropolis by nineteenth-century architectural historian Auguste Choisy, and, using Choisy's notes, he draws the analogy between the arrangement of buildings in the Acropolis ("an architectural ensemble") and cinematic montage:

> We just presented in detail the issue of montage computation within an architectural ensemble. The Acropolis of Athens was at stake. The notes Choisy devoted to it give a magnificent picture of the construction and the computation of such a montage from *the point of view of the moving spectator. But if the spectator cannot move, he has to gather in one unique point the elements of that which is dispersed in reality, unseizable to a single gaze, scattered about,* but which the author must absolutely juxtapose, for it is in taking in all these elements that the spectator will obtain an impression of the object or—moreover—the impression which the author wishes to induce in transforming the relationships of reality, that which he wants to inscribe for the perception. *Cinematographic montage is, too, a means to "link" in one point—the screen—various elements (frag-*

ments) of a phenomenon filmed in diverse dimensions, from diverse points of view and sides.[83]

This discussion of the moving spectator's "point of view" in architectural space versus the diverse points of view on the screen faced by the immobile spectator is embedded as an aside in an essay on the painter El Greco. Eisenstein describes the peripatetic movement through the architectural space of the Acropolis in further detail in his 1938 essay "Montage and Architecture."[84] As Yve-Alain Bois points out in his insightful analysis of this text, Eisenstein's writing was full of oxymorons, paradoxes, and oppositions with "heuristic potential."[85] Given his attraction to polemical pairings, Eisenstein was naturally drawn to the paradoxical relation between the mobility of the architectural spectator and immobility of the cinematic viewer.

For Eisenstein, the Acropolis provides "the perfect example of one of the most ancient films."[86] "It is hard to imagine a montage sequence for an architectural ensemble more subtly composed, shot by shot," Eisenstein writes, "than the one that our legs create by walking among the buildings of the Acropolis."[87] Eisenstein, who continually sought out analogies for cinematic montage—from the Chinese ideogram to Sharaku masks, haiku, Kabuki theater, and the Hegelian dialectic—found nascent montage in ancient architecture. Legs moving, shot-by-shot, through the Acropolis, the peripatetic body is a movie camera following a "montage plan." Looking at literature, painting, and theater through the lens of cinema, Eisenstein superimposes film montage onto architecture.

"In the past," he writes, "the spectator moved between a [series of] carefully disposed phenomenon which he absorbed sequentially with his visual sense."[88] But that was "in the past." "Nowadays," he writes, "it is the imaginary path followed by the eye and the varying perceptions of an object that depend on how it appears to the eye. Nowadays it may also be the path followed by the mind across a multiplicity of phenomena, far apart in time and space, gathered in a certain sequence into a single meaningful concept; and these diverse impressions pass in front of an immobile spectator."[89] The unacknowledged historical undertow to Eisenstein's distinction between "the past" and "nowadays" (which for him was 1938) is the assumption that modern visuality is implicitly cinematic. In the past, a walking spectator "absorbed sequentially," and the "spectator moved," whereas "nowadays . . . diverse impressions pass in front of an immobile spectator." The analogy between the architectural spectator on foot and the film spectator seated in the cinema theater is premised on a particular form of filmic construction—one, of course, seen and theorized by Eisenstein himself: montage. The full force of this analogy suggests that the very nature of filmic construction—camera movement and the sequentiality of editing (what Eisenstein refers to as the "imaginary path followed by the eye")—guides the spectator to witness a uniquely constructed ordering of the world as "the multiplicity of phenomena far apart in time and space."[90]

Here it should be pointed out that montage technique—readable in some "architectural ensembles" (like the Acropolis)—is not present in every piece of architecture, nor should the architectural ensemble be considered coterminous with itinerant movement through urban space. Historic attempts to the contrary, the city is not a planned *promenade architecturale.* Rather, as every situationist will attest, the city is a prime site for a more fluid itinerary, a *dérive,* which includes a key element that makes the city-walker unlike the cinema spectator: chance. Chance is a key experiential element as the body moves through the city, but it is not a factor in (conventional) cinematic spectatorship. (Exceptions prove the rule: surrealist interventions and recent interactive movies challenge the otherwise legislated convention of cinematic form—where each film is repeatable in identical fashion, a metonymy of repeated sameness.)

As we draw Eisenstein into our discussion of the material and mobile paradoxes of spectatorship, let us note that he targets the fixity of the screen. ("Cinematographic montage is, too, a means to 'link' in one point—the screen—various elements (fragments) of a phenomenon filmed in diverse dimensions, from diverse points of view and sides.") Hence, in order to establish a parallel between the peripatetics of the viewer of architecture and (*virtual*) peripatetics of the film spectator, two key elements must be disavowed: (1) the reduction of movement—of camera, of editing shot-to-shot, of sequence—to the fixed confines of a screen; and (2) the shifted temporalities of film viewing, where the implicit time travel of spectatorship means that everything seen is from "the past" as the film's virtuality invents a new form of temporal monumentality.[91] For the architectural spectator, the materiality of architecture meets the mobility of its viewer; for the film spectator, the immateriality of the film experience meets the immobility of its viewer. Hence, the bodily, haptic, phenomenological perception of an itinerant and peripatetic viewer operates as an entirely different visual system once the itinerary becomes framed, an optical "imaginary path" with boundary and limit.

It was this quality of the filmic that Soviet filmmaker Lev Kuleshov explored with his famous "experiments" of "creative geography" and "creative anatomy." When Kuleshov followed a shot of a street in Moscow with a shot of the White House in Washington, his example not only sutured an imaginary geopolitical space, but illustrated how the film image, in its framed immateriality, could produce an improbable "creative" geography, anatomy, or architecture.[92]

Fast-forward fifty years from the architectural and montage work of Le Corbusier and Eisenstein: in *L'espace critique* (1984; translated as *Lost Dimension,* 1991), Paul Virilio also addresses "this sudden confusion between the reception of images from a film projector and the perception of architectonic forms."[93] As Virilio describes the dimensional transfer that is performed: "three dimensions of constructed space are translated into the two dimensions of a screen, or better of an interface."[94] In evaluating the consequences of this transfer, Virilio conducts a subtractive arithmetic of space: as the materiality of three-dimensional space is "translated" into the two-dimensional space of the screen, the "lost dimension" brings us, Virilio proclaimed, to the "zero degree of architecture."[95] But here, instead of emphasizing the paradoxical transfer from the mobility of the architectural spectator to the immobility of the film spectator, Virilio's analysis emphasizes the second paradox—the transfer from the materiality of architectural space to the immateriality of the filmic image. (I explore Virilio's discussion of the screen as the locus of lost dimensions of space and technological transformations of time in "Lens IV: Virilio's Screen.")

In Virilio's writing, architecture dematerializes, and dimensions are lost; there is an "aesthetics of disappearance" as "telematics replaces the doorway"[96] and the "pixel replaces the bolt."[97] Virilio began to diagnosis the architectonic consequences of the immaterial "opto-electronic" "interface" of computer terminals and video monitors in the early 1980s, describing video as an architectonic element: "It's the new window," he proclaimed, a "cathode window."[98] In Virilio's metaphor, the window is the television screen, a media-specific figure for the opening to "technological space-time."[99] Virilio is particularly astute about the temporal implications of this telematically mediated view: "These viewpoints are simultaneously time-points in the tele-topological continuum of long-distance projection and reception."[100]

Virilio's early 1980s discourse of architectonic "disappearance" recirculates in his writing of the 1990s with the addition of the term "virtual." Architectural materiality dissolves, as the title of a 1993 interview indicates, into "the Age of Its Virtual Disappearance":[101] "Architecture will 'take place' in the literal sense of the word, in both domains: in real space (the materiality of architecture) and virtual space (the transmission of electromagnetic signs). The real space of the house will have to take into account the real time of transmission."[102] Echoing the writing of Giedion and Kepes on the dematerialization of glass, Virilio's discourse of dematerialization and disappearance foretold a new logic to the visible, to the immaterialities and immobilities of a visuality, framed and virtual.

> *Whatever its other technical qualities (including color and 3-D which will one day be available), the television picture will always retain its mediocre legibility, it will also remain a product essentially consumed in the family circle, and as such, it will continue to be limited to a small screen.*
>
> —André Bazin, "Will CinemaScope Save the Film Industry?"

Much of the early competition between film and television centered around screen size, since the ten-to-twelve-inch television screen was tailored to the domestic scale of the home. Movie producers and exhibitors competed by differentiating their offerings with color, 3-D, and wider screen formats. Drive-in "roofless" theaters, or "ozoners," catered to the mobility and domestic encapsulation of the automotive spectator; "four-walled" or "hardtop" theaters introduced Widescreen and Cinerama formats to supply what the small black-and-white screens of television could not.[103] As the editor of the "Better Theaters" section of *Motion Picture Herald* declared after the 1952 preview of *This Is Cinerama!*: "Cinerama is an expansion of the theatre's motion picture, as televised films are a contraction of it."[104]

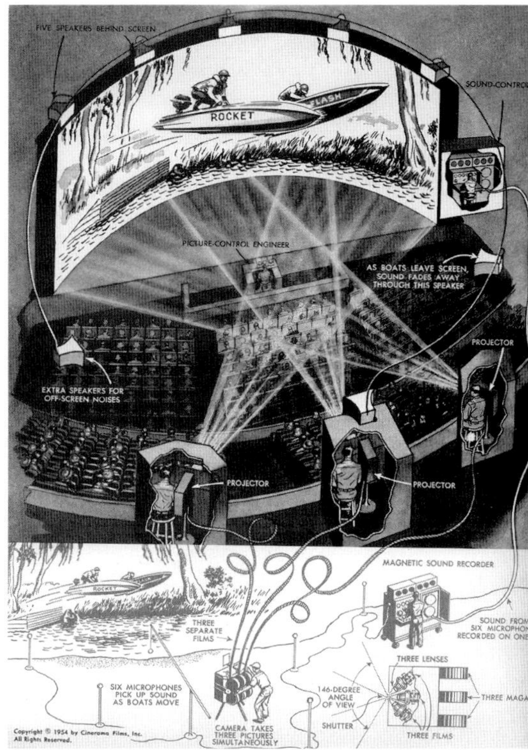

4.14 *This Is Cinerama!* promotional brochure, 1954.

Cinerama was only one of several subsequent and more successful screen formats—CinemaScope (1953), Todd-AO (1954), and VistaVision (1955)—designed to present an immersive illusion of depth through screens wide enough to fill peripheral vision.[105] In the opening credit sequence for the 1956 CinemaScope *The Girl Can't Help It* (dir. Frank Tashlin, 1956), Tom Ewell addresses the audience in a frame that snugly fits him in 1.33:1—and then, realizing that the image is not in the "grandeur" of CinemaScope, he "extends" the frame to stretch the image to 2.55:1 aspect ratio. A year later in another Tashlin film, *Will Success Spoil Rock Hunter?* (dir. Frank Tashlin, 1957), Tony Randall "breaks the frame" by directly addressing the audience and then, in a sequence often remarked upon as paradigmatic of the frame-size competition between theatrically exhibited movies and domestically ensconced television, the CinemaScope frame shrinks to a 4:3 aspect ratio, and goes from Technicolor to scratchy black and white, as Randall describes the remarkable invention of television. Both of Tashlin's films luxuriate in the sumptuous embellishments of CinemaScope and Technicolor.

The movie industry's mid-1950s campaign to counter the threat of television is exemplified by a 1957 advertising campaign mounted by a Los Angeles-based publicity company, Hallmark of Hollywood, to contrast the discomforts of television stay-at-home viewing with the compensations of "going out" to the movies. Ads extolled the virtues of screen size ("the gigantism of 330 times!") and the "fresh air" respite of leaving the domestic confinement of "4 walls." (This rhetorical strategy was laced with irony, because the very theaters that represented leaving the "4 walls" of home for "fresh air" were referred to in the trades as "4 wallers" in contrast to the outdoor drive-in theaters, which were known as "ozoners.")[106]

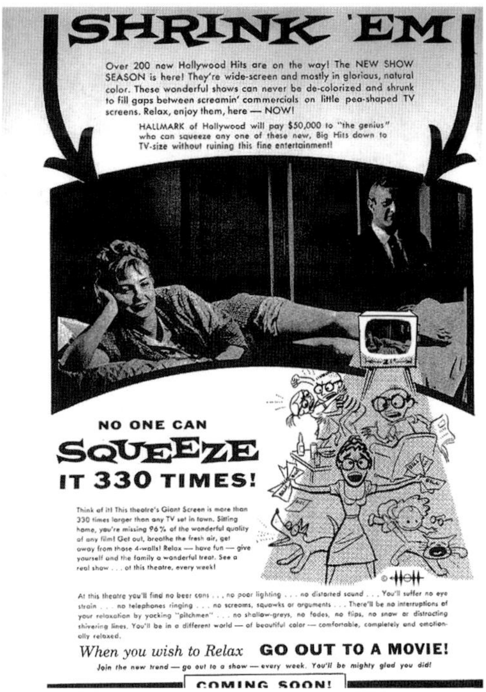

4.15 "Shrink 'Em" ad campaign.

The image here relies on the horizontal sprawl of Joanne Woodward (with Lee J. Cobb lurking behind) in a still from the 1957 CinemaScope (2.35:1 formatted) *Three Faces of Eve.* A tiny TV set contains the same image pitifully cropped, with a small "21 inch" arrow measuring its size. The TV seems to radiate a haze of benday dots: a barking dog, some fighting children, a crawling baby, a woman clutching bills, and an armchair-ridden man—all bespectacled (including the dog), no doubt due to eyestrain—become the cartoon of the suffering that the shrunken screen produces. The ad copy boasts:

> The NEW SHOW SEASON is here! They're widescreen and mostly in glorious natural color. These wonderful shows can never be *de-colorized* and *shrunk* to fill the gaps between *screamin commercials* on *little pea-shaped* TV *screens.*
>
> Hallmark of Hollywood will pay $50,000 to "the genius" who can squeeze any one of these new, Big Hits down to TV size without ruining this fine entertainment.
>
> NO ONE CAN SQUEEZE IT 330 TIMES![107]

John Belton argues that the "*shape* of the screen in this period can be said to be less significant in terms of the subsequent development of widescreen cinema than the *size* of the screen."[108] The commercial introduction of television in 1948 produced what was called, in the popular press, "the Lost Audience." In the years between 1947 and 1957, movie attendance had dropped by one half, while 90 percent of the American population acquired a television.[109] And although much of the early competition between film and television centered around screen size,[110] the dominant use of expanded screen real-estate was, as I will argue in the next chapter, to extend the frame and not to multiply the images or perspectives within it.

Despite the many debates about the size, shape, and format of screen size—from Sergei Eisenstein's call for a "Dinamic Square" in 1930 to widescreen, Cinerama, and CinemaScope in the 1940s and 1950s—the architectural arrangement for the proscenium of the framed image remained the same.[111] The cinema screen emerged as a piece of newly *immaterial* architecture in nickelodeons, palaces, and multiplexes.

Sounding very much like André Bazin in 1953 ("The television picture will always retain its mediocre legibility"), in 1975 Raymond Williams described television as an "inferior kind of cinema."[112] When Williams imagined the "developing technology" of television from his 1975 vantage, he forecast that "the major development of the late seventies may well be the large screen receiver: first the screen of four-by-six feet which is already in development; then the flat-wall receiver."[113] Williams's analysis incisively targeted the concept of televisual "flow" to explain television's liquid continuousness, its ever-present presence as an aspect of its spatial and social role. His account foretold what subsequent television scholars would regard as standard markers of the television's screenic role: "liveness" and "presence."[114]

And as Lynn Spigel's writing on the television "set" and its place in the postwar American home demonstrates, the television screen played a key role in the transformation of domestic architectural space in the 1950s. Spigel situates the TV "set" amid the picture windows and sliding glass doors that became the domestic vernacular of the suburban home.[115] Contrary to this welcoming discourse that gleefully pictured the television as a "window on the world," Lee Friedlander's series of black-and-white photographs of television sets (1961–1963) casts the TV as an ominous surveillant look back into the home, more of a claustrophobic closed circuit than a ventilating aperture.[116]

While to some (from the theater-owners campaigning to reclaim lost viewers to the film theorists like Bazin to early television theorists like Raymond

Williams), television may have seemed an "inferior cinema screen," it nevertheless functioned as a virtual window. No longer dependent on the projective features of the camera obscura, the screens of television and the computer are light-emanating surfaces, always already full of light. Recently Microsoft has expanded the reach of Windows to the Microsoft XP Media Center. This convergent "home entertainment system" converts TV to computer, allows the user/viewer to rewind and control "live" TV, record multiple programs at once, burn DVDs of recorded TV, archive and sort by title and date. As the television screen has changed its aperture—from a broadcast receiver to cable- and VCR-enabled to the more recent satellite and DVR exponents and wired connections codependent on the computer screen—the cinema screen may soon be seen as an inferior television, an inert computer display.[117] The very term "spectatorship" has lost its theoretical pinions—as screens have changed, so have our relations to them.[118]

PARADOX 1 REDUX: MATERIAL SPACE MEETS VIRTUAL SPACE

Another way of thinking about this tension between the material and immaterial is by means of a question often asked in spectator theory: "*Where* are we?" or "*When* are we when we watch film or television or sit at the computer?" Theorists have answered this in a variety of ways. The answer might be something like*: in a subjective elsewhere, in a virtual space, a virtual time.* If we adopt a psychoanalytic approach (as apparatus theorists Metz, Baudry, and others have), we would say we are in the "imaginary," a place of psychic regression produced by cinema's apparatical effect:

> The arrangement of different elements—projector, darkened hall, screen—in addition to reproducing in a striking way the *mise-en-scène* of Plato's cave (prototypical set for all transcendence and the topological model of idealism) reconstructs the situation necessary to the release of the "mirror stage" discovered by Lacan.[119]

If we choose a phenomenological approach (as Vivian Sobchack, Steven Shaviro, and Laura Marks have), we might describe how

> The experience of watching a film remains stubbornly concrete, immanent, and pre-reflective: it is devoid of depth and interiority. Sitting in the dark, watching the play of images across a screen, any detachment from "raw phemonena," from the immediacy of sensation or from the speeds and delays of temporal duration, is radically impossible. Cinema invites me, or forces me, to stay within the orbit of the senses.[120]

If we adopt a *Kulturkritik* approach, as some of the German critical theorists have, we might describe the spectator's sense of space (*Raumgefühl*). In Siegfried Kracauer's writing, the terms "space" (*Raum*) and "surface" (*Oberfläche*) are consistent indications of his interest in the spatial tensions between surface and depth. In "Cult of Distraction" (1926), he pits the two-dimensionality of the film screen against its three-dimensional material surrounds.[121] Another Berlin-based journalist, Herman G. Scheffauer, writing at a moment when the "true art form for the film had not yet been invented or evolved," excitedly noted how the "sixth sense of man, his feeling for space or room—his *Raumgefühl*—has been awakened and given a new incentive":

> Space—hitherto treated as something dead and static, a mere inert screen or frame, often of no more significance than the painted balustrade-background at the village photographer's—has been smitten into life, into movement and conscious expression. A fourth dimension has begun to evolve out of this photographic cosmos.[122]

If we adopt a more literal architectural approach, we could describe the space of the movie theater and its material and technical specifications as Frederick Kiesler did:

> The most important quality of the auditorium is, on the one hand, its power of suggesting concentration of attention. Even more important is its power of destroying the sensation of confinement which may be involved in the focal concentration of the spectator upon the screen. I mean that the Reflex which the film creates in the psyche of the spectator must make it possible for him to lose himself in imaginary, endless space, to feel himself alone in universal space, even though the projection surface, the screen, implies the opposite.[123]

Whether large and wide or small and narrow, black-and-white or bright color, projected light or the electronic light of the cathode-ray tube or plasma screen—the space of the screen is a virtual space, an elsewhere that occupies a new dimension. In the next chapter, we will consider the computer display, and trace how it has followed television's lead from CRT to LCD and plasma: ever thinner, flatter, and even mountable on a wall.

The changing technologies of "delivery" alter the effect of moving images in "display." As the advertisement in figure 4.16 declares: "He loves 19th century works. I prefer 20th. We agreed on a piece from the next century." Whatever form a "piece from the next century" will take, we still need to ask questions about the altered and altering effects of screens that are mobile and fixed, that bring images and sounds in varied sizes and shapes, that permeate our spaces public and private, that sit on our desktops, in our living rooms, on our laps, or are hand-held, accompanying us on airplanes, in automobiles, to desert islands—with us here, there, everywhere.

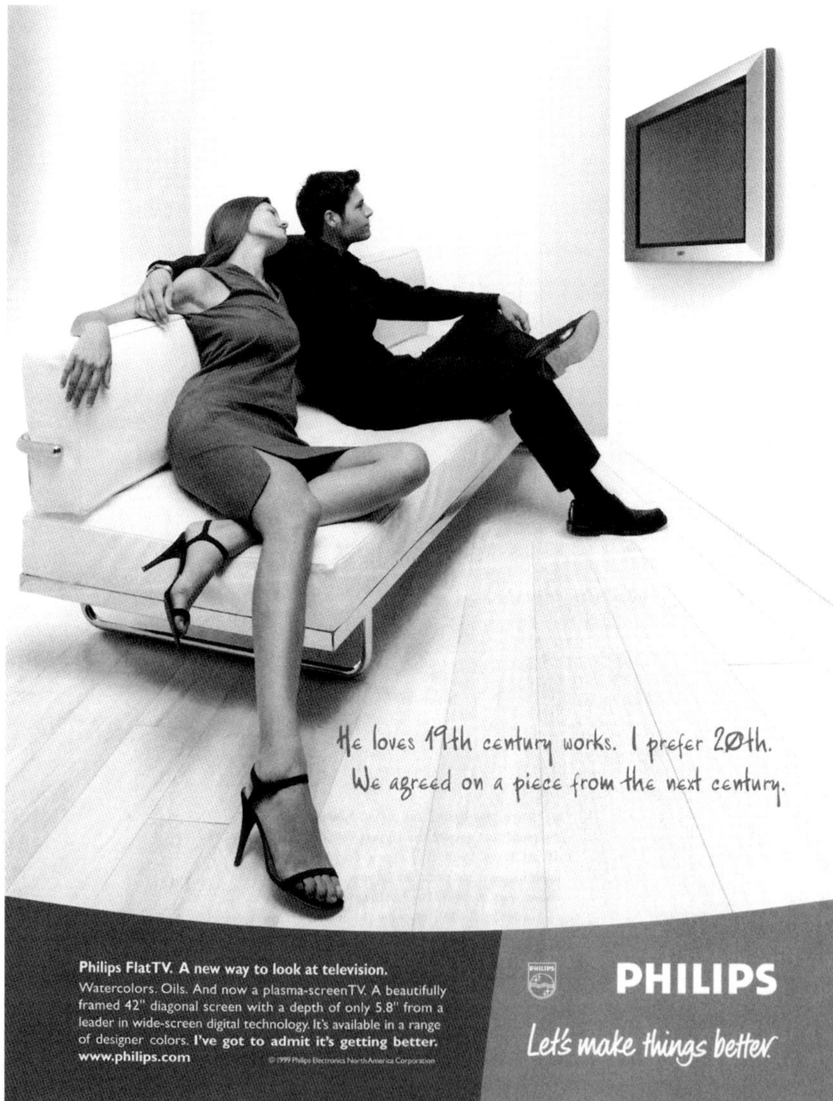

4.16 Philips ad for flat-screen TV, 1999.

LENS IV

VIRILIO'S SCREEN

In some way, you can read the importance given today to glass and transparency as a metaphor of the disappearance of matter. It anticipated the media buildings in some Asian cities with facades entirely made of screens. In a certain sense, the screen became the last wall. No wall out of stone, but of screens showing images. The actual boundary is the screen.

—Paul Virilio, 1993 interview, "Architecture in the Age of Its Virtual Disappearance"

VIRILIO'S screen: Is it a cinema, television, or computer screen? Does Virilio parse the media specificity of these screens, or does he subtly elide their differences? More importantly: in an era of technological convergence, does it matter? If Virilio does not theorize the technological differences between film, television, and the computer, it is because, for him, the screen remains in a metaphoric register, a virtual surface that overrides any specificities of its media formation. Known for his theorization of the logic of speed, the technologies of war, and for the "opto-electronic" mutation in the logistics of human perception produced by both, Virilio posits a new metaphysics: the screen is the locus of lost dimensions of space and technological transformations of time. It modifies our relation to space, a surface-mount for its "accelerated virtualization."[1]

But first: in order to place Paul Virilio's writing in its intellectual trajectory—as part of a cumulatively built missile of twentieth-century cultural critique—I suggest we return to an earlier writer who also incisively attempted to pinpoint the spatial and temporal consequences of modern technology. Equally French, uncannily prescient, reducible to the same initials—the paraph *PV*—the writings of Paul Valéry form an augury of a V-2, Paul Virilio.

In a 1928 essay, "Conquest of Ubiquity," Valéry imagined a future moment when, in push-button ubiquity, "works of art" would "appear and disappear at the simple movement of the hand": "Works of art will acquire a kind of ubiquity. . . . They will not merely exist in themselves but will exist wherever someone with a certain apparatus happens to be. . . . Just as water, gas, electricity are brought into our houses from far off to satisfy our needs in response to a minimal effort, so we shall be supplied with visual and auditory images, which will appear and disappear at the simple movement of the hand, hardly more than a sign. . . . I don't know if a philosopher has ever dreamed of a company engaged in the home delivery of Sensory Reality."[2]

Walter Benjamin uses a lengthy quote from Valéry as an epigrammatic launch to his own essay on the changing epistemology of "works of art." "The Work of Art in the Age of Mechanical Reproduction" (1936) opens with Valéry's proclamation: "For the last twenty years, neither matter nor space nor time has been what it was from time immemorial."[3] In Valéry's loose historiography, the first two decades of the twentieth century foretold "profound changes." While Benjamin's "Work of Art" has since acquired its own ubiquity, one that has exceeded Paul Valéry's work, Virilio channels both authors, taking their forecasts of the "profound change" affecting works of art to a more quotidian exponent. Virilio cites Valéry's passage in which "visual and auditory images . . . appear and disappear" as an "augury of telecommunications."[4] For Virilio, new vectors of space-time-speed are produced as a result of transport and transmission technologies: ubiquity meets instantaneity. Both Benjamin and Valéry emphasize the apparatus of delivery more than the site of display; Virilio's discourse of dematerialization and disappearance has foretold a new logic to the visible, framed, and virtual, on a screen.

Virilio began to diagnose the architectonic consequences of the immaterial "interface" of television screens, computer terminals, and video monitors in the early 1980s. His writing is full of neologisms ("teletopographical," "opto-electronic," "the optic foyer," "the cathode window"), paradoxes ("without necessarily leaving, everything 'arrives'"[5]; "one day the day will come when the day won't come"[6]), and some of the irritating unevenness manifest in polemics by Baudrillard or McLuhan. Phrases appear and disappear in a fugal weave of intermittent and episodic argumentation; words are placed in italicized and bolded fonts for emphasis. In a tone of fin-de-siècle hyperbole fraught with loss and disappearance, Virilio casts the screen as the site of "the passage from something material to something that is not."[7]

Virilio initiated his account of these changes in *The Aesthetics of Disappearance,* a svelte volume published in 1980 (translated to English in 1991) which targets the cinema's innate capacity to defer time, to dissolve material space. "The deferred time of the cinematographic motor," he writes, "empties the present world of appearances, the ubiquity allows millions of spectators that haunt the auditoriums . . . to forget their material plight."[8] Laced with references to filmmakers Méliès, Cohl, Gance, and Clair, as well as to Welles and Disney, *The Aesthetics of Disappearance* marks the cinema as an instrument of a new logic of visibility. The cinema,

Virilio points out, relies on a "picnoleptic" ellipse, the gap of what is invisible between frames, between shots, a disappearance that produces a new register of appearance. Writing of Méliès's stop-action trick: "What science attempts to illuminate, 'the non-seen of the lost moments' becomes with Méliès *the very basis of the production of appearance,* of his invention, what he shows of reality is what reacts continually to the absence of the reality which has passed" (his emphasis).[9]

As an architect struck by the manner in which the cinema substitutes material space for a new immateriality, Virilio remarks: "now in the time of cinematographic factitiousness; literally as well as figuratively, from now on *architecture is only a movie*" (his emphasis).[10] The movie house was a transitional space for this transubstantiation: "the evolution of moviehouses may be revealed as useful for analysis of the cities . . . from now on architecture is only a movie . . . the city is no longer a theatre (agora, forum) but the cinema of city lights."[11] While Virilio asserts the specificity of cinema's perceptual process in *The Aesthetic of Disappearance,* he also foresees a gradual ellision of difference between the screens of cinema, television, and computer screen. Situating the computer screen as a descendant of cinema, he writes: "We're still here in the domain of cinematic illusion, of the mirage of information precipitated on the computer screen."[12]

In *The Aesthetics of Disappearance,* the "cinema" is the instigator of architectonic dissolution, and yet Virilio does not attend to its screen except as a site of "luminous emission."[13] Soon after he published *The Aesthetics of Disappearance,* the television screen began to appear more prominently in his writing. In retrospect it seems as if Virilio wrote *The Aesthetics of Disappearance* on the cusp of cinema's own disappearance. While the dates of English translations of Virilio's work may disguise this fact (*Lost Dimension* [1984] and *Aesthetics of Disappearance* [1980] both appeared in English in 1991), Virilio changed his description of the screen as a result of two marked developments in television delivery and reception: CNN and the VCR. Ted Turner's Atlanta-based twenty-four-hour cable news network CNN—launched in June 1980—inaugurated a new mode of televisuality. "In the interface of the screen," Virilio comments, "everything is always already there, offered to view in the immediacy of an instantaneous transmission. In 1980, for example, when Ted Turner decided to launch Cable News Network as a round-the-clock live news station, he transformed his subscribers' living space into a kind of global broadcast studio for world events . . . the instantaneity of ubiquity."[14] The twenty-four-hour presence of CNN induced Virilio's insight about the screen as the site of architectonic disappearance: "The contour of daily living and the framing of viewpoint in an architectonic constructed of doors and doorways, windows and mirrors are replaced by a cathode framework, an indirect opening in which the electronic false-day functions like a camera lens, reversing the order of appearances to the benefit of an imperceptible transparence, and submitting the supremacy of certain constructive elements to that cathode window that rejects both the portal and the light of day."[15] The architectural metaphor of "the cathode window" began to appear in many of Virilio's interviews in the period soon after the CNN launch. In an interview with *Cahiers du cinéma* in 1981, Virilio described the cathode tube of the video screen as serving as an architectonic element: "It's the new window," he proclaims, a "cathode window."[16] In this frequently cited interview, it is the newly marketed videocassette recorder, which creates an additional "false-day," that seems to have changed Virilio's thinking about the television screen.

Lost Dimension (*L'espace critique,* 1984, translated 1991) was the book-length culmination of Virilio's speculations about the changing dynamics of televisual space. In *Lost Dimension,* Virilio describes the dimensional transfer performed as "three dimensions of constructed space are translated into the two dimensions of a screen, or better of an interface."[17] As the materiality of three-dimensional space is "translated" into the two-dimensional space of the screen, the "lost dimension" brings us, he proclaims, to the "zero degree of architecture."[18] Virilio charts the transformation of the constructed environment due to an "integral cinematism" in which "diverse projection apparatuses—magic lanterns, the phenakistoscope, the kinetoscope and all the cinemascopes" led to the "architectural mutation of a wall-screen."[19] The transfer from the materiality of architectural space to the immateriality of the screenic image pivoted on a "sudden confusion between the reception of images from a film projector and the perception of architectonic forms."[20] Architecture was dissolving, mutating into the hyphenate "wall-screen."

In "The Overexposed City," the opening section of *Lost Dimension,* Virilio sets up a polemic about the "disappearance" and "loss" of architectonic dimension. The screen is an "interface" that relies on a visibility "devoid of spatial dimension," a "visibility without any face-to-face encounter in which the *vis-à-vis* of the ancient streets disappears and is erased."[21] As punctuation, Virilio stresses: "With the interfacing of computer terminals and video monitors, distinctions of *here* and *there* no longer mean anything" (his emphasis).[22] The polis, agora, and forum have been replaced by the screen.

In *Lost Dimension,* the screen is variably described in relation to its media formation—cinema, television, computer. The cinema screen and the television screen differ only in scale: "The situation of the 'tele-spectator' or the 'tele-laborer' at home is the same as that of the audience in the darkened theaters of Pagnol, yet with one major difference of scale, one which affects, more than the dimensions of the projection room, the space-time of the metropolitan concentration."[23]

As a television screen, the "cathode-ray screen" becomes the "third window."[24] (The first window is the door, the second is the window itself, the third is the screen.) Virilio asserts, "In the new trellis of lines, 625 or 819 lines, of imperceptible subtlety, the pixel replaces the bolt and the rivet." And yet the screen is also a computer screen: "The office, which was once an other-place, an architectural aside, has now become a simple screen."[25]

In the section of *Lost Dimension* entitled "Improbable Architecture," Virilio conducts an elliptical excursis through Walter Benjamin's "Work of Art," expanding upon Benjamin's most vivid and explosive image of "the film." "Then came the film," Benjamin famously wrote, and "with the dynamite of its tenths-of-a-second" it burst apart the spatial materials of modernity—its taverns and city streets, offices and furnished rooms, railway stations, and factories.[26] Virilio extrapolates on the further consequences of the "constitutive dispersal" in the far-flung spatial and temporal exponents of contemporary *tele*communications. "Benjamin relied on the metaphor of explosion," Virilio notes; in his writing, explosion is replaced by a slow dissolve. Architecture dematerializes, dimensions are lost. In the "aesthetics of disappearance," "telematics replaces the doorway," and the "pixel replaces the bolt."[27]

Another book Virilio published in 1984 demonstrates that his account of the television screen was developing alongside his insights about the (fatal) interpenetration of military and cinematic technologies. In *War and Cinema: The Logistics of Perception,* Virilio elaborates on the disappearance of direct vision in battle, of sight machines, surveillance, and camouflage. (In a 1997 interview, Virilio noted that *War and Cinema* was published in the same year as William Gibson's *Neuromancer* and the coinage of the term "cyberspace.")[28] In this account, the screen recedes as the camera, a sight machine of eyeless vision ("the soldier's obscene gaze . . . his art of hiding from sight in order to see"), serves as the instrumental coterminus of perception and destruction, of "looks can kill."[29]

War and Cinema predicted, in an advance-guard of seven years, the military logistics of the yet-to-be-waged first Gulf War, its "derealization" of military engagement and the use of images as ammunition. *L'écran du désert: Chroniques de guerre* (1991; translated as *Desert Screen: War at the Speed of Light*), written during and after the war of images in Operations Desert Shield/Desert Storm, took the logistics of military perception to its logical extreme—the screen of their display: "War henceforth takes place in a stadium, the squared horizon of the screen, presented to spectators in the bleachers."[30] The stadium—not the screen—is the metaphor here: the screen has become the real theater of military operation. When asked in 2000, why he used the title *Desert Screen* for his collection of writings about the Gulf War, Virilio returned to the "mirage" of cinema, in an echo of *Aesthetics of Disappearance*: "The screen is the site of *projection of the light of images*—MIRAGES of the geographic desert like those of the CINEMA" (his emphasis).[31] As he wrote in *Desert Screen,* the screen has a mutational power: "It is almost as if the image in the mirror were suddenly modifying our face: the electronic representation on the screen, the radar console, modifies the aerodynamic silhouette of the weapon, the virtual image dominating in fact 'the thing' of which it was, until now, only the 'image.'"[32]

Virilio began to note how the square of the screen (*au carré*) replaced the horizon of real space, a geometric measure used as the vanishing point of Quattrocento perspective. The horizon of the screen (*L'horizon au carré*)[33] forms, in Virilio's coinage "a real time perspective": "Just as the perspective of the event in real time in the *square* of the screen is no longer the perspective of the real space of the *line* of the horizon, so also the moment of *live* reception, *"the real moment,"* is no longer the present moment, that of everyday experience, but a moment falsified by immediacy itself (his emphasis)."[34] Virilio's early 1980s discourse of architectonic "disappearance" re-circulated in his writing of the 1990s with the addition of the term "virtual." Architectural materiality dissolved, as the title of a 1993 interview indicates, into the "Age of Its Virtual Disappearance." In this interview, Virilio argues, "Architecture will 'take place' in the literal sense of the word, in both domains: in real space (the materiality of architecture) and virtual space (the transmission of electromagnetic signs). The real space of the house will have to take into account the real time of transmission."[35] In *Open Sky,* Virilio doubles back over his earlier writing as the "acceleration of communications tools" and "teleaction technologies coming on top of the technology of mere conventional television" further the split between "virtual and actual realities" and the "apparent horizon and transapparent horizon of a screen."[37] He describes how the "transapparent horizon of a screen" has taken over from the apparent horizon of quattrocento perspective: "a 'transappearance' that eliminates the normal boundary of the horizon line, exclusively promoting the screen frame."[37]

By the time he wrote *The Information Bomb* (1998), Virilio was asserting a teleology from Hollywood movie-making to a catastrophe of a metaphysical scale: "what began with the grand-scale Hollywood of the 1920s was . . . the catastrophe of the derealization of the world."[38] Walter Benjamin's explosive metaphor for the cinema as an epistemological TNT becomes, in Virilio's precision-guided critique, an "information bomb": the "presentation of reality that is both accelerated and augmented" on screens that display the "instantaneous superimposition of actual and virtual images."[39] As Virilio's screens have multiplied in global extension, distinctions between them have disappeared, are lost.

5

THE MULTIPLE

Cubism breaks with Renaissance perspective. It views objects relatively: that is from many points of view, no one of which has exclusive authority. And in so dissecting objects it sees them simultaneously from all sides—from above and below, from inside and outside.

SIGFRIED GIEDION, *SPACE, TIME AND ARCHITECTURE*

Cubism, by seizing on instant total awareness, suddenly announced that *the medium is the message*. Is it not evident that the moment that sequence yields to the simultaneous, one is in the world of structure and configuration?

MARSHALL MCLUHAN, *UNDERSTANDING MEDIA: THE EXTENSIONS OF MAN*

5 FROM SEQUENCE TO MULTIPLICITY[1]

Cubist painting, as described in the epigraphs to this chapter, not only fractured the single viewpoint but also placed disparate objects on the same spatial plane, adjacent and simultaneous. In striking contrast to the many modes of representation that shattered the fixity of single-point perspective, the media of film and television—in their dominant forms through most of the twentieth century—were viewed in a single frame, seen on a single screen. Variations of scale, position, and camera angle from shot to shot may alter the positioned fixity of the camera's view, but these shifts in "perspective" are *sequential* and do not occur on the same picture plane as in cubist painting, chronophotography, or dadaist collage.[2] As moving images follow each other in sequence—frame-by-frame, shot-by-shot—they are held within the fixed frame of a screen, a surface that holds its constancy regardless of the continuous or radically discontinuous spatial and temporal relation between shots. In this way, the prevailing format for moving-image media did not follow literary, painterly, or even architectural challenges to the perspectival frame but held on much longer to the strictures of its "symbolic form." In the century-long history of film and the half-century-long history of television, there are only limited examples of either multiple-screen display or multiple-screen composition within the single frame.[3] That is, until recently. With the advent of digital imaging technologies and new technologies of display in the 1990s, the media "window" began to follow painting's and architecture's lead in the challenge to a fixed perspective.

Hyperboles invite a challenge: there were, of course, exceptions to the dominant single-frame, single-screen paradigm. Experiments by filmmakers who toyed with layers of superimposition, split screens, and multiple-screen projections—from Richter to Ruttman, from Brakhage to Warhol, from Abel Gance to Charles and Ray Eames, from Zbigniew Rybczynski to Mike Figgis—provide a catalog of resistance to the dominant form of screenic display. But these exceptions also prove the rule. The rapid and recent remaking of cinematic, televisual, and computer-based forms of imaging and display force us to note, in retrospect, the remarkable historical dominance of the single-image, single-frame paradigm as an intransigent visual practice.

The televisual image largely followed the cinema's conventions of a single-screen format and sequential flow, but once the televisual apparatus became a multiple-channel receiver with the capacity for switching channels at will, aided and accelerated by a remote-control device, television added a new axis of spatial and temporal depth to the cinema's fixed sequentiality. The armchair televisual viewer is a *montagist,* composing a sequenced view from a database of channels and delivery formats, a random set of synchronic alternatives to the single-screen view. And as recent televisual features (programming style cluttered with text crawls and inset frames; monitors enabled with "picture-in-picture" display) facilitate multiple-screen insets, televisual "windows" have become multiple and simultaneous receivers of a variety of programming.[4]

In the short span of the last two decades, the introduction of computer-generated images and digital display technologies has radically transformed the space of the screen.[5] Before digital imaging, the virtuality of representation was measured in brushstrokes, by the use of color and shadow, and was eased by perspectival techniques, by drawing aids like the camera obscura, and by varying levels of artistic skill. Digital imaging technologies not only make it easier to conduct "cut-ups" and collages, to construct seamless substitutions and simulation effects, but also ease the use of inset framing devices, to facilitate multiple "windowed" screens. Digital multiples are readily cloned and easily deployed; gravity-defying digital effects change the physical and temporal laws of the computer-rendered environment. If the digital image is postphotographic; the digital moving-image is postcinematic.[6]

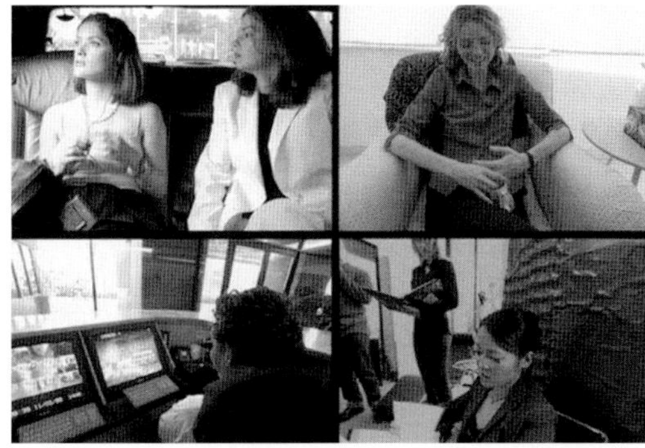

5.1 Frame still from *Time Code,* directed by Mike Figgis, 2000.

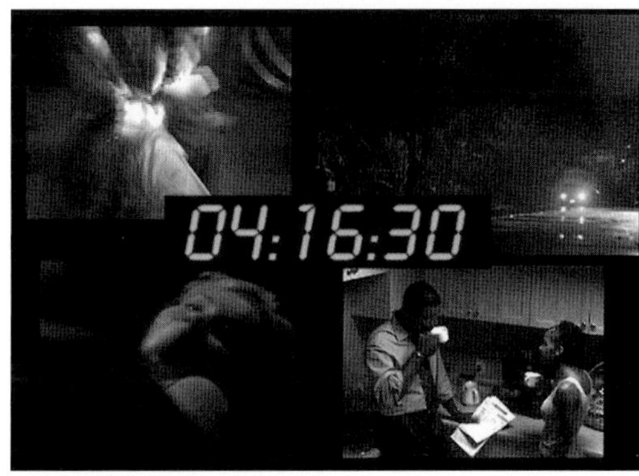

5.2 Frame still from *24* (Fox Television, 2001).

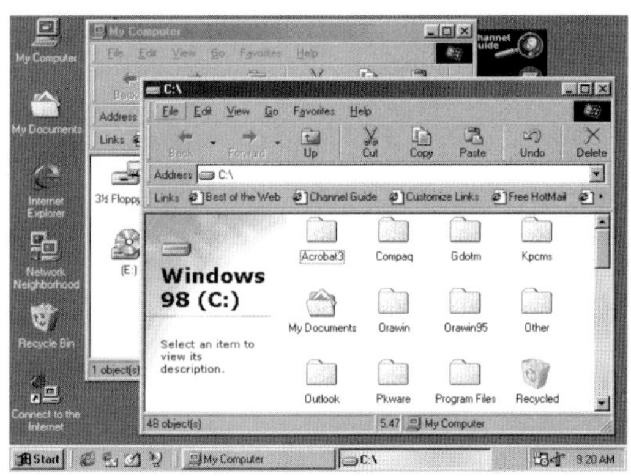

5.3 Screen shot, computer window with Windows.

And yet the markers of these changes are recent. As I will describe in this chapter, they have emerged alongside the developing display interface of the computer screen. The "graphical user interface" (GUI) transformed the computer screen from a surface with glowing symbols and text to one which displayed icons and, later, digital images. The GUI display introduced an entirely new visual system—a text or image in one "window" meeting other texts or images in other "windows" on the same screen. The multiple framed images of Muybridge (seen in sequence) and the silkscreen multiples of Andy Warhol (seen in repetition) contained images that exist in relation to each other, whereas the "windows" of the computer may not. Cinema and television screens, the once sacrosanct domain of the single image, have been invaded by text crawls, inset screens, pop-up windows. Multiple-frame images are a readable new visual syntax, a key feature in the contemporary remaking of a visual vernacular.

If we follow Panofsky's assertion that perspective was a "symbolic form"—a way of apprehending the world through a mental apparatus—then the representational postulates of perspective have met their end on the computer screen. And, if we accept Panofsky's further argument that perception is conditioned by representational habits, then our new mode of perception is multiple and fractured. It is "postperspectival"—no longer framed in a single image with fixed centrality; "postcinematic"—no longer projected onto a screen surface as were the camera obscura or magic lantern; "post-televisual"—no longer unidirectional in the model of sender and receiver.

THE MOVING IMAGE AND THE MULTIPLE FRAME IN FILM AND TELEVISION

> *Painters had discovered that one observation point, in spite of emphasis by distortion, was not sufficient to give the spatial essence of the object. . . .* Painters shifted the point of vision into a kind of cinematographic sequence, and represented the projection of several points of view in one picture.
>
> —Gyorgy Kepes, *Language of Vision* (emphasis added)

> *The spectator is not just responsive to what is moving but also to what stays in place, and the perception of movement supposes fixed frames.*
>
> —Pierre Francastel, "Espace et illusion"

As Gyorgy Kepes suggests in the above epigraph, in the single-spatial plane of cubist painting, "Painters shifted the point of vision into a kind of cinematographic sequence, and represented the projection of several points of view in one picture."[7] Kepes's introduction of the cinematic metaphor describes the stuttering representation of movement, a "cinematographic sequence" seen arrayed on one spatial plane, as well as the polyscenic, multiple time-frame found in cubist and futurist paintings such as Picasso's *Les demoiselles d'Avignon* (1907), Giacomo Balla's *Dynamism of a Dog on a Leash* (1912), and Marcel Duchamp's *Nude Descending a Staircase, No. 2* (1912). Pierre Francastel reminds us of another aspect of the cinematographic sequence, one that remains insistent through most of the cinematic century: the perception of cinematic movement "supposes" the fixed frame of the screen.[8]

THE SINGLE FRAME, THE SINGLE SCREEN

In Charles Musser's account, the "history of screen practice" was marked by several major technological transformations: the development of the magic lantern in the 1650s, the adaptation of photographic slides for projection around 1850, and the projection of chrono-photographic images around 1895.[9] These technical turning points in the emergence of a "screen practice" mark the addition of photography to magic lantern projection. Yet an examination of the emerging cultural practices of image projection will also indicate what remained constant during these changes: viewers faced projected images on a screen, and most commonly, these images were projected sequentially rather than arrayed adjacently.[10] This practice was not determined by the limits of existing technology but, instead, by the representational convention of the single image in a single frame. Multiple lanterns were routinely used by phantasmagoria exhibitors to create composite effects; two projectors could have been placed side by side from the earliest moments of screen practice.

Although the popular mid-nineteenth-century term for slide projection—the "stereopticon"—might seem to indicate a system for two-slide projection, the term was adapted because of the common practice of transferring stereoscope views to ground glass, cutting the double image in half, and selling them separately as lantern slides.[11] Even before lantern slide images began to rely on photography around 1850, the prevailing exhibition practice was to project single-frame images despite discontinuities in the image (its angle, its distance) as slides were projected in sequence.[12]

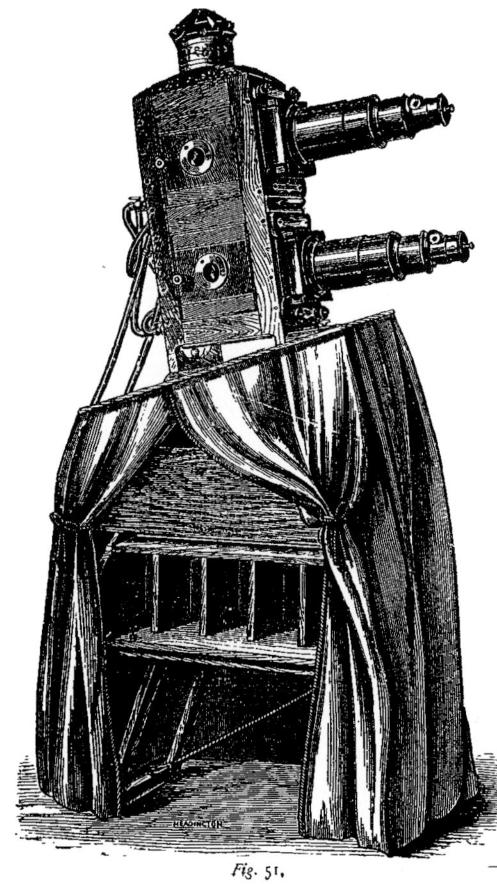

5.4 Malden Bi-Unial lantern, from W. J. Chadwick, *The Magic Lantern Manual* (London: Frederick Warne, 1878).

As an exemplary indication of late-nineteenth-century magic lantern technique, the 1878 handbook *The Magic Lantern Manual* details a variety of lantern types and instructions for their use. Its author describes the operation of the Malden Bi-Unial Lantern (figure 5.4): "[it] combines two lanterns in one, having their optical systems placed one over the other.

This form of Dissolving View seems the one most in general use at the present time."[13] The "Bi-Unial" lantern had two separate optical systems and technically could have projected images in multiple array. Instead, the standard practice involved using the two lenses to dissolve between images—one on top of the other—in the appearance of a single frame.

In this regard, the emerging use of projected lantern slides in art history lectures formed an important contrast to the predominant forms of late-nineteenth-century entertainment and the emerging format for moving images. The comparative method of the double-slide lecture became one of the pedagogical mainstays of German art historian Heinrich Wölfflin soon after he began to lecture at the University of Berlin in 1901. Wölfflin's predecessor at the University of Berlin, Hermann Grimm, had used slides extensively in his lectures in the late 1890s. Wölfflin began to use two slide projectors, arranged side by side, so that he could compare different images or show details alongside the principal image. The use of double-slide projection allowed the viewer to consider one image in relation to another image—to compare an image to one of an earlier time, to a closer detail, to a contrasting style. The conclusions drawn from this method were comparative and analytic.[14]

By contrast, the emerging mode of moving-image projection retained the singularity of one image, one screen. As lantern images were projected in increasingly rapid succession (with apparatuses like L. S. Beal's 1866 choreutoscope or Coleman Sellers's 1861 kinematoscope, or Muybridge's 1880 photographic-based zoopraxiscope), images were projected in sequential dissolve.[15] Between 1896 and 1900, many different inventors, manufacturers, filmmakers, exhibitors, and entrepreneurs struggled to define the format and venue for moving images, but there was a remarkable consistency in the form of single-screen projection.[16] The technical systems for projection available by 1896—the Lumières' Cinématographe, R. W. Paul's animatographe and Theatrograph, Jenkins and Armat's Phantoscope, Edison's Vitascope, but also Lyman H. Howe's animotoscope, W. Watson's motograph, William Paley's kalatechnoscope, Herman Casler's Biograph, Charles Urban's bioscope, and Latham's eidoloscope—all had different capabilities and relied on different patents and construction, but they had one common element: all projected single-screen images, seen in a single frame.[17]

Even so, the many systems for exhibiting moving images demonstrated the uncertainty about what the predominant form of the medium would be. At the Paris 1900 Exhibition, Raoul Grimoin-Sanson's ten-projector Cinéorama provided spectators with an unframed 360-degree view of projected moving images, while the Lumières' Grand Écran/Cinématographe Géant projected a program of films and color slides onto an immense screen that could be viewed from both sides.[18] The size and format of single-screen projection, viewed by spectators in fixed seats facing the screen, was not yet the dominant form. The cultural practice that emerged for the projection of moving images on a screen did not deploy multiple projectors but, instead, cast a single image on a single screen.

THE MOVING IMAGE IN A SINGLE FRAME: THE COMPOSITE SHOT

The first recorded moving images evidenced a broad range of camera angles, camera distances, and locations—the Lumière brothers' outdoor *actualités* of workers leaving the Lumière photographic plate factory (*Sortie d'usine,* filmed directly facing the action), the arrival of a train at the station (*Arrivée d'un train à La Ciotat,* filmed from a dynamic diagonal angle), and the baby eating breakfast (*Repas de bébé,* filmed from a closer camera position), or the in-studio films of W. K. L. Dickson and Thomas Edison, which staged action against flat black backgrounds inside of the "Black Maria" (*The Leonard-Cushing Fight,* filmed in six separate one-minute "rounds" for separate ten-cent kinetoscope view; *The Kiss; The Corbett-Courtney Fight*). Whatever the differences were in the first single-shot films, their action was contained within the bounds of a single frame and was projected onto a single screen.

Even when filmmakers discovered the stop-action trick (the camera was stopped during filming and a substitution was made before the camera commenced filming again), this special effect relied on maintaining the continuity of the frame. The one-shot film *The Execution of Mary Queen of Scots* (1895, made by Arthur Clarke for the Edison Manufacturing Company) provides a simple example. An actor dressed as Queen Mary posed with his head on the execution block, the camera stopped, a mannequin was substituted, and the camera recommenced filming as the guillotine made its cut. The resulting film displays the regicidal decapitation within the seeming continuity of one shot. The "ontological cut" here was invisible, in the missing time between frames. Films by Georges Méliès, Ferdinand Zecca, and others relied on this stop-action trick to enact a new visual system based on disappearances, substitutions, reappearance, and the "seamless" cut.

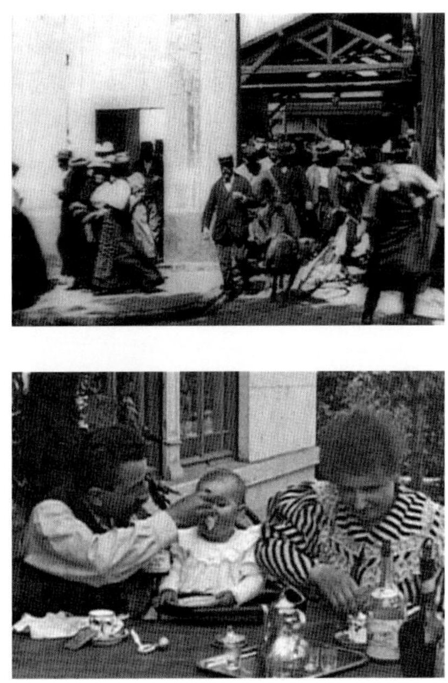

5.5 Single image, single frame: frame enlargements from Lumière *actualités,* 1895.

Early filmmakers were also quick to exploit the potential of "double exposures," exposing portions of the film more than once. Following the magic lantern tradition of dissolving views between slides, in-camera double exposures were used to supply dissolve transitions between two separate "shots." Yet the resulting superimposition of two different images—a predigital compositing technique—would still be seen in a single frame. By exposing only a portion of the film during one "take" and another portion during a subsequent "take," filmmakers could also produce the effect of a split screen. Edwin S. Porter's *The Twentieth Century Tramp* (1902), for example, used the technique of split exposure to add the New York skyline to the lower portion of the frame while the upper portion showed a "tramp" pedaling on a flying bicycle-contraption above it.[19] The title seems to pun on the double meaning of "tramp"—describing both a vagrant and an excursion by foot—and implied a wild new mobility for drifters in the new century.

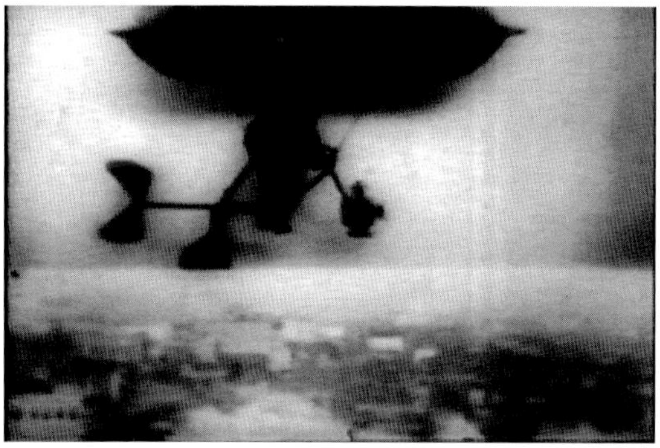

5.6 Split-screen image from *Twentieth Century Tramp,* Thomas Edison Company, directed by Edwin S. Porter, 1902.

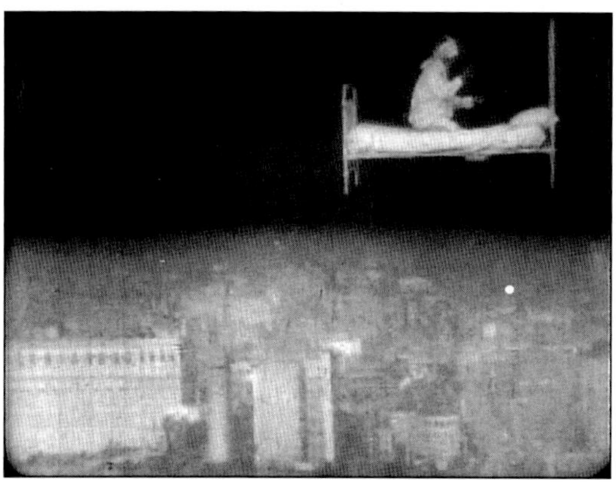

5.7 Split-screen image from *Dream of a Rarebit Fiend,* Thomas Edison Company, directed by Edwin S. Porter, 1906.

Another Edwin S. Porter/Thomas Edison film, *The Dream of a Rarebit Fiend* (1906), relied on a similar split-screen technique to indicate that the dreamer in his bed was flying over the city. Based on an episode of Windsor McCay's comic strip *Little Nemo in Slumberland, The Dream of a Rarebit Fiend* used a panoply of trick devices—superimpositions, stop-motion tricks, split-frame superimpositions—to visualize the drunken dream state resulting from overindulgence in beer and cheese rarebit. In both of these instances, the split screen was intended to help viewers visualize a fantastical world by meshing the two parts seamlessly rather than drawing their attention to the split in the frame of the shot.

Like the polyscenic painters of the quattrocento, early filmmakers could manipulate the spatial and temporal components of a single shot by using stop-action or split-frame double exposure, by layering the image into a polyscenic composite as either a directly visible or hidden effect. And as filmmakers began to have one shot follow another, the logic of shot-to-shot sequentiality—the ordering of images one after another, not one adjacent to another—became a basic constraint of cinematic construction. Histories of film style—whether they imply an evolutionary model, or assume that the cinema developed according to its essential characteristics, or imply a relation to historical, cultural specificities—all must account for the dominance of the single-frame image.

THE MOVING IMAGE IN A SINGLE FRAME: THE SPLIT SCREEN

Edwin S. Porter used a simple two-way split screen in *The Twentieth Century Tramp* (1902) and *Dream of a Rarebit Fiend* (1906), but the split was intended to provide a seamless rend, an early instance of a compositing "special effect." In Lois Weber and Phillips Smalley's 1913 Rex film *Suspense,* the screen is visibly split into a triptych of three triangles, showing three simultaneous actions not sequentially, but within one frame. The title of the film indicates its primary narrative function: to suspend the spectator in the midst of dramatic action, uncertain of its narrative outcome. *Suspense* tells a familiar story, one quite common to one-reel threat-and-resolution narratives: a wife is home alone while her husband is off on business, and a burglar tries to break into the house. D. W. Griffith's 1909 *The Lonely Villa* has a nearly identical setup; but his one-reel narrative relied on cross-cutting—the sequential back-and-forth between several lines of action—to build suspense: the viewer watches the woman fretting inside her domestic sanctum while a menacing burglar threatens from the outside. A call to the husband, who is far from home in a third, more distant space, initiates a rush to the rescue. In *The Lonely Villa,* the viewer is literally suspended from seeing developments in one line of action while viewing the action of the "meanwhile." The telephone is used to link two separate spaces in simultaneity.[20] In contrast, in *Suspense,* instead of cross-cutting between the three spaces, Weber and Smalley chose to portray the suspenseful narrative moment within the confines of one shot, one frame.

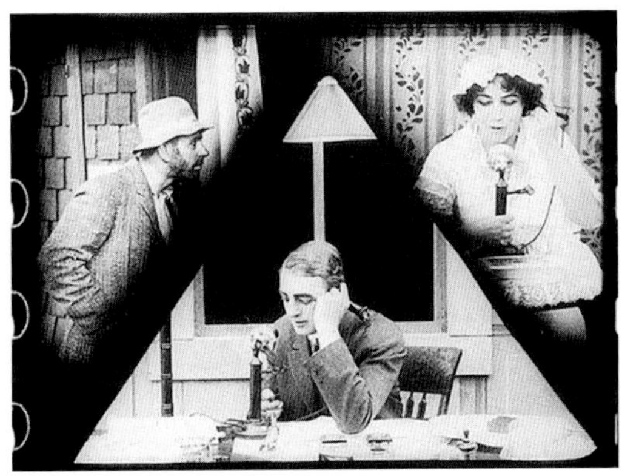

5.8 Split-screen frame enlargement from *Suspense,* directed by Lois Weber and Phillips Smalley, 1913. Museum of Modern Art Film Library.

Suspense offers an early example of the narrative function of split-screen composition. The suspense occurs across the orthogonals that divide the shot. The split screen forms a bold contrast to the perspectival agenda of representing the near and far along the axis of depth. Instead, it places the near and far on the same spatial plane, flat and adjacent, like the moment, described by McLuhan in the epigraph at the start of this chapter, when "sequence yields to the simultaneous, one is in the world of structure and configuration."[21]

FRAMES WITHIN FRAMES

> *Doors, windows, box office windows, skylights, car windows, mirrors, are all frames. The great directors have particular affinities with particular secondary, tertiary, etc. frames. And it is by this dovetailing of frames that the parts of the set or of the closed system are separated, but also converge and are reunited.*
>
> —Gilles Deleuze, *Cinema 1: The Movement-Image*

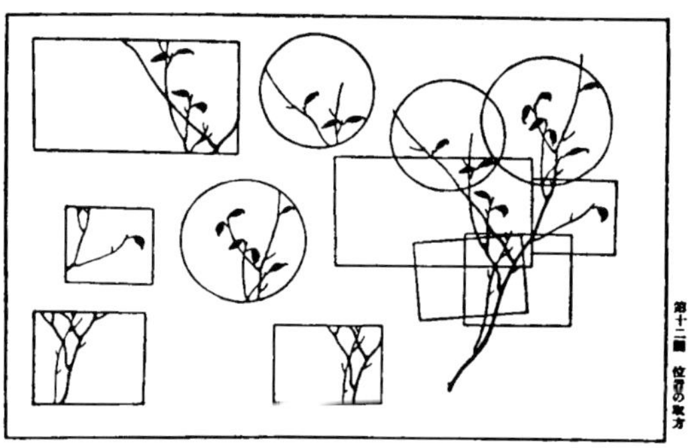
THE CINEMATOGRAPHIC PRINCIPLE AND THE IDEOGRAM 41

Here's the branch of a cherry-tree.[9] And the pupil cuts out from this whole, with a square, and a circle, and a rectangle—compositional units:

He frames a shot!

5.9 Diagram of variable framing of branches, from Sergei Eisenstein, *Film Form: Essays in Film Theory* (New York: Harcourt, Brace and World, 1949).

Although my discussion so far has emphasized early filmmaking and the emerging conventions of moving-image representation, allow me to now turn to several contemporary French theorists who have analyzed the preponderance of frame-within-a-frame compositions. Gilles Deleuze, in his first volume of film theory, *Cinema 1: The Movement-Image,* broke the moving image into its constituent frames.[22] While Deleuze's discussion of the frame (*cadre*) and framing (*cadrage*) pivots on the polarities between the contents of the frame—full versus empty, rarefaction versus saturation—it is his discussion of the boundary of the frame that interests me here. For Deleuze, following Bergson, the frame is an "immobile section" that gives "false movement." As Deleuze notes, silent filmmakers experimented with the boundaries of the frame: "The iris method in Griffith, which isolates a face first of all, then opens and shows the surroundings; Eisenstein's researches inspired by Japanese drawing, which adapt the frame to the theme; Gance's variable screen which opens and closes 'according to the dramatic necessities,' and like a 'visual accordion'—from the very beginning attempts were made to test dynamic variations of the frame. In any case framing is limitation."[23]

Deleuze maintains that framing determines the closed system of the shot: "[I]n the final analysis, the screen, as the frame of frames, gives a common standard of measurement to things which do not have one—long shots of the countryside and close-ups of the face, an astronomical system and a single drop of water—parts which do not have the same denominator of distance, relief or light. In all of these senses the frame insures a deterritorialization of the image."[24] The container of the screen—as the master frame—translates the variables of distance and angle, light and depth, into a "common standard of measurement to things which do not have one." Deleuze supplies a catalog of films that use inset frames for dramatic effect (Fritz Lang's films *Thousand Eyes of Dr. Mabuse* and *Woman in the Window* are key examples), yet he is keen to note that these compositional framing devices or partial frames still remain within the boundaries of the screen. Deleuze's insistence that the screen "as the frame of frames" is the grand denominator of what it contains supplies profound support for an analysis of the screen as a closed visual system. As a close corollary to his attention to the frames within the master frame, his insight—"All framing determines an out-of-field [*hors-champ*]"[25]—posits a radical elsewhere, always unseen.

In a later essay, "L'écran second, ou le rectangle au carré" (The Second Screen, or the Rectangle Squared), Christian Metz also addresses the representational practice of using frames within frames: "The film presents us with a spectacle as if through a frame, door, window, etc. which is itself enframed at the same time by the rectangle of the screen."[26] The shot within a shot is a familiar figure of cinema. It plays a central role in the intrigue and continuity of certain films: at the same time, it is emblematic in the very name of these films—*Rear Window* (dir. Hitchcock, 1954), *Secret Beyond the Door* (dir. Fritz Lang, 1948), *Woman in the Window* (dir. Fritz Lang, 1944)—in which the window of the title is itself redoubled in the framing of a photograph and also in another film again; or the interior screen materializes under special variables—windshields of automobiles, a torn curtain, different demarcations of the view.[27]

Metz engages an argument made elsewhere by film theorist Marc Vernet that such secondary framing—framing within the frame—is a self-reflexive strategy engaged in the diegetization of the apparatus (*diégétisation du dispositif*).[28] While Metz's discussion is largely devoted to the compositional *mise en abyme* performed by framing devices that enact a secondary screen, he concludes his essay with a description of the use of the split screen in Brian De Palma's *Sisters* (1973), describing how De Palma deployed this technique to present the shot and its countershot simultaneously.[29]

As is evident in Metz's description of *Sisters* (and as we will see in some of the examples discussed below), the shot-countershot can occur in the same master frame in a multiple-frame, multiple-screen format. Separate "points of

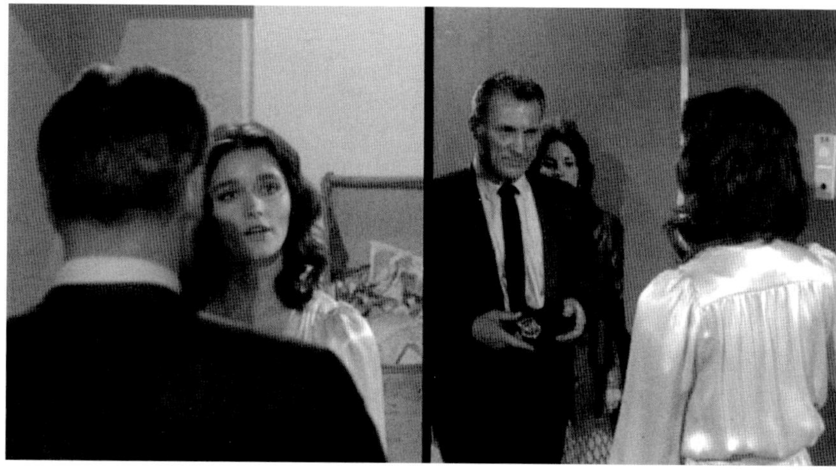

5.10 Shot/countershot on two screens, from *Sisters,* directed by Brian De Palma, 1973.

view"—of seeing and being seen—can be combined, compared, placed simultaneous and adjacent. In terms of theories of suture, replacing the sequence of shot/countershot with this form of nonsequential simultaneity skews the sense that the spectator is somehow sutured into the film, between the shots.[30] While the single-screen moving image offers multiple perspectives through the sequential shifts of montage and editing, the multiple-frame or multiple-screen moving image offers the same via adjacency and contiguity.

MULTIPLICITY: A TAXONOMY OF VARIABLES

Considering the differences between the split screen (fracturing the screen within the master frame), the multiple frame (frame within a frame), and the use of multiple screens (multiplying the number of screens, often requiring multiple projection devices), a taxonomy of variables begins to emerge, each with its own historical lineage: (1) Films that use the split screen to vividly demarcate separate spaces, as exemplified in the split screens of *Suspense* (1913) and later in films such as *It's Always Fair Weather* (1955), *Pillow Talk* (1959), *Grand Prix* (1966), *Boston Strangler* (1968), *The Thomas Crown Affair* (1968), *Woodstock* (1968), and *Sisters* (1973); (2) films that use a frame-within-a-frame of a master shot or an inset screen as an element within the fictional world (a "diegetization of the apparatus") as found in examples from *Uncle Josh at the Moving Picture Show* (1902) to *Sherlock Junior* (dir. Buster Keaton, 1924) to *Purple Rose of Cairo* (dir. Woody Allen, 1985); (3) films that were projected onto multiple screens, from Abel Gance's three-projector Polyvision system for *Napoléon* (1926) to the multiscreen exhibits of Ray and Charles Eames; Francis Thompson and Alexander Hammid's triple-screen exhibit *To Be Alive* at the 1964 New York World's Fair and their six-screen *We Are Young* at Expo '67 in Montreal; Andy Warhol's two-screen projections *Inner and Outer Space* (1965), *Lupe* (1965), *The Chelsea Girls* (1966); and other experiments at world exhibitions like Expo '67 and by experimental filmmakers Harry Smith (four-screen *Mahagonny,* 1970–1980) and Sally Potter (two-screen projects *Black and White,* 1969, and *Play,* 1971). These multiple-screen practices "expanded" cinema to venues outside of the commercial movie theater.

Experiments in screen format have occurred at critical crossroads in the history of moving-image technology. Eisenstein proposed a "dinamic screen" amid the reformulation of aspect ratio in the wake of the late 1920s transition to sound. In the early 1950s, in response to another set of economic and technological challenges to the film industry (divestiture, the commercial introduction of television), a variety of new screen formats were introduced. The expanded screen aspect ratios of Cinerama and CinemaScope challenged filmmakers to use the expanded horizontal scope of the frame. Despite the following catalog of split-screen and multiple-screen projects, these examples remain rare exceptions to dominant screen practice.

SPLIT SCREENS, MULTIPLE SCREENS

In the 1950s, filmmakers took advantage of the new aspect ratio to divide the screen into component screens. In the opening prologue of *This Is Cinerama!,* the feature-length travelogue produced for Cinerama's initial commercial demonstration in 1952, Lowell Thomas narrates a familiar teleology of motion picture history, tracing the desire to "reproduce nature" from cave paintings to magic lanterns, nickelodeons and silent movie-making. As Thomas begins his account, he is seen on a screen with the standard Academy 4:3 aspect ratio. And then, as the screen dramatically expands its format and widens to Cinerama's wider aspect ratio, Thomas announces: "This is Cinerama!"[31]

Although the patented Cinerama process involved recording with a three-lens camera and projecting with three projectors onto a concave screen, Cinerama was largely deployed for seamless continuity between the three screens.[32] With the exception of the occasional loss of registration (as in the three-legged woman who appears in Saint Mark's Square in Venice, a freak byproduct of a mistake in camera alignment), most of the film's eleven segments rely on the scope of the elongated rectangular frame to demonstrate the wrap-around immersion of the wide screen. The roller coaster at Rockaway's Playland, a helicopter trip over Niagara Falls, a bullfight in Madrid, and the canals of Venice are filmed in three-screen registration to demonstrate the panoramic expanse of the 146-degree Cinerama screen. One sequence of the film, however, divides the panoramic display into its three constituent segments, in a manner similar to Gance's Polyvision. Set in Florida's proto–theme park, the Cypress Gardens segment exploits a three-way split of the screen. Speedboats pull "Aquabelles" and "Aquabats" on water skis through the canals of Florida's Lake Eloise in an elaborate triptych choreography. The three-screen split shows the race not in a sequential cross-cut but in multiple simultaneous juxtaposition.[33] Nevertheless, the predominant use of the three-projector Cinerama system was to hide the "seams" between each screen and give the illusion of an expansive, continuous panoramic display. As indicated in the promotional brochure accompanying *This Is Cinerama!*: "Not only has the screen a new shape and dimension, but now there are three projection booths simultaneously throwing the image on the screen—a clear, bright image that almost imperceptibly merges into one great, panoramic picture."[34]

As another example of splitting the expanded horizontal aspect ratio of the widened frame, several sequences of the anamorphic widescreen CinemaScope film *It's Always Fair Weather* (1955, dir. Gene Kelly and Stanley Donen) split the screen into a triptych. The three-way split forms the perfect analog to the film's narrative about the separation and reunion of three World War II war buddies (Gene Kelly, Dan Dailey, Michael Kidd). At the end of the war, Kelly tears a dollar bill into three pieces, one for each of the buddies. Each veteran goes his separate way. (John Belton also notes that the aspect ratio of the American dollar bill is "by strange coincidence" almost exactly the same shape as CinemaScope: 2.35:1).[35] In the musical number "I Shouldn't Have Come," Donen uses a three-way split screen to show the three protagonists as they separately regret their reunion. Like many 1950s films that addressed the threat of television by incorporating it into its plot, the final brawl is at a TV studio but seen through the windows of the control booth and in the multiple-screen display of the studio's television monitors. Whether or not, as Belton suggests, Donen's use of a three-way split screen "playfully parodies" the three camera/three projector system of Cinerama, *It's Always Fair Weather* used the single-projector CinemaScope format to fracture simultaneous action into comparative adjacent display.

Another CinemaScope (2.35:1) film, *Pillow Talk* (dir. Michael Gordon, 1959), used a two-way split screen to establish both the separation and the connection between its two protagonists—the single career woman played by Doris Day and the playboy songwriter played by Rock Hudson. Day and Hudson share a party line; Day can't receive or make calls when Hudson is on the line romancing his many girlfriends. The screen is split to reveal their two separate habitats

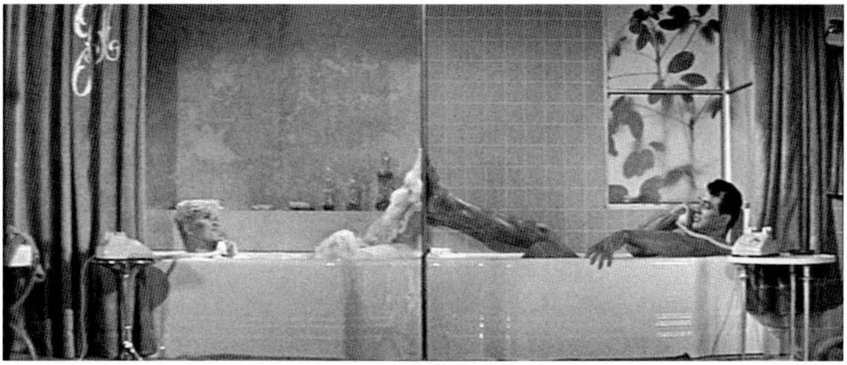

5.11 Frame enlargement from *Pillow Talk,* Universal Pictures, directed by Michael Gordon, 1959.

and the telephonic link between them. In the still shown in figure 5.11, the frame edge is playfully eroticized. As Day and Hudson each recline, nude in separate bathtubs, each places a bare foot on the wall.[36] The two sections of the split screen abut in the center of the frame, and Day's and Hudson's feet touch along the boundary that separates them. As in Weber and Smalley's *Suspense,* the telephone links these separate spaces, seen here in temporal, not spatial, contiguity.

The use of the split screen for its narrative possibilities continued into the 1960s. In some cases, filmmakers were directly inspired by multiple-screen exhibitions seen at world's fairs. For the 1959 Moscow World's Fair, the U.S. Department of State commissioned designer George Nelson and the Los Angeles-based team of Ray and Charles Eames to design a multimedia exhibit on American life. The sheer number of images (2,200) displayed the abundance of life in the United States—automobiles, lawnmowers, washing machines, televisions, a plenitude magnified by the multiple (seven) screens.[37] The exhibit's coy title, *Glimpses of the USA,* suggested that, in one swift but multiplied glimpse, the United States was a land of abundant consumer durables, skyscrapers, housing projects, expansive highways, and the shiny and happy people who use them. The Eameses drew upon a repertoire of images from their database of more than 350,000 slides, and the multiple-screen presentation multiplied the impression of scale. As Beatriz Colomina has suggested, the Eameses' multiple-screen technique was organized with the logic of data compression, condensing a large quantity of information into a compressed physical space.[38] Seven twenty-by-thirty-foot screens were mounted inside an expansive geodesic dome designed by Buckminster Fuller.[39] After the success of *Glimpses* (it was seen by three million Soviet citizens and received wide critical acclaim), the Eameses received another government commission for a multiscreen (six-screen) presentation at the 1962 World's Fair in Seattle. And for the IBM Pavil-

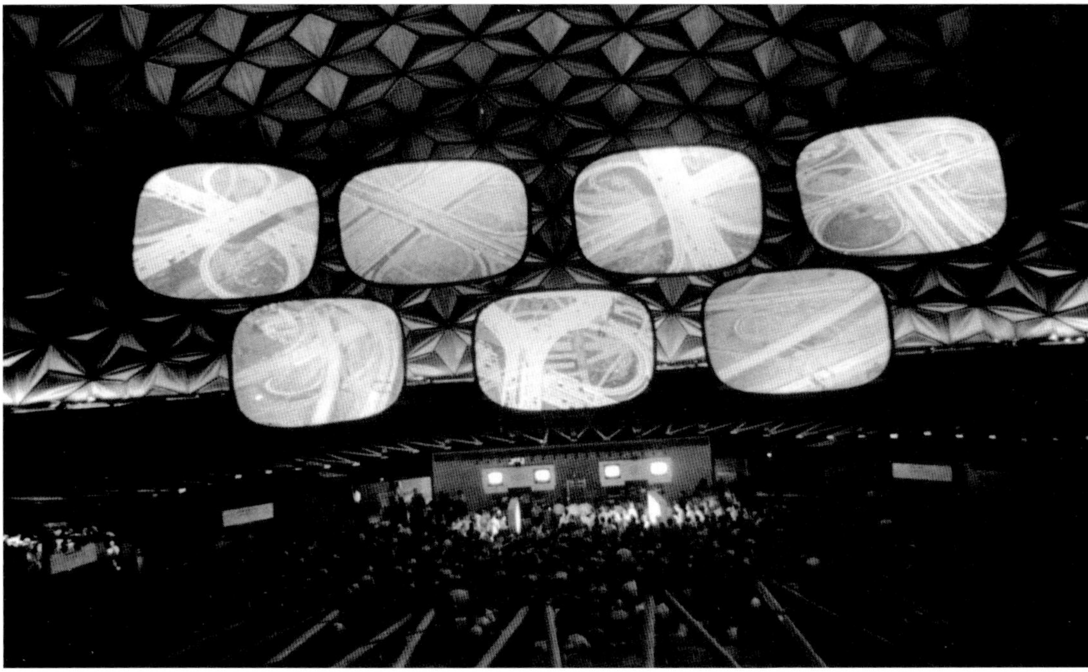

5.12 Ray and Charles Eames, *Glimpses of the USA* (Moscow, 1959). Image courtesy of the Eames Archive, Los Angeles.

ion at the 1964 New York World's Fair, *Think,* the Eameses' multimedia paean to the virtues of the computer, increased the number of screens to fourteen.[40]

While the Eameses are certainly the best-known designers of multiple-screen visual displays, other filmmakers were drawn to this form of display. Another corporate pavilion at the 1964 New York World's Fair featured a three-screen film (18 minutes, for the Johnson Wax pavilion). Filmed on location in Africa, Europe, and the United States by filmmakers Francis Thompson and Alexander Hammid, *To Be Alive* won the 1965 Academy Award for Best Documentary Short Subject.[41] When *To Be Alive* received publicity from its Academy award, a number of feature filmmakers took inspiration from it. In 1966, John Frankenheimer, who had seen the Thompson/Hammid exhibit, used a three-way split screen for his 70mm Super-Cinerama film *Grand Prix* about the French auto race.[42] Frankenheimer and cinematographer Lionel Lindon mounted specially constructed cameras on racing cars, combined dynamic point-of-view racing footage with helicopter footage from above. Although *Grand Prix* was not projected onto multiple screens like the Thompson/Hammid project that inspired it, its tripartite split of the screen's wide-aspect ratio was a notably new narrative technique.

"EXPANDED CINEMA"

In the fall of 1965, a survey entitled *Expanded Cinema* was screened at the Film Maker's Cinematheque in New York City. "There were artists working with sound-light-multiple projections for a good ten years," wrote reviewer Jonas Mekas, "but thcy remained in experimental, semi-private stages until the Expanded Cinema Survey."[43] Between corporately sponsored projects for world's fair pavilions and "expanded cinema" performances that included film projection alongside other forms of light-play—slide shows, searchlights with color gels, strobe lights, mirror-balls—multiple-screen projection became a marked visual display practice of the 1960s.[44]

ANDY WARHOL AND THE MULTIPLE SCREEN, 1965–1966

In 1965 and 1996, Andy Warhol, whose serial painted portraits and silk-screen multiples placed repeated images in serial display, began to also place moving images in multiple array.[45] In *Outer and Inner Space* (1965, black and white, 33 minutes), Warhol doubled the frame of the film screen by placing a video screen in the shot and then doubled the frame again by projecting two reels of film side-by-side.[46] As if in a mixed-media update of Edwin S. Porter's *Uncle Josh at the Moving Picture Show,* Warhol framed his blonde superstar Edie Sedgwick in front of her framed prerecorded video image. In a clever confrontation between the two competing media formats—video/television and film—Sedgwick's image was multiplied, quadrupled, in a mirrored *mise en abyme.* In the video inset, Sedgwick is framed in profile conversing with someone just offscreen, off-frame. But within the film frame, the video monitor is placed in the back of the shot, and Sedgwick faces toward the film camera as if she is talking to someone just offscreen, off-frame. On the few occasions when Sedgwick faces the inset screen, she faces herself as if in a mirror but with a time delay. (Although the sound is at points garbled, Sedgwick's portrait is also an aural one. At points she mocks herself, mouthing her words as she hears them and sees them on the video monitor.) As portraiture, the multiplication of Sedgwick's image gives the effect of a quadrupled Edie, talking about fame and celebrity in an empty feedback loop. Warhol's title, *Outer and Inner Space,* names the complex spatial and temporal play that occurs between the outside and inside of the frame of the TV set and the frame of the film screen as it touches another screen in its multiple adjacent display. One might think that Maurice Merleau-Ponty, in his 1945 lecture on film and the "new psychology," had anticipated the philosophical gravity of Warhol's experiment: "if philosophy is in harmony with the cinema, if thought and technical effort are heading in the same direction, it is because the philosopher and the moviemaker share a certain way of being, a certain view of the world which belongs to a generation. It offers us yet another chance to confirm that modes of thought correspond to technical methods and that, to use Goethe's phrase, 'What is inside is also outside.'"[47] In many of his films with stationary camera setups, Warhol kept his performers in the claustrophobic frame of the shot, often addressing someone, perhaps the camera operator, just off-frame. In *Blow Job* (1964), for example, the edge of the frame and the action just off-frame or off-camera become as erotically charged as the frame-line between Doris Day and Rock Hudson in *Pillow Talk.*

In another double-screen project with Edie Sedgwick, *Lupe* (1965, color, 36 minutes), Warhol has Sedgwick reenact the 1944 suicide overdose of Hollywood "Mexican Spitfire" actress Lupe Velez. As in *Outer and Inner Space, Lupe* uses the doubling of two screens in adjacent display to suggest the fractured subjectivity of Sedgwick/Velez. In a morbid forecast, Sedgwick's performance in *Lupe* mirrored her own death by overdose in 1971.[48]

Warhol's most ambitious two-screen project, *The Chelsea Girls* (1966, 210 minutes), projected twelve single-take film reels in double-screen display. Jonas Mekas describes the four-hour "epic movie-novel" filmed in the Chelsea Hotel as "a series of rooms at the Chelsea Hotel, two rooms projected side by side at the same time, with different people in different rooms, or sometimes, overlapping."[49] And although Mekas doesn't linger on this model of double-screen projection as a dollhouse in axonometric cross-section, he claims: "As the time goes, this gallery of people and lives grows into a complex human hive. The film in its complex and overlapping structure, in its simultaneity of lives before our eyes, comes closest to Joyce. Forgive me this sacrilegious comparison—really this is the first time that I dare mention Joyce in connection with cinema. This is the

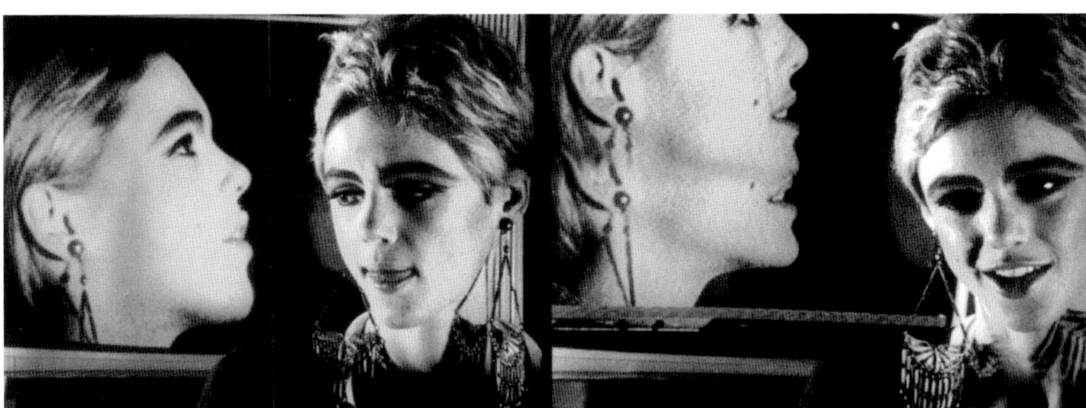

5.13 *Outer and Inner Space,* directed by Andy Warhol, 1965. Image source and permission from Andy Warhol Museum, Pittsburgh, Pennsylvania.

first time I see in cinema an interesting solution of narrative techniques that enable cinema to present life in the complexity and richness achieved by modern literature."[50] Warhol's double-screen projects may have been edgy because of their unexpurgated content (although perhaps not as overtly hardcore as that of *Blow Job, Couch, Harlot,* or *Vinyl*), and yet as formal experiments with the conventions of projection, they also directly challenged the cultural strictures of the single screen. Double-screen projection widened the visual field and, like the art historical double-slide projection, increased the opportunity for formal and analytic comparison. Placing two 16mm projectors side-by-side, one image would comment on the other, space was more complexly fractured, and the temporality of past and present could interact in simultaneity.[51] As Warhol quipped: "I put two things on the screen in *Chelsea Girls* so you could look at one picture if you were bored with the other."[52]

Multiple-screen projection also became a standard feature of the multimedia "light shows" of the *Exploding Plastic Inevitable* and musical performances by The Velvet Underground and Warhol's "superstar" Nico in 1966 and 1967. *EPI* performances included three to five movie projectors, slide projectors, strobe lights, and moving spotlights with color gels, creating an expanded sensorium of light, sound, and movement.[53] In their 1967 book *The Medium Is the Massage,* Marshall McLuhan and Quentin Fiore include an illustration of an *EPI* performance: a close-up of Nico's face looms as backdrop in multiple-screen projection. McLuhan's text precedes the two-page spread: "[t]he audience becomes a participant in the total electric drama" (McLuhan used the word "electric," not "electronic"): "The ear favors no particular 'point of view.' We are enveloped by sound. It forms a seamless web around us. . . . We hear sounds from everywhere

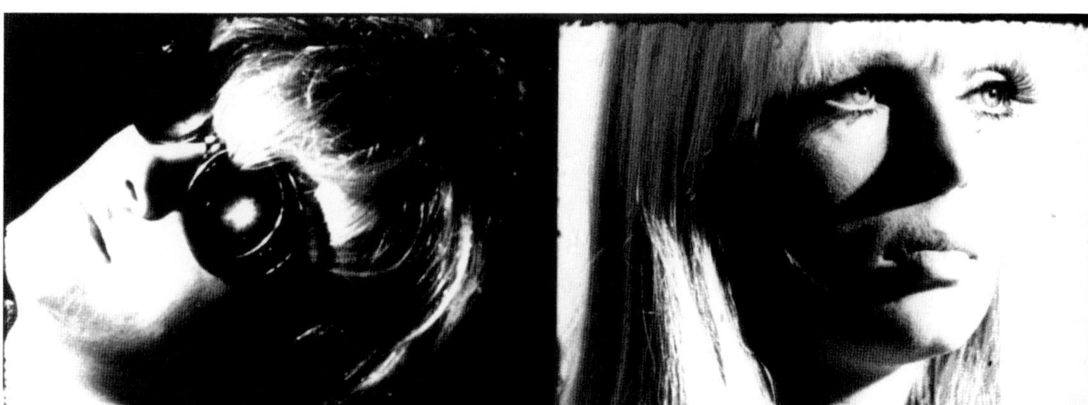

5.14 *The Chelsea Girls,* directed by Andy Warhol, 1966. Image source and permission from Andy Warhol Museum, Pittsburgh, Pennsylvania.

without ever having to focus. Sounds come from 'above,' from 'below,' from in 'front' of us, from 'behind' us, from our 'right' and from our 'left.'"[54]

McLuhan emphasizes the auditory aspects of this immersive participation, but he also incisively targets the shift from a fixed perspectival vantage to a multiple viewpoint, which could equally describe the use of multiple-screen projection: "The main obstacle to a clear understanding of the effects of the new media is our deeply embedded habit of regarding all phenomena from a fixed point of view. . . . The method of our time is to use not a single but multiple models for exploration."[55]

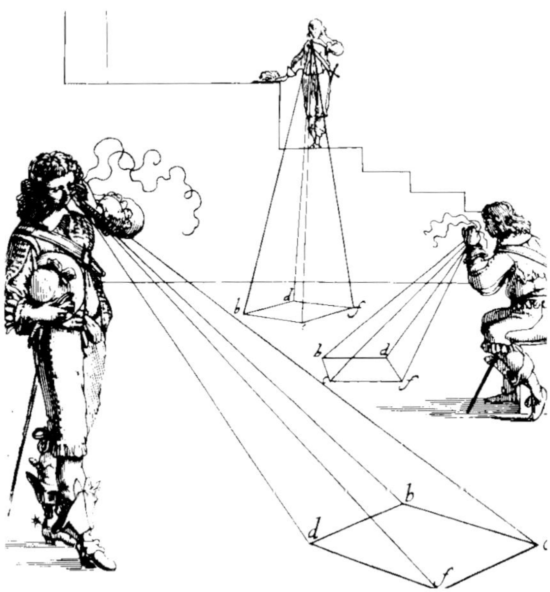

5.15 Drawing from Marshall McLuhan and Quentin Fiore, *The Medium Is the Massage* (New York: Random House, 1967).

McLuhan's instincts about this shift in media were rooted in his thinking about the instantaneous and continuous aspects of "electric circuitry." In the text of *The Medium Is the Massage,* McLuhan assesses a break with the deeply embedded perspective paradigm: "Since the Renaissance the Western artist perceived his environment primarily in terms of the visual. Everything was dominated by the eye of the beholder. His conception of space was in terms of a perspective projection upon a plane surface consisting of formal units of spatial measurement. He accepted the dominance of the vertical and horizontal—or symmetry—as an absolute condition of order. This view is deeply embedded in the consciousness of Western art."[56] In opposition to visual space, McLuhan placed "primitive" acoustic, horizonless, boundless, olfactory space. Although his analysis of the nonvisual aspects of the primitive seems counterintuitive, his claims about the postperspectival multidimensional models of "new media" seem prescient: "Electric circuitry is recreating in us the multidimensional space orientation of the 'primitive.'"[57]

The participant-spectators at "expanded," "exploded" multimedia performances were enveloped by sound but also bombarded by light. In a 1966 piece "More on Strobe Light and Intermedia," Jonas Mekas questioned Steven Durkee, one of the producers of the USCO "light shows," about the effect of the strobe light. Durkee commented: "*Strobe is the digital trip.* In other words, what the strobe is basically doing, it's turning on and off, completely on and completely off. . . . It creates a discontinuance so that it looks like the flicks." The invocation of the "digital trip" inspired Mekas to muse further on the subjective consequences of this lighting effect: "You become a particle, a grain of the movie. Maybe that's what it is. We are cut by strobe light into single frames, to eight frames per second or whatever the strobe frequency is, on and off. . . . *You know, we started with a simple screen and one-long-take images; then we started superimposing images; triple superimpositions; then two, three, eight screens;* single frames; superimpositions were further atomized, spiritualized by silk screens and colored veils and sound tracks. Now we've left the screen, the film and we come down to ourselves, with strobes we cut ourselves into single frames, like some symbolic or magic gesture or ritual."[58]

POLYMORPHOUS, POLYSCENIC POLYVISION: EXPO '67

In the spirit of world expositions as phantasmagorias, the pavilions of Montreal's Expo '67 displayed a wide variety of multiple-screen exhibits, with names that emphasize the expanded field of vision: CircleVision, Polyvision, Diopolyecran. Following on the success of the Academy Award–winning three-screen *To Be Alive* for the 1964 New York World's Fair, Thompson and Hammid produced the six-screen *We Are Young* for Expo '67.[59] For the "Canada '67" exhibit at Expo '67, the Canadian telephone companies commissioned a nine-projector, 360-degree CircleVision film. Recalling Raoul Grimoin Sanson's ten-projector *Cinéorama* at the Paris 1900 Exposition, CircleVision used nine projectors concealed in the space between screens to project a circular image, while twelve synchronized sound channels enveloped the audience in sound.

The most ambitious multiple-screen projects at Expo '67 were found at the Czechoslovakian pavilion.[60] Czech set-designer and inventor Josef Svoboda's "*Polyvision:* Czechoslovakia—The Automated Country" used twenty slide projectors, ten motion-picture screens, and five mobile projection screens for an eight-minute panorama of Czech industrial life. Another Czech invention, Emil Radok's Diopolyecran, a mobile multiple-screen slide show, had viewers sit on a carpeted floor facing a wall of 112 separate cubes. From inside each cube, two Kodak Carousel slide projectors projected slides onto the front of the cubes. Each cube could move into three separate positions within a two-foot range, giving the effect of the flat surface turning into a three-dimensional surface and back again. In all, there were fifteen thousand images in the eleven-minute show.

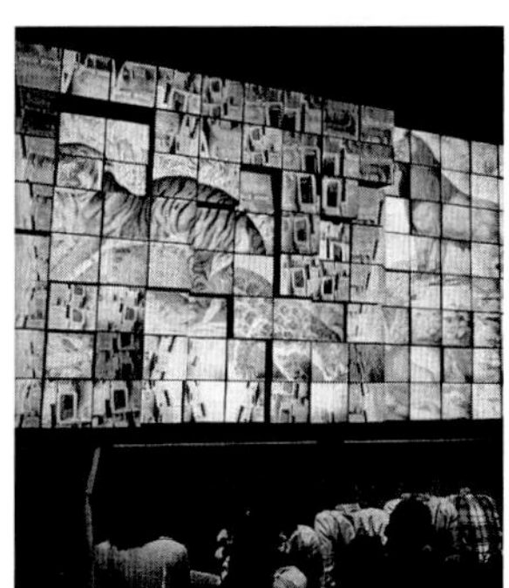

5.16 Emil Radok, Diopolyecran, Expo '67, Montreal.

In addition to the two multiple-screen exhibits at the Czech pavilion, an interactive narrative film, *Kino-Automat* (developed by cinematographer Radúz Činčera), had viewers vote on the outcome of a film narrative. Instead of random juxtaposition of multiple-screen display, the narrative linearity of *Kino-Automat* was split into branching alternatives, dependent on the majority vote.

In the weeks before he began shooting *The Thomas Crown Affair* (1968), Norman Jewison took his cinematographer Haskell Wexler and editor Hal Ashby to Expo '67 to see another multiple-screen project, Christopher Chapman's *A Place to Stand.* Jewison credits Chapman's "multi-screen technique" as an inspiring model for his complex use of multiple inset screens in *The Thomas Crown Affair:* "We were trying to tell five stories," Jewison recounts, claiming "we used the multiple screen as a story-telling device . . . long before digital effects and computerized technology."[61] Another film from 1968, *The Boston Strangler* (dir. Richard Fleischer), used multiple inset screens (in different sizes and combinations) as a storytelling device. Fleischer split the screen into multiple views showing the precautions that Boston residents take—locking their doors, buying guns, walking in twos or threes at night—and to display, for example, the shot and reverse-shot of a victim at her intercom and a point-of-view shot of the intercom while she hears the strangler's voice.

As I've already discussed, Brian De Palma's *Sisters* (1973) used the two-way split-screen technique to show both shot and countershot in adjacent display. A voyeuristic neighbor (Jennifer Salt) sees a murder in an apartment across the way (à la Hitchcock's *Rear Window)* and calls the police. On one screen, we see Salt trying to convince the police to investigate, while we watch the murder being covered up on the other. In side-by-side parallel editing, by the time the police arrive, there is no evidence.

In addition to these examples from mainstream filmmaking, experimental filmmakers continued to toy with the potentials of multiple-screen projection.[62] Harry Smith's unfinished *Mahagonny* (1970–1980) was an ambitious four-projector, four-screen project. Restored in 2002, *Mahagonny* carries with it the force of some of the great *projets maudits* of the last century—Walter Benjamin's *Passagenwerk,* Sergei Eisenstein's film of *Das Kapital*—equal in its grandiose aspirations, but destined to remain incomplete.[63] As Smith declared, *Mahagonny* was "a mathematical analysis of Duchamp's *La Mariée mise à nu par ses célibataires* expressed in terms of Kurt Weill's score for *Aufsteig und Fall der Stadt Mahagonny* with contrapuntal images (not necessarily in order) derived from Brecht's libretto for the latter work."[64]

Like Warhol's *Chelsea Girls, Mahagonny* was shot in and around the Chelsea Hotel in New York City. But unlike Warhol's double-screen projects that played with random juxtaposition, Smith's color four-screen project had a complex plan for its formal structure. Mapping his plans in charts, diagrams, and index cards, Smith deftly curated his filmed images, placing them in groups of four, each image raised to its formal exponent in relation to the others and to the soundtrack of the Brecht/Weill opera.[65] In the four-screen structure, *Mahagonny* adheres to the organizing principle of the four sides of a rectangular screen. The projection splits the rectangular frame into quadrants, with each screen becoming a picture block, a montage element poised for its combinatory power. Like the Eameses' deck of colorful still images *House of Cards* (1952), Smith's images form a building set, an encyclopedia of objects, landscapes, and portraits to be dealt in recombinant juxtapositions. Color forms a matrix, a quilt, breeding kinship and symmetries between deep reds, glaring yellows, and muted pastels. Smith had a numerological system for the four-screen organization—twenty-four shots in each reel, twelve reels, four images at a time. Images were placed in a four-image grid—top left, top right, bottom left, bottom right—sometimes paired vertically, sometimes paired horizontally, sometimes mirroring each other in bilateral symmetry. The disposition and place of each screen image amplifies its singular force; placed together, the four moving images exceed the burden of their singular frames. Smith also spatialized his montage; the cut between shots is visible across the seam of the frame line. *Mahagonny*'s structural ambitions foretold its own difficult destiny. The film was rarely projected as Smith intended.

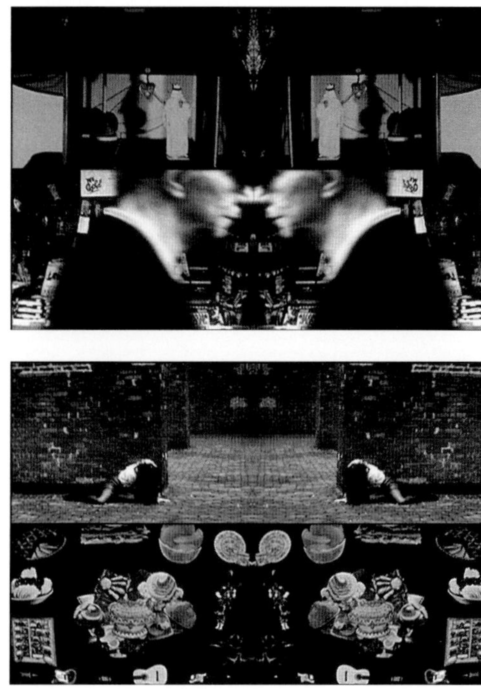

5.17 Frame enlargements from *Mahagonny*, directed by Harry Smith, 1970–1980. Image courtesy of Harry Smith.

MULTISCREEN BUT ALSO MULTIMEDIA: VIDEO AS MEDIUM

The formal confrontation between filmic and televisual media took a variety of forms in the 1950s and 1960s. The expanded scope of the film screen was an attempt to win back viewers from the competing format of television; the split-screen fractures of the widescreen were filmmakers' strategies to more fully utilize the new real estate of the widescreen frame. In the same manner that films of the 1950s *(It's Always Fair Weather, Will Success Spoil Rock Hunter?)* took television as an object of narrative, films of the 1960s and 1970s began to use video as an inset medium. Warhol's *Inner and Outer Space* (1965) not only doubled the screen into a two-screen projection but, in each screen, Sedgwick confronted her prerecorded video image on a video monitor placed next to her.[66] But more expansively, as video was introduced as an emerging art medium, a wide array of video artists—Nam June Paik, Bruce Nauman, Vito Acconci, Linda Benglis, John Baldessari, Bill Viola, Gary Hill, and others—used multiple monitors to experiment with the fracturing of time and the multiplication of the video image.[67] Frank Gillette and Ira Schneider's *Wipe Cycle* (1969), for example, displayed a wall of nine monitors with a mix of live broadcast, videotape, and closed-circuit shots of people in the gallery. Bruce Nauman's *Live-Taped Video Corridor* (1969–1970) placed two video monitors at the end of a narrow corridor, one on top of the other. One monitor displayed a live image from a video camera at the entry to the corridor, while the other showed a prerecorded video from the same position. Like Sedgwick confronting her video self in *Inner and Outer Space,* the two monitors enact the confrontation of video-liveness with the time shift of video playback.

Nam June Paik's playful repurposing of the video cabinet led him to new configurations for the cathode-ray monitor. Whether it be his interactive deconstruction of the video image with electromagnets in *Magnet TV* (1965) or the baring of the apparatus in *Zenith (TV Looking Glass)* (1974), Paik eviscerated the materiality of the electronic image, questioning television as a *dispositif.*[68] For *Zenith (TV Looking Glass),* Paik removed the cathode-ray tube from a Zenith television cabinet and replaced it with a Sony video camera. The set was placed in front of a window, with the camera and the empty glass monitor screen framing portions of the view outside. When a viewer looked into the monitor screen, she saw what the camera recorded facing the "window on the world," its liveness self-reflexively bared.

A fuller examination of video art is outside the scope of this study, but as artists and activists began to use the cathode-ray "monitor" box in single or multiple array, video entered the art world as a sculptural, time-based extension of painting in much the same ways that the kinetic aspects of film were explored by artists like Hans Richter and László Moholy-Nagy in the 1920s. Gallery-based "installation" assumed a different configuration of spectator and screen. Video monitors had, at first, the force of a signed urinal—a piece of everyday plumbing, now framed as art. More recent museum and gallery installations have freed video art from the confines of its box, with video images being projected via the beams of high-resolution data-projectors onto the wall.[69] Video—once only an "inferior cinema"—is now its brightly luminous equal. The material specificity of video—its small screen, its scanned image, its liveness—has been lost as the medium has expanded to include film, video, and computer display in what is now referred to as "time-based media." With video projection and ever-flatter LCD or plasma screens, the video image–art form, display technology, closed circuit, broadcast, cable, or satellite program—becomes a virtual window on the wall. As Rosalind Krauss recently suggested, after several decades of video art: "[video] proclaimed the end of medium-specificity. In the age of television . . . we inhabit a post-medium condition."[70]

NUMÉRO DEUX (DIR. JEAN LUC GODARD, 1976)

In his 1976 film *Numéro deux,* Jean Luc Godard made bold use of an inset video screen. Godard placed two video screens in the black expanse of a 35mm CinemaScope frame. The two screens—one large, one small—produce a range of formal variables that enact the literal dialectic of doubling and division, flatness and depth, film and video. To make *Numéro deux,* Godard shot 16mm footage of a fictional working-class family engaged in everyday domestic activities, transferred these segments to videotape, and rephotographed the video images as they were displayed on monitors, using 35mm film. In this way, Godard could use both the techniques of film editing (in 35mm) and the video effects of key and matte overlay. Within the grand denominator of the full screen, Godard used the full panoply of possible combinations—only one small screen, both screens in dialectic display, both screens with the same image, with sync sound, nonsync sound, silence. At one point in the film, as if to suggest a zero-point of the film's style, the two inset screens contain only the static graininess of video "snow" against the empty black background of the film's frame.

Godard opens *Numéro deux* with a full-frame shot taken in the video control room of his studio in Grenoble. We see Godard standing next to a film chain, a film projector that projects directly into a video camera. In the framing of this shot, Godard's head is cropped and offscreen, severed by the frame edge, but it is resutured into the shot, appearing on the video monitor next to him in a simultaneous playback. Offscreen cinematographic space (the *hors-champ* that Deleuze writes about) is transmuted into on-screen video space. Godard is visible on both the full screen and the inset screen, controlling the production of his own image. (In fact, we are aware of Godard's presence in every aspect of *Numéro deux.* At one point, as the sync sound

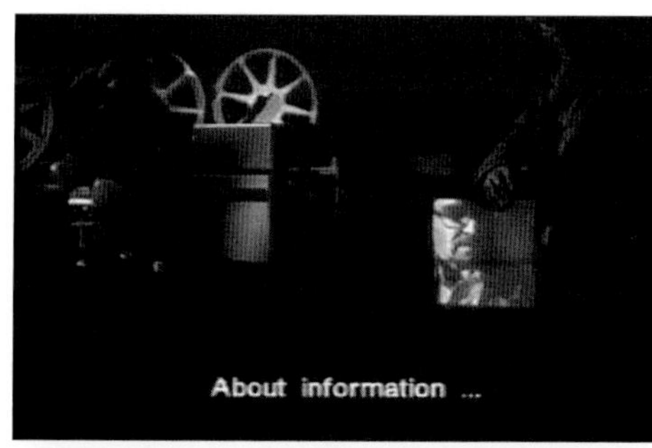

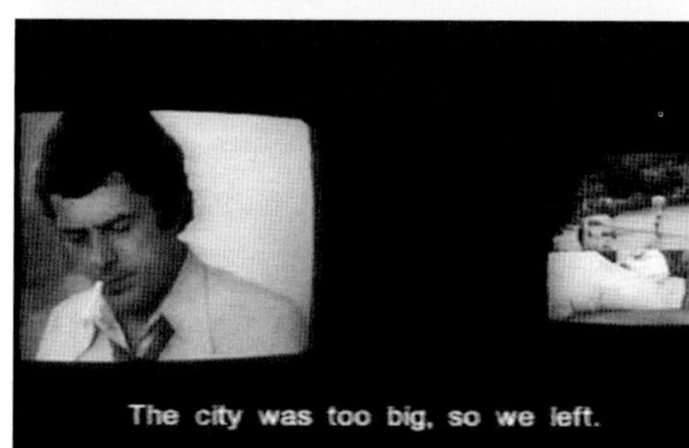

5.18 Frame enlargements from *Numéro deux,* directed by Jean Luc Godard, 1976.

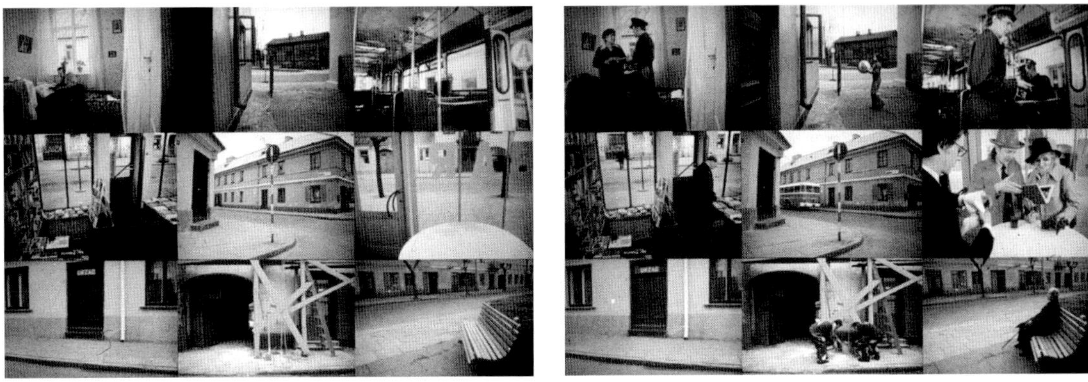

5.19 Frame enlargements from *Nowa książka* (New Book), directed by Zbigniew Rybczynski, 1976. Image courtesy of Zbig Vision Ltd.

is interrupted by a music track, we even hear his voice, as sound mixer, saying "merde" at this slip.) In full-blown self-reflexivity, Godard asserts control of every shot and its combination—images are not juxtaposed in a random dialectic as in Warhol's *Chelsea Girls*.[71] While Godard's use of the multiple inset screen both uses and exposes the machinery of video production, we see the video cameras and monitors, but we never see the 35mm scope camera that has filmed the film. The cinema camera remains invisible, the still mystified source of the cinematic image, but the video monitor is exposed, visible as an instant feedback loop making the reception and projection of an image simultaneous.

In *Outer and Inner Space* and in *Numéro deux*, Warhol and Godard multiplied the frame by using the video monitor as an inset medium. Not only did these films enact a formal confrontation between filmic and televisual media, they both imply the spatial context of video as the inner (domestic) space and film as the outer (public) space of reception.

In another film from 1976, *Nowa książka* (New Book), Polish filmmaker-inventor Zbigniew Rybczynski divided the screen into nine squares, each shot displaying actions in a cubist fracture of contiguous space. The film is like a puzzle: we follow various characters (a man in an orange coat, a postman in uniform, a man with a violin, a boy on a scooter) as they move from one space to another (on a bus seen from its inside, off the bus seen from its outside). The separate frames are loosely stitched together: the space of each shot is only roughly contiguous with the adjacent one. Following the movement of people through the nine separate frames, we assume that the action in each frame is occurring in real time (at one point, a sudden jolt occurs in each frame—an earthquake, perhaps) and that the separate spaces are united in simultaneous response.[72] Like *Numéro deux, Nowa książka* was made before digital technology could aid in its filming, editing, and postproduction effects.[73]

Peter Greenaway, another filmmaker to explore the syntax of the inset frame in his films, used video effects to produce multiple-screen images, letter-boxed frames, overlaid texts, and writing superimposed on images. In *Prospero's Books* (1991) and *Pillow Book* (1996), Greenaway was an early adopter of digital technology for postproduction special effects. A history remains to be written of the accretion of digital minutes invading film and television production, leading to the "born digital" films of the present.

THE DIGITAL MOVING IMAGE: MULTIPLE IMAGING AND DISPLAY

> *Digital cinema offers formal solutions to "tense" limitations of mechanical cinema. Past, present and future can be spoke in the same frame at once.*
>
> —Gene Youngblood, "Cinema and the Code"

As evidenced in the 1966 discussion between Steve Durkee and Jonas Mekas, the concept of the "digital" began to creep into discourse about representation and experience in the mid-1960s, but it had not yet figured as a technology for image production or postproduction. Here, a taxonomic question remains an important one. At what point did the specificity of "film" as a medium become irreparably altered by digital technology? In a slow accretion since the first use of computer-generated images (was it the infrared point of view of Yul Bryner's gunslinger in *Westworld* in 1973?) to the growing number of on-screen minutes given over to CGI (culminating perhaps in *Toy Story* [1995], the first CGI feature-length animation) to *Sky Captain and the World of Tomorrow* (2004, the first film with all-CGI background and live actors)—film has become its digital other. *Sky Captain and the World of Tomorrow* was born on hard drives, developed on microchip, with no sets, no locations, only the blue screen. Like a James Turrell light box, the blue screen is the foundation for a new screen reality.

TIME CODE (DIR. MIKE FIGGIS, 2000)

In *Time Code,* Mike Figgis's four-camera digital video project, the screen is split into quadrants. For a deftly choreographed ninety-three minutes, starting at 3 PM on November 19, 1999, on Sunset Boulevard near the Los Angeles bookstore Book Soup, four hand-held digital video cameras followed four separate "lines" of action. Each camera filmed in "real-time" in one ninety-three-minute-long, unedited take.[74] In the final film, the four camera views are shown in four screens, quadrants of a full-size movie screen. The action—although in real time—is fictional, acted and loosely scripted. For the viewer, each quadrant displays simultaneous but not sequential action, a flattened fracturing of a moment into four "perspectives." As in *Suspense* (1913), *It's Always Fair Weather* (1955), *The Boston Strangler* (1968), *Sisters* (1973), and *Numéro deux* (1976), the sequential spatiality and cross-cut temporality of single-screen film-making has been replaced by simultaneous nonsequential display.

As the film commences, each quadrant of the screen starts up sequentially: first, in the top right, a close shot of a woman (Saffron Burrows) in a therapy session; second, in the upper left, Lauren (Jeanne Trippelhorn) scampers out to a parked BMW to let the air out of the tires; third, in the lower right, a massage therapist arrives at the offices of a film production company. The lower left screen shows the fractured screens of video surveillance. At first, we are not certain of the spatial relation between these screens, whether they are contiguous or distant. Like the other split-screen films I've discussed, *Time Code* links its spaces with telephonic simultaneity. In one scene, Kyle McLachlan is on the phone with Alex (Stellan Skarsgard) inside the offices while Lauren sits in her stretch limo outside listening to an audio-bug she has placed in the bag of her lover, Rose (Salma Hayek). McLachlan is seen through the back window of the limo, framed in the deep space of one shot, while on another screen, he is seen from the front. The four separate screens abut each other. Characters from one screen may wander into the space of another, seen from two perspectives. Another indication that the four screens are all displaying simultaneous lines of action occurs when an "earthquake" conjoins the separate screens as we suddenly react to the jolt. Figgis has projected the film with a variety of sound mixes, changing the level of priority of sound and image.[75]

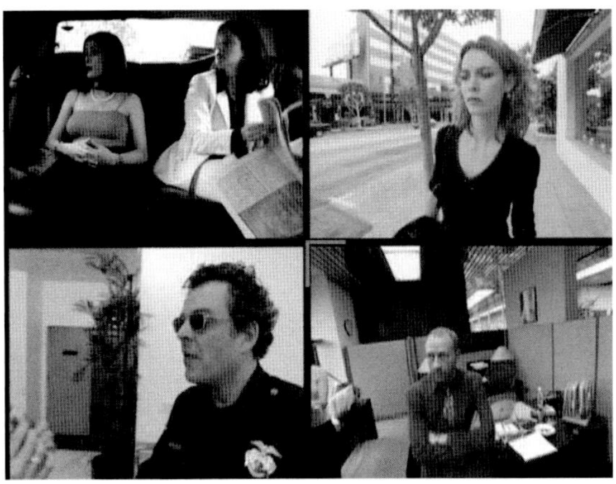

5.20 Frame enlargement from *Time Code,* directed by Mike Figgis, 2000.

The *Time Code* website declared: "Technology has arrived. Digital video has arrived. For the first time, a film shot in real time. Who do you want to watch? A story that could only be told in four dimensions."[76] Despite the assumption that even in multiple display one watches only one screen at a time, we actually watch all of the screens at the same time. Rather than demonstrate our split attention, the film demonstrates our ability to follow all four screens.

The multiple-screen idiom has taken hold in the world of video art as well: Sam Taylor-Wood's seven-screen piece *Third Party* (1999) peels away the dynamics of a cocktail party by filming the event with seven cameras in real time and projecting with seven 16mm projectors; Isaac Julien and Javier de Frutos's *The Long Road to Mazatlán* (1999), a triple DVD projection, plays with a full panoply of formal variables of the triptych split of images; and French artist Pierre Huyghe's double-screen piece *The Third Memory* (2000) parallels excerpts from Sidney Lumet's *Dog Day Afternoon* with Huyghe's own film of the bank robber, John Woytowicz, thirty years later, reenacting the crime with actors on a set.[77] Iranian artist Shirin Neshat uses two screens in a trilogy of films, *Turbulent* (1998), *Rapture* (1999), and *Fervor* (2000), to vividly convey the rigid divisions in gender between Iranian men on one screen and Iranian women on another.[78] Doug Aitken's *Electric Earth* (2000) used three rooms with multiple screens to display his protagonist's stroll through the electric landscape of a Los Angeles night; Christian Marclay's four-screen *Video Quartet* (2002) combines component clips from hundreds of movie scenes depicting musical performances;[79] and in Barbara Kruger's *Twelve* (2004), the artist installed four screens in the Mary Boone Gallery to surround the gallery viewer—each screen has a close shot of a dining scene as a text band crawls along the bottom of the screen.

For contemporary artists who experiment with the representational possibilities of flat-screen digital video, the multiple-image, multiple-frame, multiple-screen format has become an accessible new idiom.[80] Filmmaker Julie Talen writes: "There's an unnamed satisfaction in stretching this newfound ability to navigate through images. We're actually hungry to use this ability, to feed it with something more substantive than frenzied Web animations and stock tickers. We crave stories. The single-channel film is the visual art form of the gaze; multi-channel is the art form of the glimpse."[81]

THE COMPUTER SCREEN AND ITS "WINDOW"

> *In front of him was the display screen. The large screen behind him could alternate between, or share, multiple views of Doug's hands, his face, the information on the display screen, and images of his colleagues and their display screens at Menlo Park. The screen could be divided into a number of "windows," each of which could display either text or image. The changing information displayed on the large screen, activated by his fingertip commands on the five-key device and his motions of the mouse, began to animate under Doug's control. Everyone in the room had attended hundreds of slide presentations before this, but from the moment Doug first imparted move-*

ment to the views on the screen, it became evident this was like no audiovisual presentation anyone had attempted before.

—Howard Rheingold, *Tools for Thought,* an account of Douglas Engelbart's demonstration at the Fall Joint Computer Conference, San Francisco Convention Center, December 9, 1968

In the 1960s, as filmmakers explored split- and multiple-screen formats, as the media of video and film began to interact as production formats, there were, at first, only subtle changes to vernacular screen media. But as the "personal computer" began to invade daily life, a new "interface" to the screen began to produce new modes of cinematic, television, and video display.

The graphical user interface (now synoptically known as GUI) has changed the way we use and imagine computers. Computing mechanisms were first room-sized mainframes, then faceless beige boxes. As they acquired display screens, the computer supplied a new "interface" with its user. "Interface"—a geometric term for the surface that forms the common boundary between two three-dimensional figures—was deployed to describe the human-computer relation once the user was literally "facing" the computer. In this way, the user's relation to the computer screen can be measured in terms that we've used for other screen formats—the representation of flatness and depth, the use of the frame, the assumed "point of view" of the viewer, etc. The metaphor of the window, so overdetermined by the connotative drag of its cultural heritage, quickly entered into the terminology for computer operating systems, as an inevitable component of computer "architecture."

But here, as we enter into the discursive terrain of computers and computing, it will become apparent that an entirely different set of terms and philosophical assumptions are at play. Computer operating systems also rely on metaphor, as if we can imagine the future only in the familiar language of the past. Metaphors, of course, are already translators. Metaphors substitute one thing for another, performing an alchemy from a material referent to the immaterial tissue of language. But computer metaphors are not just descriptive figures, aloft in language; they are integral to the conversion of binary bits of information into words and images. A computer metaphor acquires near-materiality as a *virtual* object.

In the history of computing devices, the use of metaphor became a direct component of the graphic display screen. In *Interface Culture* (1997), Steven Johnson eloquently details the ways in which the graphical user interface transformed the spatial imagination. Johnson convincingly argues that visual metaphors (of the desktop, the window, but also of the personal assistant, shopping mall, town square, and living room) have served as key cultural accommodations to a "digital revolution" and to an interface with a new "space" of information.[82]

The earliest computing devices—Blaise Pascal's calculator, the Pascaline (1642), and Charles Babbage's Difference Engine (1820)—were brass instruments crafted with the same precision mechanics of clocks, watches, and automata. One can easily imagine the user's engagement with such intricate pieces of design. These early computing apparatuses were prosthetic devices, offloading the calculations of the human brain to the delicate workings of a machine. As the machinery of computing grew to room-sized mainframes, the human user was dwarfed by the sheer scale of the machine. Contact with these gargantuan machines became an awkward interaction via knobs and dials, plugs and circuits, punch-tapes and punch-cards.

One way to conceptualize the changing "interface" with computing machinery is to consider the barriers between humans and machine. John Walker, founder and CEO of the computer design company Autodesk, charts five successive "user interaction generations" in terms of the intermediaries placed between the human and the computer: front panel, countertop, terminal, menu, screen.[83] In Walker's account, the "first generation" was clumsy but direct: "the user went one-on-one with the computer, in the computer room, operating the computer at the switch and knob level. Since the user was the operator of the machine and controlled it with little or no abstraction, there was essentially no mediation between the computer and its expert user."[84]

In the rapid set of technological changes that led to the advent of the personal computer in the early 1980s, the acquisition of a display screen as the visual

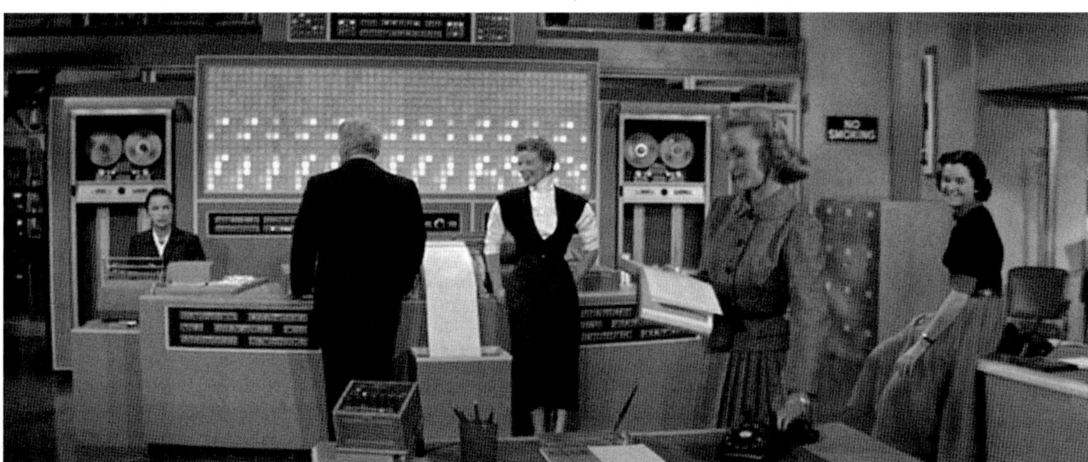

5.21 Frame enlargement from *Desk Set,* 1957.

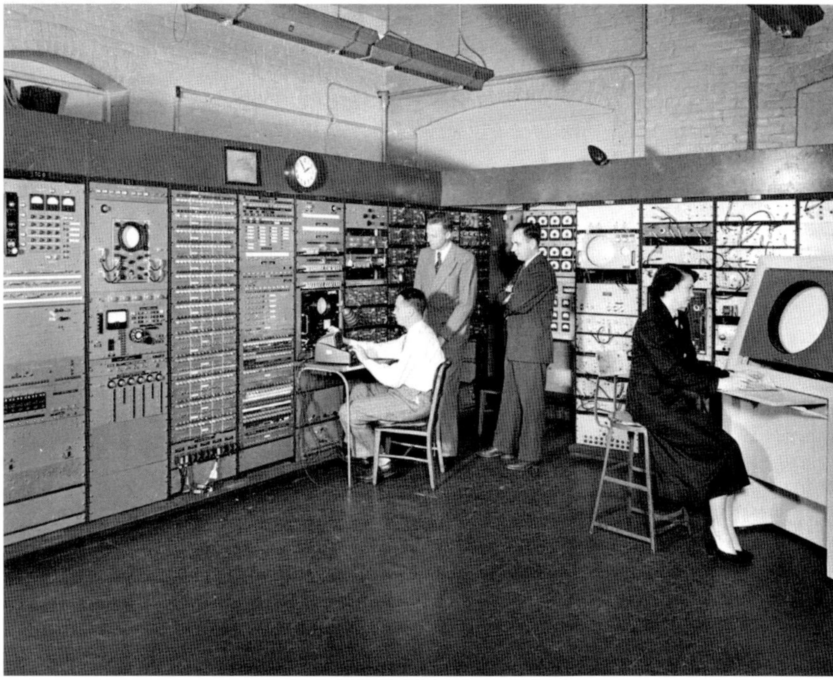

5.22 MIT Whirlwind, 1951.

interface with a computing mechanism and the switch from alphanumeric "command lines" to a screen with icons and images were the two key developments that brought the computer closer to the other predominant forms of visual imaging.[85] Add an Internet-enabled World Wide Web to this graphic-display screen, and the computer window opened itself to convergences with the cinema and television screen.[86]

In 1951, the Whirlwind, an Air Force-funded military computer at MIT, used a circular CRT screen equipped with a light pen and a keyboard for input into its mainframe. Modeled directly on a radar screen, the Whirlwind's CRT screen was more of a porthole than a rectangular frame.[87] Although the screen served as a surface for entering information into a large mainframe, it was, as is apparent in figure 5.22, one of several means of input at the front panel of the massive device.

The image quality of radar monitors and early computer CRT screens, far from the pixels of today's display, was not sharp enough or bright enough to display details of characters and fonts.[88] When, as a researcher at the Stanford Research Institute, Douglas Engelbart first hooked video terminals to computer mainframes, his specially designed monitors had small, fuzzy black-and-white screens.

The exact origin of the first use of the term "window" as a metaphor for an inset framed section of the computer screen is difficult to pinpoint. Douglas Engelbart may not have used the exact term "window" to describe his multiple-screen "TV approach" to the computer interface, yet his "Augmented Human Intellect Study" contained a prototype for the form. In a 1962 project description, "Augmenting the Human Intellect? A Conceptual Framework," Engelbart declared his Enlightenment goals for the computer: "By 'augmenting human intellect' we mean increasing the capability of a man to approach a complex problem situation, to gain comprehension to suit his particular needs, and to derive solutions to problems."[89] As Engelbart summarized some of the conclusions to be drawn from his study: "We see the quickest gains emerging from (1) giving the human the minute-by-minute services of a digital computer equipped with computer-driven cathode-ray-tube display, and (2) developing the new methods of thinking and working that allow the human to capitalize upon the computer's help."[90]

To illustrate computer-aided "intellect augmentation," Engelbart supplies an example that uncannily draws us back to Alberti and his 1452 architectural treatise *De re aedificatoria* (On the Art of Building). Engelbart imagines an architect designing a building at a computer workstation. The system imagined has "a visual display screen some three feet on a side" which is his "working surface."
The display screen is controlled by a computer ("his 'clerk'") that the architect runs "by means of a small keyboard and various other devices." Engelbart describes the architect's work process, which begins with a "perspective view": "he has just coaxed the clerk to show him a perspective view of the steep hillside building site with the roadway above, symbolic representations of the various trees that are to remain on the lot, and the service tie points for the different utilities. The view occupies the left two-thirds of the screen. With a 'pointer,' he indicates two points of interest, moves his left hand rapidly over the keyboard, and the distance and elevation between the points indicated appear on the right-hand third of the screen."[91] The "perspective view" occupies only a portion of the screen; the other portion displays specifications of distance and elevation. As the architect's work proceeds, he enters specifications for the building using a keyboard and pointer: "Now he enters a reference line with his pointer, and the keyboard. Gradually the screen begins to show the work he is doing (a neat excavation appears in the hillside) revises itself slightly, and revises itself again. After a moment, the architect changes the scene on the screen to an overhead plan view of the site, still showing the excavation."[92] The perspective view—undifferentiated from its Renaissance forebear—shifts with the stroke of a finger to an overhead view. The imagined depth of the screen surface, deep toward a vanishing point at one moment, shifts

to the flat surface of the view from above. Prior to Renaissance perspective, painterly representation did not imply a singular fixed point; the view was from both above and below. While the exact details of the screen and its component portions are not described in Engelbart's 1962 proposal, his intentions for what he would call a "TV approach" to a multiple-screen display are prototypically clear.

Engelbart worked on this interface through the mid-1960s, but his ninety-minute multimedia demonstration of networked computing at the Fall Joint Computer Conference in San Francisco on December 9, 1968, was to the computer window what the Lumière brothers' December 28, 1895, showing at the Grand Café was to the cinema: it provides a dramatic markable date, more symptomatic than exact, and only to be qualified by corrections and exceptions.[93] Film historians debate the "first" public projection of moving images: was it the Lumière brothers' scientific demonstration in March 1895, or their December 1895 showing at the Grand Café; or the November 1895 public projection by the Skladanosky brothers at the Winter Garden in Berlin? Equally, the computer graphic display window was demonstrated in a variety of venues, all of which are described with a dramatic weight equivalent to the writing of protocinematic history—Engelbart's 1968 display at the Fall Joint Computer Conference, Charles P. Thacker's April 1973 demo of the Alto at Xerox PARC, Steve Jobs's 1979 visit to Xerox PARC, the 1984 Super Bowl ad that introduced the Apple Macintosh.

In the report that accompanied the 1968 demo, Engelbart describes the components of his display system. He emphasizes the limitations of the system (he used small black-and-white CRTs), but also defends the cost features of this "TV approach":

> *5c3a* The display systems consists of two identical subsystems, each with display controller, display generator, 6 CRT's, and 6 closed-circuit television systems.
>
> *5c3b* The display controllers process display-command tables and display lists that are resident in core, and pass along display-buffer contents to the display generators.
>
> *5c3c* The display generators and CRT's were developed by Tasker Industries to our specifications. Each has general character vector plotting capability. They will accept display buffers consisting of instructions (beam motion, character writing, etc.) from the controller. Each will drive six 5-inch high-resolution CRT's on which the display pictures are produced.

5c3c1 Character writing time is approximately 8 microseconds, allowing an average of 1000 characters on each of the six monitors when regenerating at 20 cps.

5c3d A high-resolution (875-line) closed circuit television system transmits display pictures from each CRT to a television monitor at the corresponding work-station console.[94]

Engelbart does not use the term "window" in this description of the 1968 demo—only the retrospective accounts do. In Howard Rheingold's description of Engelbart's 1968 show, for example, Rheingold uses the word: "The screen could be divided into a number of 'windows,' each of which could display either text or image. The changing information displayed on the large screen, activated by his fingertip commands on the five-key device and his motions of the mouse, began to animate under Doug's control."[95] It is not clear whether the term "window" was actually used at SRI or whether now, in recovered memory, the inset screen was believed to always already have been a window.

But after Engelbart's demo, there is a clear instance in which the window metaphor was invoked. In his 1969 dissertation at the University of Utah, Alan Kay described a graphical "object orientation system" that had "VIEWPORTS" and "WINDOWS."[96] The figure of a "viewport" is only slightly different from a window and could equally have become the proprietary trademark. Both imply an aperture, a visual porthole onto the graphic expanse of a screen that simultaneously represents and masks the workings of the computer's code. In this form of "object-oriented" programming, anything could be an object—a number, a word, a picture—and hence it was assumed to be a multimedia display. Kay imagined the computer as just such a metamedium able to incorporate other media, a convergence device waiting to happen.

As computer operating systems were developed through the 1970s and into the 1980s and as the "personal" computer was marketed as a consumer appliance, the use of a screen was not an immediately apparent advance. While other contemporaneous developments (the military roots of ARPANET and the eventual Internet) were expanding the potentials of networked communication, the emerging conventions for computer display took place in the laboratories of corporate research and development.[97]

In April 1973, the Alto computer was demonstrated to a group of researchers at Xerox PARC. The Alto's eight-and-a-half-by-eleven-inch CRT screen displayed an "animated test pattern" of the *Sesame Street* character Cookie Monster in digital ones and zeros. The computer screen was "bit-mapped," given a face but not yet a window. The Alto was an in-house computer at PARC, not released to the market. But the competition with old media was clear; to viewers accustomed to 70mm widescreen films and colorful high-resolution television images, the computer display was still a dim relative.

The Alto screen was shaped like an upright letter-sized piece of paper, so the implicit metaphor of this interface was that of typing onto a page. Other members of the PARC group were developing crucial components of what would become a display screen with inset "windows."[98] In 1975, Dan Ingalls wrote a display algorithim that provided the means to move whole rectangles of bitmap from one location to another. "BitBlt" (an abbreviation for bit boundary block transfer) became the root algorithim for overlapping "windows": part of the screen could be hidden by a block that appeared on top of it, as if the screen display had layers. Not only could the screen be divided into separate movable inset frames, but each one could run a different application—one displaying a text program, one filled with pure code, one with a drawing. The overlapping window changed the metaphor ever so slightly. The surface windowpane now had depth and defied gravity, since windows could also be stacked. The user would manipulate from a position as if in front and also above. The window interface did, however, rely on the idea of a dynamic square—a resizable, dragable, motile frame, with a scroll bar to navigate within its boundaries. The computer window is like a screen where the contents move but the frame stays stable.

The graphical user interface developed at Xerox PARC emphasized the metaphoric nature of computer usage—"mice" that scurry under our fingers at the fluid command of wrist and palm; "desktops" that defy gravity and transform the horizontal desk into a vertical surface with an array of possible documents and applications; "icons" that represent objects or, more exactly, object-oriented tasks. This interface became known as the WIMP interface—Windows, Icons, Mouse, Pull-down Menus.[99]

The bitmap screen introduced a new layer to the user interface. In the graphic interface, the user directly manipulates a *virtual* version of what she intends to command—the user selects, drags, drops, opens, closes, copies, deletes, puts in the trash. The user can see the documents and applications on the "desktop" and in the "windows" of the screen. By contrast, the user of the "command line" interface may be "conversing" with the computer, giving it commands to perform a task, but she must speak to it in its code. Instead of translating a three-dimensional material world to a two-dimensional virtual representation as painters and photographers and filmmakers have done, the bitmap computer display constructs its virtual world entirely from digital information. The bitmap screen performs a different translation: from the nondimensional immateriality of bits to a visual (graphically iconic) mapping of metaphor onto the virtuality of a two-dimensional screen.

The computer "window" referred to any enclosed, rectangular area on a display screen. In a 1982 book *Principles of Computer Graphics,* the "window manager" and the term "window" were nonproprietary idioms: "Many system and user programs on the ALTO employ a *window manager* to control multiple, typically overlapping windows, i.e., areas on the screen in which a page or piece of a page may be displayed. Each window is in essence a variable-size virtual screen that reflects the progress of some activity. The general effect is one of looking at a small desk with papers of varying size lying partially on top of one another."[100] The "window" here refers to a "variable size virtual screen" but is also a component of a mixed metaphor: a window and a desk. The desktop metaphor of a stack of papers, in overlapping array, implies a view from above. The window metaphor implies looking into or out of an aperture, a "perspective" position facing an upright perpendicular surface. Stacking windows on top of each other, piling documents in layers, meant that the user could maximize the limited "real estate" of the relatively small screen. The space mapped onto the computer screen was both deep and flat. It implied a new haptics in the position of its user: in front of and above.

The window-based interface allowed the user to open more than one window, introducing the concept of multiple tasks, applications, views to the computer user. "A computer is just one machine," writes Yale computer scientist David Gelernter, "a screen is a single plot of real estate, but windows allow you to create as many communication channels as you choose between yourself and your running program."[101]

In December 1979, Steve Jobs—the twenty-four-year-old cofounder of Apple, the manufacturer of Apple I and Apple II personal computers—visited Xerox PARC. Apple II and Commodore home computers both were configured to use TV screens as monitors. The 1981 IBM PC used a monochrome CRT screen but not GUI display. Retelling the import of Jobs's tour of Xerox PARC with the full narrative intrigue of industrial espionage, Michael Hiltzik describes Jobs's visit as a "daring raid."[102] (According to another writer, Jobs traded $1 million in stock options in Apple for the visit.)[103] At Xerox PARC Jobs saw the graphical user interface used on the Alto and the Star. The GUI-run Xerox Star was introduced to the market two years later, in 1981, but its price was too high for the home computer market. Jobs used both the Alto and the Star as models for the 1983 Apple Lisa,[104] the first *personal* computer with GUI. Although the Lisa

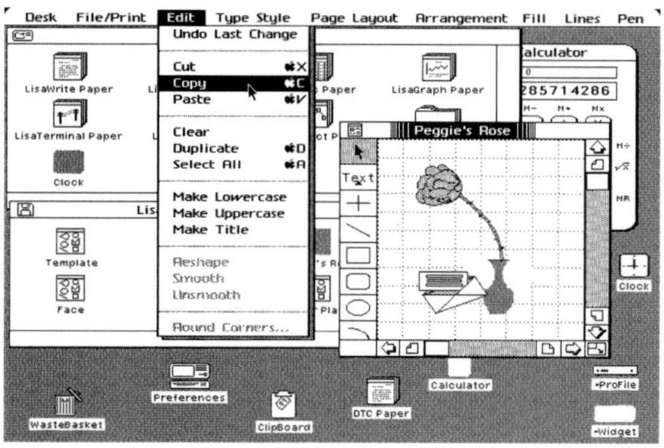

5.23 Screen shot of Apple Lisa, 1983.

didn't sell well (it was priced at $9,995 and aimed at the business market), Apple's next product was introduced less than a year later, with a dramatic ad campaign that drew its strength from the historical confluence of anti-Soviet cold war rhetoric and the Orwellian year, 1984.

In a now-historic sixty-second spot, placed during half-time of Super Bowl XXL on January 22, 1984, Apple unveiled its new computer, the Macintosh.[105] The ad, produced by Los Angeles-based ad firm Chiat/Day and directed by *Blade Runner* director Ridley Scott, opened onto a monochromatic future city connected by tubes full of conformist worker drones marching as if in robotic obedience to unseen commands. They march in lockstep into a large auditorium where a Big Brother preaches in monotones from a giant TV screen. Suddenly a lone woman, in a white tanktop and red running shorts, bursts into the auditorium and sprints down the center aisle carrying a large hammer. She runs at the screen and tosses the hammer toward it, shattering it with a blaring explosion of light as the voice-over announces: "On January 24th, Apple Computer will introduce the Macintosh. And you'll see why 1984 won't be like *1984.*" With this dramatic introduction, the Apple Macintosh triggered what Neal Stephenson deemed a "sort of holy war in the computer world."[106] The Macintosh, priced at a much more reasonable $2,495, was a personal computer with an operating system based on graphic display instead of the "command line" interface.

PROPRIETARY WINDOWS

In his 1995 memoir, *The Road Ahead,* Bill Gates recalls the transition from the command line to graphic interface. Gates describes his intention, as early as 1983, to develop graphical interface and to abandon MS-DOS: "Our goal was to create software that would extend MS-DOS and let people use a mouse, employ graphical images on the computer screen, and make available on the screen a number of 'windows,' each running a different computer program."[107] In Gates's account, the other two personal computer systems that had graphical interfaces in 1983, the Xerox Star and Apple Lisa, were proprietary and expensive: "Microsoft wanted to create an open standard and bring graphical capabilities to any computer that was running MS-DOS."[108] Despite the rhetoric of an "open standard," Microsoft attached a proprietary trademark to the term "window" and in November 1985 introduced graphical computing to IBM PCs (and their "clones") with a product called Windows 1.0. In the fall of 1987, Windows 2.0 added icons and resizable, overlapping windows. The software war had begun. In 1988, Apple sued Microsoft for copying the "look and feel" of the Macintosh's graphic display, but the term "windows" now belonged to Microsoft as Windows.™[109] By 1993, Windows 3.0, which was released in 1990, had sold 25 million copies. And as the media-saturated campaign for Windows 95 emphasized, by the end of its first decade, Microsoft's Windows became the most widely used operating system.[110] As David Gelernter writes: "Pushing beauty instead of old-fashioned DOS ugliness, Microsoft emerged as the uncontested leader of the desktop computing world."[111]

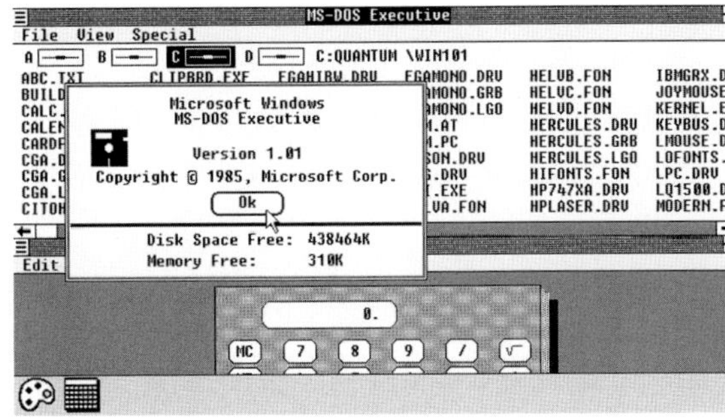

5.24 Screen shot of Windows 1.0, 1985: windows are "tiled" and cannot be overlapped.

Like the Mac OS, the "interface" of Windows extends screen space by overlapping screens of various sizes; each "window" can run a different application; the user can scroll through a text within a "window," arrange "windows" on the screen in stacked or overlapping formations, decorate "windows" (with wallpapers, textured patterns), and conduct new forms of "window shopping."[112] The "windows" trope is emblematic of the collapse of the single viewpoint; it relies on the model of a window that we don't see through, windows that instead overlap and obscure, and are resizable and movable.

Consider the following shift in discourse from the Albertian metaphor. *Webopedia,* an online dictionary of new media terms, defines "window" as distinctly polyscenic:

> An enclosed, rectangular area on a display screen. Most modern operating systems and applications have graphical user interfaces that let you divide your display into several windows. Within each window, you can run a different program or display different data.
>
> Windows are particularly valuable in *multitasking environments,* which allow you to execute several programs at once. By dividing your display into windows, you can see the output from all the programs at the same time. To enter input into a program, you simply click on the desired window to make it the foreground process.[113]

Why are we rejecting explicit word-based interfaces, and embracing graphical or sensorial ones—a trend that accounts for the success of both Microsoft and Disney?
—Neal Stephenson, *In the Beginning Was the Command Line*

Before Microsoft adopted a graphical user interface for its Windows operating system, the "holy war" between the MAC and the MS-DOS "command line" interface was described by Umberto Eco as a struggle between Macintosh/Catholicism ("the essence of revelation is dealt with via simple formulae and sumptuous icons") and MS-DOS/Protestantism ("To make the system work you need to interpret the program yourself: a long way from the baroque community of revelers, the user is closed within the loneliness of his own inner torment").[114] The religious war between a command line and a graphic display interface pitted the word and the text against the image and icon.

In his polemical treatise *In the Beginning Was the Command Line* (1999), cyber-novelist Neal Stephenson rails against a growing global "interface culture," a monoculture with a computerized visual interface.[115] Stephenson compares the Macintosh and Windows interface: the Macintosh is "not only a superb piece of engineering but an embodiment of certain ideals about the use of technology to benefit mankind," while Microsoft's Windows equivalent is "a pathetically clumsy imitation and a sinister world domination plot rolled into one."[116] And yet, despite the competition between the Mac and Windows operating systems, Stephenson holds both systems accountable for millions of computer users becoming accustomed to a graphical interface.[117]

By mapping code onto a graphic display, the GUI interface conceals its workings, hides its code. In Stephenson's account, the graphical interface "introduced a new semiotic layer" between human and machine: "GUIs use metaphors to make computing easier, but they are bad metaphors."[118] Stephenson compares this to the Disney model of "putting out a product of seamless illusion." (Stephenson's diatribe carries with it an implicit critique of icon-based graphics as reductive cartoons.) In this way, both the Mac and Windows operating systems are in the same business: that of "short-circuiting laborious, explicit verbal communication with expensively designed interfaces."[119] Alternatively, Stephenson champions the Linux operating system because its workings are exposed and it can be customized by its user, like a tuner-car. An obvious analogy occurs here: both the Mac OS and Windows interface operate like classical Hollywood film style—concealing its workings, aiming for unreflexive illusionism—while the Linux OS operates more like an independent or avant-garde film, self-reflexive, its substrates and premises exposed. The Linux OS is computing with distanciation, as if it were an operating system designed by Bertolt Brecht. But Stephenson's polemic holds a prescient command of the global effects of interface culture, for GUIs have become the "meta-interface" found on almost any screenic device—VCRs, cell phones, car navigational systems, gaming consoles, and my favorite new screen-enabled appliance, the Samsung "Internet refrigerator."[120]

While the scale and domestic place of the television may have prepared us for the screens of the "personal" computer, computer "users" are not spectators or viewers. Immobile, with attention focused on a screen, the "user" interacts directly with the framed screen image using a device—keyboard, mouse, or in the case of touch-screens, finger—to manipulate what is contained within the parameter of the screen. Computer interfaces may have been designed to become dyadic partners in a metaphysical relationship, but complaints about the awkwardness of this liaison have targeted the interface. Brenda Laurel proclaims: "Using computers is like going to the movie theater and having to watch the projector instead of the film."[121]

OLD METAPHORS, NEW SCREENS

For Alberti, the metaphor of the window implied direct, veridical, and unmediated vision, transparency of surface or aperture, and transmitted light. The computer "window" implies its opposite: the visual field seen through a computer "window" is rarely direct (although webcams play on this function); it is mediated to a high degree through its proprietary or trademarked "software"; and its representational function is highly iconic. Computer "windows" coexist on the flat surface of a computer display. They open onto flatness or depth, image or text, moving or still content. Some "windows" open onto networked systems, some only refer to the hard drive of its base. Although computer "windows" can be "open" at the same time, they rarely serve, as the art historical double-slide projection did, as a means for comparative analysis.

So let's consider the computer user who navigates the "windows" of screen space. In the mixed metaphor of the computer screen, the computer user is figuratively positioned with multiple spatial relations to the screen. "Windows" stack *in front of* each other (if one is looking into the screen perpendicularly, as if through a window) or *on top of* each other (if one is looking into the screen as if its perpendicular is in a gravity-defying ninety-degree rotation of an angle overhead). As either a "page" or a "window," a mobile switch of position is implied in the mixed metaphor: the user switches between a recumbent (desktop view) and an upright (window) view. The desktop metaphor implies background and foreground layers, but seen from above. The gravity-defying space of the computer screen accustoms us to the antigravity of CGI in films such as *Crouching Tiger, Hidden Dragon,* and *The Matrix.* The computer user may switch back and forth between these layers, open and close "windows," switch activities at will. The user may not be able to see each "window" in the stack on the desktop, but this doesn't mean the program isn't there or is no longer active. The computer may be "thinking" about several things at once, it may have several applications open, different programs running in separate "windows."

Of course, the icons of the graphical user interface are reductively simple, far from high art, farther even from the screens of popular culture. The Microsoft version of the window interface did not even draw on the "deep beauty" that David Gelernter finds in software that is "simple and powerful."[122] And yet, on the fractured plane of the computer screen, the metaphor of the window has retained a key stake in the technological reframing of the visual field. The Windows interface is a postcinematic visual system, but the viewer-turned-user remains in front of (*vorstellen*) a perpendicular frame.

MULTITASKING, THE COMPUTER "WINDOW," AND THE MULTIPLE SCREEN

> *The distracted person (*der Zerstreute*), too, can form habits. More, the ability to master certain tasks in a state of distraction proves that their solution has become a matter of habit. . . . Reception in a state of distraction . . . finds in the film its true means of exercise.*
>
> —Walter Benjamin, "The Work of Art in the Age of Mechanical Reproduction"

In an oft-cited passage from "The Work of Art in the Age of Mechanical Reproduction," Walter Benjamin draws a distinction between the modes of "reception" of painting, film, and architecture. "Painting invites the spectator to contemplation/concentration," Benjamin explains, while "Architecture has always represented the prototype of a work of art the reception of which is consummated by a collectivity in a state of distraction." The film meets this mode of reception "halfway."[123] Architectural theorists have often bridled at Benjamin's dismissive generalization about the experience of architecture and, equally, film theorists have debated this assessment of the film spectator. But "reception in a state of distraction" now seems to provide a prescient model for the multitasking computer user.

For cinema spectators, the conventions of film narrative and the protocols of theatrical exhibition encouraged cognitive focus and engagement. (Spectators who eat loudly, make out, talk on their phones—or otherwise multitask—are targets of social opprobrium.) Although the instances of split-screen and multiple-screen filmmaking described at the beginning of this chapter suggest that the film spectator was increasingly equipped to engage with such fractures in attention, televisual spectatorship much more directly encouraged the habits of a split-attentive viewer. The television's domestic site encouraged housewives to iron and fold laundry in front of the set, families to eat dinner with the TV on in the background, children to play with toys while watching cartoons. Channel switching, aided by accessory devices like the remote, implied the inherent potential to engage in a "mode switch." By contrast, the computer user must engage with the computer screen directly, as it only responds to the user's interactive "input." Yet the computer user can—and easily does—split focus and attention to multiple tasks, since computers can now routinely run multiple applications, each open in a different window.

Multiple "windows" made computer "multitasking" possible.[124] As one Web dictionary defines "multitasking," it is "working with various computer programs at one time in order to increase your productivity and reach your intended goal."[125] The windows interface made it easy for the user to switch back and forth between two documents or two applications. In order to theorize the subjective consequences of computer multitasking, we need to first consider the technical base of multiple-screen "windows." For a computer to multitask, the computer does tasks not simultaneously but serially, and yet at a high speed. (Even a slow computer with a hundred-megahertz processor can execute a million instructions between each pair of keystrokes.) While a computer microprocessor can keep many programs running at the same time (parallel processing), the user still "crosscuts" between one or more programs in selective sequence. Just as the instrumental base for the moving image—the retinal retention of successive virtual images—produced a newly virtual representation of movement and a complex new experience of time, the instrumental base for multiscreen multitasking poses new questions about the computer user's experience of time.

Computer multitasking makes it possible to combine work with leisure—running an Excel spreadsheet while checking email or shopping on eBay—and hence serves to equate productivity with a fractured subjectivity.[126] A 1998 *New York Times* article reported the following statistic: "Microsoft says the average office user of Windows 95 has more than three programs running at a time. At home, more than 10 million American households now have a television and a personal computer in the same room."[127]

Screen-based multitasking is only one form of multitasking. Using multiple screens (computers and TVs) or engaging in multiple activities (talking on the phone while "watching" TV) has extended the meaning of "multitasking" to a more pervasive cultural mode. In a study of American leisure time habits in 2000, an MTV Networks/Viacom Study of Media, Entertainment, and Leisure Time reported that Americans spend time with media and entertainment 4.7 hours a day. For 2.9 of those hours, the average American simultaneously reads magazines and watches TV, listens to CDs and sends email. The results, the study reports, imply that a multitasker's average day has 29.8 hours of activity.[128] However, as another critic assesses the psychic liabilities of technologically enabled multitasking: "Technology didn't give us more time, it just upped the expectations of what we could do in the same time."[129] As a further indication of the effects of multitasking on styles of learning and thinking, consider the following advice on time management offered to college students: "Multi-window, multi-task activity is the norm for today's students. E-mail, games, and web searches are routinely managed simultaneously with writing papers or completing research assignments. Students have learned to value the pace and accessibility of video presentations and sound-bite synopses of popular culture. The slow, linear process of reading a book or attending a lecture may challenge a student's time management skills and attention to detail. While multi-tasking can be a valuable tool, so are focused attention and concentration. All are required for success in college."[130]

A George Washington University website offers the following recommendations:

> Multi-window, multi-task activity breaks concentration and consumes time rapidly.
>
> - Turn off or minimize your pop up windows. Avoid screen clutter and eliminate distractions.
> - Break tasks into manageable time blocks and stick to them.
> - Plan the hours of your day (or study periods) in advance. Schedule a time to return e-mail.
> - Control interruptions or even schedule 10 minute breaks for 50 minute study periods.
> - Make allowances for periods of relaxation.
> - Exercise and strengthen your ability to sustain concentration and absorb information by gradually increasing your study time and effort until you reach an established goal.
> - Create a variety of study aids to help focus your attention (e.g., index cards, tables, diagrams.)
> - Allow time to stop and think about connections among course materials, facts, and findings.[131]

This discussion of multitasking implies the direct cognitive effects of multitasking behaviors. Is the fractured subjectivity of multitasking in service of productivity and efficiency? Is it a mode of technologically enhanced labor-saving for the "human motor"? Does the liberatory rhetoric associated with multitasking (you can work where you want; take your computer to the beach or the café) merely mask the increased expectations of 24/7 productivity? (Do you really want your laptop at the beach?) Just as "alibi servers" help to evade surveillance, enacting a technological illusion of being elsewhere, computer "windows" can be alibi servers for identity. In *Life on the Screen,* Sherry Turkle describes how computer windows work to produce an identity with "distributed presence": "Windows provide a way for a computer to place you in several contexts at the same time . . . your identity on the computer is the sum of your distributed presence."[132] Turkle portrays the computer user as a "decentralized self" who, cycling between different windows, has a fractured but multiple identity.[133] She ascribes this screen life its theoretical analogs:

> [M]ore than twenty years after meeting the ideas of Lacan, Foucault, Deleuze, and Guattari, I am meeting them again in my new life on the screen. But this time the Gallic abstractions are more concrete. In my computer-mediated worlds, the self is multiple, fluid, and constituted in interaction with machine connections; it is made and transformed by language; sexual congress is an exchange of signifiers; and understanding follows from navigation and tinkering rather than analysis. And in the machine-generated world of MUDs, I meet characters who put me in a new relationship with my own identity.[134]

As a screen-based visual system, the "windows" interface subtly exponentiates what Erwin Panofsky described as the "unique and specific possibilities" of the cinema: the *dynamization of space* and the *spatialization of time.* On the computer, we can be two (or more) places at once, in two (or more) time frames, in two (or more) modes of identity, in a fractured post-Cartesian cyberspace, cybertime.

AUGURIES OF CONVERGENCE

The screen featured in a 1995 ad faces its audience: the regimented rows of a computer keyboard, each key in the fixed position of a cinema spectator. The image—of the transformative moment in *Metropolis* when the metallic robot Maria is infused with the life force of electricity—suggests another moment of transformation: the cinema screen has been replaced by its digital other, the computer screen.

By now, the once distinct material differences between cinematic, televisual, and computer screens have vanished.[135] Televisions have become more like computers: hard-disk video recorders (DVRs such as TIVO, Replay TV) record television signals onto an auxiliary hard-drive; HDTV-ready TVs use chips running mega-MIPS. Conversely, computers have become more like televisions: MPEG and QuickTime "movies" and "streaming" videos flash across and through Web browser pages. Networked multimedia home stations (Microsoft's X-box, Nintendo's Game Cube, Sony's Playstation 2) combine the functions of telephone, television, and gaming console with the computer, and further confound the technical differentiation of film, television, and the computer.

The segregation of histories of telephony, moving-image, and computing technologies appears—in postmillennial retrospect—to have been a set of arbitrary separations that disregarded the intermedial complexity of technological development. To write a "history" of these new media formations is to encounter many familiar historiographical challenges.[136] As Stephen Heath warned in an earlier historical moment (1978), when the "cinematic apparatus" seemed a dominant technological form: "Technological determinism substitutes for the social, the economic, the ideological, proposes the random autonomy of invention and development, coupled often with the vision of a fulfillment of an abstract human essence—and some of the wildest versions of this latter are to be found in accounts of the (then aptly named) 'media.' . . . [Cinema's] history is a history of the technological and social together, a history in which the determinations are not simple but multiple, interacting, in which the ideological is there from the start."[137] While careful not to overstate the determinations of technological development, Heath and other apparatus theorists attempted to provide an account of the technological and social specificities of the cinema as a single medium.

In this way, we may wish to regard Marshall McLuhan as the first apparatus theorist. Back in 1964, when McLuhan proclaimed, "the medium is the message," his sound-bite aphorism drew attention—not only to the *media*tion that the media implied, but also to the specificity of each separate medium. McLuhan inveighed against a content-based study of the media: "The 'content' of any medium," he writes, "blinds us to the characteristics of the medium."[138] Instead, McLuhan prescribes an analysis of the effects—"the change of scale or pace or pattern"—that each particular medium might produce. While McLuhan analyzed the interrelatedness of media in an evolutionary scheme ("The content of any medium is always another medium"),[139] he also insisted

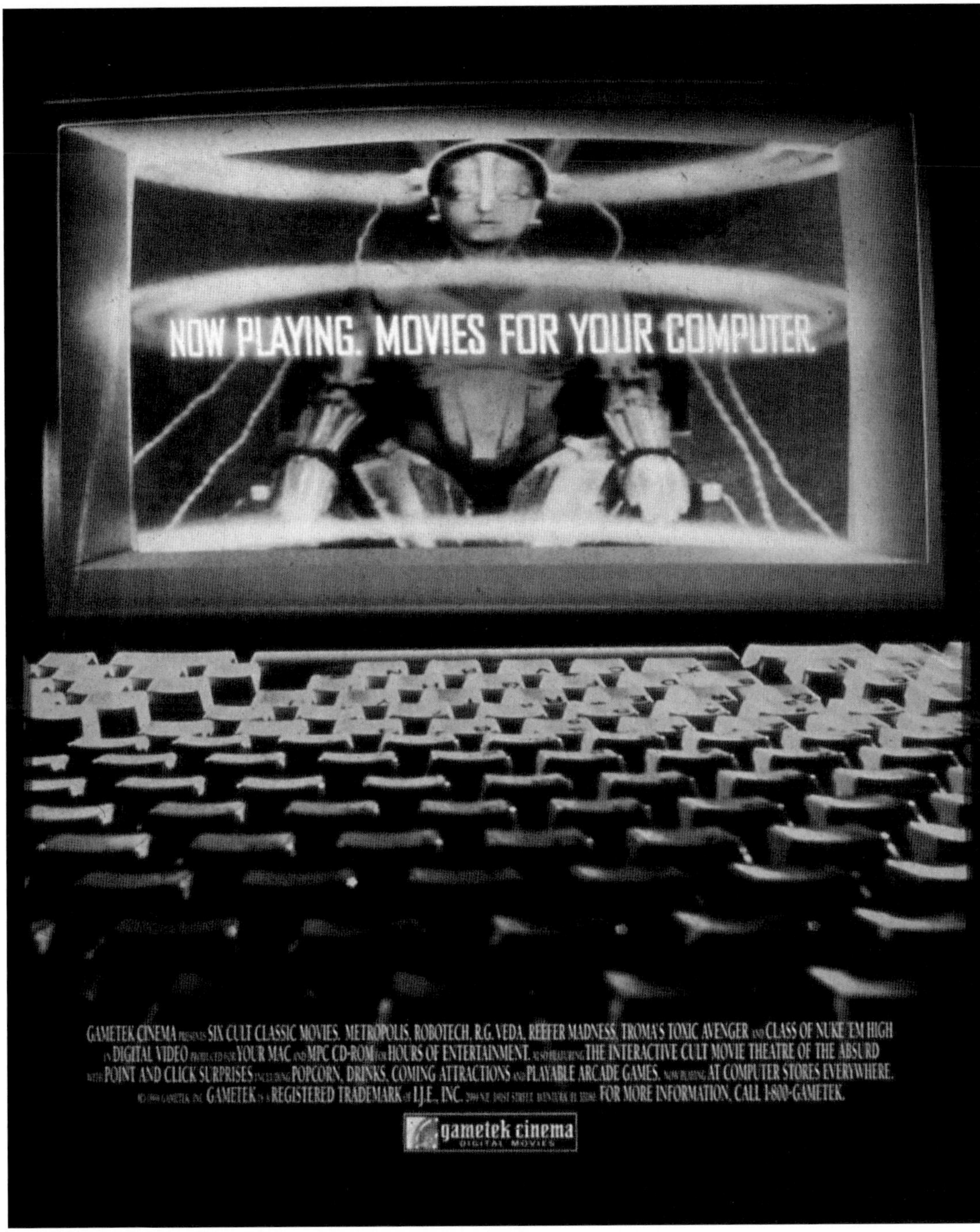

5.25 "Now playing. Movies for your computer," 1995 ad from Gametek Cinema/Digital Movies. Gametek presents six classic cult movies: *Metropolis, Robotech, R. G. Veda, Reefer Madness, Troma's Toxic Avenger,* and *Class of Nuke 'em High.*

that each new medium would "institute new ratios, not only among our private senses, but among themselves, when they interact among themselves."[140] How, then, do we account for the "new ratios" produced by the rapid and recent changes in the screens and interfaces of moving-image media?

Nicholas Negroponte, another McLuhan-styled media prognosticator, offers a counterpolemical aphorism, turning McLuhan's "The medium is the message" on its head. Negroponte declares: "The medium is not the message in the digital world. It is an embodiment of it. A message might have several embodiments automatically derivable from the same data."[141] For Negroponte, digital technology dissolves the specificity of individual media: digital imaging, delivery, and display effectively erase the messages implicit in the source medium. Negroponte proclaims: "The basic difference between today's TVs and PCs has nothing to do with location, social habits, or our need to relax. It has to do with how the bits arrive."[142] If we follow Negroponte's axiom ("the medium is not the message in the digital world"), we arrive at a newfound determinism: digital technology inherently implies a convergence of all media forms.

German media theorist Friedrich Kittler anticipated this loss of media specificity when he wrote (in 1986), "The general digitalization of information and channels erases the difference between individual media."[143] Yet Kittler predicted that the installation of fiber-optic cable—and not the phone wires of the Internet or the wireless future of the Web—would be the technology to turn film, television, music, and phone calls into a "single medium."

The changes in screens and our "interfaces" with them have occurred at the speed of fast-forward. But have the screens of cinema, television, and computer really lost their apparatical distinctions? A recent sales website for flat-screen monitors conflates the multiple functions of the screen—TV, movie display, Internet browser—now displayed within the same electronic picture frame:

> Hanging on a wall they look more like art rather than a TV set. When you're not watching TV, DVD videos, surfing the net or reading your e-mail, there is no need to switch the plasma panel off. It can be used as an electronic picture frame, with a continuously changing selection of artworks of your choice: An endless art collection![144]

Or, as the Consumer Electronics Association predicted in 2002:

> In the ultimate living room, TVs and music don't stand alone; they interact with each other, with the Internet, with the PC in the home office or the electronic game equipment in the family room.[145]

Auguries of convergence always suggest a teleology: some media are seen as transitional, while others seem destined to evolve into the next species. A media paleontologist could examine the fossil remains: the VCR may have begun to erode the differences between televisual and cinematic viewing; the DVD may have became the delivery format to serve the displays of computers and televisions alike. New-generation gaming consoles offer features that include DVD players, output jacks for HDTV, broadband connections, and hard drives for storing music and games. While newer iterations of the gaming console seem poised to further bridge the gap between the digital world of the personal computer and the analog world of television, one cannot predict what delivery or display format will survive the vicissitudes of the consumer market. There have been earlier attempts at marketing the convergence of television, computer, and cinema screens that failed. In 1993, Apple introduced the "Macintosh TV," a convergence appliance that anticipated a hybrid computer-user/television-viewer who would use the same CRT screen as a television receiver and computer display. But Apple decided the market wasn't there: the Mac TV was discontinued almost before it began.[146] In 1996, "WebTV," an Internet appliance marketed to users who might want to access the Web on their television screens, imagined a convergence that bypassed the personal computer. The convergent screen of Microsoft's XP Media Center is positioned to fulfill these earlier promises. The television screen (big screen, plasma screen, LCD screen) is now coequal with the pixels of computer "display."

"New" media imply the ever-obsolescence of the "old." As Antonio Gramsci put it: "the old is dying and the new cannot be born; in this interregnum a great variety of morbid symptoms appear."[147] And yet, amid these morbid symptoms, the continued engagement with a "virtual window" seems somehow assured.

CONCLUSION

THE FUTURE OF WINDOWS:

SMART GLASS, STREAMING PORTALS, AND SCREENLESS IMAGES

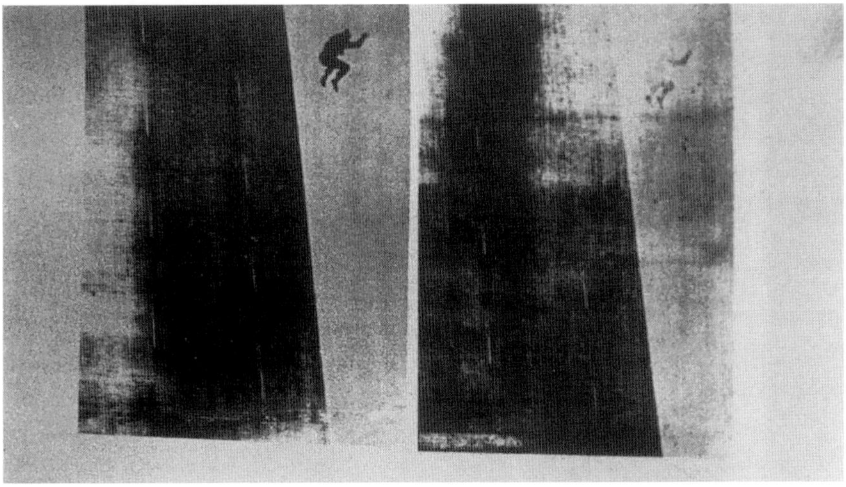

C.1 Andy Warhol, *Suicide,* 1963. Synthetic polymer paint and silkscreen ink on canvas. © The Andy Warhol Foundation for the Visual Arts/ARS, NY. Photo: The Andy Warhol Foundation, Inc./Art Resource, New York.

S'est défenestré.

—French radio announcement of the death of Gilles Deleuze

IN NOVEMBER 1995, philosopher Gilles Deleuze committed suicide by throwing himself or jumping out of the window of his Paris apartment. We might recall some of Deleuze's own writing about the window, the closed system of the frame and the "out-of-field" (*hors-champ*) of representational space as we ask, What was the fatal lure of penetrating the space of the window into the great beyond?[1]

"Doors, windows, box office windows, skylights, car windows, mirrors, are all frames," wrote Deleuze in *Cinema 1: The Movement-Image.* "The great directors have particular affinities with particular secondary, tertiary, etc. frames," he continues. "And it is by this dovetailing of frames that the parts of the set or of the closed system are separated, but also converge and are reunited."[2] The frame of the screen is a closed system, a primary container for inset secondary and tertiary frames that may recede in *mise en abyme,* but also converge to reunite within a grander but still bounded frame. Yet, for Deleuze, there is always a beyond, outside this frame, an "out-of-field," a more "radical elsewhere." "All framing determines an out-of-field [*hors-champ*]": "In one case, the out-of-field designates that which exists elsewhere, to one side or around; in the other case, the out-of-field testifies to a more disturbing presence, one which cannot even be said to exist, but rather to 'insist' or 'subsist,' a more radical elsewhere, outside homogeneous space and time."[3] In his death, Deleuze found this elsewhere, outside of the frame.

For the rest of us—left facing the window, the frame, the screen—we might wonder: Is there a new logic to vision as our windows, frames, screens are ever more fractured and virtually multiplied? Which technologies will break through the frame and have us climb through the virtual window? And which will have us stay fixed—nose to the glass (or as the French say about window-shopping, *lécher les vitrines,* "to lick the windows")—in front of the windows, caught in the hold of an image, framed in display?[4]

This book took shape while the screens of cinema, television, and computer began to converge, gradually losing their apparatical distinctions.[5] Now, a variety of screens—long and wide and square, large and small, composed of grains, composed of pixels, lit by projected light, cathode-ray tube, plasma, LCD—compete for our attention without any convincing arguments about hegemony. Screens are "display and delivery" formats—variable in versions of projection screen, TV screen, computer screen, or hand-held device. "Film" is a "storage" medium—variable in versions of video, DVDs, computer hard drive, databank, online server. Spectators are "users" or "players" with an "interface"—variable in versions of remotes, mice, keyboards, touch screens, joysticks, goggles and gloves and body suits. Just as the chemically based, analog images of photography have been replaced by digital images, the "cinema" has been displaced by systems of circulation and transmission that abolish the projection screen and link the screens of the computer and television with the dialogic interactivity of the telephone.

In the "cinematic century"—seen now in the 20/20 of retrospective "vision"—the viewer remained immobile in front of the frame of the screen. As we begin this new century, the "postcinematic" "post-televisual" viewer has new forms of ever-virtual mobility—new speeds of access to deep histories of images and text, newly mobilized screens that travel in airplanes and automobiles, screens that can be hand-held and wireless. As public buildings and domestic spaces boast image-bearing glass skins, as large-screen televisions are big enough and flat enough to substitute for real windows, as "windows" within our computer screens stream images from multiple sources, as virtual reality technologies expand from the gaming world into entertainment or daily services, the "virtual window" has become a ubiquitous portal—a "wormhole"—to pasts and futures.

In 1915, D. W. Griffith imagined a future library where one could sit in front of a "properly adjusted window" and "actually see what happened" in the past:

> Imagine a public library of the near future, for instance. There will be long rows of boxes or pillars, properly classified and indexed of course. At each box a push button and before each box a seat. Suppose you wish to "read up" a certain episode in Napoleon's life. Instead of con-

sulting all the authorities, wading through a host of books, and ending bewildered without a clear idea of exactly what did happen, *you will merely seat yourself at a properly adjusted window in a scientifically prepared room, press the button and actually see what happened. . . . There will be no opinions expressed. You will merely be present at the making of history.*[6]

Griffith's prediction captured an insight about his century's "new" technology for storing time, yet he imagined a "properly adjusted window" as ideologically transparent—he did not acknowledge any mediations to the "history picture" it would record.

Alberti's fifteenth-century metaphor of the window served to frame the geometric, geophysical world, arranging the above, below, ahead, and behind on the flat framed plane of representation. Alberti's window was not a transparent "window on the world," but it provided us with a Renaissance root for a "windowed elsewhere"—a virtual space that exists on the virtual plane of representation. In Alberti's schema, there was no absolute size, only proportions relative to the human measure: "Large, small, long, short, high, low, wide, narrow, light, dark, bright, gloomy, and everything of the kind [*magnum, parvum, longum, breve, altum, infimum, latum, arctum, clarum, obscurum, luminosum, tenebrosum et huiusmodi omni*], which philosophers termed accidents, because they may or may not be present in things, all these are such as to be known only by comparison."[7]

The screens of the twenty-first century are large, small, long, short, high, low, wide, narrow, light, dark, bright, gloomy, and known by their relative measure to the human scale. And yet, as the display screens of movies, television, and the computer begin to grow more similar to each other, a new logic to framed visuality takes hold. The window's metaphoric boundary is no longer the singular frame of perspective—as beholders of multiple-screen "windows," we now see the world in spatially and temporally fractured frames, through "virtual windows" that rely more on the multiple and simultaneous than on the singular and sequential.

This book has engaged in a split optic, a historical parallax. Renaissance perspective negotiated a new relation between the near and the far, organized along the vanishing point of a single line of vision. By analogy, this book negotiates the now and the then, the near and the far of technology refracted through the foreshortened focal length of the present. In this way, I've brought fifteenth-century theories of perspective, seventeenth-century theories of optics and the mind, nineteenth-century devices and visual practices, and twentieth-century moving-image media onto the flattened plane of the present, held next to each other and yet seen through a kaleidoscope of critical lenses. Descartes's window, Heidegger's frame, Bergson's virtual, and Virilio's screen combine to give us an optic through which we can see these changes in modern visuality. Rather than simply provide a technological account, they give us a philosophical and subjective sense of those changes—and of their consequences.

Meanwhile, the next generation—today's ten-year-olds—are transfixed in front of screens full of images driven by X-Boxes or PlayStations or GameCubes, with "controllers" in their hands. Or they multitask—doing homework assignments, researching on the Web, redesigning their *my space* page, while IMing with friends. They are living deep in their own virtually rendered elsewheres, and yet, like the generations before them, they sit in front of the frame of a "window." Their interaction with the screen may be different, but if it is, it makes the intransigence of the frame a chilling constant, one with inexorable cultural power.

Or perhaps, as films like *ExistenZ, The Matrix,* and *Strange Days* predict, the screen may dissolve; images and data will be "uploaded" directly, bypassing the eye and the optics of vision. This new circuitry takes us beyond and through the window, a defenestration that has new risks and pleasures. In this vision, the "age of windows"—and by extension, the age of screens—has, as H. G. Wells predicted, reached its end.

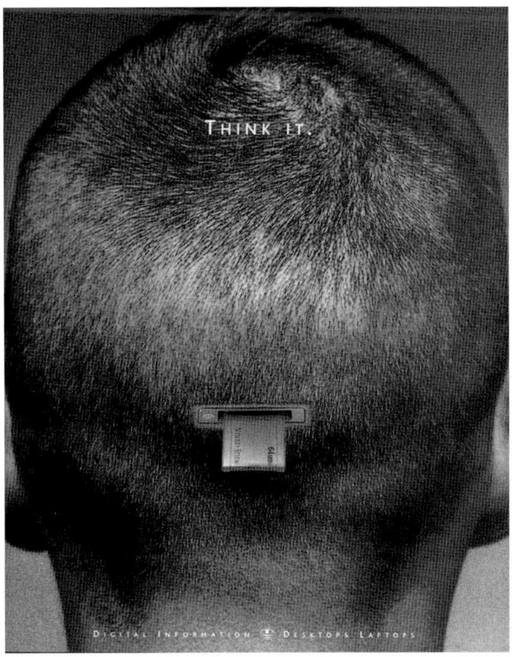

C.2 Sony Memory Stick ad, 1999.

POSTLOGUE 2005

It is difficult to write about the immediate of media, difficult to analyze the pervasive present ever slipping away. This book was written amid the hyperspeed of technological change; it began long before our television screens began to look like websites, before our computer screens routinely contained moving images, and before movies looked like both. As time wore on and the technological snapshot of the present kept changing, I found it necessary to add richer historical and theoretical detail, taking some steps backward from the digital present to detail how the past presses its nose up against the glass of the future.

But this book was also written in an era of "posts"—the post- to modernity, the post- to colonialism, the post- to the millennium, the post- to 9/11—as if the present can be understood only as an epilogue itself, an ending after the end. We can know the past only in terms of how it has been constructed for us, in terms of how evidence appears to us now, mediated through the lenses of the present. This book has tried to provide an account not of how we got to here, but of where we've come from.

When I wrote *Window Shopping,* I wanted to argue how deeply moving-image media had permeated our consciousness, how they had changed our access to history and to the past. I argued that postmodernity could be understood only as a consequence of the creeping centrality of mediated modes of visuality and in terms of the virtual mobilities in everyday life. I offered an account of subjectivity—a temporally confused subjectivity—in the media-saturated first world, a world where the commodity fetish set the rule of culture. But the "mobilized and virtual gaze" was not—*and is not*—the global norm. Nor are there easy generalizations to make about consciousness itself. An individual's relation to space and to time is mediated by a range of determinants—including geographical place in the world, access to media, religious belief, psychological state.

This book, like *Window Shopping,* attempts to provide an account of the subjectivities of people in the most mediated provinces of the first world. I have been drawn to philosophies that attempt to conceptualize the ways in which our bodies and minds move and think in the everyday. The drives of technophilia—lust for efficiency, mobility, accelerated modes of experience—produce changes that are both gradual and dramatic. Yet these changes require that we confront the sad truth of their price—a consequence that has been termed a "digital divide" but is less about the digital than about another more deeply rent divide.

All agonistic accounts require a theory of rupture, an account of the break. The collapse of the World Trade Towers provided a dramatic visual turning point, a break that forced a change in all accounts of the interdependence of global and technological change. The disintegration of two massive towers of glass and steel had an explosive epistemological charge. As the writer A. M. Homes recounted in the *New York Times:* "I see the plane, and I see the plane crash into the building. I see the buildings burn, and I see the buildings fall down. I see imagery that until now did not exist in reality, only in the fiction of film. Seeing it with your own eyes, in real time—not on a screen, not protected by the frame of a television set, not in the communal darkness of a movie theater—seeing it like this is irreconcilable, like a hallucination, a psychotic break."[1] A. M. Homes was unprotected by the frame or by the screen. While many wished that the images of 9/11 were only a movie or television special effect, the towers of glass and steel remain only in the immaterial archive of memory and in the archive of photographs and films that retain them. The film remains after the building fades: the ephemeral materiality of the Twin Towers—and the lives extinguished inside them—has been imparted to the archival immateriality of photographic, filmic, and television images.

In many ways, this implosive inversion of our technologies—aircraft turned into missiles against buildings on our own shores—is more and more possible as fear has lost its borders. Terrorism is made possible by modern media—funded by a transnational credit economy, organized by the decentered networks of the Internet. Chemical agents can be sent through the postal system. Diseases can cross borders and refute the metaphors of quarantine. The only way to counter the rhetoric of fear is to deconstruct it, to teach cynicism and doubt and critical reading.

Here, I've struggled to add an appropriate epilogue to this book, one written from the cusp of new realizations about how the frame functions, about the collapse of borders and boundaries, and about how mobility has changed its valence. As a book-writer at the end of the twentieth century, I found that my writing process was facilitated—or perhaps hindered—by word-processing software that encouraged holding each chapter open in overlapped windows, with easy "copy" and "paste" changes made without regard to linear logic. Computer-assisted writing is further enabled (or disabled) by the easy switch between the deep desktop of "offline" applications and "online" sources with search engines and text archives available on the very same screen. The blank "page" is now an upright screen, but not a blank screen. It has toolbars and desktop icons and many "windows." In fact, one of the inset frames on my computer screen contains a little Microsoft mascot—an inset "window" that opens to a cartooned computer with its own belly-like screen—a foggy blue eyeball in the socket of a monitor with feet. This creature taps its foot and nods, yawns and dozes, sits and wiggles its toes—an impish avatar of the computer's solipsistic pull. In daily screeds, I fomented against the liabilities of multitasking and the toll that it was taking on my ever-more fractured subjectivity. If the *flâneur* and *flâneuse* were models for the subject in nineteenth- and twentieth-century modernity, the multitasker is their twenty-first-century heir. Despite my own wild technophilia, I developed a reactionary nostalgia for the fixity and simplicity of a single-window view.

My argument in this book largely sidesteps the new configurations of global, transnational, and borderless networks, of how the border and boundaries of nation-states no longer control the sovereignty of peoples. Glassmaking was invented in the sands of Mesopotamia—now Iraq. Islamic research into optics was of determinant importance to all subsequent optical theory. The dematerializations made possible by solid yet transparent planes of glass take on a new significance as we look into newly mediated windows, with new *istoriae* to be seen.

NOTES

INTRODUCTION: THE VIRTUAL WINDOW

I have used the terms "vision" and "visuality" throughout this book and need to define these terms at the outset. "Vision" here refers to the perceptual experience of sight; "visuality" refers to the social, psychical, and historical habits of vision. Both of these terms were set into question by the Dia Foundation Discussions in Contemporary Culture in 1988. The proceedings of this conference were published as a slim volume, *Vision and Visuality,* edited by Hal Foster (Seattle: Bay Press, 1988).

1 As Alberti writes: "Let me tell you what I do when I am painting. First of all, on the surface on which I am going to paint, I draw a rectangle of whatever size I want, *which I regard as an open window through which the subject to be painted is seen.*" This quotation is taken from section I.19 of the 1435 Latin text: "quod quidem mihi pro aperta finestra est ex qua historia contueatur." Leon Battista Alberti, *On Painting and On Sculpture: The Latin Texts of De pictura and De statua,* trans. Cecil Grayson (London: Phaidon, 1972), 55.

2 The upright vertical spatiality implied by the "window"—looking through—is confounded by the implied horizontal surface of the "desktop," where stacked documents defy the laws of gravity.

3 Hubert Damisch, *The Origin of Perspective,* trans. John Goodman (Cambridge: MIT Press, 1995), 28.

4 In *Space, Time and Architecture: The Growth of a New Tradition* (1941; Cambridge: Harvard University Press, 1976), Sigfried Giedion argued that buildings by a new generation of architects—Walter Gropius, Le Corbusier, Mies van der Rohe—exemplified new forms of "transparency," the same nonperspectival spatial innovations as cubist painting. For an important reexamination of the relation between cubist painting and modern architecture, see the collection of essays edited by Nancy J. Troy and Eve Blau, *Architecture and Cubism* (Montreal: Centre Canadien d'Architecture, 1997; Cambridge: MIT Press, 2002).

5 In Anthony Vidler's incisive reading of the "warpings" and pathologizing of domestic and public spaces in modernity, he describes the perspectival space of the computer screen:

> *little has changed in the framing of space itself over the modern period. Perspective is still the rule in virtual reality environments. . . .* Ostensibly there is as little to distinguish Alberti's window from a computer screen as there is to differentiate an eighteenth-century axonometric by Gaspard Monge from a wire-frame dinosaur generated by Industrial Light and Magic. *What has changed is the technique of simulation and, even more importantly, the place, or position, of the subject or traditional "viewer" of representation.* Between contemporary virtual space and modernist space there lies an aporia formed by the autogenerative nature of the computer program, and its real blindness to the viewer's presence. *In this sense the screen is not a picture, and certainly not a surrogate window, but rather an ambiguous and unfixed location for the subject* [emphasis added].

If, as Vidler maintains, "What has changed is the technique of simulation and, even more importantly, the place, or position, of the subject or traditional 'viewer' of representation," the differences between the "simulation" techniques of painting, photography, cinema, television, and computer-based representation require distinctions of historical and media specificity. In all of these instances, the "traditional 'viewer' of representation" must confront her position in relation to the "unfixed location" of virtual space. The space of the screen—whether it contains montage and the special effects of a cinematic simulation, the postproduction digital effects of a television image, movements determined by the auto-generative computer algorithm of a VR environment, or a screen image responsive to the user's input device—remains a *virtual* space. And, given the fractured frames found in many recent examples of film, television and computer display, I would argue that *much* has changed in the framing of that space. Anthony Vidler, *Warped Space: Art, Architecture, and Anxiety in Modern Culture* (Cambridge: MIT Press, 2000), 7–8.

6 These anomalies will be further detailed in chapter 5. Despite the exceptional examples of multiple-screen experiments (Abel Gance's three-screen *Napoléon* of 1926; multiple-screen installations of Ray and Charles Eames, Frances Thompson, and Alexander Hammid; Andy Warhol's double-screen projections) and split-screen special effects (in films like *It's Always Fair Weather* [1955], *Pillow Talk* [1959], and later *The Boston Strangler* [1968]), the dominant screen practice through most of the cinematic century was to project single-frame, single-screen moving images.

7 The implications of my argument hang in the balance between the nuanced distinctions of coincidence and causality; either (1) the multiple-frame image became more common *coincident with* the development of the computer display window, or (2) the multiple-frame image became more common *because of* the common use of the computer display window.

8 William Mitchell has maintained that photography was itself a rampant site of image alteration; Henry Peach Robinson's and Oscar Reijlander's "combination prints" were photocomposites using predigital techniques of image manipulation. William J. Mitchell, *The Reconfigured Eye: Visual Truth in the Post-Photographic Era* (Cambridge: MIT Press, 1992), 10–15. Lev Manovich offers a moderated account of the break between film-based and digital photography in a short 1995 essay, "The Paradoxes of Digital Photography": "The logic of the digital photograph is one of historical continuity and discontinuity. The digital image tears apart the net of semiotic codes, modes of display, and patterns of spectatorship in modern visual culture—and, at the same time, weaves this net even stronger. The digital image annihilates photography while solidifying, glorifying and immortalizing the photographic." Lev Manovich, <http://www.manovich.net/TEXT/digital_photo.html>.

9 This argument, which blurs the agonistic distinction between predigital and digital imaging strategies, can also be found in Gene Youngblood (with Peter Weibel and Woody Vasulka), "Cinema and the Code," in Jeffrey Shaw and Peter Weibel, eds., *Future Cinema: The Cinematic Imaginary after Film* (Cambridge: MIT Press, 2003), 156–161. Youngblood acknowledges his essay as a "working draft" based on conversations about digital imaging with Peter Weibel and Woody Vasulka since 1986. In their definition, "cinema" is "the art of organizing a stream of audiovisual events in time" and includes film, video, holography, and structured digital code (156). The digital distinction blurs as they assert that "there are no new classes of images, there are only new variations and new epistemological and ontological conditions for generating and witnessing those variations."

10 Nicolas Negroponte, *Being Digital* (New York: Alfred Knopf, 1995), 71.

11 Siegfried Zielinski, *Audiovisions: Cinema and Television as Entr'actes in History* (1988), trans. Gloria Custance (Amsterdam: Amsterdam University Press, 1999).

12 This list is a synoptic selection of twentieth-century writers on media and technology and, as written, may draw as many charges of omission as questions of inclusion.

13 Indeed, it is important to credit the nonproprietary, pre-trademarked use of the term "window" for computer display. Douglas Engelbart at the Stanford Research Institute, Alan Kay at Xerox PARC, and Steve Jobs and the Apple pioneers were the discursive forebears to Microsoft's trademark of the window metaphor.

14 The term "ontological cut" is taken from Victor Stoichita's *The Self-Aware Image: An Insight into Early Modern Meta-Painting* (Cambridge: Cambridge University Press, 2001). Stoichita uses it to refer to the separation of the portable panel painting from the wall and describes how seventeenth-century painting was obsessed by the "ontological cut" made by the frame of the painting. I am indebted to Lisa Pon, a fellow Getty Scholar-in-Residence 2001–2002, for introducing me to this text and for productive conversations about the historiography of Renaissance art.

15 This is a précis of a more detailed account of the emergence of a "mobilized and virtual gaze" put forth in my earlier book, *Window Shopping: Cinema and the Postmodern* (Berkeley: University of California Press, 1993). The technologies that led to the moving image emerged, I argued, as a convergence of two visual practices developed in the nineteenth century: those produced by machines of mobility (trains, steamships, bicycles, elevators, escalators, moving walkways—all apparatuses that changed the relation of sight to bodily movement and hence produced a *mobilized* visuality) and those produced by contrivances for an ever-more *virtual* visuality (evidenced in representational devices like the panorama and the diorama, but most dramatically produced by photography's indexical record). Although *Window Shopping* situated the spatial immobility of the cinema spectator in terms of new forms of virtual mobility—the virtual *flânerie* that moving-image spectatorship offered—a crucial component of my argument concerned the effects on spectator's temporality as a result of cinema's exploitation of a mobilized and virtual visuality.

I coined the phrase "mobilized gaze" without knowledge of Jacques Aumont's parallel formulation in his book, *L'Oeil interminable: Cinéma et peinture* (Paris: Séguier, 1989). After *Window Shopping* was published, James Lastra brought Aumont's book to my attention. I found to my surprise, and delight, that Aumont's account of the "mobilized gaze" had many tangents with mine, particularly regarding the development of the cinematic apparatus in relation to the mobile machines of railroad and transport. A key difference, however, can be found in my emphasis on the *virtuality* of the cinema's "mobilized gaze." The second chapter of the Aumont book has since been published as "The Variable Eye, or the Mobilization of the Gaze," trans. Charles O'Brien and Sally Shafto in Dudley Andrew, ed., *The Image in Dispute: Art and Cinema in the Age of Photography* (Austin: University of Texas Press, 1997), 231–258.

16 Indeed, Raymond Williams's 1975 insight into the "cultural form" of television was defined in terms of the "new needs" created in the wake of the transformation of industrial society and a long history of capital accumulation: "An increased awareness of mobility and change, not just as abstractions but as lived experiences, led to a major redefinition, in practice and then in theory, of the function and process of social communication" (22). Williams describes television technology as a communication form that addressed these new configurations of "mobile privatization." In the following passage, Williams offers an explanation of how social mobilities and immobilities led to television's size and format in the formal competition between the cinema and television screen:

> Higher-definition systems, and colour, have still only brought *the domestic television set, as a machine, to the standard of a very inferior kind of cinema.* Yet most people have adapted to

this inferior visual medium, in an unusual kind of preference for an inferior immediate technology, because of the social complex—and especially that of the privatised home—within which broadcasting, as a system, is operative. The cinema had remained at an earlier level of social definition; it was and remains a special kind of theatre, offering specific and discrete works of one general kind. Broadcasting, by contrast, offered a whole social intake: music, news, entertainment, sport. The advantages of this general intake, within the home, much more than outweighed the technical advantages of visual transmission and reception in the cinema, confined as this was to specific and discrete works. While broadcasting was confined to sound, the powerful visual medium of cinema was an immensely popular alternative. *But when broadcasting became visual, the option for its social advantages outweighed the immediate technical deficits.*

Raymond Williams, *Television: Technology and Cultural Form* (New York: Schocken Books, 1975), 28–29 (emphasis added). Williams reacts to the two most common positions that theorize a technology and its effects—either technological determinisms that claim technologies produce/determine cultural change or accounts of technology that claim its development as a symptomatic response to social, political, or cultural change—by negotiating a more complex account of this relation, arguing that technologies are intentional and direct responses to social needs.

Vivian Sobchack takes a perceptual and phenomenological approach to the same questions in "The Scene of the Screen: Envisioning Cinematic and Electronic Presence," writing: "historical changes in our contemporary 'sense' of temporality, spatiality, and existential and embodied presence cannot be considered less than a consequence of correspondent changes in our technologies of representation" (138). Sobchack constructs a taxonomy of the "materialities" of "presence" embodied in photographic, cinematic, and "electronic" media but with a cautionary tone, warning that "electronic presence suggests that we are all in danger of becoming merely ghosts in the machine" (153). Vivian Sobchack, "The Scene of the Screen: Envisioning Cinematic and Electronic Presence" (1994), reprinted in John Thornton Caldwell, ed., *Electronic Media and Technoculture* (New Brunswick: Rutgers University Press, 2000), 137–155.

17 My use of the term "frame" is quite different from Gregory Bateson's "bracketing" or Erving Goffman's "frame analysis," where "frame" refers to the organization of experience (social and natural). Instead, I am referring to the material frame—the painterly frame as panel painting developed in the thirteenth century, the window as it developed as an opening in architectural space, and the various frames that form virtual analogs of both—the screens of movie, television, and computers. As a measure of the frame's metaphysical consequence, it will be necessary to question both the discursive and material practices of "framing" the visual field. See Erving Goffman, *Frame Analysis: An Essay on the Organization of Experience* (Cambridge: Harvard University Press, 1974). Goffman's use of "framing" is based on Gregory Bateson's "bracketing" in the essay "A Theory of Play and Phantasy," first published in *Psychiatric Research Reports 2,* American Psychiatric Association (December 1955), and reprinted in Bateson, *Steps to an Ecology of Mind* (New York: Ballantine Books, 1972).

18 In this regard, as I will argue later in this volume, Gilles Deleuze's discussion of the "time-image" and the cinematic temporality in the post–World War II films of Rossellini, DeSica, Fellini, Godard, Resnais, Antonioni, Pasolini, Rohmer, Ophuls, and others posits a diegetic temporality but does not address the temporality produced by the repeated viewing of films of widely divergent times and temporalities *over* time—in the true sense of Bergsonian *durée.* See Gilles Deleuze, *Cinema 2: The Time Image* (1985), trans. Hugh Tomlinson and Robert Galeta (Minneapolis: University of Minnesota Press, 1989). David Rodowick's careful analysis of Deleuze's work productively rescues Deleuze's project from its inherent limits as a periodizing history of filmmaking, and explores the potential for reading the "time-image" as a philosophical construct for the imaging of thought. See David Rodowick, *Gilles Deleuze's Time Machine* (Durham: Duke University Press, 1997).

19 In *Window Shopping* (1993), I argued that this form of detemporalized subjectivity was not merely a symptom of "postmodern" subjectivity, but was one of its contributing causes: "Rather than proclaiming a single distinct moment of rupture—when the modern ended and the postmodern began—I suggest a gradual and indistinct epistemological tear along the fabric of modernity, a change produced by the increasing cultural centrality of an integral feature of both cinematic and televisual apparatuses*: a mobilized 'virtual' gaze*" (1–3). At the time I wrote *Window Shopping,* the critical debates about the "postmodern" were an important subtending animus to my discussion of the temporalities of cinematic spectatorship.

20 An *episteme,* as Michel Foucault sets forth in the preface to *Order of Things,* "is the epistemological field, the *episteme* in which knowledge, envisaged apart from all criteria having reference to its rational value or to its objective forms, grounds its positivity and thereby manifests a history which is not that of its growing perfection, but rather that of its conditions of possibility." Michel Foucault, *The Order of Things* (New York: Vintage Books, 1970), xxii.

21 This project developed with a debt to a variety of methodological models that, in turn, sustain its broader claims. As German image scholar Horst Bredekamp has recently shown, the German and Austrian tradition of *Bildwissenschaft* (image study) included a range of media and never separated the "high" from the "low," while the tradition of *Kunstgeschichte* (art history) practiced more broadly in Anglo-American contexts has relied on the separation of high art media—painting and sculpture—from media that may not be part of the canon—photography, movies, television, new media. The founders of art history—Grimm, Lübke, Springer, Burkhardt, Wölfflin, and Panofsky—not only valued photographic slides and image projection as research tools, but also took "non-art" images seriously. Aby Warburg defined himself as a "picture historian" (*Bildhistoriker*) rather than as an art historian, and argued that art history should include "images in the broadest sense." The emerging disciplinary model of visual studies expands the study of images both diachronically and synchronically—across the perpendicular axes of history and media—to draw upon a deeper history of visual practices and image production as well as to construct a broader comparative analysis of a range of media and visual practices. For me, and for a number of recent scholars, it has been important to contextualize the study of film and other media in relation to a deeper history of visual representation and within a broader conception of the practices of vision and visuality. See Horst Bredekamp, "A Neglected Tradition? Art History as Bildwissenschaft," *Critical Inquiry* 29 (Spring 2003): 418–428. Two recent studies—James Elkin's monograph *Visual Studies: A Skeptical Introduction* (New York: Routledge, 2003) and Margaret Dikovitskaya, *Visual Culture: The Study of the Visual after the Cultural Turn* (Cambridge: MIT Press, 2005)—address the debates about the emerging disciplines of visual studies and visual culture studies.

22 See Mizuko Ito, Daisuke Okabe, and Misa Matsuda, eds., *Personal, Portable, Pedestrian: Mobile Phones in Japanese Life* (Cambridge: MIT Press, 2005), for a model interrogation of the *keitai,* the Japanese term for the mobile phone, meaning roughly, "something to carry with you." See also Heidi Cooley, "It's All about the *Fit:* The Hand, the Mobile Screenic Device and Tactile Vision," *Journal of Visual Culture,* special issue on Televisual Space (Summer 2004), 133–155.

23 *Webster's Third New International Dictionary Unabridged* (1993), s.v. "virtual" (emphasis added). Full citation:

> **virtual** adj. [ME, fr. ML *virtualis,* fr. L *virtus* strength, virtue + -alis -al—more at *virtue*] 1. *obs.* of, relating to, or possessing a power of acting without the agency of matter. 2. notably effective. 3. being functionally or effectively but not formally of its kind.

A bit of etymological usage is important here: Webster's 1913 edition lists: "having the power of acting or of invisible efficacy without the agency of the material or sensible part" as the first meaning of the term. The *Oxford English Dictionary* lists this meaning—"that is so in essence or effect, although not formally or actually"—as the fourth meaning after "1. Possessed of certain physical virtues or capacities" (which it cites as "now rare") and "2. Morally virtuous. 3. Capable of producing a certain effect or result." The *Online Etymology Dictionary* traces "virtual" to the fourteenth century: "influencing by physical virtues or capabilities," from medieval Latin *virtualis,* from Latin *virtus* "excellence, potency, efficacy (see *virtue*)." The meaning of "being something in essence or fact, though not in name" is first recorded 1654.

24 Gilles Deleuze writes to reverse the Platonic distrust of images—as simulacral "false claimants" to truth—and to reclaim the simulacrum from its detractors:

> *Copies* are second-hand possessors, well-grounded claimants, authorized by resemblance. *Simulacra* are like false claimants, built on dissimilitude, implying a perversion, an essential turning away. . . . The simulacra is not a degraded copy. It harbors a positive power which denies the *original and the copy, the model and the reproduction.* At least two divergent series are internalized in the simulacrum—neither can be assigned as the original, neither as the copy. . . . There is no longer any privileged point of view except that of the object common to all points of view. There is no possible hierarchy, no second, no third. . . . The same and the similar no longer have an essence except as *simulated,* that is as expressing the functioning of the simulacrum.

See Gilles Deleuze, "Plato and the Simulacrum," trans. Rosalind Krauss, in *October* 27 (1984): 48, 53, 45–56; Michael Camille, "Simulacrum," in Robert S. Nelson and Richard Shiff, eds., *Critical Terms for Art History* (Chicago: University of Chicago Press, 1996), 31–44. Jean Baudrillard also reversed the Platonic dichotomy between model and copy more radically in his argument about the "precession of simulacra" and the hyperreal: "It is no longer a question of imitation, nor even of parody. It is rather a question of substituting signs of the real for the real itself." Jean Baudrillard, "The Precession of Simulacra," in *Simulacra and Simulations,* trans. Paul Foss, Paul Patton, and Phillip Beitchman (New York: Semiotext(e), 1983), 2. Others may argue that the use of the term "virtual" serves an ideological agenda, that is, to *conceal* the connection between the material and the immaterial.

25 Johannes Kepler, *Optics: Paralipomena to Witelo and the Optical Part of Astronomy,* trans. William H. Donahue (Sante Fe, N.M.: Green Lion Press, 2000); Euclid's *Optics* is the earliest surviving work on geometrical optics. There were a number of medieval Latin translations, which became of new importance in the fifteenth century for the theory of linear perspective. See Margaret Atherton, *Berkeley's Revolution in Vision* (Ithaca, N.Y.: Cornell University Press,

1990); David C. Lindberg, *Theories of Vision from al-Kindi to Kepler* (Chicago: University of Chicago Press, 1976); Nicholas Pastore, *Selective History of Theories of Visual Perception, 1650–1950* (London: Oxford University Press, 1971); A. I. Sabra, *Theories of Light from Descartes to Newton* (Cambridge: Cambridge University Press, 1981); A. Mark Smith, "Knowing Things Inside Out: The Scientific Revolution from a Medieval Perspective," *American Historical Review* 95 (1990): 726–744.

26 For a further discussion of Descartes's reference to the camera obscura, see "Lens I: Descartes's Window," in this volume.

27 The term "virtual" in optics, according to the OED, meant "the apparent focus or image resulting from the effect of reflection or refraction upon rays of light."

28 The OED traces the first English usage of "virtual" in optical treatises as follows:

> 1704 J. HARRIS *Lex. Techn.* I, *Virtual Focus,* or *Point of Divergence* in a Concave Glass. 1728 CHAMBERS *Cycl., Point of Dispersion,* is that wherein the Rays begin to diverge; usually call'd the Virtual Focus. 1808 J. WEBSTER *Nat. Philos.* 185. They issued from the virtual focus in the axis of the lens. [Sir David Brewster uses the term in his writings about the principles of refraction:] 1831 BREWSTER *Optics* i. 11 The point A', behind the mirror is called their *virtual focus,* because they only tend to meet in that focus . . . 1831 BREWSTER *Optics* ii. 18 In convex mirrors the image is always a virtual one formed behind the mirror. 1859 PARKINSON *Optics* (1866) 130 A familiar instance of a *virtual* image is that formed by a common looking-glass of an object in front of it:—the image of an object under water is virtual.

Oxford English Dictionary, 2d ed., s.v. "virtual."

29 A variety of late-nineteenth-century detective and science fictions identify a murderer by recuperating the last image on the victim's retina. In Rudyard Kipling's 1891 short story "At the End of the Passage," in Villiers de l'Isle-Adam's philosophical tale *Claire Lenoir* (written in 1867 and revised in 1887), in an 1897 detective story by Jules Claretie entitled *L'accusateur,* and in Jules Verne's science-fiction adventure *Les Frères Kip* (1902), the optogram, or retinal photograph, reveals the last thing seen before death. For excellent discussions of the optogram in fiction, see Arthur B. Evans, "Optograms and Fiction: Photo in a Dead Man's Eye," *Science Fiction Studies* 20, no. 3 (November 1993): 341–361, and Andrea Goulet, "South Sea Daggers and the Dead Man's Eye: Foreign Invasion in Fin-de-Siècle Optogram Fiction" <http://www.mfo.ac.uk/Publications/actes1/goulet.htm>.

The optogram registers the inscription of light onto the inner chambers of the eye. Although this form of retinal evidence is not the same as a photographic record, an 1877 court case, Eborn v. Zimpleman, 47, 503, s.c. 26 Am. Rep. 315, uses the logic of the retinal image to argue for the acceptance of photography as evidence:

> Until photography was discovered, nothing in nature was exactly like any other thing, except that thing's image reflected in a polished surface, which disappeared when the object was removed. Until this discovery there was, therefore, reason in tile rule which required the production of the original paper writing as the best evidence of its appearance. Science now steps forward and relieves the difficulty, by making permanent, and materializing with minute exactness the reflected image. What reason thus remains why a discovery which destroys the foundation for a rule should not be used as proposed in the ascertainment of right? *Every object seen with the natural eye is only seen because photographed on the retina. In life the impression is transitory; it is only when death is at hand that it remains*

permanently fixed on the retina. Thus we are secure in asserting that no witness ever swore to a thing seen by him without swearing from a photograph [emphasis added]. What we call sight is but the impression made on the mind through the retina of the eye, which is nature's camera. Science has discovered that a perfect photograph of an object, reflected in the eye of one dying, remains fixed on the retina after death. (See recent experiments stated by Dr. Vogel in the May number, 1877, of the *Philadelphia Photographic Journal.*) Take the case of a murder committed on the highway; on the eye of the victim is fixed the perfect likeness of a human face. Would this court exclude the knowledge of that act from the jury, on the trial of the man against whom the glazed eye of the murdered man thus bore testimony? In other words, would a living eye-witness, whose memory only preserved the fleeting photograph of the deed, be heard, and the permanent photograph on the dead man's eye be excluded? We submit that the eye of the dead man would furnish the best evidence that the accused was there when the deed was committed, for it would bear a fact, needing no effort of memory to preserve it. It would not be parol evidence based on uncertain memory, but the handwriting of nature, preserved by nature's camera.

I am indebted to Howard Rodman for pointing out this legal case detailing the role of the photographic record in analogy to the retina of the recently dead.

30 Elizabeth Grosz, "Cyberspace, Virtuality, and the Real," in her *Architecture from the Outside: Essays on Virtual and Real Space* (Cambridge: MIT Press, 2001), 79.

31 See Henri Bergson, *Matter and Memory* (1896), trans. N. M. Paul and W. S. Palmer (New York: Zone Books, 1990), and *Creative Evolution* (1907), trans. Arthur Mitchell (1911; reprint, New York: Dover Publications, 1998).

32 "Virtual, this memory can only become actual by means of the perception which attracts it. Powerless, it borrows life and strength from the present situation in which it is materialized." Bergson, *Matter and Memory,* 127.

33 See Deleuze's 1956 essay "Bergson's Conception of Difference," trans. Melissa McMahon, in John Mullarkey, ed., *The New Bergson* (Manchester: Manchester University Press, 1999), 42–65; Gilles Deleuze, *Bergsonism* (1966), trans. Hugh Tomlinson and Barbara Habberjam (New York: Zone Books, 1988); Gilles Deleuze, *Difference and Repetition,* trans. Paul Patton (New York: Columbia University Press, 1995); Gilles Deleuze, *Cinema 1: The Movement-Image,* trans. Hugh Tomlinson (Minneapolis: University of Minnesota Press, 1986); and Gilles Deleuze, *Cinema 2: The Time Image.* Other recent writers on Gilles Deleuze—such as David Rodowick, Ronald Bogue, Paul Douglass, Michael Hardt, John Mullarkey—have provided extensive analysis and elaboration of Deleuze's relation to Bergson. See *Deleuze: A Critical Reader,* ed. Paul Patton (Oxford: Blackwell Publishers, 1996); Rodowick, *Gilles Deleuze's Time Machine;* Mullarkey, *The New Bergson;* Ronald Bogue, *Deleuze on Cinema* (New York: Routledge, 2002); Keith Ansell-Pearson, *Philosophy and the Adventure of the Virtual: Bergson and the Time of Life* (London: Routledge, 2002).

34 Deleuze, *Bergsonism,* 98. Jean-Luc Nancy describes Deleuze's philosophy as a "virtual philosophy," but takes the meaning of "virtual" to be "a universe formed entirely of images": "Gilles Deleuze's philosophy is a virtual philosophy, in the sense in which we use this word today when we speak, in a strangely indifferent way, of virtual reality or image—designating a universe entirely formed from images, and not only images as high quality illusions of the real, but rather, those that leave no place for the opposition between the real and the image." Jean-Luc Nancy, "Deleuzian Fold of Thought," in Patton, *Deleuze: A Critical Reader,* 110.

35 Deleuze, *Bergsonism,* 100.

36 Félix Guattari, *Chaosmosis: An Ethicoaesthetic Paradigm,* trans. Paul Bains and Julian Pefanis (Bloomington: Indiana University Press, 1995).

37 Pierre Lévy, *Becoming Virtual: Reality in the Digital Age,* trans. Robert Bononno (New York: Plenum Trade Press, 1998).

38 For a discussion of the use of "virtual" in Virilio's writing, see my "Virilio's Screen: The Work of Metaphor in the Age of Technological Convergence," in *Journal of Visual Culture* 3, no. 2 (August 2004): 179–190, and Lens IV in this volume.

39 Howard Rheingold's two popular books, *Virtual Reality: The Revolutionary Technology of Computer-Generated Artificial Worlds and How It Promises to Transform Society* (New York: Simon and Schuster, 1992) and *The Virtual Community: Homesteading on the Electronic Frontier* (New York: Harper Perennial Paperback, 1993), helped to assure the conflation of "virtual" with "computer-generated" and "electronic." McKenzie Wark's *Virtual Geography* (Bloomington: Indiana University Press, 1994) examined the implications of emerging computer-generated "spaces."

40 The *Oxford English Dictionary* (2d ed.) lists the computer-related uses for "virtual" with its first usage cited in 1959:

> Not physically existing as such but made by software to appear to do so from the point of view of the program or the user; spec. applied to memory that appears to be internal although most of it is external, transfer between the two being made automatically as required.
>
> 1959. *Proc. Eastern Joint Computer Conf.* xvi. 82/2 The sole function of the virtual memory is to increase machine speed. 1966 R. ADAIR et al. *IBM Cambridge Scientific Center Rep.* No. G320–2007 (*title*) A virtual machine system for the 360/40. 1966 *IBM Systems Jrnl.* V. 79 A virtual-storage computer (VSC) can decode addresses that are longer than those of its memory. The longer address is treated . . . as a virtual address that must be transformed to the actual, shorter memory address. . . . The virtual addressing of the word in external storage triggers a procedure that automatically brings the addressed word into memory. 1972 *Computer Jrnl.* XV. 199/2 Our system runs in a virtual machine, which is implemented by an interpreter. We can therefore easily add new instructions to our virtual hardware, merely by extending the interpreter. 1973 P. B. HANSEN *Operating System Princ.* i. 3 An operating system makes a virtual machine available to each user. . . . The simultaneous presence of several users makes the virtual machines much slower than the physical machine. 1981 POHL & SHAW *Nature of Computation* vi. 198 The Algolic language defines an Algolic virtual machine that may be implemented on a variety of computers. The Algolic machine could be constructed with the following software on a particular machine. 1982 G. LEE *From Hardware to Software* xxvi. 444 In a multiprogramming system, several programs are being executed "at once.". . . Thus the operating system has to make available to each user a virtual store, of which he appears to be the sole user. 1983 *80 Microcomputing* Feb. 232/2 Virtual-memory systems have been prevalent in main-frames and large minicomputers for at least a decade. 1985 *Which Computer?* Apr. 54/1 No doubt this is a side effect of using the disc as a virtual memory.

41 Brian Massumi, "Line Parable for the Virtual (On the Superiority of the Analog)," in John Beckmann, ed., *The Virtual Dimension* (Princeton: Princeton Architectural Press, 1998), 309.

Massumi's definition of the virtual may contradict my own reliance on the term for describing an image. To Massumi, the virtual refuses its own imaging: "It is virtual because you cannot effectively see it or exhaustively diagram it. It is an image because you can, for all of that, figure it, more or less vaguely, in the imagination. Imagination is the mode of thought most precisely suited to the vagueness of the virtual" (306). See also Brian Massumi, *Parables for the Virtual: Movement, Affect, Sensation* (Durham: Duke University Press, 2002).

42 See, for example, Mark Poster, "Theorizing the Virtual," in *What's the Matter with the Internet* (Minneapolis: University of Minnesota Press, 2001). Poster's account provides a useful concordance to Baudrillard's use of the term "virtual" and its interchangeability with his use of the term "simulation," but Poster assumes that the virtual is inherently an experience that is electronically mediated. In this regard, Poster uses the term "virtual" for all electronically mediated experiences. Within this, he does not distinguish between text-based (MUDs and MOOs) and image-based (goggles and gloves) virtual reality.

43 In his study *Virtual Art: From Illusion to Immersion,* Oliver Grau points out that while Baudrillard's discussion of "mimesis without foundation" is commonly taken to refer to electronic and postelectronic media, it forms a description applicable to older image-producing media. See Oliver Grau, *Virtual Art: From Illusion to Immersion,* trans. Gloria Custance (Cambridge: MIT Press, 2003), 11 n., 19–20 n. 16.

44 N. Katherine Hayles, *How We Became Posthuman: Virtual Bodies in Cybernetics, Literature, and Informatics* (Chicago: University of Chicago Press, 1999), 13–14. See also N. Katherine Hayles, "The Condition of Virtuality" in Peter Lunenfeld, ed., *The Digital Dialectic* (Cambridge: MIT Press, 1999), 68–94.

45 Hayles begins with Alan Turing's classic 1950 test to distinguish human from computational machine. For Hayles, an "erasure of embodiment" occurs as the material body of the computer user becomes the "represented body" in a teletyped text. While such turning of bodies into information may perform a written or textual masquerade, this masquerade is not much different from the kind performed by Balzac or Barthes in the telling of *Sarrasine,* a form of textual virtuality that preceded post–World War II cybernetics. And such a textual dematerialization of the body is a very different process from the conversion of the flesh of a material body into a dematerialized virtual image or screen representation, where representational indexicality is more direct.

46 Grau, *Virtual Art,* p. 13. See also Oliver Grau, "Kunst als Inspiration medialer Evolution. Intermediale Etappen des Virtuellen im 20. Jahrhundert," in the e-zine *mtg* [Medien/Theorie/Geschichte] 4.0 (1999), <http://waste.informatik.hu.berlin.de/mtg/mtg4/grau.html>.

47 In this way, for example, the framed proscenium of the diorama with its moving platform of spectators became a fixed-frame system for the spectator amid the expansive peripheries of the panorama. See my discussion of the diorama and panorama in *Window Shopping,* 20–29.

48 The concept of virtuality links television, media art, and computer culture in Margaret Morse, *Virtualities: Television, Media Art, and Cyberculture* (Bloomington: Indiana University Press, 1998). For a deeply historical root to the discourse of "cyberspace," see Margaret Wertheim, "The Medieval Return of Cyberspace," in John Beckmann, ed., *Virtual Dimension,* 46–61; and her book *The Pearly Gates of Cyberspace* (New York: Doubleday, 1999).

49 "Metaphor" is from the Greek *metapherein,* to transfer. See Michel de Certeau, "Spatial Practices," from *The Practice of Everyday Life* (1974), trans. Steven Randall (Berkeley: University of California Press, 1988), 91–130.

50 *Ekphrasis* defines the bidirectional relation of text to image and image to text by taking the side of language used to represent or evoke images. Horace said that "painting is mute poetry and poetry a speaking picture." See W. J. T. Mitchell, *Iconology: Image, Text, Ideology* (Chicago: University of Chicago Press, 1986); W. J. T. Mitchell, *Picture Theory: Essays on Verbal and Visual Representation* (Chicago: University of Chicago Press, 1994); Murray Krieger, *Ekphrasis: The Illusion of the Natural Sign* (Baltimore: Johns Hopkins University Press, 1992); and Wendy Steiner, *The Colors of Rhetoric: Problems in the Relation between Modern Literature and Painting* (Chicago: University of Chicago Press, 1982).

51 It is not my project to trace the painterly use of the window, or to argue the effect of changes in technology on strategies of painterly representation. For studies of the window motif in painting, see Carla Gottlieb, *The Window in Art: From the Window of God to the Vanity of Man* (New York: Abaris Books, 1981); Lorenz Eitner, "The Open Window and the Storm-Tossed Boat: An Essay in the Iconography of Romanticism," *Art Bulletin* 37 (1955): 281–290; Kyra Stromberg, "The Window in the Picture—The Picture in the Window," *Daidalos* 13 (1984): 54–63; and Bruno Reichlin, "The Pros and Cons of Horizontal Windows: The Perret-Le Corbusier Controversy," *Daidalos* 13 (1984): 65–78. For related discussions of the literary figure of the window, see Robert Greer Cohn, "Mallarmé's Windows," *Yale French Studies*, no. 54 (1977): 23–31; Ellen Eve Frank, *Literary Architecture: Essays toward a Tradition: Walter Pater, Gerard Manley Hopkins, Marcel Proust, Henry James* (Berkeley: University of California Press, 1983); Heinz Brüggemann, *Das andere Fenster: Einblicke in Häuser und Menschen* (Frankfurt am Main: Fisher Taschenbuch Verlag, 1989).

52 "Hence one must know—this is a fundamental presupposition, presupposing what is fundamental—how to determine the intrinsic—what is framed—and know what one is excluding as frame *and* outside-the-frame. We are thus *already* at the unlocatable center of the problem. And when Kant replies to our question: 'What is a frame?' by saying: it's a *parergon*, a hybrid of outside and inside, but a hybrid which is not a mixture or half-measure, *an outside which is called to the inside of the inside in order to constitute it as an inside*." Jacques Derrida, *Truth in Painting* (1978), trans. Geoff Bennington and Ian McLeod (Chicago: University of Chicago Press, 1987), 63 (emphasis added).

53 Ibid., 45.

54 Ibid., 60–61; emphasis added.

55 In his discussion of "The Psychology of Styles," Ernst Gombrich writes: "We may ask whether there is a link between a painting and its frame." His formulation of the "organic unity" between these separate elements resembles Derrida's *parergon:* "or more specifically," Gombrich writes, "between all the elements of a Gothic altar, the shrine with its sculptures, the wings with their reliefs and painted panels and the architectural detail of its fretwork setting." The figure that Gombrich attaches to illustrate this question—the high altar of the Klosterkirche in Blaubeuren, Germany (1493–1494)—displays an altar with panel paintings, placed below a Gothic cove of three arched leaded-glass windows. An examination of the stylistic relation of the frame to its painting to nearby window frames cannot be addressed in the scope of this volume, but would be an important study to undertake. See Ernst Gombrich, "The Psychology of Styles," chapter 8 of *The Sense of Order* (1979), reprinted in *The Essential Gombrich: Selected Writings on Art and Culture*, ed. Richard Woodfield (London: Phaidon Press, 1996), 264.

56 Derrida, *Truth in Painting*, 40, 41.

57 In his reading of Derrida's reliance on architectural metaphor, Mark Wigley provides a detailed account of the complex codependency between philosophy and architecture. See Mark Wigley, *Architecture of Deconstruction: Derrida's Haunt* (Cambridge: MIT Press, 1996).

58 This plate is found on page 72 of Derrida, *Truth in Painting,* and on page 84 of the French text, Jacques Derrida, *La vérité en peinture* (Paris: Flammarion, 1978).

59 See Derrida, *Truth in Painting:* "It begins by enclosing the theory of the aesthetic in a theory of the beautiful, the latter in a theory of taste and the theory of taste in a theory of judgement" (69). And: "If one applies to it the rule defined in the 'Clarification by Examples,' and if it becomes in its turn an example of what it allows us to consider as an example [frame described in the frame], then one can act as though the content of the analytic of judgement were a work of art, a picture whose frame, imported from the other *Critique,* would by virtue of its formal beauty play the role of *parergon*" (71–73).

60 My definition of this ekphrastic reversal refers to images that, like the Derrida illustration from *The Truth in Painting,* render a philosophical or textual concept in visual terms. A description of a visual object rendered in words (ekphrasis) is rendered in analogy to a visual object (reverse ekphrasis). This is somewhat different from the argument that media philosopher Mark Taylor attempts to perform in his work. Taylor's graphic polemic implores the need to philosophize with images not written concepts. See Mark Taylor, *Imagologies: Media Philosophy* (New York: Routledge, 1994). Sergei Eisenstein maintained that a series of images could articulate a philosophical point; his construct of "dialectical" montage demonstrates that he thought images could follow in sequence like the dialectical flow of ideas. See Sergei Eisenstein, "A Dialectic Approach to Film Form," in *Film Form: Essays in Film Theory,* trans. Jay Leyda (New York: Harcourt Brace, 1949).

61 In a different context, Jay David Bolter describes the reversal of priority of word and image: "Today, as the visual and the sensual are emerging out of verbal communication, images are given the task . . . of explaining words, rather than the reverse." See Jay David Bolter, "Ekphrasis, Virtual Reality and the Future of Writing," in Geoffrey Nunberg, ed., *The Future of the Book* (Berkeley: University of California Press, 1996), 264. In this regard, the agonistic debate over the future of literacy and the book often turns to a indictment of moving-image media.

62 For one example of the priority of metaphoric language for philosophy, see Hans Blumenberg, "Light as Metaphor for Truth," in *Modernity and the Hegemony of Vision* (Berkeley: University of California Press, 1993); for a discussion of metaphor in digital discourse, see Ken Hillis, "Space, Language, Metaphor," in *Digital Sensations: Space, Identity and Embodiment in Digital Culture* (Minneapolis: University of Minnesota Press, 1999).

63 See for example Christian Metz, *The Imaginary Signifier: Psychoanalysis and the Cinema,* trans. Celia Britton et al. (Bloomington: Indiana University Press, 1982).

64 Antonio di Tucci Manetti, *The Life of Brunelleschi* (1475), ed. Howard Saalman, trans. Catherine Enggass (University Park: Pennsylvania State University Press, 1970), 4.

65 Damisch notes: "to paint with the aid of a mirror (as in executing a self-portrait), or to bring in a mirror *a posteriori,* the better to judge a painting or, in the present instance, to submit it to a kind of *autopsy*—quite literally; these are two very different things" (*The Origin of Perspective,* 138). Damisch also draws a distinction between Brunelleschi's *tavoletta* device and the camera obscura and telescope, both optical instruments that were directed toward an exterior, whereas the *tavoletta* was "closed in on itself" (128).

66 In the history of photography, the mirror and the window have also been marked discursively, paired/compared as metaphors for styles of photographic practice. See John Szarkowski, *Mirrors and Windows: American Photography since 1960* (New York: Museum of Modern Art, 1980). More recently, these two metaphors have been remediated to describe styles of digital practice. See Jay David Bolter and Diane Gromala, *Windows and Mirrors: Interaction Design, Digital Art, and the Myth of Transparency* (Cambridge: MIT Press, 2003).

67 Vivian Sobchack, *The Address of the Eye: A Phenomenology of the Film Experience* (Princeton: Princeton University Press, 1992), 14–17.

68 The binary opposition of formalist/"formative" and realist film theory structures André Bazin's 1951–52 account of "The Evolution of the Language of the Cinema." Bazin separates "two broad and opposing tendencies" of "directors with faith in the image" versus "directors with faith in reality." See Andre Bazin, "The Evolution of the Language of the Cinema," in *What Is Cinema?* vol. 1, trans. Hugh Gray (Berkeley: University of California Press, 1967). This opposition also became the organizing principle for Dudley Andrew's *The Major Film Theories: An Introduction* (New York: Oxford University Press, 1984). Andrew divides his book by separating formative, realist, and contemporary traditions. The "formative" tradition (film's capacity to transform reality) includes Münsterberg, Arnheim, Eisenstein, and Balazs, while the "realist" tradition (film's capacity to mirror reality) includes Kracauer (the postwar writings) and Bazin. This schematic historiography has limitations once you add film theorists like Dziga Vertov (who is both formative and realist) and the Frankfurt school writing of Benjamin and Kracauer (whose early work does not conform to the realist tradition).

69 Sobchack, *The Address of the Eye*, 15.

70 Ibid.; emphasis added.

71 Ibid., 131.

72 Ibid., 134.

73 And, as we will see, virtuality complicates the body's relation to its senses.

74 Robert D. Romanyshyn, *Technology as Symptom and Dream* (New York: Routledge, 1989), 42. While Romanyshyn's use of the window as a figure to illustrate the separation between perceiver and world is in accordance with my discussion here, Romanyshyn expands his analysis to another metaphoric exponent, which is not: "The vanishing point is the launchpad of the modern world . . . we have all become astronauts" (33–34). See also Robert D. Romanyshyn, "The Despotic Eye and Its Shadow: Media Image in the Age of Literacy," in David Michael Levin, ed., *Modernity and the Hegemony of Vision* (Berkeley: University of California Press, 1993), 339–360.

75 Ron Burnett questions Romanyshyn's description of "media spectacles," which function to separate the spectator and which "freeze viewers into positions that they cannot control or change." Burnett argues that the window trope could be used for a different model of vision: "It will be crucial to subjectify the window, to give it a personality, to recognize the productive consequences of our paradigmatic manipulation of its form and shape and content." See Ron Burnett, *Cultures of Vision: Images, Media and the Imaginary* (Bloomington: Indiana University Press, 1995), 4–8.

76 Stanley Cavell, *The World Viewed: Reflections on the Ontology of the Cinema* (New York: Viking Press, 1971), 24.

77 Sigmund Freud, "Screen Memories" (1899), in *The Standard Edition of the Complete Psychological Work of Sigmund Freud,* ed. and trans. J. Strachey (London: Hogarth Press, 1953–

1974), 3:301–322. While the Strachey and Brill translations of many of Freud's German terms have been questioned, I found only a few English language references to the original German title "Über Deckerinnerungen," and have not located any discussions of the translation of this phrase as "screen memories."

78 See Harvey Roy Greenberg, *Screen Memories: Hollywood Cinema on the Psychoanalytic Couch* (New York: Columbia University Press, 1993).

79 Although Lacan's famed account of subject formation as a scenario of vision, found in his 1949 mirror-phase essay ("The Mirror Stage as Formative of the Function of the *I* as Revealed in Psychoanalytic Experience"), is commonly thought of as his key contribution to theories of visuality, the metaphor of the mirror is not how Lacan formulates his concept of "the gaze." Rather, it is in the sequence of seminars in 1964 entitled "Of the Gaze as *Objet Petit a*" that Lacan defines the gaze. See Jacques Lacan, Seminar XI, "Of the Gaze as *Objet Petit a*," in *The Four Fundamental Concepts of Psycho-Analysis,* trans. Alan Sheridan (New York: W. W. Norton, 1977), 67–119. Originally published as *Les quatre concepts fondamentaux de la psychanalyse,* vol. 11 of *Le séminaire de Jacques Lacan* (1964; reprint, Paris: Editions du Seuil, 1973), 79–135.

There are two English words that correspond to the French *le regard*—"the look" and "the gaze." While these terms are largely interchangeable, they have acquired different connotations. Sartre's use of *le regard* in *Being and Nothingness* has been translated (by Hazel E. Barnes) as "the look," while Lacan's use has been translated (by Alan Sheridan) as "the gaze." The English language appropriation by British (and later American) film theorists slips without an organizing rigor between "the gaze" and "the look." Lacan's "Of the Gaze as *Objet Petit a*" begs to be read with the Sartre text, which Lacan calls "one of its most brilliant passages" (84). In their separate accounts of *le regard,* both Sartre and Lacan make the distinction between the eye and the look; both claim that the self is constituted by the gaze of the Other; both claim that *le regard* is manifest through its effects, not its source. But Sartre's schema differs in that he maintains that the look has a binary of power, either in the position of mastery (the man at the keyhole) or in the position of a slave (once he is "surprised" by the look of the Other); Lacan concretizes the gaze through the metaphor of the camera and maintains that it is always predicated on lack or castration. See Jean Paul Sartre, "The Look," trans. Hazel E. Barnes, in *Being and Nothingness: An Essay on Phenomenological Ontology* (London: Metheun, 1957), 340–400; Jacques Lacan, "Of the Gaze as *Objet Petit a*"; and Norman Bryson, "The Gaze and the Glance," in *Vision and Painting: The Logic of the Gaze* (New Haven: Yale University Press, 1983), 87–131.

80 These diagrams are widely polysemic, open to a variety of readings. I mention them here to establish the metaphoric use of the term "screen." The first diagram (Lacan, "Of the Gaze as *Objet Petit a*," 91) mimics the commonly ascribed geometry of perspective, a triangular diagram of orthogonals radiating from the vertex of the viewer/painter's "geometral point."

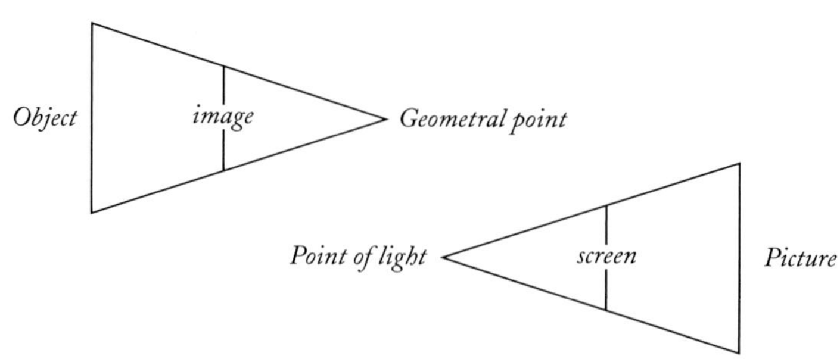

The "image" in the first diagram corresponds to the picture plane that mediates between the geometral apex of the triangle and its base, which corresponds to the objects perceived in the scopic field of the viewer. In the second diagram, the vertex corresponds to the point of light. The third diagram, a double dihedron that superimposes the schemas of the first two, suggests the reciprocity of vision, the imbrication of seeing while being seen.

The cover of the French edition of *Les quatre concepts* has a reproduction of Holbein's *The Ambassadors* (1533), a painting that Lacan uses to illustrate *anamorphosis,* a concept which supplies an optical metaphor for his critique of the perspectival fixity of the subject: "not that punctiform being located at the geometral point from which perspective is grasped" ("Gaze as *Objet Petit a,*" 96).

81 Kaja Silverman, *The Threshold of the Visible World* (New York: Routledge, 1996), 125–227. Silverman devotes several pages to an explication of the geometric diagrams from Lacan's *Four Fundamental Concepts* in order to expand upon this notion of the screen in the field of vision. In an earlier book, *Male Subjectivity at the Margins* (1992), Silverman relied upon these Lacanian diagrams to define the screen as a metaphor for a "culturally generated image or repertoire of images through which subjects are constituted" (150). In *The Threshold of the Visible World,* she adjusts this definition a bit but keeps it within the same metaphoric register as "the conduit through which social and historical variability is introduced" (135). See also Kaja Silverman, *Male Subjectivity at the Margins* (New York: Routledge, 1992).

82 Silverman, *The Threshold of the Visible World,* 134. Silverman is engaged in a polemic about the historicity of vision, using Lacan's "transhistorical account" to "offer an invaluable corrective to the extreme historical relativism of *Techniques of the Observer.*" Her corrective intends to sort out "what is and what is not historically variable" while still relying on a Lacanian account of vision as "ahistorical," i.e., unaffected by changing paradigms of visuality, historically specific visual technologies, or habits of vision. "Thus," she writes, "Lacan provides a transhistorical account not only of the gaze but also of the entire field of vision, which for him includes the look and the screen" (133). The Lacanian metaphor of screen (*écran*) as a metaphor for intersubjective mediation also suggests another psychoanalytic metaphor, one not addressed by Lacan or Silverman—projection.

83 Silverman cites Jonathan Crary's definition of the camera obscura as "a discursive formation (that) intersects with material practices" as a methodological model, yet her discussion of the screen relies on the Lacanian metaphor within the psychic register and does not describe its use in material practice. Kaja Silverman, *The Threshold of the Visible World,* 136; quoting Jonathan Crary, *Techniques of the Observer* (Cambridge: MIT Press, 1990), 30–31.

84 Friedrich Kittler, "Perspective and the Book," *Grey Room* 05 (Fall 2001): 38–53. Kittler's argument hinges upon several key conflations. Relying on the account of the biographer Vasari a century after Alberti in 1570, Kittler assumes that Alberti used a camera obscura as an instrument to devise his mathematical formulas for linear perspective. Alberti's knowledge of the camera obscura is a matter of scholarly speculation. Mention of the principles of pinhole projection was found in the writings of the Arabic scholar Alhazen in the tenth century and in John Pecham's perspective treatise of 1279—both texts to which Alberti may have had access—but the device is not mentioned in Alberti's 1435 treatise on perspective, *De pictura.* Hence, there is a bit of sleight of hand to equate the optical device of the camera obscura with Alberti's geometrical treatise on perspective. Kittler also conflates the device of the *velo* and its grid with camera obscura—two very different instruments and methods for the tracing of perspectival depth—and he conflates the technologies of computer-writing with computer-reading. (Kittler contests the assumption put forth by media theorists Marshall McLuhan and Vilem Flusser that writing is linear and one-dimensional while the image is two-dimensional. Instead, he argues, writing was never simply linear.) Theories of perspective had been passed through generations by the circulation of manuscripts and university teaching. Paradoxically, printed editions of works of Euclid, Alhazen, and Pecham produced a revival of interest in perspective.

85 Kittler, "Perspective and the Book," 53. Such a leap assumes a phylogenic relation between the analog image of the photographic camera and the digital icons and images of a computer screen.

86 "(And today the book is already, as the present mode of scholarly production demonstrates, an outdated mediation between two different filing systems. For everything that matters is to be found in the card box of the researcher who wrote it, and the scholar studying it assimilates it into his own card index.)" Walter Benjamin, "One-Way Street," in *Reflections: Essays, Aphorism, Autobiographical Writings,* ed. Peter Demetz, trans. Edmund Jephcott (New York: Harcourt Brace Jovanovich, 1978), 78–79.

87 Ibid., 77–78; emphasis added.

88 Benjamin's coy list of admonitions for writers, the instructive "Principles of the Weighty Tome, or How to Write Fat Books," did not seem to help him in his own struggle with book writing (Benjamin, "One-Way Street," 78–79). The handwritten manuscript pages to his unfinished "Arcades Project" were left unindexed as alphabetized "convolutes," a palimpsest of quotations and commentary with only a blueprint—in the form of several "drafts" or "exposés"—of the book's massive architecture. Despite his intention to find a method for history writing commensurate with the optical metaphors of "telescoping [of] the past through the present" [N7a3] and "literary montage," his writerly method was *bricolage,* collecting a hodge-podge of things and themes—boredom, mirrors, conspiracies, exhibitions, advertising, the doll, the automaton, prostitution, a theory of progress. As he noted, "Method of this project: literary montage. I needn't say anything. Merely show" [N1a8]. Walter Benjamin, "N [On the Theory of Knowledge: Theory of Progress]," in *The Arcades Project,* trans. Howard Eiland and Kevin McLaughlin (Cambridge: Harvard University Press, 1999), 460, 471. See my extended discussion of the dialectical images (*dialektische Bilder*) and montage principle in *Passagenwerk* in *Window Shopping,* 47–53.

89 At stake here is an underlying conviction that computer technology has profoundly changed the relation of writer to text. The subjective consequences—for both writers and readers—of computer-assisted writing technologies remain a topic of much debate. Christina Haas, for example, has questioned the effects of computer technology on the "embodied process" of writing: "How is it that material tools can shape mental processes? And what is the relationship of material tools to the culture in which they are embedded?" Christina Haas, *Writing Technology: Studies on the Materiality of Literacy* (Mahwah, N.J.: Lawrence Erlbaum Associates, 1995), 224. Haas outlines two inherent dangers—a Scylla and Charybdis—to answering these questions. On one hand, a "transparency myth" assumes that writing "is not changed in any substantive way by the transparent medium through which it passes" and erases the role of technology in the agency of writing; on the other hand, "postmodern theories of technology" assume that technology is overdeterminant. For these writers, "postmodernism's insistent move away from any kind of agency means technology must be posited as self-determining, if not all-powerful. . . . Theory and technology exist in a kind of circular relationship, which theory used to somehow legitimate modern technology, which itself is seen as underscoring the aptness of contemporary theory" (44). Here, I would agree with Haas that technologies have a materiality and that we need "to understand how material technologies both constrain and enable acts of mind, on the one hand, and how cultures produce, adapt and are affected by material technologies, on the other hand" (27).

90 In the 1970s and 1980s, the de-historicizing impulse of film theory may have led to some arterial narrowing at the heart of the discipline. In the last decade, historical writing on cinematic "origins" has reached most deeply into history and most broadly in comparison to other visual practices. See Vanessa Schwarz, *Spectacular Realities: Early Mass Culture in Fin-de-Siècle Paris* (Berkeley: University of California Press, 1998), and Vanessa Schwarz and Leo Charney, *Cinema and the Invention of Modern Life* (Berkeley: University of California Press, 1995). Laurent Mannoni's "multi-century trajectory"of optical devices and projected images, *The Great Art of Light and Shadow,* proclaims: "Even the most serious author, Jacques Deslandes, absolutely refused to travel back further than the nineteenth century." Laurent Mannoni, *The Great Art of Light and Shadow: Archeology of Cinema,* trans. Richard Crangle (Exeter: University of Exeter Press, 2000), xvi.

91 Alberti, *On Painting and On Sculpture,* 55.

CHAPTER 1: THE WINDOW

1 The bibliography on perspective is voluminous, testimony to the wide debate about its emergence, discovery, and theorization. See Cecil Grayson, introduction to Leon Battista Alberti, *On Painting and On Scuplture: The Latin Texts of De pictura and De statua,* trans. Cecil Grayson (London: Phaidon, 1972); Erwin Panofsky, *Perspective as Symbolic Form* (1924–1925), trans. Christopher S. Wood (New York: Zone Books, 1991); William M. Ivins, *Art and Geometry: A Study in Space Intuition* (New York: Dover, 1946); M. H. Pirenne, *Optics, Painting and Photography* (Cambridge: Cambridge University Press, 1970); Samuel Y. Edgerton, *The Renaissance Rediscovery of Linear Perspective* (New York: Basic Books, 1975); Svetlana Alpers, *The Art of Describing: Dutch Art in the Seventeenth Century* (Chicago: University of Chicago Press, 1983); Michael Kubovy, *The Psychology of Perspective and Renaissance Art* (Cambridge: Cambridge University Press, 1986); Martin Jay, "Scopic Regimes of Modernity," in Hal Foster, ed., *Vision and Visuality* (Seattle: Bay Press, 1988), 3–23; Martin Kemp, *The Science of Art: Optical Themes in Western Art from Brunelleschi to Seurat* (New Haven: Yale University Press, 1990); James Elkins, *The Poetics of Perspective* (Ithaca: Cornell University Press, 1994); Hubert Damisch, *The Origin of Perspective,* trans. John Goodman (Cambridge: MIT Press, 1994); Alberto Pérez-Gómez and Louise Pelletier, *Architectural Representation and the Perspective Hinge* (Cambridge: MIT Press, 1997); and Karsten Harries, *Infinity and Perspective* (Cambridge: MIT Press, 2001).

2 Elkins, *The Poetics of Perspective.* Elkins's dense account of the metaphorization of perspective charts the separate discursive treatments of perspective as "positivist" and "poststructuralist," pitting the positivist writing of Kemp, Edgerton, and others against the philosophical discourse of Damisch and Derrida. Attuned to what he describes as the "battalion of opposites," Elkins lists the oppositional terms that writers have used to describe the pictured surface and the picturing mind: objective/subjective; distance/nearness; unity/infinity, present/past; realism/idealism; individual/collective; viewer/viewed; master/slave; active/passive; interiority/exteriority; literal/figurative; knowledge/illusion; Aristotle/Pythagoras.

3 A lengthy note on the extensive scholarship on Alberti and the invention/discovery/rediscovery of the techniques of perspective is required here. Alberti (1404–1472) was the son of an exiled Florentine merchant banker; he received a doctorate in canon and civil law from the University of Bologna in 1428. In 1428–1430 he wrote *On the Advantages and Disadvantages of Letters and Scholarship,* a critique of the social position of the classical scholar, arguing that the scholar is unequipped for living. In 1434, the exile of Alberti's family was lifted and Alberti returned to Florence, where he became familiar with the work of Brunelleschi, Donatello, Masaccio, and Ghiberti. He wrote *De pictura* in 1435 in Latin, and then in 1436 he composed an Italian (Tuscan) version that he dedicated to the Florentine architect Filippo Brunelleschi (1377–1446). *De pictura* applied the optical laws of vision Alberti had learned as a classical scholar to the techniques of painterly representation. See Anthony Grafton, *Leon Battista Alberti: Master Builder of the Italian Renaissance* (New York: Hill and Wang, 2000).

Many scholars credit Brunelleschi's experiments in perspective in 1425—his mirror painting of the Florence Baptistry—for initiating the techniques of linear perspective in painting, while others credit Alberti's treatise as the first theoretical elaboration of these techniques. For example, Samuel Edgerton calls Brunelleschi "the midwife, if not the father, of linear perspective in the Western World" (*Renaissance Rediscovery,* 4), and Martin Kemp asserts, "Linear perspective was invented by Filippo Brunelleschi" (*The Science of Art,* 9), while Cecil Grayson declares Alberti to be "the inventor of the theory of fixed-point perspective in painting" (introduction to Alberti, *On Painting,* 13). In a letter to Brunelleschi that precedes the 1436 version, Alberti proclaims his admiration for the artistry of the Florentines: "But after I came back here to this most beautiful of cities from the long exile in which we Albertis have grown old, I recognized in many, but above all in you, Filippo, and in our great friend the sculptor Donatello and in the others, Nencio, Luca and Masaccio, a genius for every laudable enterprise in no way inferior to any of the ancients who gained fame in these arts" (*On Painting,* 33). Alberti admired Brunelleschi's vaulted dome for the cathedral of Santa Maria del Fiore: "such an enormous construction towering above the skies, vast enough to cover the entire Tuscan population with its shadow, and done without the aid of beams or elaborate wooden supports" (*On Painting,* 33). In this regard, scholars have speculated that Alberti must have also known about Brunelleschi's perspective experiments, and that he was familiar with the paintings of Masaccio and the sculptures and reliefs of Donatello and Ghiberti before he wrote his treatise with mathematical formulas for fixed-point perspective. In spite of Brunelleschi's practical precedents, Alberti codified his procedures in a treatise that was, as Kemp asserts, "the first written account of one-point perspective." Kemp, *The Science of Art,* 21.

The writings of Cecil Grayson, Martin Kemp, Samuel Edgerton, Erwin Panofsky, Hubert Damisch, and James Elkins provide detailed scholarship on Alberti and the defining origins of perspective. While many of these scholars take issue with each other, many also take issue with the "platitudinous discourse" (Damisch, *The Origin of Perspective,* xiv) or the frequent reductive caricatures of "Renaissance perspective."

4 Alberti, *On Painting,* I.1, p. 37; emphasis added.

5 *De pictura* was a pre-Gutenberg manuscript. Its 1435 text was a handwritten and hand-copied manuscript and was not printed until 1540. A century later, in treatises like Dürer's

Underweysung der Messung (1525), the instructions for perspectival technique could be illustrated and easily reproduced by supplying woodcut illustrations as engravings reproduced with the text.

Alberti scholar and architectural historian Mario Carpo eloquently assesses the fifteenth-century transition from script to print, a technological transformation that largely occurred in Alberti's lifetime. As Carpo details, Alberti was keenly aware of the technologies of reproducibility available to him, and suggests: "there is a vast amount of evidence that Alberti was vividly aware of the conditions of reproducibility specific to all the different formats and media he used—languages, alphabets, ciphers, numeric notations, manuscripts, drawings, and, some years later, also print, and even three-dimensional objects." Before the advent of print, manually copied drawings were not the most assured manner of transmitting knowledge or information. Carpo describes Alberti's "digital map" of Rome (dated between 1448 and 1459), which was not drawn as an image but given as a code. Rather than include a drawing, Alberti published a list of numbers or coordinates, and explained how to use these coordinates to draw a map. As in his formula for perspectival drawing, Alberti supplied the formula, not the image. In this way, Carpo suggests Alberti "invented" the digital image, transformed ekphrasis to algorithm. See his discussion in Mario Carpo, *Architecture in the Age of Printing,* trans. Sarah Benson (Cambridge: MIT Press, 2001), 122–124, and in his "Alberti's Vision and a Plan of Rome: A New Edition and Three New Translations of Alberti's *Descriptio urbis Romæ,*" in *Albertiana* 6 (2003). See also *Leon Battista Alberti, Descriptio urbis Romae,* ed. and trans. Martine Furno and Mario Carpo (Geneva: Droz, 2000), 65–97.

Alberti biographer Anthony Grafton finds it odd that Alberti did not include diagrams for *De pictura,* given that he did provide illustrations for his work on sculpture, *De statua.* See Grafton, *Leon Battista Alberti,* 100.

6 *De re aedificatoria,* or *On the Art of Building in Ten Books*—reviving/rewriting Vitruvius's ancient text *De architectura*—was begun in 1443, finished in 1452.

7 Alberti, *On Painting* I.19, p. 55; emphasis added.

8 Alberti writes, "It is usually said that vision operates by means of a triangle, whose base is the quantity seen, and whose sides are those same rays which extend from the extreme points of that quantity" (*On Painting* I.6, p. 41). Alberti's training as a scholar of classics familiarized him with the ancient science of optics in Euclid, Pliny, and Alhazen. His historical knowledge of the classical past allowed him to link antiquity with contemporary trends and practices. Kemp, Edgerton and others detail Alberti's knowledge of earlier optic theorists: Euclid's *Optica* (300 B.C.), the Islamic scholar Alhazen (1000 A.D.), and John Pecham's *Perspectiva communis* (1279).

9 Alberti acknowledges but avoids an ancient debate about the physiology of vision—whether vision is based on extromission (a visual force emitted from the eyes) or intromission (picture-like effluxes that are emitted from objects and embed in the surface of the eye): "Indeed among the ancients there was considerable dispute as to whether these rays emerge from the surface or from the eye. This truly difficult question, which is quite without value for our purposes, may here be set aside" (*On Painting* I.5, p. 41). And he similarly evades whether "sight rests at the juncture of the inner nerve of the eye, or whether images are created on the surface of the eye, as it were in an animate mirror. I do not think it necessary to speak here of all the functions of the eye in relation to vision" (*On Painting* I.6, p. 41). Grayson sums up the Albertian formulation as "an empirical, geometrical explanation of monocular vision as a practical basis for pictorial representation. Whilst it is, therefore possible to indicate the sources for this in Euclidean optics and geometry and in the late medieval version of, and commentaries on, Arabic work on optics, this stripping down of those theories to a simple working system, and their transfer from the realm of physiology, philosophy and theology to that of painting is really what constitutes Alberti's originality. His is the first deliberate and rational application of a theory of vision to the art and technique of painting." Grayson, introduction to Alberti, *On Painting,* 12–13.

10 Edgerton, *Renaissance Rediscovery,* 32. Alberti's mathematical formulas were technical aids, but also served to demystify the illusion of perspective by supplying its laws.

11 Alberti, *On Painting* I.12, p. 48.

12 Here the substitution of the Italian term "prospettiva" for the technique of *perspectiva* emphasizes the forward-facing aspect of perspective.

13 Walter Benjamin, "One-Way Street," in *Reflections: Essays, Aphorism, Autobiographical Writings,* ed. Peter Demetz, trans. Edmund Jephcott (New York: Harcourt Brace Jovanovich, 1978), 77–78.

14 Jacques Aumont describes the "noteworthy metonymy" by which the geometric point of perspective becomes coextensive with the eye of the painter as a "point of view." See Jacques Aumont, "The Point of View," trans. Arthur Denner, *Quarterly Review of Film and Video* 11 (1989): 1–22. Translated from "Le point de vue," *Communications* 38 (1983).

15 "In the Founding Perception, the gaze of the painter arrests the flux of phenomena, contemplates the visual field from a vantage-point outside the mobility of duration, in an eternal moment of disclosed presence; while in the moment of viewing, the viewing subject unites his gaze with the Founding Perception, in a perfect recreation of that first epiphany." Norman Bryson, *Vision and Painting: The Logic of the Gaze* (New Haven: Yale University Press, 1983), 94.

Bryson describes the "dyadic reversibility" of the two visual pyramids formed by these "gazes" with a logic that follows Lacan's discussion of the "gaze" in Jacques Lacan, "Of the Gaze as *Objet Petit a,*" in *The Four Fundamental Concepts of Psycho-Analysis,* trans. Alan Sheridan (New York: W. W. Norton, 1981), 106. Bryson writes:

> The centric ray constitutes a return of the gaze upon itself: the cone of lines emanating from the Albertian eye is redoubled in its opposite, a cone radiating towards it out of that point from which all the architectonic lines radiate. . . . At the picture plane, the two cones intersect; which is to say that the single vanishing point marks the installation within the painting of a principle of radical alterity, since its gaze returns that of the viewer as its own object: something is looking at my looking: a gaze whose position I can never occupy, and whose vista I can imagine only by reversing my own, by inverting the perspective before me, and by imagining my own gaze as the new, palindromic point of disappearance on the horizon. (*Vision and Painting,* 106)

16 Binocular vision implies that two separate two-dimensional images are seen by two separate eyes; the mind combines them to produce the illusion of three-dimensional depth. Binocular parallax is subsumed by this monocular paradox. Panofsky emphasizes this monocular "assumption" as an essential element of single-point perspective: "It forgets that we see not with a single fixed eye but with two constantly moving eyes" (*Perspective as Symbolic Form,* 31). See also M. H. Pirenne's discussion of binocular vision and the perspective picture: "When we look binocularly at a flat picture, the visual angles involved are not quite the same for the two eyes, since the eyes are at different positions. This is clear for instance with regard to the frame of the picture; and it is this largely which enables us to locate the position of the picture with its frame" (*Optics, Painting and Photography,* 77).

17 Alberti, *On Painting,* I. 12, p. 49.

18 *The Literary Works of Leonardo da Vinci,* ed. J. P. Richter, vol. 1 (London: Oxford University Press, 1939), 150.

19 Pirenne, *Optics, Painting and Photography,* 74.

20 Leonardo, quoted in Kim H. Veltman, *Linear Perspective and the Visual Dimensions of Science and Art: Studies on Leonardo da Vinci,* vol. 1 (Munich: Deutscher Kunstverlag, 1986), 56. Veltman describes Leonardo's drawings as "perspectival windows" but emphasizes the relation—for Leonardo—between the window and the net. The earliest drawing in the Codex Atlanticus has no text but shows a rather cumbersome perspective frame. A later drawing shows simply an eye and a translucent plane. See Veltman, *Linear Perspective,* 107–109.

21 In a later chapter, I will return to the size and shape of the "rectangle" in the debates about the standardized "aspect ratio" of the movie screen.

22 In *De re aedificatoria* (On the Art of Building), Alberti lists many openings that function to distinguish between a wall (*paries*) and its opening. Architecture has six elements: region (*regio*), ground (*area*), organization (*partitio*), wall (*paries*), ceiling (*tectum*), and opening (*apertio*). See Werner Oechslin, "Leon Battista Alberti's *Apertio*—the Opening Absolute," *Daidalos* 13 (1984): 29–38.

23 Leon Battista Alberti, *On the Art of Building in Ten Books,* trans. Joseph Rykwert, Neil Leach, and Robert Tavernor (Cambridge: MIT Press, 1988), I.12, 28. Alberti began *De re aedificatoria*—his homage to Roman architect Vitruvius's *Ten Books on Architecture*—in 1443 and finished it in 1452, but it was not published until 1486. Although there are no surviving paintings that can be attributed to him, Alberti received a number of architectural commissions between 1450 and 1470. See also Robert Tavernor, *On Alberti and the Art of Building* (New Haven: Yale University Press, 1998).

24 Alberti, *On the Art of Building in Ten Books,* 7.12.

25 Ibid., 7.15; emphasis added.

26 Alberti's treatise, *De re aedificatoria,* may have been intended to describe a way of building inspired by antiquity and not the way buildings were being built in Florence or Rome, where some elements of glazing were used.

27 While limited evidence of glazing is evident in Rome and Florence, glass for windows was not common or transparent. See Fernand Braudel, *Capitalism and Material Life 1400–1800,* trans. Miriam Kochan (New York: Harper and Row, 1973), 121, 124.

28 In *The Poetics of Perspective,* James Elkins describes Alberti's appeal to metaphor as a "tropological enrichment" to his otherwise "dry argumentative mode" of discourse (31). For more on Albertian metaphors, see Martin Kemp, *The Science of Art,* 10. In *De pictura,* Alberto describes "visual rays" as "like extended very fine threads gathered tightly in a bunch at one end" (*On Paniting* I.5, p. 41); Edgerton mentions Alberti's metaphor for the geometric concept of a "plane" as "many lines joined closely together like threads in a cloth" and for a concave surface as like "the inner surface of eggshells" (*Renaissance Rediscovery,* 82). A closer look at section I.4 of *On Painting* also reveals that Alberti describes the surface as "like a skin stretched over the whole extent" and like "clear water."

29 *Historia* was more of a style of painting than simply a painted subject. In his introduction to *On Painting,* Cecil Grayson supplies detailed notes to the various manuscripts of *De pictura* and to the Latin text and Italian texts. (See also Cecil Grayson, "The Text of Alberti's *De pictura,*" *Italian Studies* 23 [1968]: 78–93.) In *De re aedificatoria,* Alberti likens looking at a painting to reading a good story (*bonam historiam*). See Michael Baxandall's discussion of *istoria* in his *Painting and Experience in Fifteenth-Century Italy* (Oxford: Oxford University Press, 1972), 45–56.

30 The Italian text of the same passage apparently does not use an equivalent for "historia." See Cecil Grayson's notes in Leon Battista Alberti, *Opera volgari,* ed. Grayson (Bari: G. Laterza, 1973), vol. 3.

31 I am aware that this has already been a point of contention for many art historians. There are many who wish to emphasize the nonnarrative, non-storytelling function of Italian painting. For example, Martin Jay describes the "de-narrativization" of Alberti as part of the increasing autonomy and abstraction of the image: "Thus the abstraction of artistic form from any substantive content, which is part of the clichéd history of twentieth-century modernism, was already prepared by the perspectival revolution five centuries earlier." See Jay, "Scopic Regimes of Modernity," 9. Norman Bryson suggests that the figural function of Italian painting overtook its storytelling function (Bryson, *Word and Image: French Painting of the Ancien Régime* [Cambridge: Cambridge University Press, 1981]). On the other hand, Svetlana Alpers describes Italian painting as "a narrative art" but only in order to contrast it with Dutch seventeenth-century painting, which she describes as predominately "descriptive" (*The Art of Describing,* xix).

32 Grayson, introduction to Alberti, *On Painting,* 12.

33 Ibid., 13.

34 Panofksy, *Perspective as Symbolic Form,* trans. Christopher S. Wood (New York: Zone Books, 1991), 27.

35 Joseph Masheck, "Alberti's 'Window': Art-Historiographic Notes on an Antimodernist Misprision," *Art Journal* 50 (Spring 1991): 34–41. Masheck also made this argument in an earlier piece, "Hard-Core Painting," *Artforum* 16 (April 1978): 46–55.

36 James Elkins argues that contemporary accounts too often posit a unified "Renaissance perspective" against which the fragmentations of modernism are defined. See Elkins, *The Poetics of Perspective,* 217–261.

37 Masheck provides ample evidence of the rhetorical use of the window as painterly metaphor—by Dürer, by Ruskin in 1885, by Panofsky, Gombrich, and Arnheim. Abstract painters—Mondrian, de Kooning, Reinhardt—struggled with the Albertian window. See Ad Reinhardt, in *Art-as-Art: The Selected Writings of Ad Reinhardt,* ed. Barbara Rose, Documents of 20th-Century Art (New York: Viking, 1975), 47–49, and Willem de Kooning, "The Renaissance and Order" in *The Collected Writings of Willem de Kooning,* ed. George Scrivani (Madras: Hanumann, 1988), 17–36. A larger history of the window as a painterly motif would require a substantial digression here. A survey would include (1) the window as a sacred motif in Renaissance religious painting (the *fenestra caeli,* "window of Heaven," in which the Virgin Mary is symbolized as a window through which the Lord endows the world with light—for incarnation—*fenestra cancellata*); (2) the secular use of the window in seventeenth-century Dutch genre painting; (3) Duchamp's ironic study of glass and transparency in *The Bride Stripped Bare by Her Bachelors, Even* (*The Large Glass*) (1915–1923) and *Fresh Widow* (1920); (4)

the flat abstractions of Klee or Albers, as only a few examples; (5) the recurrent literal metaphor of the window for representation in Magritte. See Carla Gottlieb, *The Window in Art: From the Window of God to the Vanity of Man* (New York: Abaris Books, 1981).

38 Alberti, *On Painting* I.19, p. 55. Roberto Rossellini devoted the third part of his historical film cycle *The Age of Cosimo de Medici* (*L'età di Cosimo*), of 1973, to a biographical portrait of Alberti: *Leon Battista Alberti: Humanism.* Michael Silverman's essay "Rossellini and Leon Battista Alberti: The Centering Power of Perspective," in *Yale French Studies* 1, no. 1 (1977), argues a parallel between Alberti's theorization of the "centering" principles of perspective and Rossellini's use of Alberti as a "centering" character. For a different reading of the Rossellini film, one that emphasizes the use of architecture as Rossellini's centering priority, see Roger McNiven, "Rossellini's Alberti: Architecture and the Perspective System versus the Invention of Cinema," in *iris,* special issue on Cinema and Architecture (Paris: Méridiens Klincksieck, 1991), 11–24. These two essays read Alberti through the lens of Rossellini's film—his choices of framing, camera movement, zooming, and shot sequence—and are less about the principles inherent in Alberti's theorization of perspective.

39 Ibid.

40 In a recent essay denoting the representational tradition of measuring deviation from human scale, Ricky Jay has noted the manner in which the doorway is used as a marker of standard human measure. See Ricky Jay, "Giants and Dwarves," in *Omnivore: A Journal of Writing and Visual Culture* (New York Institute of the Humanities; Autumn 2003): 47–54.

41 Panofksy, *Perspective as Symbolic Form,* 69.

42 The possibility that Renaissance artists might playfully incorporate representational metaphors is argued by Michael Kubovy in *The Psychology of Perspective and Renaissance Art* in terms of a different but frequently cited metaphor—the arrow in the eye (1–16).

43 Lew Andrews, *Story and Space in Renaissance Art: The Rebirth of Continuous Narrative* (Cambridge: Cambridge University Press, 2001), 35.

44 Dagobert Frey, *Gotik und Renaissance: Als Grundlagen der modernen Weltanschauung* (1929), translated in W. Sypher, ed., *Art History: An Anthology of Modern Criticism* (New York, 1963), 164. Quoted in Andrews, *Story and Space in Renaissance Art,* 5.

45 Ibid., quoted in Andrews, *Story and Space in Renaissance Art,* 5.

46 Ibid., 35.

47 In Martin Kemp's extensive history of mechanical instruments for perspective, *The Science of Art,* he is doubtful about the role that perspective machines played in pictorial practice and holds that they served mostly as exercises and intellectual toys made prominent in the writing of Dürer, Dante, and Cigoli: "Linear perspective machines, for all their intellectual charm and mechanical ingenuity, do not seem to have brought any major transformations in artistic practice at any point in their history, and they eventually underwent progressive extinction." Martin Kemp, *The Science of Art: Optical Themes in Western Art from Brunelleschi to Seurat* (New Haven: Yale University Press, 1990), 188. The machines are wonderfully wrought specimens of the Renaissance urge for instrumentation: Cigoli's perspectograph (made and described circa 1650–1750), the pantograph, a parallelograms of levers, and the optigraph.

In May 2002, the Getty Research Institute held a symposium and exhibition entitled "The Geometry of Seeing: Perspective and the Dawn of Virtual Space." Papers were given by Hubert Damisch, Martin Kemp, Christopher Wood, Mario Carpo, and others.

48 Michael Kubovy argues that the viewer was not always in the same position as the painting might imply (*The Psychology of Perspective and Renaissance Art,* 16).

49 As Steinberg points out, the center of projection in *The Last Supper* is around fifteen feet from the floor—nearly three times the height of the average Italian. See Leo Steinberg, "Leonardo's *Last Supper,*" *Art Quarterly* 36 (1973): 297–410.

50 Alpers describes the flat materiality of Dutch/northern painting—its relation to Baconian empiricism and to mapping—as a grid without a positioned viewer. In Alpers's account, Dutch art can be characterized in terms of "the absence of a prior frame—that rectangle or framed window which Alberti offers as his initial definition of the picture—so that the image spread out on the pictorial surface appears to be an unbounded fragment of the world" (*The Art of Describing,* 27). Alpers draws a distinction between the narrative "perspectival" art of Italy and the more descriptive "optical" art of the north. Dutch art de-emphasizes the frame—its frames operate more like a "random cut" (Bryson's term in *Vision and Painting,* 25), with an interest in surface not depth.

In a different vein, Jonathan Crary discusses two paintings by Vermeer, *The Astronomer* (1668) and *The Geographer* (1668–1669), which depict the scientist at his desk studying his globe and map, respectively, as rays of light come through the leaded glass window and cast light on his work. As Crary reads these paintings: "each has his eyes averted from the aperture that opens onto the outside. The exterior world is not known by direct sensory examination but through a mental survey." Jonathan Crary, *Techniques of the Observer* (Cambridge: MIT Press, 1990), 44–46. In both of these paintings, the leaded glass window is a gridlike *velo,* but its view does not attract the astronomer or the geographer, who know the world on different terms than window-gazing.

51 Alberti, *On Painting* II.31, p. 69.

52 Ibid.

53 The conversion of digital data in the form of a single "bit"—either zero or one—to a pixel (picture element) of an illuminated CRT screen was a process developed by researchers at Xerox PARC in the 1960s. As "bits" are "mapped" onto a screen, the grid of pixels forms a graphic two-dimensional representation of digital information. I discuss "bit-mapping" and the graphical interface further in chapter 5.

54 Richter, *Literary Works of Leonardo da Vinci,* 523.

55 See Mario Carpo's discussion of Alberti's reinvention of digital imaging in *Architecture of the Age of Printing* (122–124), and in his "Alberti's Vision and a Plan of Rome."

56 Panofksy, *Perspective as Symbolic Form,* 27. Panofksy's essay opens with this citation from *Dürers schriftlicher Nachlass* (Halle, 1893). "Die Perspektive als 'symbolische Form'" was first published in *Vorträge des Bibliothek Warburg,* 258–330; it was reprinted in Erwin Panofsky, *Aufsätze zu Grundfragen des Kunstwissenschaft* (Berlin: B. Hessling, 1964), 99–167. See also Michael Ann Holly, *Panofsky and the Foundations of Art History* (Ithaca: Cornell University Press, 1984).

57 Rosalind Kraus describes a very different trajectory for the use of a grid to structure a "picture." As Krauss writes in a catalog essay accompanying a 1978 Pace Gallery show featuring works by Piet Mondrian, Paul Klee, Josef Albers, Ad Reinhardt, Ellsworth Kelly, Andy Warhol, and others, grids are "emblems of all that is quintessentially modern in art." The grid was "flattened, geometricized, ordered, it is anti-natural, anti-mimetic, anti-real." Krauss notes, however, that while the grid conveyed "by its very abstraction . . . the separation of the perceptual screen from that of the real world," it also surfaced in symbolist art in the form of windows and their mullions. Caspar David Friedrich's *View from a Painter's Studio* (1818) and Odilon Redon's *Le jour* (1891) take the image of the window "in an explicitly modernist direction" because it is "experienced as simultaneously transparent and opaque." See also John Elderfield, "Grids," *Artforum* 10 (May 1972): 52–59.

58 Bryson compares Western representational oil painting with Chinese painterly traditions, where the brushstroke is displayed as an extension of the painter's bodily presence, a work in "real time" (*Vision and Painting,* 88–89).

59 Kemp, *The Science of Art,* 169. Kemp notes Alberti's apologetic qualifications about the use of the *velo* in *De pictura:* Alberti writes he "will not listen to those who say it is no good for a painter to get into the habit of using these things, because, although they offer him the greatest help in painting, they render the artist unable to do anything without them" (*On Painting,* 68–69). Kemp also quotes Leonardo: "There are some who look at the things produced by nature through glass, or other surfaces or transparent veils. They trace outlines on the surface of the transparent medium. . . . But such an invention is to be condemned in those who do not know how to portray things without it, nor how to reason about nature with their minds" (*The Science of Art,* 163).

The 2000–2001 uproar over Philip Steadman's and David Hockney's claim that Renaissance painters regularly relied on optical devices like the camera obscura hinged on the rhetoric, in accusation and defense, of "cheating": "Mr. Hockney insists he is not accusing artists of cheating. A device like a camera lucida, he said, is difficult to use and is 'just a tool—it doesn't paint the picture.'" Mel Gussow, "Old Masters Pursued by Artistic Gumshoes: Debating Whether Artists Used Optics," *New York Times,* November 29, 2001, E1, E4.

60 Panofsky's hypothesis that Greek and Roman representational systems conceived of the world as curved was based on his argument—which he claimed was a tenet of ancient optics—that the eye perceives the world as curved, not with straight rays of vision. This component of Panofsky's study has been widely challenged. See Joel Snyder, "Picturing Vision," *Critical Inquiry* 6, no. 3 (Spring 1980). Christopher S. Wood comments on Panofsky's exploitative slippage in the double entendre of *Weltanschauung.* See Christopher S. Wood, introduction to Erwin Panofsky, *Perspective as Symbolic Form.*

61 Panofsky, *Perspective as Symbolic Form,* 41. See Ernst Cassirer, *Philosophie der symbolischen Formen,* vol. 1, *Die Sprache* (Berlin, 1923); English translation, *The Philosophy of Symbolic Forms* (New Haven: Yale University Press, 1955–1957). For an account of Panofsky's use of Cassirer's term, see Holly, "Panofsky and Cassirer," in *Panofsky and the Foundations of Art History,* and Damisch, *The Origin of Perspective,* 6–20. Damisch positions Panofksy's essay as a "threshold text," calling it "the inescapable horizon line and reference point for all inquiry concerning this object of study and all related matters" (4).

62 Panofsky, *Perspective as Symbolic Form,* 29.

63 Ibid., 31. This "discrepancy," Panofsky asserts, "is also true . . . for the entirely analogous operation of the camera." Panofksy argues that, with perspective, the "aggregate space" of antiquity is replaced by the "systematic space" of modernity (*Perspective as Symbolic Form,* 42).

64 In Panofsky's words: "Thus the great *evolution* from aggregate space to systematic space" (*Perspective as Symbolic Form,* 65; emphasis added). The cultural or historical "discovery," "invention," or "evolution" of perspective remains a matter of much debate. In Samuel Edgerton's account, the "perceptual revolution" of linear perspective was a historical invention that produced, over the centuries, an "innate" geometry in our eyes" (*Renaissance Rediscovery of Linear Perspective,* 4).

Although not directly targeting Edgerton by name, Hubert Damisch takes great issue with the methodologies of Edgerton and other scholars who attempt to construct a cultural history of perspective: "This crude evolutionist notion of the emergence of cultural formations takes no account of the curiously paradoxical nature of those objects and structures I would call paradigmatic, which traverse history—or collide with it" (*The Origin of Perspective,* xx).

65 Panofsky, *Perspective as Symbolic Form,* 56.

66 Ibid., 34.

67 Lacan will remark: "what is at issue . . . is simply the mapping of space, not sight" ("Of the Gaze," 86).

68 Panofsky, *Perspective as Symbolic Form,* 66.

69 Ibid., 67; emphasis added. Panofsky's reference here to the "distancing and objectifying sense of the real" in "contemporary philosophy" may well have been to Heidegger's writing about the standing-outside-of position in respect to the "standing-reserve" (*Bestand*).

70 Ibid., 49.

71 Ibid., 68.

72 Ibid., 66.

73 See Thomas Kuhn, *The Structure of Scientific Revolutions* (Chicago: University of Chicago Press, 1962); Michel Foucault, *The Order of Things* (New York: Vintage Books, 1970); Martin Jay, "Scopic Regimes of Modernity"; Christian Metz, "The Passion for Perceiving," trans. Ben Brewster, in *Imaginary Signifier: Psychoanalysis and the Cinema* (Bloomington: Indiana University Press, 1982).

When Ernst Gombrich weighs in on perspective as a new *Weltanschauung,* he is less certain about its symbolic form:

> Much, perhaps too much, has been written about perspective and the claim has been made in various forms that this new style reflects the new philosophy, the new *Weltanschauung,* centered on man and on a new rational conception of space. But cannot Occam's Razor be applied to these entities? Can it not be argued that perspective is precisely what it claims to be, a method of representing a building or any scene as it would be seen from a certain vantage point? If it does, Brunelleschi's perspective represents an objectively valid intervention, no less valid than the invention of spectacles a century earlier. Nobody has yet claimed that to look at the world through lenses to correct bad eyesight is due to a new *Weltanschauung,* though we may claim that it is due to inventiveness.

Sir Ernst Gombrich, "From the Revival of Letters to the Reform of the Arts: Niccolò Niccoli and Filippo Brunelleschi" (1967), in *The Essential Gombrich: Selected Writings on Art and Culture* (London: Phaidon, 1996), 430–431.

74 Erwin Panofsky, "On Movies," *Princeton University, Department of Art and Archeology, Bulletin* (1936): 5–15; "Style and Medium in the Moving Picture," *transition* 26 (1937): 121–133; "Style and Medium in the Motion Pictures," a later version of the essay, was first published in *Critique: A Review of Contemporary Art* 1 (1947): 5–28; reprinted in Panofsky, *Three Essays on Style,* ed. Irving Lavin (Cambridge: MIT Press, 1995), 93–126. In his introduction to the 1947 version, "Style and Medium in the Motion Pictures," Irving Lavin remarks on the various titles in each version of Panofsky's essay—"movies" (1936), "moving picture" (1937), and "motion picture" (1947). Lavin suggests that the first, most informal version of the essay took the colloquial term "movies" to argue that movies were a folk art and, even if they attained higher aesthetic import, they retained a base in popular entertainment. See Irving Lavin, introduction to Panofsky, *Three Essays on Style*, 3–14. Lavin's introduction examines the development of Panofsky's analysis from "personal chat" to a "proper theoretical essay," while it retains an unchanging "impish grace and wit" as Panofsky moves "in a genre limbo somewhere between personal reminiscence, high journalism, formal art criticism, and professional art history" (*Three Essays on Style*, 9–12).

75 Thomas Y. Levin, "Iconology at the Movies: Panofsky's Film Theory," *Yale Journal of Criticism* 9, no. 1 (1996): 27–55. In Levin's vivid account of Panofsky's newfound interest in the "movies," he suggests that Panofsky did not apply his rigorous analysis of representational form to his discussion of "the movies" and that he was more concerned with cinematic content—its nascent iconology—than with its form. In this regard, only Lavin, Levin, and Horst Bredekamp have attempted an analysis of the relation between the Panofsky's film essay and his art historical writing. Lavin suggests that the American Panofsky—who learned English only after moving to the United States at age forty-one—may have had a different "academic persona" than the German Panofsky. See Lavin, introduction to *Three Essays on Style*, 9–12; Levin, "Iconology at the Movies," 27–55; and Bredekamp, "A Neglected Tradition? Art History as *Bildwissenschaft*," *Critical Inquiry* (Spring 2003): 426–428.

76 Panofsky, "Style and Medium in the Motion Pictures," 93.

77 Levin, "Iconology at the Movies," 6.

78 Panofsky, "Style and Medium in the Motion Pictures," 96.

79 Panofsky, *Perspective as Symbolic Form*, 65. Christopher S. Wood suggests in his introduction to the perspective essay that Panofsky was always drawn to the reconciliation of opposites. See Wood, introduction to Panofsky, *Perspective as Symbolic Form*, 23. Panofsky's claim for the twin "triumphs" of perspective—"distance-objectifying" and "distance-denying"—has a formal similarity to if not a direct evolutionary root in his twin diagnostic phrases—"spatialization of time" and "dynamization of space—for the "motion picture."

80 Horst Bredekamp has suggested that Panofsky may have known Benjamin's essay—which was published and available in New York in its French version in 1936—or perhaps had access to it in the MOMA film library, where Jay Leyda had attempted to commission an English translation of the German version. Bredekamp also points out that Benjamin reread Panofsky's essay on perspective to prepare for his defense of his "Work of Art" essay in 1935. See Bredekamp, "A Neglected Tradition?" 418–428.

In addition, the two essays share parallel histories of revision and republication. Benjamin's essay, entitled "Das Kunstwerk im Zeitalter seiner technischen Reproduzierbarkeit," was published in French as "L'ouevre d'art à l'époque de sa reproduction mécanisée," in *Zeitschrift für Sozialforschung* 5, no. 1 (1936). Benjamin revised the essay, but the revision was published only posthumously in the collection *Schriften*, ed. Gretel and Theodor Adorno (Frankfurt: Suhrkamp, 1955). Harry Zohn's translation, "The Work of Art in the Age of Mechanical Reproduction," in Hannah Arendt's edited collection of Benjamin's writings, *Illuminations* (New York: Schocken Books, 1969), was translated from the version of the essay in *Schriften* but retains the title of the French translation, not the German original. See Susan Buck-Morss, *The Origin of a Negative Dialectics* (New York: Free Press, 1977), 286.

81 Benjamin, "The Work of Art," 222; emphasis added.

82 Ibid., 250, n. 19.

83 Panofsky, "Style and Medium in the Motion Pictures," 119. The cathedral analogy is most frequently drawn into debates about the algebra of authorship. Panofsky's knowledge of the cooperative nature of medieval art production allowed him to see "the role of the producer corresponding, more or less, to that of the bishop or archbishop; that of the director to that of the architect in chief; that of the scenario writers to that of the scholastic advisers establishing the iconographical program; and that of the actors, cameramen, cutters, sound men, makeup men, and the diverse technicians to that of those whose work provided the physical entity of the finished product, from the sculptors, glass painters, bronze casters, carpenters, and skilled masons down to the quarry men and woodsmen" (119–120).

84 "Buildings are appropriated in a twofold manner: by use and by perception—or rather touch and sight." Benjamin, "Work of Art," 240.

85 Anthony Grafton describes Panofsky's critical "vision": "he had the panoramic vision of the parachutist and the microscopic attention to detail of the trufflehunter." Grafton, "Panofsky, Alberti and the Ancient World," in Irving Lavin, ed., *Meaning in the Visual Arts: Views from the Outside, a Centennial Commemoration of Erwin Panofsky (1892–1968)* (Princeton: Institute for Advanced Study, 1995), 124.

86 Christopher S. Wood's introduction to his translation of Panofsky's *Perspective as Symbolic Form* describes Panofksy's "spectacular moments of irresponsible synthesis" (18).

87 Jay performs this conflation in order to argue against those who have invoked it as "*the* reigning visual model of modernity" (his emphasis, 5): "Let me begin by turning to what is normally claimed to be the dominant, even totally hegemonic, visual model of the modern era, that which we can identify with Renaissance notions of perspective in the visual arts and Cartesian ideas of subjective rationality in philosophy. For convenience, it can be called 'Cartesian perspectivalism'" (Jay, "Scopic Regimes of Modernity," 4).

88 Ibid., 10.

89 Ibid., 8.

90 "Scopic regime" is a term used by film theorist Christian Metz to describe cinematic visuality; Jay's retronymic appropriation here has transformed the term into one that provides a visual corollary to Foucault's episteme. See Christian Metz, "The Passion for Perceiving," in *The Imaginary Signifier: Psychoanalysis and Cinema,* trans. Ben Brewster (Bloomington: Indiana University Press, 1982), 61.

91 The conflation of the epistemic assumptions of the fifteenth and seventeenth centuries poses a set of historiographical questions. Norman Bryson asserts, "Alberti's conception of the subject is already Cartesian in its reduction of the space of the painting to dimensionless punctuality." Bryson's description of the "Founding Perception" also contains the language of this equation: "The only position for the viewing subject proposed and assumed by the image will be that of the Gaze, a transcendent point of vision that has discarded the body of labour and exists only as a disembodied punctum" (*Vision and Painting,* 103, 107).

92 Descartes wrote, "As regards judgment of distance by size, shape, colour, or light, perspective pictures show how easy mistakes are. For often things depicted in them appear to be farther off than they are because they are small, or their outlines are more confused, or their colours are darker or fainter, than we imagine they ought to be." "Dioptrics," in *Descartes: Philosophical Writings,* trans. and ed. Elizabeth Anscombe and Peter Thomas Geach (London: Thomas Nelson and Sons, 1954), 256. Also see Karsten Harries, "Descartes,

Perspective, and the Angelic Eye," *Yale French Studies* 49 (1973): 28–42; and Harries, *Infinity and Perspective.*

93 The idea of the world as measurable object has led some writers to extrapolate a teleology that leads to apprehending the world as "information." For example, "As a spectacle, an object of vision, it is already well on the way to becoming a bit of data, observable, measurable, analyzable, and readable as a computer print-out, for example, or as a blip on a radar screen." Robert D. Romanyshyn, *Technology as Symptom and Dream* (New York: Routledge, 1989), 42.

94 Elizabeth Grosz has productively questioned the frequent equation between virtuality and disembodiment: "If we don't just have bodies but are bodies (as I have argued elsewhere), there can never be the threat of displacing body in favor of mind or abandoning the real for the virtual. Rather, Cyberspace, virtual worlds, and the order of computer simulation—whether imagistic or computational—show that our notions of real, of body, and of the physical or historical city need to be complicated and rethought to accommodate what they seem to oppose." See Elizabeth Grosz, "Cyberspace, Virtuality, and the Real," in *Architecture from the Outside: Essays on Virtual and Real Space* (Cambridge: MIT Press, 2001), 86. See also Elizabeth Grosz, *Volatile Bodies: Toward a Corporeal Feminism* (Bloomington: Indiana University Press, 1994). Equally, phenomenological accounts of the embodiment of the viewer have forcefully challenged the idea that spectatorship enacts a disembodiment. See Vivian Sobchack, *The Address of the Eye: A Phenomenology of Film Experience* (Princeton: Princeton University Press, 1991), and *Carnal Thoughts: Embodiment and Moving Image Culture* (Berkeley: University of California Press, 2004); Laura U. Marks, *The Skin of the Film: Intercultural Cinema, Embodiment, and the Senses* (Chapel Hill: Duke University Press, 2000), and *Touch: Sensuous Theory and Multisensory Media* (Minneapolis: University of Minnesota Press, 2002); and Steven Shaviro, *The Cinematic Body (Theory Out of Bounds)* (Minneapolis: University of Minnesota Press, 1993).

"Cyberspace" is frequently described as post-Cartesian space because, in the metaphor of virtual space, one is "in" it, not outside of it, watching it. My argument will assign a different meaning to "post-Cartesian" space. Instead of suggesting that the outside/looking-in position will be overcome by placing the viewing subject "inside" the experience, I underline how the viewing subject's relation to the screen maintains an outside/looking-in separation while the relationship with the screen has changed in a variety of bodily ways. Screen size, scale, and format, interactive interface, and multiple-screen interaction necessitate changes in the theorization of the spectator/viewer/user in relation to a monologic single-frame moving image.

LENS I: DESCARTES'S WINDOW

1 Descartes's treatise on optics was an appendix to his *Discourse on Method,* a methodological introduction to three "specimen essays" demonstrating the application of his philosophical method to the natural sciences and mathematics, titled in full: *Discourse on Method of Rightly Conducting Reason and Reaching the Truth in Science, with the Optics, Meterology and Geometry.* There were ten "discourses" in *The Dioptrics:* Discourse II sets out the laws of refraction; Discourse VII is on the improvement of vision with optical instruments, Discourse X is on the grinding of lenses. René Descartes, "Extracts from *The Dioptrics,*" in *Descartes: Philosophical Writings,* trans. and ed. Elizabeth Anscombe and Peter Thomas Geach (London: Thomas Nelson and Sons, 1954), 245.

2 Ibid., 245–246; emphasis added. Descartes wrote *Discourse on Method* in French, his native language, as he comments at the end of his draft, "rather than in Latin, the language of my teachers, because I hope for a better judgement of my opinions from those who use only their natural reason . . . than from those who only trust old books" (*Descartes: Philosophical Writings,* 56).

3 Translators Elizabeth Anscombe and Peter Thomas Geach add a note at the word "shutter" in the passage I've quoted to indicate that in the French version Descartes uses the word "fenestre." While they note this, they also suggest "'window" would hardly do, since this *fenestre* lets in no light except through the hole where the eye is, even though Descartes goes on to say: "No light must enter the room except through the eye." Descartes, "Extracts from *The Dioptrics,*" 245–246.

4 Johannes Kepler, *Optics: Paralipomena to Witelo and the Optical Part of Astronomy,* trans. William H. Donahue (Sante Fe, N.M.: Green Lion Press, 2000). See also Wilbur Applebaum, ed., *The Encyclopedia of the Scientific Revolution: From Copernicus to Newton* (New York: Garland Publishing, 2000); David C. Lindberg, *Theories of Vision from al-Kindi to Kepler* (Chicago: University of Chicago Press, 1981); A. I. Sabra, *Theories of Light from Descartes to Newton* (Cambridge: Cambridge University Press, 1981); and A. Mark Smith, "Knowing Things Inside Out: The Scientific Revolution from a Medieval Perspective," *American Historical Review* 95 (1990): 726–744.

5 Descartes was intensely engaged in optical questions in the 1620s and was familiar with the key writings about perspective and geometric optics. Stephen Gaukroger and A. Mark Smith assert that Descartes was familiar with Kepler's *Ad Vitellionem,* Pecham's *Perspectiva communis,* Roger Bacon's *Perspectiva,* and Witelo's *Perspectiva.* See Stephen Gaukroger, *Descartes: An Intellectual Biography* (Oxford: Clarendon Press, 1997), 139–146; A. Mark Smith, "Descartes' Theory of Light and Refraction: A Discourse on Method," *Transactions of the American Philosophical Society* 77, no. 3 (1987), 1–92.

6 See Dalia Judowitz, "Vision, Representation and Technology in Descartes," in David Michael Levin, ed., *Modernity and the Hegemony of Vision* (Berkeley: University of California Press, 1993).

7 Descartes, Discourse V, "Extracts from *The Dioptrics,*" 244.

8 *Descartes: Philosophical Writings,* 152, 165–166.

9 René Descartes, *Meditations on First Philosophy* (1641) in *Descartes: Philosophical Writings,* 73. Maurice Merleau-Ponty cites this passage in his "The Film and the New Psychology," in order to conclude that "even objects right in front of me are not truly seen but merely thought." Maurice Merleau-Ponty, "The Film and the New Psychology," trans. Herbert L. Dreyfus and Patricia Allen Dreyfus, in *Sense and Non-Sense* (Chicago: Northwestern University Press, 1964), 50.

10 A century later, automatons continued to explore the very mind-body dualities that Descartes set forth. In 1740, Jacques de Vaucanson constructed an automaton duck that performed the trick of defecation in front of assembled salon patrons. Pierre Jaquet-Droz (1773) produced a writing automaton that would write "Cogito ergo sum" and "We are androids." Both are mentioned in Horst Bredekamp, *The Lure of Antiquity and the Cult of the Machine* (Princeton, N.J.: Marcus Weiner Publishers, 1995), 4. See also Jessica Riskin, "The Defecating Duck, or, the Ambiguous Origins of Artificial Life," *Critical Inquiry* 29, no. 4 (Summer 2003): 599–634, and Jessica Riskin, "Eighteenth-Century Wetware," in *Representations,* no. 83 (Summer 2003): 97–125.

11 Gaukroger, *Descartes: An Intellectual Biography,* 294.

12 Genevieve Lloyd, *Man of Reason: "Male" and "Female" in Western Philosophy* (Minneapolis: University of Minnesota Press, 1985), 50.
13 The lure of automata that was evident in Descartes's thinking in the seventeenth century and in Vaucanson's duck in the eighteenth, was also felt powerfully by Thomas Edison in the nineteenth century. See Gaby Woods, *Edison's Eve: A Magical History of a Quest for Mechanical Life* (New York: Alfred A. Knopf, 2002). While seventeenth- and eighteenth-century inventors were fascinated by the differences between the animal and the artificial machine, twentieth-century thinkers such as Norbert Wiener, who coined the term "cybernetics" in his *Cybernetics, or Control and Communication in the Animal and Machine* (Cambridge: MIT Press, 1948), and John von Neumann, who developed the theory of "self-reproducing automata" in a *Scientific American* article in April 1953, were concerned with the relation between humans and thinking machines.
14 A. M. Turing, "Computing Machinery and Intelligence," *Mind, a Quarterly Review of Psychology and Philosophy* 59, no. 236 (October 1950): 433–460.
15 Ibid., 434.
16 N. Katherine Hayles, *How We Became Posthuman: Virtual Bodies in Cybernetics, Literature, and Informatics* (Chicago: University of Chicago Press, 1999), xi.
17 Yet Hayles's account sidelines another loss—the body of Turing, who was convicted of "gross indecency" (homosexuality) and sentenced to twelve months of "organo therapy" (chemical castration) before he committed suicide at age forty-one. See Andrew Hodges, *Alan Turing: The Enigma of Intelligence* (New York: HarperCollins, 1985).
18 See Ken Goldberg, ed., *The Robot in the Garden: Telerobotics and Tele-epistemology in the Age of the Internet* (Cambridge: MIT Press, 2001).

CHAPTER 2: THE FRAME

1 Alberti's knowledge of the camera obscura remains a matter of speculation. Biographer Anthony Grafton suggests that Alberti's demonstrations of the "miracles of painting" may have employed a small box device like the camera obscura. See Anthony Grafton, *Leon Battista Alberti: Master Builder of the Italian Renaissance* (New York: Hill and Wang, 2000). Nevertheless, contemporary accounts have emphasized the conceptual relation between Alberti's *De pictura* and the camera obscura. Norman Bryson, for example, asserts that the camera obscura "provides a conceptual framework for *De pictura*" and that "both Alberti and Vermeer theorize painting around the camera obscura." See Norman Bryson, *Vision and Painting: The Logic of the Gaze* (New Haven: Yale University Press, 1983), 107, 111.
2 For an account of the camera obscura's discursive history, see Jonathan Crary, "The Camera Obscura and Its Subject," in *Techniques of the Observer* (Cambridge: MIT Press, 1990), 30–31. Crary's is careful to describe the camera obscura as a "complex social amalgam" of technical and discursive practices, and he situates its discursive and epistemic status in the writings of Descartes, Newton, Locke, and Leibniz. See also Crary's earlier essay, "Modernizing Vision," in Hal Foster, ed., *Vision and Visuality* (Seattle: Bay Press, 1988), 29–44.

For accounts of the camera obscura as a drawing tool, see J. H. Hammond, *The Camera Obscura: A Chronicle* (Bristol: Adam Hilger, 1981); Martin Kemp, *The Science of Art: Optical Themes in Western Art from Brunelleschi to Seurat* (New Haven: Yale University Press, 1990); Helmut Gernsheim with A. Gernsheim, *The History of Photography: From the Camera Obscura to the Beginning of the Modern Era* (London: Thames and Hudson, 1955); Arthur K. Wheelock,

Perspective, Optics, and Delft Artists around 1650 (New York: Garland, 1977); and Janice L. Neri, "Camera Obscura," in Jonathan Dewald, ed., *The Dictionary of Early Modern Europe* (New York: Scribners, forthcoming).

For the role of camera obscura in relation to the history of projected light and shadow, see Laurent Mannoni, *The Great Art of Light and Shadow: Archeology of the Cinema,* trans. Richard Crangle (Exeter: University of Exeter Press, 2000).

3 Leon Battista Alberti, *On Painting and On Sculpture: The Latin Texts of "De Pictura" and "De Statua,"* trans. Cecil Grayson (London: Phaiden, 1972), 69; emphasis added.

4 The camera obscura produced a number of paradoxical transformations of inside and outside. Kim H. Veltman suggests that the camera obscura, although theoretically suited for making representations of both exterior and interior spaces, was in practice more often used for the painting of interiors. Veltman also suggests that the tradition of ceiling painting that became known as *quadratura* "interiorized" the central atrium-like courtyard of the Renaissance home and functioned as a window into the sky above. Kim H. Veltman, *Linear Perspective and the Visual Dimensions of Science and Art,* Studies on Leonardo da Vinci, vol. 1 (Munich: Deutscher Kunstverlag, 1986). When camera obscuras were large enough to be full-sized rooms or tents, the architectural function of its tiny window opening was only for admitting focused light. The aperture reduced the window's function for ventilation to metaphor.

5 The term "natural magic" is taken from Giambattista della Porta's 1558 text *Magiae naturalis.* Della Porta's 1589 Latin edition of this text was translated and published in English as *Natural Magick in Twenty Books,* in London in 1658. The chapters include instruction on changing metals, counterfeiting gold, perfuming, production of new plants, strange cures, beautifying women, and invisible writing. Book 17, on "strange glasses," contains the discussion of "catoptrick" glasses and the "wonderful sights to be seen by them." For a discussion of the role of optics in the "natural sciences," see Thomas L. Hankins and Robert J. Silverman, "Instruments and Images: Subjects for the Historiography of Science," in *Instruments and the Imagination* (Princeton: Princeton University Press, 1995), 3–14; Barbara Maria Stafford, "Revealing Technologies/Magical Domains," in Barbara Maria Stafford and Fran Terpak, *Devices of Wonder: From the World in a Box to Images on the Screen* (Los Angeles: Getty Research Institute, 2001), 1–142; and Mannoni, *The Great Art of Light and Shadow: Archeology of the Cinema.*

6 *Selections from the Notebooks of Leonardo da Vinci,* ed. Irma A. Richter (Oxford: Oxford University Press, 1977), 115–116. In optical terms, the problem of inversion was not solved until Kepler described his theory of the retinal image in 1604. See David C. Lindberg, *Theories of Vision from al-Kindi to Kepler* (Chicago: University of Chicago Press, 1976). Leonardo compared the eye to the camera obscura, but, according to Lindberg (*Theories of Vision,* 164), he never asserted that the retina function as a screen onto which images are projected. Lindberg describes the magnitude of Kepler's achievement in terms of his innovation of a theory of the retinal image and asserts that Kepler was the first to use the term *pictura* to refer to the inverted image on the retina: "For this is the first genuine instance in the history of visual theory of a real optical image within the eye—a picture, having an existence independent of the observer, formed by the focusing of all available rays on a surface" (*Theories of Vision,* 202). While Kepler's description of "radiation through apertures" and his punctiform analysis of rays of vision were based upon medieval perspectivists and he did not, at first, depart from their accounts of the geometry of vision, Kepler needed to investigate and understand lenses and their refraction in order to account for the inversion of the image. The correction of the image's inversion came later and was performed by the use of mirrors.

The camera lucida—a drawing device invented much later—is quite different from the camera obscura. While the name "camera lucida" may suggest a relation to the camera obscura, is does not involve a chamber (*camera*) at all but is instead a glass prism on a stand which refracts light to a perpendicular surface where the artist can trace the image.

7 Johannes Kepler, *Ad Vitellionem paralipomena* (Frankfurt, 1604) and Kepler, *Dioptrice* (Augsburg, 1611). Many historical accounts describe the use of the camera obscura in earlier epochs. Although the optical properties of projective light had been known, the name of the device had not yet been coined. See Paula Findlen, ed., *Athanasius Kircher: The Last Man Who Knew Everything* (New York: Routledge, 2004); and Lindberg, *Theories of Vision.*

8 "Therefore vision occurs through a picture of the visible thing [being formed] on the white, concave surface of the retina. And that which is to the right on the outside is portrayed on the left side of the retina; that which is to the left is portrayed on the right; that which is above is portrayed below; that which is below is portrayed above." Kepler, *Ad Vitellionem paralipomena* (1604), quoted in Lindberg, *Theories of Vision,* 200. Kepler did not illustrate his retinal theory with a drawing, but Descartes supplied an illustration of the retinal inversion in his *La dioptrique* (1637).

9 The Italian Girolamo Cardano may have been the first to introduce lenses in 1550: "If you care to see what goes on in the street when the sun is bright, place in your windows a glass disc and the window having been closed [shuttered] you will see images projected through the aperture onto the wall." From G. Potonniée, *The History of the Discovery of Photography,* trans. E. Epstean (New York: Tennant and Ward, 1936), 14. Otherwise, it is generally agreed that della Porta (in his 1589 edition) suggested the use of a lens in the opening to improve the quality of the projected image. Giovanni Battista della Porta, *Natural Magick* (reprint, New York, 1957), 363–364.

10 René Descartes, Discourse V, "Extracts from *The Dioptrics,*" in *Descartes: Philosophical Writings,* trans. and ed. Elizabeth Anscombe and Peter Thomas Geach (London: Thomas Nelson and Sons, 1954), 245. In *Magiae naturalis* (1558, 1589) della Porta popularized the camera obscura as an entertainment device. In his work on optics, *De refractione* (1593), he suggested the eye was a miniature camera obscura. See Lindberg, *Theories of Vision,* 182–184.

11 For an excellent account of the use of optical devices in scientific illustration, see Janice L. Neri, "Fantastic Observations: Images of Insects in Early Modern Europe," Ph.D. diss., University of California, Irvine, 2003. Despite Robert Hooke's claim in his preface to *Micrographia* that it took "a sincere hand, and a faithful eye, to examine and to record the things themselves as they appear," Neri demonstrates that he also relied on a variety of pictorial strategies to carefully craft both the specimen and the image.

12 See Barbara Maria Stafford, "Magnifying," in *Body Criticism: Imaging the Unseen in Enlightenment Art and Medicine* (Cambridge: MIT Press, 1993). While Dutch lensmakers Hans Lippershey and Hans Jansen had versions of a device that used convex and concave lenses in a tube in 1609, it was Galileo who made the device famous. After the publication of his 1632 book *Dialogue Concerning the Two Chief World Systems, Ptolemaic and Copernican,* Galileo was called to Rome, found guilty of heresy, and put under house arrest for the remainder of his life. For sources on the history of the telescope—its combination of lenses, astronomical and terrestrial uses, and its field of magnification—see Henry King, *The History of* *the Telescope* (London: Griffin, 1955), and Albert van Helden, "The Invention of the Telescope," in *Transactions of the American Philosophical Society* 67, no. 4 (1977). In Max Horkheimer's skeptical reading, these dioptric devices did not enhance vision but were blinding: "As their telescopes and microscopes, their tapes and radios become more sensitive, individuals become blinder, more hard of hearing, less responsive." Max Horkheimer, *Dawn and Decline* (New York: Seabury Press, 1978).

13 Lewis Mumford, *Technics and Civilization* (New York: Harcourt, Brace, 1934). This quotation serves as a caption to an illustration plate between pp. 180 and 181.

14 Ibid., 131.

15 See the discussion "Microscopes," in Stafford and Terpak, *Devices of Wonder,* 205–214. Microscopes were used in upper-class drawing rooms and museums and, in this way, were part of a visual culture that prized exhibition and display. The stereoscope and the camera obscura were also used as entertainment as much in the drawing room as in the laboratory. *Devices of Wonder* is an illustrative compendium of such devices.

16 See Hammond, *The Camera Obscura;* Kemp, *The Science of Art;* Gernsheim and Gernsheim, *The History of Photography;* and Wheelock, *Perspective, Optics, and Delft Artists.* In his book *The Great Art of Light and Shadow: Archeology of the Cinema,* Laurent Manonni challenges many "erroneous attributions" in the histories written about the camera obscura and magic lantern tradition. He pointedly objects to historians who wrongly attribute its invention to Giovanni Battista della Porta (c. 1535–1615). In fact, della Porta merely published a description of it in his *Magiae naturalis* printed in Naples in 1558. The mistaken paternity is found repeated in supposedly authoritative works, such as the *Leçons de physique* of Abbé Nollet (1743) and the *Encyclopédie* of Diderot and d'Alembert (1753), among other sources (Mannoni, *The Great Art,* 8). Kepler uses "window" to describe camera obscura opening: "When a screen with a small window is placed in front of the globe within the limit of the sections of the parallels, and the window is smaller than the globe, a picture of the visible hemisphere is projected on to the paper, formed by most of the rays brought together behind the globe at the limit of the last intersection of the rays from a luminous point. The picture is inverted, but purest and most distinct in the middle." Johannes Kepler, "On Vision/*De modo visionis,*" trans. A. C. Crombie, chapter V, proposition XXIII <http://web.clas.ufl.edu/users/rhatch/pages/03-SCI-REV-Home/resource-ref-read/vision/08sr-visnkplr.htm>.

17 In January 2000, Lawrence Wechsler published an article in the *New Yorker* describing David Hockney's theory about the use of lenses by the old masters. In December 2001, the New York Institute for the Humanities held a public symposium entitled Art and Optics: Toward an Evaluation of David Hockney's New Theories Regarding Opticality in Western Painting of the Past Six Hundred Years. See Lawrence Wechsler, "The Looking Glass," *New Yorker,* 31 January 2000; Mel Gussow, "Old Masters Pursued by Artistic Gumshoes: Debating Whether Artists Used Optics," *New York Times,* 29 November 2001: E1, E4; and Sarah Boxer, "Paintings a Bit Too Perfect? The Great Optics Debate," *New York Times,* 4 December 2001: E1, E4.

18 For accounts of Vermeer's use of the camera obscura, see Charles Seymour Jr., "Dark Chamber and Light-Filled Room: Vermeer and the Camera Obscura," *Art Bulletin* 46 (1964): 323–331; Daniel A. Fink, "Vermeer's Use of the Camera Obscura: A Comparative Study," *Art Bulletin* 53 (1971): 493–505; Wheelock, *Perspective, Optics, and Delft Artists;* and Philip Steadman, *Vermeer's Camera: Uncovering the Truth behind the Masterpieces* (London: Oxford University Press, 2001). Svetlana Alpers is less insistent on the use of the camera obscura in Dutch painting. See Svetlana Alpers, *The Art of Describing: Dutch Art in the Seventeenth Century* (Chicago: University of Chicago Press, 1983), 13. As Crary points out about the Vermeer debate, the art historical interest in the camera obscura has focused on its effects on the stylistics of painting, and not on techniques of observation (*Techniques of the Observer*, n. 45, 43–46).

19 Steadman, *Vermeer's Camera*, 155.

20 See David Hockney, *The Secret Knowledge: Rediscovering the Lost Techniques of the Old Masters* (New York: Viking Press, 2001). In formal terms, Hockney's method of research and argumentation was based on his collage construction of a "Great Wall" of painting, a comparative array of historical representation. If considered in overall form, this collage of art history bears a resemblance to Hockney's own collage forms. See my footnote 59 in chapter 1.

21 Hockney argues that Holbein could have used Dürer's drawing device for the lute seen on the bottom shelf but that the other curved objects in the painting—the curtains, the globe, and most emphatically, the musical score—suggest the use of optical tools (Hockney, *The Secret Knowledge*, 56–57, 100). Martin Kemp's lecture "Painting with Light or with Geometry: Looking into David Hockney's Secret Knowledge" questioned the "cliché" of a split between the use of light (by southern or Italian painters) and the use of optics (by northern or Dutch painters). Martin Kemp, lecture, 3 May 2002, Getty Research Institute.

22 Alpers, *The Art of Describing*, 31. Alpers writes: "The problem is that although many sixteenth and seventeenth-century treatises that discuss the artistic use of the camera obscura recommend tracing its image, we have no evidence of cases in which artists actually did this. The argument from use, rather than from analogy, has had to proceed therefore by trying to establish specific phenomena present in paintings that are not seen by unaided vision and that, it is concluded, must result from the use of the camera obscura" (*The Art of Describing*, 30).

23 Ibid., 27.

24 Ibid., 51.

25 Ibid., 138. Alpers maintains that Dutch paintings do not adhere to the Albertian concept of a picture as "a framed surface or pane situated at a distance from a viewer who looks through it at a substitute world."

26 Ibid., 51, 32.

27 "It is less the nature or use made of the camera obscura," Alpers writes, "than the trust placed in it that is of interest to us in understanding Dutch painting" (*The Art of Describing*, 33).

28 Ibid., xxv. Alpers characterizes the geographically defined styles as "visual culture," citing Michael Baxandall, *Painting and Experience in Fifteenth-Century Italy: A Primer in the Social History of Pictorial Style* (Oxford: Oxford University Press, 1972).

29 Ibid., 26, 32.

30 In this regard, Jonathan Crary astutely points out that Kepler may not be representative of only northern visual culture and that the camera obscura held a transregional importance in the writings of Leibniz, Newton, Locke, and Descartes. See Crary, *Techniques of the Observer*, 35.

31 Samuel van Hoogstraten's perspective box (c. 1660) established a fixed viewpoint for the viewer, who must look into the deep space of the box with one eye: "From at least the time of Alberti there had been adaptations of the *camera obscura* principle to create miniature rooms. The seventeenth century brought new portable versions of the *camera obscura*, as well as developments by Dutch artists to create peep shows (the *perspectifkas*) into perspectival rooms and interiors. The eighteenth century extended this idea to create optical glasses (*optiques* or zograscopes) and show-boxes (*Guckkasten*), the latter sometimes with moving images." Veltman, *Linear Perspective and the Visual Dimensions of Science and Art,* 80–84.

Alpers mentions Hoogstraten's peep-box as "an unframed sequence of rooms or vistas successively viewed," "which provides the viewer with an eye-hole through which to look at an interior illusionistically depicted on the inner surfaces of the box." Alpers, *The Art of Describing,* 62, 35.

32 Alpers, *The Art of Describing,* 13; emphasis added.

33 Crary, *Techniques of the Observer,* 34; emphasis added.

34 Ibid., 39. Crary uses the Kircher illustration on the same page.

35 John Baptist Porta [Giambattista della Porta], *Natural Magick in Twenty Books* (London, 1658), 364; emphasis added. Manuscript in special collections, Getty Research Institute Library.

36 Johannes Zahn, *Oculus artificialis teledioptricus sive telescopium* was principally devoted to the telescope, but as its illustrations attest, it also contained discussions of the magic lantern as a projection device and the camera obscura as a drawing device.

37 Crary, *Techniques of the Observer,* 5. The "history of the observer is not reducible to changing technical and mechanical practices any more than to the changing forms of artworks and visual representation" (8).

38 Ibid., 5. The importance of Crary's insight is twofold: Besides shifting from the traditional art historical analysis of the art object to the practices and habits of vision of an "observing subject," Crary productively questions the oversights produced in the familiar and reductive teleologies that form the core narratives of modernism and photography. Both of these elements have turned his work into a central and admirable example of a "visual studies" methodology.

39 Crary challenges the core narrative of modernism—that the classical strictures of painting were in place until late in the nineteenth century, when impressionist painters broke with perspectival models of vision and ruptured classical space and mimetic codes that had been in place since the Renaissance. More importantly here, however, is Crary's challenge to the core narrative of photography—that it represented a continuous tradition of realist strictures which also had been in place since the Renaissance. Crary argues for an earlier moment of rupture—in the 1820s and 1830s, before the invention of photography and before the stylistics of impressionism and cubism.

40 See W. J. T. Mitchell's incisive critique of Crary's "failing to heed many of his own warnings about overgeneralization and categorical truth claims," in "The Pictorial Turn," *Artforum* 30, no. 7 (March 1992): 89–94. Architectural historians Alberto Pérez-Gómez and Louise Pelletier also find Crary's Foucault-derived rupture problematic. They argue that Crary overstates the importance of the camera obscura in the seventeenth and eighteenth centuries without discussing its precedents in *perspectiva naturalis.* Though many indeed were fascinated by the camera obscura because of its capacity to represent a resonant, magical image, its application in the arts is still highly speculative:

> Crary's study can be seen, in fact, as a radical antithesis to the "progressive" history of optics and painting that is the premise of Martin Kemp's *Science of Art.* Both of these recent works on problems of representation in the European tradition take extreme positions that appear very problematic. Such complex questions, with great repercussions for our own artistic and architectural practice, demand a different kind of thinking and can-

not be reduced to either a simplistic progressive continuity or a radical historicity. In our opinion, the epistemological discontinuities of vision must be acknowledged without disregarding a continuity in the history of European science and philosophy.

Alberto Pérez-Gómez and Louise Pelletier, *Architectural Representation and the Perspective Hinge* (Cambridge: MIT Press, 1997), 67–68.

41 Crary, *Techniques of the Observer*, 27. Crary posits a radical rupture in genealogies that trace a continuous Western visual and philosophical tradition of an ideal, centered "observer" from Renaissance perspective onward to the birth of photography and the cinema. Crary's argument posits two broad and opposing epistemes, two very separate models of vision with two very different "observers." In the seventeenth and eighteenth century, Crary locates the "camera obscura model of vision" as the "dominant" paradigm for "explaining human vision, and for representing the relation of a perceiver and the position of a knowing subject to an external world." The "observer" in the seventeenth and eighteenth centuries was, in Crary's account, at a distance from the object of vision. In this model, vision was separate, outside of the body, "incorporeal." In the nineteenth century, a "sweeping transformation" of social practices and optical devices produced a fundamental change to this "apparatically produced" model of vision. In the 1820s and 1830s, as optical researchers studied human vision and produced optical devices that demonstrated the "physiological optics" of binocular parallax and persistence of vision, the "observer" was retooled, Crary asserts, as an active producer of optical experience. In his rush to fit optical devices into the epistemes of tidily contained centuries (the disembodied "camera obscura" of the seventeenth and eighteenth centuries versus the "physiological optics" of the nineteenth), Crary elides the differences between nineteenth-century devices that rely on binocular parallax—like the stereoscope—and those relying on persistence of vision—like the phenakistoscope—devices which produce quite different optical and hence subjective effects. Devices like the stereoscope and the phenakistoscope demonstrated these new optical principles; the visual effects produced by these devices occurred in the "body" of the observer. In Crary's account of this new regime of vision, the observer had a new "carnal density" and "corporeality." Although Crary terms this a "physiological optics" and emphasizes the bodily produced sensations, he does not account for the body's position in relation to the eye—the relation of sight to bodily movement—or for the optical and hence subjective differences between binocular parallax and persistence of vision. Crary's account of the "body of the observer" is not an account of a socially constituted or gendered body.

42 Ibid., 33; emphasis added. Crary's dismissal of the magic lantern as a "counter-deployment" of the camera obscura seems odd because he supplies more evidence for its use as a device of illusion than as a drawing device.

43 Two recent books have elaborated this history: Laurent Mannoni, *The Great Art of Light and Shadow* (2000), and Deac Rossell, *Living Pictures: The Origins of the Movies* (Albany: State University of New York Press, 1998). Mannoni's book was first published in French as *Le grand art de la lumière et de l'ombre: Archéologie du cinéma* (Paris: Editions Nathan, 1994).

44 See Martin Quigley Jr., *Magic Shadows: The Story of the Origin of Motion Pictures* (New York: Quigley, 1960); Olive Cook, *Movement in Two Dimensions* (London: Hutchinson & Co, 1963); C. W. Ceram, *Archeology of the Cinema* (New York: Harcourt, Brace & World); Charles Musser, "Toward a History of Screen Practice," in *The Emergence of Cinema: The American Screen to 1907* (New York: Charles Scribner's Sons, 1990), 15–54; Jac Remise, Pascale Remise, and Regis van de Walle, *Magie lumineuse: Du théâtre d'ombres à la lanterne magique*

(Paris: Balland, 1979); and H. Mark Gosser, "Kircher and Lanterna Magica—A Reexamination," *Journal of the Society of Motion Picture and Television Engineers* 90 (October 1981): 972–978.

45 In Mannoni's corrective account of the "magic lantern," German Jesuit Athanasius Kircher was "its pseudo-inventor" and Dutch Protestant Christiaan Huygens "its true father" (34). Kircher's 1646 edition of *Ars magna lucis et umbrae* claimed many inventions, and Mannoni writes, "some of the most serious historians have been deceived into believing (some still to this day) that his was the invention of the magic lantern" (*The Great Art,* 23). The "magic lantern," Mannoni claims, was invented in 1659 by Christiaan Huygens and was properly named in 1668 by Italian mathematician Francesco Eschinardi (*The Great Art,* 3–73).

46 The discovery of chemicals to fix the camera's image made it possible to retain the writing of light on a surface, to *photo-graph.* Once light writes its image on a surface, the image out its window—its tiny aperture—is fixed as its two-dimensional virtual other. The flight of birds, the movement of trees in the wind, the gestures of humans were of great fascination to the viewers of the camera obscura, but the photograph could not record the movement in two dimensions. In order to reconstitute movement, a different apparatus with different mechanics needed to be developed: movement had to be recorded onto separate frames on a strip of light-sensitive film, and the strip of separate images had to be moved quickly past a light source. See Cook, *Movement in Two Dimensions.* The size of the image was dependent on its distance from the aperture, but the shape of the projected image, as noted by commentators as early as Aristotle, was always circular. Roger Bacon tried a square aperture, but the image was still circular, leading him to conclude that it was a property of light.

47 Mannoni, *The Great Art,* 264.

48 The recent facsimile reprint of a two-volume set of nineteenth-century precinematic documents provides many texts and treatises as evidence of the vibrancy of the practice in the late nineteenth century. Stephen Herbert, *A History of Pre-Cinema,* 3 vols. (New York: Routledge, 2000), includes W. J. Chadwick, *The Magic Lantern Manual* (1878).

49 Karl Marx and Friedrich Engels, *The German Ideology,* ed. C. J. Arthur (New York: International Publishers, 1970), 47.

50 For an exegesis of the camera obscura and other figurative language in Marx, see W. J. T. Mitchell, "Rhetoric of Iconoclasm: Marxism, Ideology, and Fetishism," in *Iconology: Image, Text Ideology* (Chicago: University of Chicago Press, 1986); Raymond Williams, "From Reflection to Mediation," in *Marxism and Literature* (Oxford: Oxford University Press, 1977); and Sarah Kofman, *Camera obscura, de l'idéologie* (Paris: Editions Galilée, 1983). Marx also invoked another optical device, the *phantasmagoria,* to decry capitalism's realm of illusion. The editors of the feminist film journal *Camera Obscura* launched their first issue with an editorial that adopted the metaphor as a convergence of ideology and representation. See editorial, "Feminism and Film: Critical Approaches," *Camera Obscura* 1 (Fall 1976): 3–10.

51 Marx and Engels, *The German Ideology,* 47.

52 Roland Barthes, *Camera Lucida: Reflections on Photography,* trans. Richard Howard (London: Vintage, 1993), 80. This point is also made by Jean-Louis Comolli in a 1978 essay, "Machines of the Visible." In a critique of French theorist J. P. Lebel, for his concern with the ideological/scientific "regulation" of cinema equated with geometral optics, Comolli writes: "he simply forgets the other patron science of cinema and photography, photochemistry, without which the camera would be no more precisely than a *camera obscura*." See Jean-Louis Comolli, "Machines of the Visible," in Teresa De Lauretis and Stephen Heath, eds., *The Cinematic Apparatus* (New York: St. Martin's Press, 1980), 125.

53 Quoted in Beaumont Newhall, *The History of Photography* (New York: Museum of Modern Art, 1964), 13. Quoted from V. Fouque, *La vérité sur l'invention de la photographie; Nicéphore Niépce* (Paris, 1867), 61. Niépce's view from his window at Le Gras is often thought to be the earliest known existing photograph. As a millennial gesture in 2000, Magnum photographer René Burri returned to Niépce's attic window and retook the photograph, which was then published in *Life* magazine. (In much the same manner of historical parallax, the 1995 film *Lumière & Co.* had contemporary filmmakers use the Lumières' 1895 Cinématographe to make short *actualitiés* one hundred years later.)

54 The "first photograph" is currently housed in its original presentational frame but encased with inert gas in an airtight steel-and-Plexiglas storage frame at the Harry Ransom Humanities Research Center, University of Texas in Austin. Photo historian Helmut Gernsheim obtained the photograph for his own collection in the 1950s and then donated the piece to the university in 1963. In 1952, Gernsheim attempted to photograph the heliographic image for a copy print. The image of the original heliograph that is commonly reproduced was made in 1952 at the Eastman Kodak Research Laboratory in Harrow, England.

55 André Bazin, "The Ontology of the Photographic Image," in *What Is Cinema?*, vol. 1, trans. Hugh Gray (Berkeley: University of California Press, 1967), 11.

56 Beaumont Newhall's *The History of Photography* (New York: Museum of Modern Art, 1964) commences with the assertion: "Camera pictures have been made since the Renaissance" (11). See also Gernsheim and Gernsheim, *The History of Photography: From the Camera Obscura to the Beginning of the Modern Era*.

57 André Bazin, "The Myth of Total Cinema," in *What Is Cinema?*, vol. 1, 20–21; emphasis added. Although both of these early essays share the assumption of a teleological impulse toward realism, the later essay is largely concerned with the technical delays in achieving the ideal of "total cinema." I would argue, counter to Bazin, that it was the fascination with *virtuality*—the *near*-approximation of the real—and not with the reality of images that has driven these inventions. In his writing on animation, Alan Cholodenko argues that the fascination for spectators was with "*the illusion of life* . . . the way in which an apparatus animates—gives movement and life to—images of peoples and things." Cholodenko emphasizes that cinema was first an "animatic apparatus," from which all forms of cinema descended. See Alan Cholodenko, ed., *The Illusion of Life: Essays on Animation* (Bloomington: Indiana University Press, 1993), 20.

58 Bazin, "Ontology of the Photographic Image," 11–13.

59 "Painting was forced, as it turned out, to offer us illusion, and this illusion was reckoned sufficient unto art. Photography and cinema, on the other hand, are discoveries that satisfy once and for all and in its very essence, our obsession with realism." Bazin, "Ontology of the Photographic Image," 15.

Here it is necessary to ground Bazin's commitment to a realist ontology in relation to his post–World War II indictment of the antirealist film aesthetics of the Soviet montagists and the German expressionists. Bazin's argument holds the Soviets and Germans—wartime enemies of the French and the Allies—as implicit rhetorical villains. In "The Evolution of the

Language of the Cinema," a composite of essays written between 1950 and 1955, Bazin's position shifted slightly from his early claims for the "integral" ontological realism of the photographic image to a more specifically stylistic realism of the long-take, deep-focus style. In this essay, Bazin attacks the montage-style of the Soviets Kuleshov and Eisenstein ("they did not give us the event, they alluded to it") and the mise-en-scène of the German school (which "did every kind of violence to the plastics of the image by way of sets and lighting"). Bazin, "The Evolution of the Language of the Cinema," in *What Is Cinema?,* vol. 1, 25–26. For a discussion of Bazin's war and postwar politics, his rejection of the Stalinism of the Communist party, see Dudley Andrew, *André Bazin* (New York: Columbia University Press, 1978). Andrew also offers a biographical account of the influence of Bergson, Malraux, and Sartre on Bazin.

60 Collections of key essays from "apparatus" theory—the writings of Jean-Louis Baudry, Jean-Louis Comolli, Stephen Heath, and Christian Metz—have been anthologized in translation in three anthologies: De Lauretis and Heath, eds., *The Cinematia Apparatus;* Phil Rosen, ed., *Narrative, Apparatus, Ideology* (New York: Columbia University Press, 1986); and Theresa Hak Kyung Cha, ed., *Apparatus* (New York: Tanam Press, 1980).

Phil Rosen's book *Change Mummifed: Cinema, Historicity, Theory* (Minneapolis: University of Minnesota Press, 2001) examines the continental and Anglo-American rejection of Bazin in 1970s film theory. Rosen finds the spatial realism of perspective to be of less importance to Bazin than issues of temporality. He takes the line from Bazin's "Ontology" essay, "For the first time, the image of things is likewise the image of their duration, change mummified as it were" (15), as the signal statement about the cinema's capacities in the "defense against the passage of time" (Rosen, *Change Mummifed,* 3–41).

61 "Apparatus" has been used as the translation for the French word *dispositif*—a device or arrangement which includes its metaphysical and metapsychological effects. The translation "apparatus" elides the distinction between the *dispositif* as arrangement and the *appareil* as machine. Although Althusser is usually credited for the derivation of the term *dispositif* for film theory, Joan Copjec asserts that apparatus theory borrowed that term from Bachelard, not Althusser. See Joan Copjec, *Read My Desire: Lacan against the Historicists* (Cambridge: MIT Press, 1997); see also Etienne Balibar, "From Bachelard to Althusser: The Concept of 'Epistemological Break,'" *Economy and Society* 5, no. 4 (November 1976): 385–411.

62 Jean-Louis Baudry, "Ideological Effects of the Basic Cinematographic Apparatus," trans. Alan Williams, in Rosen, ed., *Narrative, Apparatus, Ideology,* 286. Baudry's two essays, "Ideological Effects of the Basic Cinematographic Apparatus" (1970) and "The Apparatus: Metapsychological Approaches to the Impression of Reality in the Cinema" (1975), offer an ideological critique of the "reality effect" of cinematic spectatorship. The earlier essay is more directly influenced by a post–May 1968 critique of the ideology of representation; the second essay is more fully in the force field of psychoanalytic theory. "Ideological Effects" was first printed in *Cinéthique,* nos. 7–8 (1970); "The Apparatus" was first printed in *Communications,* no. 23 (1975): 56–73. Both have been reprinted in translation in Cha, ed., *Apparatus,* as well as in Rosen, ed., *Narrative, Apparatus, Ideology.*

63 Baudry, "Ideological Effects," in Rosen, ed., *Narrative, Apparatus, Ideology,* 288.

64 Ibid., 288–299.

65 Marx and Engels, *The German Ideology,* 47.

66 Diagram from Jean-Louis Baudry, "Ideological Effects of the Basic Cinematographic Apparatus," in Rosen, ed., *Narrative, Apparatus, Ideology,* 288:

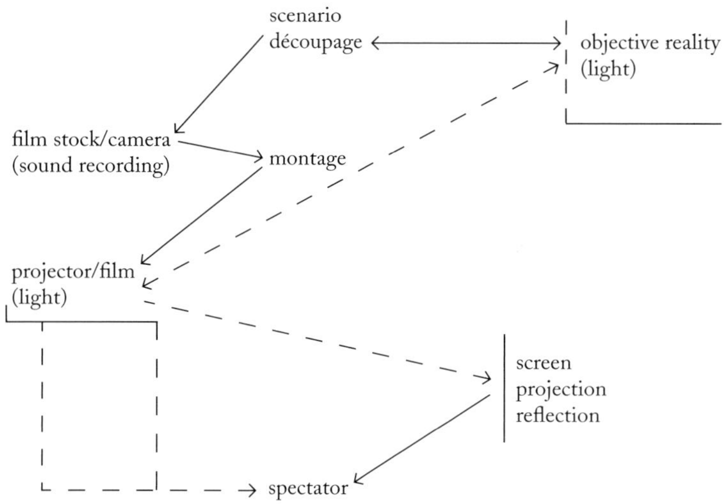

The disposition of elements and the broken lines indicating the ideological process are clarified in the text.

67 Hubert Damisch, *The Origin of Perspective,* trans. John Goodman (Cambridge: MIT Press, 1995), xiv–xv.

68 Ibid.; emphasis added.

69 Ibid., xvii.

70 A recent collection of writings—Michael O'Pray, ed., *The British Avant-Garde Film 1926 to 1995: An Anthology of Writings* (London: Paul & Co., 2003)—includes determinative essays on the structuralist-materialist project: Peter Gidal, "Theory and Definition of Structuralist/Materialist Film"; Stephen Heath, "Repetition Time: Notes around 'Structuralist/Materialist Film'"; Malcolm Le Grice, "The History We Need"; and Lis Rhodes, "Whose History?"

71 Stan Brakhage, *Metaphors on Vision,* special issue of *Film Culture,* 1963. Certainly Brakhage's project as a filmmaker explored the apparatical limits of the materials of filmmaking and challenged habits of perception and vision. David James suggests: "Brakhage's compositional attention to the entire frame, especially to its edges, produces the 'all-over' decenteredness of abstract expressionism rather than the centered subjectivity of perspective painting." See David E. James, "Stan Brakhage: The Filmmaker as Poet," in *Allegories of Cinema: American Film in the Sixties* (Princeton: Princeton University Press, 1989), 47, n. 11.

72 Christian Metz, "Le signifiant imaginaire," in *Communications,* no. 23 (1975): 3–56. This special issue of *Communications,* entitled "Psychanalyse et cinéma," contained pieces by Metz, Baudry, Kristeva, Guattari, Barthes, Kuntzel, Bellour, and Nick Browne. Four of Metz's essays were collected and published in the 10/18 series as *Le signifiant imaginaire: Psychanalyse et cinéma* (Paris: Union Générale d'Editions, 1977). The cover of the 1977 paperback has a nineteenth-century drawing of a projecting praxinoscope casting images onto a screen. This volume was translated as Christian Metz, *The Imaginary Signifier: Psychoanalysis and Cinema,* trans. Celia Britton, Annwyl Williams, Ben Brewster, and Alfred Guzzetti (Bloomington: Indiana University Press, 1982), 49.

73 Quoted in Stephen Heath, "Narrative Space," in *Questions of Cinema* (London: Macmillan, 1981), 29, n. 9. From Marcelin Pleynet, interview with Gérard Leblanc, *Cinéthique*, no. 3 (1969). Heath's essay was originally printed in *Screen* 17, no. 3 (Autumn 1976): 68–112. The quotes from Heath that follow are taken from the *Questions of Cinema* version.

74 Ibid., 28. Marcelin Pleynet's work formulated this idea directly: "a camera productive of a perspective code directly constructed on the model of the scientific perspective of Quattrocento" (quoted in Heath "Narrative Space," 28). Heath's premises in this essay were challenged in a lengthy and zealous attack by Noël Carroll in "Address to the Heathen," *October* 23 (Winter 1982), to which Heath responded in "Le Père Noël," in *October* 26 (Fall 1983): 63–115. While much of Carroll's animus is directed toward his rejection of Heath's Lacanian-Althusserian premises, Carroll's rejoinder to Heath's account of perspective as ideological is to claim instead the accuracy of perspectival representation as "not a dissimulation/counterfeit replica of vision, but the most accurate means of rendering information about spatial appearance" ("Address to the Heathen," 114).

75 Heath, "Narrative Space," 28. The camera represented autonomous vision, vision that did not depend on the human organ for sight.

76 Ibid., 28–29. Heath emphasizes central perspective's "ceaseless confirmation of the importance of centre and position" and insists, "What must be more crucially emphasized is . . . the ideal of a steady position, of a unique embracing center." The "cost of such fixed centrality" is the anamorphic distortion caused when the eye is not centered.

77 Ibid., 28. Although Heath mentions the Latin *istoria* in parentheses here, he does not suggest how *istoria*—the Latin for "narrative" or "holy story"—is related to "framed, centred, harmonious." In the larger logic of his essay, Heath argues that narrative serves to fulfill the functions that perspective does: centering and framing.

78 Ibid., 34; emphasis added.

79 Ibid., 30.

80 Ibid., 31.

81 Claus Grimm, *The Book of Picture Frames* (New York: Abaris Books, 1992), 25. Grimm writes of these periods, "Certainly there were few pictures serving as movable furnishings for any and every private room. But in stately secular rooms there were already areas painted with illusionistic pictures, which were surrounded with ornamental bands and painted friezes; this is proved by the late classical wall painting." While the beginnings of the painterly frame are not exact, the end of the picture frame is within recent memory. Malevich preferred no frame; Mondrian rejected the frame. When in 1954 Frank Stella left the edge of the canvas visible and used thicker canvas supports, the material support of the painting was revealed. See also Piers and Caroline Fretham, *The Art of Framing* (New York: Clarkson Potter, 1997); and Desmond MacNamara, *Picture Framing: A Practical Guide from Basic to Baroque* (London: David and Charles Publishers, 1986).

82 A recent collection of essays examines the boom in panel painting in Italy from the middle of the thirteenth century onward. Panel painting was not confined to altarpieces, but also transformed existing object types, including painted crosses, altar frontals, and monumental panels of the Virgin and Child, and brought on new surfaces for painting, lunette-shaped panels for architectural settings, small-scale panels for personal devotion, and painted chests for private homes. See Victor M. Schmidt, ed., *Italian Panel Painting of the Duecento and Trecento* (New Haven: Yale University Press, 2002).

83 Grimm, *The Book of Picture Frames,* 26. There are many questions about the history of the frame that I will not pursue here: the relation of the frame to its architectural surround, to the ornamentation found on adjacent doors and windows, the relation of framing motifs to book cover motifs, the difference between frames of text and frames of image, frames as architectonic structures separating the multipartite sequences in triptychs and polyptychs, the relation of the pictorial frame to the theatrical proscenium frame, etc.

84 See Ernst Gombrich's discussion of the relation between painting, frame, and architectural surround in "The Psychology of Styles," chapter 8 of *The Sense of Order* (1979), reprinted in *The Essential Gombrich: Selected Writings on Art and Culture,* ed. Richard Woodfield (London: Phaidon Press, 1996), 264.

85 The painter could carry his easel into the landscape. Evidenced in many Renaissance paintings—such as Rembrandt's self-portrait *Artist in His Studio* (1629) and Velázquez's *Las meninas* (1656–1667)—the presence of the easel marked the painter's activity.

86 John Berger, *Ways of Seeing* (London: Penguin Books, 1972), 109. Michael Baxandall also described the painting as a "deposit" when, in the first sentence of his 1972 study *Painting and Experience in Fifteenth Century Italy,* he proclaims: "A fifteenth-century painting is the deposit of a social relationship" (1). Baxandall's work describes the pleasures of possession, and the contract between painters and their clients. Baxandall, *Painting and Experience in Fifteenth Century Italy: A Primer in the Social History of Pictorial Styl*e (Oxford: Oxford University Press, 1972), 1.

87 Heath, "Narrative Space," 34.

88 Ibid., 35.

89 Damisch, *The Origin of Perspective,* 170.

90 Lew Andrews, *Story and Space in Renaissance Art: The Rebirth of Continuous Narrative* (Cambridge: Cambridge University Press, 2000).

91 Metz, *Imaginary Signifier,* 49.

92 Heath, "Narrative Space," 32; emphasis added.

93 Baudry, "Ideological Effects," 292.

94 Kaja Silverman, *The Threshold of the Visible World* (New York: Routledge, 1996), 125. See also my account of the primary, secondary, and tertiary registers of identification: Anne Friedberg, "A Denial of Difference: Theories of Cinematic Identification," in E. Ann Kaplan, ed., *Psychoanalysis and Cinema* (New York: Routledge, 1989), 36–45.

95 Jean-Pierre Oudart's essays on "suture" in *Cahiers du Cinéma* in 1969, 1970, and 1971 were written in the context of many post–May '68 film debates in the French journals *Tel Quel, Cinéthique,* and *Cahiers du Cinéma* which engaged with Althusserian concepts of ideology and Lacanian psychoanalysis. Oudart's writing was translated into English in the British journal *Screen* in 1977–1978. Using Lacan's notion of the subject "suturing" the "lack," Oudart adapted the metaphor of suture to his account of the spectator's reaction to shot transitions. Oudart describes the spectator's switch from enjoying the plentitude and *jouissance* of an image to the discovery of its frame. He maintains that this realization reveals the absent space outside of the frame and exposes the film as constructed/enunciated operation. Once the spectator notes the frame, the spectator asks: whose point of view? For the dossier of debate on "suture," see Jacques-Alain Miller, "Suture (Elements of the Logic of the Signifier)," *Screen* 18, no. 4 (1977–1978): 29–34; Jean-Pierre Oudart, "Notes on Suture," *Screen* 18, no. 4 (1977–1978): 35–47; Stephen Heath, "Notes on Suture," *Screen* 18, no. 4 (1977–1978): 48–76; Daniel Dayan, "The Tutor-Code of

Classical Cinema" (1974), in Leo Braudy and Marshall Cohen, eds., *Film Theory and Criticism*, 5th ed. (New York: Oxford University Press, 1999), 118–129; William Rothman, "Against the System of the Suture" (1975), in Braudy and Cohen, eds., *Film Theory and Criticism*, 130–136.

96 "It is the differences in frame between film and painting that are generally emphasized: film is limited to a standard screen ratio (the three to four horizontal rectangle)." Stephen Heath, "On Screen, in Frame: Film and Ideology" (1975), first published in *Quarterly Review of Film and Video* 1, no. 3 (August 1976): 251–265, and reprinted in Heath, *Questions of Cinema* (London: Macmilllan, 1981), 10. Heath's interest in frames and screens makes a fugal reappearance in other essays: "Narrative Space" (1976), and "Screen Images, Film Memory," *Edinburgh '76 Magazine* (1976): 33–42. In "Narrative Space," Heath writes: "In a sense, moreover, the constraint of the rectangle is even greater in the cinema than in painting: in the latter proportions are relatively free; in the former, they are limited to a standard aspect ratio (Frampton's 1.33 to 1 rectangle, the aptly named 'academy frame') or as now, to a very small number of ratios." *Questions of Cinema*, 35.

I will discuss the postwar expansion of the frame's rectangle—in CinemaScope and Cinerama—as important indications of the changing notion of the screen as "window" in chapter 4.

97 Vivian Sobchack provides a critique of film theory's use of the metaphor of the frame and the metaphor of the window and the metaphor of the mirror along phenomenological lines. See Vivian Sobchack, *The Address of the Eye: Phenomenology and the Film Experience* (Princeton: Princeton University Press, 1992).

98 Apparatus theory met with theoretical challenges on a number of fronts. Feminist film theorists challenged the ungendered accounts of visuality implicit in theories of the apparatus that assumed a spectator unaffected by its gendered body or psyche. In her "feminal" essay "Visual Pleasure and Narrative Cinema" (1975), Laura Mulvey qualifies the relation between spectator and screen by introducing a specific equation between the viewing position of "man as bearer of the look" and the "spectacle" of "woman as object of the look." See Laura Mulvey, *Visual and Other Pleasures* (Bloomington: Indiana University Press, 1989), 3–26. Other critiques of the implicit gendering of the conventions of "looking" can be found in Sandy Flitterman-Lewis, "Woman, Desire, and the Look: Feminism and the Enunciative Apparatus in Cinema," *Ciné-Tracts* 2, no. 1 (1978): 63–68; Linda Williams, "Film Body: An Implantation of Perversions," in Rosen, ed., *Narrative Apparatus, Ideology*, 507–534; Lucy Fisher, "The Image of Woman as Image: The Optical Politics of Dames," in Rick Altman, ed., *Genre: The Musical* (London: Routledge and Kegan Paul, 1981), 70–84; and Kaja Silverman, *The Subject of Semiotics* (New York: Oxford University Press, 1983), 222–236. For a sustained analysis and nuanced critique of Metz and Baudry, see Mary Ann Doane, *Femmes Fatales: Feminism, Film Theory, Psychoanalysis* (New York: Routledge, 1991).

On another front, apparatus theory was vigorously challenged by Noël Carroll, David Bordwell, and others for its Lacanian-Althusserian premises. See David Bordwell and Noël Carroll, eds., *Post-Theory: Reconstructing Film Studies* (Madison: University of Wisconsin Press, 1996). Jacques Aumont stages a veiled attack on apparatus theory, positing a change between 1780 and 1820 in the switch between the *ébauche* (the sketch) and the *étude* (the study). Jacques Aumont, "The Variable Eye, or the Mobilization of the Gaze," trans. Charles O'Brien and Sally Shafto, in Dudley Andrew, ed., *The Image in Dispute: Art and Cinema in the Age of Photography* (Austin: University of Texas Press, 1997), 231–258.

99 While Lacan invoked the mirror as a model for the visual scenario of identity formation, his most elaborate theorization of the constitutive scenarios of vision rely on the metaphor of the screen (*écran*). Apparatus theories seemed more taken by the mirror metaphor than the screen. See note 79 in the Introduction.

100 David Bordwell, *Narration in the Fiction Film* (Madison: University of Wisconsin Press, 1985), 107.

101 Ibid., 107–109.

102 Ibid., 4–15. Bordwell divides theories of narration into two broad categories, those which involve "showing" and those that involve "telling." While this is a useful distinction, he also equates "mimetic theories of narration" with showing and "diegetic theories of narration" with the telling. This reader finds these latter categories to confuse the issue rather than to provide further clarification. "Mimetic" implies the realism of imitation, not the fictional status of the image in visual narration; and although "diegetic" refers to a fictional world, "fictional" does not imply a mode of telling rather than showing. One can certainly have a diegetic spectacle, i.e., a purely visual fictional diegetic world. See also David Bordwell, *On the History of Film Style* (Cambridge: Harvard University Press, 1997).

103 Bordwell, *Narration in the Fiction Film,* 5.

104 Ibid., 4, 7.

105 The theoretical standoff between psychoanalytically inflected apparatus theory and the cognitive reformation of post-70s film theory was acted out in the debate between Stephen Heath and Noël Carroll in subsequent issues of the journal *October* in 1983. Carroll and Bordwell both took up the banner of refuting the claims of apparatus theory in their book *Post-Theory.* Despite the theoretical posturing of difference, there are marked similiarities to be found in the writing of Heath and Bordwell.

106 Bordwell misses this important distinction. He writes: "Perspective (from the Italian *prospettiva*) means, we are reminded often enough, 'seeing through'" (5). He has the terminological definition wrong. *Perspectiva* relies on the prefix *per* (Latin for "through") and means "seeing through"; *prospettiva* relies on the prefix *pro* (Latin for "before or in front of") and means "seeing in front of."

107 Richard DeCordova has argued this point with fine-tuned historical specificity in "From Lumière to Pathé: The Break-up of Perspectival Space," in Thomas Elsaesser, ed., *Early Cinema: Space, Frame, Narrative* (London: BFI, 1991), 76–85. First published in *Cine-Tracts* 4, nos. 2 and 3 (Summer, Fall 1981): 55–63.

108 In *Cinema 1: The Movement-Image* (1986), Gilles Deleuze breaks down the moving image (*movement-image*) into is constituent frames and examines and expands upon these variables in analytic detail. One of Deleuze's categories, which I will examine in the final chapter, is a framed moving image that contains another frame. Gilles Deleuze, *Cinema 1: The Movement-Image,* trans. Hugh Tomlinson (Minneapolis: University of Minnesota Press, 1986).

109 Baudry, "Ideological Effects," 290.

110 Ibid.

111 Ibid., 290, 293.

112 Noël Carroll's objection to Heath is based on Heath's claims for narrative as a perspective system, for the equation of perspective and narrative. See Carroll, "Address to the Heathen."

113 Heath, "Narrative Space," 44; emphasis added. Heath's arguments about narrative are also closely related to the core of Tom Gunning's "cinema of attractions" argument—that the fascination with pure movement subsided as narrative took over. While Gunning doesn't address perspective, the framing of movement, or the tension between the movement of the virtual image and the stasis of the spectator, his argument about the emergence of narrative suggests that storytelling aspects exceeded and/or instrumentalized story-showing aspects in service of narrative logic. See Tom Gunning "The Cinema of Attractions: Early Film, Its Spectator and the Avant-Garde," in Elsaesser, ed., *Early Cinema,* 56–62.

114 In this regard, the revisionist film histories of the last two decades (Rossell, Manoni, Gunning) have recast the considerations of early cinema from its development as a form of storytelling to its place in the radically new perceptual habits (of movement, of illusion, of life/virtuality). See Mannoni, *The Great Art of Light and Shadow,* and Rossell, *Living Pictures.*

115 Quoted in Heath, "Narrative Space," 27. (Quoted from "Espace et illusion," *Revue internationale de filmologie* 2, no. 5 [1948]: 66.) Heath makes a complex claim for cinematic specificity, claiming that the "partial unreality of film" ("something between" two dimensions and three) is what makes this construction of space possible.

116 Ibid., 44.

117 Kristin Thompson, "Classical Narrative Space and the Spectator's Attention," in David Bordwell, Janet Staiger, and Kristin Thompson, *The Classical Hollywood Cinema: Film Style and Mode of Production to 1960* (New York: Columbia University Press, 1985), 214.

118 Ibid., 215. Elsewhere in the same volume, David Bordwell describes how cinematic space is tailored to the demands of narration: "Classical narration of space thus aims at orientation: The scenography is addressed to the viewer. Can we then say that a larger principle of 'perspective' operates here—not the adherence to a particular spatial composition but a general 'placing' of the spectator in an ideal position of intelligibility?" David Bordwell, "Space in the Classical Film," in Bordwell, Staiger, and Thompson, *Classical Hollywood Cinema,* 54. In a footnote to this passage, Bordwell references Stephen Heath.

119 "There are no jerks in time and space in real life. Time and space are continuous." Rudolf Arnheim, *Film as Art* (Berkeley: University of California Press, 1971), 21.

120 André Bazin, "The Evolution of the Language of the Cinema," in *What Is Cinema?* vol. 1, 23–40.

121 As I will argue in more detail in chapter 5 of this book, although there are scattered exceptions, through most of the century that constitutes the history of the moving image, the frame was most often a single frame. The conventions of editing that developed to stitch the separate spaces together in a logic of successive continuity relied on a single-framed image.

122 While phenomenological accounts of film spectatorship that insist on the body of the observer may seem, at first, to be congruent with Crary's claims for the "carnal density" of vision, his argument is based on the retinal properties of the viewing with devices like the stereoscope and phenakistoscope, and not on bodily effects of viewing.

123 Gordon Hendricks, *The Kinetoscope: America's First Commercially Successful Motion Picture Exhibitor* (New York: The Beginnings of the American Film, 1966).

124 Although I am drawing a broad contrast here between the implicit viewing systems of the kinetoscope and the Cinématographe, the exacting details of the many patented inventions and inventors leads to a much more nuanced account. The "first" public projection is a matter of historical debate: Max Skladanovksy debuted his Bioskop film projection device in the Berlin Wintergarten in November 1895. And although it was not intended for public display, in 1892 Marey had a design for a primitive projection mechanism to display his images of analyzed motion. In their 13 February 1895 patent, Auguste and Louis Lumière first deemed their device a "projecting chronophotographe." The March patent renamed the device "Cinématographe." See Marta Braun, *Picturing Time: The Work of Etienne-Jules Marey (1830–1904)* (Chicago: University of Chicago Press, 1992), 407, n. 69; French patent 245,032. See also Mannoni, *The Great Art of Light and Shadow,* and Rossell, *Living Pictures.*

125 Crary, *Techniques of the Observer,* 1.

126 Hollis Frampton, "Eadweard Muybridge: Fragments of a Tesseract," *Artforum* (March 1973): 43–52. Special issues of the journal *October* have explored Frampton's exceptionally rich oeuvre of films and writings. See *October* 32 (Spring 1985) and *October* 109 (Summer 2004). A tesseract (Gk: *tessares,* four + *aktis,* ray) is a three-dimensional hypercube taken to the next exponent, the fourth dimension, time.

127 Three recent books should be noted. Marta Braun's detailed research and analysis of the work of Etienne Jules Marey, *Picturing Time,* forcefully decontextualizes Marey from his previous historical position as merely a "precursor" to futurism, the cinema, and the scientific management studies of Frank Gilbreth and places Marey's project and commitments in terms of nineteenth-century positivism and scientific thought. Rebecca Solnit dramatizes Muybridge's "annihilation of time and space" in a recent biography, *River of Shadows: Eadweard Muybridge and the Technological Wild West* (New York: Viking, 2003). In her deeply theorized historical account *The Emergence of Cinematic Time: Modernity, Contingency, the Archive* (Cambridge: Harvard University Press, 2002), Mary Ann Doane situates the work of Marey and Muybridge in relation to the emergent cinematic modes of restructuring of time and contigency.

128 E. J. Marey, *Animal Mechanism: A Treatise on Terrestrial and Aerial Locomotion* (New York: D. Appleton, 1874). This volume has 117 plates, etchings, and charts, no photographs.

129 In 1882, Marey wrote to his mother: "I have a photographic gun [*fusil photographique*] that has nothing murderous about it and that takes pictures of a flying bird or running animal in less than 1/500 of a second." Quoted in Braun, *Picturing Time,* 57.

130 Ibid., 64; emphasis added. In calling the shutter aperture a "window," Marey seems to have used the same phrasing as Descartes.

131 My discussion of Marey is briefly reductive of his single-plate chronophotography. As detailed by Braun, Marey also built a multiple-lens camera to allow for each lens to sequentially expose onto the same plate. See Braun, *Picturing Time,* 85–91. Marey's work at the Station Physiologique on human locomotion and fatigue is analyzed in a different light by Anson Rabinbach, *The Human Motor: Energy, Fatigue and the Origins of Modernity* (Berkeley: University of California Press, 1992).

132 Sigfried Giedion makes a distinction between the two methods of recording movement in *Mechanization Takes Command* (New York: Oxford University Press, 1948), 14–30. Marta Braun draws exacting distinctions between the goals and methods of Marey and Muybridge: "Marey wanted to give a visible expression to the continuity of movement over equidistant and known intervals . . . and to do so within a single image" (*Picturing Time,* xvii). Muybridge's photographs, Braun argues, were not "scientific depictions of movement, but fictions" (xvi). Braun's contrast of Muybridge and Marey centers on their separate valuation of the realist/positivist aspects of the camera. Marey, she argues, "used his camera to work directly against a code of perspective, built on the model of the scientific perspective of fifteenth-century Italy," while Muybridge's "narrative fantasies" duplicated "exactly those illusions Marey tried all his life to avoid" (254–255).

133 For analysis of Muybridge and his gendered subjects, see Linda Williams, *Hard Core: Power, Pleasure and the Frenzy of the Visible* (Berkeley: University of California Press, 1989). For a further discussion of Muybridge and cinematic illusion, see Mieke Bal, "The Gaze in the Closet," in Teresa Brennan and Martin Jay, eds., *Vision in Context* (New York: Routledge, 1996).

134 Doane, *The Emergence of Cinematic Time,* 172–205. Doane returns to the paradox of Zeno (cited in early theorizations of the cinema by philosopher Henri Bergson and filmmaker Jean Epstein) in order to contend with the paradox of the cinematic image—that movement is produced from static images.

135 As Marey wrote: "Cinema produces only what the eye can see in any case. It adds nothing to the power of our sight, nor does it remove its illusions." Etienne-Jules Marey, preface to Charles-Louis Eugène Trutat, *La photographie animée* (Paris: Gauthier-Villars, 1899), ix. Quoted in Braun, *Picturing Time* n. 413, 32.

136 Kuntzel describes *défilement:*

> *Défilement* . . . means, in the vocabulary of cinema, "progression, the sliding of the film-strip through the gate of the projector" and, in military art, the use of the terrain's accidents or of artificial constructions to conceal one's movements from the enemy. In the unrolling of the film, the photograms which concern us "pass through," hidden from sight what the spectator retains is only the movement within which they insert themselves. . . .
>
> Between the space of the film-strip and the time of the projections the film *rubs out:* movement erases its signifying process, and eventually conceals some of the images which pass too rapidly to be "seen."

Thierry Kuntzel, "The Défilement: A View in Close-Up," trans. Bertrand Augst, *Camera Obscura,* no. 2 (Fall 1977): 56; reprinted in Cha, ed., *Apparatus,* 233–241.

137 In *Window Shopping,* this was a central aspect of my argument about the fluid temporalities and "proto-postmodernity" of the "mobilized virtual gaze." The coincidence of H. G. Wells's publication of his time-travelling novel *The Time Machine* and British inventor R. W. Paul's application for a patent for a device to travel through time in 1895 marked the cinema as an apparatus for time travel. See my *Window Shopping,* 91–94; 104–106.

138 Vachel Lindsay, *The Art of the Moving Picture* (1915; reprint, New York: Modern Library Paperback Edition, 2000).

139 In fact, Panofsky's own instability about the title of his essay, "On Movies" (1936)—"Style and Medium in Moving Pictures" (1937, 1940), and "Style and Medium in Motion Pictures" (1947)—is an indication of the mobility of terminology around the medium's specificity of movement. Erwin Panofsky, "On Movies," *Princeton University, Department of Art and Archeology, Bulletin* (1936): 5–15. See chapter 1, note 74 in this volume.

140 As discussed in chapter 1, when Panofsky's incisive isolation of these two specificities is held up to his writing on perspective as a "symbolic form," he seems to be approaching—but not yet willing to assert—the "motion picture" as a postperspectival "symbolic form."

141 In *Open Sky,* Paul Virilio opens his account with the horizon and the limitless blue sky above: "Besides, the entire history of Quattrocento perspectives is only ever a story of struggle, of the battle of geometers vying to make us forget the 'high' and the 'low' by pushing the 'near' and the 'far,' a *vanishing point* that literally fascinated them even though our vision is actually determined by our weight and oriented by the pull of earth's gravity, by the classic distinction between *zenith* and *nadir*." Paul Virilio, *Open Sky*, trans. Julie Rose (London: Verso, 1997), 1.

LENS II: HEIDEGGER'S FRAME

1 Martin Heidegger, "Der Grundvorgang der Neuzeit ist die Eroberung der Welt als Bild" (1938), published trans. as "The Age of the World Picture," in Heidegger, *The Question Concerning Technology and Other Essays*, trans. William Lovitt (New York: Harper and Row, 1977), 134. "The Age of the World Picture" was Heidegger's published version of a lecture entitled "The Establishing by Metaphysics of the Modern World Picture" given on June 9, 1938. Many of its concepts were revised, repeated in four lectures given in Bremen in 1949–1950—"Das Ding" (The Thing), "Das Ge-stell" (Enframing), "Die Gefahr" (The Danger), "Die Kehre" (The Turning)—and in the lecture "Die Frage nach der Technik" given in Munich on November 18, 1955. The German text, "Die Zeit des Weltbildes," appears in Heidegger, *Holzwege* (Frankfurt am Main: Vittorio Klostermann, 1950), 69–104. I have relied on both the German text and the Lovitt translation. The notes that follow emphasize the importance of reading Heidegger's writing in the original German.

2 "[T]he fact that the world becomes picture at all is what distinguishes the essence of the modern age." Heidegger, "Age of the World Picture," 130. As Lovitt explains, he translates Heidegger's "der Neuzeit"—more literally, "New Age"—as "modern age." Heidegger's questioning of the word "picture" (*Bild*) exemplifies that it does not mean "copy" (*Abbild*) or "imitation" (*Abklatsch*) and emphasizes instead the representedness (*Vorgestellheit*) of the world: "Hence world picture, when understood essentially, does not mean a picture of the world but the world conceived and grasped as picture" ("Age of the World Picture," 129).

3 René Descartes, *Meditations on First Philosophy with Selections and Objections and Replies*, trans. J. Cottingham (Cambridge: Cambridge University Press, 1986). Heidegger explicitly cites Descartes's *Meditations:* "What it is to be is for the first time defined as the objectiveness of representing, and truth is first defined as the certainty of representing in the metaphysics of Descartes" ("Age of the World Picture," 127). Lovitt translates the German word *Gegenständlichkeit* as "objectiveness" rather than making the meaning of the "standing outsideness" of representation more direct.

4 Heidegger, "Age of the World Picture," 132. ("Daß die Welt zum Bild wird, ist ein und derselbe Vorgang mit dem, daß der Mensch innerhalb des Seienden zum Subjectum wird" ["Die Zeit des Weltbildes," 85].) In a long appendix on Descartes, Heidegger expands upon the relation between thought and representation: "Thinking is representing, setting-before, is a representing relation to what is represented" ("Age of the World Picture," 149). This representation (*Vorstellung*)—what we "set-before" (*vorstellen*)—is also structured by us.

5 Heidegger, "Age of the World Picture," 134. ("Die Zeit des Weltbildes," 84.)

6 As Lovitt points out, *Gebild* is a Heideggerian neologism, with the overtones of a "structured picture." (Heidegger, "Age of the World Picture," 134.)

7 Heidegger entitled his second Bremen lecture "Das Gestell." This lecture was again reworked into Heidegger's now oft-cited and yet frequently misunderstood canonical text, "The Question Concerning Technology," in *The Question Concerning Technology and Other Essays*, trans. William Lovitt (New York: Harper and Row, 1977), 3–36. The German text,

"Die Frage nach der Technik," appears in *Vorträge und Aufsätze* (Pfullingen: Günther Neske Verlag, 1954), 13–44. The essay is translated by Samuel Weber as "Questing after Technics." *Gestell* has been translated variously as "enframing" (Lovitt) and "emplacement" (Weber). See Samuel Weber, "Upsetting the Set Up: Remarks on Heidegger's 'Questing after Technics,'" *Modern Language Notes* 105, no. 5 (December 1989): 977–991.

8 Heidegger, "The Age of the World Picture," 129.

9 Translations efface the verbal matrices and linguistic connotations implicit in Heidegger's German. For a discussion of the difficulties of translating Heidegger, see Samuel Weber, "Upsetting the Set Up." *Das Gestell* is the nominalized form of the German verb *gestellen* (to place, to frame, to trap)—a component of the matrix of verbs from the root *stellen* (to set, to place, to set into place), including *bestellen* (to order, to command), *vorstellen* (to represent), *darstellen* (to present or exhibit), and *gestellen* (to place, to frame, to trap)—which are deployed by Heidegger to interrogate the metaphysical relationship between thought and representation. Heidegger makes the distinction between traditional/preindustrial technics and modern technics by suggesting the historical shift from the German word *bestellen*—the peasant *bestellt* (tilled, worked, but also cherished) the land—to *gestellen*. For the modern farmer, the land is *gestellt* (placed, trapped, framed). As Weber points out, *stellen* is an important spatializing verb. The Lovitt translation of *Gestell* as "enframing" effaces the apparatical sense of the word and its mixture of movement and stasis; Lacoue-Labarthe translates *Gestell* as "installation," while Weber prefers "emplacement." In a footnote to the translated volume of Luce Irigaray's *L'oubli de l'air chez Martin Heidegger* (The Forgetting of Air in Martin Heidegger), trans. Mary Beth Mader (Austin: University of Texas Press, 1999), 183, Mader, the translator, points out that the French translations of Heidegger's *Gestell* are, variously, *arraisonnement* and *dispositif* (183 n.). The French term *dispositif*—which also was used to describe the cinematic apparatus—indicates that *Gestell* connotes an apparatus with metapsychological and metaphysical effects.

10 See David Michael Levin, "Decline and Fall: Ocularcentrism in Heidegger's Reading of the History of Metaphysics," in David Michael Levin, ed., *Modernity and the Hegemony of Vision* (Berkeley: University of California Press, 1993), 186–215. Levin centers his analysis of Heideggers's critique of vision and its discourses on *Being and Time* (1927) and *Introduction to Metaphysics* (1935) rather than on the later writings, "The Age of the World Picture" (1938) and "The Question Concerning Technology" (1949–1955). See also "Das Ge-stell: The Empire of Everyday Seeing," in David Michael Levin, *The Opening of Vision: Nihilism and the Postmodern Situation* (New York: Routledge, 1988).

11 Heidegger, "The Question Concerning Technology," 16; emphasis added. ("Die Frage nach der Technik," 15.)

12 Robert Smithson,"The Monuments of Passaic," *Artforum* 6 (December 1967): 49 (emphasis added); quoted widely but not in relation to this passage by Heidegger. See Craig Owens, "Toward a Theory of Postmodernism," in Scott Bryson et al., eds., *Beyond Recognition: Representation, Power and Culture* (Berkeley: University of California Press, 1992), 27; and Kaja Silverman, *The Threshold of the Visible World* (New York: Routledge, 1996), 204.

13 Martin Heidegger, "The Turning," in *The Question Concerning Technology and Other Essays*, 48.

14 Martin Heidegger, "The Thing," trans. Albert Hofstadter, in Heidegger, *Poetry, Language, Thought* (New York: Harper and Row, 1971), 165.

15 See Richard Dienst, "The Dangers of Being in a Televisual World: Heidegger and the Ontotechnological Question," in *Still Life in Real Time: Theory after Television* (Durham: Duke University Press, 1994), 103–127. Dienst suggests that television has become the most disturbing version of enframing (117).
16 Erwin Panofsky, *Perspective as Symbolic Form,* trans. Christopher S. Wood (New York: Zone Books, 1991), 67.

CHAPTER 3: THE "AGE OF WINDOWS"

1 In H. G. Wells's film script, the line reads, "I love history and history pictures! It's so exciting to see how the world has changed." See Leon Stover, *The Prophetic Soul—A Reading of H. G. Wells' Things to Come* (Jefferson, N.C.: McFarland, 1987), 159. See also H. G. Wells, *The Shape of Things to Come* (New York: Macmillan, 1933), 13–28; and H. G. Wells, script treatment of *Things to Come* (London: Cresset Press, 1935), 9–47.
2 I use the word "alongside" because the implications of my argument hang in the balance between the nuanced distinctions of coincidence and causality, either (1) the architectural role of the window changed coincident with the development of the window's virtual analogs, or (2) the architectural role of the window changed because of the development of the window's virtual analogs.
3 Clifford Howard, "What of the Future?," *Close Up* (March 1929): 76. The international film journal *Close Up* was published between 1927 and 1933. See James Donald, Anne Friedberg, and Laura Marcus, eds., *Close Up: Cinema and Modernism* (Princeton: Princeton University Press, 1998). Howard's 1929 account reads remarkably like André Bazin's 1945 essay "Myth of Total Cinema." Buoyed by the "advent of the talking picture" and other technical changes that would enhance cinematic realism, Howard writes: "Our modern world is a world of realism: and no art form yet invented has so closely approximated the realistic as will that of the cinema of the near future." His conception of the future includes sound, color, and three dimensions: "Dialogue and music will be but a part of the cinema of tomorrow. Their effectiveness will be enhanced by color and by a three-dimensional screen. The actors will have the semblance of living beings. The present flat presentments in colorless shades will be replaced by reflected actualities." Howard even predicts new forms of exhibition, viewing in the home: "Screening will be by means of reflection in place of direct projection. Homes will be equipped with phonographs and radios, and moving-picture rolls will be as cheaply bought or rented as are books or gramophone records." ("What of the Future?," 73–78.)
4 Le Corbusier, "Techniques Are the Very Basis of Poetry," in *Precisions on the Present State of Architecture and City Planning,* trans. Edith Schreiber Aujame (Cambridge: MIT Press, 1991), 52. Paul Virilio's telescoped history of windows selects many of the same examples and leads to the "televisual window":

> consider the evolution and three-dimensional extension of the light-providing opening from the ancient cloister, through the mullion windows of the Middle Ages, the great lancet and rose windows, past the special effects of gothic architecture, to the bow-windows and the great metal spokes of the last century and beyond, and up to the glass facades of our present skyscrapers, and the curtain-walls that were themselves contemporaries to the invention and development of the cathode opening. All of this helps explain the importance of this transmutation of appearances, the subsequent supremacy of the

televisual window over the door and other traditional means of access, a supremacy that already contributes to the decline of public space and the decrease of collective venues.

Paul Virilio, "Improbable Architecture," in *Lost Dimension,* trans. Daniel Moshenberg (New York: Semiotext(e), 1991), 90–91.

5 By far the most comprehensive account of the history of glass in architecture can be found in Raymond McGrath and A. C. Frost, *Glass in Architecture and Decoration* (1937; revised, London: Architectural Press, 1961). See also Frances Rogers and Alice Beard, *5000 Years of Glass* (New York: J. B. Lippincott, 1937); Ada Polak, *Glass: Its Makers and Its Public* (London: Weidenfeld & Nicholson, 1975); R. W. Douglas and Susan Frank, *A History of Glassmaking* (Oxfordshire: G. T. Foulis, 1972); Chloe Zerwick, *A Short History of Glass* (New York: Corning, 1980); Hugh Tait, ed., *5,000 Years of Glass* (New York: Harry N. Abrams, 1991); and Alan Macfarlane and Gerry Martin, *Glass: A World History* (Chicago: University of Chicago Press, 2002).

6 In the seventeenth century, three influential glassmaking treatises were written and broadly circulated. Florentine Antonio Neri's *L'arte vetraria* (1612) describes techniques for making crystal glass and colored glass. The book was reprinted three times, and was translated into English in 1662 under the title *The Art of Glass* by Christopher Merritt. The Merritt-Neri volume was translated into Latin (1668), German (1678), French (1697), and Spanish (1776). German glassmaker and scientist Johann Kunckel published *Vollständige Glasmacherkunst* in 1679.

7 As I noted earlier, a history of the window motif in painting would require a separate study. For an example of an attempt to write such a comprehensive history, see Carla Gottlieb, *The Window in Art: From the Window of God to the Vanity of Man* (New York: Abaris Books, 1981).

8 Regional availability of materials determined the types of glass produced. Lime gave stability, magnesia gave off a pinkish tint, metal oxides would produce brilliant colors, lead offered high refraction. The chemistry of glass involved experimenting with the variable combination of oxide elements: silica = silicon dioxide, SiO_2; soda = sodium oxide, Na_2O; lime = calcium oxide, CaO; potash = potassium oxide, K_2O.

9 See Hans Blumenberg's 1954 "metaphorology" on the metaphorics and metaphysics of light, "Light as a Metaphor for Truth," in David Michael Levin, ed., *Modernity and the Hegemony of Vision* (Berkeley: University of California Press, 1993), 30–62. Although Blumenberg details a metaphoric history of light, the comment about the absence of glass windows in the Dark Ages is my own.

10 The trade in glass and traveling glaziers, who brought materials and skills, may explain why stained-glass windows can be found in locations where there was little glassmaking. In England and Scandinavia, for example, colored glass must have been imported.

11 See Gianfranco Toso, *Murano Glass: A History of Glass* (Verona: Arsenale Editrice, 2000); Macfarlane and Martin, *Glass: A World History,* 21–24.

12 Samuel Y. Edgerton, *The Renaissance Rediscovery of Linear Perspective* (New York: Basic Books, 1975), 134–135.

13 See Sabine Melchior-Bonnet, *The Mirror: A History,* trans. Katherine H. Jewett (New York: Routledge, 2002). To Melchior-Bonnet, the plane mirror was part of a "new philosophy of representation" and "reflected the humanist's new relationship with knowledge" (128). See also Diana I. Agrest, "Architecture of Mirror/Mirror of Architecture," in *Architecture from Without: Theoretical Framings for a Critical Practice* (Cambridge: MIT Press, 1991), 139–155.

14 Johannes Zahn, *Oculi artificialis teledioptrici sive telescopii fundamentum III, Practico-mechanicum fabrica* (1675), 1–218. Manuscript in the Getty Research Institute Library.
15 Lewis Mumford, *Technics and Civilization* (New York: Harcourt, Brace, 1934), 180–181.
16 Denis Diderot's and Jean Le Rond d'Alembert's *Encyclopédie, ou Dictionnaire raisonné des sciences, des arts des métiers et* (published between 1751 and 1772) comprised seventeen volumes of text and eleven volumes of plates—with hundreds of engravings depicting mechanical processes that were transforming the world. One volume of engravings was dedicated to the techniques for the making of sheet glass, *Art du verre, fabrication des glaces.* A contemporary reprint edition of this volume was published in 2002. Diderot and D'Alembert, *L'Encyclopédie, Art du verre/fabrication des glaces* (Tours, France: Bibliothèque de l'Image, 2002). See also Barbara Maria Stafford, *Artful Science: Enlightenment Entertainment and the Eclipse of Visual Education* (Cambridge: MIT Press, 1994).
17 David C. Lindberg, *Theories of Vision: From Al-Kindi to Kepler* (Chicago: University of Chicago Press, 1976).
18 William III introduced a window tax in England in 1697. Houses with ten to twenty windows were charged four shillings a year; houses with more than twenty were charged eight shillings. In 1747, the tax was changed to charge ten to fourteen windows at 6d per window, fifteen to nineteen windows at 9d, and twenty or more windows at 1s. In 1825 the tax was lessened and houses with fewer than eight windows became exempt. The excise duty on glass—levied by weight—was officially repealed in 1845. The window tax was repealed in July 1851, just in time for the opening of the Crystal Palace, which used one million square feet of glass. See W. R. Ward, "The Administration of the Window and Assessed Taxes," *English Historical Review* 67 (1952): 522–542.

Daniel Defoe worked in the British government's Glass Duty office between 1695 and 1699 during the window tax. Hence, it is no surprise that in his *Complete English Tradesman* (1725), Defoe was attentive to the changes in glass and its uses for windows: "It is true," writes Defoe, "that a fine shew of goods will bring customers; . . . but that a fine shew of shelves and glass windows, should bring customers, that was never made a rule in trade 'till now." Daniel Defoe, *The Complete English Tradesman,* in *Familiar Letters* (London, 1725), 315. The British window tax is mentioned in Dickens, *Pickwick Papers* (1837): "The windows were looked out of often enough to justify the imposition of an additional duty upon them." Meanwhile, in the American colonies, the Townshend Acts of 1767 imposed import duties on tea and glass. In response to agitation by the American colonists, the British Parliament withdrew all duties in 1769, except the nominal one on tea.
19 The manufacture of the glass "bulb" for electric light was dependent on the development of glassblowing machines. The artificial light of electricity displaced light as a natural source of illumination and transformed it into a medium to be contained in glass. See Wolfgang Schivelbusch, *Disenchanted Night: The Industrialization of Light in the Nineteenth Century,* trans. Angela Davies (University of California Press, 1988); Carol Marvin, *When Old Technologies Were New: Thinking about Electric Communication in the Late Nineteenth Century* (New York: Oxford University Press, 1988); and David E. Nye, *Electrifying America: Social Meanings of a New Technology* (Cambridge: MIT Press, 1992). As Carol Marvin describes, "Early in its career, electric light was not well known as an illuminator of private spaces" (*Old Technologies,* 162). Domestic interiors were more commonly lit by gaslight; and the introduction of electrical illumination into homes was a luxury well into the 1890s.

20 Dolf Sternberger discusses the "störende Fenster" in his *Panorama of the Nineteenth Century* (Oxford: Basil Blackwell, 1977), 156 ff (translated from *Das Panorama oder Ansichten vom 19 Jahrhundert* [Hamburg: Goverts Verlag, 1938]). See also Georg Kohlmaier and Barna von Sartory, *Houses of Glass: A Nineteenth-Century Building Type* (Cambridge: MIT Press, 1986), 21–24, for a discussion of the nineteenth-century ambivalence toward the window.

21 By the early 1900s, handmade methods were replaced by mechanized sheet glass production. Ribbons of molten glass were poured from a furnace onto rollers. Also see Richard Sennett, *The Conscience of the Eye* (New York: Alfred A. Knopf, 1990), 106–114, for his discussion of plate glass.

22 The exchange of trade secrets and processes between French and English glassmakers involved the exchange of information on sheet glass for windows and optical glass for lenses. The French glass technologist Georges Bontemps began to work with British brothers Lucas and William Chance in 1832. The Chance brothers also developed processes for optical glass. In 1851, the Chance Brothers displayed inside the Crystal Palace a twenty-nine-inch disk of flawless optical glass. See Douglas and Frank, *A History of Glassmaking*, 79–81.

23 John Ruskin did not receive the "new order of architecture" heralded by the Crystal Palace with as much enthusiasm as many of his contemporaries. Ruskin's affront was less about glass per se than about the cultural priorities that led to ephemeral structures like the Crystal Palace being preserved while great paintings rotting in Venice and monuments of Christian architecture were being destroyed. In 1854, the Crystal Palace from the 1851 Exhibition was disassembled from its Hyde Park location and reassembled in Sydenham in South London with great fanfare. Ruskin was not convinced by the mechanical ingenuity of its construction or by its scale: "we suppose ourselves to have imagined a new style of architecture, when we have magnified a conservatory." See John Ruskin, "The Opening of the Crystal Palace Considered in Some of Its Relation to the Prospects of Art" (1854), in *The Works of John Ruskin*, vol. 12 (London: Longmans, 1904).

24 Lothar Bucher, *Kulturhistorische Skizzen aus der Industrieausstellung aller Völker* (1851), quoted in Daniel Boorstin, "Walls Become Windows," in *The Americans: The Democratic Experience* (New York: Random House, 1973), 341; emphasis added. In a different context, in Paul Virilio uses Bucher's description as indicative of "the advent of buildings stripped of any optic center, in which the structural architectonic of iron and glass behaves as the later image-form will behave in the computer terminals and televised sequences. In the new trellis of lines, 625 or 819 lines, of imperceptible subtlety, the pixel replaces the bolt" ("Improbable Architecture," 93).

25 Although the Crystal Palace opened the building to large expanses of glass, Pierre Francastel challenges Giedion and others who claim that it represented a radical new use of glass as a material: "the architect remained faithful to the greenhouse model. He did not realize that the glass panel cleared the way for new types of volumetric systems." Pierre Francastel, *Art and Technology in the Nineteenth and Twentieth Centuries*, with a foreword by Yve-Alain Bois, trans. Randall Cherry (New York: Zone Books, 2000), 91.

26 See my discussion of the role of window display (and L. Frank Baum's trade journal *The Show Window*) in my *Window Shopping* (Berkeley: University of California Press, 1993).

27 Bill Evans and Andrew Lawson, *A Nation of Shopkeepers* (London: Plexus, 1981), 120–121.

28 Molly Nesbit describes the client list for Atget's "documents"—architects, decorators, building trade workers, antiquarians—who used Atget's photographs as if they were docu-

ments or technical drawings. Molly Nesbit, "What Was an Author?" *Yale French Studies,* no. 73 (1988): 229–257.

29 Sigfried Giedion, *Space, Time and Architecture* (Cambridge: Harvard University Press, 1991), 195.

30 Paul Scheerbart, *Glass Architecture* (with Bruno Taut's *Alpine Architecture*), ed. Dennis Sharp (New York: Praeger Publishers, 1972), 41, 74. These two pronouncements form the alpha and omega of Scheerbart's manifesto *Glass Architecture*—the first, Aphorism #1, and the last, #111.

31 Scheerbart, *Glass Architecture,* 41. Scheerbart's manifesto extolled the transformative powers of glass, including the prismatic properties of colored glass not just clear crystalline glass.

32 Ibid., 52.

33 Paul Scheerbart, *Glasarchitektur* (Berlin: Verlag der Sturm, 1914), quoted in Reyner Banham, "The Glass Paradise," *Architectural Review* (London, February 1959), 88.

34 See Kenneth Frampton, "The Glass Chain: European architectural Expressionism 1910–24," in *Modern Architecture: A Critical History* (London: Thames and Hudson, 1986), 116–129; Iain Boyd White, *The Crystal Chain Letters: Architectural Fantasies by Bruno Taut and His Circle* (Cambridge: MIT Press, 1985); Banham, "The Glass Paradise," 87–89.

35 For an account of Banham's challenges to the histories of the modern movement by Pevsner and Giedion, see Panayotis Tournikiotis, *The Historiography of Modern Architecture* (Cambridge: MIT Press, 1999).

36 Frank Lloyd Wright, "VI. The Meaning of Materials—Glass" (July 1928), in *In the Cause of Architecture,* ed. Frederick Gutheim (New York: Architectural Record, 1975), 171.

37 Ibid., 197.

38 Ibid., 201. Both Wright and Scheerbart assumed that glass was a fireproof building material. The catastrophic 1936 fire in the Crystal Palace in Sydenham seems to prove this belief wrong.

39 Ibid., 197.

40 Ibid., 198.

41 Ibid., 199.

42 Walter Benjamin, "Paris, Capital of the Nineteenth Century," in *Reflections,* trans. Edmund Jephcott (New York: Harcourt Brace Jovanovich, 1979), 147. See also Detlef Merten, "The Enticing and Threatening Face of Prehistory: Walter Benjamin and the Utopia of Glass," *Assemblage* 29 (April 1996): 7–23.

43 Peter Behrens (AEG turbine factory, 1910), Walter Gropius (Fagus shoe works, 1911; Bauhaus building, 1926), Mies van der Rohe (project for glass tower, 1921; Lake Shore Drive Apartments, 1952), Le Corbusier (Villa Savoye, 1921), etc. In his building for the Fagus shoe factory (1911), Gropius writes, "the role of walls is restricted to that of mere screens stretched between the upright columns of the framework to keep out rain, cold and noise . . . glass is assuming an ever greater structural importance." The glass is joined at the corners without masonry piers. Walter Gropius, *The New Architecture and the Bauhaus* (1937), quoted in Giedion, *Space, Time and Architecture,* 482.

44 Anthony Vidler, "Transparency," in *The Architectural Uncanny* (Cambridge: MIT Press, 1992), 217–225; also 125–127; 168–170. In the eighteenth century, the meaning of "transparency" as a philosophical ideal was epitomized in Jean-Jacques Rousseau's ideal of the heart as "transparent as crystal." See Jean Starobonski, *Jean-Jacques Rousseau: Transparency and Obstruction,* trans. Arthur Goldhammer (Chicago: University of Chicago Press, 1971), 254–267; also *Journal of Architectural Education* 56, no. 4 (May 2003), special issue on Transparency.

45 Sennett, *The Conscience of the Eye,* 108. "Sight," Sennett writes, "is routinely insulated from sound and touch and other human beings" (109). In his earlier "Paean to Plate Glass," Sennett describes an epiphany he had about plate glass:

> For the first time in a building by Mies, I felt comfortable leaning back against the glass. I don't want to make too much of this moment, only that it gave me an intimation, through the material, of what the phrase modern might truly and positively imply. It was just a sense of the inherent ambiguity of glass; more than a metaphor, it was a field on which the exchange between inner and outer occurs, a field reflecting the violation of space but also enclosing and protecting. And I suppose this is why plate glass is so interesting: now a window on nothing, a mirror of solitude, its possibilities have yet to be explored in the practice of an ambiguous, permeable, violating, warm and thus truly modern art.

Richard Sennett, "Paean to Plate Glass," in Richard Poirier, ed., *Raritan Reading* (New Brunswick: Rutgers University Press, 1990).

46 Giedeon, *Space, Time and Architecture,* 237.

47 See Tournikiotis, *The Historiography of Modern Architecture.*

48 Giedion, *Space, Time and Architecture,* lvi.

49 A further clue to how Giedion conceives this "optical revolution" can be found in his introduction to Gyorgy Kepes's 1944 study *Language of Vision.* Giedion writes of Kepes: "His main object is to demonstrate just how the optical revolution—around 1910—formed our present-day conception of space and the visual approach to reality." Sigfried Giedion, introduction to Gyorgy Kepes, *Language of Vision* (Chicago: Paul Theobald, 1944), 7.

The year 1910 recurs in Giedion's account: "about 1910," he writes, "the method of presenting spatial relationships which the cubists developed led up to the form-giving principles of the new space conception" (*Space, Time and Architecture,* 434). In a footnote, he asserts: "we shall treat contemporary movements in art here only so far as their methods are directly related to the space conceptions of our period, and in order to understand the common background of art, architecture, and construction." Giedion continues this methodological project in his 1948 sequel, *Mechanization Takes Command* (New York: Oxford University Press, 1948).

The year 1910 also is of striking significance to Henri Lefebvre in *The Production of Space:*

> The fact is that around 1910 a certain space was shattered. It was the space of common sense, of knowledge (*savoir*), of social practice, of political power, a space hithero enshrined in everyday discourse, just as in abstract thought, as the environment of and channel for communications; the space, too, of classical perspective and geometry, developed from the Renaissance onwards on the basis of the Greek tradition (Euclid, logic) and bodied forth in Western art and philosophy, as in the form of the city and town. . . . This was a crucial moment. Naturally, "common-sense" space, Euclidean space and perspectivist space did not disappear in a puff of smoke without leaving any trace in our consciousness, knowledge or educational methods; they could not more have done so than elementary algebra and arithemetic, or grammar, or Newtonian physics.

Henri Lefebvre, *The Production of Space,* trans. Donald Nicholson-Smith (Oxford: Blackwell Publishers, 1991), 25.

50 Giedion, *Space, Time and Architecture,* 435.

51 As Eve Blau and Nancy J. Troy maintain in the introduction to their collection of essays exploring the links between cubist painting and architecture: "Most often the connections between cubist painting and modern architecture were construed analogically, by reference to shared formal qualities such as fragmentation, spatial ambiguity, transparency, and multiplicity; or to techniques used in other media such as film, poetry, and photomontage. Cubist space itself remained two-dimensional; with the exception of Le Corbusier's work, it was never translated into the three dimensions of architecture. Cubism's significance for architecture also remained two-dimensional—a method of representing modern spatial experience through the ordering impulses of art." See Eve Blau and Nancy J. Troy, eds., *Architecture and Cubism* (Cambridge: MIT Press, 1997), 12.

52 As an apt pupil of Heinrich Wölfflin, Giedion drew upon the methodological fundamentals of German art history for his account of architectural history. Henry-Russell Hitchcock's *Painting toward Architecture* (New York: Duell, Sloan & Pearce, 1948) continued Giedion's methodology, by comparing Frank Lloyd Wright, Le Corbusier, Gropius, and Mies van der Rohe to cubist painters Léger, Mondrian, Arp, and Klee. Hitchcock declares that these developments in painting were *direct* determinants to architectural change.

53 Giedion, *Space, Time and Architecture,* 436.

54 Giedion references Hermann Minkowski's 1908 concept of "space-time." On 21 September 1908, Minkowski began his famous lecture at the University of Cologne with these words: "The views of space and time which I wish to lay before you have sprung from the soil of experimental physics, and therein lies their strength. They are radical. Henceforth space by itself, and time by itself, are doomed to fade away into mere shadows, and only a kind of union of the two will preserve an independent reality" (quoted in Giedion, *Space, Time and Architecture,* 14).

55 Giedion, *Space, Time and Architecture,* 497.

56 Ibid., 495, 497. Giedion champions this feature, which had not been exploited by previous generations who had "used it either for practical purposes or had stained it or painted it" (497). Elsewhere he also remarks on how the only form to capture this new architecture was film: "still photography does not capture them clearly. One would have to accompany the eye as it moves—only film can make the new architecture intelligible" (Sigfried Giedion, *Bauen in Frankreich* [Leipzig: Klinkhardt & Biermann, 1928], 92).

57 Giedion, *Space, Time and Architecture,* 493; Picasso's painting is reproduced full-page on page 494 and, in mirror fashion, a photograph of the Dessau Bauhaus is full-page on page 495.

58 Kiesler was writing about Duchamp's "plate glass picture": "It is architecture, sculpture and painting in ONE." Frederick Kiesler, "Design—Correlation: Marcel Duchamp's Large Glass," first published in *Architectural Record* 81, no. 5 (May 1937); republished in Anthony Hill, ed., *Duchamp: Passim* (Australia: Gordon and Breach Arts International, 1994).

59 Kepes, *Language of Vision,* 77. A painter, photographer, designer, and typographer, the Hungarian-born Kepes (1906–2001) was a friend of—and collaborator with—fellow Hungarian Bauhaus photographer László Moholy-Nagy. Moholy-Nagy invited Kepes to teach at the New Bauhaus in Chicago, where Kepes taught from 1937 to 1943. In 1946, Kepes joined the faculty at MIT, where he founded the Center for Advanced Visual Studies (CAVS) in 1967.

60 Ibid., 78–79. Kepes declares his debt to the perceptual studies of Gestalt psychologists Max Wertheimer, Wolfgang Köhler, and Kurt Koffka in his acknowledgments and footnotes.

In his introduction to *Language of Vision,* Kepes writes: "Vision is primarily a device of orientation; a means to measure and organize spatial events. . . . To grasp spatial relationships and orient oneself in a metropolis of today, among the intricate dimensions of streets, subways, elevated and skyscrapers, requires a new way of seeing" (p. 14).

61 The publisher, Paul Theobald, was based in Chicago where Bauhaus exiles had congregated to form the New Bauhaus in 1937. *Language of Vision* has over three hundred reproductions of paintings, drawings, and photographs. Kepes's essay is broken into small sections, each with multiple illustrations: "Breakdown of Fixed Perspective" is the section title on p. 93; "Final Elimination of the Fixed Perspective Order" is the section title on p. 107.

62 Ibid., 91: Kepes writes, "Vision unchained by the photographic camera was able to explore hitherto untouched territories of perspective," and "The invention and perfection of the camera was by no means the only factor tending to break down the absolute validity of linear perspective" (93).

63 Ibid., 91.

64 Ibid., 95.

65 Ibid., 90, where Kepes uses the section title "Multiple, Simultaneous Perspective."

66 The writing, rewriting, and publishing history of this text are described in Colin Rowe and Robert Slutzky, *Transparency,* with a commentary by Bernhard Hoesli and introduction by Werner Oechslin (Boston: Birkhäuser Verlag, 1997). The transparency discussion needs to be placed in the context of an underlying intellectual history of influence and debate. As professors at the University of Texas at Austin, Slutzky and Rowe were familiar with the writing and polemics of many of the Bauhaus exiles, including Giedion, Moholy-Nagy, and Kepes. See also Colin Rowe and Robert Slutzky, "Transparency: Literal and Phenomenal" (1955–1956), in Rowe, *The Mathematics of the Ideal Villa and Other Essays* (Cambridge: MIT Press, 1976), 159–184; Colin Rowe and Robert Slutzky, "Transparency: Literal and Phenomenal II," in Joan Ockman, ed., *Architecture Culture, 1943–1968: A Documentary Anthology* (New York: Rizzoli, 1993).

67 Rowe and Slutzky, "Transparency: Literal and Phenomenal II," 167.

68 And here there is long list of artists who "experimented" with moving images—Léger, Richter, Eggeling, Moholy-Nagy, Salvador Dalí. See Standish Lawder, *The Cubist Cinema* (New York: New York University Press, 1975). Although the cause may be the technical difficulty of fracturing the image in a single frame, it is striking to see how infrequently filmmakers actually fractured the frame of the image, split the screen, or used inset frames. While skewed camera angles (in *Accident*) and angular set design (as in *The Cabinet of Dr. Caligari*) were often used to indicate a nonperspectival image (and often equated with psychic disequilibrium), the use of a multiple image in a single frame was rare. Dziga Vertov's *Man with a Movie Camera* (1929) and Walter Ruttman's *Berlin: Symphony of a City* (1929) used the split screen to represent the visual jumble of the city.

69 Boorstin, "Walls Become Windows," 336–345.

70 Le Corbusier, *Precisions,* 54.

71 This controversy has become well known in architectural histories. See Bruno Reichlin, "The Pros and Cons of the Horizontal Window: The Perret–Le Corbusier Controversy," *Daidalos* 13 (September 1984): 65–78; Beatriz Colomina, *Privacy and Publicity: Modern Architecture as Mass Media* (Cambridge: MIT Press, 1994); and Karla Britton, *Auguste Perret* (New York: Phaidon Press, 2001).

72 In her recent monograph on Perret, Karla Britton describes him in terms of the tensions between his "filiative roots" as the scion of a construction company and his "affiliative grounding in the cultural landscape" (*Auguste Perret,* 35). His filiative roots gave him a commitment to materials: Perret trained in his father's Parisian construction firm. When he took over the family business with his brother after their father's death in 1905, their sign indicated their signature commitment to concrete as a building material: "Perret Frères, architects, constructors, reinforced concrete." His affiliative roots, on the other hand—his architectural influences—Viollet-le-Duc, Choisy, Gaudet—and his wide circle of artist compatriots—Valéry, Poiret, Ozenfant, Gide, Apollinaire—provided Perret with his moral dedication to architectural form. Britton quotes Le Corbusier: "Perret is divided into two men; on the one hand he is a constructor in the highest, most worthy sense of the term; on the other he defends outworn methods in an unexpectedly and inconceivably rhetorical attitude of opposition, thus sitting between two stools" (*Auguste Perret,* 42).

73 Le Corbusier wrote a blunt biographical sketch of Perret for a special issue of *Architecture d'Aujourd'hui* in 1932. See Le Corbusier, "Perret," *Architecture d'Aujourd'hui* 7, special issue on Perret (October 1932): 7–9; reprinted in English as "Auguste Perret" in *Architectural Education* 1 (1983): 7–21.

74 For example, the massive vaulted interior to his Esders sewing factory in Paris (1919–1920); the reinforced concrete frames for the apartment building at 25 bis rue Franklin (1903), and for Théâtre des Champs-Elysées (1911–1913).

75 Perret describes the virtues of concrete: "construction in concrete is among the oldest of building methods; and at the same time is one of the most modern. . . . Putting iron into concrete makes it flexible; in other words, the iron acts like a sinew within the concrete. This property has made it resistant to decay, fire and frost. A STRUCTURAL FRAME with an indefinite lifespan. . . . And now reinforced cement concrete, invented in France, is spreading all over the world." Reproduced from a manuscript found in the Perret archives, in Britton, *Auguste Perret,* 245.

76 In the second half of the seventeenth century, windows "rose from the floor to almost ceiling level and had double valves (sometimes termed French windows), in which the casements pivoted from the jamb. . . . When wood frames replaced the stone transoms and mullions and with rectangular panes it was possible for the casements to open outward." Robbie G. Blakemore, *History of Interior Design and Furniture* (New York: Van Nostrand Reinhold, 1997), 164.

77 See "Modern Machines: From the Virgin to the Widow," in David Joselit, *Infinite Regress: Marcel Duchamp 1910–1941* (Cambridge: MIT Press, 1998); and Molly Nesbit, "Ready-Made Originals: The Duchamp Model," *October* 37 (1986).

78 "M. Auguste Perret nous parle de l'architecture au Salon d'Automne," *Paris Journal* (1 December 1923), 5. Translated and quoted in Britton, *Auguste Perret,* 136. Perret also is quoted as saying that the horizontal window "condemns us to a view of an unending panorama," and that "I detest panoramas."

79 Guillaume Baderre, "Une visite à Le Corbusier-Saugnier," *Paris Journal* (14 and 28 December, 1923). Quoted in Britton, *Auguste Perret,* 137.

80 "Fine French tradition" is quoted in Reichlin, "The Pros and Cons of the Horizontal Window," 71.

81 Le Corbusier, *Precisions,* 54, quoted in Colomina, *Privacy and Publicity,* 311.

82 Le Corbusier, *Une petite maison—1923* (Zurich: Editions d'Architecture, 1954), 30–31.
83 Reichlin, "The Pros and Cons of the Horizontal Window," 65.
84 Ibid., 75.
85 For her discussion of the Perret/Le Corbusier debate, see Colomina, *Privacy and Publicity,* 128–139; 306–312. Colomina compares the flat frontality of Ozenfant's purist drawing with the use of surface in Le Corbusier's window.
86 Ibid., 133. Colomina supports this analogy of house as camera by demonstrating that Le Corbusier relies on a photographer's chart for exposure times to measure proper illumination (133, 311).
87 Ibid., 311.
88 Ibid.
89 Ibid., 134.
90 Ibid.
91 Deleuze separates the "shooting" of the movie camera from the "projection" onto a screen. Gilles Deleuze, *Cinéma I: L'image-mouvement* (Paris: Editions de Minuit, 1983), 12; *The Movement-Image,* trans. Hugh Tomlinson and Barbara Habberjam (Minneapolis: University of Minnesota Press, 2001), 3.
92 These tensions were, of course, famously discussed by Walter Benjamin. In his "Work of Art" essay, Benjamin draws the distinction between the "polar opposites" of distraction and concentration for the spectator of the painting, the film, and architecture: "Architecture has always represented the prototype of a work of art the recepton of which is consummated by a collectivity in a state of distraction," while "Painting invites the spectator to contemplation/concentration." See Walter Benjamin, "The Work of Art in the Age of Mechanical Reproduction," in *Illuminations,* ed. Hannah Arendt, trans. Harry Zohn (New York: Schocken Books, 1969), 239, 238.

Soviet filmmaker Sergei Eisenstein also addressed this relation in his 1938 text "Montage and Architecture"; see my discussion in chapter 4.
93 My discussion of Eisenstein's "dinamic square" and the debates about screen size and format was a component of this project at its earliest stages. I am indebted to Sylvia Lavin for pointing me toward its parallels with the Perret–Le Corbusier debate.
94 "The Dinamic Square" was based on a speech Eisenstein made at a special meeting of the technician's branch of the Academy devoted to the Wide Film. The Academy members were in the midst of an extensive debate about how to manage variable camera and projector apertures. The 17 September 1930 invitation-only meeting was held at the Café de Paris at Fox Hills Studios. More than one hundred requests for reservations had to be refused. Lee DeForest and Karl Struss were scheduled speakers; Eisenstein spoke from the floor. As recorded in the *Academy of Motion Picture Arts and Sciences Bulletin:* "Discussion was limited to the advantages and disadvantages of different proportions of screen image and to the adjustments in production technique which will be necessary for photography upon any larger negative, whatever its exact dimensions. . . . The meeting of the technician's Branch was similar to the Academy meetings two years ago during the period in which sound was modifying production technique" (*Academy of Motion Picture Arts and Sciences Bulletin,* no. 35 [1 October 1930]: 4). Eisenstein sent a typescript entitled "The Dinamic Square" to the Academy secretary, Lester Cowan, with the following impassioned introduction: "For a shudder takes me when I think that, by not devoting enough attention to this problem, and permitting the standardization of a new

screen shape without the thorough weighing of all the pros and cons of the question, we risk paralyzing once more, for years and years to come, our compositional efforts in new shapes as unfortunately chosen as those from which the practical realization of the Wide Film and Wide Screen now seems to gives us the opportunity of freeing ourselves" (typescript, Special Collections, Margaret Herrick Library, Academy of Motion Picture Arts and Sciences).

The "dinamic square" forecasts the contemporary screen wars about "letterboxing" the image, a debate that has been resolved on television monitors that allow setting for or changing multiple aspect ratios.

Eisenstein's reception in Hollywood was paradoxically warm and respectful and wildly dismissive. During his stay in Hollywood in 1930, the Academy extended Eisenstein and his entourage (which included Ivor Montagu, his assistant Alexandrov, and his cameraman Eduard Tisse) a variety of courtesies, which included a dinner hosted by Academy president William DeMille, a luncheon with the Executive Committee of the Directors Branch, and a joint banquet of the Directors and Writers branches, followed by a screening of *Potemkin* and *The Old and the New.* Eisenstein became a member of the Director's branch. See *Academy of Motion Picture Arts and Sciences, September Bulletin,* no. 24 (12 September 1930): 2. See also Ivor Montagu's memoir, *With Eisenstein in Hollywood* (London: International Publishers, 1969).

95 S. M. Eisenstein, "The Dinamic Square," *Close Up* 8, no. 1 (March 1931): 4–5.

96 Ibid., 5.

97 Ibid., 6: "So neither the horizontal nor the vertical proportion of the screen alone is ideal for it. Actuality, as we saw, in the forms of nature as in the forms of industry, and in the encounters together of these forms, we have the fight, the conflict of both tendencies. And the screen, as faithful mirror, not only of conflicts emotional and tragic, but equally of conflicts psychological and optically special, must be an appropriate battle ground for the skirmishes of both these optical-by-view but profoundly psychological-by-meaning space tendencies of the spectator."

98 W. K. L. Dickson first used 35mm film by dividing Kodak 70mm film stock in two. The 35mm-wide filmstrips they used followed the 4:3 rectangle (first called "Edison size"). But there were already a variety of widths, unique to the variety of apparatuses manufactured by early inventors: 54mm (2⅛"), Friese-Greene in 1887; 54mm paperfilm (2⅛"), Le Prince, 1888; 54mm, Skladanowsky, 1895; 60mm, Prestwich and Demeney, 1893 for the Demeny Phonoscope, and 1896 for the Gaumont-Demeny Chronophotographe; 38mm, Casimir Sivan/E. Dalphin, Geneva, 1896; 63mm, Veriscope, 1897; 65mm, Hughes Moto-Photoscope, 1897; 68mm, Biograph 1897 camera; 70mm unperforated experimental film, Birt Acres 1894. John Belton provides a detailed account of the standardization of film gauge to the 4:3 or 1.33:1 aspect ratio. See John Belton, *Widescreen Cinema* (Cambridge: Harvard University Press, 1992).

99 Reese V. Jenkins, *Images and Enterprise: Technology and the American Photographic Industry 1839–1925* (Baltimore: Johns Hopkins University Press, 1975).

100 Stephen Heath, "On Screen, in Frame: Film and Ideology," in *Questions of Cinema* (London: Macmillan, 1981), 1–18.

101 The aspect ratio of 4:3 (also known as 1.33:1), the proportion first established by Edison in 1889, remained in use until 1928, when movie-tone sound-on-film added an optical track to the side of the film image, consequently reducing the image from 4:3 to a near square 1.15:1.

In 1929, the Academy of Motion Picture Arts and Sciences made a preliminary recommendation to establish a standard format for camera and projector apertures. After extensive research and review of information supplied by the studios, laboratories, and equipment manufacturers, the Academy moved to establish a standard aspect ratio.

A standard format would resolve problems vexing both exhibitors and producers since the addition of sound: theaters could do away with screen masks, aperture plates, and lenses during projection; cinematographers would no longer need to set up compositions for separate apertures—sound-on-disk, sound-on-film—and could be assured that the film would be projected as shot. The "Academy standard" became effective on 15 February 1932. In March 1932, the Academy bulletin announced: "By the new plan the shape of theatre screens will tend away from the square and toward an oblong of approximately three by four proportions. The aperture dimensions agreed on are .631" by .868" for cameras . . . For projectors the agreed figures are .600" by .825"." *Academy of Motion Picture Arts and Sciences Bulletin,* no. 43 (25 March 1932). In July 1932, the Academy published a supplemental Technical Bulletin, "Uniform Aperture Specifications: Recommendations of the Academy for Dimensions of Picture Image Frame for Use on 35mm Film," *Academy of Motion Picture Arts and Sciences, Technical Bulletin,* supplement no. 6 (1 July 1932).

The "Academy standard" held until 1953, when the Academy—facing the competition of television—decided to allow for "wider" movies. See Belton, *Widescreen Cinema,* 44–45.

102 In an essay about the Paris 1900 Exposition, I discuss the Grimoin-Sanson system and other devices—the Mareorama and Stereorama—intent on presenting a virtual mobility. See Anne Friedberg, "*Trottoir Roulant:* The Cinema and New Mobilities of Spectatorship" in Jan Olsson and John Fullerton, eds., *Allegories of Communication: Intermedial Concerns from Cinema to the Digital* (London/Sydney: John Libbey, 2004), 263–276.

103 Richard Abel provides a detailed descriptive analysis of the final reel of the film. Although I saw the reconstructed hand-tinted film in its Radio City premiere in 1981, I rely on Abel's description, not my memory. See Richard Abel, *French Cinema: The First Wave, 1915–1929* (Princeton: Princeton University Press, 1984), 441–446. For a discussion of the film's reconstruction, see Kevin Brownlow, *The Parade's Gone By* (New York: Alfred A. Knopf, 1968), and *Napoleon: Abel Gance's Classic Film* (New York: Alfred A. Knopf, 1983).

104 The contemporary shopping mall has no exterior windows; its fenestration is turned toward the interior—windows are deployed functionally as walls to separate individual shops from the shared space of the mall and serve as glass vitrines and a surface for product display.

105 In his 1984 essay "The Cultural Logic of Late Capitalism," Fredric Jameson argues that the Bonaventure Hotel, like the Eaton Center in Toronto or the Beaubourg in Paris, "aspires to being a total space, a complete world, a kind of miniature city; to this new total space, meanwhile, corresponds a new collective practice, a new mode in which individuals move and congregate, something like the practice of a new and historically original kind of hypercrowd." Jameson suggests that human subjects "do not possess the perceptual equipment to match this new hyperspace . . . because our perceptual habits were formed in that older kind of space I have called the space of high modernism." He reads this new architecture as an "imperative to grow new organs, to expand our sensorium" to contend with new disjunctions between body and the built environment. Fredric Jameson, "The Cultural Logic of Late Capitalism," first published in *New Left Review* 146 (1984); reprinted and expanded in Fredric Jameson, *Postmodernism, or, The Cultural Logic of Late Capitalism* (Durham, N.C.: Duke University Press, 1991), 1–54.

106 Spectatorship is a figurative "ship," transporting the viewer to a time and place at odds with the moment of viewing, also at odds with the moment of the film's production—a third time, in a fictional future or fictional other world. All films may exist in this third time, because the question of "when are we" while watching a film requires us to coin some new descriptors. See my discussion in *Window Shopping* (104–106) of the coincidence of H. G. Wells's 1895 *Time Machine* and the R. W. Paul patent for a moving-image apparatus to travel in time. British writer George Herbert Wells (1866–1946) predicted control over time in his 1895 novel *The Time Machine.* Unlike earlier science fictions that suggest time travel (in Washington Irving's *Rip Van Winkle,* the character sleeps for years; in Louis Sébastien Mercier's 1770 *Mémoires de l'an 2440* a Parisian travels in a dream to 2440; in Edward Bellamy's 1888 novel *Looking Backward,* his character enters a "mesmeric sleep" in a subterranean sleeping chamber and wakes up in the year 2000), in the Wells novel, the Time Traveler enters the future on a machine. In October 1895, months after reading Wells's utopian novel, the British inventor Robert W. Paul applied for a patent for a "novel form of exhibition" in which "spectators have presented to their view scenes which are supposed to occur in the future or past, while they are given the sensation of voyaging upon a machine through time." Quoted in Terry Ramsaye, *Million and One Nights* (New York: Simon and Schuster, 1926), 152–161.

107 All quotations are from the DVD version of *Things to Come* (Image Entertainment, 2001). *Things to Come* may have been a box office failure in 1936, but it was remembered only a few years later for its vivid prediction of World War II's aerial bombing of London. (The image of a swarm of planes flying over the cliffs of Dover was particularly chilling.)

108 The production budget ($1,400,000) for *Things to Come,* in 1936, marked it as the most expensive science fiction film to date. In Wells's treatment, the year was 2054; in the Cameron Menzies film, it was changed to 2036. Vincent Korda had ambitious plans for the "work" sequence of rebuilding Everytown—including a transition from black and white to color, from the standard aspect ratio to a wider screen.

109 Christopher Frayling, who had access to the British Film Institute dossier of materials on the film, provides an account of the film's production design that offers more detail than previous sources, which claim that László Moholy-Nagy designed the sets. See Christopher Frayling, *Things to Come* (London: BFI, 1995), 62–75.

110 Sybil Moholy-Nagy provides an account of Moholy-Nagy's participation on the film. She writes: "The fantastic technology of the Utopian City of the future would, so Moholy dreamed, eliminate solid form. Houses were no longer obstacles to, but receptacles of, man's natural life force, light. There were no walls, but skeleton of steel, screened with glass and plastic sheets." See Sybil Moholy-Nagy, *Moholy-Nagy: Experiment in Totality* (Cambridge: MIT Press, 1950), 129. British interior designer Oliver Hill had exhibited a glass bed, couch, and table in the well-publicized Exhibition of British Industrial Art in 1933. Hill's designs for glass furniture were, in many ways, a fulfillment of the principles of Scheerbart's *Glasarchitektur.*

111 Cinematic set design could posit imaginary new spaces without the material constraints of the built world. *Things to Come* has functioned as a key example in histories of modern architecture and design that describe the role of film in disseminating the image of the "modern" to a broad audience. Donald Albrecht, for example, argues that modern design usually appears in the bathrooms and bedrooms of the promiscuous, in the apartments of the wealthy, in nightclubs, hotel lobbies, ocean liners, and skyscrapers but not in the average home. The virtual worlds of science fiction from 1930s films, MGM's Cedric Gibbons, RKO's Van Nest Polglase in the 1940s, and *The Fountainhead* of 1948 posited spaces that could be entered only through the vicarious visuality of spectatorship. For discussions of film design, set design, and the use of architecture within the film frame, see Donald Albrecht, *Designing Dreams: Modern Architecture and the Movies* (London: Thames and Hudson, 1987); Dietrich Neumann, *Film Architecture* (New York and Munich: Prestel Verlag, 1996); and Mary Corliss and Carlos Clarens, *Designed for Film*, exh. cat. (New York: Museum of Modern Art, 1978).

112 Lawder describes this "videoscope machine" in *The Cubist Cinema.*

113 As Thomas Elsaesser has suggested, "Lang makes himself the ironic archivist of the pleasures and dangers of assisted sight." See Thomas Elsaesser, "Fritz Lang: Illusion of Mastery," *Sight and Sound* (January 2000). See also Tom Gunning, "The Grand Enunciator and the Power of the Gaze," *The Films of Fritz Lang: Allegories of Vision and Modernity* (London: British Film Institute, 2000), 108–113.

114 Interview with Friedrich Kiesler in *Progressive Architecture* 42 (July 1961): 105–123, quoted in Lawder, *The Cubist Cinema*, 112.

115 Described in Jennifer Gough-Cooper and Jacques Caumont, "Frederick Kiesler and *The Bride Stripped Bare . . .* ," first published in Dieter Bogner, ed., *Frederick Kiesler* (Vienna: Locker Verlag, 1988); republished in Hill, ed., *Duchamp: Passim.*

116 Hans Ulrich Gumbrecht's *In 1926: Living at the Edge of Time* (Cambridge: Harvard University Press, 1997) takes the year 1926 as a historical cross-section that arrays Jorge Luis Borges, Ernest Hemingway, and Martin Heidegger; Fritz Lang, Alfred Hitchcock, and Leni Riefenstahl; Josephine Baker, Gertrude Stein, and Greta Garbo. I am indebted to Vivian Sobchack for introducing me to this remarkable example of intermedial historiography.

117 Timothy Egan, "It Takes Time to Build a Xanadu for Citizen Gates," *New York Times*, 12 January 1995, B1.

LENS III: BERGSON'S VIRTUAL

1 See especially Keith Ansell-Pearson, *Philosophy and the Adventure of the Virtual: Bergson and the Time of Life* (London: Routledge, 2002); Constantine V. Boundas, "Deleuze-Bergson: An Ontology of the Virtual," in Paul Patton, ed., *Deleuze: A Critical Reader* (Oxford: Blackwell, 1996), 81–106.

Although much of this bibiliography was listed in the introduction, I repeat it here: Deleuze's 1956 essay "Bergson's Conception of Difference," trans. Melissa McMahon, in John Mullarkey, ed., *The New Bergson* (Manchester: Manchester University Press, 1999), 42–65, and Deleuze's 1966 volume *Bergsonism*, trans. Hugh Tomlinson and Barbara Habberjam (New York: Zone Books, 1988); Gilles Deleuze, *Difference and Repetition*, trans. Paul Patton (New York: Columbia University Press, 1995); Gilles Deleuze, *Cinema 1: The Movement-Image*, trans. Hugh Tomlinson (Minneapolis: University of Minnesota Press, 1986); Gilles Deleuze, *Cinema 2: The Time Image*, trans. Hugh Tomlinson and Robert Galeta (Minneapolis: University of Minnesota Press, 1989); David Rodowick, *Gilles Deleuze's Time Machine* (Durham: Duke University Press, 1997); and Ronald Bogue, *Deleuze on Cinema* (New York: Routledge, 2002).

2 Bergson's *Essai sur les données immédiates de la conscience* (1889) was translated in 1910 as *Time and Free Will.* Henri Bergson, *Time and Free Will: An Essay on the Immediate Data of Consciousness*, trans. F. L. Pogson (London: George Allen and Unwin, 1910).

3 Henri Bergson, *Matter and Memory*, trans. N. M. Paul and W. S. Palmer (New York: Zone Books, 1990), 36–37; emphasis added.

4 Ibid., 127.

5 Ibid., 13.

6 Ibid., 9.

7 The structure of *Matter and Memory* demonstrates Bergson's concern with "images." The chapters titles are "The Selection of Images for Conscious Presentation," "Of the Recognition of Images," "Of the Survival of Images," and "The Delimiting and Fixing of Images."

8 Bergson, *Matter and Memory*, 38; emphasis added.

9 Ibid., 38–39; emphasis added.

10 Henri Bergson, *Matière et mémoire: Essai sur la relation du corps à l'esprit* (Paris: Presses Universitaires de France, 1939), 36.

11 Bergson, *Matter and Memory*, 133–134; emphasis added.

12 Deleuze, *Bergsonism*, 56.

13 Marta Braun, *Picturing Time: The Work of Etienne-Jules Marey (1830–1904)* (Chicago: University of Chicago Press, 1992), 278–282.

14 Henri Bergson, *Creative Evolution*, trans. Arthur Mitchell (1911; reprint, New York: Dover Publications, 1998), 272, n. 1.

15 The Lumière catalog between 1895 and 1907 listed 1,427 "vues": 337 scenes of genre, 247 trips to foreign countries, 181 official ceremonies, 125 French military reviews.

16 Bergson, *Creative Evolution*, 304–305.

17 Ibid.; emphasis added.

18 Ibid., 305.

19 Bergson was familiar with the optical explanation of persistence of vision (from Peter Mark Roget's 1824 account) and was not yet privy to the subsequent challenges to this optical physiology—Max Wertheimer's 1912 explanation of the *phi phenomenon* or, later, J. J. Gibson's Gestalt work.

20 Deleuze, *Cinema 1*, 2. The "official birth of the cinema" occurred between Bergson's discussion of the photograph in *Matter and Memory* and of the cinematograph in *Creative Evolution*. Mary Ann Doane describes "Bergson's adamant rejection of the cinema" while suggesting that the "cinema emerges as a philosophical machine for the demonstration of duration in its truth" and that Bergson's philosophy was "consonant with the cinema." Mary Ann Doane, *The Emergence of Cinematic Time: Modernity, Contingency, the Archive* (Cambridge: Harvard University Press, 2002), 175–176. In his essay "Bergson and Cinema," Paul Douglass tries to reconcile what he also deems as Bergson's implicit critique of cinematic technology with the easy adaptation of his writing on *durée* to cinematic theory. Douglass argues against Deleuze's reading that Bergson knew only films with fixed views and no moving camera (Lumière, Méliès, Edison). Paul Douglass, "Bergson and Cinema: Friends or Foes?," in Mullarkey, ed., *The New Bergson*, 209–227.

21 Deleuze, *Cinema 1*, 3.

22 Ibid., xiv.

23 Ibid., 3.

24 As Deleuze asserts: "The notion of the virtual will come to play an increasingly important role in Bergsonian philosophy. . . . For, as we shall see, the same author who rejects the concept of *possibility* . . . is also he who develops the notion of the *virtual* to its highest degree and bases a whole philosophy of memory and life on it" (*Bergsonism*, 43).

25 Henri Bergson, *Duration and Simultaneity*, ed. Robin Durie, translation of supplementary material by Mark Lewis and Robin Durie (Manchester, England: Clinamen Press, 1999).

26 A translation of the transcript of this event (originally published in *Bulletin de la Société française de Philosophie* 22, no. 3 [July 1922]) is added as Appendix V to Bergson's *Duration and Simultaneity,* 154–159. A young Merleau-Ponty was also in the room for this dramatic encounter. See Maurice Merleau-Ponty's account, "Einstein and the Crisis of Reason," in *Signs,* trans. R. C. McCleary (Evanston: Northwestern University Press, 1964).
27 Appendix V of Bergson, *Duration and Simultaneity,* 158–159.
28 Deleuze, *Bergsonism,* 116, 117.
29 The virtual mobility that moving images offer, transformed the material space of spectatorship itself into a (new) ship of sorts, a ship of virtual transport. The relativity of this process, in fact the theory of relativity itself, assumes an important new role when seen in terms of the distinct modalities of movement and relative mobilities that prefigure Einstein's theories of a newly relativized space-time. Einstein's first paper on the Special Theory of Relativity was given June 30, 1905. His example for his "system of coordinates" was based on the observation of movement from two positions: "I stand at the window of a railway carriage," Einstein writes, "which is traveling uniformly and drop a stone on the embankment without throwing it. A pedestrian who observes the misdeed from the footpath notices that the stone falls to earth in a parabolic curve." Einstein uses the railway carriage and the footpath on the embankment as the two coordinates for his calculations on the relativity of simultaneity and the velocity of light, but the subjectivity of the passenger and the pedestrian are never merged, never crosscut into a virtual simultaneity. Albert Einstein, *Relativity: The Special and the General Theory* (1916), trans. Robert W. Lawson (New York: Crown Publishers, 1961), 9.

CHAPTER 4: THE SCREEN

1 A range of recent architectural projects add cameras, screens, and moving images as key components of a mediated reformulation of the architectural experience. For example, Diller + Scofidio's permanent installation project *Facsimile,* at the Moscone Center in San Francisco, combines the architectural experience of space with mobile forms of film and video spectatorship. As Diller + Scofidio describe their project:

> A 16' high by 27' wide video screen is suspended by a vertical structure that rides on a horizontal tracking system. Several live video cameras are fixed along the height of the structure pointed into and away from the building. The structure travels slowly along the surface of the exterior facade and broadcasts live and pre-recorded video imagery to the screen as it moves. While the live images naturally correspond with the speed and direction of the scanning motion, the pre-recorded programs (fictional vignettes, virtual transparencies into fictional office buildings) are constructed to simulate the same speed. The apparatus could be seen as a scanning device, a magnifying lens, a periscope (a camera at a high elevation looks toward the city), and as an instrument of deception substituting impostors for actual building occupants and spaces.

See <http://www.arcspace.com/architects/DillerSchofidio/moscone/>. Edward Dimendberg has written about Diller + Scofidio's ongoing deployment of electronic mediation to the built environment. See Dimendberg, "Blurring Genres," in Aaron Betsky, ed., *Scanning: The Aberrant Architectures of Diller + Scofidio* (New York: Whitney Museum of Art, 2003), 67–80.
2 I've taken the term "architecture of spectatorship" from the title of a panel organized by Sylvia Lavin for the College Art Association Conference in Los Angeles in 1999. The panel

had three papers: Beatriz Colomina on the Eames exhibit at the New York World's Fair, Sylvia Lavin on Neutra's Crystal Cathedral and the drive-in, and my paper on automotive visuality and the postwar screens of Los Angeles: drive-ins and the Cinerama Dome.

3 Donald Albrecht's 1987 study *Designing Dreams: Modern Architecture and the Movies,* for example, describes how cinematic set designers (MGM's Cedric Gibbons; RKO's Van Nest Polglase) were able to construct architectural space without the material constraints of the built world. In Albrecht's argument, the imaginary spaces seen on the cinema screen helped to disseminate images of the "modern." For discussions of set design and the use of architecture within the film frame, see Donald Albrecht, *Designing Dreams: Modern Architecture and the Movies* (London: Thames and Hudson, 1987); Dietrich Neumann, ed., *Film Architecture* (New York and Munich: Prestel Verlag, 1996); Leon Barsacq, *Caligari's Cabinet and Other Grand Illusions: A History of Film Design* (Boston: New York Graphic Society, 1976); Mary Corliss and Carlos Clarens, *Designed for Film,* exh. cat. (New York: Museum of Modern Art, 1978). A special issue of *iris* (Paris: Méridiens Klincksieck, 1991) on Cinema & Architecture contains essays and book reviews that interrogate the ampersand of this relation. Françoise Penz and Maureen Thomas, eds., *Cinema and Architecture: Méliès, Mallet-Stevens, Multimedia* (London: BFI Publications, 1997), collects papers from a 1997 conference at Cambridge University. Mark Lamster's anthology *Architecture and Film* (New York: Princeton Architectural Press, 2000) also contains essays about set design, the filming of landscape and architecture, the characterization of architects in film narratives. The rapidly expanding bibliography on film and architecture demonstrates an increasing crossover attraction: architectural historians and theorists have been drawn to media history and theory and, conversely, media historians and theorists have been drawn to architectural history and theory. This chiasmic exchange may indeed be a symptom of the encounter between the architectonics of material space and the technologies of the virtual.

4 In an original and subtle argument about the complex relation between the "cycle" of films deemed *film noir* and the architecture and spaces of the "built environment" in U.S. cities between 1939 and 1959, Edward Dimendberg capably reads the two-dimensional spaces of film against the three-dimensionality of urban lived space. Edward Dimendberg, *Film Noir and the Spaces of Modernity* (Cambridge: Harvard University Press, 2004). See also Anthony Vidler, "Metropolitan Montage: The City as Film in Kracauer, Benjamin, and Eisenstein," in *Warped Space: Art, Architecture, and Anxiety in Modern Culture* (Cambridge: MIT Press, 2002); David B. Clarke, *The Cinematic City* (New York: Routledge, 1997); James Donald, *Imagining the Modern City* (Minneapolis: University of Minnesota Press, 1999); and Mark Shiel and Tony Fitzmaurice, eds., *Screening the City* (London: Verso, 2003).

5 As discussed in chapter 3, Beatriz Colomina theorizes the relation of the movie camera to the architectural work of Adolf Loos and Le Corbusier. Beatriz Colomina, *Privacy and Publicity: Modern Architecture as Mass Media* (Cambridge: MIT Press, 1994).

6 Anthony Vidler, "The Explosion of Space: Architecture and the Filmic Imaginary," in Neumann, ed., *Film Architecture,* 13. Vidler postulates that architecture is the "fundamental site of film practice . . . the indispensable real and ideal matrix of filmic imagery" (14).

7 Beatriz's Colomina's study of modern architecture's engagement with mass media offers an exemplary parallel, if inverse, model for this study. In her book *Privacy and Publicity,* Colomina approaches the architecture of the two modern architects Le Corbusier and Adolf Loos in terms of their engagement with "mass media." Colomina writes: "The window in the age of mass communication provides us with one more flat image. The window is a screen" (334). She concludes: "this screen undermines the wall. But here it is not, as in Loos's houses, a physical undermining, an occupation of the wall, but a *dematerialization* following from emerging media. The organizing geometry of architecture slips from the perspectival cone of vision, from the humanist eye, to the camera angle. It is precisely in this slippage that modern architecture becomes modern by engaging with the media" (335).

My study approaches architecture and media from the other side—not "modern architecture as mass media" but, perhaps to twist the terms: modern media as mass architecture. Instead of arguing, as Colomina does, that the "physical undermining" and "dematerialization" of modern architecture are results of an architect's "engagement" with media, I emphasize how the mediated screens of cinema, television, and computer serve as architectonic elements that impart a different sense of space through the virtual "window" of the screen.

8 Once light writes its image on a surface, the image outside its window—its tiny aperture—is fixed as its two-dimensional virtual other. The flight of birds, the movement of trees in the wind, the gestures of humans were of great fascination to the viewers of the camera obscura, but the photograph could not record the movement in two dimensions. In order to reconstitute movement, a different apparatus with different mechanics needed to be developed: movement had to be recorded onto separate frames on a strip of light-sensitive film, and the strip of separate images had to be moved quickly past a light source. See Olive Cook, *Movement in Two Dimensions* (London: Hutchinson, 1963).

9 Hans Blumenberg, "Light as a Metaphor for Truth," in David Michael Levin, ed., *Modernity and the Hegemony of Vision* (Berkeley: University of California Press, 1993), 30–62. Also see Victor I. Stoichita, *A Short History of the Shadow* (London: Reaktion Books, 1997).

10 The history of projected light entertainments is covered in detail by Laurent Mannoni in *The Great Art of Light and Shadow: Archeology of Cinema,* trans. Richard Crangle (Exeter: University of Exeter Press, 2000).

11 See my discussion of the lure of this disavowal—"I know it is artifice, yet I believe it is real"—in the experience of the *phantasmagoria, eidophusikon,* panorama, and diorama in *Window Shopping,* 20–29. Charles Musser maintains that Jesuit theorist and practitioner Athanasius Kircher sought to demystify the illusion of the projected image. Even if, to the contrary, Kircher's text trained a new legion of mystifiers, these spectacles relied on the deep pleasures of acknowledgment and its countering disavowal. Charles Musser, *The Emergence of Cinema: The American Screen to 1907,* vol. 1 (New York: Scribner's, 1991), 31.

12 Wolfgang Schivelbusch, *Disenchanted Night: The Industrialization of Light in the Nineteenth Century,* trans. Angela Davies (Berkeley: University of California Press, 1988); emphasis added.

13 Paul Virilio, *Lost Dimension,* trans. Daniel Moshenberg (New York: Semiotext(e), 1991), 88.

14 Manonni, *The Great Art,* 416; emphasis added.

15 Douglas Gomery, *Shared Pleasures: A History of Movie Presentation in the United States* (Madison: University of Wisconsin Press, 1992), 7.

16 Vachel Lindsay, *The Art of the Moving Picture* (1915; New York: Modern Library Paperback Edition, 2000), 163, 95; emphasis added. "Architects would send forth publicity films which are not only delineations of a future Cincinnati, Cleveland, or St. Louis, but whole counties and states and groups of states could be planned at one time" (163). "Here we have this great instrument, the motion picture, the fourth largest industry in the United States, attended daily by ten million people, and in ten days by a hundred million, capable of interpreting the largest conceivable ideas that come within the range of the plastic arts, and those ideas have not been supplied" (164).

17 Ibid., 111.

18 Hugo Münsterberg, *Film: A Psychological Study* (New York: Dover Publications, 1970), 19. Long out of print, Münsterberg's volume was republished recently as *Hugo Münsterberg on Film: The Photoplay—A Psychological Study and Other Writings,* ed. Allan Langdale (New York: Routledge, 2002).

19 Münsterberg, *Film,* 21.

20 Ibid., 22.

21 Ibid., 23.

22 Ibid., 30.

23 Rudolf Arnheim, *Film as Art* (1932; Berkeley: University of California Press, 1971), 28.

24 Ibid., 20.

25 Gertrud Koch, "Rudolf Arnheim: The Materialist of Aesthetic Illusion—Gestalt Theory and the Reviewer's Practice," *New German Critique,* no. 51 (Fall 1990): 177.

26 In "An Aesthetic of Astonishment: Early Film and the (In)Credulous Spectator," Tom Gunning interrogates the sources and assumptions behind this oft-repeated anecdote. Gunning cites Georges Sadoul's *Histoire générale du cinéma* (1948) as the most commonly cited source of this legend. Tom Gunning, "An Aesthetic of Astonishment: Early Film and the (In)credulous Spectator," *Art & Text* 34 (Spring 1989): 31–45; reprinted in Leo Braudy and Marshall Cohen, eds., *Film Theory and Criticism: Introductory Readings,* 5th ed. (New York: Oxford University Press, 1991), 818–832. Lynne Kirby, in her excellent study of the relation between the mobilities of train and cinema technologies, *Parallel Tracks: The Railroad and Silent Cinema* (Durham: Duke University Press, 1997), quotes a French 1896 source from *L'Illustration* that describes panicked audiences. See also Stephen Bottomore, "The Panicking Audience? Early Cinema and the 'Train Effect,'" *Historical Journal of Film, Radio and Television* 19, no. 2 (June 1999): 177–216. Bottomore summarizes the positions of Gunning, Tsivian, Metz, and Loiperdinger in the debate.

27 Gunning, "An Aesthetic of Astonishment," 822.

28 Ibid., 832.

29 Arnheim, *Film as Art,* 61. Bottomore discusses the size of the screen in many of the earliest projection occasions—the Lumière screen in the Grand Café projection was two meters wide; however, an illustration in a 1897 *Scientific American* of a Biograph show has a screen that appears to be larger, around four meters wide ("The Panicking Audience?," 187).

30 Arnheim, *Film as Art,* 17.

31 André Bazin, "Theater and Cinema," in *What Is Cinema?* vol. 1, trans. Hugh Gray (Berkeley: University of California Press, 1976), 105.

32 David Bordwell describes the development of "continuity" editing: "Classical continuity editing . . . reinforces spatial orientation. Continuity of graphic qualities can invite us to look through the 'plate-glass window' of the screen. From shot to shot, tonality, movement, and the center of compositional interest shift enough to be distinguishable but not enough to be disturbing. . . . In sum, the intelligible orientation created within the single shot is kept consistent across shots by positing a spectator that can be moved only within the limits of a theatrical space of vision." David Bordwell, "Space in the Classical Film," in *The Classical Hollywood Cinema: Film Style and Mode of Production to 1960* (New York: Columbia University Press, 1985), 55, 56. Theorists of a "system of suture" (Jean-Pierre Oudart, Daniel Dayan) argue that the two-shot sequence of shot/countershot functioned as a means to "suture" the spectator into the space of the film. Using the Velázquez 1656 painting *Las meninas,* which was in the forefront of French intellectual discourse in the wake of Foucault's analysis of it in the opening of his *Order of Things* (1968), Oudart describes the filmic field in analogy to the *Las meninas* model: it poses the question of who is watching. Is it an absent viewer whose presence is implied in a correspondent absent field? The film spectator, in Oudart's account, occupies the position of the "absent one" in the first shot of the two-shot sequence. In the second shot of this sequence—the countershot—the field of vision/point of view is attributed to a fictional character. The effect of this shift or cut between the shot and its countershot is to "suture" the spectator into the fictional space of the film. For Oudart, the first shot in this sequence is pleasurable until the spectator notices the frame of the shot, and realizes that there is an absent space outside the frame. Oudart's articles, first published in *Cahiers du cinéma* in 1969, 1970, and 1971, were translated as "Notes on Suture" in the British journal *Screen* 18, no. 4 (1977–1978): 48–76. William Rothman takes issue with the universality of this system of "enunciation" and with the account that filmic enunciation is ideology-laden; he points out that it is really a three-shot sequence, not two. William Rothman, "Against 'The System of the Suture'" (1975), in Braudy and Cohen, eds., *Film Theory and Criticism,* 130–136.

See also Daniel Dayan, "The Tutor Code of Classical Cinema" (1974) in Braudy and Cohen, eds., *Film Theory and Criticism,* 106–117; and Kaja Silverman, "Suture" (1983), in *The Subject of Semiotics* (New York: Oxford University Press, 1983), 194–236.

33 This follows from my discussion in chapter 2. Richard DeCordova has argued this point with fine-tuned historical specificity in "From Lumière to Pathé: The Break-up of Perspectival Space," in Thomas Elsaesser, ed., *Early Cinema: Space, Frame, Narrative* (London: BFI, 1991), 76–85.

34 Tom Gunning, "The Cinema of Attractions: Early Film, Its Spectator and the Avant-Garde," in Elsaesser, ed., *Early Cinema: Space, Frame, Narrative,* 56–62, and Gunning, "An Aesthetic of Astonishment."

35 Erwin Panofsky, "Style and Medium in the Motion Pictures" (1947), in *Three Essays on Style,* ed. Irving Lavin (Cambridge: MIT Press, 1998), 93.

36 Ibid., 96–98; emphasis added.

37 Erwin Panofsky, "Style and Medium in the Motion Pictures" (1947), and "On Movies" (1936). As a scholar who so carefully dissected the frame of perspectival painting, it is striking that Panofsky did not address the frame of the "motion picture."

38 Although the term "ontological cut" is taken from Victor Stoichita's *The Self-Aware Image: An Insight into Early Modern Meta-Painting* (Cambridge: Cambridge University Press, 2001), where it is used to refer to the separation of the portable panel painting from the wall, it also provides an incisive description of the relation between the moving-image screen and the wall.

39 *Uncle Josh* is an early instance of an attempt to play with the relation between a diegetic character and a diegetic screen, a *mise en abyme* that is enacted in a set of films from *Sherlock Jr.* (Buster Keaton, 1924) to *Les carabiniers* (Jean Luc Godard, 1963) and *Purple Rose of Cairo* (Woody Allen, 1985).

40 In Charles Musser's description, the film "lampoons a rube farmer who confuses what he sees on the screen with real life and becomes more and more involved with the images" (*Emergence of Cinema,* 321).

41 Edwin Porter had reworked the "Edison Projecting Kinetoscope" in 1901—and this self-referential announcement of the projecting apparatus also served as an advertising plug for Edison's patented device.
42 *Uncle Josh* may offer itself to a more elaborate psychoanalytic reading of spectatorship—both in terms of the transgendered pleasures of identification and the psychic threat of the split subjectivity of all identification with the mirrored others on the screen.
43 Although the opacity of the screen surface was a necessary requirement for projection, the emerging conventions of a single-sided surface were still not in place in 1900. At the 1900 Paris exposition, the Lumière brothers showed their Cinématographe films on a *grand écran,* an enormous screen hung in the center of the Salle des Fêtes which could be viewed from either side. In Michael Snow's *Two Sides to Every Story* (1974), the recto and verso of the screen surface can be moved around, walked behind, but never entered.
44 A variety of devices at the 1900 Paris exposition supplied exhibition-goers with virtual voyages.

The Maréorama, an elaborate, noncinematic virtual voyage, surrounded the spectator with the sensations of sea travel. The spectator sat on the bridge of a ship and—amid the smell of salt air and the gentle swaying motion of the ship—watched views of a Mediterranean voyage from Nice to Venice to Constantinople. Conceived by Hugo d'Alesi, a painter of posters for railway and shipping companies, the Maréorama relied on two screens—one on the port side, one on the starboard—that were unrolled painted canvas panoramas.

The Stéréorama relied on an immobile spectator who stood looking out the frame of a window from inside the cabin of a steamer sailing along the Algerian coast. The ship's window looked into a moving panorama, emphasizing the motion of the waves, that was painted on forty-four-inch-tall concentric sheet metal screens which were moved up and down by an electric motor. The effect of a sea voyage was produced by the relative mobility of a static spectator and a framed and mobile image.

Another exhibit, the Trans-Siberian Express, provided a moving spectator with a moving view through a train window. In this attraction, presented by the international railway company Compagnie Wagons-Lits, the spectator sat in an actual railway carriage (equipped with dining-rooms, smoking rooms, bedrooms, bars). As the car moved eighty meters from the Russian pavilion to the Chinese pavilion, painted canvases rolled past its windows.

The Cinéorama relied on moving-picture film. Engineered by French cinema inventor Raoul Grimoin-Sanson, the Cinéorama placed the spectator inside of a balloon basket to watch a 360-degree cinematic projection (ten synchronized 70mm projectors) of a balloon ascent over Paris. The execution of this plan proved to be difficult: the ten projection apparatuses needed a central mechanism to synchronize the action, and a large platform with three men to operate the projectors at the speed of sixteen frames per second was required. For a further discussion of the bodily and virtual mobilities of spectators at the 1900 Paris exposition, see my "*Trottoir Roulant:* The Cinema and New Mobilities of Spectatorship," in Jan Olsson and John Fullerton, eds., *Allegories of Communication: Intermedial Concerns from Cinema to the Digital* (London: John Libbey, 2005), 263–276.
45 Stephan Oetterman's *The Panorama: History of a Mass Medium,* trans. Deborah Lucas Schneider (New York: Zone Books, 1997), provides an excellent comprehensive history of the painted panorama.

46 Most of the films from the Thomas Edison Company are in the Library of Congress's Paper Print Collection of more than 3,000 titles. When they were deposited for copyright from 1894 to 1912, these films were printed as positive pictures frame by frame on long rolls of paper. In recent years, in order to serve the goals of access and preservation, the Library of Congress has been copying the paper rolls onto 35mm motion picture negative film. Next, a positive film print is made from the 35mm negative and this is transferred to Betacam SP videotape to produce the master for digitization. To present an authentic record of the paper prints as artifacts, some of the edging and perforations evident on the originals have been left in the digital frame. Likewise, original labels, titles, and other tagging documentation has been retained, as well as other imperfections.

The motion pictures chosen for digitization were all black-and-white and silent, whether originating from the paper prints or from early film copies in other collections. The original motion pictures were shot with hand-cranked cameras at varying frame rates, generally at sixteen frames per second (fps). (In fact, the frame rate may vary within a single title.) In the video mastering process, the playback speeds were adjusted to present the appearance of natural motion to the greatest degree possible.

James Henry White had been hired to head the "kinetograph department" of the Edison Manufacturing Company in October 1897. He was credited as producer for many of Edison's static indoor films photographed at the Black Maria, but White also "produced" many outdoor scenes, such as *Shooting the Chutes at Coney Island* (1896) and *Passaic Falls* (1896). (The cameraman for these was William Heise.) White frequently mounted the camera on means of transport, and his films are records of his interest in the relative movement. In May 1900, a month before he left for Paris, White filmed the Whirlpool Rapids at Niagara Falls in *Panorama of Gorge Railway,* as a "phantom ride." The Edison films catalog reports: "The camera in securing this picture was placed at the front end of a train ascending the grade at a very rapid rate of speed. The combined motion of the train in one direction and the water in the opposite direction, the latter impeded and interrupted in its course by the rocky path through which it flows, sending beautiful masses of spray and foam many feet in the air, makes an impression on the audience long to be remembered." "Inventing Entertainment: The Motion Pictures and Sound Recordings of the Edison Companies," Library of Congress.

47 Edison films catalog, Library of Congress Collection.

48 Gunning, "The Cinema of Attractions" and "An Aesthetic of Astonishment."

49 An excellent example of this can be found in Thomas Edison's films of the Pan-American exposition in Buffalo in 1901. Two short films, *Circular Panorama of Electric Tower, Pan-American Exposition, 1901* and *Circular panorama of Electric Tower, Pan-American Exposition at Night, 1901* were taken from a panning-head tripod, laterally panning in 360 degrees. Another was taken from a hot-air balloon, but the effect is the same.

50 A similar argument has been suggested by Paul Virilio: "If last century's revolution in transportation saw the emergence and gradual popularization of the dynamic motor vehicle (train, motorbike, car, plane), the current revolution in transmission leads us in turn to the innovation of the ultimate vehicle: The static audiovisual vehicle, marking the advent of a behavioral inertia in the sender/receiver that moves us along from the celebrated retinal persistence which permits the optical illusion of cinematic projection to the bodily persistence of the terminal-man; a prerequisite for the sudden mobilization of the illusion of the world, of a whole world, telepresent at each moment, the witness's own body becoming the last urban frontier." Paul Virilio, "The Third Interval," in *Open Sky*, trans. Julie Rose (London: Verso, 1997), 11.

51 *Merriam-Webster's Third New International Dictionary* gives the etymology as: "the·ater *or* the·atre from: Middle English *theatre*, from Middle French, from Latin *theatrum*, from Greek *theatron*, from *theasthai* to view, from *thea* act of seeing." See also Martin Jay, *Downcast Eyes: The Denigration of Vision in Twentieth-Century Thought* (Berkeley: University of California Press, 1993), 23. For a further etymological history of the relation between "theater" and "theory," Jay cites David Michael Levin, *The Opening of Vision: Nihilism and the Postmodern Situation* (London: Routledge, 1988), 99f.

52 Sir Banister Fletcher, *A History of Architecture on the Comparative Method*, 16th ed. (New York: Charles Scribner's Sons, 1958), 117–118; 172–173.

53 These are broad generalizations of the development of theater architecture. For a more detailed historical account, see Gaelle Breton, *Theaters* (New York: Princeton Architectural Press, 1989); George C. Izenour, *Theater Design*, 2nd ed. (New Haven: Yale University Press, 1996). Alberto Pérez-Gómez and Louise Pelletier describe a temporary theater at Versailles (1672) constructed so that the king could occupy the central point of perspective; see Alberto Pérez-Gómez and Louise Pelletier, *Architectural Representation and the Perspective Hinge* (Cambridge: MIT Press, 1997), 57.

54 The relation between "stage" and "screen" has commonly been conceptualized in terms of the adapted elements of narrative, set design, and staging and in terms of differing acting styles for live audiences and for the camera. A. Nicholas Vardac's classic *Stage to Screen: Theatrical Origins of Early Film: David Garrick to D. W. Griffith* (Cambridge: Harvard University Press, 1949) provides the standard historical inscription of the proto-cinematic nature of nineteenth-century narrative and staging techniques. More recently, in *Theatre to Cinema: Stage Pictorialism and the Early Feature Film* (New York: Oxford University Press, 1997), Ben Brewster and Lea Jacobs emphasize the influence of the pictorial tradition of staging action on the mise-en-scène of early feature films. Comparative studies of "stage" and "screen" acting contrast acting styles for the camera and for a live audience. Also see the discussion of the differences between stage and screen acting in Walter Benjamin's "The Work of Art in the Age of Mechanical Reproduction," in *Illuminations*, ed. Hannah Arendt, trans. Harry Zohn (New York: Schocken Books, 1969); and Leo Braudy's *The World in a Frame: What We See in Films* (New York: Doubleday, 1976).

55 The kinetoscope was an upright four-foot-high wooden cabinet with a peephole at the top; inside the box was an elaborate threading mechanism that pulled a fifty-foot film loop over a series of spools via an electrically driven sprocket wheel. Beneath the film was an electric lamp modulated by a shutter as the film passed over it. Ten of the first twenty-five kinetoscopes manufactured were shipped to Andrew Holland for the opening of a kinetoscope parlor at 1155 Broadway, New York, on April 14, 1894. See David Robinson, *From Peepshow to Palace: The Birth of the American Film* (New York: Columbia University Press, 1997). W. K. L. Dickson delivered ten films (one for each machine), including *Wrestling*, *Horse-shoeing*, and *Barbershop*. In this venue, customers paid twenty-five cents to view a row of five kinetoscopes. Edison equipped other models of the kinetoscope with nickel-slot attachments for their installation in arcades, barrooms, hotels, and restaurants. His plan to combine the phonograph and the Kinetograph, as the Kineto-phonograph, followed the logic of combining the individual apparatuses in the same venue. Gordon Hendricks, *The Kinetoscope: America's First Commercially Successful Motion Picture Exhibitor* (New York: Beginnings of the American Film, 1966).

56 For accounts of movie theater architecture and the developing spatial habits of spectatorship, see Ina Rae Hark, ed., *Exhibition: The Film Reader* (London: Routledge, 2002); Gomery, *Shared Pleasures;* Maggie Valentine, *The Show Starts on the Sidewalk: An Architectural History of the Movie Theater Starring S. Charles Lee* (New Haven: Yale University Press, 1994); Morton Shand, *Modern Picture Houses and Theaters* (Philadelphia: J. B. Lippincott, 1930); Charlotte Herzog, "The Movie Palace and the Theatrical Sources of Its Architectural Style," *Cinema Journal* 25 (Spring 1981): 15–37; and Ben Hall, *The Best Remaining Seats: The Story of the Golden Age of the Movie Palace* (New York: Clarkson N. Potter, 1961).

57 Robert Allen argues that technical underpinnings of projection systems had determinant effects on exhibition practice. The Lumière Cinématographe was hired out to theaters as a package—with a traveling cameraman and projection operator—whereas Edison's Vitascope projector was developed to be used by showmen/projectionists—and hence worked best in fixed-site cinemas. See Robert C. Allen, "Vitascope/Cinématographe: Initial Patterns of American Film Industrial Practice," in John L. Fell, ed., *Film before Griffith* (Berkeley: University of California Press, 1983), 144–152; Charles Musser and Carol Nelson, *High Class Moving Pictures: Lyman Howe and the Forgotten Era of Traveling Exhibition 1880–1920* (Princeton: Princeton University Press, 1991); and Charles Musser, *Before the Nickelodeon: Edwin S. Porter and the Edison Manufacturing Company* (Berkeley: University of California Press, 1991).

58 There is a broad bibliography on these early struggles for competition and control. See, for example, Jeanne Thomas Allen, "The Industrial Context of Film Technology: Standardization and Patents," in Stephen Heath and Teresa de Lauretis, eds., *The Cinematic Apparatus* (London: Macmillan, 1980), 26–36; Alan Williams, "The Lumière Organization and 'Documentary Realism,'" in Fell, ed., *Film before Griffith,* 153–161; and Tino Balio, *The American Film Industry* (Madison: University of Wisconsin Press, 1976).

59 Jean Louis Baudry, "The Ideological Effects of the Cinematic Apparatus," trans. Alan Williams, in Phil Rosen, ed., *Narrative, Apparatus, Ideology* (New York: Columbia University Press, 1986), 293.

60 Dziga Vertov, *Kino-Eye: The Writing of Dziga Vertov,* ed. Annette Michelson, trans. Kevin O'Brien (Berkeley: University of California Press, 1984), 15.

61 Hans Belting, "Theaters of Illusion," in Hiroshi Sugimoto, *Theaters* (New York: Sonnabend Sundell Editions, 2000), 8–17.

62 In an essay entitled "The Virtual Image," Sugimoto gives the following account of the photograph image:

> The structure of the photographic camera is, in sum, perhaps a "copy" of the structure of our eyes. Historically at around the same time as painters began developing perspective drawing in the fifteenth century, the study of the structure of human eyes evolved. Out of this came about the "camera obscura," a device that projects, through a pinhole, the outside scenery inside the dark box. The lens continued to gain greater precision, rather implicitly, to cater to the pleasure of then legally banned astronomical observation. At last in the nineteenth century, thanks to the discovery of the photosensitivity of silver, the area of photography came to fruition.

Hiroshi Sugimoto, "The Virtual Image," in Sugimoto, *Theaters,* 17.

63 Russell Merritt's "Nickelodeon Theaters, 1905–1914: Building an Audience for the Movies" examines the strategies theater operators used to lure a middle-class audience. In Balio, ed., *The American Film Industry;* reprinted in Ina Rae Hark, ed., *Exhibition: The Film Reader* (London: Routledge, 2002).

64 Gunning, "The Cinema of Attractions," 56–62.

65 Two indispensable texts on the economic and social history of film exhibition are Douglas Gomery, *Shared Pleasures: History of Movie Presentation in the United States,* and Ina Rae Hark, ed., *Exhibition: The Film Reader,* both cited earlier.

66 Charlotte Herzog traces the architectural evolution from the penny arcade, kinetoscope parlor, store theaters, nickelodeon, and small-time vaudeville theaters to the "movie palace." Herzog, "The Movie Palace and the Theatrical Sources of Its Architectural Style," 15–35. For an insightful examination of the marked recent changes in film exhibition, see Charles R. Acland, *Screen Traffic: Movies, Multiplexes, and Global Culture* (Durham: Duke University Press, 2003).

67 Here Gunning's description of "the cinema of attractions," which "directly solicits spectator attention, inciting visual curiosity, and supplying pleasure through an exciting spectacle. . . . Theatrical display dominates over narrative absorption," matches a description of the nonnarrative aspects of the theatrical space for film exhibition. The theater was itself a destination where "theatrical display dominates over narrative absorption" ("Cinema of Attractions," 59).

68 My own account in *Window Shopping* emphasizes the relation between the mobile visuality of the *flâneur* and *flâneuse* and the virtual mobility of the cinema spectator. See also Giuliana Bruno, *Streetwalking on a Ruined Map: Cultural Theory and the City Films of Elvira Notari* (Princeton: Princeton University Press, 1993); Vanessa Schwartz's discussion of boulevard culture and public visits to the morgue, wax museums, and panoramas and dioramas in *Spectacular Realities: Early Mass Culture in Fin-de-Siècle Paris* (Berkeley: University of California Press, 1998); Douglas Gomery, "Movie Audiences, Urban Geography, and the History of the American Film," *Velvet Light Trap* 19 (1982): 23–29; and Gomery's *Shared Pleasures.*

69 Roland Barthes, "Upon Leaving the Movie Theater," in *Communications* 23; reprinted in Theresa Ha Kyung Cha, ed., *Apparatus* (New York: Tanam Press, 1980), 1. Barthes compares the "urban darkness" of the movie theater to the "opposite experience" of television, where the space is "familar, organized, . . . tamed."

70 Siegfried Kracauer, "On Employment Agencies: The Construction of a Space," trans. David Frisby, in Neil Leach, ed., *Rethinking Architecture* (London: Routledge, 1997), 60.

71 Siegfried Kracauer, "Cult of Distraction: On Berlin's Picture Palaces" (1977), trans. Thomas Y. Levin, in *The Mass Ornament: Weimar Essays* (Cambridge: Harvard University Press, 1995), 323–328.

72 Siegfried Kracauer, "Kult der Zerstreuung: Über die Berliner Lichtspielhäuser,"in *Das Ornament der Masse: Essays* (Frankfurt am Main: Suhrkamp, 1977), 312.

73 Kracauer, "Cult of Distraction," 325–326.

74 Ibid., 328.

75 Ibid.

76 Heide Schlüpmann, "Kracauer's Phenomenlogy of Film," *New German Critique,* no. 40 (Winter 1987): 97–114. Miriam Bratu Hansen has productively examined the trajectories in Kracauer's writing from the 1920s to his 1960 volume of film theory, in her exemplary introduction to the reprint of Kracauer's *Theory of Film: Redemption of Physical Reality* (Princeton: Princeton University Press, 1997).

77 Fredrich Kiesler, "100 Percent Cinema," *Close Up* (August 1928): 36.

78 Ibid., 16.

79 Fredrick J. Kiesler, "Building a Cinema Theatre," *New York Evening Post* (February 1929), 16–18. The Film Guild Cinema was described in an article in the special "Better Theatres" section of *Exhibitor's Herald-World.* See Douglas Fox, "The Film Guild Cinema: An Experiment in Theatre Design," *Exhibitor's Herald-World,* 16 March 1929, 15–19.

80 A. V. Pilichowski, *Close Up* 10, no. 1 (March 1933): 69.

81 A. C. Hardy and R. W. Conant, "Perspective Considerations in Taking and Projecting Motion Pictures," *SMPTE Journal* 12, no. 33 (1928): 117–125; emphasis added. While this article deals with "optical perspective considerations only," it notes the need to produce an equivalent "acoustical perspective" when sound is added to the picture. The authors conclude, after a calculation of focal lengths and distances, that "the correct distance for viewing a motion picture production is obtained by multiplying the projection distance in the theater by the ratio of the focal length of taking the camera to the focal length of the projector" (121). Put simply, they conclude that the best seat in the auditorium would be two-fifths of the distance of the projector from the screen.

82 Sigfried Giedion, *Bauen in Frankreich* (Leipzig: Klinkhardt & Biermann, 1928), 92.

83 Yve-Alain Bois quotes this excerpt from Eisenstein's essay "El Greco y el cine" (written around 1937) in his introduction to Sergei M. Eisenstein's "Montage and Architecture," in *Assemblage,* no. 10 (December 1989): 111; emphasis added here. In a footnote, Bois notes that Eisenstein's El Greco essay and the "Montage and Architecture" piece are also mentioned by Hubert Damisch in his discussion of Le Corbusier's "storyboard" plans for Algiers and Rio in *Précisions* (1930). See Damisch, "Les Tréreaux de la vie moderne," in *Le Corbusier: Une encyclopédie* (Paris: Centre Georges Pompidou, 1987), 253–255.

84 Sergei Eisenstein, "Montage and Architecture," *Assemblage,* no. 10 (December 1989). This essay was reprinted in volume 2 of *Selected Works: S. M. Eisenstein,* ed. Michael Glenny and Richard Taylor, trans. Michael Glenny (London: BFI Publishing, 1991), 59–81. As Bois points out in his *Assemblage* introduction to "Montage and Architecture," in this essay Eisenstein "is no longer concerned with movement in its virtuality, but with the real movement of the beholder in space" (113). Subsequent references to this essay are from the *Assemblage* version.

85 Bois, introduction to "Montage and Architecture," 112. Anthony Vidler, Yve-Alain Bois, and Giuliana Bruno have all profitably drawn upon Eisenstein's essay. In her recent book *Atlas of Emotions* (New York: Verso, 2002), Bruno follows the spectatorial logic of Eisenstein's "imaginary path": "There is a mobile dynamics involved in the act of viewing films, even if the spectator is seemingly static. The (im)mobile spectator moves across an imaginary path, traversing multiple sites and times. Her fictional navigation connects distant moments and far-apart places" (55–56). Bruno's wide-ranging and eloquent argument underlines the mobility, if not the framed containment, inherent in the spectator's imaginary traversal.

86 Eisenstein, "Montage and Architecture," 117.

87 Ibid. Eisenstein quotes Auguste Choisy's 1889 description of the Acropolis in his *Histoire d'architecture.* Choisy asserts: "equally strong however is the calculation of a montage effect, that is, the sequential juxtaposition of those shots."

88 Eisenstein, "Montage and Architecture," 116.

89 Ibid.

90 Eisenstein reads the Bernini coat of arms from St. Peter's as "eight shots, eight montage sequences of a whole montage scenario." He suggests that Bernini's practical joke/satiric message was not easily readable because the "true image of this montage statement only emerges in the sequential juxtaposition of its constituent frames." (One wonders whether this montage fooled Pope Urban VIII? If so, does this explain how Bernini got away with the orgasmic St. Teresa? "Each shield in itself means nothing," Eisenstein writes. "Viewed in isolation, it is dumb.") Eisenstein concludes with a number of examples of how several Russian magazines (one called *Zritel* [The Spectator]) cleverly dodged the vigilant censorship imposed by the tsarist government after the abortive 1905 revolution by applying a "disassociated display of images that only acquired significance through the montage technique of sequential juxtaposition"; pictures shown separately to the censor could be passed as harmless and later put into montage context. Here montage was employed to hide or conceal a subversion where mise-en-scène is innocent ("each shield means nothing"); meaning is produced in *mise en cadre.* (A contemporary reversal of this logic is found in the revelations about workers for Pope Disney who apparently concealed their subversions in the static frames of *Roger Rabbit.* Invisible in the *mise en cadre* of animated motion, and only visible in the freeze-frame mise-en-scène made possible with laser disk technology, are revealing parts of Jessica Rabbit's anatomy and also a frame with a graffiti that reads, "For a good time call Alyson Wonderland," and allegedly supplying Michael Eisner's home phone number. Just as with Bernini, the subversion here is negotiated over female anatomy.) See Eisenstein, "Montage and Architecture," 121–129.

91 Yve-Alain Bois discusses Choisy's use of axonometry because it does not imply a fixed view but is more akin to the "cinematic perception of architecture" (introduction to "Montage and Architecture").

92 "Khoklova is walking along Petrov Street in Moscow near the 'Mostorg' store. Obolensky is walking along the embankment of the Moscow River—at a distance of about two miles away. They see each other, smile, and begin to walk toward one another. Their meeting is filmed at the Boulevard Prechistensk. This boulevard is in an entirely different section of the city. They clasp hands, with Gogol's monument as a background, and look—at the White House!—for this point, we cut in a segment from an American film, *The White House in Washington.*" Lev Kuleshov, "The Art of the Cinema," in *Kuleshov on Film: Writings of Lev Kuleshov,* trans. and ed. Ronald Levaco (Berkeley: University of California Press, 1974), 52.

93 Paul Virilio, "Improbable Architecture," in *Lost Dimension,* trans. Daniel Moshenberg (New York: Semiotext(e), 1991), 69.

94 Ibid., 73. This chapter of *Lost Dimension* makes the most sense if read in tandem with Benjamin's "Work of Art" essay. Unless one is familiar with the order and logic of Benjamin's essay, Virilio's intermittent references to it are somewhat cryptically inscribed. Virilio also seems to be skimming the surface of Sigfried Giedion's *Space, Time and Architecture.* Although *Lost Dimension* begins with a discussion of Walter Benjamin and the cinematic, Virilio makes no apparatical distinction between cinema and television—and refers to both as "televised interface."

95 Ibid., 100.

96 Ibid., 13.

97 Ibid., 93.

98 Paul Virilio, "The Third Window: An Interview with Paul Virilio," trans. Yvonne Shafir, with a preface by Jonathan Crary, in Cynthia Schneider and Brian Wallis, eds., *Global Television* (Cambridge: MIT Press, 1988), 191. Originally published as "La troisième fenêtre: Entretien avec Paul Virilio," *Cahiers du Cinéma,* no. 322 (April 1981): 35–40.

99 Although the television "window" may appear on the film screen—as filmmakers began to include television sets as elements of mise-en-scène—for Virilio it shows up only in American films, and occasional Wenders films, but rarely in French cinema.

100 Virilio, *Lost Dimension,* 76.

101 This is the title of a 1993 interview, "Architecture in the Age of Its Virtual Disappearance: An Interview with Paul Virilio," in John Beckman, ed., *The Virtual Dimension: Architecture, Representation, and Crash Culture* (New York: Princeton Architectural Press, 1998), 176–187.

102 Ibid., 182–183.

103 For a discussion of the relation between automotive visuality and the post–World War II widescreen formats, see Anne Friedberg, "Urban Mobility and Cinematic Visuality: The Screens of Los Angeles—Endless Cinema or Private Telematics," *Journal of Visual Culture* 1, no. 2 (2002): 183–204.

104 George Schutz, "Cinerama and the Future," in *Motion Picture Herald,* 4 October 1952. Cinerama was first developed for the military during wartime and used by the Air Force as a gunnery trainer in simulated combat conditions. It was pioneered by inventor Fred Waller, financed by Laurence Rockefeller, and promoted by his business partner, radio commentator Lowell Thomas. Seven films were made with the Cinerama process: *This is Cinerama!, Cinerama Holiday, Seven Wonders of the World, Search for Paradise, South Seas Adventure, Wonderful World of the Brothers Grimm,* and *How the West Was Won.*

105 Charles Barr, "Cinemascope: Before and After," *Film Quarterly* 16, no. 4 (Summer 1963): 4–24.

106 Hallmark of Hollywood publicity campaign, in clippings file, Margaret Herrick Library, Academy of Motion Picture Arts and Sciences, Los Angeles.

107 Ibid.

108 John Belton, *Widescreen Cinema* (Cambridge: Harvard University, 1992), 34.

109 These statistics are from Balio, ed., *The American Film Industry,* and Gomery, *Shared Pleasures.*

110 The 1948 Supreme Court decision on the antitrust suit *U.S. v. Paramount Pictures, Inc. et al.* ruled that the "Big Five" movie studios had to divest themselves of their theater holdings; the "Divestiture Decision" effectively separated film production from exhibition. The film industry—with its producers and exhibitors now divorced from each other and operating sometimes at cross-purposes—had two strategies to combat the commercial introduction of television. One was to compromise—by adjusting to the spectatorial advantages of television—and the other was to compensate—by offering larger screen size, color images, and the immersive spectatorship that television could not supply. In an early attempt to broker a compromise between the new programming available on television screens and the out-of-the-home theater-going audience, in 1947 and 1948 theaters began to have TV-viewing lounges, using fifteen-by-twenty-foot screens. Anna McCarthy has explored the role of television outside the domestic arena—the barstool audience in taverns ("'The Front Row Is Reserved for Scotch Drinkers': Early Television's Tavern Audience," *Cinema Journal* 34, no. 4 [Summer

1995]: 31–49) and the boxing audience for theater television ("'Like an Earthquake!' Theater Television, Boxing, and the Black Public Sphere," *Quarterly Review of Film and Video* 16, nos. 3–4 [1994]: 307–323); see also Anna McCarthy, *Ambient Television: Visual Culture and Public Space* (Durham: Duke University Press, 2001).

111 A small historical aside here: in the Salles des Fêtes of the Paris 1900 exhibition, the Lumières' Cinématographe Géant was double-sided, viewed by spectators on both sides—hence it had bilateral directionality of movement within the frame—and it was also of an enormous scale. Stephen Heath writes: "it is important that the Lumière brothers should set the screen as they do in the Grand Café and not with the audience on either side of a translucent screen, that cinema architecture should take its forms in consequence." Stephen Heath, "Narrative Space," in *Questions of Cinema* (New York: Macmillan Press, 1981), 37. Michael Snow's *Two Sides to Every Story* (1974) projected a 16mm film loop onto both sides of a screen.

112 André Bazin's 1953 article, "Will CinemaScope Save the Film Industry?," originally published in French as "Cinémascope: sauvera-t-il le cinéma? (*Esprit* 21, nos. 207–208 [October-November 1953]) and translated in André Bazin, *Major Reviews from the Forties and Fifties,* ed. Bert Cardullo (NewYork: Routledge, 1997). As I've described earlier, Williams negotiates an account of the development of television technology that avoids the common technological determinism or technology-as-symptom arguments, and instead maintains that television technologies develop in response to new social and cultural needs. Hence his description of "mobile privatization" and "flow," both highly original and incisively prophetic, remains a salient analysis of the cultural form. Raymond Williams, *Television: Technology and Cultural Form* (New York: Schocken Books, 1975), 22; 28–29.

113 Ibid., 136.

114 Jane Feuer, "The Concept of Live Television: Ontology as Ideology," in E. Ann Kaplan, ed., *Regarding Television* (Los Angeles: American Film Institute, 1983). Vivian Sobchack's "The Scene of the Screen: Envisioning Cinematic and Electronic Presence" (1994) compares the concept of "presence" in cinematic and "electronic" (read televisual) media. Vivian Sobchack, "The Scene of the Screen: Envisioning Cinematic and Electronic Presence" (1994), reprinted in John Thornton Caldwell, ed., *Electronic Media and Technoculture* (New Brunswick: Rutgers University Press, 2000), 137–155.

115 See especially Lynn Spigel, "Installing the Television Set: Popular Discourses on Television and Domestic Space, 1948–1955," in Lynn Spigel and Denise Mann, eds., *Private Screenings: Television and the Female Consumer* (Minneapolis: University of Minnesota Press, 1992), 3–38. Spigel offers a sustained account of the space of reception, the television "set" in the private sanctum of the home. See Spigel's "The Home Theater," in *Make Room for TV: Television and the Family Ideal in Postwar America* (Chicago: University of Chicago Press, 1992), 99–135, and her subsequent work, *Welcome to the Dreamhouse: Popular Media and Postwar Suburbs* (Durham: Duke University Press, 2001). A new volume examining the transitional technologies of a "post-television" era, Lynn Spigel and Jan Olsson, eds., *Television after TV: Essays on a Medium in Transition* (Durham: Duke University Press, 2004), appeared as this book was going to press.

As a complementary account of the television screen outside of the home, Anna McCarthy's *Ambient Television* describes the television screen in the public spaces of taverns, department stores, and airports. See also Anna McCarthy, "From Screen to Site: Television's Material Culture and Its Place," *October,* no. 98 (Fall 2001): 93–11; and Anna McCarthy and

Nick Couldry, eds., *Media/Space: Place, Scale and Culture in a Media Age* (London: Routledge, 2004).

116 For an excellent examination of artists' reaction to and incorporation of television in the 1960s see John Alan Farmer, *The New Frontier: Art and Television 1960–65* (Austin: Austin Museum of Art, 2000).

117 Ellen Seiter, "Television and the Internet" (1999), in *Television and New Media Audiences* (London: Oxford University Press, 1999); reprinted in John Thornton Caldwell, ed., *Electronic Media and Technoculture* (New Brunswick: Rutgers University Press, 2000), 227–243.

118 See Anne Friedberg, "The End of Cinema: Multimedia and Technological Change," in Linda Williams and Christine Gledhill, eds., *Reinventing Film Studies* (London: Arnold Publications, 1999), 438–452; reprinted in Leo Braudy and Marshall Cohen, eds., *Film Theory and Criticism*, 6th ed. (New York: Oxford University Press, 2004), 914–926.

119 Baudry, "Ideological Effects of the Basic Apparatus," 294.

120 Steven Shaviro, *The Cinematic Body* (*Theory Out of Bounds*) (Minneapolis: University of Minnesota Press, 1993), 31.

121 For a discussion of Kracauer and the "surface" in Weimar culture, see Janet Ward, *Weimar Surfaces: Urban Visual Culture in 1920s Germany* (Berkeley: University of California Press, 2001).

122 Herman G. Scheffauer, "The Vivifying of Space," *Freeman* (24 November–1 December 1920); reprinted in Lewis Jacobs, ed., *The Introduction to the Art of the Movies* (New York: Noonday Press, 1960), 76.

123 Frederick Kiesler, "Cinema Manifesto," *Close Up* (August 1928).

LENS IV: VIRILLIO'S SCREEN

1 Paul Virilio, *The Information Bomb*, trans. Chris Turner (London: Verso, 2000), 16.

2 Paul Valéry, "The Conquest of Ubiquity," in *Aesthetics*, trans. Ralph Mannheim (New York: Pantheon Books, 1964), 226. "La conquête de l'ubiquité" was first published in *De la musique avant toute chose* (Paris: Editions du Tambourinaire, 1928).

3 Walter Benjamin, "The Work of Art in the Age of Mechanical Reproduction," in *Illuminations*, ed. Hannah Arendt, trans. Harry Zohn (New York: Schocken Books, 1969), 217.

4 Virilio misattributes Valéry's "augury of telecommunications" to 1936, the year of Walter Benjamin's essay, collapsing the two works as coincident rather than sequential. Paul Virilio, *Lost Dimension*, trans. Daniel Moshenberg (New York: Semiotext(e), 1991), 72.

5 Ibid., 15; repeated as epigraph to "The Third Interval" chapter in *Open Sky* (*La vitesse de libération* [Paris: Galilée, 1995]), trans. Julie Rose (London: Verso, 1997), 9.

6 Used as opening epigraph to Virilio, *Open Sky*.

7 Paul Virilio, interview with Jerome Sans in *Flash Art* (1988), reprinted in *Virilio Live: Selected Interviews*, ed. John Armitage (London: Sage Publications, 2001), 116. In *Virilio Live*, Armitage has compiled the most comprehensive bibliography to date of Virilio's work in French and English.

8 Paul Virilio, *Esthetique de la disparition* (Paris: Balland, 1980); *The Aesthetics of Disappearance*, trans. Philip Beitchman (New York: Semiotext(e),1991), 55. (Virilio uses an epigram from Marcel L'Herbier as chapter banner: "Film is a new age for humanity.")

9 Virilio, *The Aesthetics of Disappearance*, 17.

10 Ibid., 65.

11 Ibid., 64–65.

12 Ibid., 46.
13 Ibid., 54, 66.
14 Virilio, *Lost Dimension,* 17.
15 Ibid., 87.
16 "La troisième fenêtre: Entretien avec Paul Virilio," *Cahiers du cinéma,* no. 322 (April 1981): 35–40; "The Third Window: An Interview with Paul Virilio," trans. Yvonne Shafir, with a preface by Jonathan Crary, in Cynthia Schneider and Brian Wallis, eds., *Global Television* (Cambridge: MIT Press, 1988), 191.
17 Paul Virilio, "Improbable Architecture," in *Lost Dimension,* 73.
18 Virilio, *Lost Dimension,* 100.
19 Ibid., 86, 88.
20 Ibid., 69.
21 "The Overexposed City" section of *L'espace critique* (1984) was translated and published separately in 1984: "The Overexposed City," trans. Hustvedt in Michel Feher and Sanford Kwinter, eds., *Zone 1/2* (New York: Urzone, 1984), 15–31.
22 Ibid.
23 Virilio, *Lost Dimension,* 75.
24 Ibid., 19, 79.
25 Ibid., 73.
26 This paragraph from "The Work of Art in the Age of Mechanical Reproduction" is oddly translated in the Daniel Moshenberg translation from Virilio's French to English. Instead of the standard Harry Zohn translation of Benjamin's *Kerkerwelt* as "prison-world," Moshenberg's translation reads: "Then came the film, and with the dynamite of its tenths-of-a-second, it blew up the *concentration-camp universe,* so that now, abandoned in the midst of its far-flung debris, we take on adventurous expeditions" (71; emphasis added).
27 Virilio, *Lost Dimension,* 13, 93.
28 Paul Virilio, "From Modernism to Hypermodernism and Beyond: Interview with John Armitage (1997)," trans. Patrice Riemens, in Armitage, *Virilio Live,* 24. Virilio said: "I got the foreboding of virtual space. . . . And the curious thing is that I published *Lost Dimension* in the same year as William Gibson published *Neuromancer.* . . . The reason why space is critical is because it is on the verge of becoming virtual space."
29 Paul Virilio, *War and Cinema: The Logistics of Perception,* trans. Patrick Camiller (London: Verso, 1989), 49.
30 Paul Virilio, *Desert Screen: War at the Speed of Light*, trans. Michael Degener (London: Athlone Press, 2001), 41.
31 "Virilio Looks Back and Sees the Future: Interview by James Der Derian (2000)," in Virilio, *Desert Screen,* 135.
32 Virilio, *Desert Screen,* 57.
33 *Au carré* can mean both "on the screen" and "squared." "L'horizon au carré" is the title of a 1990 article (published in *Libération,* 29 September 1990) about the relation between the screen and the horizon for fighter pilots who maneuver missions on the basis of looking at a screen and not at the horizon line of the earth below. A section of *Desert Screen* titled "The Squared Horizon" (dated 2 September 1990) opens with a list of the dramatis personae in the impending television war: "How can we fail to recognize, after a month of standoff, that the true intervention force in the Gulf is television? And more precisely CNN, the Atlanta net-

work. Saddam Hussein and George Bush, certainly, but also Ted Turner, the owner of Cable News Network" (20).

34 Virilio, *Desert Screen,* 57.

35 "Architecture in the Age of Its Virtual Disappearance: An Interview with Paul Virilio (1993)," in John Beckman, ed., *The Virtual Dimension: Architecture, Representation, and Crash Culture* (New York: Princeton Architectural Press, 1998), 181–182.

36 Virilio, *Open Sky,* 9, 37.

37 Ibid., 41.

38 Virilio, *The Information Bomb,* 25.

39 Ibid., 119.

CHAPTER 5: THE MULTIPLE

1 "Multiplicity," an awkward back-construction of an adjectival term into its noun form, is taken from Henri Bergson. In *Time and Free Will* (1889), Bergson introduces the term to distinguish between duration and the prospect of a single objective time. My use here carries some overtones of Bergson's, but is largely invoked to contrast two forms of time-based representation: the single-frame image, seen in sequence, and the multiply framed image, seen in adjacency and simultaneity.

Another use of "multiplicity" can be found in Heinrich Wölfflin's 1915 *Kunstgeschichtliche Grundbegriffe* (Principles of Art History). Wölfflin used five opposing stylistic categories—linear vs. painterly, plane vs. recession, open vs. closed forms, multiplicity vs. unity, absolute vs. relative clarity—to distinguish between High Renaissance and baroque. Multiplicity, to Wölfflin, was associated with the dispersed, isolated compositional style of Renaissance painters. Heinrich Wölfflin, *Principles of Art History: The Problem of the Development of Style in Later Art* (1915), trans. M. D. Hottinger (1932; reprint, New York: Dover Publications, 1950).

2 In his 1982 study *History of Bourgeois Perception,* Donald M. Lowe offers an account of the wide perceptual and philosophical paradigm shift "from linearity to multi-perspectivity" in the "perceptual revolution of 1905–1915." Lowe asserts: "In a number of quite different, unrelated disciplines visual rational linearity was overthrown" and replaced by a "new perceptual field" of "multi-perspectivity." Lowe claims: "The perceptual transformation from bourgeois society to the bureaucratic society of controlled consumption, during the decade of 1905–1915, was as fundamental as that from the Renaissance to estate society in the early 17th century, or that from estate society to bourgeois society in the last third of the 18th century. There is no continuity from one period to the next; each is a different world" (109). Although Lowe differentiates his study from Foucault's concept of historical discontinuity and the *episteme,* his distinction is both subtle and profound: "Foucault is studying the changing historical rules of *discourse,* whereas I am concerned with the history of *perception*" (9). Lowe's study asserts a broad phenomenological shift in the perceptual dynamics of temporality, spatiality, and embodiment which registered in the phenomenology of Edmund Husserl; the philosophy of Henri Bergson; the physics of Einstein and Minkowski; the cubist painting of Picasso, Braque, Léger, and others; the music of Arnold Schönberg; the writing of Henry James, Dorothy Richardson, Gertrude Stein, James Joyce, and Marcel Proust; and in the architecture of Adolf Loos, Walter Gropius, and Frank Lloyd Wright. In a ten-page section on the spatiotemporality of film, Lowe argues that "camera and editing constitute the multi-perspectivity of film, being more dynamic than the visual perspective of a painting or narrator in a novel"

(124). Lowe's discussion of the spatiotemporal specificity of film focuses on familiar distinctions between the categories of fictional, factual, and experimental film and the relation between representation and reality in each of these broad categories. In this regard, Lowe's study does not follow through with its promise to provide an account of how the cinema figured in the break with linearity in its new terms of sequential spatialities and cross-cut temporalities. See Donald M. Lowe, *History of Bourgeois Perception* (Chicago: University of Chicago Press, 1982).

3 There are, of course, many examples of compositional framing devices—doors, mirrors, windows—that suggest a frame within a frame. I will discuss these elements later in this chapter, but here I mean the use of two or more framed images, split screens, or multiple screens.

4 The changes in television reception and display—from cable, the VCR, remote of the 1980s to picture-in-picture display, TIVO, Web-linked intermedia-interaction in the 1990s—have turned the television viewer into a user, an interlocuter in viewing habits, making choices of program type and viewing time. See the recent collection of essays on the transitional technologies of a "post-television" era, Lynn Spigel and Jan Olsson, eds., *Television after TV: Essays on a Medium in Transition* (Durham: Duke University Press, 2004).

In his description of "televisuality," John Caldwell suggests that in the 1980s, in reaction to economic competition from cable and new networks (MTV, CNN, Fox), television became more conscious of its visual style. Caldwell argues that television, which began as a format driven by "word based rhetoric and transmission," went through a "structural inversion" in the 1980s as it began to include cinematic directors and styles and also to take advantage of new CGI techniques for logos and effects. Caldwell's 1995 account largely prefigures the routine use of digital technology for television production and postproduction. John Thornton Caldwell, *Televisuality: Style, Crisis, and Authority in American Television* (New Brunswick, N.J.: Rutgers University Press, 1995).

5 In 1992, with the first marketing of a digital camera, the computer-processed digital image began supersede the silver-based photographic image. In 1993, less than half a dozen feature films used computer graphics; by 2004 there were perhaps only a half dozen that *didn't* use computer graphics. Computer imaging is now commonly used from the smallest films and commercials to the largest big-budget extravaganza. As director James Cameron said after the success of *Titanic* in 1995: "We're on the threshold of a moment in cinematic history that is unparalleled. . . . [A]nything you can imagine can be done." See William Mitchell, *The Reconfigured Eye: Visual Truth in the Post-Photographic Era* (Cambridge: MIT Press, 1992).

6 As this book was nearing completion, MIT published a remarkable volume of essays accompanying an equally remarkable exhibition, "Future Cinema: The Cinematic Imaginary after Film," curated by Jeffrey Shaw and Peter Weibel at the Center for Art and Media in Karlsruhe in 2003. Although other writers had begun to address many of the changes in screen technologies, *Future Cinema* has quickly emerged as canonical—a brilliantly curated intervention marking the transformation of the cinematic to the postmedial condition of moving-image media. See Jeffrey Shaw and Peter Weibel, eds., *Future Cinema: The Cinematic Imaginary after Film* (Cambridge: MIT Press, 2003). See also Philip Hayward and Tana Wollen, eds., *Future Visions: New Technologies of the Screen* (London: BFI Publishing, 1993); Andrew Darley, *Visual Digital Culture: Surface Play and Spectacle in New Media Genres* (London: Routlledge, 2000); and Martin Rieser and Andrea Zapp, eds., *New Screen Media: Cinema/Art/Narrative* (London: BFI Publishing, 2002).

7 Gyorgy Kepes, *Language of Vision* (Chicago: Paul Theobold, 1944), 95.

8 Pierre Francastel, "Espace et illusion," *Revue internationale de filmologie* 2, no. 5 (1948): 66; cited in Stephen Heath, "Narrative Space," *Questions of Cinema* (New York: Macmillan, 1981), 27, n. 7.

9 Charles Musser, "Toward a History of Screen Practice," in *The Emergence of Cinema: The American Screen to 1907* (New York: Charles Scribner, 1990). Musser quotes C. Francis Jenkins (1908) describing the "animated picture" as a "lantern equipped with mechanical slide changer," and Henry Hopwood (1899) describing a "living picture" as a "multiple lantern slide" (15).

10 In the heading of this section, by "single frame" I mean the frame as the framed shape to the screen, not the film frame as sequentially arrayed on the film strip and projected at a speed that belies the discrete separation between frames.

11 Musser, *The Emergence of Cinema,* 30.

12 In 1850, William and Frederick Langenheim invented a technique for developing a positive photographic image on a glass slide. The Hyalotype (*hyalo* is Greek for "glass") slides were black and white but were frequently hand-tinted.

13 W. J. Chadwick, *The Magic Lantern Manual* (London: Frederick Warne, 1878), 69. Chadwick asserts: "Many different ways of applying the Magic Lantern present themselves perhaps none more pleasing than its adaptation to Dissolving Views." Reprinted in Stephen Herbert, ed., *A History of Pre-Cinema,* vols. 1 and 2 (London: Routledge, 2000), 9.

14 By 1873, Bruno Meyer, an art historian at the Polytechnic Institute in Karlsruhe, was using projected lantern slides in art history lectures. Meyer also began to manufacture what he called *Glasphotogramme,* which he sold at two marks a piece. In an article published in 1897, Hermann Grimm a professor at the University of Berlin, reports how lantern slides permitted the full-size projection of works or allowed small works or fragments to be enlarged to colossal scale. Grimm's enthusiasm for slide projection may have been aided by the introduction of electric lanterns projectors in 1892.

See Howard B. Leighton, "The Lantern Slide and Art History," *History of Photography* 8, no. 2 (April–June 1984): 107–119; Robert Nelson, "The Slide Lecture, or The Work of Art History in the Age of Mechanical Reproduction," *Critical Inquiry* 26, no. 3 (Spring 2000): 414–434; Heinrich Dilly, *Kunstgeschichte als Institution: Studien zur Geschichte einer Diziplin* (Frankfurt am Main: Suhrkamp, 1979); Heinrich Dilly, "Lichtbildprojektion—Prothese der Kunstbetrachtung," in Irene Below, ed., *Kunstwissenschaft und Kunstvermittlung* (Giessen: Anabas, 1975), 153–172; Heinrich Dilly, "Die Bildwerfer. 121 Jahre kunstwissenschaftliche Dia-Projektion," *Rundbrief Fotographie,* n.s. 5 (1995): 39–44; Silke Wenk, "Zeigen und Schweigen: Der kunsthistorische Diskurs und die Diaprojektion," in Sigrid Schade et al., eds., *Konfigurationen. Zwischen Kunst und Medien* (Munich: Wilhelm Fink Verlag, 1999). I am indebted to Karen Lang for an illuminating discussion of this practice and for these references.

15 For example, Musser describes the twelve-slide Joseph Boggs Beale rendition of Edgar Allan Poe's "The Raven" (1890)—the first four slides in the series each show a slightly different angle: "The perspective shifts, 'moving in' and 'panning' from right to left for the first three slides and 'pulling back' for the fourth." Musser, *The Emergence of Cinema,* 34–36.

16 See Deac Rossell's final chapter, "Multiple Questions: the Many Cinemas of 1896–1900," in *Living Pictures: The Origins of the Movies* (Albany: State University of New York Press, 1998), 133–163.

17 Laurent Mannoni's *The Great Art of Light and Shadow: Archeology of Cinema,* trans. Richard Crangle (Exeter: University of Exeter Press, 2000) and Deac Rossell's *Living Pictures* provide ample evidence of the continued cultural and epistemic centrality of the projection of light and images. Rossell is particularly pointed about Thomas Edison's inability to envision the full potential of the kinetoscope and its next step into projection: "Like Marey in France, he was a dedicated scientist who had no inclusion in any technological frame that embraced optics, the magic lantern, projected narratives, showmanship, or entertainment. Not only was nothing in Edison's past linked to Charles Musser's 'history of screen practice,' his outlook was also one where large enterprises were able successfully to control the introduction and diffusion of technology" (*Living Pictures,* 100).

18 See Anne Friedberg, "*Trottoir Roulant:* The Cinema and New Mobilities of Spectatorship," in Jan Olsson and John Fullerton, eds., *Allegories of Communication: Intermedial Concerns from Cinema to the Digital* (London/Sydney: John Libbey, 2004), 263–276; and Siegfried Zielinski, *Audiovisions: Cinema and Television as Entr'actes in History* (1988), trans. Gloria Custance (Amsterdam: Amsterdam University Press, 1999), 28–28.

19 Not that Porter was the first to use this technique; as Musser points out, it may have been indebted to Ferdinand Zecca's *A la conquête de l'air.* See Charles Musser, *Before the Nickelodeon: Edwin S. Porter and the Edison Manufacturing Company* (Berkeley: University of California Press, 1991), 193.

20 See Tom Gunning, "Heard over the Phone: *The Lonely Villa* and the de Lorde Tradition of the Terrors of Technology," *Screen* 32, no. 2 (Summer 1991): 184–196. Split-screen compositions are frequently reliant on the telephone as a link. *Pillow Talk* (1959), *Bye Bye Birdie* (1963), and *The Boston Strangler* (1968) link action seen in separate inset frames by using the telephone (or in the case of *The Boston Strangler,* the apartment intercom) to visualize the near and the far in one spatial plane.

21 Marshall McLuhan, *Understanding Media: The Extensions of Man* (Cambridge: MIT Press, 1994), 13.

22 Gilles Deleuze, *Cinema 1: The Movement-Image,* trans. Hugh Tomlinson and Barbara Habberjam (Minneapolis: University of Minnesota Press, 1986), 14. In his analytic model Deleuze supplies his own taxonomy of terms, drawing upon C. S. Peirce and Henri Bergson. See David Rodowick's concordance to Deleuze's writing on cinema, D. N. Rodowick, *Gilles Deleuze's Time Machine* (Durham: Duke University Press, 1997).

To be a bit picky about the translation in the epigraph to this section, Deleuze writes that doors, windows, etc. are "cadres dans le cadre"—not just *frames,* but *frames within* the frame. See Gilles Deleuze, *Cinéma 1: L'image-mouvement* (Paris: Editions de Minuit, 1983), 26.

23 Deleuze, *Cinema 1,* 13.

24 Ibid., 14–15.

25 Ibid., 15.

26 Christian Metz, "L'écran second ou le rectangle au carré," in *L'enonciation impersonnelle ou le site du film* (Paris: Méridiens Klincksieck, 1991), 71–79. The translation is mine. I am indebted to Dana Polan for both mentioning this essay and loaning me its text.

27 Ibid.

28 Marc Vernet, *De l'invisible au cinéma—Figures de l'absence* (Paris: Cahiers du Cinéma, Editions de l'Etoile, 1988).

29 I will return to De Palma's *Sisters* later in this chapter: the fictional conceit of the film involves Siamese twins Danielle and Dominique (both played by Margot Kidder) who have been separated and—as their split has rendered them separate—one is always menacing the other, but from off-frame. Often deliberate in his concretization of metaphor, De Palma may have intended to use the separated twins as a metaphor for the radical ontological cut of the frame in split screen. (As another example of De Palma's deliberate concretization of metaphor: *Blow Out,* De Palma's "remake" of Antonioni's *Blow-Up* (1966), took Antonioni's narrative about the evidentiary use of photographic enlargement ("blow up") and adapted it to a narrative pivoting on the audio analysis of the sound recording of a tire ("blowout").

30 See chapter 2, note 95.

31 *This Is Cinerama!* (dir. Llowell Thomas and Merian C. Cooper, 1952) was restored and reconstructed for a retrospective of widescreen films at the Hollywood ArcLight/Cinerama Dome in 2002.

32 To prevent the projection light from bouncing back from the concave screen surface, inventor Fred Waller devised a louvred screen with 1,100 vertical bands of perforated tape, forming a surface like vertical venetian blinds. Waller also devised a means to obscure the join lines between the three separate images when projected: "Tiny comblike bits of steel are fitted into each projector at the side of the film gate. Jiggling up and down along the edges of the film at high speed, they fuzz the edges of the picture and minimize the lines between them." From "This Is Cinerama!," promotional brochure (Stanley Warner Cinema Corporation, copyright 1954), 2.

33 Waller, the inventor of Cinerama, also "invented" water skis. The Cypress Gardens sequence, filmed by nature documentarian Merian C. Cooper and co-producer Robert Bendick, commanded an inventive multiscreen technique to capture the choreography of Dick Pope's water carnival of "Aquabelles" and motor boats.

34 "This Is Cinerama!," 1.

35 John Belton, *Widescreen Cinema* (Cambridge: Harvard University Press, 1992), 223.

36 In a different context, Richard Meyer has written about the "unflagging hygiene" associated with Hudson's star persona in many of his fanzine poses, including a 1959 *Photoplay* "pin-up" of Hudson reclining in a bathtub. See Richard Meyer, "Rock Hudson's Body," in Deborah Bright, ed., *The Passionate Camera: Photography and Bodies of Desire* (London: Routledge, 1998), 341–360. The 1963 film adaptation of the stage play *Bye Bye Birdie!* used the split screens to illustrate the fractured but connected bedrooms of teenage girls as they chat on the phone.

37 See Pat Kirkham, *Charles and Ray Eames: Designers of the Twentieth Century* (Cambridge: MIT Press, 1995); Donald Albrecht, *The Work of Charles and Ray Eames: A Legacy of Invention* (Harry N. Abrams, 1997); and Beatriz Colomina, "Enclosed by Images: The Eameses' Multimedia Architecture," in *Grey Room* 02 (Winter 2001): 5–29. In a 1977 interview, Charles Eames explained why they decided to use the multiple of seven: "We wanted to have a credible number of images, but not so many that they couldn't be scanned in the time allotted. At the same time, the number of images had to be large enough so that people wouldn't be exactly sure how many they have seen. We arrived at the number seven. With four images, you always knew there were four, but by the time you got up to eight images you weren't quite sure. They were very big images—the width across four of them was half the length of a football field." Owen Gingerich, "A Conversation with Charles Eames," *American Scholar* 46, no. 3 (Summer 1977): 331. Quoted in Beatriz Colomina, "Enclosed by Images," 19.

38 Colomina's remarkable essay contextualizes the varied design projects of the Eameses—their furniture, exhibitions, films—as movable frameworks in an architecture of a new "space of information." See "Enclosed by Images," particularly pp. 18 and 20. Colomina describes this "space of information" as multiple-screen: "We are surrounded today, everywhere, all the time, by arrays of multiple, simultaneous images. . . . The idea of a single image commanding our attention has faded away" (7).

39 As Colomina notes, the Fuller dome was an integral part of the Eameses exhibit: "The huge array of suspended screens defined a space within a space. The Eameses were self-consciously architects of a new kind of space. The film breaks with the fixed perspectival view of the world. In fact, we find ourselves in a space that can only be apprehended with the high technology of telescopes, zoom lenses, airplanes, nightvision camera, and so on, and where there is no privileged point of view" ("Enclosed by Images," 11). If Fuller's geodesic dome became associated with these 1960s redefinitions of architectural space, it also became associated with the redefinitions of and expansions to the cinema screen. In 1964, the Cinerama Dome in Hollywood (a project of Welton Beckett, the Los Angeles firm that also designed a glass pavilion for the 1959 Moscow exhibit) encased its expanded Cinerama/CinemaScope screen inside a Fuller-designed geodesic dome.

40 The Eameses had been making educational and promotional films for IBM since the early 1950s, and so they were keenly aware of the growing importance of the computer. Their 1953 film for IBM, *A Communications Primer,* was an early encounter between the film medium and the newly marketed computer. IBM became a key sponsor of their multimedia shows. In 1957, the Eameses made *The Information Machine* for the IBM pavilion at the Brussels world's fair. And at their 1959 *Glimpses* exhibit in Moscow, an IBM computer was on hand to answer questions about the United States. Pat Kirkham suggests that the success of the Eameses' 1961 IBM commission for *Mathematica: A World of Numbers and Beyond* at the Chicago Museum of Science and Industry gave the corporate sponsor the confidence to hire them for the 1964 New York World's Fair IBM Pavilion (*Charles and Ray Eames,* 299). In 1972, the landmark exhibition *A Computer Perspective* mounted a graphic history of computing. See Charles and Ray Eames, *A Computer Perspective: Background to the Computer Age* (1973; reprint, Cambridge: Harvard University Press, 1990).

41 Alexander Hammid (Czech-born Alexander Hackenschmidt) was Maya Deren's husband and a key collaborator and cameraman on her *Meshes of the Afternoon* (1943) and *Choreography for the Camera* (1945).

42 Super-Cinerama was the printed film format for a select number of films—including *It's A Mad, Mad, Mad World* (1963), *The Greatest Story Ever Told* (1965), and *Khartoum* (1966)—shown in a small number of specially equipped theaters.

43 Jonas Mekas, "On the Plastic Inevitables and the Strobe Light," *Village Voice,* 26 May 1966; reprinted in *Movie Journal: The Rise of a New American Cinema 1959–1971* (New York: Collier Books, 1972), 242. In his 1967 introduction to *Introduction to the American Underground Film,* Sheldon Renan uses the term "expanded cinema" to describe the performative expansions of spectatorship that appeal to a fuller sensorium of experience. Sheldon Renan, *Introduction to the American Underground Film* (New York: Dutton, 1967). In *Expanded Cinema* (1970), Gene Youngblood also writes: "We are tragically in need of a new vision: expanded cinema is the beginning of that vision. We shall be released. We will bring down the wall. We'll be united with our reflection." Gene Youngblood, *Expanded Cinema* (New York: E. P. Dutton, 1970), 49.

44 Liz Kotz has addressed the historiographic challenges of writing about multiscreen and and "paracinematic" performative cinema, insisting that these practices be situated within a wider history of kinetic sculpture and multimedia architecture. See Liz Kotz, "Disciplining Expanded Cinema," in Museum Moderner Kunst Stiftung Ludwig Wien and Matthias Michalka, eds., *X-Screen: Film Installations and Actions in the 1960s and 1970s* (Cologne: Verlag der Buchhandlung Walther König, 2003), 44–56, 51.

45 Warhol's use of the multiple has remained one of the most commonly discussed elements of his work. See Kynaston McShine, ed., *Andy Warhol: A Retrospective* (New York: MOMA, 1989); and Benjamin H. D. Buchloh, "Andy Warhol's One-Dimensional Art, 1956–1966," in McShine, *Andy Warhol: A Retrospective.* Warhol's early relation to television was also multiple. As he famously quipped: "So in the late 50s I started an affair with my television which has continued to the present, when I play around in my bedroom with as many as four at a time." *The Philosophy of Andy Warhol (From A to B and Back Again)* (New York: Harcourt Brace Jovanovich, 1975), 26.

For further discussion of Warhol's film projects, see Steven Koch, *Stargazer: Andy Warhol's World and His Films* (New York: Praeger, 1973); David E. James, "Andy Warhol: Producer as Author," in *Allegories of Cinema* (Princeton: Princeton University Press, 1989), 58–84; and Michael O'Pray, ed., *Andy Warhol: Film Factory* (London: BFI, 1989). A note on seriality: Warhol displayed his early short films in a looped fashion (such as his installation at Lincoln Center): the film loop suggests a sequential seriality rather than the simultaneous seriality of the multiple screen. In *Sleep,* Warhol's turn to filmmaking demonstrated his interest in duration. Between 1964 and 1966, Warhol filmed five hundred black-and-white "screen tests" with each subject filmed in excruciating close shot in front of a static camera.

46 This was Warhol's first double-screen projection and also his first use of video. Callie Angell, the curator of the Andy Warhol Film Project at the Whitney, provides excellent detail of Warhol's pioneering use of video and his experimentation with the double-screen format. In the summer of 1965, the Norelco Company loaned Warhol a portable video-recording system using a "slant scan" video format. (Angell suggests that Warhol's use of video predated Nam June Paik's first use in October 1965.) Although Warhol videotaped around 11½ tapes of video, the only remaining versions of this material exist on the films, like *Outer and Inner Space,* that Warhol made using the prerecorded video. Angell also suggests that Warhol's use of video in the making of *Outer and Inner Space* (1965) led to his subsequent use of a double-screen format in *The Chelsea Girls* (1966). In her analysis of the doubling of the image, Angell draws an analogy to his serialized multiples on silk-screen, using video to link to his practices as a painter:

> Warhol is particularly fascinated by the ability of video playback to double the image of his subject—to place a person in the same frame with his or her own image. And it seems to me this doubling of a person's image would naturally have reminded Warhol of his own paintings, in which he often silk-screened multiple images of the same face onto the same canvas. And once he had doubled the image of his subject, Edie Sedgwick, by filming her in the same frame with her video image, it would seem an obvious step to further multiply her image by adding a second film screen to the first, just as he often multiplied the repeated images in his paintings by adding on additional panels or canvases. So, I think that is what you see happening in this film—the medium of video provides Warhol with a link back to his own practice as a painter, and his practice as a painter then suggests ways

to further expand his filmmaking into the new formats of double- and multi-screen projection which will dominate so much of his later film work.

See Callie Angell, "Doubling the Screen: Andy Warhol's *Outer and Inner Space*," *Millennium Film Journal*, no. 38 (Spring 2002). See also Callie Angell, "Andy Warhol's *Outer and Inner Space*," in Thomas Y. Levin, Ursala Frohne, and Peter Weibel, eds., *CTRL[SPACE]: Rhetorics of Surveillance from Bentham to Big Brother* (Cambridge: MIT Press, 2002), 278–281. In *Stargazer*, Steven Koch devotes an entire chapter to *The Chelsea Girls* but includes *Inner and Outer Space* in a long list of films lost or "bad to a degree that is barely credible" (65).

Warhol's title, *Outer and Inner Space*, also forms the title of a traveling exhibition and catalog of video art that explores video art's preoccupation with the conditions of spectatorship and the aesthetic, psychological, and philosophical relation between outside and inside, surface and depth. See John B. Ravenal, ed., *Outer and Inner Space: Pipilotti Rist, Shirin Neshat, Jane & Louise Wilson, and the History of Video Art* (Richmond: Virginia Museum of Fine Arts, 2002).

47 Maurice Merleau-Ponty, "The Film and the New Psychology," in *Sense and Non-sense* (1948), trans. Hubert L. Dreyfus and Patricia Allen Dreyfus (Chicago: Northwestern University Press, 1964), 59. Or, as Warhol said about pop art: "I can't tell you what Pop Art is: it's too involved; it's just taking the outside and putting it on the inside or taking the inside and putting it on the outside, bringing the ordinary object into the home." *I'll Be Your Mirror: Collected Andy Warhol Interviews*, ed. Kennedy Goldsmith (New York: Carroll & Graf, 2004), 90.

48 The formal doubling of the screen was complexly mirrored in the "doubling" of Warhol through his identification with his superstars. Wayne Koestenbaum has suggested that Sedgwick was a doppelganger for Warhol in his "homo-erotics of repetition and cloning." See Wayne Koestenbaum, *Andy Warhol* (London: Wiedenfeld, 2001); reviewed by Hal Foster, "Andy Paperbag," in *London Review of Books* 24, no. 6 (21 March 2002).

49 Jonas Mekas, "On *The Chelsea Girls*," *Village Voice*, 29 September 1966; reprinted in *Movie Journal*, 256.

50 Ibid.

51 The use of the double screen might intensify rather than distract, producing the same effect as repetition. As Thomas Crow writes: "the argument could be offered that the repetition of the photographic image within the pictorial field can increase rather than numb sensitivity to it, as the viewer works to draw the separate elements into a whole." Crow, "Saturday Disasters: Trace and Reference in Early Warhol," in *Modern Art in the Common Culture* (New Haven: Yale University Press, 1996), 61.

52 Quoted in 1969 interview with Joseph Gelmis, reprinted in *I'll Be Your Mirror*, 166.

53 See Branden W. Joseph, "'My Mind Split Open': Andy Warhol's Exploding Plastic Inevitable," *Grey Room* 08 (Summer 2002): 80–107, and David Joselit, "Yippie Pop: Abbie Hoffman, Andy Warhol, and Sixties Media Politics," *Grey Room* 08 (Summer 2002): 62–79 for a fuller contextualization of Warhol's multimedia experiments. As a document of EPI performances, Ronald Nameth's 1966 film *Andy Warhol's Exploding Plastic Inevitable with The Velvet Underground* attempts to capture the expanded sensorium of performative "happenings" in a single-screen film.

54 Marshall McLuhan and Quentin Fiore, *The Medium Is the Massage*, produced by Jerome Agel (New York: Simon and Schuster, 1967). This portion of the text has no pages numbers so it is difficult to reference.

55 Ibid., 68.

56 Ibid., 56–57. As if to illustrate the reversal of this Renaissance mode, the text is printed upside-down on these two pages.

57 Ibid., 57.

58 Jonas Mekas, "More on Strobe Light and Intermedia," *Village Voice,* 16 June 1966; reprinted in *Movie Journal,* 246; emphasis added.

59 Thompson and Hammid produced multi-image and giant-screen films for other world expositions after the New York Word's Fair, including HemisFair '68 in San Antonio, Texas, and Expo '82 in Knoxville, Tennessee. In 1975, Francis Thompson's company was commissioned by the Smithsonian Institution to produce the premiere film for its new National Air and Space Museum. Thompson chose to produce *To Fly!* in the newly invented 70mm IMAX large-format film system.

60 Two recent essays accompanying the 2003 "Future Cinema" exhibition in Karlsruhe offer accounts of the Czech-based tradition of film experimentation. See Michael Bielicky, "Prague—A Place of Illusionists," and Vít Havránek, "Laterna Magika, Polyekran, Kinoautomat: Media, Technology and Interaction in the Works of Set Designers Josef Svoboda, Alfréd Radok and Radúz Činčera, 1958–1967," in Shaw and Weibel, *Future Cinema,* 96–101; 102–109.

61 In the DVD release of *The Thomas Crowne Affair* (1968), Norman Jewison supplies a voice-over commentary detailing many aspects of the film's production (MGM DVD, 1999). Chapman's "multiple screen technique" in *A Place to Stand* proved to Jewison that you "could take in more than one image at the same time as long as there wasn't a lot of sound."

62 In some of her earliest works, British experimental filmmaker Sally Potter made multi-screen pieces: the two-screen project *Black and White* (eight minutes, 1969) and the double-screen *Play* (15 minutes, 1971) both play with cinematic space. Other experimental filmmakers with double-screen experiments include William Raban and Chris Welsby, *River Yar;* David Parsons, *Mechanical Ballet;* Chris Welsby, *Wind Vane;* David Crosswaite, *Choke;* and Malcolm Le Grice, *Castle Two.*

63 *Mahagonny* was screened for ten performances at Anthology Film Archives in 1981. The film has been lovingly restored by Rani Singh, curator of the Harry Smith Archive, with assistance from the Getty Research Institute, Michael Friend, Simon Lund, and Balázs Nyari. In a carefully thought-out choice, Singh took the many reels of picture elements and struck a single-screen 35mm print that is divided into four quadrants, much like *Time Code.* Smith's original project required four synchronized projectors; for the purposes of preservation, the film takes the four screens and combines them as quadrants for a one-screen, one-projector exhibition.

Sergei Eisenstein's project for a film of Marx's *Das Kapital*—sketched in notes from 1927–1928 "with its formal side dedicated to Joyce"—was a conceptual marriage of literary stream-of-consciousness and cinematic intellectual montage, also left unconsummated.

64 Harry Smith, "*Mahagonny* (Film #18), a Description." Smith describes his eleven hours of filmed material, compiled and presented on four screens, as a two-hour-and-twenty-one-minute presentation synchronized to the Brecht/Weill opera. See also Harry Smith, "On *Mahagonny,*" in P. Adams Sitney, ed., *The Avant-Garde Film: A Reader of Theory and Criticism* (New York: Anthology Film Archives, 1987), 103–109.

65 As Singh explains, Smith divided the images into categories—animation, portraits, nature, and symbols (A, P, N, S). Rani Singh, program notes "The Getty Research Institute presents Harry Smith's Film #18, *Mahagonny,*" 2002.

66 Warhol's use of Sony's newly released portable half-inch videotape recorder and player (the Portapak) allowed him to bypass television in its dominant broadcast mode. The Portapak opened a new medium for artists and activists to experiment with and challenge the existing forms of moving-image media. Video was less expensive than film, and provided an alternative to broadcast television (already controlled by large media corporations).

67 A select bibliography on video art since the 1970s includes Gene Youngblood, *Expanded Cinema* (New York: E. P. Dutton, 1970); Ira Schneider and Beryl Korot, eds., *Video Art: An Anthology* (New York: Harcourt Brace Jovanovich, 1976); Michael Shamberg and the Raindance Foundation, *Guerrilla Television* (New York: Holt, Rinehart, and Winston, 1971); Gregory Battcock, ed., *New Artists Video: A Critical Anthology* (New York: E. P. Dutton, 1978); John Hanhardt, ed., *Video Culture: A Critical Investigation* (Layton, Utah: Gibbs M. Smith, Inc., Peregrine Smith Books; and Rochester, N.Y.: Visual Studies Workshop Press, 1986); Doug Hall and Sally Jo Fifer, eds., *Illuminating Video: An Essential Guide to Video Art* (New York: Aperture Press, 1991); Michael Renov and Erika Suderberg, eds., *Resolutions: Contemporary Video Practices* (Minneapolis: University of Minnesota Press, 1996); and Erika Suderberg, ed., *Space Site Intervention: Situating Installation Art* (Minneapolis: University of Minnesota Press, 2000).

68 John G. Hanhardt, *The Worlds of Nam June Paik,* exh. cat. (New York: Harry N. Abrams, 2000). In this catalog to the Paik retrospective at the Guggenheim Museum in New York in 2000, Hanhardt argues that Paik's video projects are a necessary reference for the study of television.

69 Liz Kotz, "Video Projection: The Space between the Screens," in Zoya Kocur and Simon Leung, eds., *Theory in Contemporary Art since 1985* (London: Blackwell Publishing, 2004), 101–113.

70 Rosalind Krauss describes the "heterogeneity" of video practice: "For, even if video had a distinct technical support—its own apparatus, so to speak—it occupied a kind of discursive chaos, a heterogeneity of activities that could not be theorized as coherent or conceived of as having something like an essence or unifying core." Rosalind Krauss, *A Voyage on the North Sea: Art in the Age of the Post-Medium Condition* (New York: Thames and Hudson, 1999), 31.

71 This discussion of *Numéro deux* draws upon an unpublished NYU graduate school paper by the author, "One Cannot Put Everything into a Paper: Godard's *Numéro Deux*" (1976). See also Jonathan Rosenbaum, "Numéro Deux," *Sight and Sound* 45, no. 2 (Spring 1976): 124–125.

72 See Siegfried Zielinski, "Zbig Vision Ltd. Miniature of Zbigniew Rybczynski," in Shaw and Weibel, *Future Cinema,* 198–201. Zielinski notes Rybczynski's "dissatisfaction with the visual possibilities of central perspective, the geometrical principles of every photo or film camera and the basis of all three-dimensional software applications." See also Paul Virilio, "The Rybczynski Phenomenon," in Shaw and Weibel, *Future Cinema,* 196–197.

73 Rybczynski made pioneering use of digital technology once it became available. Recipient of many awards for his experiments with visual effects, Rybczynski's 1983 *Tango* won an Academy award for Best Short Film.

74 Figgis used the Sony DSR-1 digital video camera, a camera that held ninety-three-minute loads and could be synched to other cameras.

75 Each performer wore a digital watch that was synchronized to the same time so that the earthquake could be enacted at the same moment in each of the four real-time takes. Unlike Warhol's *Outer and Inner Space,* in which Warhol lurks off-camera, as Sedgwick waits for cues and directions from offscreen, in Figgis's *Time Code* the hermetic boundary of the diegesis is nearly complete. The director's "directions" remain invisible, as in the example of the synchronized watches that cued the actor's simultaneous responses to the earthquake.

76 The website for *Time Code* has been removed, but the promotional tagline to the film, found on all VHS copies and on IMDB is: "Who Do You Want to Watch?"

77 Huyghe provides a spatial description of the two-screen projection in Pierre Huyghe, "The Third Memory," trans. Sarah Clift, in Shaw and Weibel, *Future Cinema,* 242–243.

78 Arthur C. Danto, "Shirin Neshat," *BOMB Magazine,* no. 73 (Fall 2000).

79 See the exhibition catalog to a 2003 exhibition of Marclay's work organized by Russell Ferguson at the UCLA Hammer Museum in Los Angeles: Russell Ferguson, curator, *Christian Marclay* (Los Angeles: UCLA Hammer Museum, 2003).

80 See Marsha Kinder, "Designing Database Cinema," in Shaw and Weibel, *Future Cinema,* 346–353. The Labyrinth Project's DVD-ROM and DVD installations of Norman M. Klein (with Rosemary Comella and Andreas Kratsky), Pat O'Neill, and Péter Forgacs have been exemplary explorations of new forms of multiscreen storytelling. See *Bleeding Through: Layers of Los Angeles 1920–1986* (Labyrinth Project DVD-ROM, 2002); *Tracing the Decay of Fiction: Encounters with a Film by Pat O'Neill* (Labyrinth Project DVD-ROM, 2002); and *The Danube Exodus: The Rippling Currents of the River* (interactive DVD installation, Karlsruhe, 2003). Lev Manovich makes a similar prediction: "I believe the next generation of cinema—broadband cinema, or macrocinema—will add multiple windows to its language." Lev Manovich, *The Language of New Media* (Cambridge: MIT Press, 2001), 324.

81 Julie Talen, "24: Split-Screen's Big Comeback," *Salon.com,* 14 May 2002 <http://archive.salon.com/ent/tv/feature/2002/05/14/24_split/index2.html>. Talen, a New York-based journalist, screenwriter, and filmmaker, has also made a "multichannel" film, *Pretend* (2003). See Cara O'Connor, "When You Cut Up the Frame: An Interview with Julie Talen," in *Senses of Cinema* Issue 30 (January-March 2004).

82 Steven Johnson, *Interface Culture: How New Technology Transforms the Way We Create and Communicate* (San Francisco: Harper, 1997). Johnson asserts the magnitude of this transformation with the following hyperboles: "Not since Renaissance artisans hit upon the mathematics of painted perspective has technology so dramatically transformed spatial imagination" (24); "The discovery of information-space may engender a social transformation as broad and as variegated as the one that followed Alberti's marvelous breakthrough" (214–215); and he asserts that the "modern interface" and the "information space" it constructs compose the "great symbolic accomplishment of our era" (215).

Johnson speculates on the displaced effects and "unintended consequences" of the graphic computer interface. He finds one effect in television programming—the proliferation of self-referential "shows about shows" as the "metaform" of media-about-media, which he sees as evidence that media has become a reality in and of itself, justifying a switch from storytelling to commentary.

83 Walker's taxonomy of the five "user interaction generations" are as follows: at the "front panel" of a gargantuan mainframe, the user would perform direct manipulations and commands. The second generation of interaction, "batch" processing, involved a more abstract and mediated relation. The "countertop" was introduced as a transactional space, a physical intermediary placed between user and mainframe. In the third generation, the user types commands using keyboard input devices to a computer "terminal" and awaits the computer's response in a typed "readout." Walker speculates that the endurance of this "command line" interface (and the endurance of DOS in the personal computer marketplace and the use of BASIC for home computers in the Commodore and Atari systems) has to do with the conceptual (albeit abstract) model of "conversational computing." A fourth generation of command-based interface, using "menus," was directed to noncomputer users, allowing the user to select from a menu of choices. The fifth and final generation in Walker's account uses "graphics," and brings the computer/user relation back to the first-generation level of directness. In the graphic interface, the user interacts with a screen. The screen is a barrier, but the user can directly manipulate what is seen on the screen (WYSIWYG) and files can be moved by "drag and drop." Walker argues that with graphic interaction the user has a more direct, less abstract relation to the machine than through the mediation of the command line. See John Walker, "Through the Looking-Glass: Beyond 'User Interface,'" in *The Autodesk File: Bits of History, Words of Experience,* 4th ed., 1994. (Walker's online and downloadable history of Autodesk, Inc., is annotated with contemporary documents and his own reflections on developments in computing hardware and software: <http://www.fourmilab.ch/autofile/>.)

84 Ibid.

85 A plenum of recent books have traced the histories of computing: Christian Wurster, *Computers: An Illustrated History* (Cologne: Taschen, 2002); Michael Hiltzik, *Dealers of Lightning: Xerox PARC and the Dawn of the Computer Age* (New York: Harper Business, 1999); Paul E. Ceruzzi, *A History of Modern Computing* (Cambridge: MIT Press, 1998); Shoshanna Zuboff, *In the Age of the Smart Machine* (New York: Basic Books, 1988); Howard Rheingold, *Tools for Thought: The History and Future of Mind-Expanding Technology* (New York: Simon and Schuster, 1985; Cambridge, Mass.: MIT Press, 2000); Paul Frieberger and Michael Swaine, *Fire in the Valley: The Making of the Personal Computer,* 2nd ed. (Berkeley: McGraw-Hill, 2000); Steven Levy, *Insanely Great: The Life and Time of Macintosh, the Computer that Changed Everything* (New York: Penguin, 1995); Steven Levy, *Hackers: Heroes of the Computer Revolution* (Garden City, N.Y.: Anchor Press/Doubleday, 1984); Sherry Turkle, *The Second Self: Computers and the Human Spirit* (New York: Simon and Schuster, 1984); Tracy Kidder, *Soul of a New Machine* (Boston: Little, Brown, 1981); and William Mitchell, *The Reconfigured Eye: Visual Truth in the Post-photographic Era* (Cambridge: MIT Press, 1992).

In the early 1970s, a spate of computer histories appeared, including Adele Goldberg, *The Computer from Pascal to von Neumann* (Princeton: Princeton University Press, 1972); John G. Kemeny, *Man and the Computer* (New York: Charles Scribner, 1972); and Charles and Ray Eames, *A Computer Perspective: Background to the Computer Age* (Cambridge: Harvard University Press, 1973). While the above histories all provide exemplary background accounts, each emphasizes a different relation between inventors, inventions, and sponsorship.

86 In the narrative of convergence, the 1993 introduction of MOSAIC—a graphic browser for the World Wide Web—brought hyperlinked graphics and text to network-enabled screens. The Web and its succession of graphic browsers—MOSAIC, Netscape, Internet Explorer, Safari—was to text-based email and Internet file transfer protocols what the bit-mapped screen was to ASCII code: that is to say, a computer screen that could now relay graphics, text, and images.

87 The Whirlwind used a radar oscilloscope screen. After Russia's detonation of an atomic bomb in 1949 and the outbreak of the war in Korea in 1950, the Air Force was eager to develop an air defense system. Under the direction of George Valley and Jay Forrester, Project Whirlwind formed the basis of the "Semi-Automated Ground Environment" [SAGE] system, which was up by 1958. Whirlwind may have been the first computer to use a video display for input. In 1960, Digital Equipment Corporation's PDP-1 used a graphics CRT display for input with a light pen. (It was on one of these computers at MIT that the first videogame, Spacewar, was run in 1962.)

Although the above accounts (note 85) of computers and computing form a composite history of the mechanisms and interfaces of computing, a singular history of the use of video display (the CRT screen; the VDM, video display module; the GDM, graphic display monitor) has yet to be written. Siegfried Zeilinski's intertwined history of cinema and television forms the other side of this intermedial development. The CRT tube was introduced in 1897 by German inventor Dr. Karl Ferdinand Braun. See Zielinski, *Audiovisions.* For an excellent illustration of the dovetailed development of the personal computer alongside video recording and display technology, see <http://www.cedmagic.com/history/>.

88 Sony introduced its high-resolution bright-screen color monitor, the Trinitron, in 1968; in 1973 the Trinitron was the first TV receiver/monitor to receive an Emmy.

89 Douglas Engelbart, "Augmented Human Intellect Study: Proposal for Research," SRI No. ESU 62–85; Extension of Contract AF 49(638)-1024 (2 October 1962). A year earlier, Engelbart wrote "Special Considerations of the Individual as a User, Generator and Retriever of Information" (1961). Many of Engelbart's papers are available online: <http://sloan.stanford.edu/mousesite/Archive.html>.

90 <http://sloan.stanford.edu/mousesite/EngelbartPapers/B5_F18_Concept_FrameworkPt1.html 1.A>.

91 Ibid.

92 Ibid.

93 In addition to inset screen "windows," Engelbart's demonstration at the Association for Computing Machinery/Institute of Electrical and Electronic Engineers-Computer Society (ACM/IEEE-CS) Fall Joint Computer Conference also debuted hyperlinks between documents and the mouse as an input device.

94 Douglas C. Engelbart and William K. English, *AFIPS Conference Proceedings of the 1968 Fall Joint Computer Conference,* San Francisco, CA, December 1968, vol. 33, 395–410; <http://sloan.stanford.edu/mousesite/Archive/ResearchCenter1968/ResearchCenter1968.html>. A ninety-minute film was made of this demonstration; segments of it are available as RealVideo streaming video clips at <http://sloan.stanford.edu/MouseSite/1968Demo.html>.

95 Rheingold, *Tools for Thought,* 190.

96 Alan Kay, "The Reactive Engine," Ph.D. dissertation, University of Utah, 1969; Alan Kay, "User Interface: A Personal View," in Brenda Laurel, ed., *The Art of Human-Computer Interface Design* (Reading, Mass.: Addison-Wesley, 1990).

97 In 1970, the chairman of Xerox, Peter McCollough, proclaimed a commitment to "architecture of information" and opened the Xerox Palo Alto Research Center (PARC). Alan Kay joined Xerox's PARC in 1971, where as a member of the Learning Research Group, he and others developed Smalltalk, a programming language based on Kay's commitment to both hiding the details of its operation and keeping the display of programming instructions compact (small). Kay's group worked on the development of the Dynabook, a book-sized personal computer with high resolution color display. The Dynabook was a prototype for the wireless laptop, with a radio link to a worldwide computer network and the inclusion of mailbox, library, telephone, and secretarial functions.

98 David Gelernter credits the Alto as a progenitor of a windows-based interface that allows the user to have multiple "channels of communication" with the machine: "The Alto played a central role in the rise of the window. Windows are a crucial piece of computing elegance because they liberate your channel of communication with the computer from the exigencies of a particular chunk of hardware. Without windows, the size of your screen limits your communication channel: human and machine communicate through a single rectangular chink in a blank-wall. But once you have windows, you have as many separate channels to the computer as you want." David Gelernter, *Machine Beauty: Elegance and the Heart of Technology* (New York: Basic Books, 1998), 77.

In *Dealers of Lightning,* Michael Hiltzik describes the Alto's demo in 1973: "Everyone's eyes focused on the screen as it flickered to life. Suddenly the pattern appeared. As the group watched, transfixed, Cookie Monster stared back at them, shaggy and bug-eyed, brandishing its goofy grin, moving across the screen while holding the letter 'C' in one hand a cookie in the other" (xxiii).

99 It is unclear who first called this interface "WIMP," but I've often fantasized that it might have been a sarcastic gesture by Adele Goldberg—one of the few female members at PARC—who worked closely with Kay on interface design.

100 Foley and Van Dam, *Principles of Computer Graphics* (Reading, Mass.: Addison Wesley, 1982).

101 Gelernter, *Machine Beauty,* 77–78.

102 Hiltzik, back cover flap to *Dealers in Lightning.* Scott Gasch described the visit in a 1996 online paper, "Alan Kay": "When Steve Jobs, Jeff Raskin, and some other Apple pioneers visited PARC in 1979, . . . they recognized immediately that Kay's ideas were the way of the future. They were impressed with the idea of a windowing GUI and were astounded with the flexibility of the Smalltalk language. Kay's work at PARC were the seeds from which the Apple Macintosh's look grew. Even Microsoft Windows, the most popular computer operating system in the world today, is a scion of Kay's ideas" <http://ei.cs.vt.edu/~history/gasch.kay.html>.

103 Adam Powell, "Web 101: A History of the GUI," *Wired News,* 19 December 1997.

104 In the 1995 PBS documentary *Triumph of the Nerds,* Jobs recalls this visit: "I was so blinded by the first thing they showed me, which was the graphical user interface. I thought it was the best thing I'd ever seen in my life. . . . They'd done it very well and within, you know, ten minutes it was obvious to me that all computers would work like this some day." Transcripts to the documentary are available at <http://www.pbs.org/nerds/part3.html>.

105 *Advertising Age* named this spot the 1980s' "Commercial of the Decade"; the ad ranked twelfth among *Advertising Age*'s Top 100 Advertising Campaigns of the 20th Century.

106 Neal Stephenson, *In the Beginning Was the Command Line* (New York: Avon, 1999), 20.

107 Bill Gates, *The Road Ahead* (New York: Viking, 1995), 53.

108 Ibid. In 1981, Microsoft was developing a software interface it called the "Interface Manager." In 1982, Microsoft added pull-down menus and dialog boxes, as used on the Xerox Star. In a 1983 announcement, the Interface Manager was renamed "Microsoft Windows."

109 Microsoft's defense in this suit was that both Apple and Microsoft actually stole from Xerox PARC.

110 Windows went through a variety of updates and improvements in its first decade: When Windows/386 was released, Windows 2 was renamed Windows/286. There were frequent criticisms of the interface: windows could be overlapped, but were instead "tiled." Windows were not allowed to cover an area at the bottom of the screen that was reserved for "iconized" programs. Windows 95 was the beginning of a new look for Microsoft. Its new graphical user interface (owing much to the Mac interface) was much more intuitive than the cascading style of Windows 3.1. Multitasking and increased network capability also made it a more powerful operating system for an office environment. Hackers called the Microsoft interface "Microsloth Windows" or "Windoze" because of its agonizingly slow speed.

111 Gelernter, *Machine Beauty,* 37.

112 Computer terminology has added a new meaning of "window shopping" to the vernacular. As defined in the Web-based *HyperDictionary,* "window shopping" is

> A term used among users of WIMP environments like the X Window System or the Macintosh at the US Geological Survey for *extended experimentation with new window colours, fonts, and icon shapes.* This activity can take up hours of what might otherwise have been productive working time. "I spent the afternoon window shopping until I found the coolest shade of green for my active window borders—now they perfectly match my medium slate blue background." *Serious window shoppers will spend their days with bitmap editors, creating new and different icons and background patterns for all to see.* Also: "window dressing," the act of applying new fonts, colours, etc.

<http://www.hyperdictionary.com/dictionary/window+shopping> (emphasis added).

113 *Webopedia* <http://www.webopedia.com/TERM/w/window.html>.

114 Eco's argument:

> The fact is that the world is divided between users of the Macintosh computer and users of MS-DOS compatible computers. I am firmly of the opinion that the Macintosh is Catholic and that DOS is Protestant. Indeed, the Macintosh is counter-reformist and has been influenced by the "ratio studiorum" of the Jesuits. It is cheerful, friendly, conciliatory, it tells the faithful how they must proceed step by step to reach—if not the Kingdom of Heaven—the moment in which their document is printed. It is catechistic: the essence of revelation is dealt with via simple formulae and sumptuous icons. Everyone has a right to salvation.
>
> DOS is Protestant, or even Calvinistic. It allows free interpretation of scripture, demands difficult personal decisions, imposes a subtle hermeneutics upon the user, and takes for granted the idea that not all can reach salvation. To make the system work you need to interpret the program yourself: a long way from the baroque community of revelers, the user is closed within the loneliness of his own inner torment.
>
> You may object that, with the passage to Windows, the DOS universe has come to resemble more closely the counter-reformist tolerance of the Macintosh. It's true: Windows represents an Anglican-style schism, big ceremonies in the cathedral, but there is always the possibility of a return to DOS to change things in accordance with bizarre decisions. . . .
>
> And machine code, which lies beneath both systems (or environments, if you prefer)? Ah, that is to do with the Old Testament, and is Talmudic and cabalistic.

This excerpt is from an English translation of Umberto Eco's back-page column "La bustina di Minerva," in the Italian newsweekly *Espresso* (30 September 1994).

115 Steven Johnson also uses that term in his *Interface Culture: How New Technology Transforms the Way We Create and Communicate* (San Francisco: Harper, 1997).

116 Stephenson, *In the Beginning Was the Command Line,* 23. Much of Stephenson's complaint about Microsoft is an aesthetic one, targeting the "aesthetic gaffes" and "white-trash stuff" of the Microsoft operating system ("Microsoft therefore bears the same relationship to Silicon Valley elite as the Beverly Hillbillies did to their fussy banker . . . they simply don't care and they are going to go on being tacky, and rich, and happy, forever"); but Stephenson also succinctly separates the Mac OS from Windows OS in terms of Apple's model of hardware monopoly compared to Microsoft's software business, which cleverly found a way of marketing a string of ones and zeros, a disk full of information in an empty box. The polemical thrust of Stephenson's essay is to unmask the GUI, and to advocate the more exposed workings of the Linux operating system.

117 There are many more distinctions to draw between the Mac version of a graphic user interface and the Windows one. In Stephenson's description, when a GUI computer crashes, the result looks like "static on a broken television set—a 'snow crash.'" But when a Windows machine crashes, "the old command line interface would fall down over the GUI like an asbestos fire curtain sealing off the proscenium of a burning opera. When a Macintosh got into trouble, it presented you with a cartoon of a bomb, which was funny the first time you saw it" (*In the Beginning,* 22).

Also, the Macintosh's technical means of running its graphical user interface led to its being built in one well-designed box that contained both the "motherboard" of its processing unit and the CRT video system that mapped computer memory and commands onto its screen. Ultimately, Stephenson finds a twisted irony in this: a Mac user "couldn't open up the hood and mess around with it. . . . Apple, in spite of its reputation as the machine of choice of scruffy, creative hacker types, had actually created a machine that discouraged hacking, while Microsoft, viewed as a technological laggard and copycat, had created a vast disorderly parts bazaar" (*In the Beginning,* 80).

118 Ibid., 64.

119 Ibid., 52.

120 Samsung's Digital Network Refrigerator (model RH2777AT) has a detachable flat-screen display that functions as photo album, message board, Internet browser, TV, and refrigerator temperature control.

121 Brenda Laurel, quoted in David Kline, "The Embedded Internet," *Wired* 4.10 (October 1996): 101.

122 Gelernter, *Machine Beauty,* 2–10.

123 Walter Benjamin, "The Work of Art in the Age of Mechanical Reproduction," in *Illuminations,* ed. Hannah Arendt, trans. Harry Zohn (New York: Schocken Books, 1969), 239–240. As Colin Rowe and Robert Slutzky write: "Painting can only imply the third dimension, architecture cannot suppress it." Colin Rowe and Robert Slutsky, "Transparency: Literal and Phenomenal," in Rowe, *The Mathematics of the Ideal Villa and Other Essays* (Cambridge: MIT Press, 1977), 166.

124 A multitasking operating system makes it possible for users to run multiple applications at the same time or to run "background" processes while conducting other tasks on the computer. At first a term for computer operating systems capable of running more than one task at the same time, "multitasking" has now come to refer to humans as operating systems juggling tasks—driving while talking on a cell phone, cooking dinner while watching TV, checking email while sitting in a meeting.

125 <http://en.wikipedia.org/wiki/Computer_multitasking>.

126 Recent research suggests that human multitasking, which at first may seem to increase efficiency, actually is less efficient than focusing on one task at a time. Rubinstein, Meyer, and Evans describe how their research revealed that for all types of tasks, subjects lost time when they had to switch from one task to another, and time costs increased with the complexity of the tasks: see Joshua S. Rubinstein, David E. Meyer, and Jeffrey E. Evans, "Executive Control of Cognitive Processes in Task Switching," *Journal of Experimental Psychology—Human Perception and Performance* 27, no. 4 (2001). After a long-term study of American's use of time, with a team of researchers at the University of Maryland, College Park, Dr. John Robinson concluded: "You can't expand time, so what you try to do is deepen time by doing more things in the same period." See John Robinson and Geoffrey Godbey, *Time for Life: The Surprising Ways Americans Use Their Time* (University Park: Pennsylvania State University Press, 1997).

127 Amy Harmon, "Talk, Type, Read E-mail," *New York Times,* 23 July 1998, late edition–final, G1.

128 The MTV Networks/Viacom Study of Media, Entertainment, and Leisure Time surveyed 4,070 Americans between the ages of four and seventy. The study also reported that TV viewers are using their computers while "watching" TV 20 percent of the time; one third of those in the study have their TV in the same room as their computer; and 28 percent have visited a Web address given on TV. See Stephen Battaglio, "TV, Napster and the 29.8 Hour Day," *inside.com* (June 2000).

129 Joanne Ciulla, *The Working Life: The Promise and Betrayal of Modern Work* (New York: Crown Business Books, 2000,) cited in "Multi-tasking to the Max," *USA Today,* 7 June 2000 (<http://www.usatoday.com/life/cyber/tech/cth787.htm>).

130 This website, run by George Washington University, offers students guidelines for computer use. *Computer Multi-tasking and Internet Interference with College Academics* <http://gwired.gwu.edu/counsel/html/virtual-handouts/computer-multi-tasking.html>.

131 Ibid.

132 Sherry Turkle, *Life on the Screen: Identity in the Age of the Internet* (New York: Simon and Schuster, 1995), 13.

133 Cognitive theorists and artificial intelligence theorists alike have challenged the concept of a unitary "self." See, for example, Marvin Minsky, *The Society of Mind* (New York: Simon and Schuster, 1986).

134 Turkle, *Life on the Screen,* 14–15.

135 In the last decade, our interfaces with the cinema, television, and computer sciences have changed markedly. In an essay written in 1997 ("The End of Cinema: Multi-media and Technological Change"), I explored the ways in which the then-new technologies challenged the discrete object of the "film," placing "the cinema" in an expanded field of screens, served by an expanded variety of production and delivery formats. In that essay, I argued that a "convergence" of film and television technology began without fiber-optic cable, occurred before the digitalization of imagery, and preceded the advent of the home computer. The VCR, I argued, was the first technology to begin to erode the historical differences between television and film, altering as it did the terms of electronic and cinematic viewing. In addition, the technologies that transformed the media environment of 1980s—the VCR, cable television, and the TV remote—not only changed our concept of film-going and television-viewing but prepared us for another "convergence"—that of the television and computer screen. Some portions of this section were taken from my recent essays: Anne Friedberg, "The End of Cinema: Multimedia and Technological Change," in Linda Williams and Christine Gledhill, eds., *Reinventing Film Studies* (London: Arnold Publications, 1999), 438–452; and "Interfacing the Screen: CDs, CD-ROMs, DVDs," in Dan Harries, ed., *The New Media Book* (London: BFI Publications, 2002), 30–39.

136 Lev Manovich's *The Language of New Media* (2001) and Erkki Huhtamo's *The Elements of Screenology: Toward an Archeology of the Screen, ICONICS*, vol. 7 (Tokyo: Japan Society of Image Arts and Sciences, 2004) trace some of the history I have just recounted; both works provide central definitional accounts of the emerging semiotic specificities of the computer screen.

137 Stephen Heath, "The Cinematic Apparatus: Technology as Historical and Cultural Form," in *Questions of Cinema* (London: Macmillan, 1981), 221–235.

138 Marshall McLuhan, *Understanding Media* (Cambridge: MIT Press, 1994), 9.

139 Ibid., 8.

140 Ibid., 53.

141 Nicolas Negroponte, *Being Digital* (New York: Alfred Knopf, 1995), 71. Negroponte imagines a media world of digital images making their way to digital display endpoints, with little or no difference in content, only a subtle "re-purposing" for display.

142 Nicolas Negroponte, "Bit by Bit, PCs are Becoming TVs. Or Is It the Other Way Around?," *Wired.com*, 1 August 1995.

143 Friedrich Kittler, *Grammophon, Film, Typewriter* (Berlin: Brinkmann & Bose, 1986); "Gramophone, Film Typewriter," *October* 41 (1986): 101–118.

144 <http://www.digitaldefinitions.co.uk/>.

145 Consumer Electronics Association (CEA) 2002, "Five Technologies to Watch," <http://www.ce.org/>.

146 The limited-edition Macintosh TV was introduced in October 1993 and terminated in February 1994. Only ten thousand were made. The Mac TV was equipped with a cable-ready TV-tuner card, and included a CD-ROM drive. It came in a black LC 520–style case. (It was one of only a few Macs to have been black.) Although the Mac TV was quickly discontinued, the TV-tuner card became a popular option on other mid-1990 Apple models, LCs, and Performas.

147 Antonio Gramsci, *Selections from the Prison Notebooks*, ed. and trans. Quintin Hoare and Geoffrey Nowell Smith (London: Lawrence and Wishart, 1971), 275–276.

CONCLUSION: THE FUTURE OF WINDOWS: SMART GLASS, STREAMING PORTALS, AND SCREENLESS IMAGES

1 Some thought of Deleuze's suicide as a philosophical gesture, an anecdote of thought occasioned by his thought: "In this respect, Deleuze's death also becomes, as [Jean-Pierre]Faye suggested, the 'terrible moment during which the ironical philosopher can no longer breathe and wants to join the air by diving towards death, from the height of a window.'" André Pierre Colombat, "November 4, 1995: Deleuze's Death as an Event," *Man and World* 29 (1996): 244.

See also Jean-Pierre Faye, "J'étouffe, je te rappellerai," *Libération* (7 November 1995): 38. The act of defenestration always carries with it a legal ambiguity (jumped? pushed?). Peter Greenaway explores death by defenestration in his 1974 film *Windows.*

Pictures taken of bodies falling (or jumping) from the windows of the World Trade Center on September 11, 2001, quickly became taboo. "There is something almost rebellious in the man's posture," writes Tom Junod of Richard Drew's photograph *Falling Man,* "as though once faced with the inevitability of death, he decided to get on with it; as though he were a missile, a spear, bent on attaining his own end. . . . In the picture, he is frozen; in his life outside the frame, he drops and keeps dropping until he disappears." Tom Junod, "The Falling Man," *Esquire* 140, no. 3 (September 2003); and Richard Drew, "The Horror of 9/11 That's All Too Familiar," *Los Angeles Times,* 10 September 2003. As Thomas Crow writes of the same type of image rendered in Warhol's *Suicide* (1962): "In the 1962 print on paper *Suicide,* the implacable facade of the building from which the victim has jumped (we can see neither its top nor its bottom) becomes an area of obscure abstraction marked only by dim ranks of unseeing windows; it is the dark complement to the bright wedge that surrounds the leaper's horrific silhouette." Thomas Crow, "Saturday Disasters: Trace and Reference in Early Warhol," in *Modern Art in the Common Culture* (New Haven: Yale University Press, 1996), 58. See also Hal Foster, "Death in America," *October* 75 (Winter 1996), reprinted in Annette Michelson, ed., *Andy Warhol,* October Files 2 (Cambridge: MIT Press, 2001), 70–88; and Peggy Phelan, "Francesca Woodman's Photography: Death and the Image One More Time," *Signs* 27, no. 4 (2002): 979–1004.

2 Gilles Deleuze, *Cinema 1: The Movement-Image,* trans. Hugh Tomlinson and Barbara Habberjam (Minneapolis: University of Minnesota Press, 1986), 15.

3 Ibid.

4 The French phrase for window-shopping (*lécher les vitrines*) has carried over to computer terminology. An online dictionary of French computers terms, *Teminologie d'Internet,* includes "*léche-vitrine virtuel,* n, Activité consistant à flâner à travers le Web, à passer d'une boutique virtuelle" <http://www.oqlf.gouv.qc.ca/resources/bibliotheque/dictionnaires/internet>.

5 My own writing about these changes in our media environment could barely keep the pace of media change. See Anne Friedberg, "The End of Cinema: Multimedia and Technological Change" (1997), in Linda Williams and Christine Gledhill, eds., *Reinventing Film Studies* (London: Arnold Publications, 1999), 438–452; reprinted in Leo Braudy and Marshall Cohen, eds., *Film Theory and Criticism,* 6th ed. (New York: Oxford University Press, 2004).

6 D. W. Griffith, "Five Dollar 'Movies' Prophesized" (1915), reprinted as "Some Prophecies: Film and Theatre, Screenwriting, Education," in Harry M. Geduld, ed., *Focus on D. W. Griffith* (Englewood Cliffs, N.J.: Prentice-Hall, 1971), 34–35; emphasis added. Quoted in Anne Friedberg, "'A Properly Adjusted Window': Vision and Sanity in D. W. Griffith's 1908–1909 Biograph Films," in Thomas Elsaesser, ed., *Space, Frame, Narrative: Early Cinema* (Bloomington: Indiana University Press, 1990), 326–335.

7 Leon Battista Alberti, *On Painting and On Sculpture: The Latin Texts of De pictura and De statua,* trans. Cecil Grayson (London: Phaidon, 1972), I.18, p. 53.

POSTLOGUE 2005

1 A. M. Homes, "Writers on Writing," *New York Times,* 24 September 2001, E1.

INDEX

Page numbers in boldface indicate illustrations.